Introduction to Paralegal Studies

Introduction to Paralegal Studies

A Critical Thinking Approach

Third Edition

KATHERINE A. CURRIER
Chair, Department of Paralegal
and Legal Studies
Elms College

THOMAS E. EIMERMANN
Emeritus Professor
Illinois State University

PUBLISHERS

76 Ninth Avenue, New York, NY 10011
http://paralegal.aspenpublishers.com

Aspen Publishers
Attn: Permissions Department
76 Ninth Avenue, 7th Floor
New York, NY 10011

Printed in the United States of America

ISBN 0-7355-5755-1

1 2 3 4 5 6 7 8 9 0

Library of Congress Cataloging-in-Publication Data

Currier, Katherine A., 1949-
    Introduction to paralegal studies : a critical thinking approach / Katherine A. Currier, Thomas E. Eimermann. — 3rd ed.
        p.   cm.
        ISBN 0-7355-5755-1
        1. Legal assistants—United States. 2. Practice of law—United States. I. Eimermann, Thomas E. II. Title.

    KF320.L4C87 2006

    340.023'73—dc22

                                                                                        2006023916

About Aspen Publishers

Aspen Publishers, headquartered in New York City, is a leading information provider for attorneys, business professionals, and law students. Written by preeminent authorities, our products consist of analytical and practical information covering both U.S. and international topics. We publish in the full range of formats, including updated manuals, books, periodicals, CDs, and online products.

Our proprietary content is complemented by 2,500 legal databases, containing over 11 million documents, available through our Loislaw division. Aspen Publishers also offers a wide range of topical legal and business databases linked to Loislaw's primary material. Our mission is to provide accurate, timely, and authoritative content in easily accessible formats, supported by unmatched customer care.

To order any Aspen Publishers title, go to *http://paralegal.aspenpublishers.com* or call 1-800-638-8437.

To reinstate your manual update service, call 1-800-638-8437.

For more information on Loislaw products, go to *www.loislaw.com* or call 1-800-364-2512.

For Customer Care issues, e-mail *CustomerCare@aspenpublishers.com*; call 1-800-234-1660; or fax 1-800-901-9075.

Aspen Publishers
a Wolters Kluwer business

*To our spouses and children
for their understanding and support*

About the Authors

Katherine A. Currier, J.D., is the chair of the Department of Paralegal and Legal Studies at Elms College. She has developed and taught many paralegal courses, including Legal Reasoning, Research, and Writing; Introduction to Legal Studies I and II; Law Office Computer Literacy; Law Office Applications; Interviewing, Counseling, and Negotiating; and Law and Literature. Her publications include articles on legal ethics as applied to paralegals and law office computing.

Professor Currier is actively involved in the development of paralegal education at both the regional and the national levels, particularly through her work with the American Association for Paralegal Education (AAfPE) and the American Bar Association Approval Commission. Professor Currier has served on the national board of AAfPE, first as its parliamentarian and then later as the elected representative of four-year paralegal programs. She served many years as the AAfPE publications chair, charged with the final responsibility for overseeing the Journal of Paralegal Education and Practice and The Educator. Professor Currier frequently speaks at both the AAfPE Northeast regional meetings and the annual AAfPE conferences on topics as diverse as the use of computer shareware, paralegals and the unauthorized practice of law, creative teaching techniques, and conducting legal research on the Internet. Professor Currier also chaired the American Bar Association Approval Commission, the body charged with conducting site visits of paralegal programs that are seeking their initial ABA approval or reapproval. Katherine A. Currier graduated magna cum laude with her B.A. in Political Science from Carelton College in 1971, with her M.A. in Political Philosophy from University of California, Berkeley, in 1973, and with her J.D. from Northeastern University Law School in 1979.

Thomas E. Eimermann is Emeritus Professor of Political Science and former Director of the Legal Studies Program at Illinois State University. Dr. Eimermann helped establish the paralegal program there in 1976 and taught Introduction to Paralegal Studies and Legal Research and Writing courses in that program.

Professor Eimermann has served as President and as a member of the Board of Directors of the American Association for Paralegal Education. He has also served on the Certification Board and the Advanced Certification Board of the National Association of Legal Assistants, as well as being a member of the Illinois State Bar Association Committee on the Delivery of Legal Services, and a member of the Hearing Board of the Illinois Attorney Registration and Disciplinary Commission. As a consultant for the Illinois Department of Corrections, he designed a Uniform Law Clerk Training Program used in Illinois prisons.

Professor Eimermann's publications include three editions of *Fundamentals of Paralegalism* and journal articles on paralegals, jury behavior, and free speech issues. He earned his B.A. in Political Science at North Central College. He went on to receive an M.A. and a Ph.D. in Political Science from the University of Illinois-Urbana/Champaign campus.

Katherine Currier and Thomas Eimermann also co-authored *An Introduction to Law for Paralegals: A Critical Thinking Approach* and *The Study of Law: A Critical Thinking Approach.*

Summary of Contents

Contents

List of Illustrations

Preface

NEW TO THIS EDITION

This third edition keeps pace with many new developments in the law and the paralegal profession. We have added new topics, expanded on others, and incorporated discussions of many recent court decisions.

Most noticeably in this edition we have made several organizational changes in order to improve readability and student comprehension. These changes involve moving the Civil Litigation and Its Alternatives chapter to Part 1 and splitting the former chapter on Civil Law into three shorter, more accessible chapters on Torts, Contracts and the UCC, and Property and Specialized Practice Areas. In the chapter on Civil Litigation and Its Alternatives, we now cover various forms of alternative dispute resolution before the discussion of civil procedure to more closely approximate the sequence of events in real disputes. The Distressed Grandfather and the Pregnant Waitress cases are also more fully integrated into the text of that chapter. Another major change is the addition of a new appendix on the fundamentals of good writing.

References to new developments include updated information on the membership of the U.S. Supreme Court and recent activities of paralegal-related professional associations. The text also incorporates references to new legislative and judicial developments involving federalism, eminent domain, reckless behavior, insanity, search and seizure, sentencing guidelines, capital punishment, and legal ethics. New developments in the law are also incorporated into Legal Reasoning Exercises, Discussion Questions, and NetNotes.

The new edition also includes the addition of three new Paralegal Profiles featuring paralegals working in the areas of intellectual property, municipal government, and paralegal management.

APPROACH

As the subtitle of this book indicates, it uses a critical thinking approach to paralegal studies. Paralegal studies focuses on the functions and duties of paralegals in the American legal system. The critical thinking approach to paralegal studies places great emphasis on the development of analytical thinking skills.

We use this critical thinking approach because we believe it is the best way for students to learn the fundamental principles of law. By learning how to read and interpret statutes, cases, regulations, and court documents, students will be better able to learn how to perform paralegal duties in a variety of specialty

areas. Therefore, this book emphasizes careful reading for detail, analytical thinking, and the written presentation of arguments.

Another key element of this critical thinking approach is the interactive nature of the book. We have included Hypothetical Cases, Discussion Questions, Legal Reasoning Exercises, Practice Tips, and Ethics Alerts to stimulate students to think about and discuss the underlying assumptions behind various aspects of the law and the ramifications of different approaches to legal problems. We purposely dispersed these items throughout the chapters so that the students would be encouraged to think about them while the material is fresh from recent reading and so as to be readily available for instructors to use as springboards for classroom discussion. While we did relegate the review questions to the end of each chapter, we have labeled them with the pages they cover so that you can easily assign just part of a chapter with its accompanying review questions.

Although this book was specifically designed to be used in introductory paralegal courses, general prelaw students, criminal justice majors, government majors, business students, and anyone wishing to know more about the law will also find it useful. It presents an overview of the legal system and covers the skills of legal research, legal writing, interviewing, investigation, and computerized case management.

ORGANIZATION OF THE BOOK

Part 1, Paralegals and the American Legal System, introduces students to the study of law, the organization of the legal system, and the role of paralegals in that system. Chapter 2, Paralegals in the Legal System, includes classification of different types of paralegals and what they do, as well as coverage of the issues of paralegal education, registration, certification, and licensure. Chapters 3 through 6 cover such topics as sources of the law, the different ways in which law is classified, the structure of the courts, and the various stages involved in litigation and alternative dispute resolution.

Part 2, Substance of the Law, introduces readers to the basic concepts involved in the areas of torts, contracts and the Uniform Commercial Code, property and specialized practice areas, and criminal law. It also includes an in-depth coverage of legal ethics, including confidentiality, conflicts of interest, and the unauthorized practice of law.

Part 3, Legal Analysis and Research, contains chapters that build the critical thinking skills students need for reading and analyzing the law. Chapters 12 and 13 cover finding and interpreting statutory law and court opinions. Chapter 14 discusses basic legal research tools, and Chapter 15 shows students how to apply what they have found to specific legal problems. Chapter 15 also discusses how to use the IRAC approach to legal analysis and how to report research findings in a legal memorandum.

Whereas Part 3 builds skills for finding and analyzing the law, **Part 4, Paralegals and the Work World,** builds skills related to gathering and managing relevant factual information. Chapter 16 focuses on interviewing while Chapter 17 covers the gathering, preservation, and use of different types of evidence.

Chapter 18 introduces readers to case management and the various types of computer programs that attorneys and paralegals can use to manage case information.

KEY FEATURES

Among the many features that set this book apart are the following:

- Discussion Questions integrated into each chapter
- Legal Reasoning Exercises
- Marginal definitions of key terms
- Practice Tips
- Ethics Alerts
- NetNotes
- Review Questions
- An appendix on the fundamentals of good writing
- A glossary, including definitions for all bold-faced words and phrases found in the text

Because this book stresses the critical thinking approach, we illustrate our points with hypothetical situations and with real case decisions that students will understand and to which they can relate. Discussion Questions and Legal Reasoning Exercises call on students to synthesize and analyze the material rather than simply recite an answer. The Practice Tips help connect the theoretical textbook learning to the reality of the work world. They provide checklists and other words of wisdom regarding practical paralegal tasks. By bringing the text to life, the Discussion Questions, Legal Reasoning Exercises, and Practice Tips all help maintain students' attention and aid in their retention of the material.

Ethics Alert boxes are placed throughout the text to draw attention to the ethical issues involved in various aspects of the law. These boxes warn students of actions that would be considered unethical; they also give advice on how to act appropriately. NetNotes provide students with handy links to key Internet resources.

Because so much of learning the law involves mastering legal vocabulary, we have included marginal notes containing key definitions. The end-of-the-chapter review questions also help students reinforce basic concepts.

Of special note are the appendices. Appendix A contains major excerpts from the U.S. Constitution. Appendix B includes the major codes of ethics with which paralegals need to be familiar. New to this edition, Appendix C provides students with a convenient and easy-to-understand primer on the basics of grammar, including verb tense, pronoun agreement, placement of modifiers, punctuation, and style. Appendix D provides a useful summary of all of the NetNotes found in the text.

An instructor's manual that includes suggested answers for all the Discussion Questions, Review Questions, and Legal Reasoning Exercises, as well as teaching tips, is available to help teachers make the most effective use

of this book. Also available is a PowerPoint presentation to assist with classroom lectures and a computerized test bank.

RELATIONSHIP TO THE AUTHORS' OTHER TEXTS

Those familiar with *Introduction to Law for Paralegals: A Critical Thinking Approach* and *The Study of Law: A Critical Thinking Approach* will recognize many similarities to this text. All three books emphasize the critical thinking approach to understanding the law. All three include discussion questions, NetNotes, practice tips, and references to ethical questions. Topics such as sources of law, classification of the law, structure of the court system, overviews of civil and criminal litigation, overviews of torts, contracts, property, and criminal law, and analysis of statutes and cases are covered in all three books.

However, *The Study of Law* is directed at a more general audience. Both the *Introduction to Law for Paralegals* and this text are specifically directed at paralegals. *Introduction to Law for Paralegals* goes into more detail in its coverage of substantive areas of the law and includes excerpts from actual court opinions. This text, *Introduction to Paralegal Studies*, expands on the discussion of the role of the paralegal by including additional chapters on interviewing, investigations, and computerized case management.

SPECIAL THANKS

Naturally, we owe a great deal of thanks to the many students, educators, paralegals, and attorneys who contributed ideas for this book. We would also like to recognize Victoria Joseph for her contribution to the criminal law chapter.

We would also like to thank the staff at Aspen Publishers for the excellent support we have received on the books we have done with them. We especially want to thank Betsy Kenny for the key role that she played in handling this third edition.

Finally, a special thank you goes to our spouses and children for their continued support and understanding of our professional activities.

Katherine A. Currier
Thomas E. Eimermann

August 2006

Acknowledgments

We are grateful to copyright holders for permission to reprint excerpts from the following items:

Abacus Data Systems

BOSTON GLOBE by MIKE BARNICLE. Copyright 1980 by GLOBE NEWSPAPER CO. (MA). Reproduced with permission of GLOBE NEWSPAPER CO. (MA) in the format Textbook via Copyright Clearance Center.

Lexis Law Publishing, United States Code Service, 42 U.S.C.S. 2000e-2, pages 449 and 452, Copyright 1989. The statute is reprinted from the United States Code Service, and is reprinted with the permission of Matthew Bender & Company, Inc. a member of the LexisNexis Group. All rights reserved.

National Association of Legal Assistants, Code of Ethics and Professional Responsibility. Copyright © 1995. Published with permission of the National Association of Legal Assistants, Inc., www.nala.org.

National Federation of Paralegal Associations, NFPA Model Code of Ethics and Professional Responsibility. Copyright © 1997. Reprinted by permission from the National Federation of Paralegal Associations, Inc., www.paralegals.org.

Shepard's, Massachusetts Citations, Case Edition, Part 4, 1993, page 318; and Northeastern Reporter Citations, Vol. 5, 1995, page 1408. Reproduced by permission of LexisNexis. Further reproduction of any kind is strictly prohibited.

Supreme Court Historical Society, photograph of the Supreme Court Justices. Collection, The Supreme Court of the United States, courtesy The Supreme Court Historical Society, photographed by Steve Petteway, Supreme Court.

West Group, Callow v. Thomas, 78 N.E.2d 637, 637–641. Reprinted with permission.

———, *Lewis v. Lewis*, 351 N.E.2d 526, 526–533. Reprinted with permission.

———, American Jurisprudence Second, Volume 41, pages 192–193. Reprinted with permission.

———, American Jurisprudence Second, Index, pages 448, 497. Reprinted with permission.

———, American Law Reports Annotated, 92 ALR3d 901, page 926. Reprinted with permission.

———, Corpus Juris Secundum, Volume 41, page 407. Reprinted with permission.

———, Massachusetts Digest, 12 Mass. Digest 2d 523; Table of Cases, page 61; Index, page 461. Reprinted with permission.

———, Massachusetts General Laws Annotated, Ch. 209 § 6, pages 351–352, 354, Pocket Part. Reprinted with permission.

———, Massachusetts General Laws Annotated, Index, page 329. Reprinted with permission.

———, Massachusetts Practice, Vol. 37, pages 259–260. Reprinted with permission.

———, West's Law Finder, page 2, National Reporter System Map. Reprinted with permission.

Introduction to
Paralegal Studies

PART

1

Paralegals and the American Legal System

Chapter 1

Introduction to the Study of Law and the Paralegal Profession

*The study of the law qualifies a [wo]man to be useful
to self, to neighbors, and to the public.*
Unknown

INTRODUCTION

You are about to embark on the study of the law, the legal system, and the paralegal profession. The purpose of this text is to give you a solid introduction to the American legal system and how paralegals and attorneys work within it. In this chapter we will give you an overview of the legal process. In the next chapter we explain what paralegals do and how one goes about becoming a paralegal. Part II of the book covers basic legal concepts that underlie our legal system, while Parts III and IV are designed to develop paralegal skills involved in legal analysis and legal research, interviewing, investigation, and case management.

In the chapters that follow, you will learn about the organization and structure of the legal system, the various forms that law takes, the procedures used in litigating civil and criminal cases, and basic legal principles that form the basis of our law in areas such as torts, contracts, and property. In addition to helping you acquire this type of basic legal knowledge, this text is designed to develop the critical thinking skills a paralegal needs to successfully conduct legal research and draft various types of legal documents. These critical thinking skills include learning how to analyze

facts, identify the appropriate legal rules, apply the rules to the facts, and report the results in a clear and understandable manner. In the remainder of this chapter, we will give you a quick introduction to those critical thinking skills in the context of two new clients who turn to the law firm of Darrow and Bryan for assistance.

The Case of the Distressed Grandfather

Approximately one year ago, Donald Drake and his six-year-old grandson, Philip, were walking down a residential road on their way home from visiting one of Philip's friends. Philip was walking on the sidewalk approximately thirty feet in front of Mr. Drake. Suddenly, a car sped past Mr. Drake, seemingly went out of control, jumped the curb, and hit Philip. Mr. Drake ran to Philip's side, but it was too late. Philip had been killed instantly. The driver of the car, Mrs. Wilma Small, was unhurt. Based on skid marks and testimony from both Mrs. Small and Mr. Drake, the police investigation following the accident determined that excessive speed was the cause of the accident.

Mr. Drake said that at the time of the accident his only concern was for the welfare of his grandson because he himself was clear of the danger. Naturally, Mr. Drake suffered a great deal of mental pain and shock because of seeing his grandson killed. While being driven home from the accident, he suffered a heart attack that necessitated a lengthy hospital stay.

One year later, he still does not feel completely recovered and often suffers from nightmares reliving the accident and his grandson's death. Following the advice of trusted friends he decided to make an appointment at the law office of Darrow and Bryan to see if he can sue Mrs. Small to recover for his hospital bills and for his pain and suffering.

The Case of the Harassed Student

Wanda Smith, a twenty-two year-old college student, was walking past a construction site on campus when several of the construction workers began to whistle and make cat calls. Wanda did not appreciate being treated as a sex object and greatly resented the way in which these construction workers were behaving.

After talking it over with a few of her friends, Wanda decided to talk to one of the attorneys at Darrow and Bryan to see if she can take legal action. She does not want other women to have to undergo similar treatment and wonders if she can collect damages for mental suffering.

A. THE CASES OF THE DISTRESSED GRANDFATHER AND HARASSED STUDENT

In addition to studying the cases of Mr. Drake and Ms. Smith in this chapter, we will refer to them again in later chapters. In fact, throughout the text we will be presenting you with short factual scenarios, similar to the cases of Mr. Drake and Ms. Smith, to illustrate how the affairs of people and businesses become

> ## P R A C T I C E T I P
>
> Everything you read in this book is wrong! Or at least it might be. Remember that law keeps changing and that it varies from state to state. Therefore, always research the law for yourself.

intertwined with the legal system. The study of law involves learning about how the legal system has developed rules to help people resolve such issues without having to resort to self-help or violence. In fact, law is sometimes viewed as the way society has developed a set of rules to help people resolve conflicts they cannot resolve on their own. Seen in that light, the study of law is the study of people and their troubles and of how society, through law, tries to resolve those troubles. However, the study of law is also the study of ways people can use legal rules to help plan their affairs so as to avoid future problems. For example, a group of entrepreneurs may seek legal advice regarding the best way to organize a new business, or a young married couple may come to an attorney for help with the purchase of their first home. Paralegals help attorneys solve people's legal problems by assisting in the gathering of factual information about the client's situation, by doing legal research to find appropriate statutes, regulations, and case law, by helping to draft various types of legal documents, and by helping to prepare and organize the information attorneys present in trials.

B. CRITICAL THINKING SKILLS

As mentioned above, in order to assist attorneys in their representation of clients, such as Mr. Drake and Ms. Smith, paralegals need to develop critical thinking skills that involve learning how to do the following:

- gather and analyze facts. This is often done through participating in the initial client interview or in drafting documents to gather information from the opposing party or witnesses.
- identify the appropriate legal rules. Normally, this is accomplished through legal research whether done in the traditional manner using law books or on-line using electronic resources.
- apply the rules to the facts. This is known as legal analysis, that is, taking the legal rule and applying it to the facts. Often this is a very straightforward process. For example, assume your firm is representing a husband seeking a divorce. He wants to know if the court will take into consideration the years his wife worked as a stay-at-home mother when it decides on the appropriate division of the marital assets. Through legal research you find a state statute that requires the court to take into account home-maker services when dividing marital property. In this case, assuming that your client's wife did indeed perform homemaking services, applying the law to your client's facts is very straightforward, and your supervising attorney would report to the husband that unfortunately for him the court will take into account her years as a homemaker when dividing

the marital assets. At other times, as we will see when we discuss Mr. Drake's case in more detail, this process is much less clear-cut. In those situations litigation often results as the two parties do not agree on how the law should be applied to their situation.

■ report the results in a clear and understandable manner. Sometimes your report will be verbal, but often your boss may want your thinking in writing.

The first skill—learning how to analyze the facts—begins when the paralegal first learns of the client's "story," often by participating in the initial client interview.

1. The Initial Client Interview and Fact Gathering

The first step in legal analysis is to gather and then review the facts. The answer to any legal question depends on the specific facts of the individual case. Even a minor change in the facts may alter the outcome of the case.

Just as a medical doctor cannot give a competent medical diagnosis without a thorough examination of the patient, a lawyer cannot render legal advice without a complete understanding of all of the relevant facts. In some areas of the law, such as those dealing with negligence or landlords and tenants, the legal outcome is particularly tied to the specific facts. For example, assume a stranger approaches an attorney at a party with questions such as: "My landlord is trying to evict me. Can he do that?" or "My husband is trying to get custody of my kids. Will he succeed?" It may be impossible for the attorney to answer without gathering a lot more information and personally reviewing key documents.

Paralegals often assist in the fact-gathering process by conducting interviews, summarizing those interviews, and reading and summarizing relevant documents. For example, when Donald Drake and Wanda Smith came to the law office of Darrow and Bryan to seek advice, they were each interviewed by Pat Harper, an attorney with the firm. Chris Kendall, one of the firm's senior paralegals, also sat in on the interviews to help take notes and to become familiar with the facts of the cases.

2. Legal Research: Identifying the Appropriate Legal Rules

After meeting with the clients, the first thing that attorney Harper needed to determine was whether either client had a basis for proceeding with a lawsuit. For

NETNOTE

One way to stay current with the changes in the law is through the Internet. You can find the latest legal news by going to the home page of Findlaw at *www.findlaw.com.* Then click on the "For Legal Professionals" tab at the top of the opening screen.

example, in Wanda Smith's case, she was clearly upset and disturbed by what had happened to her. However, that does not mean she has a legal remedy. Her lawyers will have to prove not only that the construction workers harassed and upset her but also that these actions violated some law. It is important to understand that not every problem is a problem for which the courts will supply a remedy.

Thus, the second stage of legal analysis involves the identification of the specific provisions of the law that are applicable to the client's situation. Because there are so many laws at the federal, state, and local levels, and because the law covers such a wide variety of topics, it is impossible for any lawyer to know everything there is to know about the law. The law is far too complex for any individual to be able to commit it all to memory. Furthermore, because the law is constantly changing, one's legal knowledge must be continually updated. Therefore, even lawyers who specialize and strive to keep current by reading legal newspapers, journals, and bar publications on a daily basis may still need to do legal research. Law books, and on-line computer databases, are the tools of the trade for the legal professional.

Legal research is a very time-consuming process, and attorneys often rely on paralegals to assist them in locating and summarizing the relevant statutes and cases they need to properly interpret the current status of the law. Because attorney Harper has not recently handled a similar case, Chris Kendall was assigned in Ms. Smith's case to research the law on sexual harassment and in Mr. Drake's case to see what law there was regarding the right to sue for emotional distress. We will discuss more about legal research in Part III.

Legal research
The process of finding the law.

3. Applying the Legal Rules to the Facts

Even after an attorney or paralegal has found the applicable legal rule through legal research, the job is far from completed. Because each client's problem is unique, simply knowing a general rule will not answer the client's problem. These general rules must be applied to the client's specific facts. We call this **legal reasoning.**

Generally, the result in a client's case will depend upon how the courts have handled similar situations in the past. In order to find out how similar situations have been handled in the past, an attorney or paralegal will examine prior court decisions and then apply them to the client's situation. If the facts of the client's situation and a prior court decision are similar, it is likely that the result in the client's case will be similar to the result reached in the prior case. If the facts are significantly different, it is likely that the result in the client's case will not be the same as the result reached in the prior case.

Legal reasoning
The application of legal rules to a client's specific factual situation; also known as *legal analysis.*

Unfortunately for Ms. Smith, Chris's research indicated that Ms. Smith did not appear to have a legal basis for suing the construction workers. If Ms. Smith had been employed as one of the construction workers and her boss had been harassing her in this way, she would have had the basis for a suit against the company. However, as a mere passerby she lacked such protection. Her facts combined with the law do not give her a right to sue.

Twenty years ago, Ms. Smith would not have been able to sue even if her employer had been the one to harass her. But as societal values change, the law usually changes as well. In recent years our society has become more sensitive to issues of gender equality and new laws have developed to provide new protections. Societal values change, and the law evolves in order to respond to those changes.

DISCUSSION QUESTIONS

1. Why do you suppose there are certain types of harm, such as the humiliation Wanda felt when the construction workers whistled at her, that courts will not help individuals resolve?

2. Do you think it is right that employees can go to court and sue their bosses for sexual harassment? Why? If the harasser were a coworker instead of a boss, how would you view the situation?

With regard to Mr. Drake's case, Chris's research proved more promising. Chris found one case in which a mother who saw her young child killed by a negligent driver was allowed to recover for the emotional distress the accident caused her. However, five years later, in another decision involving a similar situation, a female bystander who happened to witness the death of a young boy was not allowed to recover for her emotional distress.

In assessing the strength of Drake's case, attorney Harper must decide whether the courts would treat a grandfather as they did the mother or as they did the bystander. Take a few minutes to list as many arguments as you can muster for each side of the debate. The most important part of legal reasoning is seeking factual similarities and differences between prior decisions and your client's case and then explaining why you think those similarities or differences matter. In that process you will find that you and your classmates often differ as to the "right" answer.

In actuality there is no "right" answer, only better or worse arguments for your client. A judge may be the final arbiter as to what the answer is in a particular case, but even then it is not the "right" answer in any cosmic sense. Any decision about what the law should be is a choice between competing values. This is why some cases go to trial instead of settling—that is, because the two litigants have differing viewpoints as to which of two competing values is the most important. The important point to remember is that your goal is to learn how to develop arguments that will help persuade the other side that your answer is more correct than theirs.

4. Reporting the Results

Throughout the legal process, attorneys and paralegals are required to commit their thoughts to writing. At some points they will take informal, working notes for their own use. At other times they will make more formal reports that are designed to be read by colleagues, clients, opposing attorneys, or judges. You will be introduced to various examples of these more specialized forms of **legal writing** throughout the text.

Legal writing
Examples of legal writing include case briefs, law office memoranda, and documents filed with the court.

C. TAKING ACTIONS ON BEHALF OF THE CLIENT

After an attorney has thoroughly analyzed the application of the law to the client's situation and has advised the client as to the options available under the law, the attorney and client may agree to take some action on the client's behalf. These actions might include drafting a letter demanding that certain action be taken, initiating a lawsuit, defending against a lawsuit, or helping a client avoid future litigation through careful planning.

Although paralegals can draft legal documents, these documents cannot be filed with the court until an attorney has reviewed, approved, and signed them.

In Donald Drake's case, attorney Harper concluded that, although victory was not assured, there were good grounds for a lawsuit. Because Mr. Drake was anxious to proceed, she directed Chris to begin preparing the documents needed to officially begin the lawsuit. After carefully reviewing these documents, Pat signed them and directed Chris to file them at the local courthouse.

Legal Reasoning Exercise

Imagine that you are interning in attorney Harper's law firm. She has asked you to give her your thoughts on Mr. Drake's case. Specifically, attorney Harper wants you to list all of the ways in which you think Mr. Drake's case is similar to that of the mother who saw her child injured. Then list all of the ways in which you think Mr. Drake's case could be likened to that of the bystander. Finally, give attorney Harper your evaluation as to why you think that a court would see Mr. Drake's case as more similar to that of the mother or to that of the bystander. Also, let her know if you think there are additional facts that you would want to gather before making a final recommendation.

SUMMARY

This chapter provided a brief introduction to the role of law in our society and the manner in which lawyers evaluate and respond to their clients' legal problems. Within this context we have noted the contributions paralegals make and the nature of the legal reasoning process.

Throughout the text we will be stressing the development of the critical thinking skills you will need to become a successful paralegal. Among these skills are the ability to analyze the facts, identify the appropriate legal rules, apply the legal rules to the facts, report the results, and take actions on behalf of the client.

Although we have presented each stage in a linear fashion, the reality is that these various stages are intertwined. Legal reasoning often reveals the need to do more

research. In the process of reporting your findings, you may discover flaws in your analysis. Thinking, researching, and writing are inseparable.

In the chapters that follow, you will learn more about the organization and structure of the legal system, the various forms that law takes, the procedures used in litigating civil and criminal cases, and basic legal principles that form the basis of our law in areas such as torts, contracts, and property. You will also learn more about the duties and responsibilities of paralegals.

Do not be dismayed if you are sometimes overwhelmed by the complexity and the sheer volume of legal concepts and materials. Learning law is a lot like learning a foreign language. Although many of these terms may be new to you now, they will become increasingly familiar to you as you progress through the text. In the end you will be amazed at how these diverse pieces end up fitting into a logical and effective system.

REVIEW QUESTIONS

Pages 3 through 7

1. Why does the study of law involve more than simply memorizing rules?
2. What is legal reasoning?
3. Why is it important to know whether your client's facts are analogous to or distinguishable from those in prior court decisions?
4. Why does law change? Should it?

Pages 7 through 9

5. Why is there no one "right" answer to a legal problem?
6. Should it be the attorney or the paralegal who signs a client letter that analyzes the law? Why?

Chapter 2

Paralegals in the Legal System

[P]aralegals are capable of carrying out many tasks,
under the supervision of an attorney, that might
otherwise be performed by a lawyer.
Justice William Brennan

INTRODUCTION

In hearing about the cases of Donald Drake and Wanda Smith, you met two of the main legal professionals from the law firm of Darrow and Bryan: Pat Harper, a senior attorney, and Chris Kendall, one of the firm's paralegals. While this book focuses on paralegals, you cannot understand or fully appreciate the role of paralegals without also knowing some basic things about attorneys.

The terms "attorney" and "lawyer" are generally used interchangeably. In its most general sense, "attorney" denotes an agent, one who is authorized to act on behalf of another person or corporation. An "attorney at law" is a person who has been officially licensed to practice law in a state or federal jurisdiction. A "lawyer" is an equivalent term for an "attorney at law."

In some contexts, people use "lawyer" to refer to a person who is authorized to practice law and use "attorney" to refer to a job title. Thus, an organizational chart may carry titles such as attorney, associate attorney, enforcement attorney, District Attorney, United States Attorney, or Attorney General.

Becoming a licensed attorney involves attaining a bachelor's degree (not required in all states, but most attorneys have one), a graduate legal education

(normally three years if attending full time or four years part time), passing a state bar exam, and passing a morals/character check. In some states, to be authorized to practice law, attorneys must also join their state bar association and fulfill annual continuing education requirements.

The term paralegal refers to a person with special qualifications who assists attorneys in ways that are discussed in this chapter. The paralegal profession emerged in the late 1960s. It established its legitimacy in the early 1970s and underwent tremendous growth in the 1980s and 1990s. According to the U.S. Bureau of Labor Statistics, there were about 224,000 paralegal jobs in 2004, and the number of these types of positions is projected to grow faster than the average for all occupations through 2014.[1]

Paralegals contribute to the legal system by enhancing the quality of legal services and by working to increase access to justice. In fact, the National Federation of Paralegal Associations' Model Code of Ethics and Professional Responsibility states that "paralegal[s] shall serve the public interest by contributing to the improvement of the legal system and [the] delivery of quality legal services."[2]

In this chapter we discuss the paralegal profession and its role in the American legal system. We explain what paralegals do and how one goes about becoming a paralegal. In the process we will discuss how paralegals differ from lawyers and other law office personnel and whether paralegals should be licensed. Finally, we will look at the types of legal settings in which paralegals are most likely to find themselves employed.

A. THE DEFINITION OF PARALEGAL

A movie produced by the Philadelphia Paralegal Association begins with interviews of passersby on a busy street corner. An anonymous reporter asks each what they think a paralegal is. Their replies range from "A paralegal, ah, isn't that like half a legal?" to "Paralegal, isn't that when there is a very difficult case so they need two attorneys? You know, a pair of legals!" Although this movie was made a number of years ago, it still depicts today's reality. There is a lot of confusion regarding the role of the paralegal. This is partly because the paralegal profession is a relatively new one and partly because it is as yet totally unlicensed and, for the most part, unregulated.

As suggested above, many people are confused as to what a paralegal is or how a paralegal differs from a legal assistant, a law clerk, or a legal technician. This confusion is compounded by the fact that there are also freelance paralegals and independent paralegals, to say nothing of document clerks, legal secretaries, legal scriveners, lay advocates, and even paralegal assistants. What these groups have in common is that they perform various legal tasks without being licensed to practice law. In this section we will examine the most often heard terms:

1. traditional paralegals and legal assistants;
2. freelance paralegals;

---

[1] U.S. Bureau of Labor Statistics, Occupational Outlook Handbook (2006-2007 ed.).
[2] NFPA Model Code of Ethics and Professional Responsibility, 1.4 (1993).

3. legal technicians, lay advocates, and document preparers;
4. independent paralegals; and
5. law clerks and document clerks.

1. Traditional Paralegals and Legal Assistants

Although there are some regional preferences, traditionally in most parts of the country the terms **paralegal** and legal assistant have been viewed as synonyms. In the past few years, however, there has been a gradual movement away from using the term legal assistant and toward using the term paralegal. For example, recently the American Bar Association renamed its Standing Committee on Legal Assistants the Standing Committee on Paralegals. This "renaming" trend can also be seen in changes to the official names for some paralegal educational programs and paralegal associations, such as the Legal Management Association (LAMA), which changed its name to the International Paralegal Management Association (IPMA). While not changing its name, the National Association of Legal Assistants now allows those who successfully complete its Certified Legal Assistant (CLA) program to designate themselves as either a "Certified Legal Assistant" or a "Certified Paralegal."

The prefix *para* carries the meanings of "near" or "beside" and "similar to" or "subordinate to." The derivation of the word therefore suggests that a paralegal is one who works near or beside a lawyer, one who is similar to a lawyer but in a subordinate position. Thus, paralegals are individuals who do specialized legal work under the supervision of an attorney.

The **American Bar Association (ABA)** is the largest and most prominent national organization of lawyers. Over the past thirty years it has taken a leadership role in recognizing the need for and helping establish the paralegal profession. As the profession has developed, the ABA has periodically modified and refined its definition of paralegal/legal assistant. Most recently in 1997 the ABA amended its officially adopted definition of a legal assistant/paralegal to read:

> A legal assistant or paralegal is a person, qualified by education, training or work experience who is employed or retained by a lawyer, law office, corporation, governmental agency or other entity and who performs specifically delegated substantive legal work for which a lawyer is responsible.[3]

Because this is a long definition, we can better understand it by dividing it into its separate components. (This process of dividing a lengthy definition into more manageable subparts is very similar to the process of statutory analysis that you will study in Chapter 12.) A legal assistant or paralegal is

1. "a person, qualified by education, training or work experience" (*focus on the background of the individual*),
2. "who is employed or retained by a lawyer, law office, corporation, governmental agency or other entity" (*focus on the nature of the employer*) and

Paralegal
A person who assists an attorney and, working under the attorney's supervision, does tasks that, absent the paralegal, the attorney would do. A paralegal cannot give legal advice or appear in court.

American Bar Association (ABA)
www.abanet.org
A national voluntary organization of lawyers.

---

[3] Adopted by the ABA House of Delegates, August 1997.

3. "who performs specifically delegated substantive legal work" (*focus on the nature of the work performed*)
4. "for which a lawyer is responsible" (*focus on the supervision provided by the employer*).

The **National Association of Legal Assistants (NALA)** and the **National Federation of Paralegal Associations (NFPA)** are the two major national associations of paralegals/legal assistants. Each association is discussed later in this chapter. For now, it is important to know that each has adopted a slightly different definition of paralegal/legal assistant. NALA declares that

> [l]egal assistants are a distinguishable group of non-lawyers who assist attorneys in the delivery of legal services. Through formal education, training *and* experience, legal assistants have knowledge and expertise regarding the legal system and substantive and procedural law which qualify them to do work of a legal nature under the supervision of an attorney.[4]

Contrast the ABA's language about paralegals acquiring their skills through either formal education "or" on-the-job training (part 1) with NALA's use of "and" as the connector for education, training, and experience. This simple change of an "or" to an "and" highlights a major issue in the paralegal profession: whether on-the-job training is sufficient or whether all paralegals must also acquire some type of formal education.

Returning to the ABA definition, it also requires that the paralegal be employed or retained by a lawyer, law office, corporation, governmental agency, or other entity (part 2) and that a lawyer be held responsible for the paralegal's work (part 4). Notice how the next definition, recommended by NFPA, does not limit employment to those situations in which an attorney supervises the work, as it also includes legal work authorized by administrative, statutory, or court authority.

> A paralegal/legal assistant is a person, qualified through education, training or work experience, to perform substantive legal work that requires knowledge of legal concepts and is customarily, but not exclusively performed by a lawyer. This person may be retained or employed by a lawyer, law office, governmental agency or other entity, *or may be authorized by administrative, statutory, or court authority to perform this work.*[5]

While there are differences among these definitions, all three suggest that paralegals perform many of the same tasks normally performed by lawyers. They gather and analyze facts relevant to legal disputes, perform legal research, draft legal documents, prepare witnesses and evidence for presentation at legal proceedings, and even represent clients in some types of administrative hearings.

Over half of the states have developed some form of definition for the term "paralegal." In some cases the definition comes from the state bar association. In others the definition is one created by the state courts or legislature. In 2001,

---

[4] This definition was first set out in the 1985 version of NALA's Model Standards and Guidelines for Utilization of Legal Assistants *(emphasis added)*.

[5] NFPA, Information You Should Know about NFPA (pamph. 1990) *(emphasis added)*.

California became the first state not only to define the term paralegal but to limit the use of that term to only those individuals who meet its statutory criteria. Specifically, the statute prohibits people from using the title of "paralegal" unless they meet the following definition.

> "Paralegal" means a person who holds himself or herself out to be a paralegal, who is qualified by education, training, or work experience, and who either contracts with or is employed by an attorney, law firm, corporation, governmental agency, or other entity, and who performs substantial legal work under the direction and supervision of an active member of the State Bar of California . . . or an attorney practicing law in the federal courts of this state, that has been specifically delegated by the attorney to him or her.[6]

The statute treats the following terms as synonymous: paralegal, legal assistant, attorney assistant, freelance paralegal, independent paralegal, and contract paralegal.[7]

Even though paralegals carry out many of the same tasks performed by attorneys, paralegals are not licensed to practice law. Therefore, they can perform many of these tasks only when working under the supervision of an attorney. In addition, even when paralegals are working under the supervision of an attorney, they are not allowed to give direct legal advice to clients or to represent clients in most types of judicial proceedings.

DISCUSSION QUESTIONS

1. Which of the definitions of paralegal—the one from the ABA, NALA, or NFPA—do you like best? Why?

2. Until August 1997, the ABA definition of legal assistant read:

> A legal assistant is a person, qualified through education, training, or work experience, who is employed or retained by a lawyer, law office, governmental agency, or other entity in a capacity or function which involves the performance, under the ultimate direction and supervision of an attorney, of specifically-delegated substantive legal work, which work, for the most part, requires a sufficient knowledge of legal concepts that, absent such assistant, the attorney would perform the task.

You will see this definition quoted in most of the court opinions decided prior to 1997 that deal with the role of paralegals. It is not certain whether the courts will continue to follow this definition or the most recently adopted one. In what ways do you think the two definitions differ from each other? Which ABA definition do you prefer? Why?

3. What do you think is a good definition of *paralegal*? Try writing a model definition that could be adopted by a court or legislature.

2. Freelance Paralegals

The term **freelance paralegals** refers to a specific subgroup of paralegals who work as **independent contractors** rather than as employees of law firms or corporations. They usually contract to do a specific job and frequently have contracts with several different lawyers at once. The advantages of being a freelance paralegal include having the capacity to choose what kinds of projects

Freelance paralegal
A paralegal who works as an independent contractor rather than as an employee of a law firm or corporation.

---

[6] Cal. Bus. & Prof. Code § 6450 (2006).
[7] Cal. Bus. & Prof. Code § 6454 (2006).

you will work on and to set your own hours. Attorneys find that in this type of contractual relationship they can use paralegals on an "as needed" basis without having to pay fringe benefits and unemployment compensation insurance and without worrying about what to do with the paralegals during a slack time in the business cycle.

||| PARALEGAL PROFILE

JENNIFER LERNER
FREELANCE PARALEGAL

Although I worked in a personal injury firm while attending school for my paralegal degree, when I graduated I found I could make more money if I contracted my services than if I remained an employee. Freelance work also enables me to decide what types of duties I want to accept and allows me to work from my home. I do personal injury work for area attorneys, with a specialty in writing demands for completed cases to be sent to insurance claims representatives. The demands are based on the medical expenses incurred and the expectation as to future medical and hospital expenses, pain and suffering, and lost wages. I take the file, investigate it, make sure all of the information is there, and then come up with the price. I present the information as persuasively as possible, using spreadsheets and including particulars, such as how many hours the client had to wait in the doctor's office each week. I do all of my work on a disk that I give to the attorney. The attorney then makes any desired changes and sends the demand to the insurance company.

I like the variety that can come at you at any time and the unpredictability. I love working with the law because the whole concept of how conflicts arise and then how people go about getting rid of conflict is fascinating. For some, arbitration or mediation is the best choice. Working as a paralegal teaches you a lot about people. For example, people have very different ways of dealing with their injuries. We are in a people business and what we do changes the lives of people.

Recently, I was also hired on a part-time basis to use my paralegal skills in an unusual way. A maritime company was interested in hiring someone to research regulations, to prepare documents for ships coming into port, to ensure that crew members have all required paper-work, and to communicate with ships at sea. Even though the company did not start out looking for someone with paralegal skills, during the interview process it became evident that those skills were exactly what they needed, and I got the job. Those skills include the abilities to sustain independent thought, understand the need to maintain confidentiality in negotiations, project a professional image, understand the intricacies of dealing with contracts and government regulations, and not make a judgment before having all of the necessary information.

Even if I didn't use any of my paralegal skills as a paralegal, the education and experience I have received have armed me for what the world may throw my way. It has helped me to deal with a lack of predictability and enabled me to reason and see both sides of issues. Rather than jumping to conclusions, I now tend to back up and think of all the reasons before choosing a course of action.

3. Legal Technicians, Lay Advocates, and Document Preparers

Even though freelance paralegals are not in an employer-employee relationship, they still operate under the supervision of a licensed attorney. The terms *legal*

technician and *lay advocate*, on the other hand, are used to describe nonlawyers who provide legal services directly to the public without being under the supervision of an attorney. A **lay advocate** is generally someone operating within the law, representing persons before administrative agencies that permit this practice. **Legal technicians,** however, are nonlawyer service providers who give legal advice to people who are representing themselves. The role of the legal technician is highly controversial; without special legislative or judicial authority, it frequently constitutes the unauthorized practice of law.[8]

There are also services that offer to prepare standardized legal documents for people who are attempting to handle their legal matters **pro se** (i.e., to handle the case on their own without using a lawyer). Individuals who provide this service are also called **legal scriveners,** forms practitioners, form preparers, and legal information specialists. If they provide only typing services, they do not run the same risks of violating the unauthorized practice of law statutes as do legal technicians.

Finally, you should be aware of what California calls "legal document assistants" and what Arizona refers to as "legal document preparers." These individuals prepare legal documents for members of the public who are representing themselves in a legal matter. Their assistance is limited to ministerial tasks and to providing general published factual information. They are explicitly prohibited from giving legal advice.[9]

Lay advocate
Generally someone operating within the law, representing persons before administrative agencies that permit this practice.

Legal technician
A nonlawyer who provides legal services directly to the public without being under the supervision of an attorney. Absent a statute allowing this activity, it constitutes the unauthorized practice of law.

4. Independent Paralegals

You may also hear the term **independent paralegal.** Usually this term refers to paralegals who work under the supervision of an attorney in a contractual relationship (freelance paralegals). Sometimes, however, you will also hear it used to refer to those who provide legal services directly to the public without being under the supervision of an attorney (legal technicians).

5. Law Clerks and Document Clerks Working under the Supervision of an Attorney

The terms law clerk and document clerk are additional terms that you may come across in the legal community. The **law clerk** title has historically been reserved to describe a law student or a recent law school graduate who has not yet passed the bar and who was hired primarily to do legal research. The term **documents clerk** is usually used to describe someone who organizes and files legal documents. While normally a clerical position, it sometimes serves as an entry-level position for recent paralegal graduates.

DISCUSSION QUESTIONS

4. What do you think would be the advantages and disadvantages of working as an independent contractor (freelance paralegal) rather than as a paralegal employee?

---

[8] To read more on the licensing of these types of paralegals, see the discussion in this chapter beginning on page 25, and see Chapter 11 for a discussion of what constitutes the unauthorized practice of law.

[9] Cal. Bus. & Prof. Code § 6400 (2006); Ariz. Code of Judicial Admin. § 7-208 (2006).

5. Some people have argued that by not being located in the law office, freelance paralegals cannot receive adequate supervision from an attorney. Do you agree or disagree? Why?

6. If nonlawyers are *not* working under the supervision of an attorney, do you think they should be allowed to give legal advice to clients?

7. Should paralegals be allowed to give legal advice if they *are* working under the supervision of an attorney?

B. PARALEGAL EDUCATION

In the previous section we discussed what a paralegal is. In this section we will explore the basic qualifications necessary to become a paralegal.

Figure 2-1 presents the differences in qualifications for becoming a paralegal and becoming an attorney. While, as mentioned above on pages 11 and 12, becoming a licensed attorney normally involves attaining a bachelor's degree, and then a graduate legal education, and passing a state bar exam, including a morals/character check, nothing prevents a person with no college credits and no paralegal training from being hired to work as a paralegal. This is true because currently there are no minimum legal requirements, such as licensing statutes would create, that must be satisfied to be able to work as a paralegal. Nor are there any informal standards universally accepted by all attorneys who hire paralegals. To become a paralegal you simply need to find an attorney who is willing to hire you and assign you that title.

Figure 2-1   Paralegal versus Attorney Qualifications

Qualifications	Paralegal	Attorney
Undergraduate education	None required (An associate's degree is rapidly becoming the minimum acceptable degree for employment; many employers require a bachelor's degree.)	Bachelor's degree
Specialized education	None required (Some employers give preference to graduates of ABA-approved paralegal programs.)	Usually a degree from an ABA-accredited law school
Testing	None required (Some employers give preference to those who pass a voluntary exam administered by one of the national paralegal associations.)	Passage of a state bar exam (Most exams have multistate and state-specific questions.)
License and morals check	None required	Must be licensed

Although it is possible for anyone to be hired as a paralegal, most employers do not wish to start from scratch in training their paralegals. Therefore, they limit their employment searches to individuals who already have experience in the field or who have completed some form of formal paralegal education they trust. For example, perhaps because attorneys in most states are required to graduate from an ABA-accredited law school, many employers limit their employment search to paralegals who have graduated from an ABA-approved paralegal program.

1. Basic Qualifications

To be an effective paralegal, one must have a great deal of specific knowledge, whether gained through formal education or on-the-job training. But in addition to a sound grasp of both substantive and procedural law, an effective paralegal should possess certain intellectual and personality traits.

Because the law is complex and often ambiguous, paralegals must be able to think analytically and logically so that they can recognize and evaluate relevant facts and legal concepts. Paralegals must then be able to effectively communicate their conclusions both verbally and, what is particularly important, in clear, concise prose.

Certain personality traits are also important for success in this field. At times paralegals work closely with attorneys, clients, and members of the public. Therefore, paralegals should be congenial and diplomatic and present a good professional image. At other times, however, they must work long solitary hours in law libraries and their offices, where they draft, organize, or digest legal documents. These activities require patience, persistence, and the ability to work with a minimum of supervision. Paralegals should function well in stressful conditions because they live in a world of deadlines and often have conflicting demands placed on their time by attorneys.

Perhaps the most important characteristics for success in the paralegal field are ingenuity and good judgment. The best paralegals are innovative and resourceful. Once they understand the nature of the problem, they develop their own solutions. Because they exercise good judgment, they know when to proceed independently and when to bring matters to the attention of their supervising attorneys.

2. Formal Paralegal Education

Before 1970 there were no formal educational programs for paralegals; the necessary skills were learned exclusively through on-the-job training. Many lawyers simply gave their secretaries a variety of paralegal tasks along with their own instructions as to how they were to be done. Occasionally a law firm brought in someone with a special skill, such as accounting, to help with a specific area of the law, such as assisting with the processing of tax returns.

The late 1960s and early 1970s saw the development of paralegal programs at both community colleges and proprietary schools. Most recently many four-year colleges and universities have also developed formal paralegal programs. The quality of paralegal programs varies widely, and many paralegals and paralegal educators have expressed concern about issues of quality control in paralegal education.

3. The ABA Approval Process

Recognizing the need for some standards for paralegal education, in 1973 the ABA formally adopted a set of standards for granting American Bar Association approval to educational programs. To date the ABA is the only official body to establish a set of standards for paralegal education.

As of 2006, the ABA had approved approximately 260 of the estimated 800 paralegal programs. This does not mean that the remaining programs could not meet the ABA requirements, although some may not be able to do so. It may simply mean that those programs have chosen not to seek ABA approval for either philosophical or economic reasons. Those programs that do meet ABA requirements but have not applied for ABA approval are often spoken of as being in "substantial compliance."

4. American Association for Paralegal Education

American Association for Paralegal Education (AAfPE) *www.aafpe.org* A national organization of paralegal programs that promotes high standards for paralegal education.

In 1981 educators from a variety of paralegal programs formed the **American Association for Paralegal Education (AAfPE)**. This national organization was chartered to promote high standards for paralegal education, provide a forum for professional improvement for paralegal educators, and promote research and dissemination of information regarding the paralegal profession and paralegal education. Its membership includes approximately 350 educational institutions offering programs at the community college, baccalaureate, and postgraduate levels.

In order for an institution to be a voting member of AAfPE, it must be in "substantial compliance" with the ABA standards. The institution need not, however, have formal ABA approval. AAfPE has developed a set of core competencies for paralegals that paralegal programs are encouraged to incorporate into their curriculums. They may eventually supplement the standards developed by the ABA.

C. PARALEGAL PROFESSIONAL ASSOCIATIONS

One sign of the growing maturity of a profession is the establishment of professional associations dedicated to meeting the needs of their members as well as educating the public. The two major national paralegal associations are the National Federation of Paralegal Associations and the National Association of Legal Assistants.

National Federation of Paralegal Associations (NFPA) *www.paralegals.org* A national association of paralegal associations.

The **National Federation of Paralegal Associations (NFPA)** was formed in 1974 as a federation of local paralegal groups. Formed in 1975, the **National Association of Legal Assistants (NALA)** is a direct membership organization.

National Association of Legal Assistants (NALA) *www.nala.org* A national paralegal association.

Both organizations seek to promote the paralegal profession and monitor activities of courts, bar associations, and legislatures that might affect their members' interests. NFPA and NALA have developed formal sets of ethical guidelines, which their members are pledged to follow. Some of their differences lie in the policy positions taken by each organization on such issues as certification, licensure, the nature of the relationship between paralegals and bar

associations, and the extent to which paralegals should be permitted to operate without being under the direct supervision of an attorney.

While the existence of competing organizations demonstrates the diversity of the profession, some observers fear that paralegals may be losing political influence because they lack a single organization to speak with one voice for the entire paralegal profession. Because each organization has its own traditions and "personality," it is highly unlikely that they will merge any time in the near future.

While NFPA and NALA are clearly the two most prominent national paralegal organizations, there are a variety of other paralegal associations at the national, state, and local levels. Membership in these other associations may be general or may be limited to a particular type of paralegal, such as paralegal managers or freelance paralegals. One notable example is the **International Paralegal Management Association (IPMA).** IPMA is an influential organization representing paralegal managers in large law firms and corporate law departments.

Now would be a good time to find out which paralegal associations are strong in your community and whether they have a special membership rate for students. Joining a paralegal association will give you the opportunity to meet working paralegals and to participate in the association's benefits by, for example, attending seminars and being listed in their job bank.

P R A C T I C E   T I P

Join your local paralegal association.

International Paralegal Management Association (IPMA) *www.paralegal management.org* A national association of paralegal managers.

PARALEGAL PROFILE

LAURIE ROSELLE
DIRECTOR OF LEGAL SERVICES
CLIFFORD CHANCE US LLP

I work at Clifford Chance US LLP, one of the largest law firms in the world. We have offices in thirty-seven countries. I work in the New York office. My official title is Director of Legal Services.

As Director of Legal Services, I supervise the managers who coordinate the full-time paralegals, the temporary paralegals and attorneys, the clerks (court filers), technology support, conflicts clearance, and records groups. I often handle facilities and space related issues and generally trouble shoot for the practice groups.

I don't think I have ever had a typical day. I generally get to the office by 7 a.m. with a "To Do" list of about five items. By 9 p.m. when I've only finished one, I declare it a victory and head home, usually by hired car so I can work for another hour before arriving home. (For you country folks, you should know that in the larger cities, such as New York, it is not uncommon to get a hired car ride home . . . which means you can work in the car and bill more time; the operative phrase there being "work and bill"!)

What I really like about my work is that the people are fabulous. They are passionate, resilient, fun, and, most of all, they take very seriously what the client needs, not what suits them. We work as hard as we play. I also like that no two days are ever alike. It's like a new three-ring circus every day.

Thinking back on my education and what best prepared me for my work, I would have to say that business, math, and statistics were the courses that have helped me the most. When those math teachers tell you that you will use basic algebra all your life, believe them. Business is all a numbers game, and the more you know how to slice and dice them, the better off you'll be.

The International Paralegal Management Association (IPMA) is a great source of information and networking for the paralegal management piece of my job. Their annual conference is always well done and timely on issues directly impacting the paralegals I supervise. The Association of Legal Administrators (ALA) is an excellent group for networking and information on a wide variety of topics that cover the myriad of other items for which I am responsible. The ALA annual conference makes me giddy like a kid in a candy shop as there are so many sessions to attend. For real estate it is all about "location, location, location" and for networking, it is all about IPMA/ALA for me.

My advice to students thinking about a career as a paralegal is to act like a sponge: soak up information on both "soft" and "legal" topics. You never know where this field will lead you, so the more information you gather, the better equipped you will be to take the next step up the ladder. Embrace technology (even though we may never really see a paperless courtroom!) and never say never. The attitude you bring to the table is what an employer is looking for ... they can teach you the legal skills, but they cannot teach you attitude. If you don't have a "can-do" attitude, legal is not the field for you. Lawyers do not want to hear the reasons why you cannot do something. They want to hear that it has been done.

In my free time I do stand-up comedy, spoil my nieces and nephews, and do volunteer work with Delta Gamma Sorority, the Smile Train (a non-profit organization committed to eradicating the problem of cleft lips and palates), and the Princess Project (a non-profit organization that distributes donated new and "gently worn" formal dresses to students who might otherwise not be able to attend their proms).

D. REGISTRATION, CERTIFICATION, AND LICENSURE

Although many employers hire only paralegals who have completed an ABA-approved or other well-established paralegal education program, the lack of formal licensing requirements allows for situations in which people with no formal training or experience can be hired and given the job title of paralegal. This situation often leads to a great deal of variation among paralegals in terms of background and quality, and that, in turn, is seen by many as harming the image of the profession. "Real" paralegals and legal assistants are justifiably upset when they find some law firms giving a paralegal or legal assistant job title to legal secretaries as a reward for loyal service to the firm, even though they will continue to do the same clerical work they have always done.

Many paralegals are therefore looking to various certification and licensing systems to set themselves apart from those who are not doing paralegal work or are not qualified to do so. However, among the various problems they face is that of how these new standards would affect those working paralegals who have attained their jobs through on-the-job training and who cannot, for whatever reason, return to school for more formal education. The possibilities include registration, certification, and licensing.

1. Registration

Registration is a process by which individuals or organizations have their names placed on an official list kept by some private organization or governmental agency. Depending on the purpose of the registration process, placing one's name on this list is either voluntary or mandatory.

    As of the writing of this edition, there are no state registration systems for paralegals. The California statute that restricts the use of the title of paralegal to those who meet certain education or work experience requirements does not require paralegals to register with any government agency. As noted above on page 17, California officially recognizes legal document assistants and requires them to register in the county in which they work.

    The primary benefit of a registration system for paralegals is being able to more easily identify and locate people doing paralegal work. However, most of those in the profession seem to think that such a benefit is not worth the cost of maintaining a registration system.

Registration
The process by which individuals or organizations have their names placed on an official list kept by some private organization or governmental agency.

2. Certification

When special qualifications are established as a requirement for registration, the system moves from registration to certification (see Figure 2-2). **Certification** refers to the formal recognition by an organization that an individual has met some predetermined set of qualifications. That set of qualifications typically includes meeting educational requirements and passing an exam. Only those who meet these criteria are allowed to claim the title that goes with the designated status (such as certified public accountant or chartered life underwriter), but a person without such certification is not legally restricted from working in that occupational area. The advantage of certification is that potential employers and clients know that the individual has met certain standards. Therefore, presumably they are more likely to employ this individual than someone who is not certified.

    In 2004, North Carolina became the first state to adopt a method for paralegal certification. According to the rules adopted by the North Carolina Supreme Court, a paralegal may use the title "North Carolina Certified Paralegal (NCCP)," "North Carolina State Bar Certified Paralegal (NCSB/CP)," or "Paralegal Certified by the North Carolina State Bar Board of Paralegal Certification" only if that person has completed a post-secondary paralegal educational program, passed a written exam designed to test the applicant's knowledge and ability, and annually maintained a minimum of six hours of continuing education.[10] The purpose of the plan is to "improve the competency of those individuals [who assist in the delivery of legal services] by establishing mandatory continuing legal education and other requirements of certification."[11]

    Both of the major paralegal organizations also provide a method by which paralegals can become certified. For example, paralegals can only call themselves "Certified Legal Assistants" or "Certified Paralegals" and use the letters "CLA"

Certified
The status of being formally recognized by a nongovernmental organization for having met special criteria, such as fulfilling educational requirements and passing an exam, established by that organization.

Figure 2-2 Increasing Levels of Regulation

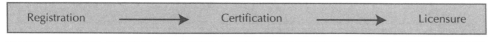

| Registration | → | Certification | → | Licensure |

---

[10] 27 N.C.A.C. 1G.0117(4) (2006).
[11] Id. at 1G.0101.

or "CP" after their names if they have completed the requirements of NALA's voluntary certification program. The terms Certified Legal Assistant and Certified Paralegal are registered trademarks of NALA.

To become a certified legal assistant or paralegal, a paralegal must pass NALA's certification exam and complete five units of continuing legal assistant education every five years. The two-day exam covers communications, ethics, legal research, judgment and analytical ability, and substantive law. A person can qualify to take the exam through either education or work experience.

For many years, NALA also offered an advanced certification in selected specialty practice areas. In 2006, NALA switched to a new curriculum-based certification that is offered online. Assessment measures are built into highly structured educational materials that are accessible via the Internet. Initial offerings were in the areas of Contracts Administration and Management, Discovery, and Business Organizations.

Until recently the two major paralegal organizations, NALA and NFPA, took opposite positions regarding certification. NFPA opposed certification, while NALA established and administers its certified legal assistant program. However, in October 1994, NFPA made a significant change in policy when it announced that it planned to develop a two-tiered proficiency exam for experienced paralegals, known as PACE. The first tier covers general legal issues, while the second tier covers legal specialties. To qualify to take the first-tier exam, a paralegal must hold a bachelor's degree, have completed a paralegal program, and have worked a minimum of two years as a paralegal. The work requirement

Ethics Alert

Even though no state has as yet licensed paralegals, paralegals must always remember that as part of the legal profession they are required to maintain demanding ethical standards. The following three points are of special importance to paralegals:

1. Paralegals are not attorneys and therefore cannot give legal advice, sign court documents, or appear in court on behalf of a client. To do so is the *unauthorized practice of law*, a crime in most states.
2. Attorneys and their staff must respect the *confidentiality* of the client-attorney relationship. You must treat anything you learn in the law firm as confidential and not discuss it with anyone—even your spouse or other family member—outside the firm.
3. Clients expect their attorneys and staff to be loyal to them. Therefore, if you change employers, you must alert your new employer to any cases with which you were involved while working for your former firm. Not to do so means running the risk of creating a *conflict of interest* for the firm.

As you read through the materials in this book, watch for potential ethical issues posed in the readings or chapter questions.

increases to four years to take the second-tier exam. Paralegals who successfully complete NFPA's certification program are authorized to use a "Registered Paralegal (R.P.)" designation.

Both the CLA exam and PACE are designed to be national exams. They test for general legal knowledge that is not state specific. NALA affiliates in California, Florida, and Louisiana have developed their own state-specific tests to complement the CLA exam. Also, the Legal Assistant Division of the State Bar of Texas administers exams on Texas law in the specialty areas of business litigation, family law, and personal injury litigation.

These certification programs are all voluntary in that certification is not a legal requirement for working in the paralegal field. However, in some regions of the country employers are more likely to employ someone who is certified than someone who is not.

To this point, our discussion has concerned certification. It is important to distinguish between being certified and being certificated. A person is **certificated** when that person receives a document verifying that he or she has successfully completed some educational program, thereby receiving a certificate of some type. In the paralegal field the term *certificated* is usually used to identify someone who has successfully completed a formal paralegal program offered by an accredited educational institution. Thus a person who has graduated from a paralegal certificate program that offers a certificate of completion, whether instead of or in addition to awarding a degree, can appropriately be called a "certificated legal assistant" or "certificated paralegal" but should not be called a "Certified Legal Assistant" or "Certified Paralegal" unless he or she has successfully completed NALA's certification requirements.

Certificated
The status of having received a certificate documenting that the person has successfully completed an educational program.

3. Licensing: Paralegals Who Work under the Supervision of an Attorney

Licensing refers to the process by which governmental agencies establish standards (or adopt those of other groups) and then prohibit those who have not met these standards from working in that occupational field. Thus a person who has not been admitted to the bar is prohibited from practicing law because he or she is not a licensed attorney. Based on the prevailing definitions of what constitutes the unauthorized practice of law, paralegals can perform a variety of legal tasks without a license to practice law as long as they work under the supervision of a licensed attorney. Some have argued, however, that a separate system of licensing should be established for paralegals in the same way that nurses are licensed separately from doctors.

Although the California statute discussed above on page 15 regulates who can use the title of paralegal, it does not qualify as a licensing statute. First, there is no requirement that those wishing to use the title paralegal register with the state. Second, although people who do not meet the established criteria cannot call themselves paralegals, it appears that the statute does not prohibit attorneys from employing anyone they choose to perform paralegal type work so long as that person does not claim to be a paralegal. Finally, there is no governing body established to review the credentials of those using the title paralegal or to investigate and punish violators.

When analyzing how the licensing of paralegals might work, one must consider what unit of governmental should be responsible for administering the licensing process. One possibility is that the state supreme courts could handle it. A second approach would involve the creation of an independent licensing agency especially for this purpose. Finally, the responsibility could be delegated to an existing agency that already handles other types of licensing. Another issue involves the extent to which standards should differ from state to state and whether states might grant reciprocity to paralegals licensed in other states.

Over the past twenty-five years, various proposals for licensing paralegals who work under the supervision of attorneys have been introduced in several state legislatures and presented to some state Supreme Courts. However, as of the time this book went to press, none has yet been formally adopted.

4. Licensing: Legal Technicians and Paralegals Who Do Not Work under the Supervision of an Attorney

Although some points overlap, the discussion of the licensing of paralegals takes on a new twist when you consider the licensing of nonlawyers who do not work under the supervision of a licensed attorney. The ABA's official definition states that a paralegal is someone who performs work "for which a lawyer is responsible." Even though freelance paralegals are independent contractors rather than employees of law firms or corporations, they are still expected to operate under the supervision of a licensed attorney. On the other hand, legal technicians, lay advocates, legal scriveners, and form preparers establish direct relationships with their clients and operate independently of any supervision by attorneys.

Legislation regarding some type of limited licensure for this group has been proposed in several states. For example, the Washington Supreme Court has adopted a rule that authorizes nonlawyers, known in that state as limited practice officers, to select and prepare certain legal documents incident to closing real and personal property transactions.[12] In California, as noted above, legislation was introduced to allow for the registration of legal document assistants. However, they are not allowed to provide direct legal services to the public and must basically limit their role to that of the scrivener discussed above. In Arizona, a hearing officer or a superior court judge is authorized to issue a cease and desist order for anyone engaging in the practice of document preparation without the required certification.[13]

Those who support these types of licensing arrangements often argue that they are needed to make legal services more accessible to the lower and middle classes. The National Resource Center for Consumers of Legal Services estimates that over 130 million people are denied legal access because the services of lawyers cost too much.[14]

Balanced against this desire to expand access to legal services is the need to protect the public from incompetent assistance. While the types of tasks proposed for legal technicians may not require all the knowledge that we require of

---

[12] Rule 12, adopted January 1, 1983.

[13] Ariz. Code of Judicial Admin. § 7-208 H.1.c. (2006).

[14] Warner, Legal Technicians—Pro and Con: Pro—Affordable Access to Law: Legal Technicians Are Part of the Solution, 5 Paralegal Educator 1 (Mar. 1991).

licensed attorneys, the tasks still do require some degree of specialized knowledge and training. Because the public cannot judge whether a specific legal technician possesses this knowledge, it is argued that the state has the responsibility to protect the public from legal technicians who may be either incompetent or unethical.

In addition, many reject the very idea of nonlawyers giving direct legal advice to the public. They argue that only licensed attorneys should be allowed to perform such functions and reject any type of limited licensing that would require less than what is currently required of attorneys. Rather than creating a new class of legal service providers, opponents argue that the unmet needs could be better served through expansion of **legal aid services** and more **pro bono work** from private attorneys.

Even those who accept the idea of licensing legal technicians still disagree regarding the nature of the licensing standards. For example, is a formal educational requirement necessary, or would that needlessly screen out members of low-income and minority groups? Should a bachelor's degree be required? How much specialized paralegal education is necessary, and what type of accreditation should be required of the program that provides that education? Should credit for on-the-job training be accepted, and if so, what kind of reasonable standards can be used to assess the quality of that training?

5. Indirect Regulation through Approval of Billing for Paralegal Time

In *Missouri v. Jenkins*,[15] the Supreme Court determined that attorneys could bill clients directly for work done by their paralegals. This is something that they cannot do for work done by secretaries and other clerical personnel. When a law firm bills its client for either paralegal time or attorney time, the firm and client negotiate the rate the client is willing to pay. However, in some cases statutes allow courts to award attorney's fees to the prevailing party. In those situations, the losing party may appeal those charges if he or she thinks the fees are unreasonable. In making that determination, a judge will determine what the reasonable charges should be, based upon the rate charged as well as whether the work done was of a substantive legal nature (as opposed to clerical work). If the work was done by a paralegal, the court will also inquire as to the paralegal's education and experience to ensure that the paralegal was qualified to handle such work. This is a fairly new area of the law. Therefore, the limitations on what constitutes substantive legal work and what qualifies someone to do that work are still in the formative stages. In the near future, we can expect to see more court decisions that will clarify what constitutes paralegal work and what types of qualifications a person has to have to do that work.

6. Conclusion

As of the year 2006, none of the fifty states had chosen to license paralegals or legal technicians. Before states begin to license nonlawyers, they must decide what types of educational standards and ethical obligations they will require paralegals to meet. In the meantime NALA operates a formal certification program through

---

[15] 491 U.S. 274 (1990).

its examination process. To take NALA's exam, the candidate must have either graduated from a sixty-credit paralegal program or attained significant work experience. NFPA administers PACE, an advanced proficiency exam. To qualify to take the PACE, the candidate must have a bachelor's degree and work experience.

DISCUSSION QUESTIONS

8. What are the strongest arguments for and against developing a certification or licensure system for paralegals? The weakest arguments?

9. Would you like to see either a certification or a licensure system developed for paralegals who work under the supervision of an attorney? Why?

E. WHAT PARALEGALS DO

Earlier in this chapter we said that when working under the supervision of an attorney, paralegals could do just about anything related to the practice of law except give legal advice to clients and represent clients in most types of judicial proceedings. In a landmark U.S. Supreme Court case dealing with the awarding of fees for paralegal work, Justice William Brennan noted that

> paralegals are capable of carrying out many tasks, under the supervision of an attorney, that might otherwise be performed by a lawyer and billed at a higher rate. Such work might include, for example, factual investigation, including locating and interviewing witnesses; assistance with depositions, interrogatories, and document production; compilation of statistical and financial data; checking legal citations and drafting correspondence. Much of this work lies in a gray area of tasks that might appropriately be performed either by an attorney or a paralegal.[16]

The tasks that paralegals perform generally fall within one of the following categories: communications with clients, research, drafting, and case management.

Ethics Alert

When talking with clients, keep in mind that everything that is said must be kept confidential. Also there may be times when you are alone with a client and the client will ask you for legal advice.

Remember that only the attorney can give that advice. For you to do so would be the unauthorized practice of law.

---

[16] Id. at 288 n.10 (1989).

1. Communications with Clients

Just as a nurse often serves as a vital link between the patient and a busy doctor, so, too, a paralegal can serve as a link between the attorney and the client. It is considered unethical for paralegals to be involved in the solicitation of clients, but once the attorney has established the attorney-client relationship, paralegals can and do play a very important role in maintaining effective communications between the attorney and the client.

Whereas many attorneys are notorious for being too busy to return phone calls to their clients, paralegals are usually far more accessible. If they are properly prepared, paralegals can relay important information about the case from the client to the attorney and vice versa. Due to their specialized training, paralegals can help explain legal procedures to the client, and they can communicate effectively with other attorneys and court officials.

2. Research

Almost all legal matters involve some sort of research. This research may involve probing into the facts or finding applicable law.

While the client will supply many of the important facts in the case, a lawyer can never rely solely on the client's perception of those facts. Invariably clients will overlook some facts, while allowing their personal prejudices and self-interest to color their perception of other facts. The paralegal can play an important role in interviewing both the client and other witnesses and then accurately recording the results of those interviews. The paralegal can also locate, analyze, and report on the existence of evidence that may be relevant to the case.

As you study more about the law, you will soon learn just how ambiguous it can be and how rapidly it changes. No lawyer, no matter how bright, can know everything there is to know about the law. That is one reason there is such a tendency for lawyers to specialize in specific areas of the law. But even if you knew everything there was to know about a very esoteric area of the law a month ago, there may have been developments in that area since the last time you studied it. Every year Congress and the state legislatures enact thousands of new laws, federal and state administrative agencies pass regulations, and federal and state judges hand down case decisions.

Therefore, attorneys and paralegals must constantly review and update their knowledge of the law. Although it is ultimately up to the attorney to judge the meaning of the law, a properly trained paralegal can locate new statutes, regulations, and court decisions that are relevant to the case at hand and provide summaries of the important changes. The techniques for finding the law and analyzing it will be presented in Chapters 12 through 15.

PRACTICE TIP

Sometimes supervising attorneys do not fully understand the type of education you are receiving. Therefore you may need to let your supervisor know the full range of responsibilities you are capable of handling.

3. Drafting

The practice of law involves voluminous exchanges of written documents. Contracts, wills, and other agreements are prepared, signed, and filed. Letters of inquiry and demands for various actions are sent. Lawsuits involve the filing of complaints, answers, motions, interrogatories, and a host of other documents. Probate actions involve the filing of numerous reports to inform the court of the distribution of the deceased's assets and the payment of appropriate taxes. In short, lawyers are responsible for the felling of a lot of trees.

Most paralegals are given responsibility for preparing drafts of legal documents for the lawyer to review. They may also be involved in drafting internal memoranda reporting the results of their legal or factual research.

4. Case Management

Paralegals play an important role in helping with the flow of paperwork involved in the preparation for a trial, a real estate closing, the probating of an estate, and so on. Even though many law offices now use computerized software packages to assist in this process, paralegals are needed to ensure that the correct data and proper instructions are being entered. They also assist in assembling the pleadings, motions, exhibits, and other documents that must be presented in court.

F. WHERE PARALEGALS WORK AND LAW OFFICE PERSONNEL

The practice of law is carried out through a variety of organizational structures and involves a variety of support personnel. Paralegals are employed in small, one-attorney law offices and in multicity mega-firms. You will also find them employed by large industrial and service corporations, governmental agencies, and nonprofit legal services organizations.

Increasingly we are also seeing paralegal graduates move into nontraditional areas of employment, becoming investigators, claims representatives, and office managers. While these positions may not carry the title of paralegal, they require similar skills and aptitudes: an ability to communicate effectively, both orally and in writing; analytical reasoning skill; top-notch research capabilities; and a sense of professionalism.

1. The Law Office Environment

Approximately 70 percent of all paralegals work in private law firms.[17] In this section we will first explore the various types of private practice arrangements. Then we will look at the people, in addition to attorneys and paralegals, who make up the law office team. Finally, we will examine the purpose of a law office procedures manual and the common practice of legal specialization.

---

[17] U.S. Bureau of Labor Statistics, Occupational Outlook Handbook (2006-2007 ed.).

a. Types of Private Practice Arrangements

Attorneys working in a private practice arrangement are self-employed or employed by other attorneys rather than by a financial institution, an insurance company, a manufacturing corporation, a trade association, or a governmental agency. There are five main types of private practice: partnerships, limited liability partnerships, professional corporations, sole proprietorships, and office-sharing arrangements.

(1) Traditional partnership

In a **partnership** arrangement attorneys work cooperatively on cases that are taken by the firm. Traditionally, lawyers who work in a partnership are designated as either associates or partners. Partners receive a share of the firm's profits rather than a set salary. The percentage of the profits received and the extent to which partners participate in the decision making for the firm depend on a variety of factors, including the amount of business they bring into the firm, the amount of fees generated by the cases they work on, the contribution they make to the management of the firm, and their longevity with the firm.

Partnership
A business run by two or more persons as co-owners.

In small partnerships most decisions are made by a "committee of the whole" comprised of the partners, who meet and discuss the matter together. As firms grow larger, however, partners are usually assigned to specialized committees in areas like fee setting and finance, recruitment of associates, lay personnel, office equipment and space utilization, and the library. The managing partner takes responsibility for seeing that the policies decided on are properly implemented.

The associate category is used for young attorneys being trained and evaluated. Associates are employees of the firm and receive a set salary, along with bonuses, for their efforts. Until very recently the policy was that after approximately five to eight years an associate either was offered a partnership or was expected to leave the firm. Many firms are starting to modify this "up or out" policy because they no longer see that policy as benefiting the attorneys, the firm, or the clients. As an alternative, they are developing a middle-level attorney tier. Such a middle tier may consist of permanent salaried attorney positions. In other firms the middle tier may simply be a way to give attorneys more time to prove themselves worthy of partnership status. Firms are using various names for the persons staffing this middle tier, including nonequity partner, of counsel, and senior attorney—titles that in the past had been reserved for older, semi-retired partners. You will still frequently see the term *of counsel* used to designate the status of a semi-retired former partner or an attorney who is affiliated with the firm on only a part-time basis.

A decided disadvantage of the partnership form is that each partner is responsible for the acts of all the other partners. For example, if one partner is sued for malpractice, every partner's personal assets are at risk. Until recently the only way to gain limited personal liability was to form a professional corporation.

(2) Professional corporation (PC)

Professional corporation (PC)
A professional entity in which the stockholders share in the organization's profits but have their liabilities limited to the amount of their investment.

Most **professional corporations** operate much as partnerships do. The law firm forms a corporation rather than a partnership in order to limit the attorneys' individual financial liability. The corporation pays salaries to all the attorneys who work for it but pays dividends only to the attorneys who are shareholders in the corporation. Attorneys who are designated as directors have a voice in controlling the corporation, and the officers are responsible for managing it. Firms organized as professional corporations usually will have the letters *PC* listed after the firm name.

(3) Limited liability partnership (LLP)

Limited liability partnership (LLP)
A professional entity in which the owners share in the organization's profits but are not liable for the malpractice of their partners.

In the early 1990s legislatures in several states created a new business form: the **limited liability partnership**. The purpose of this form is to give small businesses the best of the partnership and corporate forms without the disadvantages of either. Specifically, a limited liability partnership allows the law firm to function as a partnership but without the partners assuming liability for each other's actions. If a law firm chooses to become a limited liability partnership, the attorneys/partners will not be held individually liable if another attorney/partner makes a mistake. However, attorneys remain liable for their own malpractice and for the actions of anyone under their supervision. Another advantage to the LLP form is that a limited liability partnership is easier to form and maintain than a corporation. Firms organized as limited liability partnerships will usually have the letters *LLP* listed after the firm name.

(4) Sole proprietorship

Several lawyers share in the profits of a partnership or corporation, but in a **sole proprietorship** one lawyer owns all the assets of the business and receives all the profits (or absorbs the losses). This form of practice usually involves a single lawyer assisted by paralegals and clerical staff. However, it also can consist of an arrangement in which the sole practitioner employs other attorneys on a regular salaried basis. Those attorneys are strictly employees, however, and do not have any rights to share in the firm's profits or participate in the management of the firm.

(5) Office-sharing arrangements

Some lawyers develop various office-sharing arrangements that may appear to outsiders to be partnerships or professional corporations but that are technically still sole proprietorships. Typically, two or more attorneys share office space, a telephone system, and a receptionist. Sometimes they share a common secretarial pool and paralegals. Each attorney is responsible for paying his or her share of these common expenses, but the fees earned by each attorney are not pooled or shared.

Another variation of office sharing among sole practitioners occurs when one attorney gives another attorney (usually a young attorney trying to start his or her own practice) office space, library use, and sometimes secretarial help in return for help on some cases. The attorney receiving these office benefits is expected occasionally to perform legal research, answer some court calls, appear at real estate closings, and otherwise cover for the first attorney when he or she has schedule conflicts or takes time off.

b. Law Office Personnel

In a law office setting, in addition to attorneys and paralegals, you are likely to find other support personnel, such as law clerks, investigators, librarians, secretaries, document clerks, file clerks, bookkeepers, and business managers. While we will be discussing these positions in the context of the law office environment, many may also be found in the legal departments of businesses or governmental agencies, to be discussed below.

(1) Law clerks, investigators, and librarians

Law clerks, investigators, and librarians are specialized positions. Although their formal training differs from that of a paralegal, they perform tasks that frequently overlap work done by paralegals.

A **law clerk** usually is a law school student who works for the firm part-time during the school year or full-time during the summer but may be a recent law school graduate who has not yet passed the bar exam. Typically, most of the clerk's time is spent doing legal research. Investigators are often former law enforcement officers who locate and interview witnesses, take photographs of accident scenes, and gather documentary evidence. Librarians are responsible for updating and maintaining the firm's law library. In large firms the librarian may have a degree in library science and sometimes joint library and J.D. degrees. In smaller firms the library may be one of several other responsibilities assigned to either a paralegal or a secretary.

(2) Clerical support

No law office can function efficiently without a skilled clerical staff. In addition to typing correspondence and legal documents, the clerical personnel answer the telephone, greet visitors, set up appointments, distribute and post mail, find and file internal office records, file documents in the courthouse, and process billing records.

In smaller offices one or two legal secretaries will perform all of the above functions. In larger offices the clerical staff will be more hierarchical and have specialized jobs, such as receptionist, file clerk, legal stenographer, and bookkeeper, as well as legal secretary.

Some experienced legal secretaries perform some paralegal duties. The key distinction between secretarial and paralegal duties is that the secretarial function involves taking dictation from, or transcribing material produced by, lawyers and paralegals, whereas the paralegal function involves actually composing part of the content of the letters, memoranda, and legal documents being produced.

(3) Managers and administrators

The titles and job descriptions of administrative positions differ widely from one law office to another. In some cases there is a professional legal administrator whose responsibilities may extend to assigning legal work among the firm's attorneys. More commonly, the administrator supervises only the business aspects of the firm. These duties typically include hiring and training the support staff, maintaining personnel records, procuring and maintaining office equipment, overseeing billing operations and bank accounts, and preparing budgets and financial statements.

Administrative positions also exist within departments or units of larger law offices. Thus there may be an office manager in charge of the secretarial pool or word processing unit, a business manager in charge of the bookkeeping department, or a paralegal manager who supervises other paralegals.

c. Office Procedures Manual

The work of these various law office personnel often overlaps, and the organizational structure of the law office can be very confusing to a new employee. One source of assistance may be the office procedures manual. Most large offices maintain a loose-leaf manual containing written copies of their basic policies and procedures. Some more technologically advanced offices may have this policy and procedures manual "on line." This manual usually explains the personnel structure found within the firm, as well as policies on such things as holidays, sick leave, vacation time, and breaks. It may also describe such diverse activities as how the filing system operates, what kinds of records must be kept, and how supplies are obtained. Some manuals include a glossary of acceptable abbreviations and checklists for handling certain types of matters.

d. Areas of Specialization

In addition to practicing in a variety of different legal settings, attorneys also often differentiate themselves by area of specialization. Although law schools prepare generalists and bar exams test all major areas of the law, most lawyers specialize in a few selected and generally related fields. Some of the most common specialties include criminal law, personal injury work, real estate law, estate planning and probate, corporate law, employment law, and family law. Attorneys doing personal injury work usually segment themselves into the plaintiff's bar and the defense bar. Within an area like family law, attorneys may further specialize in an area like adoptions.

2. Other Forms of Practice

Although most paralegals work in a private practice setting, the fastest growing segment of the paralegal market involves working for corporate legal departments, insurance companies, banks, and governmental agencies.[18] These types of positions usually provide more predictable hours and compensation, greater security, and relief from the pressure to generate new clients for the firm.

a. Legal Department of a Business

All businesses need legal advice from time to time, legal assistance in filing various forms with governmental agencies, or legal representation when they are involved in litigation. They can obtain this legal assistance by either contracting for the services of a law firm or hiring lawyers as their own employees. Depending on the nature and size of the business, there are advantages and disadvantages to each approach, but because internal legal departments frequently offer greater economy, more responsive service, and greater integration with management, most large corporations hire lawyers as regular salaried employees.

---

[18] Id.

The top legal position in most companies is that of general counsel, and the position is usually placed at the vice-presidential level. This office has responsibility for advising corporate officials on how to minimize legal risks and how to respond to legal difficulties. The general counsel's office monitors proposed regulations and legislation that might affect the company's operations and then organizes appropriate lobbying efforts supporting or opposing the proposed changes.

In centralized legal departments all staff attorneys report to the general counsel and usually are located in the corporate headquarters building. In decentralized systems staff lawyers are organized into smaller units and located in operating divisions and regional offices. They may report to the vice-president of finance or the vice-president for research and development rather than the general counsel.

b. Legal Departments in Governmental Agencies

Governmental agencies—from a town manager's office to the Federal Trade Commission—also need legal assistance. If their needs are very limited, they usually retain a private law firm on a limited basis, but if their workload justifies it, they also hire lawyers as full-time employees just as businesses do. These in-house law firms closely parallel those of the private sector. They advise agency officials on the requirements of the law, keep them informed regarding proposed legislation and regulations that might affect the agency, and manage any litigation involving the agency as a party. Agency lawyers and paralegals frequently enjoy civil service protections.

In some cases an entire governmental agency is formed for the specific purpose of providing legal services. The federal Justice Department and a local district attorney's or public defender's office provide examples of agencies designed solely for such a purpose. These types of agencies also employ attorneys on a salaried basis, but they function very much like private law offices.

PARALEGAL PROFILE

MARYANN K. BRUNTON
COMPLIANCE OFFICER
MASSACHUSETTS COMMISSION AGAINST DISCRIMINATION

The MCAD is an administrative agency that investigates and prosecutes complaints of discrimination by people who charge they have been discriminated against based on their race, color, religion, national origin, ancestry, sex, sexual orientation, age, or disability. The commission hears complaints in the areas of employment, housing, places of public accommodation, education, credit, services, and mortgage lending. My job is to investigate these complaints and to enforce the state and federal laws and regulations regarding unlawful discrimination.

Once a complaint is filed with the commission, an investigation is initiated. The investigation entails written submissions filed by the parties regarding their respective positions. As part of the investigative process, I draft interrogatories and requests for production of docu-

ments, hold investigative conferences whereby the parties present their legal arguments, conduct witness interviews, conduct on-site visits, and draft affidavits.

The education I received as a paralegal student has equipped me with the knowledge and training I use every day to carry out my responsibilities as a compliance officer. Although the job is at times difficult, it is also rewarding. I have the opportunity to investigate and obtain evidence when individuals have been subjected to egregious harassment and discrimination. The education I received as a paralegal student has enabled me to pursue a career where I can help to correct some of society's injustices.

c. Other Variations

Legal clinic
Usually organized as either a partnership or a professional corporation, law clinics provide low-cost legal services on routine matters by stressing low overhead and high volume.

In addition to the forms of practice discussed above, attorneys may be employed in the legal departments of private nonbusiness organizations, such as labor unions, trade associations, consumer groups, and charities. Although the parent organization may have varying goals, the function and operation of the legal department parallel those of a business corporation or a governmental agency.

The terms *legal clinic* and *legal services office* are frequently used incorrectly and interchangeably. **Legal clinics** provide low-cost legal services on routine matters by stressing low overhead and high volume. They frequently operate out of store-front offices and make extensive use of paralegals. The attorneys who operate the clinic, however, are usually organized as either a partnership or a professional corporation. **Legal services offices** usually are legal aid services designed to help poor people and are affiliated with the federal government's **Legal Services Corporation**. The attorneys who work in such offices are salaried employees of a not-for-profit corporation that receives both public funds and private donations to provide free legal services to the poor. They hold positions similar to attorneys working for a public defender's office, except that they handle civil rather than criminal cases. Such offices frequently rely heavily on the assistance of paralegals, as much of the work of a legal services office involves representation before administrative agencies, an area where paralegals are usually allowed to practice without running afoul of the unauthorized practice of law statutes.

Legal services offices
Affiliated with the federal government's **Legal Services Corporation**, these offices serve those who would otherwise be unable to afford legal assistance.

DISCUSSION QUESTIONS

10. From an attorney's or a paralegal's perspective, what are the advantages and disadvantages of the various forms of practice? How do you think their perspectives might differ?

11. Job titles and duties are not always well defined in many law offices. Discuss the extent to which the work of various support personnel frequently overlaps that of attorneys, as well as that of those in other positions within the office.

SUMMARY

In this chapter we have discussed the ambiguities inherent in the word *paralegal*. Because formal education for paralegals began only in the 1960s, we have yet to see a well-defined understanding of what the professional role of paralegals should be. In fact, in addition to

traditional paralegals, we are now seeing other nonlawyer legal providers, such as freelance paralegals and legal technicians. In an attempt to establish some standards for nonlawyers, attorney and paralegal associations are working to develop educational and testing standards. These efforts include the ABA paralegal program approval process, the NALA certification program, the NFPA advanced proficiency exam, and AAfPE's core competencies. Various state legislatures are also investigating the possibility of registration or licensure requirements.

The most common legal work environments are private practice arrangements, such as partnerships, limited liability partnerships, corporations, sole proprietorships, and office-sharing arrangements. Lawyers and paralegals can also be found in the legal departments of businesses and governmental agencies. In addition to attorneys and paralegals, a number of other personnel, such as law clerks, investigators, librarians, and clerical support, may serve as part of the legal team.

NETNOTE

As you may have noticed by reading the marginal definitions, all of the major associations mentioned in this chapter have web sites. Take a few minutes to visit each.

American Association for Paralegal Education (AAfPE):

www.aafpe.org

American Bar Association (ABA):

www.abanet.org

National Federation of Paralegal Associations (NFPA):

www.paralegals.org

National Association of Legal Assistants (NALA):

www.nala.org

International Paralegal Management Association (IPMA):

www.paralegalmanagement.org

‖‖‖ REVIEW QUESTIONS

Pages 11 through 18

1. What are the names of the two major paralegal associations?
2. How do traditional paralegals differ from freelance paralegals?
3. How do freelance paralegals differ from legal technicians?
4. True or false:
    a. *Paralegal* and *legal assistant* are usually seen as synonymous terms.
    b. The term *independent paralegal* can sometimes refer to freelance paralegals and sometimes to legal technicians.

Pages 18 through 20

5. What are the requirements for becoming an attorney?
6. What are the requirements for becoming a paralegal?
7. When did formal paralegal education begin?
8. What role does the ABA play in paralegal education?

Pages 20 through 28

9. What is involved in the process of registration?
10. What are the major differences between certification and licensure?
11. Who has the right to use the title Certified Legal Assistant?
12. What are the three ethical issues of which paralegals must be particularly aware?

Pages 28 through 36

13. What are the four basic tasks that most paralegals perform?
14. What are the differences among a partnership, a professional corporation, and a limited liability partnership? Between a sole proprietorship and an office-sharing arrangement? Describe the advantages and disadvantages of each arrangement.
15. For a paralegal or an attorney what are the major alternatives to working in a private law practice?

Chapter 3

Functions and Sources of Law

We hold these truths to be self-evident...
Declaration of Independence

INTRODUCTION

No modern society can exist without a strong legal system, and when a person has a problem or is trying to avoid a problem, that person frequently turns to lawyers and the legal system for help. In this chapter we explore the role of law in American society and the sources of that law. As we begin that discussion, let us first introduce you to a client, Diane Dobbs, who met with attorney Pat Harper of the law firm of Darrow and Bryan. She related the following story.

The Case of the Pregnant Waitress

Ms. Diane Dobbs had been employed by the Western Rib Eye Restaurant for the past three years. Throughout that time her work record had been exemplary. Customers often spoke to the manager to tell him how Diane's service and personality contributed to their especially enjoyable dining experience at the restaurant.

Six months ago Diane, who is not married, found out that she was pregnant. When she approached her manager, Ben, to discuss arrangements for a maternity leave, instead of the favorable reception she had expected, Ben reached over, patted her stomach, and said, "Well, I guess we can't have you working for us any longer." Ben then grabbed her by the arm and escorted

her out of the restaurant. Diane protested and asked to be allowed to collect her personal belongings from her locker, but the manager just laughed and said she was "history." When Diane began to cry, he softened his demeanor a little and said, "Look, we simply can't have a pregnant lady working here. It just wouldn't be good for business."

Although she has been actively looking, Diane has not yet been able to find suitable employment.

When a client presents a problem to an attorney, the attorney may feel confident that the legal system can provide a remedy, but that will not always be so. As we indicated in Chapter 1, not every problem can be resolved by the legal system. In order to better appreciate why this is so, we need to study the function of law, the history of our American legal system, and the sources of our laws. You also need to understand the sources of law in order to do legal research and analysis.

A. FUNCTIONS AND THEORIES OF LAW

The development and enforcement of the law are essential governmental functions in all developed societies. Although the laws themselves sometimes differ, they serve the same essential functions in all fifty states and at the federal level.

1. Definition of Law

Laws
Rules of conduct promulgated and enforced by the government.

It is our **laws**—rules of conduct promulgated and enforced by the government—that define the types of conduct that are either prohibited or required. For example, a criminal code usually prohibits the unauthorized taking of property that belongs to someone else. Tax laws require that certain types of individuals or corporations give part of their income to the government. The laws can apply to the behavior of individuals, businesses, and even governments themselves. Thus municipalities may be prohibited from dumping raw sewage into lakes and rivers and the police prohibited from conducting unreasonable searches and seizures.

To be considered laws, these rules of conduct must be promulgated and enforced by the appropriate governmental bodies. For example, only the U.S. Congress can make federal statutory law, and only a state's highest court can authoritatively interpret the meaning of that state's laws.

These rules of conduct also carry with them certain sanctions that can be imposed on those who fail to follow the rules. When individuals violate a section of the criminal law, they may be fined, sent to prison, or in some cases even suffer loss of life. Persons who are found liable under the civil law may be forced to pay various penalties or damage awards or to perform some action, such as carrying out the terms of a contract. Police who conduct illegal searches and seizures may be denied the right to use in court any evidence they find and may even be forced to pay damages to the injured parties. Even presidents can be cited for contempt of court if they fail to turn over subpoenaed materials.

2. Functions of Law

While there may be a great deal of debate over the wisdom and appropriateness of a particular law (as there is, for example, over a mandatory seat belt law), there is general agreement that laws themselves are necessary. As the Task Force on Law and Law Enforcement reported to the National Commission on the Causes and Prevention of Violence:

> Human welfare demands, at a minimum, sufficient order to insure that such basic needs as food production, shelter and child rearing be satisfied, not in a state of constant chaos and conflict, but on a peaceful, orderly basis with a reasonable level of day-to-day security. . . . When a society becomes highly complex, mobile, and pluralistic; the beneficiary, yet also the victim, of extremely rapid technological change; and when at the same time, and partly as a result of these factors, the influence of traditional stabilizing institutions such as family, church, and community wanes, then that society of necessity becomes increasingly dependent on highly structured, formalistic systems of law and government to maintain social order. . . . For better or worse, we are by necessity increasingly committed to our formal legal institutions as the paramount agency of social control.[1]

It has thus been increasingly left to the legal system to define and enforce the rules of society. Some of these rules, such as restrictions on abortions, pornography, and gambling, are heavily influenced by the religious and moral beliefs of various groups in the society, while others, such as traffic regulations, have no moral content at all. In either case they help to provide the type of order and predictability that are essential elements of our modern society.

DISCUSSION QUESTIONS

1. Do you agree with the statement "Laws are necessary"? Why or why not?

2. Do we have too many laws? If you think we do, which laws would you like to see eliminated?

3. Do we need additional laws in some areas? What types of laws would you like to see added?

4. One of the basic principles of a theory known as "natural law" is that people should not have to obey an unjust law. Do you agree? Should it be left to the individual or to a judge to determine when a law is unjust? If it is left to the judge, what criteria should the judge use?

B. SOURCES OF LAW

Most people can recall something from their high school civics class about the legislature making the law, the executive branch enforcing the law, and the courts interpreting the law. The truth is that the legislative, executive, and judicial branches are all involved in making the law.

---

[1] J. Campbell, J. Sahid & D. Strang, Law and Order Reconsidered: Report of the Task Force on Law and Law Enforcement to the National Commission on the Causes and Preventions of Violence 3, 5 (1970).

1. Constitutional Law

The United States was the first nation to adopt a written constitution, and it is that Constitution that provides the framework within which all our laws are made. The first major function of the federal Constitution is to establish an organizational structure that allocates governmental powers. On the national level, the Constitution divides governmental powers among the legislative, executive, and judicial branches. This is commonly referred to as the **separation of powers.**

Separation of powers
The division of governmental power among the legislative, executive, and judicial branches.

The separate branches of government share power and have the ability to limit the actions of the other branches. In the Federalist Papers, James Madison explained that this system of **checks and balances** is designed to guard against "a gradual concentration of the several powers in the same department." Under the Constitution, Congress has the power to make laws, but the President has the power to veto them. The executive branch is responsible for administering the law, but it cannot spend money to do so unless Congress provides for the appropriate funding in the budget.

The Constitution also divides governmental power between the national government and the states. This division of power between the national government and the states is referred to as **federalism.** Certain powers are explicitly granted to the federal government, while all others are reserved to the states and the people.

Federalism
A system of government in which the authority to govern is split between a single, nationwide central government and several regional governments that control specific geographical areas.

The second major function of the Constitution is to protect individual rights from governmental overreaching. Because our founding fathers perceived a lack of such protection in the Constitution, as soon as it was ratified, the first Congress began work on the first ten amendments, commonly known as the **Bill of Rights.** These ten amendments include protections for freedom of speech and press, freedom of religion, a privilege against self-incrimination, the right to an attorney and a trial by jury, and protections against unreasonable searches and seizures. Along with the Thirteenth, Fourteenth, and Fifteenth Amendments (added during the Civil War), these amendments serve to prevent state or federal government officials from interfering with our civil rights and liberties.

Bill of Rights
The first ten amendments to the U.S. Constitution.

The Constitution and its amendments constitute the "supreme law of the land." To be enforceable, all other laws must not conflict with the principles laid down in the Constitution. When there is a challenge to the constitutionality of a law, it is the courts that determine whether or not the law is valid. The process by which the courts make these types of judgments is referred to as **judicial review.**

Power of judicial review
A court's power to review statutes to decide if they conform to the federal or state constitution.

It could be argued that since the Constitution established three coequal branches, each branch should be free to interpret the Constitution as it sees fit. However, there are times in which there is disagreement among the three branches about the interpretation of the Constitution, and in those situations, someone has to have the final say.

In *Marbury v. Madison*[2] the U.S. Supreme Court claimed this power for itself. The Court held it was inherent in the nature of a court's work to have to resolve conflicting interpretations of the law before it can carry out its assigned task of applying the law. If a Court determines that a statute does not conform to the Constitution, then the statute is invalid and the court cannot enforce it.

---

[2] 5 U.S. (1 Cranch) 137 (1803).

Over the years, the U.S. Supreme Court has used this power of judicial review to invalidate a number of federal and state laws that it found to be in conflict with the U.S. Constitution. Some of the most controversial of the more recent applications of judicial review include decisions invalidating state laws involving racial segregation, abortions, and school prayer.

In addition to determining the constitutionality of statutes, the courts are often called upon to determine the meaning of the Constitution itself. The Constitution was written more than two hundred years ago and uses broad sweeping terminology such as "freedom of speech," "establishment of religion," "unreasonable searches and seizures," and "cruel and unusual punishment." It is often difficult to determine the meaning of such ambiguous phrases, especially when applied to a specific situation. Under the power of judicial review, the U.S. Supreme Court has the final say regarding the interpretation of those ambiguous constitutional provisions.

Each of the fifty states also has a written constitution that defines the organization and powers of its government. Most also include an equivalent of the federal Bill of Rights. In the past many attorneys tended to ignore their own state's constitutional provisions. Recently, however, there has been an increase in litigation based on state constitutional law. This is partly because many state constitutions provide for more protection of individual rights than does the federal Constitution. The highest state court is the final arbiter of what its state constitution means.

NETNOTE

You can read the full text of the Declaration of Independence, the Constitution, and the Bill of Rights at the National Archives web site: *www.archives.gov.*

The Declaration of Independence:

> *www.archives.gov/national_archives_experience/declaration.htm*

The Constitution:

> *www.archives.gov/national_archives_experience/constitution.html*

The Bill of Rights:

> *www.archives.gov/national_archives_experience/bill_of_rights.html*

You can also view the Constitution and the Bill of Rights at Findlaw:

> *http://caselaw.lp.findlaw.com/data/constitution/articles.html*
> (Note: The address does not start with www.)

> *http://caselaw.lp.findlaw.com/data/constitution/amendments.html*

2. Statutory Law

As explained above, federal and state constitutions delineate the general framework within which the government must operate. Although these documents do list some major substantive and procedural rights, they were not designed to contain the types of detailed laws and regulations we need to operate in today's complex society. Rather, the federal and state constitutions specifically delegate the power to make these laws to the legislative branches of government.

At the federal level, the legislative power rests with the U.S. Congress. At the state level, it is exercised by state legislatures and a variety of local bodies such as city councils and village boards. Congress and state legislatures enact **statutes,** while city councils and village boards enact **ordinances.**

These statutes and ordinances lay down general rules that govern future conduct. They are general in the sense that they apply to broad categories of people rather than to specific individuals. Furthermore, the requirements they impose generally cannot be applied to actions taken *before* the law went into effect.

The formulation of such future oriented rules is a difficult task, because legislatures cannot foresee all the possible circumstances that might arise. Statutes therefore often contain general prohibitions that are somewhat ambiguous and open to differing interpretations. Ambiguity in statutes can also result from sloppy draftsmanship or be intentionally inserted to avoid creating conflicts among the legislation's supporters.

An example of the ambiguity contained in statutes can be found in the following excerpt from Title VII of the 1964 Civil Rights Act. It states:

> It shall be an unlawful employment practice for an employer (1) to . . . discriminate against any individual . . . because of such individual's race, color, religion, sex, or national origin.[3]

Recall the situation of Diane Dobbs mentioned at the beginning of the chapter. Was the restaurant manager discriminating against Diane Dobbs because of her sex when he fired her for being pregnant? While the statute clearly states that employers cannot discriminate on the basis of sex, it is not clear what types of actions should be considered sex discrimination. After the enactment of Title VII some people argued that pregnancy discrimination should be considered a form of sex discrimination because only women can become pregnant. Others argued that it should not be considered sex discrimination because the differential treatment is based on the condition of being pregnant rather then on the employee's sex. Although only women can become pregnant, the employer was legitimately differentiating between two different types of women—those who were pregnant and those who were not—rather than discriminating between women and men.

As with ambiguities in constitutional provisions, when disagreements such as this arise over the meaning of a statute, a court must resolve the ambiguity. Thus in *Gilbert v. General Electric*,[4] the U.S. Supreme Court was called upon to determine if discrimination based on pregnancy was a form of sex discrimination

Statute
A law enacted by a state legislature or by Congress.

**P R A C T I C E
T I P**

In areas having to do with individual rights, sometimes a state constitution will give more protection than the U.S. Constitution.

---

[3] 42 U.S.C. § 2000e-2(a) (2006).
[4] 429 U.S. 125 (1976).

under Title VII. The Supreme Court ruled in *Gilbert* that Title VII allowed employers to discriminate based on pregnancy.

The Supreme Court's interpretation would have left Diane without a remedy under the statute. However, luckily for her, if the legislative branch disagrees with the interpretation a court gives to one of its statutes, Congress can always introduce new legislation that amends the original statute to make clear that a different result or interpretation was intended. If this new legislation passes, the court's interpretation is superseded by the new statute. In this instance, Congress reacted by amending the statute to include pregnancy discrimination with the definition of sex discrimination.[5] Thus, under the amended statute it was unlawful for Diane's employer to fire her based upon her pregnancy.

Note, however, the difference between interpreting a statute and making a determination that it is unconstitutional. Whereas the legislative branch can amend one of its statutes to override a judicial interpretation, the courts retain the final authority with respect to deciding whether it is constitutional.

3. Administrative Law

Administrative agencies create administrative law. **Administrative law** is similar to statutory law in that it lays down rules designed to regulate future conduct. However, these rules are usually drawn more narrowly and directed to a more specialized group. Often the legislative branch intentionally leaves it to the executive branch and to independent regulatory agencies to "fill in the details" of the law within a general structure set down by the legislature. Through the process of filling in these details the executive branch is actually making the law.

Administrative law
Rules and regulations created by administrative agencies.

Assume a taxpayer wins $50 in the lottery. Must he pay taxes on it? The Internal Revenue Code, a federal statute, provides that he must pay tax on income but only includes general categories of income. The Internal Revenue Service (IRS), a federal agency, has developed **regulations** that define in much more detail what the word *income* means. Without the IRS, Congress would be forced to make constant revisions in the federal tax laws and would be hard-pressed to see that they were enforced.

Regulation
A law promulgated by an administrative agency.

Other examples of federal agencies include the Occupational Safety and Health Administration (OSHA), which oversees the federal statute requiring safe working conditions, and the Environmental Protection Agency (EPA), which oversees the federal statute governing the environment.

Just as the courts are drawn into the lawmaking process when they must interpret constitutions and statutes, so, too, are they called on to be the final arbiters of the meaning of administrative regulations. If someone disagrees with the administrative interpretation of a statute, the dissatisfied party can go to court to challenge the agency's interpretation. The court must support the agency's interpretation unless the court determines that the regulation is outside the authorization Congress gave to the administrative agency or that the regulation is unconstitutional. To determine whether the agency has stepped out of the bounds created for it by Congress, the court will examine the **enabling act**, the

Enabling act
A statute establishing and setting out the powers of an administrative agency.

---

[5] Bennett Amendment, 42 U.S.C. § 2000e(k) (2006).

PRACTICE TIP
Your understanding of a statute may be incomplete without also checking for related regulations. For example, policies such as the right of the police to conduct breathalizer tests may be set by state statute. However, how those policies are to be implemented (e.g., how a breathalizer test is to be conducted) may be set by administrative regulation.

statute that created the agency. The court will also seek to determine the underlying legislative intent of the statute that the agency is attempting to interpret through its regulations.

Returning once again to the case of our pregnant waitress, attorney Pat Harper may also wish to consider suing Diane Dobbs's employer for sexual harassment. A sexual harassment case would be based on the same federal statute, Title VII, that we discussed above. The statute makes no specific reference to sexual harassment. However, the Equal Employment Opportunity Commission (EEOC), acting under authority given to it in the statute, has declared that acts of sexual harassment are a form of sex discrimination. One of its administrative regulations states:

> Unwelcome sexual advances, requests for sexual favors, and other verbal or physical conduct of a sexual nature constitute sexual harassment when (1) submission to such conduct is made either explicitly or implicitly a term or condition of an individual's employment, (2) submission to or rejection of such conduct by an individual is used as the basis for employment decisions affecting such individual, or (3) such conduct has the purpose or effect of unreasonably interfering with an individual's work performance or creating an intimidating, hostile, or offensive working environment.[6]

Note how much more specific the wording of the regulation is in comparison to the wording of the statute.

Recall that Diane Dobbs alleged that the manager patted her on the stomach as he was firing her for being pregnant. Do you think that is sufficient to support a claim of sexual harassment? Is there any language in the regulation that could support such a claim?

In addition to their power to promulgate regulations, and as part of their enforcement powers, most agencies have investigatory and adjudicative powers. For example, if Diane Dobbs wants to pursue her claim of sexual harassment, Title VII mandates that she first take her complaint to the EEOC or a comparable state agency. The agency will investigate her case and, if it deems it appropriate, will hold a hearing to determine the truth of her claims. If she or her employer is not satisfied with the results they obtain at the agency, they can then take the case to court. Ultimately, the court would be the final arbiter of whether Diane Dobbs's situation fits within the agency definition of sexual harassment.

Because administrative agencies combine legislative, executive, and judicial functions, they are sometimes referred to as the **fourth branch of government.**

---

[6] 29 C.F.R. § 1604.11 (2006).

4. Judicial Interpretation and the Common Law

As we have noted above, courts play a vital role in interpreting constitutions and the laws created by the legislatures and agencies. The courts also apply and interpret the **common law** when there is no statute, administrative regulation, or constitutional provision governing the case they are adjudicating.

Common law
Law created by the courts.

The common law consists of various legal principles that have evolved through the years from the analysis of specific court decisions. Ultimately, these principles can be traced back to early medieval England, though they have been modified through the years by various state courts. When a legal dispute involves a subject that is not adequately covered by the other types of law, the judge applies the principles of the common law. In other words, in the absence of pronouncements from the constitution or a legislative or administrative body, the judge looks to the earlier decisions of other judges in similar circumstances.

Indeed, courts existed in England long before there was a democratically elected legislature to enact legislation. The roots of the court's power to create law go back to the eleventh century and the Norman Conquest. Although reading about medieval history may seem irrelevant to your study of the modern American legal system, the principles followed by our American legal system originated in England in 1066. Until 1066 Anglo-Saxon kings ruled England. There was no central legislature or centralized court system. Disputes were decided locally based on local custom. In 1066 the king, Edward the Confessor, died without children. This left the succession to the throne to either his brother-in-law, Harold, a powerful English baron, or his French cousin, William, Duke of Normandy. Harold was elected king. Immediately William assembled an army of soldiers, knights, and horses.[7]

In the fall of 1066 William landed on the south coast of England with his soldiers and knights, mounted on horseback. The mounted Norman knights overwhelmed the English foot soldiers, defeating the English army. On Christmas Day, 1066, William, the Duke of Normandy, had himself crowned king of England.

England became a country where everyone who spoke English owned no land and was impoverished. The king and the upper classes spoke French and used French in the courts. As a result, one enduring reminder of the Norman Conquest was the infusion of French words, such as **acquit** and **voir dire,** into our legal vocabulary. In addition, Norman kings used Latin in their written documents, so many Latin words, such as **certiorari** and **actus reus,** were incorporated into our legal language.

The Norman Conquest left a much greater legacy, however, than the French and Latin words in our legal vocabulary. It created an entirely new method for resolving disputes. Before the Conquest most disputes were decided locally, and the "law" would vary from town to town. As part of unifying England, the English kings wanted to create a common law throughout the land.

---

[7] This is a good illustration of what occurs when there is no established governmental structure for settling disagreements. The disputants resort to violence.

Stare decisis
The doctrine stating that normally once a court has decided one way on a particular issue, it and other courts in the same jurisdiction will decide the same way on that issue in future cases given similar facts unless they can be convinced of the need for change.

Codification of the common law
The process of legislative enactment of areas of the law previously governed solely by the common law.

Derogation of the common law
Used to describe legislation that changes the common law.

Equity
Fairness; a court's power to do justice. Equity powers allow judges to take action when otherwise the law would limit their decisions to monetary awards. Equity powers include a judge's ability to issue an injunction and to order specific performance.

Injunction
A court order requiring a party to perform a specific act or to cease doing a specific act.

Specific performance
A requirement that a party fulfill his or her contractual obligations.

How was this uniformity created? Remember that there was no central legislature. The solution was for the king to appoint judges and establish a court system so that disputes could be settled in a uniform manner. Initially, the "courts" were simply individual judges appointed by the king to "ride a circuit" around the countryside, settling disputes in the name of the king. Over time the judges realized that rather than deciding each case as though it were the first of its kind, it would be more efficient to share the results of their prior decisions with each other so that similar cases could be decided similarly. The resulting court-made law became known as the common law.

Unless a good reason dictated otherwise, it became the policy to follow the rules laid down in prior decisions. This was how the doctrine of **stare decisis** developed. Once courts had determined the law in an area, other courts followed that rule unless a court thought there was a good reason to change it.

By about 1200 the main structure of the common law system was in place. A body of centrally appointed judges applied a common law throughout the country, and a tradition of following precedent had been established. The commencement of a series of Year Books, each collecting cases from the most important courts for that year, further solidified this development. In 1535 this system was replaced by reporters, collections of court opinions as "reported" by various authors. Finally, in 1865 this process culminated in the United States with the practice of publishing official law reports.

Meanwhile, the common law had come to America and had formed the basis for our legal system. There are areas of the law that are still totally governed by the common law, such as most matters dealing with torts. However, over the years more and more areas of the common law have been enacted into statutes; that process is known as the **codification of the common law**. When the common law has been changed through legislation, the statute is said to be in **derogation of the common law**.

Before abandoning our history lesson, there was one more development in the English court system that has had a great impact on our system, and that was the development of equity courts. The courts we have discussed up to now had the power to settle disputes by requiring one party to compensate the other with money damages. But there are times when money is not what the litigants want. Rather they would like the court to order the other party to do something, such as living up to contractual obligations, or to cease doing something, such as having loud parties in the wee hours of the morning. In response to this need, the English created the **equity** courts.

Judges in the equity courts used their powers to "do justice." For example, equity powers allow judges to take preventive action when the law would otherwise limit their decisions to monetary awards after the damage has been done. Equity powers include a judge's ability to issue an **injunction** or to order **specific performance**. An injunction is a court order requiring someone to act or to refrain from acting. Specific performance requires that a party fulfill his or her contractual obligations. In the 1800s most states merged their law and equity courts. Therefore, today judges have the power to give either monetary awards or equitable relief or both, as they deem appropriate.

DISCUSSION QUESTIONS

5. Assume Congress enacted a statute making it a federal crime for "anyone" to kidnap children and take them across state lines. Assume further that the U.S. Supreme Court decided that the word *anyone* did not include a parent. If it wanted to do so, could Congress amend the statute to say that the word *anyone* does include parents? Why?

6. Assume Congress enacted a statute making it a federal crime to have an abortion. Assume further that the U.S. Supreme Court declared the statute to be unconstitutional because it interfered with a woman's constitutional right to privacy. If it wanted to do so, could the executive branch prosecute women for violating the statute? In other words, does Congress or the Supreme Court have the final word on what is constitutional? Why?

7. For each of the following, which source of law—a constitution, a statute, an administrative regulation, or a court opinion—would be best able to handle the problem and why?

  a. A requirement that all motorcycle riders wear helmets.
  b. A rule making a bar owner liable for any injuries caused by a patron to whom the bar sold drinks.
  c. A rule that all semi-trailers traveling on interstate highways use concave mud flaps.
  d. A requirement that employers not discriminate on the basis of religion or sexual orientation.
  e. A requirement that no more than a certain percentage of a known pollutant be released by factory smokestacks.
  f. A question as to whether a person not wearing a seat belt should be able to recover for injuries that person sustained in an automobile accident that was not his fault.
  g. A law prohibiting government from interfering with an individual's right to freedom of speech.

SUMMARY

Our country was the first to adopt a written constitution, and it is our federal constitution that provides the framework within which all our laws are made. Similarly, states' constitutions provide the legal basis for their governments to act.

Even though traditionally we say that the legislature makes the law, the executive branch enforces the law, and the courts interpret the law, the truth is that the legislative, executive, and judicial branches, as well as administrative agencies, are all involved in making the law. Legislatures create law by enacting statutes, agencies create law by promulgating regulations, and appellate courts create law through their written opinions known as court decisions. In addition, the executive branch occasionally creates law through executive orders.

The example with which we began this chapter provides a good illustration of how statutory, regulatory, and court-made law work together. Congress enacted a statute that prohibited "sex discrimination." Because this phrase is so broad, the EEOC, an administrative agency, has issued regulations that more clearly define some types of sex discrimination, such as sexual harassment. Finally, even the most detailed regulation

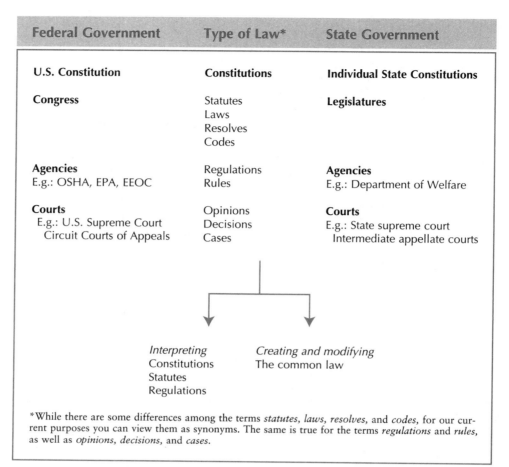

Federal Government	Type of Law*	State Government
U.S. Constitution	**Constitutions**	**Individual State Constitutions**
Congress	Statutes Laws Resolves Codes	**Legislatures**
Agencies E.g.: OSHA, EPA, EEOC	Regulations Rules	**Agencies** E.g.: Department of Welfare
Courts E.g.: U.S. Supreme Court Circuit Courts of Appeals	Opinions Decisions Cases	**Courts** E.g.: State supreme court Intermediate appellate courts

Interpreting
Constitutions
Statutes
Regulations

Creating and modifying
The common law

*While there are some differences among the terms *statutes, laws, resolves,* and *codes,* for our current purposes you can view them as synonyms. The same is true for the terms *regulations* and *rules,* as well as *opinions, decisions,* and *cases.*

Figure 3-1   Sources of Law

cannot cover every individual case. Therefore, the courts are constantly called on to interpret the meanings of both statutes and regulations.

Where no constitution, statute, or administrative regulation applies, the courts rely on the common law to resolve the problem. But it is in their role as interpreters of constitutional, statutory, and administrative provisions that courts have the greatest power: By interpreting the law, the courts end up creating the law. Figure 3-1, above, summarizes the major sources of law.

REVIEW QUESTIONS

Pages 39 through 43

1. What are the two primary functions of the U.S. Constitution?
2. What is the power of judicial review, and why is it so important to our legal system?
3. Read the excerpts from the U.S. Constitution and the Bill of Rights located in Appendix A. Then answer the following questions:

    a. Which article deals specifically with the legislature? With the executive? With the judiciary? (This may seem like trivia necessary only for Jeopardy contestants, but lawyers often refer to Article I, Article II, or Article III powers.)

    b. Which amendment states that the powers not specifically delegated to the federal government are reserved to the states?

    c. Make a list of the rights protected by the first ten amendments.

Pages 44 through 45

4. Why do constitutions and statutes frequently include ambiguous language?
5. How do courts become involved in the legislative process?
6. Who has the final say as to what a statute means, the legislature or the courts?
7. Who has the final say as to the constitutionality of a statute, the legislature or the courts?

Pages 45 through 46

8. How are statutes and administrative regulations similar? How do they differ?
9. Why are administrative agencies referred to as the fourth branch of government?

Pages 47 through 49

10. What impact did the Norman Conquest have on the American legal system?
11. What is the common law?
12. Why were equity courts created, and what special powers were they given?

Chapter 4

Classification of the Law

Logically, everything ought to come first.
Jean Jacques Rousseau

INTRODUCTION

In this chapter we will discuss the most common ways in which lawyers have traditionally categorized law. However, keep in mind that although it is necessary to categorize a client's legal problem in order to help the client, do not fall into the trap of seeing a client as only a set of legal problems that can be neatly sorted into predefined categories. Remember that there is a person behind every legal problem. Nonetheless, before attorneys can take legal action on behalf of that person, they must determine what the real cause of the problem is and what, if any, legal options are available to resolve the problem.

In the previous chapter, we explained how law is made not only by legislatures, but also by administrative agencies and courts. Based on its source, we classified law in terms of constitutional, statutory, administrative, or common law. You can classify law based on whether it involves

1. state, federal, or local law (every state as well as the federal government has its own laws);
2. civil and/or criminal law (**civil law** deals with harm against an individual—for example, a broken contract—whereas **criminal law** deals with harm against society as a whole—as when violence leads to someone's death); and

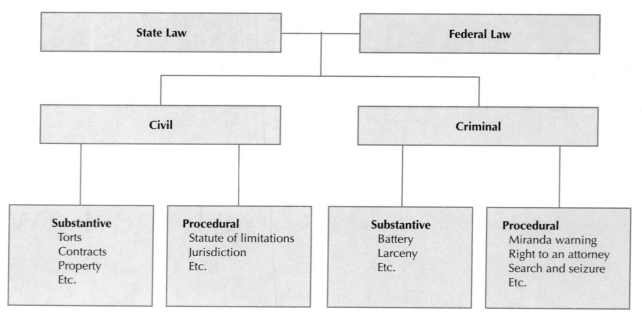

Figure 4-1 How Lawyers Classify the Law

3. substantive and/or procedural law (**substantive law** defines our legal rights and duties—for example, the duty to obey speed limits and the right of freedom of speech—whereas **procedural law** is comprised of the rules that govern how the legal system operates).

Knowledge of these classification schemes is a necessary part of organizing your legal research plan. For example, depending upon how an attorney categorizes a problem, that attorney may decide to start research in state instead of federal law or to look at statutes instead of court opinions. Often these classifications will be obvious to an experienced attorney or paralegal. There will be times, however, when the categorizations are not so obvious.

Recall the case of Diane Dobbs, the pregnant waitress introduced at the beginning of the last chapter. In analyzing Diane's story, an attorney would think in terms of the three categories we just listed. While it is not necessary to proceed in any particular order in applying the three categories listed above to Diane's situation, all three must be evaluated. First, do Diane's problems relate to state or federal law? Are both state and federal laws involved? Second, does her situation involve any criminal laws, or does only civil law apply? Third, in addition to examining the substantive law issues, what procedural issues might be involved? As we proceed through the chapter, we will discuss each of these classifications.

Note that these are not mutually exclusive categories. A client's situation may involve both federal and state laws, both civil and criminal issues, and procedural as well as substantive questions. Figure 4-1 illustrates how these different categories relate to each other. At this point do not be concerned about understanding all of the terms listed in the figure. As the chapter proceeds, we will discuss each term in more detail.

A. FEDERAL VERSUS STATE LAW

Each of the fifty states, along with the federal government, has its own legal system. Each determines how its court system will be organized and what laws it will enforce. Although the laws of one state are often similar to the laws of another, each state ultimately decides for itself what those laws will be. This is because, as we mentioned in the last chapter, the United States operates under a system of government known as **federalism.** In our federal system the power to make various types of laws is divided between the federal government in Washington, D.C., and the fifty state governments. A client's problem may involve state law or federal law or both state and federal law.

Federalism
A system of government in which the authority to govern is split between a single, nationwide central government and several regional governments that control specific geographical areas.

1. Federal Law

You will be in an area covered by federal law if the client's problem deals with any of the following:

1. a U.S. constitutional issue (such as freedom of speech or the rights of a criminal defendant);
2. a federal statute (such as the Internal Revenue Code); or
3. regulations of a federal agency (such as the IRS).

When a client's problem is covered by one of these three areas, you will hear attorneys referring to this as raising a federal issue or a federal question. As we will see later in the chapter on civil litigation, categorizing a legal problem in this way is very important as generally federal courts can only hear cases that either involve parties from different states or that raise a federal question.

When you hear people complaining about what they believe to be the excessive reach of the federal government, they are frequently referring to the second area of federal law, federal statutes. However, despite its growth in recent years, it is not true that eventually all areas of the law will be governed by federal law. The Constitution imposes important limits on the scope of Congress's law making power. Congress can enact legislation only if the Constitution has given Congress the power to legislate in that particular area. These delegated powers can be found in Article I, Section 8. In addition, several constitutional amendments, such as Section 5 of the Fourteenth Amendment, have provisions enabling Congress to pass legislation necessary to enforce that amendment.

For example, Congress could and does enact legislation regarding taxation because Article I, Section 8, provides that "[t]he Congress shall have Power To lay and collect Taxes, Duties, Imposts and Excises." On the other hand, Congress could not enact a national divorce law, as there is nothing in the Constitution to give Congress that power. Further, under the Tenth Amendment any power not specifically given to Congress by the Constitution is reserved to the people or to the states.

It is important to note, however, that after enumerating powers such as those to lay and collect taxes, establish post offices and post roads, raise armies, and declare war, Section 8 states that Congress has the power "to make all Laws which shall be necessary and proper for carrying into Execution" the specifically enumerated powers. The U.S. Supreme Court broadly interpreted this last clause

Doctrine of implied powers
Powers not stated in Constitution but that are necessary for Congress to carry out other, expressly granted powers.

in the 1819 case of *McCulloch v. Maryland*.[1] Even though the Constitution did not explicitly delegate to Congress the power to create banks, the Court ruled that Congress could create and operate a national bank as part of the exercise of its expressly delegated powers to collect taxes and to borrow money. This is known as the **"doctrine of implied powers."**

In addition, Congress has sweeping powers under Article I, Section 8. That section provides: "Congress shall have power to regulate commerce . . . among the several states." This has come to be known as the "interstate commerce clause." Originally, the courts interpreted "interstate commerce" to mean exactly that: the movement of goods across state lines. However, in *Gibbons v. Ogden*[2] the Supreme Court interpreted this clause as giving the federal government the authority not only to regulate products that actually travel in interstate commerce, but also to regulate anything that has an "effect upon" interstate commerce.

In the 1930s, Congress used this expansive reading of the interstate commerce clause as the basis for much of its "New Deal" economic legislation. This included the Unfair Labor Standards Act (controlling the hours and wages of employees who manufactured goods destined for interstate commerce) and the National Labor Relations Act (creating the National Labor Relations Board and authorizing it to enjoin unfair labor practices).

A major challenge to Congress's use of the commerce clause powers came in the 1960s, following Congress's passage of the 1964 Civil Rights Act. In Title II of the Civil Rights Act, Congress made it unlawful to discriminate in a place of public accommodation on the basis of race, color, religion, sex, or national origin. When this provision was challenged in *Heart of Atlanta Motel, Inc. v. United States*,[3] the Court held that the law was within the scope of the commerce clause because the existence of racially discriminatory practices made it more difficult for racial minorities to travel from one state to another and this had a negative impact on the free flow of interstate commerce. In a related case, *Katzenback v. McClung*,[4] the Court found that even a small, local, family-owned restaurant catering to local customers had enough of an impact on interstate commerce to justify Congress's actions in prohibiting discrimination.

From the 1960s through the 1990s, this expansive reading of the commerce clause allowed Congress to address a wide range of social problems through federal statutes. It was not until the 1995 case of *United States v. Lopez*[5] that the U.S. Supreme Court began striking down federal statutes on the basis that they had exceeded congressional power under the interstate commerce clause.

In *Lopez*, the Court reversed a conviction under a federal statute that made it a federal crime to possess a firearm in a school zone. The Court found that the interstate commerce clause did not give the federal government authority to regulate the possession of guns on public school grounds because Congress had failed to show a sufficient connection between the unlawful possession of guns near schools and an economic impact on interstate commerce. Five years later, in *United States v. Morrison*,[6] the Supreme Court struck down a federal

---

[1] 4 Wheat. 316.
[2] 9 Wheat. 1 (1824).
[3] 379 U.S. 241 (1964).
[4] 379 U.S. 294 (1964).
[5] 514 U.S. 549 (1995).
[6] 529 U.S. 598 (2000).

statute, the Violence Against Women Act of 1994, aimed at protecting women from acts of criminal violence, holding that Congress had exceeded its powers under the commerce clause. The Court held that Congress had overstepped its powers because gender-motivated crimes were not the kind of *economic* activity that Congress has the power to regulate.[7]

Many commentators thought the *Lopez* and *Morrison* decisions signaled the Court's return to a more conservative judicial philosophy that stressed the limitations of federal powers and the preservation of state's rights. But then in 2005, in *Gonzales v. Raich*,[8] the Court held that the commerce clause gave the federal government the power to prohibit the cultivation and use of marijuana, even when the marijuana was grown and used within a single state for medical purposes, pursuant to a physician's orders and authorized by state law. The Court reasoned that the marijuana used for local, medicinal purposes could find its way into the interstate market and therefore had an economic effect on interstate commerce.[9]

In addition to validating Congress's use of its commerce clause power to regulate the intrastate noncommercial use of marijuana, the Court in *Gonzales v. Raich* held that the California laws, providing for the medicinal use of marijuana, could not be used to protect California residents from federal prosecution. The Constitution's Supremacy Clause "unambiguously provides that if there is any conflict between federal and state law, federal law prevails."[10] In other words, there are some areas of law where not only does the federal government have the power to legislate, but it alone can do so. This occurs when uniformity across state line is necessary. In those areas the federal law is said to "preempt" state law.

This **doctrine of preemption** allows the federal government to prevent the states from passing conflicting laws and sometimes even to prohibit states from passing any laws on a particular subject. For example, it would create chaos if every state could individually regulate railroad safety. Instead, under the Federal Railroad Safety Act,[11] the federal government created uniform standards related to railroad safety, such as maximum train speed and train length. However, even in areas generally preempted by federal law, if there are areas left unregulated, the states may still enact "gap filler" legislation. In addition, if a state law would not conflict with federal law, nor unreasonably burden interstate commerce, it may co-exist with federal laws. For example, as we have seen, a federal statute prohibits employers from discriminating on the basis of race or sex if that employer employs fifteen or more employees. While no state may through its statutes allow such discrimination, they may create more stringent standards. For example, in Massachusetts no employer of six or more employees may so discriminate.

In summary, when you are faced with a situation in which you need to decide whether federal law, or state law, or both govern, keep these three possibilities in mind.

Preemption
The power of the federal government to prevent the states from passing conflicting laws, and sometimes even to prohibit states from passing any laws on a particular subject.

---

[7] Id. at 618.

[8] 545 U.S. 1 (2005).

[9] Id. at 2229.

[10] Id. at 2212.

[11] 49 U.S.C.A. § 20106 (2006).

- First, there are some areas in which only the states can legislate—areas reserved to the states—such as divorce. In those cases you could limit your research to state law.
- Second, there are some areas in which both the states and Congress can legislate—such as criminal behavior that crosses state lines. In those cases your research should cover both state and federal law.
- Third, there are a few areas in which only Congress can legislate—areas of total preemption—such as certain safely issues involving trains traveling across state lines. In those cases your research can be limited to federal law.

2. State Law

Whereas the federal government must trace all of its powers back to a specific constitutional authorization, the states are allowed to make any laws they deem appropriate for the health, welfare, safety, and morals of their citizens as long as those laws are not prohibited by the U.S. Constitution.[12] Typical examples of areas covered by state law are criminal behavior, contracts, torts, property, marriage, and family matters. While much of the law from one state to the next is quite similar, the states are free to create their own unique laws. Where one state may choose to legalize gambling, another may not; where one state may choose to allow no-fault divorces, another may not.

Some see this diversity as one of the great strengths of our political system. They argue that it encourages experimentation and innovation by allowing the residents of Georgia, for example, to establish rules of conduct that differ from those established by the residents of Nevada. Critics, on the other hand, point to the problems it creates for interstate business and travel—for example, forcing large corporations and other out-of-state parties to hire local attorneys and making it difficult for an attorney to move a practice from one state to another. They also point out that states are sometimes reluctant to impose needed regulations (in areas such as environmental protection and worker safety) for fear that the affected businesses will move to another state with fewer restrictions.

As we become an ever more interdependent nation, however, state laws are tending to become more and more uniform, especially in the area of commercial law. Businesses with dealings in more than one state do not like having to worry about a multiplicity of state laws. Therefore, most states have voluntarily moved to adopt uniform laws in areas such as commercial sales.

Finally, both federal and state laws cover some areas, such as employment discrimination. From our discussion above regarding preemption, you will recall that a state cannot pass laws that conflict with federal laws. However, if there is no conflict between state and federal law, a state is free to legislate in that area. For example, a Massachusetts statute states that an employer of six or more employees may not discriminate on the basis of race, color, religion, sex, or national origin. This is perfectly valid as it does not conflict with the federal statute, Title VII, that states an employer of fifteen or more

---

[12] The Tenth Amendment to the U.S. Constitution declares that "powers not delegated to the United States by the Constitution, nor prohibited by it to the States, are reserved to the States respectively, or to the people."

employees may not discriminate on the basis of race, color, religion, sex, or national origin.

DISCUSSION QUESTIONS

1. For each question determine whether you think the law involved is federal, state, or both.
   a. A person is liable for slander if that person intentionally says that someone is a thief when she knows it is not true.
   b. To be valid, a contract for the sale of real estate must be in writing.
   c. Trucks traveling on interstate highways must be equipped with concave mud flaps.
   d. No employer with ten or more employees may discriminate on the basis of race, color, religion, sex, or national origin.
   e. A manufacturer of inherently dangerous products will be liable for any defective product that causes injury.
2. Can you think of any areas of the law that are not now regulated on a federal level but should be? What are those areas, and why do you think the federal government should take on a more active role?
3. Can you think of any areas of the law that should be left solely to state and local governments? If so, what are they, and why do you think the federal government should not be involved?
4. In what areas of the law do you think there should be uniformity across all of the states? In what areas should there be diversity? Why?

B. CRIMINAL VERSUS CIVIL LAW

Another major classification within the law is the division between criminal law and civil law. Both provide mechanisms for addressing violations of the law, but they differ regarding the procedures you must use and the types of sanctions or remedies that are available. In this section we will first compare criminal and civil law. Next we will take a quick look at the major substantive areas of criminal and civil law. We cover substantive civil law in more depth in Chapters 7, 8, and 9 and criminal law in Chapter 10.

1. A Comparison of Criminal and Civil Law

Some of the major differences between criminal and civil law are listed in Figure 4-2 on page 60.

a. Type of Harm

Civil law is invoked when one individual harms another. When an individual violates a part of the **criminal law**, society considers itself the offended party and takes an active role in the sanctioning process. Thus if Peter Jones burglarizes Sam Smith's home, the criminal law views that act as an offense against society itself rather than simply as a matter between Smith and Jones.

Civil law
Law that deals with harm to an individual.

Criminal law
Law that deals with harm to society as a whole.

But what determines when an act such as burglarizing someone's home is a wrong against society as a whole? It is up to the legislative branch of government to decide when the consequences of certain acts are viewed as grave enough to classify the act as a crime against the state. Thus when the legislature perceives that a particular act, such as drunk driving, has that broader impact, it can criminalize such behavior.

b. Names of the Parties and the "Prosecutor" of the Claim

Plaintiff
A person who initiates a lawsuit.

The person who brings the civil suit (also known as a civil action or a civil lawsuit) is known as the **plaintiff,** and the person sued is called the **defendant.** For example, recall the situation involving the pregnant waitress presented at the beginning of Chapter 3. If Diane Dobbs were to sue the restaurant, she would be the plaintiff. Both the corporation that owns the Western Rib Eye Restaurant and the restaurant manager would probably be named as defendants. Although civil suits are usually between individuals, a governmental unit (federal, state, or local) can become a plaintiff in a civil suit. In a criminal case, the case is listed as *People v. Jones* or *State v. Jones*. Governmental attorneys prosecute the accused party (the defendant), and the victim is merely a witness.

Defendant
In a lawsuit the person who is sued; in a criminal case the person who is being charged with a crime.

c. Standard of Proof

Because of the serious consequences of violating criminal laws, the standard of proof is different from that used in civil cases. On the criminal side, the

Figure 4-2 A Comparison of Civil and Criminal Law

	Civil	Criminal
Type of harm	Private injury	Harm to society
Names of the parties	Plaintiff/defendant	State*/defendant
"Prosecutor" of the claim	Usually an individual; sometimes the government	Government
Standard of proof	Preponderance of the evidence	Beyond a reasonable doubt
Judgment	Liable/not liable	Guilty/not guilty
Sanctions/remedies	Damages/injunction	Imprisonment/fines/death
Source of law	Common law/statutes	Statutes

*The State may also be referred to as the Commonwealth or the People. Although the state is the named party, it is actually a government employee, the **prosecutor** (also known as the **district attorney**, **state's attorney**, or **attorney general**), who brings the lawsuit as the state's representative.

prosecution is required to prove its case **beyond a reasonable doubt.** In civil actions the plaintiff need only meet the **preponderance of the evidence** standard. Judges usually explain the beyond a reasonable doubt standard to jurors as the degree of doubt that causes a reasonable person to refrain from acting. The proof must be so conclusive and complete that all reasonable doubts regarding the facts are removed from the jurors' minds. A preponderance of the evidence, on the other hand, is usually understood to mean that the facts asserted are more likely to be true than not true. One study showed that judges equate "beyond a reasonable doubt" with a median probability of approximately 8.8 out of 10. Jurors averaged approximately 8.6 out of 10. The judges interpreted preponderance of the evidence as a median probability of 5.4 out of 10. For jurors the median was 7.1 out of 10.[13] These results indicate that although judges and jurors may disagree as to the precise meaning of the standards, they agree that the criminal law requires a greater degree of proof before its sanctions can be applied.

d. Judgment

The result of the court's actions in a civil suit is a finding of liability or no liability. Do not use the term *guilty* when referring to a civil defendant. In a criminal case we say that the defendant was found guilty or not guilty.

e. Sanctions/Remedies

The typical remedy in a civil case is either **damages,** where the defendant pays the plaintiff for the harm he or she has done, or an **injunction,** where the court orders the defendant to take some specific action or to cease acting in a specific way. For example, in Diane's situation she might ask to be paid for the time she has been out of work (damages) and request a court order requiring the restaurant to rehire her (an injunction).

While the focus of civil law is on redressing the losses of the plaintiff, in the criminal law the sanctions are designed to punish the offender and deter future offenders. If a court of law determines that a provision of the criminal law has been violated, it may impose two broad types of sanctions—loss of liberty and financial penalty. The loss of liberty can range from receiving unsupervised probation to spending a few days in the county jail to serving several years in a state penitentiary to receiving the death penalty. The fines assessed as part of the criminal process become the property of the state rather than the victim. Only occasionally will a negotiated settlement with a criminal defendant contain some provisions for restitution for the victim. Usually, if the victim wishes to receive money from the criminal defendant to compensate her for the harm done to her, she must hire a lawyer and initiate a civil suit.

Beyond a resonable doubt
The standard of proof used in criminal trials. The proof must be so conclusive and complete that all reasonable doubts regarding the facts are removed from the jurors' minds.

Preponderance of the evidence
The standard of proof used in civil trials. The proof must indicate that it is more likely than not the defendant committed the wrong.

Damages
Monetary compensation, including compensatory, punitive, and nominal damages.

---

[13] Simon & Mahan, Quantifying Burdens of Proofs, 5 Law & Socy. Rev. 319 (1971).

PRACTICE TIP

Even though we sometimes talk about civil versus criminal law, keep in mind that the same facts may give rise to both civil and criminal lawsuits. If a potential defendant in a civil case has been convicted at a criminal trial, that will make it easier for the plaintiff to win a civil case. However, even if the defendant was acquitted at the criminal trial, because of the different standards of proof and evidentiary requirements the plaintiff may still win in a civil case.

---

f. Sources of Law

A final difference relates to the sources of criminal and civil law. Criminal law is almost entirely statutory, while civil law is rooted in the common law (court-made law). Gradually, however, this distinction is being eroded as more and more areas of the civil law are becoming controlled by statutory law.

A single event can become the basis for actions in both the criminal and the civil courts. For example, the victim of a battery could sue the attacker for civil damages at the same time the state is prosecuting the attacker on a criminal charge. The driver of an automobile involved in a traffic accident may receive a traffic ticket from the police and at the same time be sued by someone else involved in the accident. In certain types of antitrust cases the government can choose between seeking criminal charges and seeking civil damages. As noted earlier regarding Diane's case, she might bring a civil action to recover money and obtain a court order. In addition, she might want to press criminal charges for the restaurant's refusal to let her collect her personal belongings. Charging a person with a criminal violation and suing that person civilly do not constitute **double jeopardy**. Double jeopardy is defined as being prosecuted twice for the same criminal offense.

Double jeopardy
A constitutional protection against being tried twice for the same crime.

In summary, common ways of differentiating criminal from civil law include the following: In a civil case the harm is to an individual, while in a criminal case the action is said to harm society itself; in a civil case the parties are labeled the plaintiff and the defendant, whereas in a criminal case they are the state and the defendant; the government prosecutes criminal cases, while individual plaintiffs initiate civil cases; in a criminal case the government must prove its case beyond a reasonable doubt, whereas in a civil case the plaintiff must prove his or her case by a preponderance of the evidence; a finding of guilt in a criminal case results in a fine or imprisonment, while a finding of liability in a civil case results in a monetary award or an injunction; and the source of law for civil cases is both court-made law and statutes, whereas almost all criminal law is based in statutes.

2. Criminal Law

Murder, robbery, and arson are examples of criminal behavior. However, it is much easier to list types of criminal behavior than it is to define the difference

between criminal and civil law. As mentioned earlier, usually it is said that a criminal act harms not just the victim but also society as a whole. That definition does not get us very far. What is a wrong against society as a whole? One way of viewing that is to say that the act hurts not only the individual victim, but also society as a whole because the act's consequences are so grave as to cause concern to the rest of the population. When the legislature perceives that a particular act such as arson has that broader impact, it enacts a statute outlining the elements of the crime and its punishment.

In this section we will discuss the major types of criminal behavior, what is necessary to prove to a court that a crime has been committed, and what defenses might be raised to try to show the court that the defendant was justified in acting as he or she did.

a. Types of Crimes

Serious crimes, such as murder, rape, armed robbery, and aggravated assault, are classified as **felonies**, and they generally involve a punishment that can include a year or more in a state prison. **Misdemeanors** include such lesser charges as disorderly conduct and criminal damage to property. When incarceration is called for in these cases, it usually is for less than one year and is served in a county jail. Today the criminal law in most jurisdictions is entirely statutory in nature, and the legislature determines whether a given act is to be considered a felony or a misdemeanor.

The criminal codes of most states typically divide crimes into the following categories:

1. crimes against persons (homicide, kidnapping, sex offenses, assault, and battery),
2. crimes against property (theft, robbery, burglary, arson, and trespass),
3. crimes against the public health or decency (drug offenses, bribery, gambling, prostitution, and disorderly conduct), and
4. crimes against the government itself (treason and official misconduct).

The focus of federal criminal law is on interstate activities and unlawful interference with a federal agency or its workers.

b. Establishing a Prima Facie Case

In order for a person to be convicted in a criminal trial, the prosecution must establish that the defendant committed an act defined as being illegal in the criminal code. This involves proving that the accused both had the requisite bad intent (called **mens rea**) and committed the requisite bad behavior (called **actus reus**). Different acts—killing someone, burning down a building, robbing a store—can give rise to different crimes. It is also true that the same act accompanied by different types of intent can give rise to different crimes. For example, the act of killing could be categorized as murder or manslaughter depending on the defendant's state of mind when he or she committed the act.

At the trial the prosecution must first present a **prima facie case**, one that establishes the elements of the crime, the requisite bad intent and bad behavior. A prima facie case contains enough evidence to support a finding of guilty if the defense presents no contrary evidence. If the prosecution fails to present a prima

Mens rea
Bad intent.

Actus reus
Bad act.

Prima facie case
What the prosecution or plaintiff must be able to prove in order for the case to go to the jury—that is, the elements of the prosecution's case or the plaintiff's cause of action.

facie case, the judge must issue a not guilty verdict without the defense even presenting its case.

DISCUSSION QUESTIONS

5. What do you think of the differences between judges' and jurors' definitions of "beyond a reasonable doubt" and a "preponderance of the evidence"? Do you think this causes any problems for our legal system?

6. Take a moment to read the following Massachusetts statute regarding larceny.

> Whoever steals . . . and with intent to steal . . . the property of another . . . shall be guilty of larceny. . . .[14]

   a. Assume Alan got into a car, knowing that it was not his, "hot wired" it, and then drove off in it. Is he guilty of violating the statute? Why?
   b. Assume Bill approached a car that he intended to steal but was scared away by a passerby. Is he guilty of violating the statute? Why?
   c. Assume Charles got into a car, thinking he was getting into his friend's car, and "hot wired" it but only meant to borrow it. Is he guilty of violating the statute? Why?

c. Defenses

If the prosecution does present a prima facie case, the defense then has the opportunity to present evidence that either contradicts that presented by the prosecutor or establishes a legally recognized justification. This evidence could involve witnesses who contradict the testimony of prosecution witnesses or evidence that establishes an alibi, self-defense, or insanity.

There are essentially two types of criminal **defenses**. The first type justifies the act. The second type negates the requisite mens rea. An example of the first type of defense, which justifies the act, is self-defense. The defendant admits killing the victim but argues that he or she had no choice. Examples of the second type of defense, which negates the requisite intent, are insanity, infancy, and intoxication. Each of these defenses has as its premise the fact that the defendant was incapable of forming the requisite intent to commit the crime.

After the defense has presented its evidence, the prosecution has a chance to respond with rebuttal witnesses to attack these defenses and reestablish the credibility of its own witnesses.

3. Civil Law

Civil law involves private actions brought by individuals to address perceived wrongs. In this section we will discuss what is necessary to prove a civil prima facie case, the defenses to a civil suit, the damages that a plaintiff can recover, and the main areas of civil law.

---

[14] Mass. Gen. Laws ch. 266, § 30 (2006).

a. Establishing a Prima Facie Case

Just as the prosecution has the burden of establishing a prima facie case in a criminal case, so, too, the plaintiff shares a similar burden in a civil case. The plaintiff has the burden of proving the various elements listed in his or her complaint that show the plaintiff has a valid **cause of action**. A cause of action is a claim that based on the law and the facts is sufficient to demand judicial action. The plaintiff must prove these elements by a preponderance of the evidence, which means it is more likely than not that the defendant committed the wrong.

Cause of action
A claim that based on the law and the facts is sufficient to support a lawsuit. If the plaintiff does not state a valid cause of action in the complaint, the court will dismiss it.

For example, assume a car and a truck collided at an intersection. The driver of the car is injured and wants to sue the truck driver, alleging the truck driver ran a red light. The car driver will be the plaintiff, and his cause of action will be based on the law of **negligence** (acting unreasonably under the circumstances) and the facts of what happened at the intersection. To succeed in a lawsuit, the plaintiff will have to present evidence that it is more likely than not that the truck driver was negligent. If the plaintiff/driver is able to do so, then he has satisfied his prima facie case. Every area of civil law has its own required elements that constitute the plaintiff's prima facie case. Later in this chapter as you read about torts, contracts, and property law, note the requirements of each for the plaintiff to prove a prima facie case.

b. Defenses

The defendant/truck driver can respond first by trying to negate the plaintiff's case. Perhaps he has a witness who will testify that the light was green for the truck driver and red for the plaintiff. In addition to attempting to negate the plaintiff's case, the defendant can raise defenses of his own, known as **affirmative defenses**. In effect, the defendant is saying this: Even if you are right and I did something wrong, I have a good excuse or a reason why my liability should be reduced.

Affirmative defense
A defense whereby the defendant offers new evidence to avoid judgment.

For example, in the accident mentioned above, the truck driver might ask the car driver's passenger to testify that the car driver was not being as attentive to his driving as he should have been. This behavior could have contributed to the accident, thereby decreasing the defendant's share of the liability.

It is very important to keep these two approaches separate: First, the defendant tries to negate the plaintiff's case. Second, the defendant raises defenses that could limit his liability even if the plaintiff's version of the law and facts is true.

Depending on the area of law different defenses will be available. For example, it might be a valid defense to a contract claim that the defendant was only fifteen years old when he signed the contract. However, being fifteen years old may not be a defense to an intentional tort, such as battery.

In some cases, statutes or constitutions protect certain classes of people or institutions from being sued by granting them either full or partial immunity. One of the oldest and most important forms of immunity is **sovereign immunity**. Historically, the doctrine of sovereign immunity prohibited injured parties from suing the government, unless the government gave its consent. This protection can be traced back to the concept of the divine right of kings and the idea that "the king can do no wrong." Later in this book we also discuss the related concepts of spousal and parental immunity.

Compensatory damages
Money awarded to a plaintiff in payment for his or her actual losses.

Punitive damages
Money awarded to a plaintiff in cases of intentional torts in order to punish the defendent and serve as a warning to others.

Nominal damages
A token sum awarded when liability has been found but monetary damages cannot be shown.

c. Damages

If a court determines that the plaintiff should recover, the issue of damages (monetary compensation) arises. There are three types of damages: compensatory, punitive, and nominal. **Compensatory damages** are intended to compensate the plaintiff for the harm done to her or him. In a tort action involving harm to a person, that might mean the cost of medical bills, lost time from work, and pain and suffering. **Punitive damages** are designed to punish the defendant and typically are awarded only for intentional torts when the court deems that the **tortfeasor** (the person who committed the tort) deserves an additional punishment beyond just compensating the plaintiff for the harm done to him or her. Finally, **nominal damages** are awarded when the law has been violated but the plaintiff cannot prove any monetary harm. As mentioned earlier, in addition to or instead of damages, the court might issue an injunction, an order to the defendant telling the defendant to do a specific act or to cease doing a specific act.

d. Areas of Civil Law

Civil law covers a very broad range of subjects, including adoption, admiralty, collections, corporate, divorce, employment, environmental, intellectual property, personal injury, probate, and real estate law. However, we believe it is helpful to think of civil law as falling into three main categories: making deals, owning property, and protecting people and property from harm. The most basic principles of each are covered in the standard law school courses of contracts, property, and torts, respectively. The various specialty fields listed above all involve applications of the principles taught in these three courses.

(1) Contracts

Contract
An agreement supported by consideration.

The formal definition of a **contract** is an agreement supported by consideration. Therefore, contract law deals with two-sided agreements or bargains. I agree to sell you my diamond ring, and you agree to give me $500 in return. We have struck a bargain, entered into a contract. If something should go wrong—if I refuse to hand over the ring or you refuse to give me the money—we would find our actions governed by contract law. For a contract to be valid there must be an offer, an acceptance of the offer, and **consideration**; that is, something of value must be exchanged. It is the consideration that differentiates a contract from a gift. Common defenses to a contract action include breach by the other side and incapacity to contract, as when one party is underage.

Consideration
Something of value exchanged to form the basis of a contract.

(2) Property

Property law
Law dealing with ownership.

Property law deals with ownership. If two neighbors have a dispute over the correct placement of the boundary separating their land, property law will resolve it. Property law is divided into two main categories: (1) **real property,** land and objects permanently attached to land, and (2) **personal property,** all other property.

Real property
Land and objects permanently attached to land.

The first issue raised in a property law case may be how to classify the property. For example, is a room air conditioner real or personal property? If it is simply sitting in a window opening and can be easily removed without damage to the window, it is personal property. But what if the window has been taken

Personal property
All property that is not real property.

You are walking along the beach and see a young child drowning. No one else is in sight. Should the law require you to try to save the child? Should it matter if you are an off-duty lifeguard?

Ethics Alert

out and the air conditioner screwed into the window frame? Is it now "permanently attached"? How you classify property is important because different rules may apply to real versus personal property.

Another common dispute that arises under property law relates to gift law. Above we noted that the difference between a contract and a gift is that a contract is two-sided (each party gives something to the other), while a gift is one-sided. The necessary elements for a valid gift include an offer, an acceptance of the offer, and delivery. Usually, the first two elements are not at issue, but the last element, delivery, can become a problem, especially when the gift is delivered symbolically, as by handing over the keys to a car. The question is, Has the car been delivered? The deciding factor is usually whether the owner has relinquished all control over the object. In the case of a car, that probably involves more than simply handing over a set of keys. This type of delivery is known as **constructive delivery.** (*Note:* A constructive delivery is one example of a **legal fiction**. Courts create a legal fiction when they need to make an assumption that is not based in fact in order to resolve a dispute. For example, courts frequently speak of corporations as though they were persons.) No actual delivery of the car is made, but the owner takes the necessary actions to allow the new owner to gain control over the gift.

Constructive
Not factually true, but accepted by the courts as being legally true.

Legal fiction
An assumption that something that is not real is real—for example, saying that a corporation is a person for purposes of its being able to sue and be sued.

(3) Torts

Issues of **tort law** arise when one person harms another person or that person's property. A tort is defined as a private wrong (other than a breach of contract) in which a person is harmed because of another's failure to carry out a legal duty. Through the common law the courts have defined legal duties as occasionally including the affirmative obligation to take action to protect others. More commonly, courts require that everyone refrain from taking actions that inflict harm on others. Torts are traditionally categorized as intentional, negligent, or the result of strict liability.

As the name indicates, an **intentional tort** occurs when someone intentionally harms a person or that person's property. If one of your classmates deliberately hits you, your classmate has committed the intentional tort known as battery. **Battery** is the intentional, harmful or offensive physical contact by one person with another person. Libel, slander, invasion of privacy, and false imprisonment are other examples of intentional torts.

Tort law
Law that deals with harm to a person or a person's property.

Intentional tort
A tort committed by one who intends to do the act that creates the harm.

Negligence
The failure to act reasonably under the circumstances.

The most common category of tort law is that of **negligence**. Negligence is the failure to act as a reasonably prudent and careful person is expected to act under the circumstances. This used to be known as the reasonable man standard but has more recently become known as the reasonable person standard.

The Case of Mr. Whipple

Your client Mr. Whipple owns a grocery store. A customer breaks a bottle of apple juice and promptly reports it to Mr. Whipple. Nonetheless, Mr. Whipple fails to have the broken jar and spilled juice cleaned up. Twenty minutes later another customer slips on the wet floor, breaking her leg.

Mr. Whipple would probably be found liable for negligence. Clearly he did not intend for the customer to slip and break her leg. Therefore, there was no intentional tort. But a jury might find that a reasonable store owner would have ordered the spill cleaned up within the twenty minutes after learning of it.

In order for a plaintiff to prove negligence, he or she must show that

1. the defendant owed the plaintiff a duty of care;
2. the defendant breached that duty;
3. the breach caused
4. the plaintiff harm.

These four basic prerequisites (elements) in a negligence case are known as duty, breach, causation, and harm. In the case just mentioned Mr. Whipple had a duty to act as a reasonable store owner would under the circumstances. The circumstances were a broken jar of apple juice about which Mr. Whipple was informed and a twenty-minute time period in which he did nothing. If the jurors believe Mr. Whipple breached his duty to act as a reasonable store owner, then they will find liability if they also think that breach caused the customer harm.

Contributory negligence
Negligence by the plaintiff that contributed to his or her injury. Normally, any finding of contributory negligence acts as a complete bar to a plaintiff's recovery.

As the store owner, Mr. Whipple would, of course, try to defend himself through rebutting the plaintiff's evidence. Perhaps it had only been two and not twenty minutes since he learned of the spill. In addition, he might try to raise an affirmative defense. As mentioned previously, an affirmative defense is a defense whereby the defendant offers new evidence to avoid or limit the judgment. The two main affirmative defenses to negligence are **contributory negligence** and **assumption of the risk**. Contributory negligence means that the plaintiff was also negligent and through that negligence contributed to his or her own injury. In Mr. Whipple's case, perhaps the customer was in a hurry and was not looking where she was going. Assumption of the risk means that the plaintiff voluntarily and knowingly subjected himself or herself to a known danger. Perhaps the customer saw the spilled juice but chose to walk through it anyway. In many states assumption of the risk is no longer a separate defense to negligence, as it has been subsumed under the more general category of contributory negligence.

Assumption of the risk
Voluntarily and knowingly subjecting oneself to danger.

Historically, any showing of contributory negligence or assumption of the risk meant that the plaintiff could recover nothing from the defendant even if the

defendant's actions were much more culpable than those of the plaintiff. Legislatures and courts in many states have tried to rectify that situation by replacing contributory negligence with a new defense known as **comparative negligence.** Under comparative negligence, instead of the plaintiff's own negligence relieving the defendant of liability, the jury compares the negligence of the plaintiff to that of the defendant and apportions the responsibility. The plaintiff's recovery is reduced by his or her degree of negligence.

Comparative negligence
A method for measuring the relative negligence of the plaintiff and the defendant, with a commensurate sharing of the compensation for the injuries.

The third category of tort law is called **strict liability.** In some cases persons or corporations can be held liable for injuries that resulted from their actions, even when their actions were reasonable under the circumstances and they did not intend to harm anyone. The doctrine of strict liability holds that persons who engage in activities that are inherently dangerous are responsible for injury that results, even though they carried out the activities in the safest and most prudent way possible. For example, someone who uses explosives or who keeps wild animals is liable for all resulting injuries, even if that person used the utmost care. In recent years many courts have held manufacturers and sellers to be strictly liable when a defective product the defendant manufactured or sold caused harm to the user or consumer, even when the user or consumer could not show that the manufacturer's negligence caused the defect.

Strict liability
Liability without a showing of fault.

DISCUSSION QUESTIONS

7. For each question decide whether the facts raise an issue of tort, contract, or property law or more than one area of law.
   a. You buy a new car. Two days later as you are driving, the brakes fail, and you go off the road, hitting a telephone pole. Luckily you are unhurt, but the car is badly damaged.
   b. You rent an apartment. One night as you are leaving the building through the central stairway, the railing gives way, and you fall down, breaking your leg.

8. For each of the following situations decide if you think liability should be found based on an intentional tort, negligence, or strict liability or whether no liability should be found.
   a. Sally was angry with Martha. One night after leaving class, she deliberately drove her car into the side of Martha's car.
   b. One night after leaving class, Sally was in a hurry. When she arrived at the stop sign at the student parking lot entrance to Main Street, she did a "rolling stop." Martha was driving by on Main Street. Sally's auto hit the side of Martha's car.
   c. One night after leaving class, Sally got into her brand new Dodge van. When she arrived at the stop sign at the student parking lot entrance to Main Street, she pressed on the brakes, but nothing happened. Martha was driving by on Main Street. Sally's auto hit the side of Martha's car.
   d. One night after leaving class, Sally got into her car. When she arrived at the stop sign at the student parking entrance to Main Street, she suddenly got a tremendous cramp in her side and momentarily lost control of her car. Martha was driving by on Main Street. Sally's auto hit the side of Martha's car.

C. SUBSTANTIVE VERSUS PROCEDURAL LAW

Substantive law
Law that creates rights and duties.

In addition to being categorized on the basis of its source, we also classify law as being either substantive or procedural. **Substantive law** refers to the part of the law that defines our rights and duties. It defines what actions will violate the criminal law and what our obligations are to each other. For example, substantive law includes the statutes that govern the legal speed limits, the circumstances under which someone can be convicted of robbery, and when a contract is enforceable. **Procedural law,** on the other hand, deals with how the legal system operates. It defines the steps that someone must go through to file a lawsuit and the procedures the police must follow in conducting a search or interrogating a suspect.

Procedural law
Law that regulates how the legal system operates.

Every case is founded in substantive law, and attorneys must determine what their client's obligations and liabilities are. However, they must be equally aware of the procedural aspects of the case. Even if the substantive law is on the client's side, the case may be lost if a claim is not filed within the time prescribed in the **statute of limitations.** The legal system imposes a limitation on how long a plaintiff has before he or she can no longer bring suit. Those limitations vary given the type of case involved. A plaintiff could also lose if the complaint, the initial document that starts a lawsuit, fails to include all the required information.

Statute of limitations
The law that sets the length of time from when something happens to when a lawsuit must be filed before the right to bring it is lost.

We have all heard of the criminal who was set free due to a "technicality." The rules of criminal procedure have their roots in the Constitution and are intended to protect the innocent from the overreaching of possibly overzealous law enforcement officials. These rules govern everything from the way in which the arresting police officer must inform a suspect of his or her rights to how evidence is introduced at trial.

Civil law is also controlled by very specific rules of procedure. Those rules of civil procedure will be the focus of Chapter 6. We discuss criminal procedure in Chapter 10.

DISCUSSION QUESTION

9. Review the hypothetical case that began Chapter 3. How would you categorize Diane's legal problems?

SUMMARY

We have seen how lawyers categorize law as either state or federal, civil or criminal, and substantive or procedural. The first category, state or federal, arises because the United States operates under a system of federalism. Under our federal system governmental authority is split between the national government and the fifty state governments. Some areas of the law, such as divorce, are reserved exclusively to the states; some are reserved to the federal government; and some are shared by the states and the federal government. If you are in doubt as to which law applies, check state law first. Federal law will be involved only if the federal Constitution, a federal statute, or a federal regulation is involved.

Civil law involves harm to an individual, while criminal law
as a whole. In both criminal and civil cases the party with the
establish a prima facie case. Once that is established, the other side
negate the prima facie case or to raise affirmative defenses. While t
ingly specialized, the main areas of civil law are contracts, property
further subdivided into those involving intentional acts, those ba
and those that result from an imposition of strict liability.

Finally, substantive law defines our rights and duties. Procedural law deals
legal system operates.

REVIEW QUESTIONS

Pages 53 through 54
1. What are the three major ways in which attorneys categorize the law?
2. What is the difference between substantive and procedural law?
• 3. In terms of the type of harm caused, what is the difference between civil and criminal law?

Pages 55 through 59
4. What is federalism?
• 5. True or false: Every state must have the same laws regarding gambling. Why?
• 6. What does it mean to say that the federal government is a government of limited powers?
. 7. Do you think Congress could (not should) enact a national divorce statute? Why?
. 8. Why are some areas of the law preempted by the federal government?

Pages 59 through 62
• 9. Name at least four ways in which civil law differs from criminal law.
. 10. When is the burden of proof "beyond a reasonable doubt" and when is it a "preponderance of the evidence"? What is the difference between them?
• 11. In a civil case if a jury is evenly split, leaning equally toward the plaintiff's and the defendant's views of the facts, who will win, the plaintiff or the defendant? Why?

Pages 62 through 66
12. What two basic elements must be established for the government to prove the prima facie case in a criminal case?
• 13. Why can the same act constitute several different crimes?
14. What are the two basic defenses to a criminal action?
• 15. In a criminal case does the government or the defendant present its case first? Why?
16. What is the general definition of a civil cause of action?
• 17. In a civil case does the plaintiff or the defendant present its case first? Why?
• 18. What are the three types of damages available in a civil case?
• 19. In addition to damages, what might a plaintiff seek in a civil case?

Pages 66 through 70
• 20. What must be present for a contract to be valid?
• 21. What is the basic difference between a contract and a gift?
• 22. What are the three main areas of tort law?
• 23. Give the general definition of negligence, and list the elements necessary to prove a prima facie case.
• 24. What are the main defenses to negligence?

Chapter 5

Structure of the Court System

Trial courts search for truth and appellate courts search for error.
Unknown

INTRODUCTION

The law provides rules about how people should behave in different types of situations and provides remedies for when those rules are broken. However, these rules are not self-enforcing. In order to enforce these rules, people often have to go to court to have a judge or jury settle it for them. A court is a unit of the judicial branch of government that has authority to decide legal disputes. **Jurisdiction** refers to the ability of a specific court to hear a particular type of case.

One major way of classifying courts is in terms of whether they are trial or appellate courts. They can also be classified in terms of whether they are federal or state courts. In this chapter we will examine the structure of the various court systems, the concept of jurisdiction, and the roles played by those who work in the court system.

A. TRIAL VERSUS APPELLATE COURTS

Most court cases begin in a **trial court**.[1] Trial courts are said to be courts of **original jurisdiction** because trial courts are where actions are initiated and heard

Jurisdiction
The power of a court to hear a case.

Trial courts
Courts that determine the facts and apply the law to the facts.

Original jurisdiction
The authority of a court to hear a case when it is initiated; as opposed to appellate jurisdiction.

---

[1] The primary exception to this pattern occurs when a dispute is adjudicated in an administrative agency and then appealed to the courts. In very rare circumstances a case can be filed directly with the U.S. Supreme Court under its original jurisdiction.

for the first time. In addition to conducting trials, much of a trial court's time is spent in far less dramatic proceedings, such as receiving plea agreements and ratifying out-of-court settlements. When a trial is held, attorneys present witness testimony and other evidence. After considering the evidence and the attorneys' arguments, trial courts have two functions. First, they must determine whose version of the facts is most credible. Second, they must apply the law to those facts to reach a decision. Therefore, trial courts must determine both questions of fact and questions of law.

Questions of fact
Questions relating to what happened: who, what, when, where, and how.

Questions of law
Questions relating to the interpretation or application of the law.

Bench trial
A trial conducted without a jury.

Questions of fact relate to the determination of what took place: Who, what, when, where, and how? **Questions of law** relate to how the judge interprets and applies the law and include such issues as how a statute is to be interpreted and whether a specific piece of evidence is admissible. In a **jury trial** questions of fact are determined by the jury, while questions of law are determined by the judge. If it is a **bench trial** rather than a jury trial, the judge will decide the factual questions as well as the legal ones.

In most cases that go to trial, the meaning of the law is clear, but the facts themselves are very much in dispute. For example, under the criminal codes of most states it is a violation of the law for a person to forcibly take someone else's property without the owner's permission. When someone is tried for robbery, the trial usually focuses on such factual questions as the identification of the alleged robber and the ownership of the property taken.

Although the primary focus of most trials is on factual issues, at times legal issues are involved as well. For example, a trial judge may have to decide if certain testimony or evidence is admissible. That is a question of law. If the judge decides that the testimony or evidence is not admissible, then the trial proceeds without it. Also, if the judge rules that a search was illegal or that disputed pictures are too prejudicial, then the objects discovered in that search or the pictures are not admitted as evidence. Based on the evidence that has been allowed, the jury then resolves the questions of fact.

Consider the following example. In most states it is a crime for someone other than a physician, pharmacist, or other authorized medical person to sell or distribute narcotic drugs. When someone is on trial for selling narcotics, the prosecution must present evidence that shows the accused did in fact sell a substance that fits the legal definition of a prohibited narcotic drug. These are issues of fact. The evidence usually consists of an undercover police agent testifying that the accused did sell the agent a substance that laboratory reports identify as a narcotic.

Entrapment
A defense requiring proof that the defendant would not have committed the crime but for police trickery.

It is possible, however, that the defendant might admit to selling the drug but then claim **entrapment**. The entrapment doctrine prohibits law enforcement officers from instigating criminal acts to lure otherwise innocent persons into committing a crime. One question of fact relating to the entrapment defense is whether the defendant ever committed such a criminal act or thought of committing such an act before. However, in addition to the factual questions and depending on the circumstances of a given case, a legal issue of what constitutes entrapment could arise. For example, assume government agents supplied the defendant with a drug and then later arrested him for selling the very same drug to another government agent. Here no one would be disputing what happened, the facts. But an appellate court could be asked to decide whether such actions legally qualify as entrapment. In *Hampton v. United States*[2] the U.S. Supreme

---

[2] 425 U.S. 484 (1976).

Court held that as long as the defendant is predisposed to commit the crime, it is not entrapment when government agents supply the defendant with a drug and then later arrest him for selling the very same drug to another government agent.

In sum, legal issues can arise in three ways. First, legal issues can arise regarding the meaning of the underlying cause of action, as in the example given above regarding whether entrapment had occurred. Second, during a trial numerous legal issues may be raised involving the conduct of the trial itself. Such issues might include whether a particular piece of evidence should be excluded because it is the product of an illegal search and seizure, whether the plaintiff's attorney should be allowed to pursue a certain line of questioning, whether the judge should present a particular set of instructions to the jury, and whether prejudicial publicity has tainted the defendant's trial—to give but a few examples. Finally, legal issues can involve challenges to the constitutionality of the law that is being applied. For example, a doctor charged with performing an illegal abortion could argue that the law he is charged with violating is itself unconstitutional.

Appellate courts review the actions taken by trial courts (and in some cases the actions of administrative agencies). The person who loses in a trial court may be able to appeal the decision to an appellate court. The party filing the appeal is called the **appellant** or the **petitioner**. The party who won in the trial court is called the **appellee** or the **respondent**. Most states and the federal government provide for one appeal as a matter of right. Additional appeals are usually at the discretion of the higher court.

Unlike trial courts, appellate courts do not hear testimony. They rely on the written record of what occurred in the trial court to determine whether the trial court made an error regarding the law. They do so because when conducting a review, appellate courts limit themselves to "legal" as opposed to "factual" issues that are specifically raised by the party who is bringing the appeal. Therefore, you can appeal a lower court decision only when you raise a valid legal issue. Appellate courts will not reconsider the facts; they will consider only whether the trial court made an error of law. The Case of the Alibi to a Murder illustrates this point.

Appellate courts
Courts that determine whether lower courts have made errors of law.

Appellant or petitioner
The party in a case who has initiated an appeal.

Appellee or respondent
The party in a case against whom an appeal has been filed.

The Case of the Alibi to a Murder

Frederick Jones could not believe it when he was arrested for murder because he thought he had an ironclad alibi.

At his trial an elderly gentleman testified that he saw Mr. Jones near the scene of the murder shortly after it took place. At one point in the trial, over the objection of the defendant's attorney, the prosecutor showed the jury bloody and gruesome pictures of the deceased victim.

Mr. Jones testified that not only did he not commit the murder, but also he was attending an out-of-town wedding at the time the murder was supposed to have taken place. Ten witnesses then took the stand in succession and testified that they had been at the wedding and seen the defendant there.

At the end of the trial the jury convicted Mr. Jones.

Do you think there is any basis for launching an appeal in Mr. Jones's case? It is a question of fact whether on the night of the murder Mr. Jones was present at the scene of the murder (as testified to by one elderly witness) or out of town attending a wedding (as testified to by ten other witnesses). Therefore, his whereabouts on the night of the murder cannot form the basis for an appeal.

On the other hand, it is a question of law as to whether the judge should allow the jury to see pictures of the victim's bloody corpse. It can be argued that the viewing of those pictures was so inflammatory as to prejudice the jury. Therefore, the showing of the pictures could form the basis of an appeal. Keep in mind that this does not mean that Mr. Jones would win at the appellate level. It simply means that he will be given the opportunity to argue his case to the appellate court.

There is one exception to the rule that appellate courts review only questions of law. Occasionally they will review a case because they believe that what the jury did was something that no reasonable jury could do. Because appellate courts review only legal issues, normally they do not engage in this type of second-guessing regarding the trial court's findings. For example, in Mr. Jones's situation mentioned above, even though ten eyewitnesses testified that Mr. Jones was out of town on the night of the murder, Mr. Jones's attorney cannot appeal on the grounds that the jury was mistaken about his whereabouts on the night of the murder. Appellate courts will accept a jury's determination as to which witnesses were most credible. Only in rare instances will appellate courts reexamine the evidence.

Harmless error
A trial court error that is not sufficient to warrant reversing the decision.

Reverse
A decision is reversed when an appellate court overturns or negates the decision of a lower court.

Remand
When an appellate court sends a case back to the trial court for a new trial or other action.

Majority opinion
An opinion in which a majority of the court joins.

Concurring opinion
An opinion that agrees with the majority's result but disagrees with its reasoning.

Dissenting opinion
An opinion that disagrees with the majority's decision and its reasoning.

If the appellate court determines that a legal error occurred but that it was minor and did not affect the result, the court labels it a **harmless error** and allows the decision to stand. If the court finds that a significant legal error was made in the way the trial was conducted, it will usually cancel the original outcome by **reversing** the trial court's decision. It may also direct that the case be retried by **remanding** the case to the trial court for further consideration.

In criminal cases a reversal of a conviction does not necessarily mean that the defendant will go free, as the government then has the option of retrying the case. However, if the appellate court rules that a key piece of evidence is inadmissible, the government may choose not to retry the defendant because it may feel that its case is too weak without the excluded evidence.

If the government chooses to proceed with a new trial, this does not violate the constitutional provision regarding **double jeopardy**. Double jeopardy occurs when a person is tried more than once for the same criminal offense. The Fifth and Fourteenth Amendments to the Constitution prohibit various forms of double jeopardy. However, when a defendant voluntarily appeals a conviction, he or she waives the right not to be retried for the same crime

Appellate court judges reach their decisions by majority vote. Someone from the majority writes the **majority opinion** explaining the court's decision and how that decision was reached. In cases where the decision is not unanimous, judges may also write concurring or dissenting opinions to explain the nature of their disagreements. In a **concurring opinion** the judge agrees with the result reached by the majority but not with its reasoning. In a **dissenting opinion** the judge disagrees with the result and with the reasoning.

In summary, there are several major differences between trial and appellate courts. At the trial-court level the parties are called the plaintiff and the

defendant in a civil case and the state and the defendant in a criminal case. At the appellate-court level the party who lost in the trial court is called either the **appellant** or the **petitioner**, while the party who won is called either the **appellee** or the **respondent**. In the trial court either a single judge or a jury decides the facts, and the judge determines the law. In the appellate court, a panel of three or more judges decides questions of law based on the attorneys' briefs (written arguments) and oral arguments. There are no witnesses who give testimony in the appellate courts and no juries. The judges merely review the trial transcript and the written briefs from the lawyers. Sometimes oral arguments from the opposing attorneys are heard, during which the judges have an opportunity to pose questions. Lower-level appellate judges usually work in rotating panels of three, while in the upper-level appellate courts all the judges jointly decide each case.

Most of these differences are directly related to the most important distinction between trial and appellate courts: Trial courts determine the facts and apply the law to those facts; appellate courts deal only with questions of law. Three basic types of legal questions can arise at the appellate level. First are those that relate to the meaning of the underlying legal cause of action or defense, such as what qualifies as entrapment. Second, one of the parties can argue that the law being applied is unconstitutional, as when the doctor challenged an abortion law. Finally, legal issues can arise that have nothing to do with the underlying legal claim but rather relate to how the trial was conducted. Figure 5-1 summarizes the differences between trial and appellate courts.

	Trial Court	Appellate Court
Parties' names	Plaintiff/defendant State/defendant	Appellant/appellee or petitioner/respondent
Decision maker	Judge and sometimes a jury	Majority vote of three or more judges
Attorney arguments	Yes	Yes
Witness testimony	Yes	No
Evidence introduced	Yes	No
Questions of fact decided	Yes	No
Questions of law decided	Yes	Yes

Figure 5-1   Comparison of Trial and Appellate Courts

DISCUSSION QUESTIONS

1. Do you think it is a good or a bad idea that only questions of law can be appealed?

2. Can you think of a situation when an appellate judge might reverse and remand a case? When a judge might reverse but not remand a case?

3. It is not always easy to know whether something is a question of fact or a question of law. In fact, there have been cases when the issue on appeal was whether something was a question of fact or a question of law. That question is itself a question of law. To see how that can happen, assume there was a negligence trial in which a grocer was sued when a customer slipped and fell. The customer testified that she slipped on a banana peel in the produce section. The grocery store owner testified that when he came to the assistance of the customer, there was no peel on the floor. One of the store employees also testified that he had mopped the floor in that area just five minutes before the accident and that there were no banana peels on the floor. Nonetheless, the jury found the store liable. Can the store appeal on the grounds that it was telling the truth and the customer was lying? Why? Can the store appeal on the grounds that the jury should not have found that it acted negligently because even if there was a banana peel, such hazards are to be expected in the produce section and the store had done all it could to make the area safe? Is that issue—that is, whether the store acted as a reasonable store should—a question of fact or a question of law?

B. FEDERAL AND STATE COURT SYSTEMS

Trial and appellate courts exist in both the federal and the state court systems. At first glance the federal and state judicial systems of this country present a confusing mixture of titles and functions. In large part this is because there are actually fifty-one different court systems (the federal system plus one for each state). To complicate matters, the same types of courts often have different names. For example, the basic trial court is called the court of common pleas in Pennsylvania, the district court in Minnesota, the circuit court in Illinois, the superior court in California, and the supreme court in New York. Although New York uses the "supreme court" designation for its trial courts, most states reserve that title for their highest appellate court. Out of this confusion we will try to create some order by discussing the basic structure of both the federal court system and a typical state court system. Although both systems can seem quite complex, the federal system, as well as most state systems, has three levels: the trial courts, the intermediate appellate courts, and one appellate court of last resort.

1. The Federal System

A simplified organizational chart of the federal court system is shown in Figure 5-2. As you can see, it follows the basic pattern described above: trial courts, intermediate appellate courts, and one highest appellate court. The federal court system also includes a variety of other less-well-known judicial bodies, such as the U.S. Court of International Trade, which are not listed here. The arrows indicate the avenues for appeals.

U.S. Supreme Court
The highest federal appellate court, consisting of nine appointed members.

The **U.S. Supreme Court** sits at the top of the federal judicial branch, where it hears appeals from both federal and state courts. However, as we will discuss more fully later in this chapter, not all state cases can be appealed to the U.S. Supreme Court. Cases are appealed from state supreme courts only when federal issues are involved.

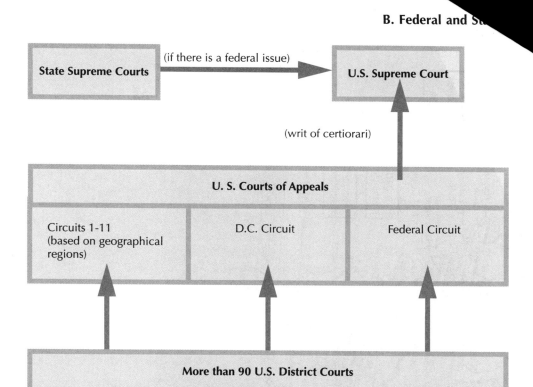

Figure 5-2 The Federal Court System

Immediately below the Supreme Court are the **U.S. courts of appeals.** Both the Supreme Court and the courts of appeals are appellate courts. The Supreme Court is the highest appellate court, while the courts of appeals are intermediate-level appellate courts. The country is divided geographically into twelve circuits, which include eleven numbered circuits and the District of Columbia as a separate circuit. The thirteenth circuit is called the Federal Circuit, where appeals in specialized cases from the entire country are heard. There is a court of appeals for each of the thirteen circuits. Most of the work, however, is done in the federal trial courts, the ninety-three **U.S. district courts** spread among the fifty states. There is at least one district court for each state. Most district court cases are appealed to the U.S. court of appeals in the circuit in which the district court is located. To gain an appreciation for how the circuits are organized, look at the map in Figure 5-3, page 80.

The basic outline for this three-tiered judicial structure is set forth in the federal Constitution. Article III, Section 1, provides that "[t]he judicial Power of the United States, shall be vested in one supreme Court, and in such inferior Courts as the Congress may from time to time ordain and establish." Those **"inferior Courts"** are the district courts and courts of appeals. Congress established the first inferior courts through the Judiciary Act of 1789. That act provided for thirteen districts and three circuits. Over the years, through further legislative action, the number of both district and federal circuits has grown to its present-day level.

U.S. courts of appeals
The intermediate appellate courts in the federal system.

U.S. district courts
The general jurisdiction trial courts in the federal system.

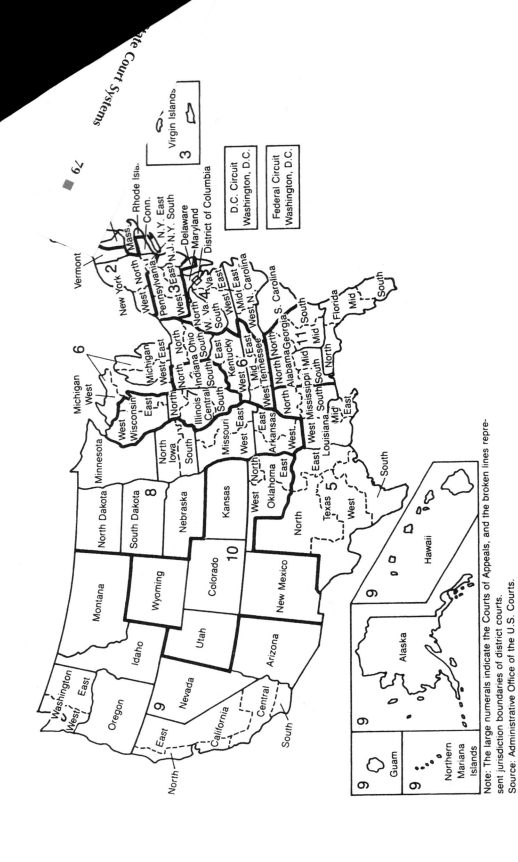

Figure 5-3 District and Circuit Court Boundaries

Note: The large numerals indicate the Courts of Appeals, and the broken lines represent jurisdiction boundaries of district courts.
Source: Administrative Office of the U.S. Courts.

a. The Primary Federal Courts

In the federal system, cases normally begin in one of the district courts, which serve as the federal trial courts. These district courts are courts of **general jurisdiction.** That means they are authorized to adjudicate all types of civil and criminal cases. Courts of **limited jurisdiction** hear only a narrow range of cases on a specific subject (such as probate, domestic relations, or traffic).

The number of judges assigned to each district varies from one to twenty-seven depending on the caseload of the district. Usually, cases are heard by a single judge or a judge and a jury. The district court judges are assisted by **magistrate judges** and **bankruptcy judges.**

The magistrate judges supervise court calendars, hear procedural motions, issue **subpoenas,** hear minor criminal offense cases, and conduct civil pretrial hearings. In some district courts the magistrate judges, with the consent of the parties involved, conduct trials and enter judgments in civil cases. Bankruptcy judges handle most bankruptcy cases entirely on their own. In a limited number of cases they conduct the trial but then must submit their proposed findings of fact to the district judge, who enters the final order or judgment.

The losing party takes an appeal from a district court decision to the appropriate court of appeals. For example, cases from California district courts are appealed to the Court of Appeals for the Ninth Circuit. Each of the twelve regular circuits has from four to twenty-three judges. In courts of appeals, a panel, normally comprised of three judges, hears appeals and reaches its decision through a majority vote. Occasionally all the judges sit together and decide a case **en banc.** This happens most frequently when the losing party in a case already decided by a panel of the court requests a rehearing before the full membership of the court.

Sitting at the top of the federal judicial system is the U.S. Supreme Court. The Court is composed of nine justices, who hear all appeals as a group. It is interesting to note that the Judiciary Act of 1789, mentioned above, provided for a Supreme Court with one chief justice and five associate justices. As with the number of courts, the number of Supreme Court justices has also grown over the years as the volume of the Court's work has increased. The Supreme Court justices also reach their decisions by majority vote. Figure 5-4 shows a picture of the U.S. Supreme Court taken in the spring of 2006.

A case seldom goes any further than a court of appeals, as the U.S. Supreme Court rarely is required to hear a case on appeal. Most cases that do reach the U.S. Supreme Court do so because the litigants have requested a **writ of certiorari.** In this writ the losing party asks the Supreme Court to review the case. The decision whether to grant a writ of certiorari is discretionary. The Supreme Court usually hears no more than 200 of the approximately 4,000 requests it receives each year. For the request to be granted, four of the nine justices must agree to hear the case. If the request is denied, this does not mean that the Court agrees with the lower court's decision. It simply means that the Court does not want to hear the case. When discussing the Court's response to a writ of certiorari, you will often hear lawyers refer to the granting or denial of cert.

All the courts discussed so far are known as **constitutional courts,** which means they were established under the provisions of Article III of the Constitution. Article II of the Constitution gives the president the power to

General jurisdiction
A court's power to hear any type of case arising within its geographical area.

Limited jurisdiction
A court's power to hear only specialized cases.

Subpoena
A court order requiring a person to appear to testify at a trial or deposition.

En banc
When an appellate court that normally sits in panels sits as a whole.

Writ of certiorari
A means of gaining appellate review; in the U.S. Supreme Court the writ is discretionary and will be issued to another court to review a federal question if four of the nine justices vote to hear the case.

NETNOTE

The official web site of the Federal judiciary is *www.uscourts.gov/*. It contains links to the U.S. Supreme Court, the U.S. courts of appeals, the U.S. district courts, and the U.S. Bankruptcy courts. Emory University's web site at *www.law. emory.edu/caselaw/* has a map of the federal circuits that allows you to link to a wide variety of information on each of the circuits. The U.S. Supreme Court's site at *www.supremecourtus.gov/* contains helpful information on the Court's procedures, its caseload, and biographies and pictures of the Justices.

appoint judges for life terms. For an appointment to become final, the Senate must confirm it. Article III, Section 1, provides that "[t]he Judges, both of the supreme and inferior Courts, shall hold their Offices during good Behaviour, and shall, at stated Times, receive for their Services, a Compensation, which shall not be diminished during their Continuance in Office." This means that "constitutional" judges are guaranteed lifetime tenure unless they resign or are impeached and are protected from any salary reductions.

Figure 5-4 The U.S. Supreme Court, 2006. **Standing, from left to right**: *Stephen Breyer*—appointed by President Clinton (D) in 1994; a former law clerk for Justice Goldberg, a law professor, and a federal appellate court judge. *Clarence Thomas*—appointed by President George H. Bush (R) in 1991; the second African-American to reach the Supreme Court and a federal appellate court judge when appointed; his confirmation hearings included the examination of charges that he had sexually harassed a female employee while he was Chairman of the U.S. Equal Employment Opportunity Commission. *Ruth Bader Ginsburg*—appointed by President Clinton (D) in 1993; the second woman to reach the Supreme Court; had been the General Counsel for the ACLU, a law professor, and a federal appellate judge. *Samuel Alito*—the most recent member to join the court, appointed by President George W. Bush (R) in 2006; was Deputy Assistant U.S. Attorney General and a federal appellate court judge. **Sitting, from left to right**: *Anthony Kennedy*—appointed by President Reagan (R) in 1988; a law professor and federal appellate judge. *John Paul Stevens*—appointed by President Ford (R) in 1975; served as a law clerk for Justice Rutledge, was an anti-trust lawyer, and served as a federal appellate court judge. *John Roberts,* Chief Justice—appointed by President George W. Bush (R) in 2005; a former law clerk to Justice Rehnquist, worked for the Justice Department during the Reagan administration, and was a federal appellate court judge. *Antonin Scalia*—appointed by President Reagan (R) in 1986; a law school professor and a federal appellate court judge. *David H. Souter*—appointed by George H. Bush (R) in 1990; a New Hampshire Supreme Court justice and a federal appellate court judge.

DISCUSSION QUESTIONS

4. Why do you think the framers of the Constitution chose to give federal judges lifetime tenure and to protect them from salary reduction? Do you think that was a wise decision?

5. Do you think it is appropriate that the Supreme Court hears no more than 200 of the approximately 4,000 requests it receives each year? What criteria should the Court use in deciding which cases it will hear?

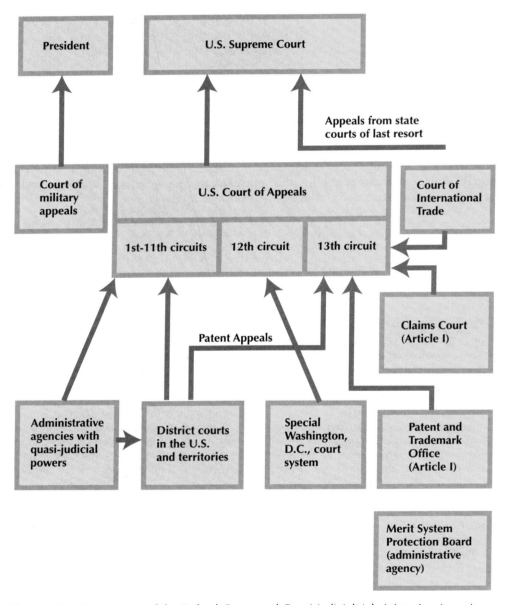

Figure 5-5   Organization of the Federal Courts and Quasi-Judicial Administrative Agencies

b. Other Federal Courts

Figure 5-5, page 84, shows where the "core" courts, shown in Figure 5-2, fit into a more complete organizational chart of the federal court system. In addition to the primary courts discussed above, Congress has created more-specialized courts, known as **legislative courts,** under Article I of the federal Constitution. These legislative courts include the U.S. Court of Military Appeals, the U.S. Tax Court, the U.S. Claims Court, and the U.S. Court of International Trade.

The U.S. Court of Military Appeals is the final appellate tribunal for court-martial convictions. The U.S. Tax Court (formerly the Board of Tax Appeals) considers challenges to Internal Revenue Service rulings. The U.S. Claims Court (formerly the Court of Claims) decides the validity of specific types of claims against the U.S. government, and the U.S. Court of International Trade (formerly the U.S. Customs Court) reviews decisions and appraisals of imported merchandise made in collecting customs duties.

Judges who serve on these courts, as well as district court magistrate and bankruptcy judges, are appointed for set terms and theoretically lack some of the independence of the constitutional judges. Magistrate judges, for example, are selected by a majority of the active judges of each district court for full-time terms of eight years or part-time terms of four years, and they can be removed for cause. Bankruptcy judges are appointed for fourteen-year terms by the court of appeals for the circuit in which the district is located.

2. State Court Systems

Due to the controversial nature of many of its decisions the U.S. Supreme Court gets the lion's share of the media coverage given to the courts on the evening news. While many important cases and significant constitutional issues are decided in the federal courts, it is in state courts where over 98 percent of all legal business occurs.[3] While paralegals may have some opportunities to work with federal courts, most will spend their time operating within state court systems.

Many states have court systems that are very similar to the federal system. Cases begin in a trial court and then proceed through one or two levels of appellate courts. Figure 5-6, on page 86, shows the organization of a typical state court system. Note how closely it parallels Figure 5-2, showing the core of the federal court system. The path for appeals in most state court systems is from the trial court to an intermediate appellate court (if one exists) and then to the state's highest appellate court (usually called the supreme court).

Rather than attempting to describe each of these fifty-one court systems, we will review some general patterns and leave it to you to search out the details for your specific state. Relatively simple explanations of most state court systems can be found in books and pamphlets published by the individual states and are usually available in the reference section of local libraries. Other sources for such information are The American Bench and the Martindale-Hubbell Law Directory, Court Calendar section.

> **PRACTICE TIP**
>
> Find the time to take a walking tour of your local courts. Note the location of the clerk's offices, the courtrooms, and the nearest law library.

---

[3] Cooke & Goodman, The State of the Nation's State Courts, Natl. L.J., Mar. 19, 1984, at 23.

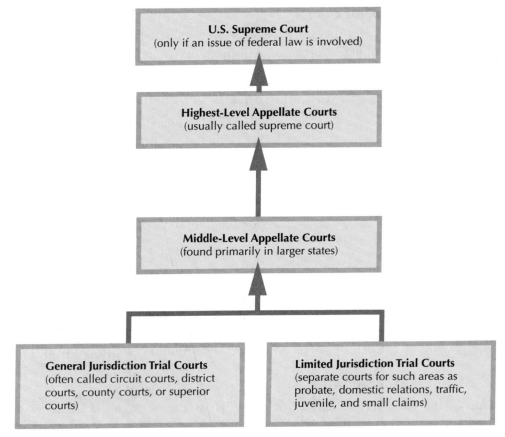

Figure 5-6   Organization of a Typical State Court System

Starting at the bottom of Figure 5-6, you will find the trial courts. In some states, below the trial courts shown in Figure 5-6 is a system of inferior courts with names such as justice of the peace, city, and magistrate courts. Those courts are not **courts of record**. No permanent record is kept of the testimony, lawyers' remarks, or judges' rulings. The absence of a record eliminates the possibility of an appeal and requires the losing party to initiate a completely new trial in a higher-level trial court if that party wishes to have the matter reconsidered.

Many states have one basic trial court, similar to federal district courts, that can hear any type of case (i.e., it has **general jurisdiction**). This court typically carries a name like circuit court, district court, county court, or superior court. On the other hand, other states have a confusing variety of specialized courts with **limited jurisdiction**. These courts hear a narrow range of cases on a specific subject (such as probate, domestic relations, or traffic) and sometimes even overlap regarding the types of cases they can hear. For example, in Massachusetts both the probate court and the superior court can hear divorce cases.

States maintain either one or two levels of appellate courts. The larger states have generally gone to a two-tiered system like that in operation at the federal level. The intermediate-level appellate courts usually sit in panels, while

Court of record
A court where a permanent record is kept of the testimony, lawyers' remarks, and judges' rulings.

the court of last resort sits en banc. On some matters appeals to the highest court are discretionary, while on others they are a matter of right. A few states have established separate courts to handle criminal versus civil appeals at the intermediate or highest level. Finally, as noted earlier in this chapter, even the name of the highest-level appellate court varies from state to state. While most states identify their highest court as the state supreme court, in New York and Maryland it is called the court of appeals.

In most cases a state's top appellate court is the end of the road because cases can be appealed to the U.S. Supreme Court only if they raise a federal issue. For example, in criminal cases state courts must accord the due process rights guaranteed by the U.S. Constitution. This can involve resolving issues regarding the right to counsel, the admissibility of evidence resulting from an allegedly illegal search, jury selection procedures, and so on. If the defendant thinks these constitutional rights have been violated, she or he may be able to appeal the case to the federal courts on the basis that a federal issue is involved. Whenever a federal law or a provision of the U.S. Constitution is involved, the federal courts have the right to make the final determination as to what that law or constitutional provision means. But remember that a criminal defendant has no right to appeal his or her conviction in a state court to a federal court unless such federal issues are raised. Under the principles of federalism the state courts are the final arbiters as to the meaning of state statutes and state constitutional provisions.

State court judges are selected in a variety of ways. In some states they are appointed by the state's chief executive or the state legislature or both. In others they are selected in either partisan or nonpartisan elections. Still other states use a modification of what has become known as the Missouri plan. These systems generally convene a special panel of lawyers and lay persons who nominate a few candidates for a vacancy. The governor then appoints from among this select group. A year or two later the person who was appointed goes before the general electorate in a special retention election. In such an election the voters are asked simply whether that judge should be retained.

3. Exclusive and Concurrent Jurisdiction

If a specific court is the only one authorized to hear a particular type of case, it has **exclusive jurisdiction.** If more than one court is authorized to hear the same type of case, they each have **concurrent jurisdiction.** Where concurrent jurisdiction exists, a case can be heard by more than one court, and the parties can select the one they wish to use.

As we mentioned in Chapter 4, the federal government is a government of limited powers. Just as Congress can legislate only if the Constitution has given it the power to do so, federal courts can hear cases only if the Constitution has given them the power to do so. Article III, Section 2, of the Constitution spells out the jurisdiction of the federal courts in terms of (1) the nature of the subject matter of the case and (2) the parties involved. Figure 5-7, on page 88, lists the requirements for federal court jurisdiction.

Two of the grounds for federal court jurisdiction require particular emphasis, as they account for the bulk of federal cases. The federal courts have jurisdiction when the case involves

Exclusive jurisdiction
When only one court has the power to hear a case.

Concurrent jurisdiction
When more than one court has jurisdiction to hear a case.

Based on the subject matter (federal question):
Any case involving the interpretation or application of
1. the U.S. Constitution,
2. a federal law or regulation,
3. a treaty, or
4. admiralty and maritime laws.

Based on the parties involved:
Any case or controversy in law and equity in which
1. the case affects ambassadors or other public ministers and counsels,
2. the United States is a party to the suit,
3. the controversy is between two or more states,
4. the controversy is between a state and citizens of another state,*
5. the parties are citizens of different states (known as diversity jurisdiction),
6. the controversy is between citizens of the same state claiming lands under grants of different states, or
7. the controversy is between (a) a state or the citizens thereof and (b) foreign states, citizens, or subjects.*

Based on the amount of money involved:
In addition to the constitutional requirements stated above, Congress has the power to add a minimum dollar value to suits between citizens of different states. The current federal statute states that the amount in controversy in diversity actions must exceed $75,000 to qualify for original federal jurisdiction.

*The Eleventh Amendment modified this to exclude situations where the suit was commenced or prosecuted against a state by an individual.

Figure 5-7   Jurisdiction of Federal Courts

Federal question jurisdiction
The power of the federal courts to hear matters of federal law.

Diversity jurisdiction
The power of the federal courts to hear matters of state law if the opposing parties are from different states and the amount in controversy exceeds $75,000.

Removal
The transfer of a case from one state court to another or from a state court to a federal court.

1. federal law. This is known as **federal question jurisdiction** and includes cases involving a federal statute, a federal regulation, or the U.S. Constitution.
2. opposing litigants from different states where the amount in controversy exceeds $75,000. This is known as **diversity jurisdiction.**

If a lawsuit does not fall within one of the categories listed in Figure 5-7, the parties have no choice but to bring the matter in a state court. Unlike the federal courts, state courts generally have the power to hear any type of case. The only time state courts are prohibited from hearing cases involving federal law is when Congress has expressly included that limitation in a federal statute.

In situations where both the state and the federal courts have concurrent jurisdiction, the plaintiff makes the initial decision as to which court to use. However, when the plaintiff selects a state court and the federal courts also have jurisdiction, the defendant may be able to **remove** the case to federal court.

Deciding whether to go to state or federal court is not the same as deciding whether the court will apply state or federal law to the case. For example, in a negligence case a federal court might have jurisdiction based on the diversity of citizenship of the parties. However, the federal court must follow state negligence law in deciding the case. If the case involves an area of unsettled state law,

the federal court must base its decision on its best guess as to what the state's highest court would do if faced with the same situation. Because the federal court is only guessing at what the state court would do, the federal court's decision is binding on the current litigants but is not binding on the state courts. Therefore, no matter how the federal court decides the case, it will still be open to the state courts to change the law in that area the next time a litigant brings a case on the same issue to the state courts. Likewise, when a state court hears a case involving a federal matter, it must follow the guidance of the federal courts.

DISCUSSION QUESTION

6. For each of these situations determine whether you think the matter should be heard in state or federal *court*. Also decide whether you think a court would apply state or federal *law*.

   a. A wife wants to divorce her husband.
   b. Martha, a Massachusetts resident, wants to sue Susan, a Massachusetts resident, for $80,000 based on breach of contract.
   c. Sam, a Massachusetts resident, wants to sue Jill, a Vermont resident, for $80,000 based on breach of contract.
   d. A teacher in a public school wants to challenge a state law requiring all teachers to start each day of class with a minute of silent prayer.

C. COURT PERSONNEL

It takes many different participants to make the judicial system work effectively. Court personnel include not only the judges and attorneys appearing before them but also court clerks, court reporters, and bailiffs.

The trial court judge is, of course, one of the most powerful members of the judicial system. Within the limits of the law the judge decides whether to dismiss a case before it reaches trial, the extent of pretrial discovery, and the amount of time the lawyers will have to prepare their cases. Once the trial is under way, the judge acts as the presiding officer, rules on objections, and determines when recesses will occur. If a jury is involved, the judge supervises its selection, removes jury members from the courtroom at key times to protect them from improper influences, and instructs them on the meaning of the law they are to apply. When a jury is not involved, the judge also acts as the fact finder and decides whether the defendant is guilty (in criminal cases) or liable (in civil cases). In criminal cases the judge is also responsible for sentencing the convicted defendant. If the litigants want to contest a trial judge's findings, they must present their arguments to appellate judges.

Some states also use **justices of the peace, court commissioners, and magistrates** in their court systems. Individuals holding these titles are lower-level court personnel who perform limited judicial duties but are not considered full-fledged judges. In some states they do not have to be lawyers to perform these duties.

In addition to being advocates for their clients, attorneys are considered officers of the court. As such, they are responsible for maintaining proper decorum in the courtroom and acting within the ethical restraints imposed on them by the courts and their profession.

Court clerks are responsible for keeping the court files in proper condition and ensuring that the various motions filed by lawyers and the actions taken by judges are properly recorded. A head clerk of the courts is usually responsible for running the central records section of the courthouse; his or her assistants are assigned to sit in on the actual courtroom proceedings.

The **court reporter** prepares verbatim transcripts of courtroom proceedings. Most reporters use a stenotype machine rather than shorthand. Because it is expensive, they prepare a written transcript only if the case is being appealed.

Bailiffs are responsible for maintaining order in the courtrooms. They are also responsible for watching over the juries when they are in recess or when they have been sequestered. When a jury is sequestered, the members sleep at a hotel and are kept isolated from the public and their families to prevent them from being exposed to prejudicial publicity, threats, bribes, or any other improper influences.

Finally, sheriffs and marshals also serve as officers of the court. They serve summonses and other court documents, collect money as required by court judgments, and otherwise help in carrying out the court's orders.

> **P R A C T I C E   T I P**
>
> When dealing with court personnel, remember that sometimes a few kind words and a professional attitude will get you the assistance you need.

SUMMARY

In this chapter we have seen that although the American legal system may seem to involve a confusing mix of names and functions, all courts can be classified in two ways:

1. They are either trial or appellate courts. Some trial courts have only limited jurisdiction; for example, they only hear cases worth less than a certain amount of money.
2. They are part of either the federal or a state system.

The federal court system and most state court systems are based on a three-tier model. At the bottom are the trial courts, which decide both factual and legal issues. Above the trial courts you will generally find an intermediate appellate court. At the top of every system is the highest appellate court. Appellate courts decide questions of law only. In the federal system the trial courts are called district courts, the intermediate appellate courts are called courts of appeals, and the highest court is the U.S. Supreme Court.

The power of a particular court to hear certain types of cases is known as its jurisdiction. The federal Constitution limits all federal courts' jurisdiction by allowing them to hear only the types of cases listed under Article III, Section 2. The two most common grounds for federal court jurisdiction are federal question and diversity of citizenship.

REVIEW QUESTIONS

Pages 73 through 77

1. What are the two basic functions of trial courts?
2. What is the difference between questions of law and questions of fact? Why is it important to know the difference?
3. Give an example of a question of fact that might arise during a murder trial. Give an example of a question of law that might arise in that same trial.
4. What is the difference between a bench and a jury trial?

5. What will an appellate court usually do if it finds that the trial court made a harmless error?
6. What is the difference between reversing and remanding a case?
7. What is the difference between a dissenting and a concurring opinion?
8. List the major differences between trial and appellate courts.

Pages 78 through 85

9. In the federal court system what are the names given to
   a. the highest appellate court,
   b. the intermediate appellate courts, and
   c. the trial courts?
10. Look at the map in Figure 5-3. How many district courts are there in your state? In which circuit is your state located?
11. If you hear that "cert."has been denied in a case, what does that mean?
12. In the federal system, what are the "inferior Courts"?

Pages 85 through 90

13. Describe a typical state court system. How is your state court system similar to or different from the "typical" state system?
14. True or false: In every state the highest appellate court is called the supreme court.
15. Jurisdiction refers to the power a court has to hear a case. Define each of the following types of jurisdiction:
    a. general jurisdiction,
    b. limited jurisdiction,
    c. original jurisdiction,
    d. appellate jurisdiction,
    e. exclusive jurisdiction, and
    f. concurrent jurisdiction.
16. What are the two major grounds for gaining federal court jurisdiction?

Chapter 6

Civil Litigation and Its Alternatives

Discourage litigation. Persuade your neighbors to compromise whenever you can. As a peacemaker the lawyer has superior opportunity of being a good man. There will still be business enough.
Abraham Lincoln

INTRODUCTION

Litigation is the process of using the courts to settle disputes. In this chapter we provide an overview of the litigation process, including the procedural steps involved in initiating, trying, and appealing civil cases. Because litigation can be a very expensive, stressful, and lengthy process, various alternatives to litigation have developed. Therefore, in addition to the litigation process, we will also look at these alternative approaches to litigation, such as arbitration and mediation, known collectively as **alternative dispute resolution (ADR)**.

We will use the cases of Donald Drake, which we introduced in Chapter 1, and Diane Dobbs, which we introduced in Chapter 3, to illustrate litigation and its alternatives. You will recall that Mr. Drake witnessed the death of his grandson, Philip, when Philip was struck by the car Wilma Small was driving. Diane Dobbs was the waitress who was fired when she announced to her boss that she was pregnant. Here are the cases again for your review.

Alternative dispute resolution (ADR) Techniques for resolving conflicts that are alternatives to full-scale litigation. The two most common are arbitration and mediation.

The Case of the Distressed Grandfather

Approximately one year ago Mr. Drake and his six-year-old grandson, Philip, were walking down a residential road on their way home from visiting one of Philip's friends. Philip was walking on the sidewalk approximately 30 feet in front of Mr. Drake. Suddenly a car sped past Mr. Drake, seemingly went out of control, jumped the curb, and hit Philip. Mr. Drake ran to Philip's side, but it was too late. Philip had been killed instantly. The driver of the car, Mrs. Wilma Small, was unhurt.

At the time of the accident Mr. Drake's only concern was for the welfare of his grandson because he himself was clear of the danger. Naturally, Mr. Drake suffered a great deal of emotional pain and shock because of seeing his grandson killed. While being driven home from the accident, he suffered a heart attack that necessitated a lengthy hospital stay.

One year later he still does not feel completely recovered and often suffers from nightmares as he relives the accident and his grandson's death. Mr. Drake would like to sue Mrs. Small to recover for his hospital bills and for his pain and suffering.

The Case of the Pregnant Waitress

Ms. Diane Dobbs had been employed by the Western Rib Eye Restaurant for the past three years. Throughout that time her work record had been exemplary. Customers often spoke to the manager to tell him how Diane's service and personality contributed to their especially enjoyable dining experience at the restaurant.

Six months ago Diane, who is not married, found out that she was pregnant. When she approached her manager, Ben, to discuss arrangements for a maternity leave, instead of the favorable reception she had expected, Ben reached over, patted her stomach, and said, "Well, I guess we can't have you working for us any longer." Ben then grabbed her by the arm and escorted her out of the restaurant. Diane protested and asked to be allowed to collect her personal belongings from her locker, but the manager just laughed and said she was "history." When Diane began to cry, he softened his demeanor a little and said, "Look, we simply can't have a pregnant lady working here. It just wouldn't be good for business."

Although she has been actively looking, Diane has not yet been able to find suitable employment.

Because this is a textbook, we have no choice but to present topics in a linear fashion. Therefore, in this chapter, we will first discuss the various alternatives to litigation and then proceed to the litigation process. However, you should keep in mind that real life does not proceed in such a straightforward manner. While informal negotiations may begin the moment a dispute arises, there is no set order in which the parties are required to proceed. They may decide to file a complaint immediately, hence initiating the litigation process, but then suspend their litigation efforts while trying to resolve the dispute through arbitration or mediation. Should those efforts not be successful, they then may pick up where they left off in the litigation process. At other times, however, the parties may turn first to an alternative dispute resolution process and only then

proceed with initiating a lawsuit if that process fails. Therefore, as you read this chapter, keep in mind that the various forms of alternative dispute resolution, including informal negotiations, mediation, and arbitration, can arise at any time: before formal litigation has begun or after a lawsuit has been filed and the litigation process is well under way.

A. ALTERNATIVE DISPUTE RESOLUTION

In general terms, litigation involves law suits whereas ADR is any other method for resolving a dispute. ADR can take many forms, ranging from very informal negotiations, which usually begin as soon as a dispute arises and may not end until the final appeal has been filed, to the more formal approaches of mediation and arbitration. Those more formal approaches require the involvement of a neutral third party, as either a mediator or arbiter. The main difference between mediation and arbitration is that in mediation, the third party acts as a facilitator who tries to help the parties reach their own resolution. In arbitration, the third party is a decision maker who acts much like a judge would at a trial. While mediation and arbitration are the most commonly used forms of formal ADR, the term sometimes includes other activities such as mini-trials and summary jury trials, which are designed to encourage out-of-court settlements.

As indicated above, ADR approaches can be used before or after litigation has begun. Recognizing that ADR can be effective after litigation has commenced, in 1998 Congress enacted legislation requiring that each U.S. district court establish and implement a plan to decrease costs and delays in the federal court system. Specifically, the legislation mandated that all district courts establish programs to offer alternative dispute resolution to litigants. In addition, nearly all of the U.S. courts of appeals have established mediation programs to assist parties in resolving their appeals. Similarly, many state and local court systems have also incorporated ADR, especially in the area of family law, where the parties are often required to participate in formal mediation regarding issues of child custody and visitation.

NETNOTE

If you are interested in learning more about various forms of ADR, there are several web sites you can visit, including the American Arbitration Association at *www.adr.org*, the Mediation Information and Resource Center at *www.mediate.com*, and the ABA Section on Dispute Resolution at *www.abanet.org/dispute*. A Particularly interesting site is that of the Victim Offender Mediation Association (VOMA) at *www.voma.org*. VOMA supports mediation between victims and offenders, so that victims are given an opportunity to have their questions answered and their emotional and other needs met, and offenders are held accountable and given an opportunity to make restitution to their victims and the community.

While such required mediation may at first appear to be a contradiction in terms, many states are now imposing such "mandatory mediation" in selected types of disputes. It is mandatory in the sense that both parties are required to engage in a formal mediation process before a court can hear the case. However, if the mediation is not successful, the parties can still end the mediation process and continue with the court proceedings.

The business community has long been a strong supporter of ADR because it is viewed as being a faster and less expensive way of settling disputes that arise in the course of doing business. It is common practice for businesses to include arbitration clauses in their contracts. Under these clauses the parties are legally bound to refer disputes over the interpretation of a contract to arbitration rather than take them to court. In addition to saving time and money, ADR often allows a company to settle a dispute without attracting the public attention that may accompany a lawsuit.

1. Arbitration

Arbitration
An ADR mechanism whereby the parties submit their disagreement to a third party, whose decision is binding.

When a dispute is sent to **arbitration**, the matter is delegated to a neutral third-party arbitrator. Both parties agree in advance to accept the arbitrator's decision. In many cases the arbitrator's decision is binding, and the dissatisfied party maynot challenge it in court unless the award was obtained by fraud.

An arbitrator functions much like a judge in a court of law, but the arbitrator follows a much simpler set of procedures that do not require as much time or expense. The arbitrator is usually selected from a panel of individuals who have special training in the area. These individuals are often affiliated with the American Arbitration Association or one of the other organizations that are set up specifically to provide arbitration services. In addition to being speedier and less expensive than traditional litigation, the results of arbitration can frequently be kept confidential.

In the field of labor law, arbitration is often used as a way of avoiding strikes. Sports fans are familiar with the role arbitration has played in determining the salaries of baseball players. Also, public employees are often required to use arbitration when state law prohibits them from striking.

The Case of the Pregnant Waitress (continued)

Many employees are members of unions and hence subject to a collective bargaining agreement negotiated between labor and management. If Diane Dobbs had been a member of a union and had filed a grievance, her union representative would first have tried to negotiate a resolution with management. If that was not successful, most likely the collective bargaining agreement would have included a mandatory arbitration clause that would require Ms. Dobbs to submit her grievance to arbitration.

Mediation
An ADR mechanism whereby a neutral third party assists the parties in reaching a mutually agreeable, voluntary compromise.

2. Mediation

Although both arbitration and **mediation** involve the disputants meeting with a neutral third party, they differ greatly with respect to the role this third party

plays. Whereas an arbitrator imposes a solution, a mediator attempts to guide the disputants toward a compromise that is voluntarily accepted by both sides.

The basic premise of mediation is that the best solution is the solution that the parties themselves devise. After all, they (not the mediator) best understand their positions, and they (not the mediator) will have to live with the solution they reach.

The mediator's role is therefore like that of a Sherpa guide. The guide's role is not to tell the explorers which mountain to climb or even whether to climb a mountain at all. The guide simply helps the climbers find the best way to reach whatever summit they have chosen to climb. In mediation the mediator helps the disputants identify the issues that divide them and explore possible solutions for bridging the divide.[1]

a. Cases Most Suitable for Mediation

Generally, some types of cases are better suited for mediation than others. Mediation is particularly appropriate in those situations where the parties will be required to deal with each other in the future, such as after a divorce when children are involved, or when the parties simply wish to have amiable future relations, such as in the case of a dispute between neighbors. It is hoped that the mediation process will not only resolve the current situation but will also improve the participants' interpersonal and conflict management skills as they continue to deal with each other in the future.

In tort cases, mediation works best in situations where liability is clear-cut and the dispute is primarily over the amount of the damages. In this type of situation, both sides can usually see the advantage to settling for an "average" damage award rather than spending a significant amount of money on trial preparation and then gambling on the outcome.

There are, of course, some situations that do not lend themselves to mediation. For example, Rosa Parks, a black woman, was arrested in 1955 for refusing to give up her seat on a city bus to a white person. Civil rights leaders used her situation to bring public attention to racial discrimination in the South and organized the famous Montgomery bus boycott. This type of political mobilization could not have happened through mediation.[2]

Mediation may also not be appropriate in situations involving domestic violence. Not only may the contact between the abuser and the victim during mediation result in further violence following the mediation session, but the victim may perceive the mediation session itself as another form of abuse. Further, as mediation works best when the parties are of fairly equal bargaining power, it is not as effective in situations of abuse, where the victim perceives herself as powerless against the abuser.

b. Mediation Process

In mediation, the role of the mediator is to encourage the parties to work together. The mediator helps the parties search for common ground. Once they have found some areas of agreement, then they can work toward creating solutions to resolve their dispute.

---

[1] See Mori Irvine, Serving Two Masters: The Obligation under the Rules of Professional Conduct to Report Attorney Misconduct in a Confidential Mediation, 26 Rutgers L.J. 155, 158 n. 13 (1994).

[2] Drew Peterson, Getting Together: Conflict Triage—Appropriate and Inappropriate Cases for Mediation, 23 Alaska Bar Rag 9 (1999).

At the initial session the mediator meets with the parties and, if the parties are represented, with their attorneys as well. The mediator starts by making some preliminary comments to inform the participants of the mediator's role as a neutral and of how the process will proceed. The mediator usually has everyone sign an agreement whereby all agree that any information divulged during the mediation session will be kept confidential. Typically, the mediator next asks each of the parties to describe the dispute from his or her point of view. The mediator identifies the different issues and sets an agenda for their further discussion.

Following this opening session, most mediators begin a series of caucuses in which the mediator meets separately with each party. As it is imperative that the parties be open with the mediator, the mediator again stresses his or her commitment to confidentiality. The mediator assures the parties that he or she will not reveal any information to the other party without the express permission of the party who revealed it. The purpose of these first private meetings is not to convince the parties to accept a solution but rather to gather information.

After the private meetings with each side, the mediator usually begins the process of floating various compromise solutions. "Would you be willing to give up_____ if you were able to get_____?" The mediator tries to get the parties to stop reacting emotionally to the situation and instead to focus on compromise.

While the parties may have entered mediation in a combative posture, if the mediation is successful, the position of the parties will change to one of collaboration whereby they can jointly construct a win-win solution. If the parties reach a resolution, they draft and sign a written agreement, which becomes a court-enforceable contract. If they do not reach an agreement, they can simply walk away from the mediation and seek other approaches to resolving their differences.

c. Mediation Training

Community groups, educational institutions, and court-annexed programs are all engaged in mediation training. This training emphasizes the need to lay aside one's personal views and to assist both sides in finding a "win-win" solution to their problems. In those cases where mediation is formally incorporated into the litigation process, some governmental agency, either the court or an administrative agency, is responsible for licensing or certifying the individuals who are designated to act as mediators. Although attorneys and retired judges frequently serve as mediators, many state and local courts also allow nonlawyers to serve as mediators. For example, clergy, psychologists, and social workers often serve as mediators in family law cases.

3. Summary Jury Trials

Summary jury trials are nonbinding mock trials in which attorneys for both sides present synopses of their cases to a jury, which then renders an advisory opinion on the basis of these presentations. Time is saved because the attorneys give summaries of what key witnesses are expected to say rather than going through complete direct and cross-examinations. It is hoped that the parties will agree to a settlement that approximates the results reached by the mock jury.

Summary jury trials
A nonbinding process in which attorneys for both sides present synopses of their cases to a jury, which renders an advisory opinion on the basis of these presentations.

If a paralegal works as a mediator, has that paralegal committed the unauthorized practice of law? If mediation is seen as the practice of law, mediation would be closed to nonlawyers, thereby leading to the loss of effective mediators. Because mediators are sometimes called upon to give legal advice and to predict the outcome should the case proceed to trial, nonlawyers engaged in evaluative mediation may be committing the unauthorized practice of law. However, if the mediator remains neutral and refrains from giving the mediator's point of view or suggesting any particular outcome to the participants, then arguably the mediator is not engaging in the unauthorized practice of law.*

---

* For a fuller discussion of this topic, see Note: Laymen Cannot Lawyer, But Is Mediation the Practice of Law?, 20 Cardozo L. Rev. 1715 (May/July 1999).

4. Role of Paralegals in ADR

Because arbitrators and mediators do not necessarily have to be attorneys, experienced paralegals may be able to qualify for such positions if they have the right mix of formal training and experience in the substantive field in which they wish to work. In addition, paralegal involvement in ADR closely parallels the functions paralegals serve in traditional litigation. They assist the attorneys in gathering and preparing information that will be presented to the arbitrator, mediator, or mock jury. They help make administrative arrangements for the ADR proceedings and schedule expert and lay witnesses. They also work to prepare clients and other witnesses for what to expect from the ADR process. Following a decision they will often prepare documents required as part of the settlement.

5. Evaluation of ADR Techniques

Proponents of ADR argue that its use saves time and avoids at least some of the expenses associated with going to court. It is also generally thought that the parties will feel better about a solution they worked out through mediation than they will about a decision imposed on them by the courts. This is especially true in child custody cases, where the parents should feel as though they "own" the decision, as they will often need to continue to have regular contact with each other and to consult with each other about the welfare of their children.

Not everyone agrees with this assessment. For example, a study conducted by the Rand Institute for Civil Justice found that ADR was not extensively used when it was voluntary and that when it was used, it did not result in great savings of time or expenses. Furthermore, its use was not found to affect the participants' views of fairness or attorney satisfaction.[3]

---

[3] Van Duch, Case Management Reform Ineffective, Natl. L.J., Feb. 3, 1997, at A3.

Nevertheless, other studies indicate that ADR participants are extremely satisfied with both the process and the result, at least when the ADR method used is mediation, not arbitration. For example, a recent survey conducted by the National Law Journal and the American Arbitration Association found that of those who responded to the survey, a majority of litigators and in-house counsel preferred nonbinding mediation over binding arbitration. Not only did mediation save money and time, but also the respondents felt it provided a more satisfactory process, as it was most likely to preserve the relationship between the disputing parties. The attorneys' complaints about arbitration included distrust of the arbiters themselves, the costs (which can approach those of litigation), and the inability to appeal an arbiter's decision.

DISCUSSION QUESTIONS

1.   If two disputants want to settle their differences other than by going to court, what options do they have?

2.   If you were involved in a dispute, which alternative dispute resolution method would you prefer?

3.   Do you think either mediation or arbitration would be appropriate in Mr. Drake's case? Why?

When alternative dispute resolution methods fail, the parties may decide to proceed to litigation. That process of litigation is the subject of the next section.

The Case of the Distressed Grandfather (continued)

Generally, attorney Harper likes to use a form of ADR whenever possible as it may save her clients time, stress, and expense. Also, if there is a chance for an ongoing relationship between the parties, mediation, because it is less adversarial than litigation or arbitration, may help to preserve that relationship. Mrs. Small's attorney, however, has refused to engage in informal negotiations or in more formal ADR methods, such as mediation or arbitration. He informed attorney Harper that it is his position that, as Mr. Drake was not Philip's parent, there is no legal basis for making Mrs. Small responsible for Mr. Drake's injuries. Attorney Harper informed Mr. Drake that they have no choice if they want to proceed but to turn to the court system and litigation.

B. LITIGATION

The procedures that govern the litigation process are spelled out in formal rules that are published under names such as the Federal Rules of Civil Procedure, Massachusetts Rules of Civil Procedure, Illinois Criminal Law and Criminal Procedure, and the Federal Rules of Evidence. Although the specific stages in

the process and the specific court documents that must be completed differ in federal and state court systems, they also have much in common. Because most state rules are based on the federal rules, the focus of this book is on the federal rules. However, even though most states base their rules on those developed for the federal system, the procedures followed in state and federal courts do vary somewhat. Therefore, you must always consult the statutes and court rules for the particular court with which you are dealing.[4] In both federal and state courts there are three basic stages of litigation: pretrial, trial, and appeal. Take a few moments to study Figure 6-1, on page 102, which provides an overview of the litigation process. Refer to it as you proceed with the remainder of this chapter to help you keep track of the various stages.

> **PRACTICE TIP**
>
> Keep a copy of your state's rules of civil procedure on your desk. It is your bible. Also check to see if your local trial courts have their own rules. If so, obtain them and keep them with your state rules.

1. The Pretrial Stage

A lawsuit officially begins when the plaintiff files the appropriate legal documents with the clerk of the court. However, before this can occur, the attorney must handle some preliminary matters:

- whether there is a legal basis for a suit,
- who should be sued,
- in which court the case should be brought,
- whether the statute of limitations has expired, and
- whether any administrative agency has to be consulted before filing suit.

Pleadings
The papers that begin a lawsuit—generally, the complaint and the answer.

Once those issues have been resolved and a determination to sue has been made, the lawsuit enters the pleadings stage. The **pleadings** are the documents each side files with the court and serves on the other side to commence the lawsuit. In order to narrow the issues, either party may file **pretrial motions**. Finally, the parties will engage in **discovery**, an attempt by both sides to gather as much information as possible. The end result of this process may be a negotiated settlement, a court determination to dismiss the suit, or a decision to proceed to the trial stage.

Pretrial motion
A motion brought before the beginning of a trial either to eliminate the necessity for a trial or to limit the information that can be heard at the trial.

a. Preliminary Matters

The decisions as to these preliminary matters are not always easy to make and may involve extensive factual and legal research in order to determine the best course of action. Paralegals are often assigned the task of locating and analyzing statutes, court rules, and cases that are relevant to these decisions. In addition, they may be called on to engage in factual investigation, such as tracing corporate ownerships or locating parties and witnesses to the suit.

Discovery
The modern pretrial procedure by which one party gains information from the adverse party.

---

[4] Local federal district court rules are available in pamphlets from the district court office. You can also find federal court rules in the annotated codes and Supreme Court digests, as well as some specialized loose-leaf services. Complete texts of the court decisions that construe the federal rules of civil and criminal procedure are published in the Federal Rules Service (a loose-leaf service of Callaghan and Co.) and the Federal Rules Decisions (a West product, containing district court decisions involving the rules of procedure not published in the Federal Supplement). At the state level you can find the jurisdictional requirements of the courts in your state's constitution and statutes.

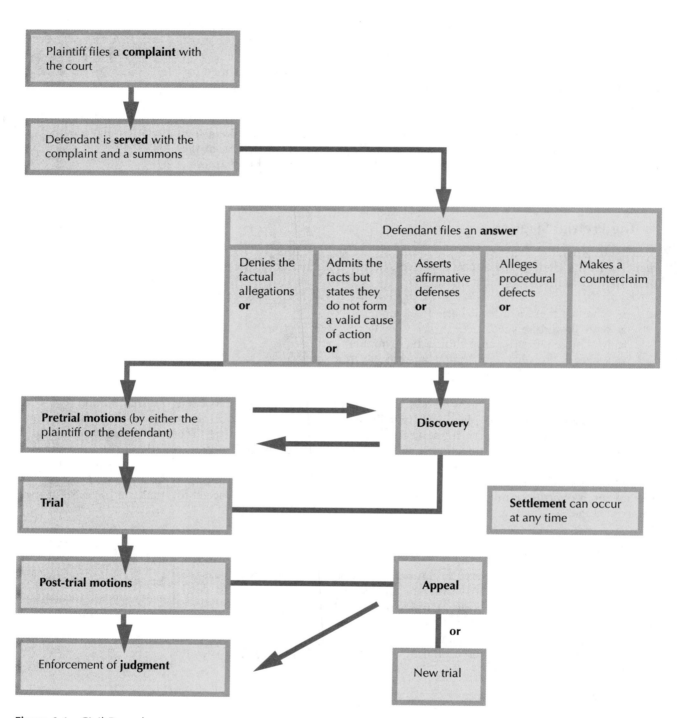

Figure 6-1 Civil Procedure

NETNOTE

On the Internet you can find all sorts of useful information about the courts—everything from their fax numbers to the location of a specific courthouse. To find the address of any state court, a good place to start is at the home page for the National Center for State Courts, *www.ncsconline.org/D_KIS/info__court_ web__sites.html*. The center maintains a complete listing for all fifty states. For information on federal courts, you can visit either the federal judiciary home page at *www.uscourts.gov* or the Federal Judicial Center home page at *www.fjc.gov*. Finally, the U.S. Supreme Court has its own web site at *www.supremecourtus.gov*.

(1) Legal grounds for the suit

As you will recall from Chapter 1, not every problem is a legal problem for which the courts can provide a remedy. Therefore, before an attorney can initiate a lawsuit, the attorney must be convinced that the client has a valid cause of action—that is, that based on the law and the facts the client's claim is sufficient to support a lawsuit. This determination involves answering two questions affirmatively. First, does the attorney believe that there are sufficient credible facts to support the plaintiff's position? Second, does the attorney believe that there is a valid legal theory to support the claim?

In determining whether their client's position is supported by credible facts, attorneys must review relevant documents and interview witnesses. They may also assign a paralegal to do much of the background research needed to determine whether a valid legal theory supports the claim.

This requirement that the attorney make a reasonable inquiry into the factual and legal bases for the claim is dictated in the federal system by Rule 11 of the Federal Rules of Civil Procedure:

> **P R A C T I C E**
> **T I P**
>
> With the use of a scanner, computers can generate realistic-looking signatures. But before you use one, keep in mind the function of a signature.

Rule 11

Signing of Pleadings, Motions, and Other Papers; Representations to Court; Sanctions

(a) **Signature.** Every pleading, written motion, and other papers shall be signed by at least one attorney of record . . . or, if the party is not represented by an attorney, shall be signed by the party.

(b) **Representations to Court.** By presenting to the court . . . a pleading, written motion, or other paper, an attorney . . . is certifying that to the best of the person's knowledge, information, and belief, formed after an inquiry reasonable under the circumstances,—

(1) it is not being presented for any improper purpose, such as to harass or to cause unnecessary delay or needless increase in the cost of litigation;
(2) the claims, defenses, and other legal contentions therein are warranted by existing law or by a nonfrivolous argument for the extension, modification, or reversal of existing law or the establishment of new law; . . . .

(c) **Sanctions.** If, after notice and a reasonable opportunity to respond, the court determines that subdivision (b) has been violated, the court may . . . impose an appropriate sanction upon the attorneys, law firms, or parties. . . .

First, notice under subsection (a) that all pleadings, written motions, and other papers must be signed by the attorney, not a paralegal. Second, under subsection (b) the attorney can sign the pleading, written motion, or other paper only after conducting a reasonable inquiry into the facts and the law. This requirement of a reasonable inquiry was added in 1983. Prior to that time an attorney's signature on a document indicated that "to the best of his knowledge, information, and belief, there is a good ground to support it." The drafters of the 1983 amendment believed that this subjective standard did not sufficiently protect the legal system from frivolous lawsuits—hence the addition of the requirement of a reasonable inquiry, a standard that can be objectively measured based on what a reasonable attorney would have done rather than simply on what the attorney actually did.

DISCUSSION QUESTIONS

4. In Mr. Drake's case, assume Massachusetts courts have allowed mothers and fathers to recover in situations similar to that experienced by Mr. Drake but have never spoken about whether they would extend the rule to allow recovery by grandparents. Several other states, however, that have directly confronted this issue have ruled against grandparents. The most common reason for not allowing recovery is the fear that to do so would encourage people to bring too many potentially frivolous lawsuits.

With that as the legal precedent do you think Mr. Drake's attorney should feel any concern in signing her name to the complaint? Why?

5. Which language do you prefer: "that to the best of his knowledge, information, and belief there is good ground to support" the claim or "that to the best of the person's knowledge, information, and belief, formed after an inquiry reasonable under the circumstances," the claim is warranted? Why?

If attorneys file lawsuits without first conducting a reasonable investigation regarding the facts of the case, they may be subject to Rule 11 sanctions.

(2) Parties to the suit

Under the legal principle called **standing**, only parties with a real stake in the outcome are allowed to participate in a lawsuit. Generally, courts are not supposed to decide abstract issues or render advisory opinions. (The one exception occurs in some states where courts are authorized to respond to requests for advice from other governmental bodies.) By requiring courts to decide concrete rather than abstract cases, they will have the benefit of parties who have a vested interest in the outcome and who will therefore vigorously argue their positions.

> Why limit lawsuits to people who have been hurt? One reason is that they're likely to marshal the strongest arguments. It brings to mind the old line about the role of the chicken and the pig in furnishing your breakfast: The chicken is involved, but the pig is *committed*. Let chickens file lawsuits against bacon-and-egg combos, and they may lack the motivation to do a good job.[5]

Because of this requirement of standing, persons and organizations cannot file lawsuits simply because they do not approve of a certain governmental policy or some corporation's building project. For example, only persons who have been sentenced to death can challenge the death penalty. If the court determines that the parties do not have standing, it simply dismisses the case without making a determination on the merits.

A classic example of how the requirement of standing affects who can sue occurred in conjunction with the litigation that led up to the famous case of *Brown v. Board of Education*.[6] While the National Association for the Advancement of Colored People (NAACP) was opposed to the Kansas policy of segregating its public school system, it had no standing on its own to challenge the constitutionality of that policy. Before it could proceed, the organization had to recruit an African-American child who was actually turned away when she attempted to enter an all-white school located in her neighborhood.[7] Eventually, the NAACP was able to find thirteen parents and their children who were willing to serve as plaintiffs in the case.

After having determined that the plaintiff has the required standing to sue, the attorney must decide who should be named as defendants. Naturally the attorney will choose to sue the person who caused his or her client harm. However, the most logical person to sue may not be worth suing because he or she may not have money to pay the damages that a court might award. This is referred to as being **judgment proof**. If there is more than one possible defendant, the plaintiff will want to make sure to include the one with the "deepest pocket" (most assets).

For example, under a theory known as **respondeat superior** an employer can sometimes be held responsible for the acts of its employees. Because employers usually have more money than employees, persons injured by an employee will frequently also sue the employer. Similarly, in an automobile accident case the plaintiff may sue the manufacturer of the auto or the governmental unit responsible for maintaining the roadway.

Standing
The principle that courts cannot decide abstract issues or render advisory opinions; rather they are limited to deciding cases that involve litigants who are personally affected by the court's decision.

Judgment proof
When the defendant does not have sufficient money or other assets to pay the judgment.

---

[5] Steve Chapman, No Decision Sometimes Best Decision, The Republican, June 22, 2004, at A9.

[6] 347 U.S. 483 (1954).

[7] Paul E. Wilson, A Retrospective of Brown v. Board of Education: The Genesis of Brown v. Board of Education, 6 Kan. J.L. & Pub. Pol'y 7 (1996).

Guardian
A person appointed by the court to manage the affairs or property of a person who is incompetent due to age or some other reason.

The attorney must also be certain that the parties to a lawsuit are legally capable of suing and being sued. For example, in many states a minor must sue or be sued through a named **guardian** or "**next friend.**" A guardian is someone who has the legal right and duty to take care of another person's property when that person is a child or is otherwise incompetent. A next friend is not the legal guardian but is a responsible party that the court recognizes as being a legitimate representative. Allowing suit by such representatives is an exception to the requirement of standing mentioned above. The guardian or next friend is not suing in his or her own right but rather as a representative for the child or incompetent person. An interesting case intertwining the principles of standing and guardianship occurred when the U.S. Supreme Court was asked to decide the constitutionality of the words "under God" in the Pledge of Allegiance. Michael Newdow had brought a suit on behalf of his daughter. His daughter attended an elementary school where each day the classes were led in a group recitation of the Pledge of Allegiance. Newdow shared physical custody of his daughter with his daughter's mother, but the mother had exclusive legal custody. Therefore, the Court determined that he lacked standing to litigate as his daughter's next friend. Because Mr. Newdow lacked standing to bring the lawsuit, the Court could make no decision as to the constitutionality of the words "under God" and dismissed the case.[8]

Compulsory joinder
When a person must be brought into a lawsuit as either a plaintiff or a defendant.

Finally, there are times when a plaintiff cannot sue one potential defendant without including the others as well. This is known as **compulsory joinder.** Where such rules do not apply, the plaintiff may be selective in deciding who should be included in the suit. The defendant, however, may later file a motion to add a defendant that the plaintiff left out. Finally, in special circumstances when a number of people have been injured, such as in an airplane crash, the plaintiff may also wish to consider the possibility of a **class action suit.** The named plaintiff brings the suit on behalf of a large class of additional plaintiffs who are in a similar situation with respect to having been wronged by the defendant.

Class action suit
A lawsuit brought by a person as a representative for a group of people who have been similarly injured.

(3) Selection of the court

The last preliminary issue requires the attorney to decide which court should hear the case. From your readings in Chapter 4 you know that lawsuits begin in a trial court and not an appellate court, but which trial court? That will depend on which trial courts have **jurisdiction** over the type of case that the attorney will be filing. Recall that jurisdiction relates to the power of a particular court to hear a case brought before it. In some cases the attorney may have the option of selecting among several different courts and must evaluate the advantages and disadvantages of using one versus the other.

Jurisdiction
The power of a court to hear a case.

In determining whether jurisdiction exists, you must consider both **subject matter jurisdiction** and **personal jurisdiction.** If a court does not have both subject matter jurisdiction and personal jurisdiction, it cannot hear the case.

Subject matter jurisdiction
The power of a court to hear a particular type of case.

(a) Subject matter jurisdiction   As the term implies, subject matter jurisdiction is determined by the subject matter of the case—that is, the type of law that is involved. Take a moment to review the material in Chapter 5 on the jurisdiction of the federal and state courts. Do you think Mr. Drake's case could be filed

---

[8] Elk Grove Unified Sch. Dist. v. Newdow, 542 U.S. 1 (2004).

in federal court? Federal courts and state courts are empowered to hear different types of cases. Generally, federal courts can hear only cases relating to federal law (such as federal constitutional or statutory issues) or cases in which the plaintiff and defendant are from different states and the amount in dispute exceeds $75,000. Rule 8 of the Federal Rules of Civil Procedure requires that the attorney filing a complaint include "a statement indicating why the federal court has jurisdiction to hear the case."

Cases involving diversity of citizenship and more than $75,000 can usually be started in either federal or state court. In deciding which court to choose, an attorney will consider matters such as filing requirements, deadline dates, the current backlog of cases, discovery procedures, the rules of evidence, and the personalities of the judges. The convenience of the physical location of the court may also be a factor.

The Case of the Distressed Grandfather (continued)

Mr. Drake's case does not involve federal law, as negligence is strictly a matter of state law. However, Mr. Drake is a resident of Massachusetts and Mrs. Small, the defendant, is a resident of New Hampshire. Because they are residents of different states, attorney Harper will be able to file the complaint for Mr. Drake's case in federal court if the amount in dispute exceeds $75,000. Recall from Chapter 5, however, that even if she brings the case in federal court, because the accident happened in Massachusetts, the federal court will apply Massachusetts state law. Attorney Harper could also commence Mr. Drake's lawsuit in state court. For his case the federal and state courts have concurrent jurisdiction. Attorney Harper is free to search for the best available forum.

(b) Personal jurisdiction   Personal jurisdiction relates to the court's power to force a person to appear before it—hence the name personal jurisdiction. Generally, for a state court to have personal jurisdiction over a defendant, the defendant must either be a resident of that state or have some **minimum contacts** with it. For example, a state court would have jurisdiction over an automobile accident that happened within its boundaries.

Personal jurisdiction
The power of a court to force a person to appear before it.

Minimum contacts
A constitutional fairness requirement that a defendant have at least a certain minimum level of contact with a state before the state courts can have jurisdiction over the defendant.

The Case of the Distressed Grandfather (continued)

Because Mr. Drake's accident happened in Massachusetts, the accident supplies the minimum contacts that Massachusetts courts need to hear the lawsuit. Mr. Drake may sue Mrs. Small in Massachusetts.

Figure 6-2   Personal Jurisdiction

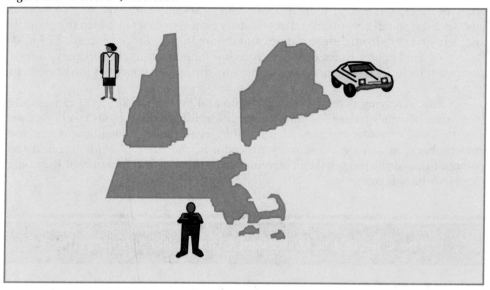

To better understand this concept of personal jurisdiction, just for a moment assume the situation had been different, as illustrated in Figure 6-2. Assume that Mr. Drake, a Massachusetts resident, had been vacationing in Maine when the accident happened and that Mrs. Small, also vacationing in Maine, was a New Hampshire resident. Then the issue of personal jurisdiction would be much more complicated. As he lives in Massachusetts, Mr. Drake would like to commence his lawsuit there. Under these revised facts, however, Mrs. Small has had no contact with Massachusetts, and as at least minimum contacts are required, Mr. Drake would not be allowed to sue her in Massachusetts. He could sue her in New Hampshire because, as a resident of that state, the New Hampshire courts would have jurisdiction over Mrs. Small. He could also sue her in Maine, as the accident in that state provides the minimum contacts necessary to satisfy personal jurisdiction.

(4) Statutes of limitations

Statutes of limitations
The law that sets the length of time from when something happens to when a lawsuit must be filed before the right to bring it is lost.

Statutes of limitations set the amount of time that a person has before he or she is forever barred from bringing a lawsuit. Such statutes vary depending on the type of situation involved. Some statutes of limitations set very shortvdeadlines. A person complaining of discrimination at work has only 180 days in which to bring a complaint. Other statutes of limitations, such as that for murder, are really without limit. Typically, persons have two years from the date of a negligent act to file a lawsuit. Mr. Drake is fortunate in that he sought legal advice well within the time frame allowed by the statute of limitations.

(5) Exhaustion of administrative remedies

If Mr. Drake's claim had involved a matter coming under the jurisdiction of an administrative agency, he might have had to consult that agency before being allowed to sue in a court of law. Such a requirement is known as the **exhaustion of administrative remedies**. The purpose behind this rule is to give the administrative agency a chance to resolve the problem without the parties having to resort to a lawsuit.

Exhaustion of administrative remedies The requirement that relief be sought from an administrative agency before proceeding to court.

The Case of the Pregnant Waitress (continued)

In employment discrimination cases, there is a requirement that an employee who has experienced discrimination at work first complain to the state or federal agency that handles such claims before being allowed to proceed with a lawsuit. Therefore, Ms. Dobbs' attorney would first instruct Diane to file a complaint with the local agency handling employment discrimination claims.

Once a person has filed a complaint with an administrative agency, that agency usually tries to resolve the issue by getting the parties to reach a mutually agreeable resolution. If those efforts are not successful, the process may proceed to a formal hearing. Such a hearing is similar to a trial but is less formal. Instead of a trial court judge, an administrative law judge oversees the proceeding. Usually there is no requirement that the rules of evidence be strictly followed. Some administrative agencies also allow for nonattorney representatives. Often, the hearing officer's decision resolves the dispute. However, if one of the parties is dissatisfied with the decision, depending on the agency, that party may have the option either to appeal the decision to a higher body within the agency itself, to appeal the decision to a court, or to start the whole process anew with a lawsuit.

PRACTICE TIP

Especially in employment cases, even before seeking an administrative remedy, there may be a contractual or union procedure that has to be followed or your client may be precluded from pursuing a remedy in court.

The Case of the Pregnant Waitress (continued)

The state agency investigated Ms. Dobbs's situation and determined that there was probable cause to believe she had been fired because of unlawful sex discrimination. The agency, however, was unable to resolve the dispute through informal negotiations with the restaurant owner. Therefore, the agency issued a right-to-sue letter so that Ms. Dobbs could proceed with a lawsuit.

The Case of the Distressed Grandfather (continued)

Mr. Drake's case against Mrs. Small does not raise any administrative law issues. Therefore, Mr. Drake's attorney did not need to involve an administrative agency prior to proceeding to litigation. However, separate from Mr. Drake's claims against her, Mrs. Small may find herself before an administrative agency, if the police determine the accident was her fault. For example, she might have to argue before a state licensing agency that her driver's license should not be revoked.

DISCUSSION QUESTIONS

6. Assume Mary was injured in an automobile accident while vacationing in California. Joe was driving the car that hit her. Mary is a resident of Michigan. Joe is a resident of Florida. In which state(s) may Mary bring suit? Why?

7. For years the federal courts have been trying to persuade Congress to eliminate diversity jurisdiction. Do you think that would be a wise decision? What purpose do you suppose diversity jurisdiction was originally meant to serve? If diversity jurisdiction is maintained, should it be tied to any jurisdictional amount, and if so, how much? Why?

The Case of the Distressed Grandfather (continued)

After reviewing the facts and the jurisdictional questions involved, attorney Harper has determined that the best court in which to proceed with Mr. Drake's case is federal district court. She directs paralegal Chris Kendall to draft a complaint to initiate the lawsuit.

Complaint
The pleading that begins a lawsuit.

Answer
defendant's reply to the complaint. It may contain statements of denial, admission, or lack of knowledge and affirmative defenses.

Counterclaim
A claim by the defendant against the plaintiff.

Cross-claim
A claim by one defendant against another defendant or by one plaintiff against another plaintiff.

Third-party claim
A claim by a defendant against someone in addition to the persons the plaintiff has already sued.

b. Pleadings

The pleadings are the documents that each side files with the court and serves on the other side in order to commence the lawsuit. Their purpose is to narrow and focus the issues involved. The initial document the plaintiff files is logically called a **complaint** because the plaintiff is the person starting the lawsuit and hence complaining of some behavior. A complaint states the allegations that form the basis of the plaintiff's case. The document the defendant files in response to the complaint is called an **answer** because it contains the defendant's answers to the charges laid out in the complaint. There are various other pleadings, including a **counterclaim** (a countersuit by the defendant against the plaintiff), a **cross-claim** (a suit by one defendant against another defendant), and a **third-party claim** (a suit by a defendant against someone not originally part of the

lawsuit), but in most litigation the pleadings are simply the complaint and the answer. Figure 6-3, below, diagrams one example of how these various pleadings might be used in litigation. Here plaintiff Smith sued two defendants, Jones and Brown, by filing a complaint against them. Defendant Jones responded with an answer to the complaint and an additional counterclaim against the plaintiff. Defendant Brown filed an answer to the complaint, a cross-claim against defendant Jones, and a third-party claim against Jim Jackson, someone whom the plaintiff had not named as a defendant in the original complaint.

(1) The complaint

The requirements for the format and the contents of the complaint are spelled out in the Federal Rules of Civil Procedure. Rule 10 outlines the form required for all pleadings and motions in federal court. Each document must begin with a **caption**, and all claims and defenses must be in numbered paragraphs. The caption must include the names of the parties, the name of the court, the title of the action, the docket file number, and the name of the pleading.

Caption
The heading section of a pleading that contains the names of the parties, the name of the court, the title of the action, the docket or file number, and the name of the pleading.

The Case of the Distressed Grandfather (continued)

Exhibit 6-1, on page 112, shows what the caption would look like in Mr. Drake's case. First, the caption would identify Donald Drake as the plaintiff and Wilma Small as the defendant. It would also indicate that the case is being filed in the U.S. District Court for the District of Massachusetts and would leave space for the eventual docket number to be entered by the court clerk. The court assigns the number at the time the attorney files the complaint.

Rule 8 determines what must appear in a claim, such as a complaint, that asks for relief. It requires that a complaint contain allegations as to why the case falls within the court's jurisdiction, the grounds that form the basis of the plaintiff's case, and the relief desired.

Figure 6-3   The Pleadings

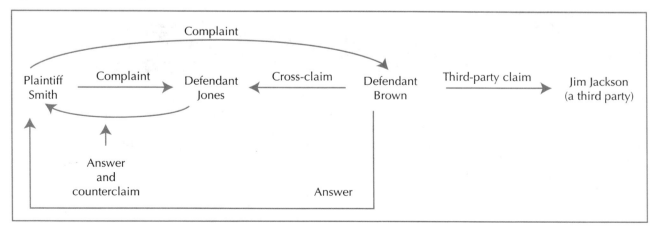

Exhibit 6-1 Caption

UNITED STATES DISTRICT COURT FOR THE DISTRICT OF MASSACHUSETTS		
		Civil Action, File Number________
Donald Drake, Plaintiff	}	
v.	}	COMPLAINT
Wilma Small, Defendant	}	

PRACTICE TIP

Find out the specific caption that is required for each of the courts with which you frequently deal. Then use your word processor to create standard captions.

Notice pleading
A method adopted by the federal rules in which the plaintiff simply informs the defendant of the claim and the general basis for it.

Rule 8

General Rules of Pleading

(a) **Claims for Relief.** A pleading which sets forth a claim for relief . . . shall contain (1) a short and plain statement of the grounds upon which the court's jurisdiction depends . . . (2) a short and plain statement of the claim showing that the pleader is entitled to relief, and (3) a demand for judgment for the relief the pleader seeks. Relief in the alternative or of several different types may be demanded.

The body of the complaint consists of the allegations of facts that constitute the cause of action. The federal rules allow for **notice pleading**; that is, the complaint must simply identify the transaction from which the plaintiff's claim arises. In many states, however, the facts being pleaded must be "ultimate" facts as opposed to conclusions of law.

The Case of the Distressed Grandfather (continued)

In Mr. Drake's case, at a minimum, the complaint must include a statement indicating why he believes the federal district court has jurisdiction, a statement showing why Mr. Drake has a valid claim against Mrs. Small, and finally what relief he would like the court to grant him. After considering all of these issues, paralegal Kendall drafted the complaint that appears in Exhibit 6-2, on page 114. Locate each of these items in the complaint.

While paralegals may draft pleadings, they may *not* sign them. To do so would constitute the unauthorized practice of law.

This sample complaint has only one **count** or basis for the lawsuit, the negligence of Mrs. Small. If the facts were different, however, the plaintiff could have alleged more than one basis for his lawsuit. For example, in Mr. Drake's case assume there were two people in Mrs. Small's car, Mrs. Small and Ms. Black. If Mr. Drake did not know which of them had been driving, he could allege in one count that Mrs. Small was the driver and alternatively allege in count two that Ms. Black was the driver. In addition, if he did not know whether the driver was simply being careless or had actually intended to hit Philip expressly to cause Mr. Drake's suffering, the complaint could include a count for the intentional infliction of emotional distress as well as one for negligence. This is known as **pleading in the alternative**.

DISCUSSION QUESTION

8. Does it seem fair to you that plaintiffs should be allowed to plead in the alternative? Why?

If a paralegal has drafted the complaint, the supervising attorney must carefully review and sign it. In some states there is a final requirement that the client verify the complaint. A **verification** consists of an affidavit signed by the client indicating that he or she has read the complaint and that its contents are correct.

Finally, the attorney or paralegal will file the complaint with the court. As provided in Rule 3, this action of filing the complaint with the court officially starts the lawsuit.

(2) The summons

The plaintiff must arrange to have the defendant notified that the suit has been filed. The plaintiff's attorney does this by preparing a **summons** and then having that summons and a copy of the complaint served on (given to) the defendant. Proper service usually requires that the local sheriff (or a U.S. marshal in federal cases) personally deliver the notice in the form of a summons to the defendant. There are occasions where proper notice can be satisfied by mailing the summons to the defendant's last known address, publishing copies of it in newspapers of general circulation, or delivering it to an authorized agent. An attorney or a paralegal must consult the federal or state civil practice act on the type of service required in each case.

Count
In a complaint, one cause of action.

Pleading in the alternative
Including more than one count in a complaint; the counts do not need to be consistent.

Verification
An affidavit signed by the client indicating that he or she has read the complaint and that its contents are correct.

Summons
A notice informing the defendant of the lawsuit and requiring the defendant to respond or risk losing the suit.

PRACTICE TIP

You can look in the Yellow Pages to find sheriffs and others who can perform service of process, but it is much more efficient to keep that list in your rolodex or computer database.

UNITED STATES DISTRICT COURT FOR THE DISTRICT OF MASSACHUSETTS

Civil Action, File Number_____

Donald Drake, Plaintiff	}	
v.	}	COMPLAINT
Wilma Small, Defendant	}	

1. Jurisdiction of this court is founded on diversity of citizenship. Plaintiff is a citizen of Massachusetts, and defendant is a citizen of Connecticut. The matter in controversy exceeds, exclusive of interest and costs, the sum of seventy-five thousand dollars.

2. The plaintiff, Donald Drake, is a natural person residing at 56 Bancroft Way, Springfield, Massachusetts.

3. The defendant, Wilma Small, is a natural person residing at 106 Hemingway Lane, Keene New Hampshire.

4. On September 1, 2006, while the plaintiff was walking on the sidewalk along a public way called Bishop Street in Springfield, Massachusetts, the defendant negligently drove a motor vehicle onto the sidewalk where the plaintiff's grandson, Philip Drake, was walking approximately thirty feet ahead of the plaintiff.

5. As a result of the defendant's negligence, the plaintiff's grandson was struck by the defendant's motor vehicle and instantly killed. The plaintiff viewed the entire accident.

6. As a direct result of viewing the death of his grandson, the plaintiff suffered a heart attack, great physical pain, mental suffering, and expenses for medical attention and hospitalization in the sum of one million dollars.

WHEREFORE the plaintiff demands judgment against the defendant in the sum of one million dollars, interest, and costs.

Plaintiff demands trial by jury.

Dated: _____

_____
Pat Harper
333 Main St.
Springfield, MA 01009
413-787-9999

Exhibit 6-2 Complaint

Courts require such **service** for reasons of basic fairness. Before a court will hear a lawsuit, it must be convinced that the defendant has received proper **notice** that the suit has been filed against her or them. The federal requirements for notice are listed in Rule 4.

Rule 4

Summons

(a) **Form**. The summons shall . . . be directed to the defendant and state the name and address of the plaintiff's attorney, ... It shall also state the time within which the defendant must appear and defend and notify the defendant that failure to do so will result in a judgment by default against the defendant for the relief demanded in the complaint.

Service
The delivery of a pleading or other paper in a lawsuit to the opposing party.

Notice
Being informed of some act done or about to be done.

The Case of the Distressed Grandfather (continued)

In addition to the complaint, paralegal Kendall prepared the summons you see in Exhibit 6-3, on page 116. This would be served along with a copy of the complaint in order to notify defendant Small of the nature of the claim.

---

(3) The answer

Upon receiving the summons the defendant has a designated time within which to file a formal answer to the complaint. For example, the summons in the *Drake* case indicates that after Mrs. Small receives the complaint and summons, she has twenty days in which to answer the complaint. In an answer a defendant can choose a combination of responses from among the following alternatives:

1. deny the facts that the plaintiff says took place,
2. admit the facts but assert that those facts do not provide the plaintiff with a legal remedy,
3. claim that additional facts give rise to an **affirmative defense**,
4. assert that there are procedural defects in the complaint, and
5. bring a claim of one's own against either the plaintiff or another defendant.

These options are not considered mutually exclusive.

A sixth alternative is simply not to respond at all—that is, not to file any documents with the court. However, the failure to take any action is viewed as an admission of the allegations contained in the complaint and creates a situation in which the plaintiff can seek a **default judgment**. In a default judgment the judge awards the judgment against the party who fails to appear in court to contest the matter. While the plaintiff must still convince the judge that the claim is legitimate, the defendant has no right either to challenge the evidence presented or to present contrary evidence. Although it is possible to have a default judgment set aside, it is a very difficult task.

Affirmative defense
A defense whereby the defendant offers new evidence to avoid judgment.

Default judgment
A judgment entered against a party who fails to complete a required step, such as answering the complaint.

UNITED STATES DISTRICT COURT FOR THE DISTRICT OF MASSACHUSETTS

Civil Action, File Number_____

Donald Drake, Plaintiff   }
                           }
            v.   }   } SUMMONS
                           }
Wilma Small, Defendant   }

To the above-named Defendant:

You are hereby summoned and required to serve upon Pat Harper , plaintiff's attorney, whose address is 333 Main St., Springfield, MA 01009 , an answer to the complaint which is herewith served upon you, within 20 days after service of this summons upon you, exclusive of the day of service. If you fail to do so, judgment by default will be taken against you for the relief demanded in the complaint.

Witness _____ , Esq.

at _____ , the _____ day of _____ 20____ .

_____
Clerk of Court

(Seal of Court)

This summons is issued pursuant to Rule 4 of the Federal Rules of Civil Procedure.

Exhibit 6-3 Summons

The specific techniques you use to assert these options differ from state to state. At the federal level the general rules for what constitutes a proper answer are laid out in Rule 8(b) and (c). Counterclaims and cross-claims (alternative 5 above) are discussed in Rule 13.

Rule 8

General Rules of Pleading

(a) Claims for Relief. . . .

(b) Defenses: Forms of Denials. A party shall state in short and plain terms the party's defenses to such claims asserted and shall admit or deny the averments upon which the adverse party relies. If the party is without knowledge or information sufficient to form a belief as to the truth of an averment, the party shall so state and this has the effect of a denial. Denials shall fairly meet the substance of the averments denied. . . .

(c) **Affirmative Defenses.** In pleading to a preceding pleading, a party shall set forth affirmatively accord and satisfaction, . . . contributory negligence . . . statute of limitations . . . and any other matter constituting an avoidance or affirmative defense.

Rule 13
Counterclaim and Cross-claim

(a) **Compulsory Counterclaims.** A pleading shall state as a counterclaim any claim which at the time of serving the pleading the pleader has against any opposing party, if it arises out of the transaction or occurrence that is the subject matter of the opposing party's claim. . . .

(b) **Permissive Counterclaims.** A pleading may state as a counterclaim any claim against an opposing party not arising out of the transaction or occurrence that is the subject matter of the opposing party's claim. . . .

(g) **Cross-claim Against Co-party.** A pleading may state as a cross-claim any claim by one party against a co-party arising out of the transaction or occurrence that is the subject matter either of the original action or of a counterclaim. . . .

After reviewing these rules, think about the type of answer you might draft if you were working for the law firm that is representing Mrs. Small, taking into account each of the alternatives mentioned above.

The Case of the Distressed Grandfather (continued)

(a) Deny the facts that the plaintiff says took place. Mrs. Small will naturally deny as many of the complaint's allegations as she can. She must be careful, however, to deny only those allegations that she truly intends to dispute. As to the other matters, she must either admit their validity or state that she is without the knowledge to form a belief as to the truth or falsity of these statements.

(b) Admit the facts but assert that those facts do not provide the plaintiff with a legal remedy. As suggested earlier, under Massachusetts law it is unclear whether grandfathers can sue for the emotional distress they experience when seeing a grandchild harmed. Therefore, Mrs. Small may want to take advantage of the second option, arguing that even if the facts as alleged are true, they do not form a basis for a lawsuit.

(c) Claim that additional facts give rise to an affirmative defense. As to the third option, in her answer Mrs. Small will also include any affirmative defense that she thinks may decrease or even eliminate her liability. In this case there does not appear to be any such defense, but let us assume the facts were different. Assume that instead of walking down the sidewalk Mr. Drake was driving his car. Assume further that just as he was approaching an intersection, the light turned from green to yellow. He might have had time to stop, but he chose to proceed through the intersection. Mrs. Small, speeding toward him from his right, ran her red light and struck his car, killing Philip. Clearly Mrs. Small was negligent, and Mr. Drake would want to sue her. However, Mrs. Small might feel that Mr. Drake was also negligent given these changed facts. Therefore, in her answer Mrs. Small would allege the affirmative defense of contributory negligence.

(d) Assert that there are procedural defects in the complaint. This option is usually raised through a separate **motion**. A motion is simply

Motion
A request made to the court.

a request made to the court, asking for a court ruling on a particular matter. The assertion that the complaint is defective will be discussed below under the heading Pretrial Motions.

(e) Bring a claim of one's own against either the plaintiff or another defendant. Finally, if Mrs. Small has a claim that she would like to bring against Mr. Drake based on the same factual situation on which he is relying, then she must bring that claim as part of her answer. In this case it does not

appear that Mrs. Small has any basis for a counterclaim. However, let us suppose the same altered facts laid out above, where both Mr. Drake and Mrs. Small were driving their own vehicles. If Mrs. Small had been injured, in addition to alleging that she does not owe Mr. Drake any money because of his contributory negligence, she might countersue Mr. Drake to try to recover some money from him to compensate her for her own injuries. As noted above, Rule 13 governs counterclaims.

Given our original facts, Mrs. Small's answer might look like Exhibit 6-4, on page 120.

c. Pretrial Motions to End Part or All of the Litigation

Sometimes the parties feel they have grounds for having the lawsuit dismissed without a trial. Therefore, in addition to or instead of filing an answer, the defendant may file a motion asking that the court immediately dismiss the case. A motion is a written request directed to the court. There are two basic motions that can end part or all of a lawsuit: Rule 12 motions, known as motions to dismiss, and Rule 56 motions, known as motions for summary judgment.

(1) Rule 12 motions to dismiss

Rule 12 outlines the basic types of pretrial motions, as well as how they are presented to the court. For example, if Mrs. Small's attorney thinks the complaint is defective, the attorney can bring a motion under Rule 12.

Rule 12

Defenses and Objections—When and How Presented—by Pleading or Motion—Motion for Judgment on Pleadings

(a) **When Presented.** . . .

(b) **How Presented.** Every defense, in law or fact, to a claim for relief in any pleading . . . shall be asserted in the responsive pleading thereto if one is required, except that the following defenses may at the option of the pleader be made by motion:

(1) lack of jurisdiction over the subject matter,
(2) lack of jurisdiction over the person,
(3) improper venue,
(4) insufficiency of process,
(5) insufficiency of service of process,
(6) failure to state a claim upon which relief can be granted,
(7) failure to join a party under Rule 19. . . .

If, on a motion asserting the defense numbered (6) to dismiss for failure of the pleading to state a claim upon which relief can be granted, matters outside the pleading are presented to and not excluded by the court, the motion shall be treated as one for summary judgment and disposed of as provided in Rule 56. . . .

Take a moment to study the various options under Rule 12. Probably the most important of the Rule 12 motions is (6), commonly referred to as a **12(b)(6) motion.** If the defendant can convince the court that she has a solid foundation for such a motion—that is, that the plaintiff has stated a claim for which the court cannot give relief—then the court will be forced to dismiss the complaint. This means that there will be no trial. No judge or jury will ever hear about the accident or about Mr. Drake's injuries. In Mr. Drake's case the defendant might very well file such a motion, arguing that, in Massachusetts, trial courts have no right to grant relief to a grandfather who suffers injury upon seeing a grandchild negligently killed.

12(b)(6) motion
A request that the court find the plaintiff has failed to state a valid claim and dismiss the complaint.

(2) Rule 56 motions for summary judgment

Another method that attorneys may use to try to end a case before trial is through filing a Rule 56 motion, known as a motion for **summary judgment.** An attorney's objective in filing a summary judgment motion is generally the same as that in filing a 12(b)(6) motion—to end the case without the need for a trial. The main difference between the two motions is that when faced with a 12(b)(6) motion, the court must make a determination based only on the facts as alleged in the complaint, and it must assume those facts are true for purposes of deciding the motion. (If the court denies the motion, all parties treat the facts as once again being in dispute.) In a summary judgment motion, however, the court will consider additional evidence as presented in documents other than the pleadings, such as depositions, answers to interrogatories, admissions on file, and affidavits. Rule 56 provides that if those documents show that

Rule 56 motion (summary judgment motion)
A request that the court grant judgment in favor of the moving party because there is no genuine issue as to any material fact and the moving party is entitled to judgment as a matter of law. It is similar to a 12(b)(6) motion except that the court also considers matters outside the pleadings.

- there is no genuine issue as to any material fact and
- the moving party is entitled to a judgment as a matter of law,

the court will grant the motion and enter judgment for the moving party.

Sometimes the parties start off with a motion to dismiss but then find that they want to present additional facts not found in the pleadings. This is permissible, and indeed Rule 12 anticipates this development by stating that when "matters outside the pleading are presented to and not excluded by the court, the motion will be treated as one for summary judgment." As with the motion to dismiss, if the court grants the summary judgment motion and there are no other unresolved factual issues, there will be no trial. This is a very important fact to keep in mind.

The Case of the Distressed Grandfather (continued)

Assume in our case that the complaint did not state that Mr. Drake is Philip's grandfather but rather had simply stated that he is a relative. The defendant's attorney could request that Mr. Drake admit he is the grandfather. With that admission in hand the defendant, Mrs. Small, could then proceed to file a summary judgment motion on the same grounds as she would have filed a motion to dismiss.

UNITED STATES DISTRICT COURT FOR THE DISTRICT OF MASSACHUSETTS

Civil Action, File Number 06-483

Donald Drake, Plaintiff   }
                           }
    v.   }   ANSWER
                           }
Wilma Small, Defendant   }

First Defense

The complaint fails to state a claim against the defendant upon which relief can be granted as there is no right to recover for the injuries suffered by a grandparent upon seeing the negligently caused death of a grandchild.

Second Defense

1. The defendant has no knowledge as to the allegations in paragraph 1.

2. The defendant has no knowledge as to the allegations in paragraph 2.

3. The defendant admits the allegations in paragraph 3.

4. The defendant admits that the plaintiff was walking on a sidewalk along a public way called Bishop Street in Springfield, Massachusetts, on September 1, 2006. The defendant denies the allegation of negligence contained in paragraph 4. The defendant is without knowledge or information sufficient to form a belief as to the truth of the remaining allegations contained in paragraph 4.

5. The defendant denies the allegation of negligence contained in paragraph 5. The defendant is without knowledge or information sufficient to form a belief as to the truth of the remaining allegations contained in paragraph 5.

6. The defendant is without knowledge or information sufficient to form a belief as to the truth of the allegations contained in paragraph 6.

Dated: _____   _____
                                               William Smith
                                               886 State St.
                                               Keene, NH 03431
                                               603-787-1111

Exhibit 6-4   Answer

(3) Appealing a summary judgment or motion to dismiss

A court's decision to grant a motion to dismiss or for summary judgment is considered a final decision and as such is appealable. If the losing party convinces the appellate court to reverse the trial court's decision, the case will then be returned to the trial court so that the parties can proceed with the litigation. In other words, having an appellate court reverse the decision to grant a motion to dismiss or a summary judgment motion does not mean that the prevailing party will have won on the merits. All the prevailing party will have won is the right to proceed with the litigation.

The Case of the Distressed Grandfather (continued)

Mrs. Small's attorney filed a summary judgment motion on the grounds that Mrs. Small owed Mr. Drake, a grandfather, no duty of care. The trial court granted this motion. Attorney Harper appealed this decision and convinced the court to reverse the trial court's decision. At that point what has she won for Mr. Drake? Only the right to continue with the lawsuit from where they left off.

Before leaving summary judgment motions, consider these two quick points. First, plaintiffs as well as defendants can bring summary judgment motions. The purpose of the motion is to avoid the necessity of a trial if there are no material facts in dispute. The purpose of a trial is to ferret out the facts. If the facts are already known, there is no need for a trial. Therefore, once the facts are known, either side can ask the court to determine that there is no need for a trial and to declare him or her the winner. Second, motions to dismiss and summary judgment motions can relate to just part of the case.

The Case of the Distressed Grandfather (continued)

Assume in Mr. Drake's situation that during her deposition Mrs. Small broke down and admitted that her speeding caused the accident. Her medical experts informed her, however, that they did not think Mr. Drake's heart attack was caused by seeing his grandson's death but rather by a combination of old age and poor eating habits. The plaintiff might be able to convince the court based on Mrs. Small's deposition testimony to grant summary judgment on the issue of the defendant's negligence. However, a trial would still be necessary in order to determine whether Mr. Drake's heart attack was caused by witnessing the accident and, if so, the amount of damages he suffered.

d. Discovery

Once the defendant files an answer, each side frequently begins using various **discovery** devices to find out more about the strength of the other side's case. The purpose of discovery is to help each side find out as much information as possible so that each can fairly evaluate the case and prepare for trial or settlement. The parties seek to discover information about the identification of witnesses, the nature of the testimony that such witnesses can be expected to provide, and the contents of relevant contracts, medical reports, and so forth. Such information is acquired through various discovery tools, including interrogatories, depositions, requests for admissions, motions to produce documents, and motions for physical and mental exams. What follows is a discussion of the most important methods.

(1) Interrogatories

Interrogatories are written questions sent by one party in a lawsuit to another party to obtain written answers in return. **Interrogatories** are used to help locate potential witnesses, establish dates, determine a person's medical or financial condition, and inquire about the existence of documentary evidence. Attorneys frequently ask their paralegals to draft interrogatories.

Rule 33 provides that "[a]ny party may serve upon any other party written interrogatories." Note therefore that interrogatories maynot be served on nonparties. Also, in the federal system the number of interrogatories is limited to twenty-five. States usually impose a similar limitation.

When a law office receives interrogatories directed to its client, the client usually is instructed to write out the answers as fully as possible. An attorney may then edit these answers and prepare the formal responses, which will be returned to the other party's attorney. When answers to a firm's interrogatories are received from the other party, a paralegal may help in analyzing and organizing them.

The Case of the Distressed Grandfather (continued)

A sample of the types of questions paralegal Kendall might draft in Mr. Drake's case can be found in Exhibit 6-5, on page 124. In addition to these questions, what other types of information do you think paralegal Kendall attempted to gather through the interrogatories?

A major advantage of interrogatories is that they are relatively inexpensive to prepare. A major disadvantage is that the answers can be closely reviewed by that person's attorney or paralegal before they are returned to the party submitting the questions.

(2) Depositions

If an attorney would like to ask questions of a nonparty, such as the doctor who treated Mr. Drake, or would like to ask questions of either a party or a nonparty in person, that attorney will consider taking a deposition. A **deposition** is sworn testimony that is taken outside the courtroom without a judge being

---

PRACTICE TIP

Because you normally are limited as to the number of interrogatories you can send: (1) Do not use them all in your first set. Hold a few back and use them after you have received the answers to your first set. (2) Keep in mind that this number usually applies to each defendant and each plaintiff. Therefore, if you are representing co-plaintiffs and each is suing two defendants, you would potentially have four times the limit.

Interrogatories
Written questions sent by one side to the opposing side, answered under oath.

Deposition
The pretrial oral questioning of a witness under oath.

present. Although a judge is not present, there is a court reporter who administers the oath and records the testimony. The format of a deposition is similar to that of a trial in that one attorney questions the witness and the opposing attorney has an opportunity to make objections and to cross-examine the witness.

Depositions are used primarily to preserve the testimony of a witness when that witness may not be available for the trial (as in the case of a physician) or when the attorney wants to ensure that the story of the individual being deposed cannot be changed. Because a person can be subpoenaed to be deposed, a statement may be obtained from a witness otherwise unwilling to talk to the attorney or to an investigator.

An attorney is responsible for asking the questions during a deposition. The advantages of a deposition over interrogatories are that the deposing attorney is not limited in the number of questions he or she can ask, the **deponent's** answers are usually more spontaneous, the deposing attorney can view the demeanor of the person answering the questions, and under certain circumstances the answers may be used later in a court trial. The major disadvantages are the time and cost involved. At a minimum a deposition requires the time and presence of both attorneys, a court reporter, and the deponent. Without a special court order the federal rules limit the number of depositions to ten.

Deponent
The person who is being asked questions at a deposition.

The Case of the Distressed Grandfather (continued)

The attorney representing Ms. Smith arranged for a deposition of Dr. Gary Booth, one of the doctors who treated Mr. Drake after his heart attack.

---

(3) Requests for admissions

A **request for admissions** is a written document that lists statements regarding specific facts for the other party to admit or deny. Once admitted, a matter cannot be contested. The purpose of the request for admissions is to clarify what is not in dispute and what therefore will not need to be resolved through a trial. Paralegals frequently draft requests for admissions.

(4) Requests for documents and physical examinations

The motion to produce documents is used to obtain documents in the possession of one of the parties. Documents in the possession of third parties can be obtained through a **subpoena duces tecum**. The motion for a physical examination is usually used in personal injury cases or other situations where the health of one of the parties is at issue.

Deponent
The person who is being asked questions at a deposition.

(5) Enforcing discovery rights

The parties to a lawsuit have an obligation to respond to discovery requests. If a party refuses to respond, the opposing attorney can go to court to seek a court order requiring the other side to comply with a valid discovery request. A plaintiff's failure to follow such a court order can result in one of the following

Request for admissions
A document that lists statements regarding specific items for the other party to admit or deny.

UNITED STATES DISTRICT COURT FOR THE DISTRICT OF MASSACHUSETTS

Civil Action, File Number 06-483

Donald Drake, Plaintiff   }

    v.   }   PLAINTIFF'S INTERROGATORIES

Wilma Small, Defendant   }   TO WILMA SMALL

[The interrogatories start with fairly standard boilerplate language. Attorneys use the word **boilerplate** to refer to standard language found in a particular type of legal document. In the case of interrogatories the boilerplate language at the beginning sets out basic information such as to whom the interrogatory answers are to be returned, the deadline for their return, and instructions for answering the interrogatories. This language is then followed by the specific questions.]

1.   State your full name, age, full address, and telephone number.

2.   At the time of the events referred to in paragraphs 4 and 5 of the complaint, did you have a valid driver's license?

3.   Has your driver's license ever been suspended or revoked, and if so, state
    a. When and where it was suspended or revoked;
    b. The grounds upon which the license was suspended or revoked. . . .

15. During the 24 hours preceding the events referred to in paragraphs 4 and 5 of the complaint, had you consumed any medicines, drugs, or alcoholic beverages of any type, and if so, state
    a. The type and amount consumed;
    b. The length of time over which the substance was consumed;
    c. The names, addresses, and telephone numbers of every person who has knowledge as to your consumption of the substance. . . .

Dated: _____   _____

                                 Pat Harper
                                 333 Main St.
                                 Springfield, MA 01009
                                 413-787-9999

Exhibit 6-5   Interrogatories

sanctions: a prohibition against using certain evidence, a dismissal of some counts, and on rare occasions a **dismissal with prejudice** of the entire case. A dismissal with prejudice means that the case cannot be refiled.

On the other hand, there are limits to the materials that each side must supply. If the judge is convinced that discovery attempts have gone beyond the bounds of reasonableness and amount to an undue burden or harassment, the judge can issue a protective order to allow the party to refuse to comply with certain types of discovery actions.

Dismissal with prejudice
A court order that ends a lawsuit; the suit cannot be refiled by the same parties.

Discussion Questions

9. If expense and time were not obstacles, would you prefer to use interrogatories or depositions? Why?

10. Some have likened the current discovery process to a guessing game whereby one side tries to guess what information the other side has and attempts to ferret it out through the clever use of interrogatories and depositions. Do you think the system would work better if all parties were automatically required to hand over all relevant information at the beginning of the lawsuit? Do you think that would be a workable system? A fair system? Recently the federal rules were amended to require automatic disclosure in certain circumstances. The change is contained in Rule 26(a)(1). It is too early to tell if the attempt to increase voluntary cooperation among attorneys will be successful.

11. If you were doing the discovery plan for Mr. Drake, what methods of discovery would you prefer? Why? Would your answer change if you were representing Mrs. Small? Why?

e. Settlement or Pretrial Conference

Most cases settle rather than going to trial. Settlement is a possibility at any time, even before the commencement of a lawsuit, but human nature being what it is, it often seems to happen on the very eve of trial. One method for trying to encourage settlement is the pretrial conference.

Pretrial conferences are informal sessions in which the opposing attorneys meet (usually in the presence of the judge) to discuss the case before it goes to trial. Such conferences focus on the issues to be presented at the trial and encourage the parties to agree to matters that they are not contesting. Such conferences make the trial more efficient and encourage out-of-court settlements. The hope is that as both sides learn more about the strengths and weaknesses of the case, they will be more likely to agree on the probable outcome of a trial and therefore reach a mutually agreeable accommodation. Such accommodations are encouraged because they serve the public interest by easing the pressure on an overburdened court system.

Dismissal with prejudice
A court order that ends a lawsuit; the suit cannot be refiled by the same parties.

If it is determined that the case will proceed to trial, various matters that relate to how the trial will be conducted may also be discussed, and the attorneys may present motions related to those issues. For example, in a case involving

Motion in limine
A request that the court order that certain information not be mentioned in the presence of the jury.

Voir dire
An examination of a prospective juror to see if he or she is fit to serve as a juror on a specific case.

sensitive material an attorney may make a **motion in limine.** A motion in limine is made to prevent reference to specific information in the presence of the jury. An attorney might also file a motion requesting that the judge allow inquiry into certain areas during **voir dire.** Voir dire is the portion of the trial during which potential jurors are questioned to determine whether they are fit to serve on a jury.

2. The Trial

If the case is not settled, then it proceeds to trial. Although the majority of lawsuits filed never reach the trial stage, the results of those that are tried influence the results of future settlements. For example, there are companies that compile and publish reports of recently decided personal injury cases in different areas of the country. When parties learn of the amount of damages being awarded in similar cases, they may see the necessity for settling their case out of court.

a. The Right to a Jury Trial

The use of juries in our legal system is a product of our English common-law heritage. The system originated as a means of limiting the powers of the English monarchy and safeguarding citizens against corrupt or biased judges and prosecutors. Today the use of the jury system is most strongly entrenched in criminal cases, but it continues to play an important role in civil cases as well.

The Seventh Amendment to the U.S. Constitution states that the right to a trial by jury shall be preserved in suits at common law where the value in the controversy exceeds $20. Although the word *preserved* might suggest that the constitutional right to a jury trial is limited to those actions tried by a jury in 1791, the right to a jury trial now extends to most types of federal civil cases. Because there is no federal right to a jury in civil cases tried in state courts, each state has defined for itself the extent to which juries are to be available in state courts. In most states you will not find juries in divorce and probate cases. But you will find juries provided for, either by statute or by constitution, in contractual and tort matters exceeding some dollar limit.

The basic function of the jury is to resolve the factual, as opposed to the legal, questions raised in the case. Generally, this comes down to deciding how much credibility to give to the often conflicting testimony of various witnesses. When damage awards are called for, the jury must decide how to measure pain and suffering in terms of dollars and cents. In cases where a jury is not used, the judge takes over the jury's function besides her or his normal duties of presiding over the trial and resolving the legal questions raised.

The right to a jury trial is the client's right, not the lawyer's or the paralegal's decision.

Finally, a word about the number of people on a jury. Under the common law a jury consisted of twelve people. However, the courts have ruled that there is nothing that is constitutionally significant about that number, and six-person juries have been used in civil cases at both the federal and the state levels. Furthermore, it is not unusual to select one or two extra jurors as alternates, especially where the trial is expected to last for more than a few days. These alternates sit in the jury box with their fellow jurors throughout the trial and are used as substitutes if regular jurors are unable to continue. An alternate does not participate in the deliberations, however, unless he or she has replaced one of the original jurors.

b. Jury Selection

The first formal step in a jury trial is the selection of individual jurors from a pool of jurors. The modern trend is to require almost everyone to serve as a juror. This process of selecting individual jurors is known as **voir dire** and marks the start of the trial. The voir dire itself consists of questioning potential jurors to determine whether they are fit to serve on the jury for that specific case. For example, a potential juror would be disqualified if he or she had some personal relationship with a party in the case or with one of the attorneys involved. Potential jurors may also be disqualified if they have been exposed to a great deal of prejudicial pretrial publicity or have been involved in similar lawsuits themselves.

Attorneys use two types of challenges when seeking to prevent specific individuals from serving on the jury in their case. The first line of attack is usually a **challenge for cause.** To exercise this challenge, the attorney must convince the judge that something about the juror's background or answers demonstrates that the person has some type of bias. If the judge agrees, the person will not be seated. There is no limit on the number of such challenges that can be raised or granted. In some well-publicized and highly controversial cases, attorneys have gone through hundreds of jurors before arriving at the final twelve.

Attorneys can also exercise **peremptory challenges.** These allow an attorney to have a potential juror removed without giving a reason for the dismissal. However, peremptory challenges are limited in number. In deciding whether to use one of these valuable peremptory challenges on a questionable juror, attorneys must weigh the risk of having to accept a worse juror later because they will have exhausted their limited supply of challenges.

DISCUSSION QUESTIONS

12. Many people argue that life and lawsuits have become too complex for the average juror. For example, how can anyone but an economist understand the intricacies of an antitrust lawsuit or anyone but a computer expert comprehend the concept of reverse engineering? Do you think there are certain types of lawsuits where the jury should be composed only of experts in that field? Should jury trials be eliminated entirely in some areas of the law?

13. When litigants have sufficient money, they often hire jury experts, people who specialize in studying the characteristics of various groups. The theory is that certain types of people will be more likely, for example, in a medical malpractice case to lean toward the doctor, while others will favor the patient. Can

PRACTICE TIP

Today there are professionals who specialize in jury selection analysis. However, if your firm cannot afford such a professional, you can perform many of the same functions by sitting at counsel table with your supervising attorney and helping spot potential problems.

Challenge for cause
A method for excusing a prospective juror based on the juror's inability to serve in an unbiased manner.

Peremptory challenge
A method for excusing a prospective juror; no reason need be given.

Cross-examination
The questioning of an opposing witness.

you think of any groups that you could characterize in this way? Do you think this is a valid approach to choosing a jury? Even if valid, should it be used?

c. Opening Statements

Once the jury is selected, the attorneys make their opening arguments, in which they outline the evidence they hope to present. In these presentations the plaintiff's and defendant's attorneys state their theories of the case and describe, from their respective points of view, what allegedly took place and to what they expect the witnesses to testify. The jury is thus presented with a framework for viewing the upcoming testimony.

Because the plaintiff has the burden of proving his or her case, the plaintiff's attorney presents the first opening argument. In most cases the defendant's attorney makes an opening statement immediately following that of the plaintiff's attorney. At other times the defense waits until the plaintiff's attorney has finished presenting the plaintiff's witnesses and exhibits and the defense is about to present its case.

d. Presentation of Evidence

After the opening statements the plaintiff's attorney presents evidence in the form of witness testimony and exhibits. The exhibits consist of such things as medical records, accident reports, and photographs of the accident scene. There are rules of evidence that dictate what types of evidence can be admitted and the manner in which witnesses can be questioned.

In considering evidence it is essential to be aware of the differences between facts and opinions. When a witness testifies that he saw the defendant's automobile strike the plaintiff's car broadside, he is testifying about a fact he observed. But when that same witness says the defendant was driving too fast for the icy condition of the road, he is stating an opinion. Generally, only expert witnesses, such as doctors and police officers, can testify as to their opinions, based on their expert knowledge.

In conducting the **direct examination** of a witness, an attorney usually cannot ask leading questions. A **leading question** is one that suggests the answer. For example, "Wouldn't you say the defendant appeared to be very angry at that point in time?" is a leading question.

Once the plaintiff's attorney has completed questioning a witness, the defendant's attorney may **cross-examine** that same witness. The cross-examination clarifies any potentially misleading statements or half-truths and attacks the credibility of the witness. Therefore, the defense attorney attempts to bring out possible biases or the inability of the witness to have seen clearly what she or he claims to have seen. On cross-examination a lawyer may ask leading questions.

The defendant's cross-examination is then followed by redirect examination, where the plaintiff's attorney has the opportunity to ask additional questions of the witness. The plaintiff's attorney uses redirect questions to rehabilitate the witness after the defense's attack on the witness's credibility. These questions cannot be used to raise new subjects or to explore topics that were not covered as part of the cross-examination. The redirect is then followed by an opportunity for recross-examination by the defendant's attorney, but that must, in turn, be limited to topics raised during the redirect. At that point the witness is finally excused, and the plaintiff's attorney then proceeds to call the next witness.

PRACTICE TIP

When accompanying your supervising attorney to court, you need to bring three essential items with you: (1) a list of the witnesses, along with their phone numbers (if a witness unexpectedly fails to appear, you can call and try to solve the problem), (2) written directions to the courthouse that you can read over the phone to that missing witness, and (3) a roll of quarters (or a phone calling card) so you can make those calls.

Direct examination
The questioning of your own witness.

Leading question
A question that suggests the answer; generally, leading questions may not be asked during direct examination of a witness.

Cross-examination
The questioning of an opposing witness.

Throughout the process of questioning witnesses and presenting evidence the attorneys must keep in mind that appellate courts usually require them to raise appropriate objections at the proper times during the trial. An attorney cannot complain later to an appellate court about something that he or she did not complain about at the proper time to the trial judge.

This requirement for "laying a proper foundation" places additional pressures on the trial attorney. A careless or incompetent attorney can simultaneously destroy the client's chances to win at the trial level and to successfully appeal an adverse decision. Attorneys will make objections for the record even when they do not expect the trial judge to accept them. This is sometimes called protecting the record or making a record for appeal.

After the plaintiff's attorney has finished calling witnesses and presenting evidence, the defense has its opportunity. Before this occurs, it is not unusual for the defense attorney to move for a **directed verdict.** This motion requests that the judge end the trial at that point and find in favor of the defendant on the basis that the plaintiff's side failed to meet its obligation of presenting a prima facie case supporting its position. The judge will enter a directed verdict if the judge concludes that the plaintiff's evidence is so weak that even considered in its most favorable light (without considering any rebuttal evidence from the defendant) it is not sufficient as a matter of law to merit a verdict in the plaintiff's favor.

Directed verdict
A verdict ordered by a trial judge if the plaintiff fails to present a prima facie case or if the defendant fails to present a necessary defense.

The Case of the Distressed Grandfather (continued)

To present the prima facie case of negligence, attorney Harper must enter evidence of each element of negligence: duty, breach, cause, and harm. If she inadvertently omits one of the elements, then there is no way for the court to find a basis for the negligence claim, and a directed verdict in the defendant's favor would be appropriate.

If the court grants the motion, the trial is over. However, it is very unusual for a judge to accept a motion for a directed verdict at this point in the trial. Typically, the judge denies the motion, and the defense attorney goes on to present his or her witnesses. The same process of direct, cross, redirect, and recross is used. The defense strategy involves presenting evidence that contradicts evidence presented by the plaintiff and possibly attempting to raise a legally accepted defense for that particular type of case.

NETNOTE

You can read about and see video clips of current trials at:

www.courttv.com

Once the defendant's case is complete, the plaintiff can ask for a directed verdict on the basis that even if the defendant's evidence is taken in its most favorable light, it would be insufficient to rebut the plaintiff's case. If the judge also denies this motion, as is usually the case, the plaintiff can present witnesses who will attempt to rebut testimony and evidence presented by the defense. After that, either side can again renew its motion for a directed verdict. If these motions are again denied, both sides then give their closing arguments.

DISCUSSION QUESTIONS

14. Do you agree with the rule that only experts should be allowed to state their opinions? Why should it matter if a witness who saw Mrs. Small stumble just before she entered her car testifies that "Mrs. Small was drunker than a skunk"?

15. One of the all-time famous leading questions is "So, when did you stop beating your wife?" What is the problem with asking your witness this type of question during direct examination?

e. Closing Arguments

Perhaps the most dramatic part of any trial is the closing arguments. Here the attorneys review and interpret the evidence in its most favorable light and develop emotional appeals. Closing arguments are their final chance to persuade the jury. Although both the plaintiff and the defendant receive equal time, in some states the plaintiff has the advantage of splitting the time and speaking both first and last. The plaintiff is given this advantage because the plaintiff also has the burden of proof to overcome.

f. Jury Instructions

Before sending the jury members out to deliberate, it is the judge's responsibility to properly instruct them about the nature of their duties and the requirements of the law. The jury's duty is to determine the facts and then apply the requirements of the law to those facts. However, the jury is composed of a group of lay persons who do not know what the law requires. Therefore, it is the duty of the judge to explain the law in terms the jury can understand.

Pattern jury instructions
A set of standardized jury instructions.

Rather than starting from scratch and risking reversal for failing to include some key element or for explaining some concept in a misleading way, judges frequently rely on **pattern jury instructions.** These are collections of instructions that have already been tested on appeal in other cases. Furthermore, the attorneys in the case have the opportunity to submit instructions they would like to see included. The judge then reviews their submissions and often discusses the issues with the attorneys in chambers before deciding which instructions to give at the trial.

Verdict
The opinion of a jury on a question of fact.

g. Jury Deliberations, Verdict, and Judgment

Mistrial
A trial ended by the judge because of a major problem, such as a prejudicial statement by one of the attorneys.

Once they have been properly instructed, the jurors retire to a special room where they deliberate in private until they reach their **verdict,** or they report they cannot reach a consensus and the judge declares a **mistrial.** In most cases the jurors must come to a unanimous agreement regarding the verdict, although

some states have provisions for less-than-unanimous verdicts in certain types of cases.

Usually, evidence is presented at the trial regarding the question of liability and the amount of damages. If the jurors find that the defendant is liable, they next consider the amount of damages. In some cases, however, a bifurcated trial is held. During the first phase of the trial the jury hears testimony regarding liability and then deliberates on that issue alone. If the jury finds the defendant liable, the trial enters a second stage, in which the jury hears evidence about the nature of the damages. The jury then deliberates regarding the amount of damages to award.

Once a verdict is reached, the court enters its official **judgment** regarding the rights and obligations of the parties involved in the case, and the clerk enters it into the record. It is this entering of the judgment that gives the parties the right to enforce the court's decision. Then, for example, if the defendant fails to pay damages that were part of the judgment, the plaintiff can request a **writ of execution.** The writ instructs the sheriff to seize the defendant's property, sell it at public auction, and then use the proceeds to pay the plaintiff. Usually, if the losing party does not appeal within a specified time period, the judgment automatically becomes effective. If the losing party does appeal, the court stays the judgment until the appellate court reaches its decision.

Judgment
The decision of the court regarding the clamis of each side. It may be based on a jur's verdict

Writ of execution
A court order authorizing a sheriff to take property in order to enforce ajudgment.

h. Post-Trial Motions

After the verdict has been announced, the losing party has a certain time period within which to file post-trial motions. The most common motions are a motion for judgment notwithstanding the verdict and a motion for a new trial.

The motion for a **judgment notwithstanding the verdict,** also known as a **judgment N.O.V.** (judgment non obstante veredicto), is a request to the judge to reverse the jury's decision on the basis that the evidence was legally insufficient to support its verdict. If the judge grants the motion, the case is over, and the moving party has won.

An attorney usually bases the **motion for a new trial** on the assertion that some procedural error has tainted the outcome. The losing party might argue, for example, that some piece of evidence was admitted that should not have been admitted or that someone made improper contacts with a juror on the case. If the court grants the motion, the case has to be retried.

Both motions are frequently made but seldom granted. Nevertheless, they are important because they may be necessary to preserve the client's right to appeal to a higher court. The doctrine of **exhaustion** requires that the trial court be given every possible opportunity to correct its own errors before the appellate courts intervene.

Judgment notwithstanding the verdict (judgment N.O.V.)
A judgment that reverses the verdict of the jury when the verdict had no reasonable factual support or was contrary to law.

Motion for a new trial
A request that the court order a rehearing of a lawsuit because irregularities, such as errors of the court or jury misconduct, make it probable that an impartial trial did not occur.

3. The Appeal

"I'll take my case all the way to the Supreme Court" is a battle cry that has been echoed by many concerned litigants. No one likes to lose, and there are few attorneys who have not dreamed of arguing a case before the U.S. Supreme Court.

On the other hand, appeals consume time and money. The client's initial desire for appeal often pales because of costs. In addition, the option to appeal may be either very limited or even nonexistent. If the attorney did not make the correct objections during the trial or if the client's case did not involve any questions of law, there will be no basis for an appeal.

a. The Timing and Filing of the Appeal

A case cannot be appealed until a final judgment has been entered. This can occur at any time during the trial if the court grants a final judgment. For example, the court can grant a motion to dismiss, a summary judgment motion, a motion for a directed verdict, or one of the post-trial motions. Most commonly a final judgment comes after a jury verdict. The party wishing to have the case reviewed must file a notice of appeal within a specified time period after the final judgment is entered.

Appellate brief
An attorney's written argument presented to an appeals court, setting forth a statement of the law as it should be applied to the client's facts.

The side bringing the appeal, the appellant, files an **appellate brief**. The brief explains the facts of the case, lists the relevant statutes and court cases, and then presents legal arguments for overturning the lower court's decisions. Then the other side, the appellee, files its brief. Finally, the appellant has the opportunity to file a reply brief in response to the appellee's argument and to any new authorities cited in the appellee's brief.

b. The Scope of the Review

When an appellate court considers a case, it does not conduct a new trial. It simply reviews the official record of the proceedings at the trial court. Moreover, it limits its review to specific **appealable issues,** for which the party appealing the case must have laid a proper foundation at the trial level.

As you know, in general appellate courts consider only legal issues. Recall that legal issues involve the interpretation and application of the law; factual issues involve the determination of whether a given event took place as alleged.

Clearly erroneous
Standard used by appellate courts when reviewing a trial court's findings of fact.

Sometimes, however, appellate courts are asked to review a trial court's findings of fact. When they do so, it is on a very limited basis. Generally, appellate courts will resolve conflicts in the testimony and questions of the credibility of the witnesses in favor of the trial judge's position. They cannot disregard a trial court's findings of fact unless they determine that the findings were **clearly erroneous**. This means not simply that the appellate court would have found otherwise but that the appellate court is convinced that the trial court made a mistake, as, for example, when the trial court did not base its findings on sufficient evidence.

However, when an appellate court reviews legal issues, it gives no deference to the trial court's findings but rather makes its own independent review. A legal issue might involve reviewing a trial judge's interpretation of a statute or legal document, such as a will or a lease. Similarly, questions about the nature of the jury instructions and the trial court's decision on the admissibility of evidence present legal issues.

Sometimes the resolution of a legal issue requires the court to review the facts. This creates a situation that is hard to categorize as either factual or legal. For example, when a party appeals based on the trial judge's decision to deny a motion for a directed verdict, the appellant is arguing that the evidence was so one-sided, it could support only one conclusion. Because it is a ruling on a

motion, it is a legal question; but to reach a decision, the appellate court must make a judgment about the strength of the evidence itself. In these mixed fact/law situations, an appellate court often does an independent review—especially if the court believes the legal aspects predominate. An appellate court uses the clearly erroneous standard when factual aspects predominate, such as in questions involving negligence.

If the appellate court decides that the trial judge made a legal error, it must determine whether that error was prejudicial or merely harmless. Errors are defined as prejudicial when they probably affected the results. **Harmless errors** are errors so minor and peripheral that they had no significant effect on the outcome. Only **prejudicial errors** are considered to be **reversible errors**.

Examples of harmless errors include (1) a mistake in the pleadings if the facts can be determined at trial; (2) errors in jury instructions unless there is reason to believe that they actually misled the jury; and (3) the failure to strictly follow the rules of evidence in a bench trial, as it is assumed a judge is unlikely to be affected by incompetent evidence.

Finally, sometimes an appeal is based upon a challenge to a trial judge's decision as to court procedure or how the case should be managed. Examples include permission to amend a complaint, denial of a request for a continuance, imposition of sanctions for filing an improper pleading, and the awarding of prejudgment interest. Because these types of decisions are generally left to the discretion of the trial judge, appellate courts review them using an **abuse of discretion** standard. They will reverse a trial court only if the appellant can prove the judge committed a clear error of judgment, lacked the authority to act, or acted with prejudice or malice.

c. Oral Arguments

Depending on the rules of the particular appellate court, the court may hear oral arguments on appeal. During oral argument the attorneys present their clients' positions. The court gives the attorneys a limited time to speak (often no more than twenty minutes), and the judges frequently interrupt the attorneys with questions. The purpose of the questioning is to probe weak points in the argument and to explore the implications of the attorney's line of reasoning.

d. The Decision and Its Publication

With or without the benefit of oral argument the judges study the matter until they reach a decision by majority vote. Usually, the case is assigned to one of the judges in the majority to prepare the official opinion of the court. As part of this process the judge's law clerks verify the authorities cited in the briefs, sometimes finding additional cases that apply. The clerks typically prepare a rough draft of the opinion for the majority judges to edit and polish. The other judges on the court have the right to prepare either concurring or dissenting opinions if they want the record to reflect their differences. You will recall that in a concurring opinion the judge agrees with the outcome but disagrees with the reasoning in the court's opinion. In a dissenting opinion the writer disagrees with both the outcome and the reasoning. The court's decision is then published in the appropriate **reporters**, lawbooks that contain all of an appellate court's opinions.

Affirm
When a higher court agrees with what a lower court has done.

Reverse
When an appellate court overturns or negates the decision of a lower court.

Remand
When an appellate court sends a case back to the trial court for a new trial or other action.

Usually, the appellate decision is either to **affirm** the lower court's action or to **reverse** and **remand** (return) the case to the lower court for reconsideration. Sometimes, based on the nature of the case, a new trial is not needed to supplement the factual record. Then the judges may simply enter a final judgment based on the existing record.

e. Further Appeals

Depending on the court structure and the nature of the case, the party that loses at the appellate level (regardless of which party lost at the trial-court level) may have the option of appealing to yet a higher-level appellate court. The general rule, however, is that there is only one right of appeal. A second appeal to a higher court is usually discretionary rather than a matter of right: The judges on the higher appellate court choose to hear only the cases that they believe have the greatest judicial significance. For example, to have a case heard by the U.S. Supreme Court, the losing party must first petition the Court and request that it grant a writ of certiorari. In support of this request the applicant will file a written brief. The purpose of the brief is not to argue the merits of the case but to convince the Court to agree to hear the case. Common reasons are the importance of the case for others beyond the immediate litigants and the need to resolve conflicts among the circuits. For example, for many years the federal courts of appeals were reaching different results in sexual harassment cases. Some courts of appeals thought such situations were covered by Title VII, while others disagreed. In a federal system, leaving such a conflict unresolved is obviously undesirable, as the outcome of a case will vary based on where it is brought. Eventually the Supreme Court agreed to hear a case involving sexual harassment and resolved the issue by deciding that such situations are covered by Title VII.[9]

If the Court grants the petition for a writ of certiorari, the litigants will then file briefs arguing the merits of the case. However, the Court denies most petitions for certiorari.

Most state courts follow a similar procedure. For example, in Massachusetts there is one right of appeal to the intermediate appellate court. If a party wishes to be heard by the state's highest court, the Massachusetts Supreme Judicial Court, that person must file an application for **leave to obtain further appellate review**. Massachusetts Appellate Rule 27.1 provides that "[s]uch application shall be founded upon substantial reasons affecting the public interest or the interests of justice." Massachusetts Appellate Rule 11 also makes it possible to bypass the intermediate appellate court and go directly to the Supreme Judicial Court if that court is convinced that the questions presented are

> (1) questions of first impression or novel questions of law which should be submitted for final determination to the Supreme Judicial Court; (2) questions of law concerning the Constitution of the Commonwealth or questions concerning the Constitution of the United States which have been raised in a court of the Commonwealth; or (3) questions of such public interest that justice requires a final determination by the full Supreme Judicial Court.

---

[9] Meritor Savings Bank v. Vinson, 477 U.S. 57 (1986).

If the higher appellate court accepts the appeal, the parties file new briefs, and the process described above begins all over again.

SUMMARY

When people have a dispute they cannot settle themselves, they typically turn to the courts to have a judge or jury settle it for them. This process of using the courts is referred to as litigation. Because it is such a complex, time-consuming, and expensive way of settling disputes, people are increasingly turning to various forms of alternative dispute resolution (ADR).

The most common types of ADR are arbitration, mediation, and summary jury trials. Increasing numbers of courts are requiring litigants to try different types of mediation before they allow a case to come to trial. Many business contracts include provisions for mandatory arbitration.

In some circumstances it may be necessary to exhaust administrative remedies prior to filing a lawsuit. Adjudicatory hearings in administrative agencies follow the general outline of a civil trial, but they are less formal and do not involve as many due process protections. A hearing officer presides over the hearing, acting much like a judge would. Although it is relatively easy to get evidence admitted into the record, the hearing officer has a great deal of discretion over the weight given to that evidence. Once all avenues of appeal within an agency have been exhausted, a party can often seek review within the judicial system.

The three main stages of litigation are pretrial, trial, and post-trial. In the pretrial stage the parties use pleadings, discovery, and pretrial conferences to identify the facts and the legal issues involved in the dispute. The majority of cases are settled "out of court" during this stage.

At the trial stage the parties present their evidence to either a judge or a jury. The rules of evidence dictate the form in which the evidence must be presented and what types of questions witnesses can be required to answer. Following the trial verdict, the losing party may challenge the trial court's decision in an appellate court.

REVIEW QUESTIONS

Pages 93 through 100

1. What are the most common forms of ADR, and how do they differ from each other?
2. What types of disputes are best suited to resolution through ADR? Which are least appropriate?
3. What do the proponents of ADR see as the advantages of ADR over traditional litigation?
4. What are the three basic stages of civil litigation?
5. What rules govern civil litigation in federal courts?
6. What issues have to be considered in deciding who should be sued?
7. How does a class action lawsuit differ from one brought by and on behalf of one individual?
8. If someone says that a particular court does not have jurisdiction over a lawsuit, what is meant by that?

9. What is the difference between subject matter jurisdiction and personal jurisdiction?
10. What is the purpose of requiring litigants to first exhaust their administrative remedies?
11. How does an administrative hearing differ from a civil trial?

Pages 100 through 118

12. What is the purpose of each of the following pleadings:
    a. the complaint,
    b. the answer,
    c. a counterclaim,
    d. a cross-claim, and
    e. a third-party claim?
13. Under the federal rules what three items must be included in a complaint?
14. What is a caption?
15. Who must sign all pleadings? Why?
16. What is the purpose of a summons?
17. What is the danger to the defendant in failing to answer a complaint?
18. What are the five basic ways that a defendant can respond to a complaint, and what is the purpose of each?

Pages 118 through 121

19. What are the grounds for a 12(b)(6) motion, and what is its purpose?
20. What is the difference between a 12(b)(6) motion and a summary judgment motion?

Pages 122 through 126

21. What is the main goal of discovery?
22. What are interrogatories and depositions, and how do they differ?
23. Besides interrogatories and depositions, what are the main discovery tools available to the parties?
24. What is the purpose of a pretrial conference?

Pages 126 through 131

25. What is the function of the jury?
26. What is a voir dire, and what is its purpose?
27. What are the differences between challenges for cause and peremptory challenges, and what is the function of each?
28. What do attorneys hope to accomplish in their opening statements?
29. Who presents evidence first, the plaintiff or the defendant, and why?
30. When can either side move for a directed verdict? What is the purpose of that motion?
31. What is the difference between a verdict and a judgment?
32. What is the difference between the motion for a judgment notwithstanding the verdict (a judgment N.O.V.) and a motion for a new trial? Give an example of when each could be used.

Pages 131 through 135

33. Describe the limitations on a litigant's right to appeal.
34. What is the difference between a harmless error and a reversible error?

PART 2

Substance of the Law

Chapter 7

Torts

The risk reasonably to be perceived defines
the duty to be obeyed.
Justice Benjamin Cardozo

INTRODUCTION

In this section of the book we introduce some of the most important legal terms and concepts a paralegal needs to know in order to have an understanding of the substance of American law. Any attempt to condense so much information into a few chapters can only begin to introduce you to such a large and complex body of knowledge. However, these chapters should give you a useful framework for understanding the basic areas of civil and criminal law and for acquiring the vocabulary you will need to do legal research.

In a previous chapter we discussed the basic differences between civil law and criminal law. Civil law can be divided into a wide variety of specialty areas, such as business organizations, commercial transactions and bankruptcy, employment law, intellectual property, estate planning and probate, family law, and administrative law. However, most of these specialty areas involve the application of basic principles found in the areas of law known as torts, contracts, and property. In this chapter we focus on the area of law called torts.

If someone injures you, slanders your reputation, or damages your property, tort law is the area of substantive civil law that can provide you with money damages or a court order to try to remedy the wrong done to you. A tort is defined as a private wrong (other than a breach of contract) in which a person or property is harmed because of another's failure to carry out a legal duty. In most instances this legal duty is an obligation to refrain from taking actions that harm

others. Occasionally, a duty will consist of an affirmative obligation to act in order to protect others.

It is important to emphasize the differences between tort and criminal law. Not every tort qualifies as a crime, but some acts if done intentionally can lead to both a criminal prosecution and civil litigation. If the government considers the act to be a public wrong, it will classify that harmful act as a crime and treat it as a offense against the state. Therefore, the government will use state resources to investigate and prosecute the offender. If convicted, the defendant is usually punished by fine or imprisonment. When a fine is levied, it goes into the government treasury. On the other hand, a tort is defined as a private wrong, and the victim must pursue a remedy by initiating a civil law suit. If the plaintiff is successful in proving that a tort has been committed, usually the result is a monetary award paid directly to the plaintiff.

Tort law has ancient roots. Over time the courts have created the rules that govern torts on a case-by-case basis. Therefore, looking to prior cases for similar situations plays an important role in any analysis of a tort problem. In addition, the courts frequently look to an authoritative secondary source, the **Restatement of the Law of Torts, Second**. Drafted by a group of legal scholars, this resource summarizes the existing common law rules in a set of black letter principles. At times, instead of simply "restating" the law, the drafters also included their vision of what tort law should become. Although the Restatement is a secondary source and is therefore only persuasive authority, you will frequently see courts citing to it and even formally adopting some of its provisions.

Despite its ancient roots, tort law has never been static. Historically, judges have seen the need to adapt the common law principles to changing conditions. Most recently, some of those conditions have included scientific advances, such as the ability to artificially create and prolong life. In addition, when the need arises, instead of simply adapting the currently existing common law rules, the courts will recognize new torts. For example, traditionally plaintiffs could recover for their emotion distress only if it was caused by another tort, such as battery. Recently courts have developed a new tort that allows plaintiffs to recover for emotional distress even absent another type of injury, so long as the intentional act that caused the emotional distress is extreme and outrageous and the emotional distress is severe. An example would be deliberately telling a mother that her eight-year-old daughter was in the hospital in critical condition when in fact that was not true.

While tort law is still predominately court-created law, legislatures are playing an increasingly active role. For example, both Congress and state legislatures have enacted "tort reform" statutes, with the purpose of modifying some of the perceived abuses of the tort system. One example is legislation to place limits on the amount of damages that can be awarded in certain types of tort cases.

Torts have traditionally been classified into three major categories: intentional acts, negligence, and strict liability. See Figure 7-1. In any one of these three areas, the person who commits the tort is known as the **tortfeasor**.

When people intentionally seek to violate a duty toward others, their purposeful conduct is classified as an **intentional tort**. Those who commit intentional torts are subject to punitive damages in addition to compensatory damages. If John intentionally drives his car into Jill's car, damaging her car and injuring Jill, John has committed an intentional tort. As we will see later in this

Restatement of the Law of Torts, Second
An authoritative secondary source, written by a group of legal scholars, summarizing the existing common law, as well as suggesting what the law should be.

Figure 7-1 Degrees of Fault

chapter, John's motive (reason) for hitting Jill's car is irrelevant. All that matters is that he intended to do so.

When the harm occurs as a result of a careless act done with no conscious intent to injure anyone, the act is classified as **negligence**. Negligent actors are subject to compensatory damages but not to punitive damages. If the reason John's car struck Jill's was not because he had intended to do so but because he had carelessly taken his eyes off the road to adjust his radio, John's behavior may be classified as negligent.

There are times when for policy reasons the defendant is held responsible even though the defendant did not act negligently nor intentionally to harm the plaintiff. These are classified as **strict liability** torts. Strict liability is usually limited to situations involving an ultrahazardous activity, such as dynamiting, or the manufacture or sale of a potentially dangerous product. For example, if the reason John ran into Jill's car was because his brakes failed, the car manufacturer may be held strictly liable.

Finally, it is important to realize that the law does not provide for compensation for all injuries. There are true accidents, when either no one is at fault or the fault rests solely with the person injured. In those situations, the injured party cannot recover damages.

A. INTENTIONAL TORTS

An **intentional tort** occurs whenever someone intends an action that results in harm to a person's body, reputation, emotional well-being, or property. Almost any harm that you can imagine if caused intentionally can be classified as an intentional tort. In this section of the chapter we will discuss just a few of the most common intentional torts. First, there are the torts that cause harm to a person's body, reputation, or emotional well-being: assault and battery, false imprisonment, defamation, invasion of privacy, and intentional infliction of emotional distress. Second, there are the torts that cause harm to a person's property: trespass, trespass to personal property, and conversion. Third, we will briefly mention a variety of other torts, including false arrest, malicious prosecution, abuse of process, fraud, and business torts.

In order to prove that an intentional tort occurred, the plaintiff must prove each of that tort's elements. The defendant then has the opportunity to raise any defenses. The primary defenses available in intentional tort cases are consent, self-defense, defense of third parties, and various types of privilege.

As we will see, one set of facts can give rise to more than one type of intentional tort. In addition, many intentional torts are also crimes. Consider the following fact scenario.

The Case of the Abused Spouse

One day attorney John Bloom asked his paralegal, Sally Green, to sit in on an initial client interview. Mr. Bloom introduced Ms. Green to the client, June Day, and explained to Mrs. Day that Ms. Green is a paralegal. Mrs. Day told them the following story:

Mrs. Day has been living with Mr. David Day for the past five years. While their marriage has never been a happy one, Mrs. Day never thought of divorce until last night. Mr. Day came home very late from an adult co-ed softball game. Mrs. Day said it was obvious that he had been drinking. They soon got into a verbal fight. Among other things, Mr. Day yelled at Mrs. Day that he had told her boss she had been skimming money from the company's petty cash drawer. Mrs. Day had never done any such thing. He also told her that he had received a call earlier in the day from the local hospital, telling him that Mrs. Day's mother had been admitted following a massive heart attack. (Later Mrs. Day found out that this was not true, but at the time she believed Mr. Day and became very upset.) The fight escalated, and Mr. Day began waving his baseball bat in front of Mrs. Day. Mrs. Day said that she was not frightened, as Mr. Day had never hit her, and she did not believe he would do so then. In fact, she turned her back on him and started to leave the room. He then yelled at her and, before she could turn around, hit her on the back of her arm with the bat, breaking her arm. Mrs. Day then fled to the bathroom, locking the door behind her. Mrs. Day remained in the bathroom for over two hours until she felt it was safe to leave. She found Mr. Day asleep on the living room couch. She fled to a neighbor's, who drove her to the hospital. The next morning Mrs. Day returned home to find Mr. Day as well as her purse gone. There was a message on the answering machine from her boss saying that she was fired.

While Mrs. Day is contemplating divorce proceedings, her more immediate concern is to learn what actions she can take to compensate her for her broken arm, emotional distress, missing purse, and lost job.

1. Assault and Battery

Assault
An intentional act that creates a reasonable apprehension of an immediate harmful or offensive physical contact.

Battery
An intentional act that creates a harmful or offensive physical contact.

In the scenario you just read, Mr. Day waved a baseball bat in front of Mrs. Day. She was not frightened and in fact turned her back on him at which point he hit her on the arm, breaking it. Do you think Mrs. Day suffered from either an assault or battery? **An assault** occurs when someone reasonably fears that he or she is about to suffer a harmful or offensive physical contact. A **battery** is the intentional harmful or offensive physical contact. While we usually think of assault and battery as one tort, in reality they are two torts. They can be present together, as, for example, when Tom first waves a fist in front of Sam's face and then proceeds to punch Sam in the nose. However, there can also be an assault with no battery whenever there is the threat of a battery but no ensuing physical contact. And there can also be a battery with no assault, as, for example, when the person being attacked does not see the threat of physical contact before it actually occurs. In the case of Mrs. Day there probably was no assault. However, there clearly was a battery when Mr. Day hit her with the baseball bat, breaking her arm.

For both assault and battery, the contact does not actually have to be physically painful. It simply must be harmful or offensive. Thus, an unwanted kiss from a stranger could qualify as an offensive contact. Also, the defendant need not actually do the touching if the defendant set the action in motion, such as by throwing a rock or ordering a dog to attack.

For a battery to occur the touching must be intentional, not accidental. For example, assume a group of college students are playing a game of touch football. If one of the players jumps up to retrieve the ball and on his way down accidentally knocks over another player, no battery has occurred. The player's intent was to grab the ball, not to touch the other player. However, if during the

course of the game, one of the players deliberately runs into another player, a battery will have occurred.

Note that the plaintiff does not need to prove that the defendant meant to cause her harm—only that the defendant intended to touch her. The extent of her injury only goes to the amount of damages she can collect and not to whether a battery occurred.

Once an injured plaintiff proves that a battery occurred, the defendant is given the opportunity to raise defenses. For example, in the case of the touch football game, the defendant might argue that the battery was excused because the other player consented to such contact by agreeing to play the game.

Indeed, consent is one of the most common justifications that can be raised as a defense to assault and battery as well as to all other intentional torts. Other available defenses include self-defense, defense of others, and sometimes defense of property. For self-defense and defense of others to be valid, the plaintiff must reasonably believe that a threat exists and then must use only as much force as is necessary to stop the battery. Self-defense, for example, could be used as a valid defense against a battery charge if the plaintiff had threatened the defendant with a knife and the defendant had defended himself with his fists. However, if the plaintiff was unarmed and struck the defendant with his fists, it might not be a valid self-defense for the defendant to stab the plaintiff with a knife.

2. False Imprisonment

False imprisonment occurs whenever one person, through force or the threat of force, unlawfully detains another person against his or her will. Issues of false imprisonment most frequently arise in situations in which store employees seek to detain suspected shoplifters or employers wish to detain and interview employees they suspect of unlawful activities. The plaintiff must actually be confined with no means of escape. For example, leaving someone alone in an unlocked office does not constitute false imprisonment.

False imprisonment Occurs whenever one person, through force or the threat of force, unlawfully detains another person against his or her will.

The most common defense to false imprisonment is that the defendant was justified in restraining the plaintiff. For example, many states have enacted statutes to protect merchants who want to question a suspected shoplifter. Usually, these statutes provide that a shopkeeper may detain a suspected shoplifter only if the shopkeeper can show probable cause to justify the delay and then may detain the suspected shoplifter only for a reasonable time and in a reasonable manner. As you can imagine, because of the way these three statutory requirements are worded, each has given rise to a great deal of litigation. For example, consider the following situation. Assume Martha, a young mother, entered the QuickMart store carrying her small child in an infant seat that she had purchased two weeks previously. The seat had cat hairs, food crumbs, and milk stains on it and a large QuickMart price tag that was still attached. She made some purchases, but just before she left the store she heard someone ask her to stop. She turned around and saw a QuickMart security guard. The security guard pulled out a store badge, showed it to her, and asked her to come back into the store, saying that he needed proof that she had purchased the infant seat. When Martha hesitated, the security guard grabbed her by the arm and led her back into the store, stopping just inside the doors. After approximately 20 minutes of heated discussion, the security guard finally told Martha she was free to go.

The first question would be whether Martha could prove that she had been detained through force or the threat of force. Assuming she could do so, the store would argue as its defense, first, that it had probable cause to believe that Martha had stolen the infant seat when they saw her trying to leave the store with an infant seat that she had not paid for and that had a price tag attached. Second, they would argue that they detained her in a reasonable manner by asking her to return to the store and then only using force when she resisted. Third, they would argue that their detention of her for twenty minutes was for a reasonable time. If you were representing Martha, what would you argue in return?

DISCUSSION QUESTION

1. Under what circumstances should merchants be able to detain a suspected shoplifter?

3. Defamation

Defamation

The publication of false statements that harm a person's repuation

Whether it is oral (slander) or written (libel), **defamation** consists of publication of false statements that cause harm to a person's reputation. The first element, publication, means that someone other than the plaintiff and the defendant must read or hear the defamatory comments. The offending material cannot harm someone's reputation if it is never seen or heard by a third party. Second, and perhaps most important, the defamatory material must be false. No matter how damaging the information, a tort of defamation has not been committed if the statement was true. As to the third element, the plaintiff must show that the publication of this false information damaged his or her reputation. This is usually established by showing that the plaintiff lost a job, a contract, or something else of value as a result of people having read or heard the defamatory material.

A special set of rules applies in situations where the alleged victim of the defamation is a public official or a "public figure." In *New York Times Co. v. Sullivan*, the U.S. Supreme Court stated:

> The constitutional guarantees require, we think, a federal rule that prohibits a public official from recovering damages for a defamatory falsehood relating to his official conduct unless he proves that the statement was made with "actual malice"—that is, with knowledge that it was false or with reckless disregard of whether it was false or not.[1]

The application of this rule was widened to cover "public figures" in 1974.[2] To qualify as a public figure, a person must either have achieved widespread fame or notoriety or be someone who became well known through involvement in a public controversy.

To prove actual malice, the plaintiff must show that the defendant either knew the material was false but went ahead and published it anyway or acted with a "reckless disregard" for whether or not it was true. This can involve an examination of the editors as to what they knew and when they knew it in reaching

---

[1] 376 U.S. 254, 279 (1964).

[2] Gertz v. Welch, 418 U.S. 323 (1974).

A famous movie star comes to your office seeking representation in what sounds like a very exciting defamation lawsuit against the local newspaper. Your boss is about to begin the initial interview when you remember that his partner represented the newspaper last year in a contract dispute it had with its paper supplier. You alert your boss. While disappointed in having to turn down the case, he appreciates your pointing out this potential conflict of interest to him.

their decision to publish the material. The courts take into consideration such factors as the nature of the news being reported, the historical trustworthiness of the source of the information, and the time constraints publishers are under to meet a deadline.

DISCUSSION QUESTION

2. Why should it be harder for a "public figure" to collect damages for libel? Where should the courts draw the line as to who is categorized as a "public figure?"

4. Invasion of Privacy

The tort of **invasion of privacy** covers a variety of different situations. They include

1. disclosure,
2. intrusion,
3. appropriation, and
4. false light.

Disclosure and intrusion best fit our common concept of what would be an invasion of privacy. **Disclosure** is the publicizing of embarrassing private affairs, and **intrusion** is the unjustified intrusion into another's private activities. Examples of intrusion include a neighbor eavesdropping and a photographer hounding a movie star by following that person everywhere he or she goes. **Appropriation** is defined as the unauthorized exploitative use of one's personality, name, or picture for the defendant's benefit. For example, Johnny Carson sued a Michigan corporation for renting and selling "Here's Johnny" portable toilets. The corporation acknowledged that "Here's Johnny" was the introductory slogan for The Tonight Show and in fact coupled the phrase with a second one, "The World's Foremost Commodian." The court determined that the defendant unfairly appropriated Carson's identity and used it for the sale of its products.[3] Finally, **false light** involves the use of a picture or some other

Invasion of Privacy
An intentional tort that covers a variety of situations, including disclosure, intrusion, appropriation, and false light.

---

[3] Carson v. Here's Johnny Portable Toilets, Inc., 698 F.2d 831 (6th Cir. 1983).

means to infer a connection between the person and an idea or a statement for which the individual is not responsible.

In cases involving invasion of privacy, truth is not considered to be a valid defense. For example, it is not considered acceptable to publicize that someone is having an affair with his or her neighbor, even if it is true. However, "newsworthiness" is a valid defense. If the material is of legitimate public interest—for example, the mayor having an affair with a member of city council—then its publication is considered to be privileged unless it was done with malice. That is why it is so difficult for movie stars to prove this tort against tabloids and gossip columnists. Finally, as with other intentional torts, consent is a defense.

5. Intentional Infliction of Emotional Distress

Traditionally, plaintiffs could only recover for their emotional distress if that distress was caused by another tort, such as battery or false imprisonment. The new tort of **intentional infliction of emotional distress** allows plaintiffs to recover for emotional distress even absent another type of injury. This tort of intentional infliction of emotional distress is sometimes referred to as the tort of outrage. In order to ensure that such claims are valid, most courts have placed severe restrictions on what the plaintiff must prove, such as requiring that the intentional act that causes the emotional distress be extreme and outrageous and the emotional distress suffered be severe. Some courts add that the emotional distress must be so severe that it results in physical injury.

DISCUSSION QUESTION

3. What constitutes "extreme and outrageous" conduct is obviously a troubling issue, as is how debilitating the emotional distress must be to be seen as "severe." Consider the facts of *Agis v. Howard Johnson Co.*, 355 N.E.2d 315 (Mass. 1976). The Howard Johnson restaurant manager called a meeting of all the waitresses, including Ms. Agis. He stated that "there was some stealing going on" and that until the identity of the thief was made known, he would start firing the waitresses in alphabetical order. The plaintiff, Ms. Agis had the misfortune of being the first one to be fired. In her complaint, she alleged that she became greatly upset and began to cry. Do you think Ms. Agis was able to prove that the manager's actions were "extreme and outrageous" and that she suffered from "severe emotional distress"?

6. Harm to a Person's Property

Intentional torts can also involve harm to property. The tort of **trespass to land** occurs whenever someone enters or causes something to enter or remain on the land of another without permission. **Trespass to personal property** occurs when someone harms or interferes with the owner's exclusive possession of the property but has no intention of keeping the property. For example, if your neighbor intentionally lets your dog loose, hoping it will never return, your neighbor has

committed the tort of trespass to personal property. Conversion involves the taking of someone else's property with the intent of permanently depriving the owner. It is the civil side of theft.

7. Other Intentional Torts

In the previous sections we briefly introduced you to some of the more commonly used intentional torts. You should know, however that there are other intentional torts, that for space considerations, we simply could not include. In fact, there is an intentional tort to cover most types of harmful behavior. For example, three torts that are designed to provide protection against misuse of the legal system include false arrest, malicious prosecution, and abuse of process. Fraud and inducing a party to breach a contract are torts related to business dealings. Figure 7-2, page 148, summarizes the elements and defenses of the most common intentional torts.

Legal Reasoning Exercise

1. Review the situation of Mrs. Day, presented at the beginning of the chapter. Think of arguments that will be raised by both Mrs. Day's attorney and Mr. Day's attorney. For example, if you represented Mrs. Day, what torts would you argue Mr. Day committed? If you were representing Mr. Day, how would you respond?

B. NEGLIGENCE

Whereas "intentional torts" involve harm to a person or property that result from an act that the tortfeasor intended to commit, negligence results from an unintentional act. Negligence is traditionally defined as the failure to act reasonably under the circumstances. It is the most common type of tort action. It is the basis for such diverse personal injury lawsuits as those arising out of traffic accidents, slip and fall cases, and malpractice actions.

PRACTICE TIP

Does the other side claim it was snowing on the date of the accident? Check it out by getting climatological data through your local airport, newspaper archives, television station records, or the Internet.

Prima Facie Case	Defenses
Assault 1. an intentional act 2. that creates a reasonable apprehension of 3. an immediate harmful or offensive physical contact	1. consent 2. self-defense 3. defense of others 4. sometimes defense of property
Battery 1. an intentional act 2. that creates a harmful or offensive physical contact	
False imprisonment 1. an intentional act 2. that caused confinement or restraint 3. through force or the threat of force	1. consent 2. justification (e.g., shopkeeper's statute)
Defamation 1. publication 2. of false statements 3. that cause harm to reputation	1. truth 2. privilege
Invasion of privacy covers a variety of different situations, including 1. disclosure 2. intrusion 3. appropriation 4. false light	1. consent 2. newsworthiness
Intentional infliction of emotional distress 1. an intentional act 2. that is extreme and outrageous 3. and causes 4. severe emotional distress	1. consent
Trespass to land 1. someone enters or causes something to enter or remain 2. on the land of another 3. without permission	1. consent 2. private necessity 3. public necessity
Trespass to personal property 1. interference with the owner's exclusive possession 2. of personal property	1. rightful retention (e.g., under a mechanic's lien) 2. necessity
Conversion 1. taking 2. personal property 3. of another 4. with the intent of permanently depriving the owner	

Figure 7-2   Summary of Intentional Torts

PRACTICE TIP

When an accident occurs, keep in mind that the media are often the first on the scene, even well before the police or the ambulances. Check to see whether local news personnel were there and whether they have it all on video.

---

1. The Elements of Negligence

To be found negligent, a person must have acted unreasonably under the circumstances. More specifically, the courts look to the following four elements to establish negligence:

1. The defendant must owe a duty to the plaintiff to act reasonably, and
2. the defendant must have breached that duty
3. thereby causing
4. the plaintiff harm.

a. Duty

The law imposes a duty to act with "due care." This due care standard is defined in terms of how a "reasonably prudent person" would act in the same situation. If the person has some specialized type of training, such as a medical degree, then that individual is expected to act not just as a reasonable person would act but also as a reasonable person with medical training would act. What legal duty you owe to others also varies depending on your relationship to that other person. The closer and more direct the relationship, the greater the likelihood that a court will find a duty. For example, a doctor clearly has a duty to use due care in treating her patients. However, does the doctor also owe a duty to the patient's family? For instance, if the doctor failed to diagnose a contagious disease and the patient transmitted that disease to his wife, should the wife be able to sue the doctor?

DISCUSSION QUESTIONS

4. Prosenjit Poddar killed Tatiana Tarasoff. Two months earlier, Prosenjit had told Dr. Lawrence Moore, a psychologist, that he intended to kill Tatiana. Dr. Moore did not warn Tatiana or her parents of Prosenjit's intention. What policy considerations would argue against finding the psychologist liable? If you represented Tatiana's parents, how would you reply to those arguments?

5. The defendant company entered a float in a parade. As the float traveled down the street, employees threw candy to the crowd. Children running to collect the candy injured a spectator. Develop an argument for why the spectator should be allowed to sue the company.

6. A grocery store customer was mugged on a sidewalk adjacent to the shopping center. The mugging occurred immediately after the customer left the store. The sidewalk was owned not by the grocery store but by the shopping

A personal injury practice can become very hectic. Missed deadlines are always a constant worry. In fact, one of the major causes of legal malpractice claims is the failure to meet a deadline. To avoid such problems, develop a tickler system. The tickler system should be computerized as well as supplemented with a manual method.

center. The grocery store knew of numerous similar muggings on the sidewalk. The store employees used the sidewalk to carry bags to customers' cars, and its lease provided that the store could hold sidewalk sales there. Analyze whether the grocery store could be held liable for the customer's injuries.

b. Breach

In order to determine if someone has breached the duty of due care, the court considers all the circumstances. In evaluating those circumstances, the actions of the defendant are measured by an objective standard. That is, the jury is asked to consider what a reasonable person would have done. In the case of professional liability the standard is what a reasonable professional would have done. Therefore, in cases involving defendants who are being sued for professional malpractice, normally the plaintiff will be required to call an expert witness to testify as to the professional standard of care and how in the expert's opinion the defendant breached that standard. For example, in a case involving alleged medical malpractice by a pediatric oncologist, the plaintiff would call as an expert witness a doctor specializing in the field.

Negligence per se
Violation of a statute as proof of negligence.

If a defendant's actions violated a statute that was designed to protect the public, some states will hold that this violation of the statute is **negligence per se**, meaning that simply violating the statue is enough to prove that the defendant was negligent. In other states violation of such a statute is only evidence of negligence and can be rebutted.

Res ipsa loquitur
"The thing speaks for itself"; the doctrine that suggests negligence can be presumed if an event happens that would not ordinarily happen unless someone was negligent.

Another concept that can sometimes be used by the plaintiff to show negligence is the doctrine of **res ipsa loquitur**—the thing speaks for itself. Res ipsa loquitur applies in those situations where the event ordinarily would not have happened unless someone was negligent, the cause of the injury was under the defendant's exclusive control, and the injury was not due to the plaintiff's actions. For example, elevators usually do not drop, panes of glass usually do not fall out of windows, and planes do not crash absent someone's negligence. In those types of situations the court will assume that the defendant was negligent without the plaintiff having to prove the precise nature of that negligence.

DISCUSSION QUESTIONS

7. Most states have statutes prohibiting the sale of alcohol to a minor. If a store sold alcohol to a minor and the minor while intoxicated drove an automobile that collided with and killed a cyclist, would the liquor store owner be held liable as to the deceased cyclist?

8. On an icy, snow-covered road the plaintiff lost control of her car, skidded across the center line, and collided with a road grader, driven by the defendant. The defendant did not have the statutorily required class-B driver's license. The plaintiff, who was severely injured in the accident, sued the defendant under the theory of negligence per se. How do you think the court ruled and why?

c. Cause

In a tort action the defendant's actions must be the cause of the plaintiff's injuries. There are two types of causation: but for and proximate. Under the "but for" standard, it is necessary to establish that if the defendant had not acted, the plaintiff would not have been injured. This is also known as the **actual cause** or cause in fact.

The second prong of the requirement that the defendant's actions "cause" the injury is known as **proximate cause**. For a defendant's actions to be considered the proximate cause, a natural and continuous causal sequence must be shown between action and harm that is unbroken by any efficient intervening cause. In deciding cases in which determining the proximate cause is a key issue, the courts frequently wrestle with unforeseeable consequences and intervening forces. For example, the courts are sometimes faced with chain-reaction situations in which a person's actions lead to an event that in turn leads to several other events that eventually impact other people. Is everyone along the chain to be held responsible under the theory that but for their actions no injury would have happened, or is it more just to say that only those actors most immediately involved in the injury should be held responsible?

This notion of proximate cause is not really about cause at all but rather represents a policy decision that at some point a defendant will not be held responsible for every consequence of every action. Just as a pebble thrown into a pond sends out ripples of ever-decreasing strength, every action sends out repercussions of ever-decreasing importance. At some point we say that the consequences are too remote from the original action to hold the actor responsible.

Assume Ms. Farmer takes a lantern with her to her barn in order to milk her cow and thoughtlessly places the lantern next to the cow, who kicks it over. The barn catches on fire. The fire spreads to the neighbor's field, which also catches on fire. No major harm is done except that the ensuing group of gawkers, as well as the multiple fire-fighting and police vehicles, blocks traffic for over an hour. As a result, Mr. Smith, who is on his way to an important appointment, misses the appointment and consequently is fired. Should the neighbor be able to sue Ms. Farmer for the damage to his field? Most certainly. Should Mr. Smith be able to sue Ms. Farmer for his lost job? Most likely no. Why? In both cases Ms. Farmer was the "but for" cause of the injury. But most courts would probably say that the foreseeability of the harm to Mr. Smith was too remote to hold Ms. Farmer accountable. They might phrase this either as a lack of duty to Mr. Smith (an unforeseeable plaintiff) or as a lack of proximate cause (an unforeseeable injury). In either case the issue boils down to one of policy; that is, is this the type of injury for which we want to hold Ms. Farmer accountable?

While in any given case, it may be difficult to decide if the issue is one of duty of care, to be resolved by a judge, or one of proximate cause, to be resolved by a jury, in practice a defendant will almost always argue it is a question of duty of care while the plaintiff will argue proximate cause. This

Actual cause
Also known as cause in fact, this is measured by the "but for" standard: But for the defendant's actions, the plaintiff would not have been injured.

Proximate cause
Once actual cause is found, as a policy matter, the court must also find that the act and the resulting harm were so foreseeably related as to justify a finding of liability.

is because it is always to the defendant's benefit to end a lawsuit as early as possible to save litigation expenses and to put the matter to rest. On the other hand, it is often to the benefit of the plaintiff to go to trial, especially when the facts may arouse the jury's sympathy. Therefore, in a negligence action whenever possible the defendant will try to argue that the defendant owed no duty to the plaintiff. As duty is a question of law, the judge can resolve the matter on a motion to dismiss. If the judge determines that there was no duty, then the plaintiff loses and the case is dismissed. However, the plaintiff will try to characterize the issue as a question of foreseeability, thereby necessitating a trial. Then the jury, after hearing all of the evidence, can resolve the issue of foreseeability as a question of fact.

Legal Reasoning Exercises

2. Two crime victims were killed, having been shot. The families wanted to sue the handgun manufacturer under the theory that manufacturers of handguns negligently marketed them in such a way as to create an underground market, making it easy to obtain the guns. However, the plaintiffs were not able to identify which specific manufacturer made the handguns used in the shootings. Should they be allowed to pursue their lawsuit and, if so, against whom?

3. An alarm company delayed calling the fire department. By the time the firefighters arrived, the fire had advanced to such a stage that one of the firefighters was killed. The firefighter's widow sued the alarm company, alleging its negligent delay in calling in the fire resulted in her husband's death. How do you think the court decided? Why?

4. Assume you are a legislator and want to draft a statute dealing with social host liability. How would you fashion such a rule? For example, would you limit liability to those cases

> where minors are involved?
> where the host knows the guest is intoxicated?
> where the host actually serves the alcohol?

How would you avoid the concern that finding liability in some cases would potentially lead to unlimited liability for social hosts?

5. Do you think a social host should be liable for accidents caused by drivers who obtained alcohol from the social host? Why? For example, consider the following facts. Margaret Davis gave her daughter, a high school student, permission to hold a party. Davis did not keep alcoholic beverages in her home, and there were none on the night of the party. Before the party began, Davis left. During the unchaperoned party a seventeen-year-old guest obtained beer brought to the party by another guest. While driving home intoxicated, the guest lost control of his car and injured Ruth Langemann. Should Langemann be allowed to sue Davis for her injuries?

d. Harm

The purpose of negligence law is to compensate the plaintiff for any harm suffered. Even if the court finds that the defendant owed the plaintiff a duty of care and breached that duty, if the plaintiff was not harmed, the plaintiff will not be able to recover for negligence.

P R A C T I C E   T I P

In some states, if you want to use medical records, you have to send certified copies along with a notice to the opposing counsel that you are planning on using them at trial. Otherwise, you may be prevented from using the records unless you go through the expense of authenticating them through witness testimony.

---

2. Defenses to Negligence

In representing the defendant in a negligence case the attorney usually attempts to rebut the plaintiff's evidence on as many of the above four elements as possible. In other words, the defense tries to show that no duty was owed to the plaintiff and that the defendant's action was not the cause of the plaintiff's injuries. Another approach to defending such cases involves raising an affirmative defense, in which it is admitted that negligence was established, but it is argued that the defendant should not be held liable because of actions taken by the plaintiff. Traditionally, the two major affirmative defenses were contributory negligence and assumption of the risk. Today most states have adopted a form of comparative negligence.

> **Contributory negligence**
> Negligence by the plaintiff that contributed to his or her injury. Normally, it is a complete bar to the plaintiff's recovery.

a. Contributory negligence

While few states still use the defense of **contributory negligence** in its pure form, it is important to understand that doctrine as it forms the basis for the modern day defense of comparative negligence. Contributory negligence asserts

---

NETNOTE

To assist you in evaluating the harm done to your client, the Internet contains many sources for medical information. For example, you can find current medical news at *www.medscape.com*. The Cancer Web at *cancerweb.ncl.ac.uk/omd/* contains an on-line medical dictionary.

that the plaintiff contributed to his or her own injuries or otherwise failed to protect him- or herself from risks that were foreseeable. In other words, it was the plaintiff's breach of a duty to protect him- or herself that was the proximate cause of the injuries. The defendant therefore is relieved of any liability connected with the defendant's negligence, no matter how great the defendant's negligence and how slight the plaintiff's contributory negligence. Under comparative negligence, to be discussed more fully below, the plaintiff is still seen as contributing to his or her injuries, but that negligence usually no longer serves as a complete bar to recovery. Rather it serves to reduce the amount of money the plaintiff can recover.

b. Assumption of the risk

Assumption of the risk
Voluntarily and knowingly subjecting oneself to danger.

Another affirmative defense involves the concept of **assumption of the risk.** According to this doctrine a plaintiff may not recover for an injury received as a result of voluntarily subjecting him- or herself to a known danger. Successful use of this defense requires proof that the plaintiff knew about the dangerous nature of the situation before voluntarily exposing him- or herself to that danger. It is argued, for example, that when people choose to attend a baseball game, they assume the risk of being hit by a foul ball.

Notice that assumption of the risk involves a subjective standard. The plaintiff must voluntarily and knowingly assume the danger; that is, he or she must actually understand the risk. This can be contrasted with contributory negligence, which is measured not by what the plaintiff was thinking but by what a reasonable person would have done.

Under the traditional view, assumption of the risk, like contributory negligence, was a complete bar to recovery. Today many states have eliminated assumption of the risk as a separate defense, having subsumed it under the defense of comparative negligence. This eliminates many of the proof problems (that is, having to prove what the plaintiff was actually thinking) and the problems of categorizing specific behavior as either negligence or assumption of the risk. For example, if you get into a car being driven by someone you know is intoxicated, is that an unreasonable act on your part (contributory negligence) or assumption of the risk (knowingly subjecting yourself to a dangerous situation)? In those states that have subsumed assumption of the risk under comparative negligence, the plaintiff's recovery can be reduced either if it can be shown that a reasonable person would have acted differently or if the plaintiff actually knew and voluntarily assumed the risk.

Exculpatory clause
A provision that purports to waive liability.

An example of an express assumption of the risk is the signing of a waiver of liability. Such waivers are frequently called **exculpatory clauses** because their purpose is to relieve tortfeasors of liability. In certain circumstances the courts have upheld such waivers, particularly when the parties are of fairly equal bargaining power and the event involves inherent danger, such as skydiving or mountain climbing. Increasingly, however, courts are refusing to enforce such waivers. Sometimes the refusal is based on the public policy argument that the parties were of very unequal bargaining power. Other times the courts have invalidated such waivers by requiring specific language or by finding an ambiguity and construing the language against the drafter. In addition, the courts usually disallow exculpatory clauses in cases of gross negligence.

Legal Reasoning Exercises

6. Mr. Alack joined a local health club. He signed a two-page, single-spaced contract that included the following language:

Member assumes full responsibility for any injuries, damages or losses and does hereby fully and forever release and discharge [the health club] from any and all claims, demands, damages, rights of action, or causes of action, present or future . . . resulting from or arising out of the Member's . . . use or intended use of said gymnasium or the facilities and equipment thereof.

One day while he was exercising, the handle of a rowing machine disengaged from the weight cable and smashed into Mr. Alack's mouth. It was discovered that the machine's handle was not connected with the necessary clevis pin and that the health club did not require periodic inspections of its equipment. If you were representing Mr. Alack, how would you argue that the release would not bar him from suing the health club for its negligent failure to maintain the rowing machine?

7. Before taking part in a horseback riding tour at the Loon Mountain Equestrian Center, Ms. Wright signed the following release:

I understand and am aware that horseback riding is a HAZARDOUS ACTIVITY. . . . I therefore release Loon Mountain Recreation Corporation . . . FROM ANY AND ALL LIABILITY FOR DAMAGES AND PERSONAL INJURY TO MYSELF . . . RESULTING FROM THE NEGLIGENCE OF LOON MOUNTAIN RECREATION CORPORATION TO INCLUDE NEGLIGENCE IN SELECTION, ADJUSTMENT OR ANY MAINTENANCE OF ANY HORSE.

While on the tour, the guide's horse kicked Ms. Wright in the leg. Ms. Wright sued for negligence, arguing that the tour guide had failed to control the horse after it had given signs it was about to "act out." If you were representing Ms. Wright, how would you argue that the release should not bar her from suing the tour company?

c. Comparative negligence

Both contributory negligence and assumption of the risk prevent a plaintiff from being compensated for very serious injuries, even when the injuries resulted from rather minor breaches when compared to the extreme negligence of the defendant. In response to the perceived unfairness of this situation, all but a handful of states, through statutes and court decisions, have moved to adopt **comparative negligence**. Under comparative negligence, negligence is measured in terms of percentages, and damages are distributed proportionately. There are three alternative theories of comparative negligence:

Comparative negligence A method for measuring the relative negligence of the plaintiff and the defendant, with a commensurate sharing of the compensation for the injuries.

1. A plaintiff can recover when the plaintiff's negligence is slight but may not recover when the plaintiff's negligence is gross.

2. Under a "pure" comparative negligence statute a plaintiff can recover actual damages less a percentage, calculated as the amount of negligence attributable to the plaintiff.
3. Under modified comparative negligence a plaintiff's recovery is reduced by the percentage of his or her own negligence if the defendant's negligence is greater than that of the plaintiff. However, the plaintiff is barred from recovering anything if the plaintiff's negligence is greater than the defendant's.

d. Immunities

Defendants may also argue immunity as a defense. For policy reasons certain defendants, even though negligent, are immune from suit. Traditionally, immunity meant a complete bar to recovery. Recently, however, the courts have been re-examining many immunities and in some instances limiting their effect or even eliminating them entirely. For example, the doctrine of charitable immunity has also been abolished or limited in most states.

The doctrine of sovereign immunity prohibits suits against the government without the government's consent. It can be traced back to the concept of the divine right of kings and the idea that the king could do no wrong. In modern times federal and state governments have passed legislation that modifies this concept. For example, at the federal level Congress has enacted the Federal Tort Claims Act (FTCA).[4] Under that statute someone can sue the government for harm caused by a government employee's negligence but not for an intentional tort or for something that resulted from a discretionary function. These limitations are a cause for much litigation, as it is often difficult to determine whether a particular action is the result of negligence or an intentional act and whether the action falls within a "discretionary function." Similarly, on the state and local level, governmental acts are often protected from suit if the public employee's action involved basic policy choices.

The elements of negligence as well as the defenses are summarized in Figure 7-3, on page 157.

3. Reckless Behavior

Recklessness
Disregarding a substantial and unjustifiable risk that harm will result.

In between the two main categories of torts that we have discussed thus far, intentional torts and negligence, is an area of liability variously described as gross negligence, or willful or wanton behavior, or **recklessness**. While there is a great deal of confusion as to the exact meaning of these terms, all three imply a *conscious* or knowing disregard of an unreasonable and substantial risk of serious bodily harm to another. While the person may not wish to cause harm, he or she is aware of the potential for harm and proceeds anyway, indifferent to the consequences. Unlike negligence, which requires merely unreasonable behavior, recklessness requires a "**conscious** choice of a course of action, with knowledge or reason to know that it will create a serious danger to others."[5]

That said, the courts have not been able to clearly define recklessness, and it is decidedly difficult to know where negligence ends and recklessness begins and,

---

[4] 28 U.S.C. § 1346 (B) (2006).

[5] Schick v. Ferolito, 767 A.2d 962, 969 (N.J. 2001) (emphasis added).

in turn, where reckless behavior ends and intentional behavior begins. For example, if a golfer carelessly forgot to check to see if anyone was in the vicinity before taking a shot, that might be negligence. However, if that golfer had looked, had seen a person in the line of sight, had yelled a warning, and then had taken a shot anyway before the person had a chance to move, some courts would find the behavior to have been reckless but others would still see it as merely negligent. Finally, if the golfer was angry at another golfer and deliberately aimed his shot at the other player intending for the ball to hit her, then the golfer's actions would amount to either an intentional tort or recklessness.

You may be asking: But why does it matter? First, it matters because the standard the court chooses to apply — negligence, recklessness, or intent — may well determine whether the plaintiff can recover. It is more difficult to prove recklessness than negligence and more difficult to prove intent than recklessness. Therefore, if the court requires a finding of recklessness, but the plaintiff only has evidence showing that the defendant acted in a careless manner, the plaintiff will

Figure 7-3   Negligence Summarized

Plaintiff's Prima Facie Case	Defenses
1. The defendant must owe a duty to the plaintiff to act reasonably, and 2. the defendant must have breached that duty 3. causing (i.e., being both the cause in fact and the proximate cause) 4. the plaintiff harm.	1. **Contributory negligence** The plaintiff fails to use due care; traditionally, this has been a complete bar to the plaintiff's suit. Most states have abandoned contributory negligence and have adopted comparative negligence. 2. **Comparative negligence** The plaintiff fails to use due care; the plaintiff's negligence is compared to the defendant's negligence, and damages are reduced accordingly. 3. **Assumption of the risk** The plaintiff knowingly and voluntarily subjects himself or herself to danger; traditionally, this has been a complete bar to the plaintiff's suit. Today assumption of the risk has been eliminated in many states that have adopted comparative negligence. 4. **Immunity** This complete bar to a lawsuit is based on policy considerations, such as preventing suits between family members and protecting charitable organizations.

lose. An example is sports injuries that occur during an athletic event when one participant harms another participant. Because some contact is inherent in most sports and because they do not want to discourage vigorous competition, most courts will apply the recklessness standard to such situations. If an injured player can only show that the other player acted carelessly, with no conscious desire to harm, then the injured player will not be able to recover.

Second, the plaintiff may wish to introduce evidence that the defendant's actions went beyond negligence and involved some level of conscious intent so as to constitute reckless or intentional behavior, in order to raise the possibility of recovering punitive damages. Finally, several courts have held that if the plaintiff can show that the defendant acted recklessly or intentionally, the plaintiff's contributory negligence cannot be used as a defense.

Legal Reasoning Exercises

6. An amateur soccer game was played between high school-aged players. Julian Nabozny was a goalie. David Barnhill was a forward for the opposing team. David was known for being a very rough player, having acquired more penalties than any other player on the team. Rather than cautioning David to play a clean game, David's coach urged all his players to play as hard as they could and to "go for the kill."

During the game David kicked Julian in the head while Julian was in possession of the ball. Contact with a goaltender while he is in possession of the ball is a violation of FIFA (International Association Football Federation—soccer's international governing body) rules, which governed the contest.

When Julian's dad saw David kick his son in the head, he jumped out of his chair, rushed onto the field, and hit David in the chin with his fist, breaking David's jaw.

Another parent, Mike Bishop, also rushed onto the field. Afraid that Julian might be hurt further, he scooped him up and carried him off the field. Unfortunately, when David had kicked Julian, he had broken his neck. When Mike picked him up, the movement caused compression in Julian's spinal cord, leaving him permanently paralyzed from the waist down.

a. Julian wants to sue David, the other player. In his complaint, which tort theory is Julian's attorney most likely to allege and what will he have to prove for Julian to be successful?

b. Julian also wants to sue the coach. In his complaint, which tort theory is Julian's attorney most likely to allege and what will he have to prove for Julian to be successful?

c. Finally, Julian wants to sue Mike, the parent who "helped" him. In his complaint, which tort theory is Julian's attorney most likely to allege and what will he have to prove for Julian to be successful?

d. For the court to allow David to recover against Julian's dad, on what tort theory will David's attorney rely?

C. STRICT LIABILITY

Negligence and intentional torts result in liability because the defendant was at fault. In the former the fault is a result of carelessness, and in the latter it is intentional. When the concept of **strict liability** is applied, however, liability is imposed even though the defendant is not at fault. The courts impose liability for the policy reason that, as between the defendant and the injured plaintiff, the defendant is in a better position to absorb the costs of the injury. The courts have applied the doctrine of strict liability in two situations: those involving inherently dangerous activities and products liability.

> **Strict liability**
> Liability without having to prove fault.

When persons engage in activities that are inherently dangerous, they may be responsible for any injuries that result, even though the activities may be carried out in the safest and most prudent way possible. In recent years the doctrine of strict liability has also been widely applied in product liability cases, in which the manufacturer is held liable for defects that occur in the product. A product is considered to be defective if it is unreasonably dangerous for use in the ordinary manner.

1. Inherently Dangerous Activities

The classic case for finding strict liability in the area of inherently dangerous activities is the use of dynamite in blasting. The rational for finding strict liability in such cases is that blasting as a business carries with it extreme risks that cannot be guarded against. Therefore, as between a for-profit company that chooses to engage in blasting and an innocent person harmed by the results of the blasting, the company should be held accountable, with the damages to be absorbed as part of the costs of doing business. Of course, any company engaging in such dangerous activities would be wise to purchase liability insurance. In addition to such dangerous business activities as using or storing explosives, courts have frequently found the owners of wild animals strictly liable for injuries the animals cause.

NETNOTE

The Consumer Product Safety Commission has a web site where you can find information on recalls and unsafe products. Start at *www.cpsc.gov.*

2. Products Liability

When a product proves to be defective, an injured party can sue under any one of three theories: negligence, breach of warranty, or strict liability. Which theory to use depends on the facts of the case and how the plaintiff's state court has chosen to categorize products liability cases. For example, a plaintiff might bring a case under a negligence theory if the plaintiff has proof of a manufacturing defect or a design defect. For example, a hockey helmet with cutouts around the ears that

> **Products liability**
> The theory holding manufacturers and sellers liable for defective products when the defects make the

allows penetration of a hockey puck is arguably defectively designed. Finally, a failure to warn of a danger known to the manufacturer but probably unknown to the user would form the basis for a negligence suit.

There are times, however, when a plaintiff cannot point to any one act of negligence. Nonetheless, the product was defective, and that defect caused an injury. In those cases the plaintiff might rely either on a warranty theory—the product failed to meet the buyer's expectations for a safe product—or on a tort strict liability theory. For example, assume you purchase a new car. One week later, as you are driving home from work, your brakes fail and, because you were unable to slow your car, you run off the road and end up in a ditch. Luckily, you are able to escape before your car bursts into flames. Because of the fire damage, there is no way to pinpoint the exact cause of the brake failure. As brand-new cars are supposed to have brakes that work, obviously the brakes were defective. However, you cannot prove the exact cause of the defect. Under negligence theory you would have been out of luck because you could not prove the precise negligence that caused the defect. However, under strict products liability you simply have to prove that the dealer sold you the car in a defective condition that was unreasonably dangerous.

The law of strict products liability was heavily influenced by the 1965 passage of Section 402A of the Restatement of the Law of Torts, Second. Under Section 402A, a manufacturer or seller is liable if it sells a defective product that harms a consumer and that defect made the product unreasonably dangerous. Unlike other provisions of the Restatement, Section 402A was not really a restatement of existing law. Rather it was the American Law Institute's vision of what the law should be. When it was passed, it had little support. Over the years that has changed, and today Section 402A has been adopted by many state courts and legislatures.

A plaintiff's contributory negligence is usually not considered a defense to strict liability. However, assumption of the risk and **product misuse** may be. For a manufacturer to assert the affirmative defense of product misuse, the manufacturer must prove that the product was not being used for its intended purpose or was being used in a dangerous manner that could not reasonably have been foreseen by the manufacturer. However, even if a plaintiff misuses a product, if that use is foreseeable, the manufacturer may be liable for a design defect. For example, in one case a young child opened a stove door in order to step on it in an attempt to reach a shelf located above the stove. Although clearly a stove is not meant to be used as a stepping stool, the court held that this misuse was foreseeable and could have been avoided by a different design.

Product misuse
When the product was not being used for its intended purpose or was being used in a dangerous manner; it is a defense to a products liability claim so long as the misuse was not foreseeable.

DISCUSSION QUESTIONS

9. A woman keeps a pit bull dog as a pet. One day the neighbor children accidentally throw a Frisbee into her yard. In attempting to retrieve the Frisbee, one of the children is severely bitten by the dog. Should the dog's owner be held strictly liable? Why?

10. Why should a company that manufactures football helmets be liable for injuries sustained by someone wearing their helmet, if they have made those helmets as safe as modern technology allows, and players choose to play even though they know it is dangerous?

11. Manuel Sanchez began smoking at the age of ten. Over his lifetime he smoked several different brands of cigarettes. At the age of fifty-three he was diagnosed with throat cancer and died within six months. His widow sued nine different cigarette manufacturers on the theory of strict liability. To win her case, what would Mrs. Sanchez have to prove? Do you think she was successful?

12. Five-year-old Daphne took a disposable lighter from her mother's purse that was stored on the top shelf of a closet in a bedroom in her grand-parents' home. While playing with the lighter, she started a fire that severely burned her two-year-old brother, Ruben. While the lighter manufacturer pro-duced lighters both with and without child safety mechanisms, this lighter did not have one. The children's mother sued the manufacturer of the lighter. If you represented the mother, how would you argue the manufacturer should be held liable for the boy's injury? How do you think the lawyers for the manufacturer would respond?

D. REMEDIES AND THE CHOICE OF WHOM TO SUE

The most common form of remedy that a plaintiff seeks in a tort action is the awarding of some form of damages. Because employers have "deeper pockets," that is, more resources to pay a large damage award, a plaintiff will often seek those damages from an employer rather than, or in addition to, the employee when hurt by an employee's negligence.

Under the doctrine of **respondeat superior**, a Latin term translated as "Let the master answer," the extent to which an employer is held accountable for the acts of a worker depends on three factors. First, was the worker an employee or an independent contractor? An employer is generally not responsible for the negligent actions of an independent contractor unless the contractor is engaged in an ultra hazardous activity, such as dynamiting. Second, if the worker was an employee, did the employee act negligently? If the employee was not negligent, then the employer cannot be held responsible. Third, at the time of the injury was the employee engaged in work of the type the employee was hired to perform? This last question requires an assessment of whether the employee was working within the "scope of employment" or, as the courts so quaintly put it, whether the employee was "on a frolic of the employee's own."

Respondeat superior
The tort theory that an employer can be sued for the negligent acts of its employees.

Once the plaintiff has decided whom to sue, the plaintiff may seek one of three types of damage awards: compensatory, punitive, and nominal. In addition to or instead of damages, the plaintiff may ask for an injunction. An injunction is a court order directing the defendant to do a specific act or to cease doing a specific act.

Compensatory damages (sometimes referred to as actual damages) are awarded to compensate the plaintiff for the harm done to him or her. In a tort action involving harm to a person, that might mean the cost of medical bills, lost time from work, and pain and suffering.

Punitive damages, also called **exemplary damages,** are designed to punish the defendant. Typically, they are awarded only for intentional torts, when the court determines that the tortfeasor deserves an additional punishment beyond just compensating the plaintiff for the harm done to him or her. Punitive awards are granted in very few cases, and the court is more likely to find that punitive damages are appropriate when the harm involves personal injury as opposed to mere property damage.

Keep in mind that the doctrine of respondeat superior binds attorney employers, too. If a paralegal fails to perform a necessary task, such as filing a document as requested by the attorney, the paralegal's negligence will be attributed to the attorney, who could then be found liable in a malpractice action.

Finally, **nominal damages** are awarded when a right has been violated but the plaintiff cannot prove any monetary harm. For example, a trespasser may have caused no harm to the land, but the landowner would still be entitled to a nominal award.

DISCUSSION QUESTION

13. Should fast food restaurants be required to pay punitive damages for serving their coffee at a temperature that they know to be hot enough to seriously burn someone if the coffee is spilled on them?

SUMMARY

A tort is a private wrong that causes harm to a person or property. Torts are generally classified as involving intentional acts, negligence, or strict liability. Intentional torts occur whenever someone intends an action that results in harm. Examples include assault and battery, false imprisonment, defamation, invasion of privacy, intentional infliction of emotional distress, and trespass. Negligence involves a breach of duty that causes harm. Cause includes both actual cause and proximate cause. Strict liability includes both ultrahazardous activities and products liability, where an unreasonably dangerous defective product is sold. Finally, in a limited number of situations, such as those involving contact sports, the courts will apply a recklessness standard. Recklessness involves a conscious decision to proceed despite a substantial and unjustifiable risk that harm will result.

Tort law is constantly evolving. The courts are still developing new torts to cover changing societal views as to what should be protected. Examples include the torts of wrongful life or birth and battered woman's syndrome.

Finally, in bringing a tort action a plaintiff is generally seeking either an injunction or damages. Damages can take the form of a compensatory, punitive, or nominal award.

REVIEW QUESTIONS

Pages 139 through 144
1. How can the same set of facts result in both a tort and a crime? Will every tort also create criminal liability?
2. How can a tort be distinguished from a contract action?
3. What are the elements of assault? Of battery?

4. How can there be an assault and no battery? A battery without an assault?

5. Review the situation of Mrs. Day presented at the beginning of the chapter. Do you think she has a valid claim for either assault or battery? Why?

6. What are the elements of false imprisonment?

7. When does a shopkeeper have a valid defense to a detained person's allegation of false imprisonment?

Pages 144 through 147

8. What are the elements of libel? The defenses?

9. In *New York Times v. Sullivan,* what limitations did the Supreme Court put on the ability of public figures to sue the press?

10. Assume Robin Barker dictates a letter to her secretary. The letter is addressed to Ms. Wanda Jones. In the letter Ms. Barker tells Ms. Jones that she thinks Ms. Jones is a thief. The secretary types and mails the letter to Ms. Jones. Can Ms. Jones sue for defamation? What element is arguably missing?

11. A grocery store employee followed a customer to the parking lot and accused her of having meat in her purse. The customer opened her purse and showed that she did not have any meat, and the employee left. Several passersby heard the remarks, but the plaintiff could not identify any of them. Should the customer be barred from proceeding with a defamation suit? Why?

12. How do the torts of defamation and invasion of privacy differ?

13. What must a plaintiff prove to win a case of intentional infliction of emotional distress?

Pages 147 through 158

14. What are the four basic elements of a negligence claim?

15. Explain the doctrine of res ipsa loquitur.

16. When might the court find that a defendant was negligent per se?

17. What is the difference between "but for" causation and proximate cause?

18. Describe the three basic affirmative defenses to negligence. How do they differ from each other?

19. A state court judge approved a mother's petition to have her "somewhat retarded" daughter sterilized. The daughter was told that she was to have her appendix removed. Later the daughter married and found out that she had been sterilized. She sued the judge. How do you think the court resolved the case?

20. A public high school required parents to sign a release-of-liability form before allowing their children to participate in interscholastic athletics. The parents objected to having to sign the form and went to court, requesting that the school district be enjoined from requiring the release. How do you think the court decided the issue?

21. State building codes set forth requirements for safe buildings. If a building inspector fails in his duty to carefully inspect a building, do you think a purchaser of such premises would have a cause of action for buying a building that was developed in violation of the governmental requirements? Why?

22. How is recklessness defined? How does it differ both from intentional conduct and negligence?

Pages 159 through 162

23. Describe the three theories that a plaintiff can use to sue a manufacturer when harmed by that manufacturer's product.

24. What are the three basic types of damages that a plaintiff can recover in a tort action, and what is the purpose of each?

Chapter 8

Contracts and the Uniform Commercial Code (UCC)

A contract has, strictly speaking, nothing to do with the personal, or individual, intent of the parties. . . . If . . . it were proved by twenty bishops that either party, when he used the words, intended something else than the usual meaning which the law imposes upon them, he would still be held.

Judge Learned Hand

INTRODUCTION

Contracts are involved in almost every aspect of our lives, from day-to-day commercial transactions to corporate mergers—from purchasing and financing a home to insuring that home, automobile, life, or health. A contract is simply an agreement, oral or written, that can be enforced in court. Contract law sets out the basic elements that must be present for an agreement to be considered legally enforceable. It also spells out when the court will excuse one of the parties for not living up to that side of the agreement. In sum, contract law reflects society's values regarding what promises we think should be kept and what excuses we will allow.

Contract law has strong common-law roots, and in areas that do not deal with the business world, the common-law rules still govern. However, if a

Uniform Commercial Code (UCC)
Originally drafted by the National Conference of Commissioners on Uniform State Law, it governs commercial transactions and has been adopted by all states, entirely or in part.

NETNOTE

The Uniform Commercial Code as revised through 1992 can be found on the Internet at:

www.law.cornell.edu/ucc/ucc.table.html

Article 1	General Provisions
Article 2	Sales
Article 2A	Leases [New]
Article 3	Commercial Paper
Article 4	Bank Deposits and Collections
Article 5	Letters of Credit
Article 6	Bulk Transfers
Article 7	Warehouse Receipts, Bills of Lading, & Other Documents of Title
Article 8	Investment Securities
Article 9	Secured Transactions
Article 10	Effective Date and Repealer

Figure 8-1 The Uniform Commercial Code

contract involves a business setting, then you may also have to consult legislation, in the form of the **Uniform Commercial Code (UCC).** The UCC is a series of model statutory provisions drafted by prominent legal scholars. It was developed with the intent that states would voluntarily incorporate these provisions into their own statutes, thus providing a uniform set of legal principles that would facilitate commercial transactions among persons in different states.

Although all states, as well as the District of Columbia, have adopted the UCC entirely or in part, it is not a federal law. That would require its enactment by Congress. The terms of the UCC are valid only if they have been adopted by the state. In addition, while most states have adopted the UCC as it was originally written, each state has the option of changing the terms. Therefore, when dealing with the UCC in a specific state be sure to check that state's precise wording.

The UCC was specially developed to make the commercial world more uniform and efficient, and there are special rules that apply only to merchants. For example, a merchant's obligation of good faith includes "honesty in fact and the observance of reasonable commercial standards of fair dealing in the trade." UCC § 2-103(b). Therefore, merchants are expected not only to deal honestly but also to be aware of the normal business practices for their trade.

The UCC is divided into ten articles. See Figure 8-1. In this chapter our discussion will focus on articles 1, 2, 3, and 9. Article 1 sets forth general provisions, such as definitions that apply to the entire UCC. Article 2 deals with the sale of goods. Note that while Article 2 of the UCC applies to some contract situations, it does not apply to all. For example, it does not apply to real estate or employment contracts because neither involves the "sale of goods."

Whenever you are faced with a contract situation, first ask yourself, does the situation involve a contract for the sale of goods? If the answer is yes, then ask whether either or both of the parties can be classified as a merchant. If yes, then be sure to check the special provisions that apply only to merchants. Finally, keep in mind the UCC's overall commitment to ensuring that all parties act in good faith and in such a way as to promote the expansion of commerce. See Figure 8-2, on page 167.

The two other articles we will be discussing in this chapter are Articles 3 and 9. Both of these articles relate to issues raised when a consumer or business is interested in borrowing money. Article 3 covers the various forms of commercial paper, such as checks and promissory notes. Article 9 deals with secured transactions, a method whereby a creditor can be assured that if the debtor fails to repay the debt, the creditor can obtain specific property as an alternative form of payment.

A. CONTRACT LAW

You will discover that contract law is very rule-bound. That is, to become an expert in contract law, you must master a vast array of technical rules. Our brief overview of contract law in this chapter is designed to help you understand the basic concepts that lie behind these rules so that you will be able to recognize a contract law problem when you are faced with one and be able to undertake research in this area.

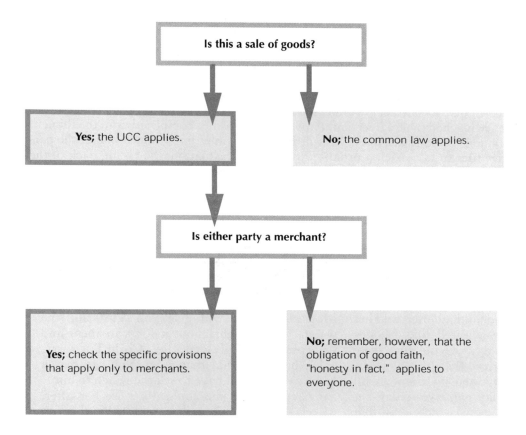

Is this a sale of goods?

Yes; the UCC applies.

No; the common law applies.

Is either party a merchant?

Yes; check the specific provisions that apply only to merchants.

No; remember, however, that the obligation of good faith, "honesty in fact," applies to everyone.

Figure 8-2   Does Article 2 of the UCC Apply?

Ethics Alert

One of the most common contracts you will find in a law firm is the fee agreement. As the only parties to the contract are the client and the attorney, a paralegal cannot establish the fee agreement. In addition, any attempt by a paralegal to set fees is considered the unauthorized practice of law.

1. The Elements of a Binding Contract

A contract can be either oral or written, but in order to be considered valid, each of its three key elements must be present:

1. An offer must be made,
2. an acceptance must be given, and
3. something of value must be exchanged (consideration).

Some writers list only two elements: an agreement and consideration. In such formulations an agreement is defined as both an offer and an acceptance, and consideration is defined as the exchange of something of value.

It is important to clearly distinguish a contract from a gift. A gift may also involve an offer (someone offers to give you something), an acceptance (you respond that you would like the gift), and the passage of something of value (the gift itself). The difference is that in a gift situation the consideration is one-sided. Only one of the parties receives something of value. On the other hand, in a contract situation each party gives up something of value. Because of this difference, a contract is completed and binding on both parties once the parties have reached their agreement. However, a gift is not completed until the thing of value is actually delivered. This difference becomes important if one of the parties tries to take back a promise. In a contract situation, the taking back of the promise creates a right in the other party to sue for breach of contract. In a gift situation, prior to delivery of the gift, the giver is free to take back the promise with no legal consequences. Consider the situation described in the following fact scenario:

The Case of "Who Owns the Watch?"

Sally, a paralegal student, had often told her friend Jill how much she admired Jill's Mickey Mouse watch. Last Monday, as the two were walking to class, Sally noticed that Jill was wearing a different watch and asked Jill about it. Jill replied that at her birthday party yesterday her boyfriend gave her this new watch. "In that case," Sally inquired, "would you be interested in selling your Mickey Mouse watch to me?" Jill replied, "I paid $200 for it, but because we are friends, I will sell it to you for $100 and will bring the watch with me tomorrow." Sally said, "Great; it's a deal." Unnoticed by Sally and Jill, Mike had overheard the conversation. "Wait," Mike said, "I have always wanted a Mickey Mouse watch. I will give you $150 for the watch." Jill thought about it for a moment and then turned to Sally and said "Gosh; I'm sorry, Sally, but I'm afraid that unless you can match Mike's offer, I will have to sell the watch to him." Sally replied that she could not raise her offer. Mike, feeling a bit guilty, told Sally that on Tuesday when he got the Mickey Mouse watch, he would no longer need his current watch and would give it to Sally. The next day Jill sold her watch to Mike. Mike, however, had a change of heart and refused to give his old watch to Sally. Sally is understandably upset by the turn of events. Does she have any legal rights against either Jill or Mike?

Looking at the first situation between Sally and Jill we see there was an agreement to exchange something of value. Recall that to form a binding contract, there must be an agreement to sell (Jill said she would sell the watch for

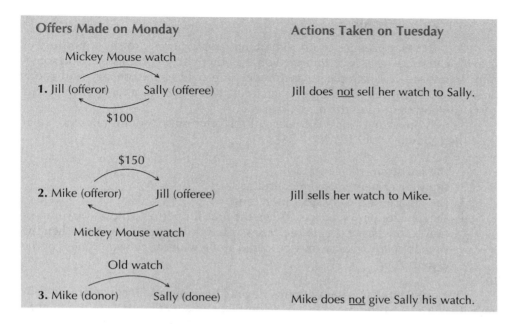

Offers Made on Monday	Actions Taken on Tuesday
Mickey Mouse watch **1.** Jill (offeror) Sally (offeree) $100	Jill does <u>not</u> sell her watch to Sally.
$150 **2.** Mike (offeror) Jill (offeree) Mickey Mouse watch	Jill sells her watch to Mike.
Old watch **3.** Mike (donor) Sally (donee)	Mike does <u>not</u> give Sally his watch.

$100 [an offer] and Sally said, "I agree" [an acceptance]); also, something of value must be exchanged (Sally was going to give $100 in return for the Mickey Mouse watch). Therefore, Sally and Jill had a binding contract. By selling the watch to someone else Jill is in breach of contract. Sally is entitled to the benefit of her bargain. However, it is unlikely that the court would order Jill to sell the watch to Sally. Such an order for specific performance occurs only when the item is unique. Instead Sally would be entitled to money damages. In this case she can purchase a similar watch, and if it costs more than the $100 she had agreed to spend, she can recover the difference.

Sometimes in analyzing contract situations it is helpful to diagram them. The arrow indicates something of value passing from one party to the other.

The second situation illustrates a fully executed contract. Mike made an offer, Jill accepted, and they agreed to exchange something of value. A binding contract was formed. Then when they fulfilled their promises, the contract was fully executed.

In the third situation, involving Sally and Mike, there was no contract. Sally did not agree to exchange anything with Mike. Mike simply offered to give Sally his old watch. For a gift to be complete, however, delivery must occur. Because Mike never handed Sally the watch, there was no completed gift, and Sally has no rights to Mike's watch.

The courts treat these situations so differently because in a contract negotiation both parties give up something of value. In the second situation, however, the transaction is one-sided. Because gift givers receive nothing in return, they should be allowed time to reconsider up until actual delivery. The delivery then provides proof that there was intent for a gift to occur.

a. Offer

Offer

In contract law, an indication of a firm desire to enter into an agreement, sufficiently definite that once accepted a contract is formed.

An **offer** is a promise to do something—for example, to sell a product or provide a service—that is conditioned on the other party's promising to do something in return—for example, to pay money or provide some other type of goods or services. The offer sets the parameters of the agreement and gives the other party the power to bind them to a contract.

To be considered valid, the terms of the offer must contain reference to at least the following four items:

1. the parties to the contract,
2. the subject matter of the contract,
3. the nature of the consideration, and
4. the time for performance. (When the time for performance is very important to the parties, as in the case of the sale of perishable fruit, then the time for performance may be stated along with the phrase "time is of the essence.")

One problem that arises with this stage of the contract is that of distinguishing between a true offer to enter into a contract and a mere statement of intent to begin negotiations. For example, assume Sam says, "I am thinking of selling my car. What would you give me for it?" If John replies, "I will give you $750 for it," Sam has made only a statement of intent, not an offer. John's reply is the offer, and it is up to Sam whether he wants to accept or not. When a person asks, "Will you buy?" or says, "I plan to sell," this also gives rise to the inference that the person was only beginning the process of negotiation but was not yet ready to be bound by the statements.

Review the facts set out in the following Legal Reasoning Exercise. Pay special attention to whether the letter sent should be seen as an offer or merely as an invitation to bid.

Legal Reasoning Exercise

1. Emma Johnson was the owner of two parcels of land. On March 27 Ms. Johnson's son-in-law, Edward Hicks, who was her agent to sell the property, wrote the following letter to James Mellon.

You will perhaps remember that we spent a pleasant visit on the breakwater at Nahant last summer. On that occasion either you or your brother-in-law expressed an interest in my Mother's property which is the Johnson cottage. . . . [Mother's] health is such that she will not be able to open the cottage this year. She has, therefore, decided that it will be best to place the property on the market; however, before turning it over to the real estate agents, I am writing to several people, including yourself, who have previously expressed an interest in the property. Our price is $7,500. This property consists of the lot and cottage on the south side of Willow Road, and also a very large plot on which a two-car garage is situated running from Willow Road clear through the block to the next street. Just how much property there is in this tract, I cannot tell you at the moment. . . . I will be interested in

hearing from you further if you have any interest in this property, for as I said before, I am advising those who have asked for an opportunity to consider it. I might just add that the property would be available for immediate occupancy. By that I mean within such time as the present furnishings could be removed and title transferred.

On March 28, Mr. Hicks received a telegram from Mr. Mellon's brother-in-law that read:

We are interested in your offer. Will look at house tomorrow. Communicate with you first of week.

On the same day shortly after the telegram was received, Mr. Hicks telegraphed Mr. Mellon:

Have heard from three interested buyers tonight which means we must accept highest bid for Nahant property. Suggest you wire or phone us Elmsford N.Y. 7292 Saturday your best offer on cash basis.

Before this was received, Mr. Mellon telegraphed Mr. Hicks:

I accept your offer on Nahant cottage. Letter in mail.

When Mr. Hicks entered into a written contract to sell the property to someone else, Mr. Mellon sued to stop the sale from being completed.

    a. Do you think an offer was ever made? Why?
    b. Do you think Mr. Mellon's suit was successful? Why?

It is important that the terms of the offer be definite so that a court can fashion a remedy and so that there is sufficient evidence that a bargain has been struck. For example, assume Sam says, "I want to sell my car," and John replies, "Done!" There is no contract because neither knows the price.

The UCC has made some major changes in this area of the law. Under the UCC a contract can be formed even if there are missing terms, so long as the quantity is specified. The missing terms are supplied by the UCC itself. For example, a missing price term becomes a reasonable price. UCC § 2-305(1).

Finally, the offer must be communicated to the offeree. Usually, this last requirement does not present any problems except in the case of rewards. Some courts have held that if a person fulfills the terms of a reward—for example, returning a lost dog to its owner—without knowing beforehand of the reward, that person cannot claim the reward, as it was never communicated to him or her.

b. Acceptance

The second element of a valid contract is **acceptance**. The UCC explicitly states that an offer can be accepted either by sending notification of such

Acceptance
In contract law, an act by the offeree indicating agreement to be bound to the contract.

acceptance or by performing the act requested. If Alice offers to pay Bruce $10 for Bruce's bicycle, Bruce's acceptance can take the form of making a telephone call stating that he will sell her the bicycle or by delivering the bicycle to her. UCC § 2-206(b).

If the offeree decides to accept, then the mirror image rule requires that the acceptance exactly mirror the offer. The offeree cannot add new terms or vary the original terms. If he or she attempts to do so, the acceptance becomes a counteroffer. A counteroffer takes away the power of the offeree to accept the original offer. For example, if John states, "I accept; please send a written contract," then there is an acceptance. However, if John says, "I accept if you send a written contract," then there is no acceptance because John has added an additional term to the contract.

The UCC has made some major changes to the mirror image rule. Basically the UCC states that if the parties intend to make a contract, then the use of additional or different terms in the acceptance will not prevent the contract from being formed. This provision recognizes that often the parties will assume they have made a contract and will act on that assumption even if the offer and acceptance do not match in every detail.

c. Consideration

Consideration

Anything of value; it must be present for a valid contract to exist, and each side must give consideration.

Consideration is the third element of a valid contract. It is defined as the exchange of something of value. The consideration can be money, services, goods, or anything else that is a benefit to one party or a detriment to the other. The key is that something of real value has to be exchanged by both parties. In other words, a contract must be distinguished from a gift. When a person promises to give something without expecting to receive anything in return, that promise does not constitute an enforceable contract.

At times it may appear as though something of value has been exchanged when in actuality it has not. For example, if someone promises to hire you and pay you "what you are worth," the phrase is so vague as to make the promise illusory. In addition, if someone makes a promise because he or she feels morally obligated to do so but receives nothing else in return, there is no consideration. For example, assume Julie is friends with Martha. Martha feels ill but does not have a doctor. Julie takes Martha to her doctor. Once Martha is cured, she refuses to pay the doctor bill. Julie may feel morally obligated to pay the bill because she took Martha to the doctor, but she is under no contractual obligation to do so.

Also, past consideration will not support a contract. Assume I volunteer to take care of your cat while you are away on vacation. When you return, if you are very pleased with the job I have done and offer to pay me for my services, no contract has been formed. I have already done my job, and there is no new consideration for me to give in return for your promise. Finally, if someone is under a pre-existing duty to act, performing that duty cannot serve as the consideration for a new contract. If your house is on fire and you offer a fire fighter $2000 to put out the fire, you will be under no obligation to pay the money. The fire fighter is already under a pre-existing duty to put out the fire.

Generally, the court will not look into the adequacy of the consideration. Simply put, the court does not care if you made a poor bargain. The philosophy behind freedom of contract is that you are free to make any bargain you like,

even a bad one. In addition, if people could sue to get out of their contractual obligations every time it turned out they had made a poor bargain, the courts would be flooded with lawsuits. Finally, the security of being able to rely on contractual performance would be gone.

2. Contract Interpretation

Sometimes even though it is clear that there is an offer, acceptance, and consideration, thus forming a valid contract, the parties disagree about the legal effect of the contract's terms. This is often due to the innate ambiguity of the English language. When such differences in interpretation arise, the parties may turn to the courts for assistance.

When asked to interpret ambiguous language, the courts generally follow many of the same guidelines that they use to interpret statutory language. We will discuss these guidelines more fully in Chapter 12. The courts usually begin by trying to give the words their plain or common sense meaning. When that is not possible, the court will try to see if the meaning of the words can be deciphered from the parties' intent as expressed in the contract. The court may also apply commonly accepted definitions from the relevant industry or business. Finally, the court may interpret the language so as to favor the party who did not draft the contract.

Legal Reasoning Exercise

2. The 2005 hurricane season spawned a number of high-profile lawsuits over the interpretation of standard homeowner insurance policies. Such policies are contracts between the insured homeowner and the insurance company to cover damage to the insured's house, home furnishings, and other types of listed property. These policies typically cover damage from high winds but exclude water damage. However, when hurricanes hit shore they usually combine high winds, heavy rain, and sometimes even tidal waves. Which of the following types of damage do you think should be considered wind damage?

   a. During the hurricane, a limb breaks off a tree and damages the roof of an insured's house.
   b. During the hurricane, water came into an insured's house through windows that had been blown out by the hurricane's winds.
   c. Rain from the hurricane caused a nearby river to overflow its banks and flood waters covered the first floor carpet.
   d. Rain from the hurricane overwhelmed the local sewer system and caused water to back up into the insured's basement.
   e. A beach house was knocked off its foundation by the tidal wave that accompanied the hurricane.

Now assume that a homeowner's policy explicitly excluded "water damage" and defined that term as "(1) flood, surface water, tsunami, seiche, over-

flow of a body of water, or spray from any of these, whether driven by wind or not; (2) water or sewage from outside the residence premise's plumbing system that enters through sewers or drains, or water which enters into and overflows from within a sump pump, sump pump well, or any other system designed to remove subsurface water which is drained from the foundation." Which, if any, of the types of damage listed above would be excluded from coverage under the terms of the policy?

3. Defenses in Contract Cases

Once the plaintiff has proven the existence of an offer, acceptance, and consideration, the defendant can raise various defenses. Those defenses include an argument that one or both of the parties lacked contractual capacity, the contract should not be enforced because it is illegal or because it violates public policy, there was no true genuineness of assent because of fraud, mistake, or undue influence, the product was defective in violation of the seller's warranties, or in some situations that the proper format was not followed, as, for example, with those contracts that must be in writing.

a. Lack of Contractual Capacity

Voidable
A contract that is invalid even if it is not repudiated by either party.

The parties to a contract can be either people or corporations. However, an individual may be considered incapable of contracting if that person is a child, is mentally retarded or mentally ill, or is under the influence of drugs or alcohol. If one of the parties is a minor, the contract may be **voidable** by the minor. Therefore, the terms of the contract are enforceable against the adult party to the contract but not against the minor party. The one exception is that minors are liable for necessaries, such as housing, food, and clothing. Minors can disaffirm the contract for necessaries, but they must pay the reasonable value of the good or services they received.

Void
A contract that is invalid even if it is not repudiated by either party.

Mental incompetence can also cause a contract to be voidable, a situation analogous to that of minors. As is true with minors, the incompetent person remains responsible for the reasonable value of necessaries. However, if someone has been adjudged mentally incompetent and the court has appointed a guardian to handle the incompetent's affairs, then that individual is without the capacity to make contracts. Instead of being merely voidable, any contract the incompetent individual tries to make is **void**. Only the guardian can enter into valid contracts.

DISCUSSION QUESTION

1. What do you think the age limit should be for being able to enter into contracts? What was your rationale for picking that age?

b. Lack of Genuineness of Assent

Another basis for challenging a contract is to assert that the parties never reached a true meeting of the minds regarding the terms of the contract. This is referred to as lack of genuineness of assent. A court will not enforce a contract if one of the parties can convince the court that fraud, mistake, undue influence, or duress interfered with a mutual understanding of the terms.

In order to prove fraud, it must be demonstrated that the other party made intentional misrepresentations or intentional nondisclosures of material facts during the course of the negotiations. Furthermore, it must be shown that the defendant did not know of the fraud and had no way to find out. Note that the misrepresentations must be material and that they must be made regarding a factual statement, not merely opinion or sales puffery. It is expected that the reasonable person engaged in contract negotiations will realize that he or she should not rely on opinions or on overblown sales statements that are obviously made simply as part of the sales pitch. However, in certain circumstances the opinion of an expert can be viewed as a fact when it is reasonable to rely on the expert's opinion, and the other party has no independent means of testing the statement's validity.

Mistakes about facts can sometimes form the basis for rescinding a contract. If the mistake is bilateral, then both parties had a different concept of what was to be included in the contract. Therefore, there never was a meeting of the minds, and the failed contract can be rescinded by either. The classic case that illustrates this principle took place in England in 1864. A buyer purchased a shipment of cotton from a seller, the cotton to be shipped on the Peerless. Unknown to either party there were two ships named the Peerless, one to depart in October and one in December. The buyer was thinking of the ship destined to leave in October and the seller the other in December. Consequently, the seller did not ship the cotton until December. By that time the buyer no longer needed the cotton. The court held that because there never was a "meeting of the minds" as to which ship was intended, no contract had been formed and the buyer was not obligated to pay for the cotton.[1] Usually, however, if the mistake is unilateral and only one party is mistaken, both parties are bound. The only exceptions are if the other party knew or should have known of the mistake and if the mistake was the result of a mathematical error.

Keep in mind that we are talking only about factual mistakes. Mistakes as to the value of the subject matter can never be the basis for rescission. For example, assume Joan contracts to sell her diamond ring to Bertha. Both think the ring is worth about $500, and they set $500 as the contract price. Later Bertha has the ring appraised and is delighted to learn that it is actually worth $5000. Joan cannot ask to have the contract rescinded on the ground that she was mistaken as to the value of the diamond. On the other hand, if Joan had contracted to sell what she thought was a zirconium ring to Bertha and upon appraisal it turned out to be a diamond ring, some courts could see that as a mutual mistake as to a fact and allow the contract to be rescinded.

Claims of **undue influence** are generally limited to situations in which there is a special fiduciary relationship between the parties. The party who is in a position of trust misuses that trust to influence the actions of another. Situations alleging undue influence are frequently brought by family members against caretakers of the elderly or ill.

A contract is also not valid if it was agreed to under duress rather than as a result of a truly voluntary action. The actions of the second party must be sufficient for the court to find that the first party was forced into the agreement.

Undue influence
When one party is in a position of trust and misuses that trust to influence that actions of another.

---

[1] Raffles v. Wichelhaus, 159 Eng. Rep. 375 (1864).

Duress is difficult to prove because the defendant must show that the pressure exerted was so great as to overwhelm his or her ability to make a free choice.

c. Illegal Contracts and Those That Violate Public Policy

Contracts can also be declared unenforceable if they are found to be either illegal or against public policy. A contract involves illegality if it calls for behavior that violates the criminal law, such as robbery, gambling, or prostitution. Contracts for an illegal purpose are void and cannot be enforced by either party.

In addition, the courts hold that some contracts are unenforceable because they are contrary to public policy. For example, covenants not to compete by their very nature are against public policy in that they restrict the right of an individual to earn a living or they tend to decrease competition. However, they can also be a form of necessary business protection. For example, if a pharmaceutical company expends a great deal of time and money training a chemist, the company will want the chemist to sign a noncompetition clause, promising not to work for another pharmaceutical plant for a certain amount of time after leaving employment with the first company. The courts are generally willing to enforce that type of covenant so long as it is tied to employment or to the sale of a business and its terms call for a reasonable time within a reasonable geographic area.

Adhesion contract
A contract formed where the weaker party has no realistic bargaining power. Typically a form contract is offered on a "take it or leave it" basis.

A second type of contract that the courts may refuse to enforce as being against public policy is an **adhesion contract**. As you will recall from our discussion of inadequate consideration, normally courts will adhere to the theory of freedom of contract and will not inquire into the fairness of the bargain. However, when a contract is formed between two parties of very unequal bargaining power and the contract is drafted by the party with the greater power and then presented to the other party, who has no opportunity to negotiate the terms, the court may view this as a contract of adhesion. The court may then hold that such a contract is unconscionable and refuse to enforce it. Generally, a contract is considered **unconscionable** if, in the context of general commercial practices and under the specific circumstances in which the contract was made, it is so one-sided as to be oppressive and grossly unfair. For example, if a poor, illiterate person were to purchase a $300 freezer, agreeing to pay 24 monthly installments of $50 each, the seller would net a $900 profit (24 × $50 = $1,200 – $300 = $900). The court might find the agreement to be so unfair as to "shock the conscience" and declare it unenforceable.

Unconscionable contract
A contract formed between parties of very unequal bargaining power where the terms are so unfair as to "shock the conscience."

d. Warranties

A common defense raised in the sale of consumer goods is that of breach of warranty. The consumer argues that he or she should not be required to pay for the item purchased because it failed to perform as expected. A **warranty** is a statement or representation, made by the seller as part of the contract of sale or implied in law, regarding the character, quality, or title of the goods being sold. If such warranted facts later prove to be untrue, the buyer is relieved of his or her obligations under the contract and the seller must compensate the buyer for any losses incurred as a result of the misrepresentation.

Warranty
A guarantee, made by the seller or implied by law, regarding the character, quality, or title of the goods being sold.

P R A C T I C E   T I P

Even if a seller states that all warranties have been disclaimed, do not assume that is true. Many states have enacted special protections for consumers that prohibit the exclusion of certain warranties.

Under the terms of the UCC Section 2-314 if a merchant is the seller, any contract of sale automatically includes an implied warranty of merchantability, an implied promise that the goods being sold will be usable for the ordinary purpose for which they were sold.

Figure 8-3   Warranties Summarized

Type of Warranty	Created by	Excluded by
Implied warranty of merchantability	the sale of goods by a merchant. The goods must be fit for their ordinary purpose.	language that includes the word *merchantability* or a disclaimer that includes the word *merchantability* or phrases such as "as is" or "with all faults." If in writing, it must be conspicuous.
Implied warranty of fitness	a seller ■ knowing the particular purpose the buyer has in mind *and* ■ being aware that the buyer is relying on the seller's expertise.	a writing that is conspicuous.
Express warranty	■ an affirmation of fact or a promise made by the seller, *or* a description of the goods being sold, including technical specifications and blueprints, *or* a sample or model *and* ■ that becomes a basis of the bargain.	words or conduct tending to limit or negate the warranty so long as such interpretation is reasonable.

Implied warranty of fitness
An implied promise that the goods being sold will satisfy a special purpose.

When a more specialized use of the goods is communicated to the seller during the course of negotiations, an **implied warranty of fitness** is also created. UCC § 2-315. This is a warranty regarding the fitness of the goods for that special purpose. For example, if you go to a hardware store and ask the clerk for electrical wiring and say nothing more, the wire will be warranted for its usual purpose of carrying household current. If instead you want the wire for outside use, you tell the clerk your special purpose, and you rely on the clerk's expertise in picking out the wire, then there will be an implied warranty of fitness for that particular purpose.

In addition to these implied warranties, a contract can create **express warranties**. UCC § 2-313. The term warranty or guarantee does not have to be used in order for a warranty to be created. However, the seller's conduct or statements must have been communicated to the buyer so that the warranty becomes part of the "basis of the bargain." UCC § 2-313(1). Express warranties can be created by an affirmation of fact or a promise made by the seller; a description of the goods being sold, including technical specifications and blueprints; or a sample or a model provided. A mere expression of opinion as to the value of an item is considered "puffing" and does not constitute a warranty.

Warranties may be excluded or modified by disclaimers. UCC § 2-316. In many states, however, merchants are limited in their ability to exclude or modify the implied warranty of merchantability when the sale is to a consumer. For each type of warranty, Figure 8-3, page 177, summarizes how it is created and what actions a seller must take to exclude the warranty.

Discussion Question

2. When should a buyer be able to rely on a salesperson's claims? What standards do you think should be used in drawing a line between "puffery" and fraud?

e. Lack of Proper Format—Writing

Statute of frauds
A statutory requirement that in order to be enforceable certain contracts must be in writing.

Even though many oral contracts are legally enforceable, it is always wiser to put them in writing because when disputes arise, it often comes down to one person's word against the other's. In addition to the fact that it simply makes sense to reduce any important contract to writing, all states have a statute known as the **statute of frauds**, which requires certain types of contracts, such as those involving transfer of real estate, to be in writing in order to be enforceable. The purpose of such statutes is to ensure that there will be reliable evidence of important or complex matters. If the contract is of the type that requires a writing and there is none, the contract is unenforceable.

Ethics Alert

Attorney Smith is always very careful to explain his contingency fee arrangement with his clients. The client is responsible for any court costs and other expenses, and attorney Smith receives 33 percent of any settlement or court award. Attorney Smith has never seen any need to put this arrangement in writing. Do you see any problems with attorney Smith's approach?

Generally, the types of contracts that must be in writing fall into one of the following categories:

1. contracts involving land, including fixtures, and documents dealing with land, such as mortgages and leases;
2. contracts that cannot be performed in one year;
3. collateral contracts, those that involve a secondary as opposed to a primary obligation, unless the main purpose is to secure a personal benefit;
4. promises made in consideration of marriage, such as prenuptial agreements; and
5. contracts for the sale of goods valued at $500 or more.

DISCUSSION QUESTION

3. Jonathan Shattuck thought he had a deal to buy a house for $1.825 million. Using e-mail, Shattuck and the seller had settled on the price. The last e-mail from the seller stated:

> Once we sign the P&S (purchase and sale agreement) we'd like to close ASAP. You may have your attorney send the P&S and deposit check for 10% of purchase price ($182,500) to my attorney. I'm looking forward to closing and seeing you as the owner of 5 Main Street, the prettiest spot in Marion Village.

Before the buyer's attorney had a chance to draw up the purchase and sale agreement, the seller informed Shattuck that he was not going to follow through on the deal as he had another buyer who was willing to pay $1.96 million. His argument is that there is no signed writing binding him to the deal. How do you think the court decided? Why?

4. Third-Party Rights

There are three circumstances in which a person or corporation who was not a party to the contract can obtain a legal interest in enforcing part of the terms of that agreement. The most common of these is through the process of assignment. Third-party rights also arise through delegation and the creation of beneficiaries.

An **assignment** occurs when one of the original parties to a contract transfers part or all of his or her interest to a third party. For example, assume a consumer signs a sales contract with a furniture store. In the contract the consumer agrees to make certain monthly payments. The furniture store then assigns the right to receive those payments to a finance company, and in return the finance company gives the furniture store ready cash. The finance company now has a legal interest in receiving the monthly payments that the consumer agreed to pay to the store.

An assignment involves an assignor, an assignee, and an obligor. See Figure 8-4, on page 180. The assignee gets the same rights that the assignor

Assignment
The transfer by one of the original parties to the contract of part or all of his or her interest to a third party.

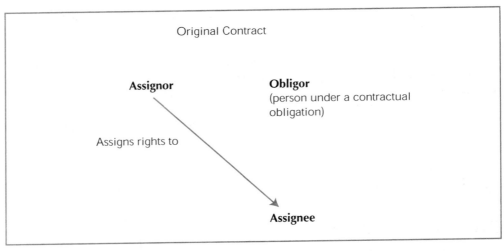

Figure 8-4   Assignment of a Contract

had, but no more. The assignee is also subject to the same defenses as could have been raised against the assignor. Assignment is usually possible unless:

1. the contract itself prohibits it,
2. the contract involves personal services, or
3. the assignment will materially alter the duties of the obligor.

Delegation
The transfer by one of the original parties to the contract of his or her obligations to a third party.

Unless the contract prohibits it, or the duty requires personal skill or special trust, contractual duties can generally be delegated to a third party. When such a **delegation** occurs, the original party remains obligated to fulfill the terms of the contract if the delegatee fails to perform. See Figure 8-5.

Assignment and delegation happen after the contract is formed. However, if at the time the contract is formed one or both of the parties want to benefit a third party, **a third-party beneficiary** relationship can be written into the contract. These beneficiaries can be either intended (creditor or donee) or incidental.

Third-party beneficiary
Although not a party to the contract, someone the contracting parties intended to benefit.

Figure 8-5   Delegation of Duties under a Contract

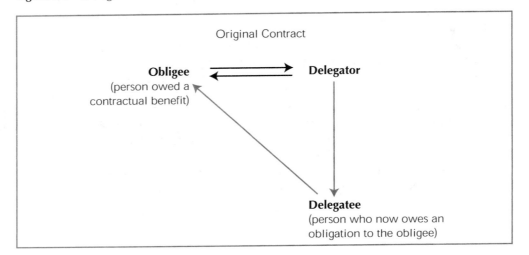

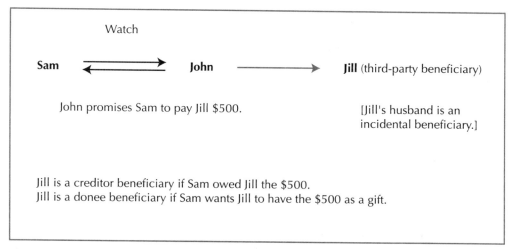

Figure 8-6 *Third-Party Beneficiaries*

An example of a creditor beneficiary occurs when a home buyer agrees to assume the seller's current mortgage. Under the terms of the sales contract, the company that holds the seller's mortgage is given a specific benefit (the right to receive money to pay off the debt) and is classified as creditor beneficiary. In a situation in which a father contracts with a bank to administer a trust fund for his children, those children would be considered donee beneficiaries.

Consider two further examples: If in return for Sam's watch, John promises Sam to pay the $500 debt Sam owes to Jill, Jill becomes a creditor beneficiary. If in return for Sam's car, John promises Sam to give a $4000 gift to Joan, then Joan is a donee beneficiary. In both cases the third party has a right to see that the contract terms are fulfilled, including the right to sue. See Figure 8-6.

An incidental beneficiary, on the other hand, is someone whom the original parties did not explicitly intend to benefit from the contract. If, in the example used above, Bill is Joan's husband and Joan plans to spend the $4000 on a vacation for her and Bill, Bill becomes an incidental beneficiary. Incidental beneficiaries cannot enforce rights under the contract, so if John fails to deliver the money, Bill has no legal right to take the matter to court.

5. Remedies for Breach of Contract

When one party fails to live up to the terms of a contract, a variety of remedies may be available to the other party, including going to court to seek either specific performance or monetary damages. **Specific performance** is a court order that the breaching party live up to the terms of the agreement. Specific performance gives the contracting party exactly the item for which the contract was formed. However, specific performance can only be used in situations where there is no alternative comparable product available, or when money alone is an inadequate remedy. Examples of when specific performance is appropriate are usually limited to items such as rare antiques or land.

Because specific performance is possible only if dollars are inadequate, courts are far more likely to award damages. Damages in contract cases are

Specific performance When money damages are inadequate, a court may use this equitable remedy and order the breaching party to perform his or her contractual obligations.

classified as compensatory, consequential, incidental, and nominal. Punitive damages are not allowed in a contract action.

The purpose of **compensatory damages** is to place the injured party in the same position that party would have been in had the contract been performed; that is, their purpose is to give the injured party the "benefit of the bargain."

In calculating compensatory damages, courts frequently use the following formula:

Promised performance minus actual performance minus mitigation plus expenses (incidental damages)

For example, if John agrees with Bill to sell Bill his watch for $500, but Bill only pays $300, John can sue Bill for $200. If Bill had paid nothing and simply reneged on the deal, John could have sold the watch to someone else and could have recovered the difference between that price and the contract price, along with any expenses incurred in finding the new buyer (incidental damages). On the other hand, if John refuses to sell the watch, then Bill has two options. First, he can try to find another watch. The UCC calls this finding of substitute goods cover. Then his damages are the cost of the substitute watch minus the contract price. For example, if Bill finds a similar watch but has to pay $700, his damages are $200. Alternatively, he can decide to forgo a new watch. In that case his damages would be the difference between the market price and the contract price.

The principle of **mitigation of damages** requires the nonbreaching party to take reasonable steps to limit his or her damages. For example, under Section 2-603 of the UCC, goods must be sold in order to minimize the seller's losses if they cannot be returned without their perishing.

Consequential damages arise out of special circumstances that must be foreseeable to the other party. Typically this is handled by notifying the other party of any such circumstances. The classic case setting forth this rule is an English case from 1854.[5] The Hadley family ran a flour mill. Their crankshaft broke, and they gave it to Baxendale to deliver to a foundry for repair. Baxendale promised to deliver the shaft the next day. However, it was not delivered for several days. Despite the common practice, the Hadleys did not have an extra crankshaft and so they were forced to keep the mill closed for those extra days. Because the Hadleys had not notified Baxendale of their lack of a spare crankshaft, he could not be held liable for their lost profits.

As in tort actions **nominal damages** are sometimes awarded when there has been a breach, but no provable damages.

In order to avoid having to litigate damage issues, some contracting parties put **liquidated damages** clauses in their contracts. Such clauses specify what will happen in case of breach. Such clauses are valid so long as they bear a reasonable relationship to the true loss and are not seen as penalty clauses.

In situations when the judge finds that the parties imperfectly expressed themselves, the court may **reform the contract**. For example, assume a covenant not to compete is included in a sale of a business. While it is limited geographically to one county, its duration is for ten years. The court might reform the contract so that the duration is for a shorter period of time.

Mitigation of damages
The requirement that the nonbreaching party take reasonable steps to limit his or her damages.

Reformation
An equitable remedy whereby the court rewrites a contract.

[5] Hadley v. Baxendale, 9 Exch. 341, 156 Eng. Rep. 14 (1854).

B. BORROWING MONEY

At some point most businesses will need to buy supplies or equipment on credit or to borrow cash. If a business writes a check to pay for new equipment or signs a promissory note promising to repay a loan, the law of **commercial paper** is involved. Whenever a supplier or creditor asks for a guarantee of repayment in the form of collateral, a **secured transaction** is created. Then if the debtor fails to repay the debt, the creditor can seize the collateral (the asset) that was used to secure the loan.

1. Commercial Paper

Commercial paper refers to a variety of instruments (written documents) used for making payments. Commercial paper has two basic functions: as a substitute for money and as a credit device. For example, if you pay for a new stereo with a check, you have just used a form of commercial paper (the check) to substitute for cash and to give yourself some free credit until the store cashes the check.

Commercial paper
A written promise or order to pay a certain sum of money.

 There are a lot of terms involved in how commercial paper is categorized. The important point is not to memorize all the terminology but to become familiar with it so that later when you encounter your first client who has a legal problem involving commercial paper, you will be conversant with the basic terms. Commercial paper is categorized in the following ways:

1. as two- or three-party instruments,
2. as orders or promises to pay,
3. as bearer or order paper, and
4. as negotiable or nonnegotiable.

 Therefore, the first way of categorizing commercial paper is by how many parties are involved. Notes only involve two parties. A **note** is a promise to pay money, whereby the **maker** signs the instrument promising to pay money to the **payee**. See Figure 8-7. These notes can be collectable either on a specific date in the future (time notes) or at any time the payee wishes to collect (demand notes). Installment notes establish a series of dates on which portions of the money are to be paid.

 Three-party instruments include drafts and checks. A **draft** is a three-party instrument in which the **drawer** orders the **drawee**, usually a bank, to pay money to the **payee**. A **check** is a specialized form of a draft in which a bank depositor names a specific payee to whom funds are to be paid from the drawer's account. See Figure 8-8, on page 184.

 Second, drafts and checks are classified as orders to pay, as each contains an order by the drawer to the drawee to pay money to the payee. Notes are promises to pay.

Figure 8-7 A Note

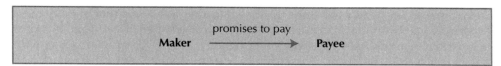

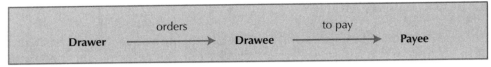

Figure 8-8   A Draft or Check. (For a check, the drawee is a bank.)

Third, instruments are also classified as being either **bearer paper** or **order paper**. Bearer paper will have written on its front a statement that it is payable to cash or payable to the bearer, or it will have a signature on the back, causing it to be indorsed in blank. An **indorsement in blank** occurs when an indorser simply signs his or her name and does not specify to whom the instrument is payable. Order paper states on its face "pay to the order of" a specific payee and has not been indorsed in blank on its back.

The fourth category, **negotiable** versus nonnegotiable, is the most essential category. Only if the paper is seen as negotiable can it be treated as a substitute for money. This is important because, as we mentioned above, one of the two main functions of commercial paper is as a substitute for cash. If the paper does not satisfy the requirements to be negotiable, that purpose has not been satisfied. Article 3 of the Uniform Commercial Code (UCC) spells out the requirements for an instrument to be negotiable. It must

1. be in writing,
2. be signed by the maker or drawer,
3. be an unconditional promise or order to pay,
4. state a specific sum of money,
5. be payable on demand or at a definite time, and
6. be payable to order or to bearer.

A person becomes a **holder** of a negotiable instrument that is bearer paper by proper delivery. If it is order paper, it must be properly delivered *and* have all necessary indorsements.

The reason all these steps are important is that if a note, check, or draft meets the requirements of negotiability, a holder can become a **holder in due course** and have the right not only to enforce the agreement but also to be exempt from some of the defenses that could have been asserted against the original payee. Under the UCC a person becomes a holder in due course only if that person receives the instrument under the following conditions. A holder in due course is someone

1. who gives value
2. in good faith (a subjective standard) and
3. without notice that the instrument is overdue or has been dishonored or has any claims against it or defenses to it (an objective standard).

Again, the main benefit of being a holder in due course, rather than a mere holder, is that a holder in due course takes the instrument free of most claims against payment. A holder, on the other hand, takes the instrument along with any defenses to its payment. Therefore, for commercial paper to truly work as a substitute for cash, it must be negotiable, and the person owning it must be a

Negotiable instrument
Commercial paper that can be transferred by indorsement or delivery. It must meet the requirements of UCC § 3–104 to be negotiable. If it does not, a transferee cannot become a holder but only gets the rights along with the liabilities of a contract assignee.

Front of the Paper	Do you have a negotiable instrument?
	▪ in writing and
	▪ signed by maker or drawer and
	▪ unconditional promise or order and
	▪ sum certain in money and
	▪ payable on demand or at a definite time and
	▪ to order or bearer
	If any are missing ≠ a negotiable instrument—STOP. If all present, continue on.
Back of the Paper	Is the transfer proper?
	▪ bearer paper—transfer alone enough
	▪ order paper—transfer plus proper indorsements
	If transfer was not proper—STOP. If transfer was proper, continue on; you have a HOLDER.
What Happened	Did the holder do all of the following?
	▪ give value
	▪ in good faith
	▪ with no notice that the instrument is overdue or has been dishonored or that there is a defense or a claim to it.
	If all were not met—STOP. If all were met, you have a HOLDER IN DUE COURSE.
Type of Defense Being Raised	Is the defense a **personal defense,** such as a defense to a breach of contract claim?
	Then the holder in due course takes the instrument clear of that defense.
	Is the defense a **real defense,** such as forgery of the instrument?
	Then the defense is good even against the holder in due course.

Figure 8-9 How to Determine Whether a Holder in Due Course Has Been Created

holder in due course. The steps by which commercial paper becomes negotiable and its owner becomes a holder in due course are outlined in Figure 8-9.

For example, assume a bakery owner signs a contract with a furniture store. The store gives the bakery owner a loan so that she can purchase new tables and chairs for her reception area. In return, the bakery owner promises to repay the loan on an installment basis. Later a finance company purchases that installment contract from the furniture store. The finance company becomes the holder in due course. Assume the furniture proves to be defective. If the store had not sold the installment contract, the bakery owner might have been able to stop paying on the loan to the furniture store by raising a defense of breach of warranty. However, the holder in due course doctrine prevents the bakery owner from being able to raise those defenses against the finance company. Therefore, even though the furniture is defective, the bakery owner will have to pay

what it owes to the finance company. It can separately sue the furniture store for breach of warranty, but the results of the lawsuit do not affect the bakery owner's obligation to pay the finance company.

2. Secured Transactions

Often a creditor will demand more than the mere promise to repay a debt. The creditor will want assurance that if the debtor fails to repay the debt, the creditor can take something of value from the debtor. Therefore, promises to repay a debt are often secured by a pledge of something of value, such as a house, an automobile, or a stock certificate, that the creditor can seize and sell if the debtor does not repay the loan. Such an arrangement is known as a **secured transaction** and is governed by Article 9 of the UCC.

Secured transaction

An arrangement whereby a creditor asks for and receives a guarantee of repayment from the debtor in the form of collateral.

A creditor who has obtained a security interest has two main concerns if a debtor defaults. First, the creditor wants to be able to obtain the secured collateral from the debtor. This is done through an **attachment.** Second, the creditor wants to have priority over other creditors who may also have rights to the same collateral. This is done through a process called **perfection.**

As to the first concern, for a creditor to have an enforceable security interest against the debtor, the following must be true:

1. The creditor must either possess the collateral or have a signed **security agreement,**
2. the creditor must have given something of value, and
3. the debtor must have rights in the collateral.

If all three requirements are satisfied, it is said that the security interest has attached. The creditor's first concern is satisfied. If the debtor fails to pay, the creditor can take the collateral from the debtor unless another creditor has a higher right to the collateral by having a perfected security interest.

For a creditor to establish priority over other creditors, the creditor must obtain a **perfected security interest** by taking additional steps. The requirements for perfection are

1. possessing the collateral, or
2. filing a **financing statement,** or
3. giving money to purchase consumer goods.

The purpose behind each of these three methods is to give third parties notice that the creditor has "first dibs" on the property. This gives the perfected creditor first rights to the collateral over other creditors.

Therefore, the difference between attachment and **perfection** is that with attachment the creditor has an enforceable security interest as against the debtor. With perfection the creditor also has priority to the collateral over other creditors. See Figure 8-10, on page 187.

A special type of perfected security interest, a **purchase money security interest,** arises when a seller gives credit to a debtor so that the debtor can purchase an item. For example, if a car dealership lets you purchase a car on credit, the dealership will have a purchase money security interest in the car you

Attachment (must occur first)	Perfection (can occur only after attachment)
Notice to the debtor that the creditor has an interest in the goods: **1a.** actual possesion *or* **1b.** a security agreement, signed by the debtor, describing the collateral *and* **2.** the creditor has received something of value *and* **3.** the debtor has rights in the collateral.	*Notice to third parties* that the creditor has an interest in the goods: **1a.** possession *or* **b.** a filed financing statement that was signed, describing the collateral, with addresses of the debtor and creditor *or* **c.** a purchase money security interest in consumer goods.

Figure 8-10   A Comparsion of Attachment and Perfection

buy. Also, if another creditor, such as a bank, gives value to a debtor so that the debtor can purchase the item, a purchase money security interest is formed. This could occur in the prior example if you obtained your loan from a credit union instead of the car dealership. The credit union would then have a purchase money security interest in your car. If you purchased the car for your own use, as opposed to that of your business, then the security interest would also be classified as a purchase money security interest in consumer goods.

While those with a perfected security interest will prevail over those whose interest has only attached, even a creditor with a perfected security interest will lose to a **buyer in the ordinary course of business**. If this were not so, once a store took out a secured loan, everyone would stop shopping at that store. For example, assume Sears took out a secured loan in order to increase its inventory of refrigerators. Without the rule protecting the ordinary buyer, if Sears failed to pay back the debt, the bank could go after customers, trying to reclaim the refrigerators they had purchased from Sears.

In sum, keeping in mind the two purposes of obtaining a security interest, to get repaid and to be first in line for the security, the general order of priorities among creditors and buyers is as follows:

1. **buyers in the ordinary course of business,**
2. perfected purchase money security interests,
3. perfected security interests,
4. lien creditors (such as a trustee in bankruptcy),
5. unperfected security interests, and
6. general creditors.

Buyer in the ordinary course of business Someone who buys a product in good faith and without knowledge that someone else has a security interest in the goods.

Finally, a security interest can be retained in collateral even when the collateral changes in character or location. For example, there can be a security interest in proceeds or after-acquired property. This is known as a **floating lien**.

Assume our four entrepreneurs introduced at the beginning of the chapter obtain a loan to purchase an oven for their bakery. In addition to getting a security interest in the oven, the creditor who loans the money for the oven's purchase can also acquire a security interest in the proceeds from the bakery sales and in property, such as a new refrigerator, that the bakery later acquires.

SUMMARY

A contract is an agreement that can be enforced in court. The basic elements of a contract are offer, acceptance, and consideration. The most common defenses are lack of contractual capacity, illegality, violation of public policy, lack of genuineness of assent, breach of warranty, and the statute of frauds. Third parties can attain contractual rights either through assignment or delegation or through being an intended beneficiary. A plaintiff bringing a contract action may be under a duty to mitigate damages and is usually seeking specific performance or compensatory or consequential damages.

While many contracts are still controlled by the common law, contracts for the sale of goods are generally governed by Article 2 of the Uniform Commercial Code (UCC). The UCC was drafted by a group of legal scholars with the hope of making commercial law more unified among the states. Most of the UCC's provisions apply to everyone, but some sections contain specific rules that apply to merchants only. Under the UCC everyone is under the obligation to act in good faith.

When a person or business borrows money, commercial paper may be involved. Commercial paper includes promises to pay, such as promissory notes, and orders to pay, such as checks. The debtor may have to guarantee repayment by supplying collateral, thereby creating a secured transaction.

REVIEW QUESTIONS

Pages 165 through 171

1. How do the courts determine if the UCC governs a contract situation?
2. What are the three basic elements of a valid contract claim?
3. What are the four basic elements that every offer should contain?
4. Juan says to Jim, "I would like to sell my watch to you." Jim replies, "Great. I will be happy to give you a fair price for it." Has a contract been formed? Why?
5. Sally offers Tom a job as a paralegal, saying she will pay him "what he is worth." Tom accepts. Has a contract been formed? Why?
6. Janet says to Joan, "I am eager to sell my antique vase to you." Joan says, "Would you consider $400 for it?" Has a contract been formed? Why?
7. We Growum, a garden center, places the following advertisement in the Sunday paper.

Spring Planting Sale
Lilac bushes $20

Tuesday John goes to the garden center. All the lilac bushes have been sold. He sues for breach of contract. Will he succeed? Why?
8. What is the name of the rule that states that the acceptance must completely agree with the terms of the offer?

9. How has the UCC changed the mirror image rule?

Pages 172 through 173

10. An uncle offers his nephew $5,000 if the nephew promises not to smoke marijuana or use other illegal drugs during the next four years while he is away at college. Has a binding contract been formed? Why?

11. John volunteers to take care of Sam's pet rabbit while he is away on vacation. When Sam returns, he is very pleased with the good care John gave his rabbit and tells him that he is going to pay him $50. When John arrives the next day to receive his money, Sam said that he has changed his mind. Is Sam under a contractual obligation to pay John for the care of his rabbit? Why?

12. Anna Sacks was an employee of the Ajax Company for thirty-seven years. The president of the company told her that (in consideration for her outstanding service) when she retired, the company would pay her $200 per month for life. Two years later she retired and began receiving the payments. Shortly thereafter, the company was sold, and the new president refused to continue the payments, arguing that there had never been a valid contract between Ms. Sacks and the company. How do you think the court resolved the case?

13. Millie requested bids from three different contractors for a price to repair the roof on her house. The bids ranged from $5,000 to $20,000. Naturally, Millie accepted the $5,000 bid from We'gottcha Roofing. On a Monday We'gottcha began work by first removing all of the old shingles. The weather prediction was for rain by the end of the week. We'gottcha told Millie she had a choice. Either she could pay them a "bonus" of $15,000 and they would continue work on her roof, or they would have to take the rest of the week to finish other jobs they had started. Millie, afraid all of her household contents would be ruined if rain hit her "deshingled" roof, agreed to the extra money. Will Millie be required to pay the $15,000 bonus? Why?

Pages 174 through 179

14. Name the six major defenses to a contract action.

15. Jim, who is sixteen years old, buys a stereo from Circuit Playground. Jim takes the stereo to the beach and ruins it when it becomes filled with sand. Jim takes it back to the store and demands the return of the money he paid for the stereo. Will the store have to refund his payment?

16. Mark and Bill are sitting at a bar drinking. They discuss the possibility of Mark selling Bill his watch for $50. Bill leaves, but Mark remains and continues to drink. Two hours later Bill calls Mark and offers him $5 for the watch. Now very intoxicated, Mark mutters, "Whatever." The next day Mark has no memory of the phone call. Will the court enforce this arrangement? Why?

17. Sara offers to sell her car to Janet for $800. Janet thinks Sara means her 1978 VW Beetle and agrees. Sara was thinking of her 1970 VW van. Has a contract been formed? Why?

18. A law firm requires all new attorneys to sign an agreement that states that if they leave the firm for any reason, they will not work for another law firm or open their own practice within a fifty-mile radius for two years. How do you think the court would treat such an agreement? Why?

19. What is the difference between a warranty of merchantability and an implied warranty of fitness? How do both of those differ from an express warranty?

20. Joan offers to buy Bill's sailboat for $2,000. Bill agrees and asks Joan to put it in writing. Joan leaves an e-mail message for her secretary, stating that she wants him to draft a contract stating that she agrees to buy Bill's sailboat for $2,000. The next day Joan changes her mind. If Bill sues for breach of contract, will he succeed? Why?

Pages 179 through 181

21. The city of Portage contracts with Get Going Builders to demolish a vacant building and replace it with a park. John Jakes is delighted, as his property is right across the street from the intended park. He envisions a significant increase in his property value. At the last minute the city decides to forgo the park in favor of increased pay for its fire fighters. John is dismayed and wants to sue the city. Will he succeed in his suit? Why?

22. Martha contracts with Sam, a noted concert pianist, to take a series of ten music lessons. After the second lesson Sam is offered the opportunity to go on a world tour. He contacts William, a lesser known pianist, to take over his lessons. Martha is upset. Does she have any grounds to complain?

23. What is the difference between an assignment and a delegation?

24. What is the difference between assignments and delegations, on the one hand, and third-party-beneficiary contracts, on the other?

Pages 181 through 182

25. When is specific performance an appropriate remedy?

26. What is cover?

27. What are consequential damages?

28. Sara Smith is a struggling young artist. Recently, however, she was "discovered" when an art dealer saw one of her paintings hanging in a local art gallery. The art dealer contracted with Sara to hold a major showing of her work in six months, November 1. Under the contract Sara was to show no less than ten original paintings. In preparation for the show Sara contracted with Paint Masters, Inc., for four cases of her favorite oil paints to be shipped no later than July 1. Sara heard nothing more from Paint Masters, Inc., until September 1 when one case arrived. Sara attempted to find the same paint from other sources but was able to procure only one more case at $200 more than she had contracted to pay Paint Masters. Because of the delay in shipment, Sara was able to complete only six paintings and the show was canceled. Sara would like to sue Paint Masters, Inc., for the lost profits she would have received from her heightened recognition had the show gone as planned, for the money she had to spend on alternate paints, and for punitive damages to teach Paint Masters a lesson. Please evaluate Sara's situation.

29. Kate contracts with Bennett to buy 100 guitars at $300 each. Kate hopes to resell the guitars for $400 each. When the time for delivery arrives, Bennett refuses to deliver the guitars. Kate then spends $100 in phone calls trying to obtain an alternate supplier. Finally, she finds substitute guitars, but has to pay $350 each for them. She saved $50, however, because in her contract with Bennett she was going to have to pay the shipping. In her new contract, the seller paid the shipping. How much is Kate owed in compensatory damages?

30. The city of Kalamazoo hired Good Builders, Inc., to build a new courthouse for $560,000. Good Builders had barely broken ground when the city notified them that it would not be able to pay for the building after all and asked Good Builders to stop all work. Good Builders refused, saying, "Hey, you guys signed a contract. We know our rights." At the time the city asked them to stop, Good Builders had expended $5,000 on materials, approximately $3,000 of which could have been returned at no loss to themselves. By completing the project, however, Good Builders expended an additional $400,000. In a breach of contract action by Good Builders against the city, how much money do you think the court should award Good Builders? Why?

Pages 183 through 186

31. Name the requirements for an instrument to be negotiable.

32. What must be satisfied for someone to be a holder in due course?

33. What are the two basic functions of commercial paper?

34. How does one become a holder of a negotiable instrument?
35. Buyer pays Seller $600 in cash for 1,000 calculators. Seller then takes the $600 and uses it to pay for a cruise.

Calculators   Cruise

Buyer ⟷ Seller ⟷ 3rd party

$600 cash $600 cash

If the calculators prove to be defective and the seller is insolvent, who loses, the buyer or the third party who accepted $600 from the seller?

36. Buyer signs a contract with Seller promising to pay $600 for 1,000 calculators on or before 6/6/07. Seller then assigns the contract to the owner of a travel agency in payment for a cruise.

Calculators   Cruise

Buyer ⟵ Seller ⟵ 3rd party

In contract Buyer   Assigns contract
promises to pay $600   to 3rd party
on or before 6/6/07

If the calculators prove to be defective and the seller is insolvent, who loses, the buyer or the third party who accepted the assigned contract rights from the buyer?

37. Buyer signs a note promising to pay Seller $600 for 1,000 calculators on or before 6/6/07. Seller then delivers the note to the owner of a travel agency in payment for a cruise.

Calculators   Cruise

Buyer ⟷ Seller ⟵ 3rd party

Buyer signs a   Delivers note
note promising
to pay $600 on
or before 6/6/07

If the calculators prove to be defective and the seller is insolvent, who loses if the note is a negotiable instrument? Who loses if the note is not a negotiable instrument? Why?

Pages 186 through 188

38. In a secured transaction what is the difference between attachment and perfection?
39. Name the requirements that a creditor must meet in order to have an enforceable security interest against a debtor (to have the interest attach).
40. How may a creditor perfect a security interest?
41. What are the two main concerns of a creditor if a debtor defaults?
42. Define a *floating lien*, and give an example.
43. Define a *purchase money security interest*.
44. What is the main benefit of being a holder in due course rather than a mere holder?
45. List the following creditors in order of priority, starting with those that have the highest level of priority: general creditors, perfected security interest holders, unperfected security interest holders, buyers in the ordinary course of business, lien creditors, and perfected purchase money security interest holders.

Chapter 9

Property and Specialized Practice Areas

In no country in the world is the love of property more
active and more anxious than in the United States.
Alexis de Tocqueville

INTRODUCTION

While many lawyers engage in a general law practice, others specialize in a specific area. We have already discussed several of the major areas of law practice: torts, including both personal injury and products liability, contract law, commercial paper, and secured transactions. This chapter begins with another major area of substantive civil law: property. Property law covers both real estate and personal property. We then discuss a variety of specialty areas, including business organizations, employment, intellectual property, estate planning and probate, and family and administrative law.

A. PROPERTY

The concept of **property** is at the heart of the American legal system. Our economic system is built on the ideas of capitalism and free enterprise, and the concept of private property rights is central to our economic success.

    Property is usually thought of as being a tangible object, such as a house or an automobile, that is "owned" by an individual, a corporation, or a government. However, in its broadest sense the legal concept of property includes any

Property
A tangible object or a right or ownership interest.

valuable right or interest that belongs to a person. Property can include promissory notes and admission tickets to concerts or sporting events. There are also circumstances under which a person can have a "property interest" in a job, an idea, or a reputation.

1. Real Property and Personal Property

Real property
Also known as *real estate*; land and items growing on or permanently attached to that land.

There are two basic types of property: real property and personal property. **Real property**, also referred to as real estate, consists of land and whatever is growing on or built on that land. It includes not only the houses, garages, sheds, and other types of buildings that are on the land but also everything that is permanently attached to those buildings—such as light fixtures, plumbing fixtures, and built-in shelves.

At times it can be difficult to determine whether something is "permanently" attached. For example, normally a room air conditioner is seen as personal property. However, if the window frame has been removed and the air conditioner bolted to the wall, it might be seen as "permanently" attached, and hence a fixture. When determining whether something should be considered a fixture, the courts look to the amount of damage that would be caused either to the item or to the underlying property if the item were removed from the premises. The courts will also take into account the intention of the parties.

In addition, real estate includes the trees and plants growing on the land, as well as the rights to gas and minerals under the land and to the air space above it. In recent years the common law right to air space has been modified so as to not interfere with modern aviation.

Personal property
All property that is not real property.

All property other than real property is classified as **personal property**, sometimes also referred to as chattel. Personal property is often classified as being either tangible or intangible. **Tangible property** consists of goods that can be touched and moved, such as automobiles, jewelry, clothing, and television sets.

Intangible property is personal property that cannot be touched, such as a stock certificate or a patent. While you can certainly touch the piece of paper that documents the stock ownership or the awarding of the patent, it is not the paper itself that has value. The term **intellectual property** is used to cover intangible assets such as trademarks, copyrights, and patents that are the product of someone's intellectual creation.

Property can change its nature from real to personal or from personal to real. For example, while oil is still in the ground, it is considered to be real property, but once it has been extracted from the ground and loaded on a tanker or sent down a pipeline, it becomes personal property. When trees are still in the forest, they are real property. When they are cut, they become personal property. It is not always easy to determine when this change occurs. For example, a mobile home on the sales lot is personal property. If it is moved to a mobile home park, has its tires removed, and is affixed to a foundation, it becomes real property. However, what if its tires are not removed and it is simply placed on the lot? Is it still personal property?

Determining whether property is real or personal can have important consequences, as the courts apply different rules to the different types of property. For example, the selling and leasing of personal property are covered by the general principles of contract law and the Uniform Commercial Code discussed in Chapter 8. The selling and leasing of real estate will be discussed in this section.

2. Ownership of Real Property

Ownership of property can rest with a single individual or be shared with others. A **joint tenancy** occurs when two or more persons simultaneously acquire equal rights in a single piece of property. A **tenancy in common** is very similar in that it also involves two or more people who share ownership of the property. The ownership shares do not have to be equal, however, nor do they have to have been acquired at the same time. In addition, on death the ownership interest of a tenant in common passes to his or her heirs, while with a joint tenancy it passes to the co-owner(s). A **tenancy by the entirety** is a special type of joint tenancy applicable only to married couples. It is essentially a joint tenancy modified by the common law theory that the husband and wife are one person. During their lifetimes neither the wife nor the husband can transfer the property without the other's consent. As with any joint tenancy, on the death of one of the spouses the other takes whole title to the exclusion of any other heirs. In some condominium arrangements the individual living units are individually owned or owned in joint tenancy, and the common halls, walks, parking lots, and garden areas are a form of tenancy in common.

The distinction between joint tenancy and tenancy in common is very important. While both represent ways to jointly own property, the part owner of property held as a tenancy in common can bequeath that share to whomever the owner pleases. However, the owner of property held in joint tenancy cannot choose to whom the property will pass on the owner's death. Even if the owner provides in a will that the property will pass to a named individual, it will nonetheless pass to the other joint tenant. In fact, you will often hear the term joint tenancy referred to as joint tenancy with a right of survivorship.

An owner's rights to use a piece of real estate can be limited by the existence of either a **restrictive covenant** or an easement. The former is a provision in a deed that prohibits specified uses of the property and commonly is added at the time a developer subdivides and improves the property before it is marketed for housing. Common provisions include requirements relating to minimum square footage, set-back, and architectural styles. Others may prohibit the installation of satellite dishes in yards or the overnight parking of boats or recreational vehicles in driveways. These covenants are recorded in the county land records and become part of the title for all subsequent owners.

An **easement** is the right to use property owned by another for a limited purpose. Utility companies acquire easements that allow them to install and maintain electrical cables and gas pipes. Another common type of easement allows a neighbor to drive over a small section of someone else's lot in order to gain access to his or her own land.

Joint tenancy
Ownership by two or more persons who have equal rights in the use of that property. When a joint tenant dies, that person's share passes to the other joint tenant(s).

Tenancy in common
Ownership by two or more people. Ownership shares do not have to be equal, but each has an undivided interest in the property. When a tenant in common dies, that person's share passes either by will or by intestate statute.

Tenancy by the entirety
A special type of joint tenancy applicable only to married couples.

Restrictive covenant
A provision in a deed that prohibits specified uses of the property.

Easement
A right to use property owned by another for a limited purpose.

DISCUSSION QUESTIONS

1. Should a condominium association that wishes to appeal to seniors be allowed to prohibit children from living in its units? What are the policy arguments for and against? How would you distinguish between children living in the unit versus those just visiting? Specifically, if you cannot discriminate on the basis of race, why should you be able to discriminate on the basis of age?

2. Sam and Mary are planning to marry and build a home. With her own money Mary plans on purchasing a piece of property. She wants Sam's name to appear on the deed as a joint tenant. Do you think this is advisable?

3. Rental of Real Property

When real estate is rented, a landlord-tenant relationship is created between the lessor (the landlord) and the lessee (the tenant). A lease is an agreement in which the property owner gives a tenant the right to use the property for a designated period of time. A leasehold is a parcel of real estate held under a lease.

The common law favored landlords over tenants. The tenant had to take the property in the condition it was in at the time that the lease was entered into, even if the tenant was not aware of defects at the time the lease was signed. The tenant also had to repair any damage resulting from natural disasters or the acts of other people, the tenant, or the tenant's family. In fact, the landlord's only obligation to the tenant was that of not interfering with the tenant's "**quiet enjoyment**" of the premises. This meant that the landlord could not interfere with the tenant's use of the property with respect to such things as what crops were planted or who was invited onto the property. The tenant's primary obligation was to pay the rent.

Over the years many state legislatures have enacted statutes that provide for a more equitable relationship between landlords and tenants. Such laws often require the owner to repair and maintain the premises at certain minimum levels. If an apartment is being rented as a residential unit, then it must come complete with running water, a working furnace, and other minimum living essentials. This requirement is present even if not written into the lease and is known as the **implied warranty of habitability**. It requires that the property be fit for the purpose for which it is being rented. These minimum standards are often equated with whatever is required in the local housing code.

State laws determine the procedures landlords must use to retake possession of their property. Under the common law a landlord could forcibly evict a tenant who was in default of any term in the lease. The landlord or the landlord's agent could go in and literally throw the tenant and the tenant's personal possessions out on the street. As a result of the hardship and the frequent violence such procedures brought about, most states now require that a landlord first give an appropriate eviction notice and then go to court to get local law enforcement agents, such as police or sheriff's deputies, to supervise the physical removal of the tenant and any possessions.

A constructive eviction occurs when the landlord does something to deprive the tenant of quiet enjoyment of the land, such as shutting off the water or changing the locks. If the tenant is forced to abandon the property, then the tenant can rely on the constructive eviction as a defense to any further requirement to pay rent. Because most state courts have held that an implied warranty of habitability defense can be used in eviction proceedings, a landlord cannot evict a tenant for failure to pay rent in situations in which the landlord has failed to maintain the premises at minimum standards.

4. Transfer of Real Property

Real property can be transferred (1) through a sales transaction, (2) as a gift, (3) as part of the probate process, (4) through a seizure by a creditor, (5) through an eminent domain proceeding, or (6) by adverse possession.

In the typical residential real estate sale's transaction, the real estate agent provides a standardized fill-in-the-blank offer form, and the buyer's agent fills in

Quiet enjoyment
The tenant's right to be free from interference from the landlord with respect to how the property is used.

Implied warranty of habitability
A requirement that property be fit for the purpose for which it is being rented. Owners are required to repair and maintain the premises at certain minimum levels.

Constructive eviction
An act by a landlord that makes the premises unfit or unsuitable for occupancy.

PRACTICE TIP

Before signing a lease, write a list describing any damaged areas and, if possible, photograph them. Have the landlord date and sign the list.

the information regarding the description of the property, the amount of money being offered, a listing of the fixtures and appliances that are to be included, and the date of possession. The offer sheet also usually contains a number of clauses that make the offer contingent on the buyer's being able to obtain financing, often at a specified interest rate; the building's passing a termite inspection; and so forth. The buyer then turns over a specified sum of money to the real estate agent as **earnest money**. This money is applied to the purchase price at the time the sale is completed and may be forfeited if the buyer defaults prior to the completion of the sale. The seller, in turn, accepts the offer, rejects it, or proposes a counteroffer. To accept the offer, the seller simply signs the appropriate line on the offer sheet. A counteroffer usually consists of a lower asking price, somewhere between the buyer's offer and the original asking price.

If an agreement is reached, the buyer arranges for financing, and the seller arranges for a title search, and sometimes title insurance. A title search is an examination of documents recording title to the property to ensure the owner has a clear title to the property. These arrangements are often handled by a paralegal working for the seller's attorney. Title companies, which specialize in providing these services, typically employ paralegals as well as attorneys.

A **real estate closing** is a meeting at which the buyer and the seller and/or their representatives sign and deliver a variety of legal documents to finalize the sale and transfer of the property. Paralegals often play a major role in drafting the documents signed and exchanged at the closing. They often assemble the required information from financial institutions and government records.

The most important part of the closing is the delivery of the deed. The deed is the legal document that formally conveys title to the property to the new owner. In most sales a warranty deed is used. With this type of deed the seller, also known as the grantor, promises "clear title" to the property, one that has no encumbrances or other defects.

At the closing the buyer signs the mortgage documents, and the seller receives the proceeds of the sale. A closing statement is prepared to itemize and allocate all costs and moneys exchanged among the various parties, including financial institutions and real estate brokers. If the actual possession of the property does not correspond to the closing date, credits are given to reflect the rent being paid by the seller to the buyer or by the buyer to the seller.

Property can also be transferred as a gift. The elements for a valid gift include an offer, an acceptance, and delivery. Wealthy parents might give a child a house as a wedding gift or elderly parents might wish to transfer ownership of a vacation condo to their children before they die rather than having it become part of their estate.

Property also changes hands when the owner dies. If the property was held as a joint tenancy, the decedent's share passes automatically to the surviving joint owner(s). Such a transaction occurs independently of any provisions in the decedent's will, and the property is not considered to be part of his or her estate. If property was owned individually or as a tenancy in common, it becomes part of the decedent's estate and is then transferred according to the provisions of the will. If the person died intestate, that is, without a will, the property is distributed according to the special procedures set out in state statutes for those who do not leave a will.

> **PRACTICE TIP**
>
> On notarized documents check the notary's seal to make sure the notary's commission was in effect at the time the document was notarized.

Ethics Alert

While some state and local jurisdictions allow paralegals to assist clients at real estate closings without the attorney also being present, most require the physical presence of the supervising attorney. The rationale for such restrictions is that the paralegal would be engaging in the unauthorized practice of law if the paralegal attempted to explain the legal consequence of the documents being signed or to negotiate a last-minute change in any of the terms of the agreement.

Foreclosure is the process by which a creditor who holds a mortgage or some other form of a lien on real property can force the sale of that property in order to satisfy the debt to the mortgagee or lien holder. Many mortgages include **power of sale clauses,** authorizing private foreclosure sales that do not require court action.

Many states protect homeowners from creditors through what is known as a **homestead exemption.** As the name "homestead" suggests, usually the exemption applies only to a primary residence. The purpose of such laws is to protect not only the homeowner but also the homeowner's family so that creditors may not force a sale of their home in order to acquire assets to pay for the homeowner's debts. In some states, a homestead exemption is automatic as soon as the property is occupied and is used as a home. In others, however, in order to gain the benefits of a homestead exemption, the homeowner must file a formal declaration, stating that the home is the declarant's principal dwelling. To find the requirements and benefits of a homestead exemption in any given state, you must research that state's statutes.

In some situations, the government can force the sale of real property through eminent domain proceedings. **Eminent domain** is the power of government to take private property for public purposes. Although the government does not need the owner's consent, it is required to provide the owner with just compensation for the property.

Eminent domain
The power of government to take private property for public purposes.

These limitations—that the property must be taken for a public purpose and that the government must pay just compensation—are found in the U.S. Constitution. The Fifth Amendment states: "nor shall private property be taken for public use without just compensation." In recent years controversies over eminent domain have centered around two issues: the use of zoning laws and what constitutes a "public use."

Through zoning laws governments can regulate the way in which property can be used, such as prohibiting the construction of a factory on land that is zoned residential. Other regulations require the owner to turn over a portion of the land as a condition of being granted a variance or special-use permit. Assuming that the government had the power to make the regulation, the issue in these cases usually focuses on whether compliance with the zoning regulation amounts to a taking so that the owner has to be compensated for the lost use of the property.

Traditionally, the concept of "public use" meant the taking for a clearly governmental purpose, such as for a new public school, a new road, or a public park. However in 2005 the U.S. Supreme Court held that "public use" also covered the taking of property so that it could be put to better economic use. The governmental body involved only had to have a rational basis for believing

the proposed economic development would benefit the public.[1] In that case, the Court held that the town of New London was justified in taking a woman's home and that of her neighbors so that a private developer could build a luxury hotel, condominiums, offices, and shops. Note, however, that there is no requirement that any local or state government exercise such sweeping eminent domain powers; only that they may do so if they wish.

Finally, property can also be transferred through adverse possession. **Adverse possession** is a situation in which someone other than the owner exercises actual, open, adverse, and exclusive use of the property for a statutorily determined number of years, usually between five and twenty. For example, assume that Greg built a fence that was actually a few feet past his property line and encroached onto his neighbor's property. If the neighbor failed to challenge the placement of that fence within the required number of years, the property inside that fence would eventually become Greg's through adverse possession. The use was actual because Greg built a fence on it. It was open because anyone could see that the fence was there. Adverse simply means that the use of the land interfered with that of the rightful owner, and the fence certainly kept the owner from using that section of his property. The fence also gave its builder exclusive use of the area.

Adverse possession
A transfer of real property rights that occurs after someone other than the owner has had actual, open, adverse, and exclusive use of the property for a statutorily determined number of years.

5. Transfer of Personal Property

Personal property changes hands in much the same way real property does. It can be sold, it can be given away, it can be seized for nonpayment of a debt, and it can become part of a person's estate. In addition, with personal property there is a distinction among lost, abandoned, and mislaid property.

Property is classified as lost if the owner has involuntarily parted with it and does not know where to find it. On the other hand, if the owner deliberately placed it somewhere and then forgot where it had been placed, it is classified as mislaid rather than lost. It is considered abandoned property when the owner left it with no intention of coming back to reclaim it.

If you find lost property, you acquire title that is good against everyone except the true owner. However, you may have to turn the property over to the police for a certain amount of time to ensure that the rightful owner does not return to claim it. On the other hand, if you find mislaid property, property that was inadvertently left behind, such as a ring next to a sink, then you acquire no ownership rights in it. Finally, if you find abandoned property, you become the owner.

When personal property is only temporarily transferred to someone other than the owner for a specified purpose, a **bailment** occurs. For example, you create a bailment when you take your clothes to be dry-cleaned or your car to be repaired. The owner is called the **bailor**, and the party taking temporary control of the property is called the **bailee**. The law imposes a duty on the bailee to exercise reasonable care toward the property while it is under the bailee's control.

Bailment
A temporary transfer of personal property to someone other than the owner for a specified purpose.

DISCUSSION QUESTIONS

3. Why should the government be able to take somebody's property without his or her consent? How should the courts determine fair market value?

4. To what extent should the government be able to restrict an owner's use of his or her property? Should a home owner be allowed to operate a beauty salon

---

[1] Kelo v. New London, 125 S. Ct. 2655 (2005).

in his or her house in a residential neighborhood? Should the government be able to prevent a landowner from building a house in the flood plain or in a wetlands area?

B. SPECIALIZED PRACTICE AREAS

In this and the previous two chapters, we have introduced the basic concepts of torts, contracts, and property. Many types of legal practice involve applications of these three main areas of civil law. For example, attorneys who specialize in areas such as business organizations, employment law, real estate, and intellectual property need to be experts in contract law. Attorneys who advise and represent corporations often get involved in areas of tort and property law. And as Karen Decrecenzo explains in her Paralegal Profile, below, attorneys who are employed by the government, such as in municipal law offices, work in a wide variety of legal areas.

PARALEGAL PROFILE

KAREN DECRESCENZO
PRINCIPAL PARALEGAL/LEGAL INTERN COORDINATOR
OFFICE OF THE CITY ATTORNEY, CIVIL DIVISION

I work in the office that services all of the legal needs for the City of San Diego. We have approximately 80 attorneys and 20 paralegals, with every four to five paralegals being supervised by one of four senior paralegals. It is my job to supervise those supervisors.

In addition, I am responsible for the process that leads to new hires. I chair the interview panels and make recommendations about whom to hire. I also hire and supervise temporary paralegals, whom we hire to cover short-term spikes in the workload. Finally, I supervise the librarian and recruit, hire, and supervise legal interns (law students). In a nutshell, my job is managing everything that relates to the paralegal staff, librarian, and law clerks, including recruitment, interviewing, hiring, training and development, utilization, workload, workflow, performance management, rewards, and recognition.

The attorneys and paralegals in our office work on a wide variety of legal issues as we handle civil litigation and advisory matters for all of the city's departments, such as police, fire, park and recreation, and water. Cases can range from allegations of civil rights violations, to trip and fall, to first amendment issues regarding sign ordinances, to collections, to condemnations, to contract disputes—really, anything about which a city can sue or be sued. Working in so many different areas means that the paralegals are called upon to engage in a lot of legal research and writing. Our paralegals particularly enjoy working on temporary restraining orders to protect city employees who receive threats from the public as the paralegals are able to appear in court for the preliminary injunctions, being careful, of course, to announce who they are and why they are there. As anyone who works for a governmental office can tell you, it's not about the money; it's about doing interesting, challenging, and rewarding work.

As with most governmental offices, ours suffers from a lack of resources. This lack of resources is both my biggest challenge and the greatest source of job satisfaction as it forces me to be creative and innovative and to use my imagination to solve problems.

I think the best preparation I had for this job was being a parent. Being a parent taught me how to juggle multiple responsibilities and how to deal with sometimes difficult personnel issues. Those skills have come in particularly handy lately, as I have been working full-time while finishing my masters in public administration.

My parting advice to students is to say that I cannot stress strongly enough the huge benefits to be gained from joining paralegal associations. It is never too early to join. Students should become active in any clubs on their campus and investigate student membership in their local paralegal association. Through that networking they will form relationships that will support and enrich them throughout their careers. Both ALA and IPMA have given me tremendous networking opportunities. I was the first and only person to work in my position. When I found IPMA, I practically cried as I walked into the meeting room and found it full of people, all of whom do what I do and understand what it takes to do my job well. The connection I formed with them has helped me throughout the years. Because of my colleagues in IPMA, I never feel isolated.

In the remaining sections of this chapter, we will briefly introduce you to some of the major "specialty areas" in which attorneys practice. These include business organizations, debt collection and bankruptcy, employment law, intellectual property, real estate, estate planning, personal injury and products liability, family law, and administrative law. We cover criminal law in the next chapter.

1. Business Organizations

When individuals are interested in starting a new business, they often consult a lawyer as to which form of organization they should use and to help them prepare and file the appropriate legal documents required to establish and maintain that type of organization.

The three classic forms of business organizations are: (1) sole proprietorship, (2) partnership, and (3) corporation. In the mid-1990s, the limited liability company and the limited liability partnership emerged as hybrids, offering the benefits of both the partnership and the corporate form. Figure 9-1, page 203, summarizes the major features of each business type.

A sole proprietorship, the most common form of business organization, is a business formed by a single owner. They are the simplest to start and maintain, requiring a minimum of paperwork and expense. However, all the owner's personal assets, regardless of whether they are related to the operation of the business, are available to satisfy business-incurred debts. For example, if the business is not able to pay its debts, in addition to seizing the assets of the business, creditors can take the business owner's home, automobiles, jewelry, or any other personal assets. Also, the owner of a sole proprietorship is often limited in funding to his or her own resources. One of the most common reasons for changing from a sole proprietorship to a partnership or corporate form is the need for additional capital to finance the business's expansion.

Under the Uniform Partnership Act a **partnership** is defined as "an association of two or more persons to carry on as co-owners a business for profit." As with a sole proprietorship, partnership assets are only taxed once as personal income to the partners.

The major disadvantage to doing business as a partnership is that every partner assumes liability for the actions of every other partner. And as with a sole partnership, personal assets can be taken to pay for business liabilities.

Agent
Someone who has the power to act in the place of another.

Principal
A person who permits or directs another person to act on the principal's behalf.

Each partner is responsible for the acts of all other partners, because each partner is an agent for the partnership. An **agent** is someone who has the power to act in the place of another. **A principal** is a person who permits or directs another person, the agent, to act on his or her behalf, subject to the principal's direction and control. When an agent is authorized to act in the principal's place, the acts of the agent become binding on the principal. Therefore, each partner's acts bind the partnership as a whole.

In order to protect their personal assets, some business owners turn to the corporate form. A **corporation** is a business entity formed by an association of stockholders. A corporation can sue, be sued, own property, and make contracts in its own name. In a corporation, the investors have the advantage of being owners without having to assume any liability beyond the cost of their individual shares. While this limitation on liability may be important in the context of lawsuits, it may be somewhat illusionary when it comes to seeking credit because banks and other creditors often require shareholders in small corporations to provide personal guarantees to secure loans. Another benefit of the corporate form is perpetual existence and transferability of shares. Unlike a partnership, it has a continuing life of its own that is not affected by the death of a stockholder or the exchange of shares of stock.

The major disadvantages of a corporation are the necessity for following certain formalities in order to ensure that the business will be viewed as a corporation and the "double taxation" involved. The corporation's profits are taxed at the corporate level before dividends are distributed to shareholders. The shareholders then are taxed again on the dividends they receive. A dividend is a distribution of the corporate profit as ordered by the directors.

Two new business forms, the **Limited Liability Company (LLC)** and **Limited Liability Partnership (LLP)** are particularly attractive to small businesses. These forms are entirely creatures of statute and offer the best of two worlds—the limited liability that is afforded by the corporate form and the single taxation that occurs in a partnership. Limited liability means that the members cannot be sued for the negligent actions of their partners. However, as is true with corporate limited liability, it cannot protect them from their own personal conduct. Professional partnerships, such as law firms, appear to be gravitating more toward the LLP form. Because this form is essentially identical to a general partnership, except for obtaining the benefits of limited liability, law firms can easily make the change to a limited liability partnership with minimal disruption of the firm's internal workings.

NETNOTE

You can find business ownership information, such as the names of the resident agent and the corporate officers, at various places on the Internet, including *www.westlaw.com* (Westlaw), *www.lexis.com* (Lexis), and many state government web sites.

Type of Business	Sole Proprietorship	Partnership	Corporation	Limited Liability Company	Limited Liability Partnership
Number of Owners	One	Two or more	One or more	Usually one or more	Two or more
Taxation	Single	Single	Double	Single	Single
Liability	Unlimited	Unlimited	Limited to capital contribution	Limited to capital contribution	Usually limited to capital contribution; sometimes liable for business debts and for own negligent acts
Ease of Formation	Very easy; nothing to file except "DBA" certificate if using fictitious name	Very easy; formed by partners' oral or written agreement; no filing required except for "DBA" certificate if using fictitious name (can also be established by partners' words or conduct— partnership by estopppel)	File articles of organization; pay annual fee; elect board of directors and officers; hold annual meetings; keep corporate records; use designation such as Corp. or Inc.	File certificate of organization; pay annual fee; use designation such as LLC	Register with the state; pay annual fee; use designation such as LLP
Managed by	Sole owner	Partners	Board of directors and officers	Manager (either an ower or a nonowner) or the owners	Usually the partners

Figure 9-1 A Comparison of the Basic Types of Business

Paralegals are often used to research corporate information and prepare various corporate records and reports. They are also frequently assigned to monitor government legislation and administrative regulations that impact on the corporation's business.

2. Debt Collection and Bankruptcy Practices

Most businesses are involved in a variety of commercial transactions that include borrowing money, buying supplies, selling and shipping products, and collecting

debts. When debts cannot be paid, creditors may seek to recover property that was used to secure the debt or the business debtor may seek relief from its financial obligations through a bankruptcy proceeding. Lawyers who work in this area find themselves applying a variety of laws including contract law, the Uniform Commercial Code, various consumer protection statutes, and bankruptcy statutes.

Depending upon the size of the businesses, it will either employ in-house attorneys (attorneys employed by the business) to do this type of legal work or retain the services of outside counsel. In addition to representing business, attorneys may focus on representing individuals who have bad debt problems or consumer complaint issues.

This is another area of law that makes widespread use of paralegals to research and identify the assets and liabilities of corporations and individuals. Paralegals also arrange for appraisals, and draft appropriate notices, petitions, schedules, pleadings, agreements, judgments, and liens.

3. Employment Law

Prior to the Industrial Revolution most workers in the United States were either self-employed or worked as part of a family unit. However, as the industrial and service economies grew, increasing numbers of people became employees.

Employees, who work without the benefit of a union contract, are considered to be employees "at will." Under traditional interpretations of the **at-will doctrine**, employers have been free to fire their employees for a good reason, a bad reason, or no reason at all so long as that reason does not conflict with specific statutes to the contrary. For example, if a paralegal reports late for work, the employer is free to fire that employee, even if this is the first instance of the paralegal's arriving late.

In recent years, however, some courts have begun to give at-will employees more protection. In some cases where employers have established employee handbooks that spell out various personnel procedures, the courts have required those employers to follow their own rules. In addition, a few courts have stated that employers owe employees an implied covenant to act in good faith. Finally, many courts have found a public policy exception that prevents an employer from firing an employee when the employer's actions are seen as harming not only the employee but also society as a whole. Examples include an employer firing an employee for asserting a legally guaranteed right, such as applying for worker's compensation; for doing what the law requires, such as reporting for jury duty; and for refusing to do an unlawful act, such as committing perjury. This is a rapidly changing area of the law so you should expect to see the rights of employers to freely fire at-will employees come under increased judicial scrutiny in the coming years.

In addition to those rights given to at-will employees by the courts, both the federal and state legislatures have enacted many statutory protections, including worker's compensation laws, antidiscrimination laws, and laws to protect the health and safety of workers. Attorneys working in this area must become conversant with the statutory provisions as well as the regulations issued by administrative agencies that have been established to enforce these laws.

One of the most important of these federal laws protecting employees from discrimination is Title VII. Until 1964, it was perfectly legal for private employers to discriminate against current and potential employees based on their race, sex, or national origin. Congress dramatically changed this with the passage of Title VII of the Civil Rights Act of 1964. With the passage of the Civil Rights Act

Congress hoped to stop all forms of discrimination, whether in voting, education, public accommodations, or employment.

Title VII of the Civil Rights Act of 1964 deals specifically with employment. It states that

> [i]t shall be an unlawful employment practice for an employer (1) to fail or refuse to hire or to discharge any individual, or otherwise to discriminate against any individual with respect to his compensation, terms, conditions, or privileges of employment, because of such individual's race, color, religion, sex, or national origin.[2]

Race, color, religion, sex, and national origin are known as protected categories. Title VII does not mean that an employer can never make an employment decision adverse to a member of a protected class. For example, an employer can refuse to hire an African American because that person lacks the skills required for the job, withhold a woman's promotion because of a bad attendance record, or fire a Muslim because that employee was caught embezzling company funds. The key is the reason behind the employer's actions. A negative action against a member of a protected class is unlawful only when the action was taken because that person is a member of a protected class.

The most difficult part of the typical employment discrimination case is the determination of the employer's true motivation behind the allegedly discriminatory action. While some employers may admit to discriminatory motives, most employers will claim that their decisions were based on legitimate considerations, such as educational credentials or work record.

NETNOTE

The EEOC home page is located at www.eeoc.gov.

In Title VII Congress also established the Equal Employment Opportunity Commission (EEOC) and delegated to it the task of developing regulations to more specifically delineate what is unlawful behavior. It also provided that persons who feel they have been discriminated against must first file claims with the EEOC or a similar state agency, before taking their cases to court.

Two other important federal statutes that provide employees protection are the Age Discrimination in Employment Act (ADEA), which prohibits discriminating against individuals 40 years of age or older, and the Americans with Disabilities Act (ADA), which prohibits employers from discriminating against those with a physical or mental impairment who are otherwise qualified to perform the job with reasonable accommodations.

Paralegals are often used to monitor changes in the government regulations affecting health and safety regulations, employee benefits, and labor relations. Paralegals working on worker's compensation cases gather information about the extent of workers' injuries and the context in which they were received. Because these cases are handled by administrative agencies rather than by the courts, paralegals in some states are authorized to represent clients at hearings.

---

[2] 42 U.S.C.S. § 2000e-2(a) (2006).

4. Intellectual Property

The term **intellectual property** is used to describe the legal protection given to a concrete manifestation of an idea. The major types of intellectual property cover patents, copyrights, trademarks, and service marks. A **patent** gives its owner the right to exclude others from making, using, or selling his or her invention. **Copyrights** give authors, composers, and artists the right to control, with certain limitations related to "fair use," the use of their writings, musical performances, and artistic creations. A **trademark** is a distinctive symbol or set of words that identify a product with a specific manufacturer, and a **service mark** is a distinctive symbol or set of words that identify a service with a particular service provider. Familiar examples include Coke, Jell-O, and "Like a good Neighbor, State Farm is there." The law gives the registered holders of these trademarks and service marks the right to control their use.

Attorneys and paralegals engaged in this type of practice research the existence of previous copyrights and related patents, and similar trademarks and service marks. They also assist in preparing and filing the forms needed to register these rights with the appropriate government agencies.

‖‖‖ PARALEGAL PROFILE

DEB MONKE
INTELLECTUAL PROPERTY ADMINISTRATOR
STATE FARM INSURANCE COMPANIES

As an Intellectual Property Administrator for one of the nation's largest insurance companies, I spend much of my time working with employees in many different areas of the company to insure compliance with company guidelines regarding the use of trademarks in advertisements and brochures. This often involves meetings, conference calls, and emails with the Brand Group, Creative Services and Marketing. As Brand Liaison for the department, I help the Brand Group develop an understanding of the proper usage of trademarks and further develop our Brand program.

Another major part of my job involves trademark, copyright, and to a lesser extent, patent registrations and infringement matters. In this context I review items involving potential infringement of State Farm's intellectual property and send out cease-and-desist letters. I am often in contact with retained counsel regarding the registration of foreign marks or an infringement matter I may have sent them for handling.

My administrative duties include the delegating and coordinating of the intellectual property workflow to a legal assistant, an Intellectual Property Technician, a secretary, and occasionally a legal assistant intern.

In order to qualify for my current position, I needed a bachelor's degree, formal paralegal training, and several years of paralegal experience in this area of law. In addition to having my CLA, I also successfully completed the Intellectual Property Specialty exam offered by National Association of Legal Assistants (NALA). I attend seminars and read journals to keep up with the changes in intellectual property.

My membership in NALA has proven very helpful. In addition to its certification program, I have benefited from the CLE courses I have taken and my experiences serving on various committees and the board of directors, and finally from my two terms as President. These activities have improved my knowledge of the paralegal profession and my management skills. I am also involved in the International Paralegal Management

Association, the International Trademark Association, the Illinois State Bar Association, and the Central Illinois Paralegal Association.

My paralegal career has been very enjoyable and rewarding. I particularly like my job because it is intellectually challenging, I am given a great deal of freedom in managing my duties, and I work with creative people.

For students considering this profession, make sure you participate in an internship, quickly establish a mentoring relationship once you begin working, keep your skills up with the changes in technology and the law, and make sure you join associations.

---

5. Real Estate

In our discussion of property law (see pages 196-199) we gave an overview of the process by which ownership of real estate is transferred from one party to another. Attorneys advise clients as to what the law requires and prepare the appropriate legal documents. Paralegals help research property ownership, liens, and other encumbrances and draft commonly used documents. Attorneys (with the assistance of paralegals) also prepare residential and commercial leases as well as the legal notices and court documents that are part of the eviction process.

6. Estate Planning and Probate

An **estate** is the total property of whatever kind, both real and personal, that a person owns at the time of his or her death, and it is **estate law** that determines how that property will be distributed. If a person dies with a valid will, the property will be distributed according to the terms of that will. If, however, a person dies without a valid will, that person is said to have died **intestate**, and the person's property is distributed on the basis of guidelines laid down by the legislature of the state in which the deceased had his or her legal residence at the time of death. These laws may not correspond to how the deceased wanted to dispose of the estate. For this reason, as well as to take advantage of potential tax savings, it is generally desirable to have an up-to-date will.

In judging the validity of a will the courts focus on three factors: whether the testator was an adult, usually eighteen or older; his or her **testamentary capacity**; and whether the testator voluntarily executed the will. As to the second requirement of testamentary capacity, all that is required is that the testator know what he or she owns, what he or she wants to do with that property, and the "natural objects of the testator's bounty" that is, the testator's spouse and other close relatives. Finally, based on the third criterion, a court can invalidate a will if it finds that due to fraud or undue influence the testator did not voluntarily sign the will.

> **PRACTICE TIP**
>
> When doing a title search check the deed to make sure the typed name and the signature of the seller are exactly the same.

> **PRACTICE TIP**
>
> Avoid these witnesses: the elderly and casual acquaintances who may disappear and therefore not be available to testify should the need arise.

> **PRACTICE TIP**
>
> Before drafting a will be sure to ask clients if they have ever been known by any other name. This can frequently occur, especially for foreign clients who have "Americanized" their names. Then include an "also known as" clause in the will.

You may also have heard the term **"living will."** A living will is not really a will, as it does not express a person's wishes as to how his or her property should be distributed upon death. Rather it is the expression of a person's desires regarding the withholding or withdrawal of life-support equipment and other heroic measures to sustain life if the individual has an incurable or irreversible condition that will cause death. These documents are also sometimes referred to as medical directives. Closely related are **health care proxies** and **durable powers of attorney**, in which individuals delegate legal authority to make medical or financial decisions for them if they are too incapacitated to make them themselves.

In addition to helping clients draft effective wills, attorneys involved in **estate planning** analyze their client's future financial needs and help the client develop strategies to meet those needs while the individual is alive, to expedite the probate process that follows death, and to avoid inheritance and estate taxes. As to the latter, modern estate planning often includes the creation of specialized trusts. A **trust** is a legal relationship in which one party holds property for the benefit of another. The property is transferred to a trust fund, where it is to be used for the benefit of a designated person or persons rather than passing directly to them as part of the probate process. The person who creates the trust is called the donor, grantor, or settlor. The person appointed to administer the trust is the **trustee**, and the person who receives the benefits of the trust is the beneficiary.

Lawyers and paralegals involved in estate planning usually work for private law firms. A major part of the paralegal's work involves gathering and organizing financial information for attorneys to review and then incorporating personal and financial information into standardized language used in wills and trust documents.

PRACTICE TIP

Before the will is signed, read it out loud to the testator. At this time clients are often too stressed to be able to read the will to themselves as carefully as they should. At the signing make sure the testator initials every page.

Probate is the process of the court overseeing the distribution of property left by someone with a will or by someone who dies intestate. The formal probate proceedings start with the filing of a petition in the probate court. A certified copy of the death certificate and the will usually accompanies this petition. After

Ethics Alert

It is a common office practice for paralegals and other office staff to act as witnesses to a will. However, most states do not address the issue of whether a paralegal can supervise the execution of a will. The Connecticut Bar Association recommends against it, while Colorado favors it. The rationale for such restrictions is that the paralegal would be engaging in the unauthorized practice of law if the paralegal attempts to explain the legal consequence of the documents being signed.

payment of the required fees, letters of testamentary are issued to give the executor or a court-appointed administrator the power to take control of the deceased's assets, pay the bills, and distribute the proceeds of the estate. Various inventories and other reports have to be filed with the court at several stages of this process.

In addition to working for private law firms and banks, paralegals working in the probate field are also employed by probate courts. In these settings they assist administrators and executors by collecting and inventorying the deceased's assets, arrange for appraisals, help locate and notify heirs, and complete and file probate and tax forms.

NETNOTE

The Uniform Probate Code has been adopted by eighteen states. You can access the text of the code as it has been adopted by each of those states by going to *www.law.cornell.edu/uniform/probate.html*.

7. Personal Injury and Products Liability

The specialty areas of personal injury and products liability primarily involve the application of tort law to a wide variety of different types of accidents and injury situations. As discussed in Chapter 7 on Torts, the principles of agency law and doctrine of **respondeat superior** often play a role in deciding whom to sue. (See page 161.)

Although nothing prevents attorneys from representing both plaintiffs and defendants, most tend to focus on either one side or the other. The plaintiff's bar usually represents individuals or groups of individuals (in class action suits) and relies on contingency fees. Defense attorneys on the other hand tend to represent insurance companies and to be compensated on an hourly fee basis.

Paralegals are used for both legal and factual research, drafting and responding to interrogatories, arranging for expert witnesses, and preparing exhibits for trial. If appeals are involved, they order and abstract copies of the record and do legal research on the issues that are involved in the appeal.

NETNOTE

You can find various uniform laws governing the family, such as the Uniform Child Custody Jurisdiction Act, the Uniform Interstate Family Support Act, the Uniform Premarital Agreement Act, and the Uniform Marriage and Divorce Act at *www.law.cornell.edu/uniform/vol9.html*.

8. Family Law

Family law, sometimes also referred to as domestic relations law, includes laws governing marriage, annulment, separation, divorce, paternity, adoption, guardianship, custody, support, childcare, abuse, and neglect. Because state statutes and the court decisions interpreting those statutes dominate family law, there is a great deal of variation from one state to the next. However, while state law is the principal source of family law, recently the federal government has enacted legislation in certain areas of family law, such as those laws assisting states with the collection of child support and trying to prevent divorced or separated parents from kidnapping their own children and taking them across state lines.

Most aspects of family law are governed by civil law, such as who can be married, how marriages take place, the property rights of marital partners, how marriages are dissolved, and how children are adopted. However, criminal statutes cover some aspects of family law, such as child and spousal abuse.

NETNOTE

"Concerned over making decisions about abused and neglected children's lives without sufficient information, a Seattle judge conceived the idea of using trained community volunteers to speak for the best interests of these children in court. So successful was this Seattle program that soon judges across the country began utilizing citizen advocates." This program is now known as CASA, Court Appointed Special Advocates. To learn more about CASA and how to train as a volunteer, go to its national web site at *www.nationalcasa.org*.

Family law is one of the most dynamic areas of the law. The very notion of what constitutes a family has become a politically and emotionally charged issue. Family law decisions go to the very heart of what we feel is important. For example, should the best interests of the child or the rights of a natural parent govern the outcome of a custody dispute? Should same-sex couples be allowed to marry? Should the courts enforce a contract whereby a woman agrees to serve as a surrogate parent? These are just a few of the issues that confront those who specialize in the area of family law.

Paralegals working in this area of the law are often engaged in meeting with clients. They gather financial information in preparation for divorce or separation

---

PRACTICE TIP

Before deciding on this practice area, you should be aware that, as with criminal law, family law raises a number of emotional issues, and the client is often unhappy no matter the results. But family law can also involve happy events, such as marriage and the adoption of children.

proceedings. Paralegals also draft petitions, discovery requests, separation agreements, and other court documents in regards to divorce and child custody proceedings.

9. Administrative Law

In Chapter 3 we explained how administrative agencies create administrative law by filling in the details within a general structure set down by the legislature. In addition to this quasi-legislative function, federal and state agencies also take on quasi-judicial functions in which they grant or deny permits, licenses, subsidies, welfare benefits, and so on. These government agencies can also assess fines for those failing to follow the prescribed rules.

Attorneys specializing in administrative law advise clients regarding the legal duties imposed by these administrative agencies and represent their clients in seeking various licenses and permits or responding to alleged violations. When dealing with agencies such as the Environmental Protection Agency, the Federal Communications Commission, the Occupational Safety and Health Administration, or a state insurance commission, the clients are usually business corporations. When dealing with agencies such as the Immigration and Naturalization Service, the Internal Revenue Service, or a state Worker's Compensation Board, the clients are more likely to be individuals. Many attorneys and paralegals are also employed by the agencies themselves to conduct investigations, prepare complaints, and represent the agency in legal proceedings.

Some agencies have provisions that allow paralegals to provide formal representation in administrative hearings. For example, the section of the federal regulations governing representation of parties at Social Security Administration hearings explicitly allows for persons other than attorneys to provide representation if they are "capable of giving valuable help" in connection with the claim.[3]

SUMMARY

Property law deals with ownership rights in real and personal property. Real property is land and anything permanently attached to land. Personal property is everything else. Property can be owned either individually or with others. Joint ownership that vests ownership rights upon death in the other co-owner(s) is known as joint tenancy with the right of survivorship. With a tenancy in common the joint owner can pass his or her share to heirs at death. Real property can be transferred through sale, at the death of the owner, as a gift, through seizure by a creditor, by eminent domain, or through adverse possession.

Residential landlords are obligated to provide habitable living areas. Tenants may sue for constructive eviction if landlords fail to do so.

Businesses must be concerned with many areas of the law, including which business form to use: sole proprietorship, partnership, corporation, or limited liability company or partnership.

[3] 20 C.F.R. § 404.1705 (2006).

Employment law is dominated by federal statutes, including Title VII of the Civil Rights Act of 1964, prohibiting discrimination based on race, color, religion, sex, or national origin; the Age Discrimination in Employment Act (ADEA), prohibiting discrimination based on age; and the Americans with Disabilities Act (ADA), prohibiting discrimination based on disability.

Intellectual property gives concrete protection to the manifestation of an idea. The major types of intellectual property are patents, copyrights, trademarks, and service marks.

Estate planning involves the analysis of a person's future financial needs and of ways to ensure that the person's desires regarding distribution of assets will be accomplished after death. Wills and trusts are two of the most common estate-planning tools. If a person dies without a will, that person is said to have died intestate, and the property passes to the decedent's heirs according to that state's statutory intestacy scheme.

Family law includes laws governing marriage, annulment, separation, divorce, paternity, adoption, guardianship, custody, support childcare, abuse, and neglect. There is a great deal of variation in family laws from one state to the next.

Some attorneys specialize in practicing before administrative agencies. Some agencies authorize paralegals to appear as representatives at adjudicatory hearings. These hearings follow the general outline of a civil trial, but they are less formal and do not involve as many due process protections. Once all avenues of appeal within an agency have been exhausted, a party can often seek review within the judicial system.

REVIEW QUESTIONS

Pages 193 through 200

1. Define the two basic types of property.
2. Why is it important to know if property is classified as personal or real?
3. Why might it be important to know whether two friends shared ownership in a house as joint tenants or as tenants in common?
4. Describe two ways in which an owner's right to use his or her property may be limited by private arrangement.
5. What is a constructive eviction, and how does it relate to the implied warranty of habitability?
6. How does someone acquire property through adverse possession?
7. According to the dictates of the Fifth Amendment, if a state wants to take private property, what must it do?
8. What is the distinction between lost and mislaid property? Why does it matter?

Pages 201 through 209

9. What are the four basic forms of business organizations, and what are the main advantages and disadvantages of each?
10. What is the most common reason for changing from a sole proprietorship to a partnership or a corporation?
11. Why might forming a limited liability company be preferable to forming either a partnership or a corporation?
12. What is employment at will?
13. What protections are afforded an employee by Title VII? the ADA? the ADEA?
14. What is intellectual property and what is it meant to protect?
15. What does it mean to say someone died intestate?
16. Why is it not a good idea to die without a will?
17. What is the purpose of a trust?

Pages 209 through 211

18. Name four areas covered by family law.
19. Is family law a fairly static or dynamic area of the law? Why?
20. Describe the quasi-legislative and quasi-judicial functions of administrative agencies.

Chapter 10

Criminal Law and Procedure

We can have as much or as little crime as we please,
depending on what we choose to count as criminal.
Herbert L. Packer

INTRODUCTION

Both torts and crimes involve acts that harm individuals. As we have seen, in tort law, harmful acts are treated as "private wrongs," while in criminal law they are treated as offenses against the state. A **crime** is therefore defined as an act that has been defined as a public wrong, that is prosecuted by the government, and that may carry a punishment of a fine or imprisonment.

Criminal law defines for society what behaviors are illegal. Many of the acts that our modern criminal code classifies as crimes were also prohibited in the English common law. In addition to putting common law prohibitions against such things as murder, robbery, and assault, into statutory form, today's criminal codes include such things as eavesdropping, wireless service theft, and computer crime.

Federal and state **rules of criminal procedure** govern everything from investigation and arrest through sentencing and appeals. The federal and state **rules of evidence** regulate what types of evidence can be used in the trial and how it must be presented.

Rules of criminal procedure
Federal and state rules that regulate how criminal proceedings are conducted.

NETNOTE

The FBI maintains a web site at *www.fbi.gov,* where you can find a great deal of information, including the "ten most wanted" list.

A. CRIMINAL LAW

Although some behavior might be considered morally or ethically wrong, it is important to understand that nothing is a crime unless the law makes it a crime. That is, no act is a **crime** unless the legislature has written a statute explicitly prohibiting that behavior. This principle is expressed by the Latin *maxim nullum crimen, nulla poena sine lege* ("there can be no crime and no punishment without the law"). In this section we will discuss how the law classifies crimes, the elements common to all crimes, the parties to crime, and defenses. We end the section with a brief discussion of the practice of criminal law. In the next section, we will discuss criminal procedure.

1. Classification of Crimes

As discussed in Chapter 4, crimes are usually classified on the basis of the type of harm done and the nature of the punishment imposed. Serious crimes are classified as **felonies,** and they generally involve a punishment that can include a year or more in a state prison. **Misdemeanors** include lesser charges, and if incarceration results it usually is for less than one year and is served in a county jail. Sometimes the same basic activity, such as drug possession, can be either a felony or a misdemeanor depending on the drug and the quantity involved. For example, while possession of a single marijuana cigarette might be only a misdemeanor, possession of a large quantity of heroin would certainly qualify as a felony. Legislators determine whether a given act is to be considered a felony or a misdemeanor at the time that they enact the statute making it a crime.

Although the state criminal code usually can be divided neatly into felonies and misdemeanors, there are some other types of quasi-criminal law situations that are also included. For example, traffic laws are usually codified in a different part of the state's statutes and do not carry the same stigma as do violations of the criminal law. Nevertheless, the judicial proceedings used to enforce these traffic laws are criminal in nature. The state takes it on itself to prosecute offenders who in turn must be found guilty "beyond a reasonable doubt." Some juvenile proceedings are also criminal in nature. Local ordinances for matters like garbage disposal and barking dogs are additional examples of quasi-criminal proceedings.

The criminal codes of most states further classify crimes according to the type of harm caused to society. Offenses involving physical harm to a person are considered more serious than offenses involving damage to someone's property. Figure 10-1 illustrates how some of the more familiar crimes fit within the major harm-based classifications. They include harm to the person, harm to habitations and property, harm to society's health and safety, and crimes against the government itself.

Offenses against the person include various types of homicides, kidnapping, and acts involving the infliction of bodily harm. A **homicide** is the killing of one

Figure 10-1   Classifications of Crime Based on Harm

Harm to Persons	Homicide crimes
	    Murder
	    Manslaughter
	    Negligent homicide
	Other crimes against persons
	    Assault
	    Battery
	    Child abandonment
	    Kidnapping
	    Rape
	    Robbery
	    Stalking	

Crimes against Habitations and Property	Arson Burglary Forgery	Receiving stolen property Shoplifting Theft Trespass
Crimes against the Public Health, Safety, or Decency	Alcohol offenses Child pornography Disorderly conduct	Drug offenses Obscenity Prostitution
Crimes Affecting Governmental Functions	Bribery Perjury Treason	

human being by another. As we will discuss further, later in this chapter, the circumstances under which the killing takes place and what the defendant was thinking at the time of the killing determine whether it was a first-degree murder, manslaughter, negligent homicide, or not a crime at all. **Battery** is a wrongful physical contact with a person that entails some injury or offensive touching. An **assault** is conduct that places another person in reasonable apprehension of receiving a battery. **Kidnapping** is similar to the tort of false imprisonment in that it involves unlawful confinement. However, in most states the victim must also be moved. **Robbery** is a theft of personal property in circumstances that involve either the infliction of serious bodily injury or the threat of such injury. **Stalking** is a relatively new crime. It is committed when a person intentionally or knowingly engages in a course of conduct that causes a reasonable person to fear the imminent physical injury or death of him- or herself or of a member of that person's family.

Crimes against habitations and property involve harm to or the taking of another's property without consent. **Arson** is the malicious burning of the house or property of another. Despite frequent misuse of the term, burglary is not synonymous with theft. **Burglary** involves breaking into and entering a building with the intent of committing a felony. That felony could be theft, but it also could be some other felony, such as rape. **Theft**, also known as **larceny**, is the act of "stealing" that is, taking property without the owner's consent. To be found guilty of receiving stolen property, the state must prove that the property was stolen, that the defendant knew the property was stolen, and that the defendant knowingly had the stolen property in his or her possession. **Forgery** involves the alteration or falsification of documents with the intent to defraud. **Trespass** is an unauthorized intrusion or invasion of the premises or land of another.

Crimes affecting the public health, safety, and decency cover a wide variety of crimes, ranging from alcohol and drug abuse to obscenity and prostitution. This is one of the most controversial areas of the criminal law. As "victimless crimes," many of the laws in this category are criticized for interfering with basic civil liberties. Offenses covering alcohol and drugs include the possession, use, and sale of these substances. Some drugs are totally outlawed, while others can be sold or possessed only when prescribed by a licensed physician. Alcohol regulation can range from the establishment of a minimum drinking age to complete prohibition. Prostitution involves participation, or offering to participate, in sexual activity for a fee, and obscenity regulations restrict the availability of sexually explicit books, magazines, movies, videos, and live performances.

Crimes affecting governmental functions include bribery, perjury, and treason. Historically, **bribery** involved offering something of value to a public official

PRACTICE TIP

Because crimes vary from state to state, never rely on a general description of criminal law. Always consult your state statutes to determine the elements of particular crimes in your state.

NETNOTE

The U.S. Department of Justice maintains statistics about crimes and victims at *www.ojp.usdoj.gov/bjs,* as does the University of Michigan through its National Archive of Criminal Justice Data (NACJD) project at *www.icpsr.umich.edu/ nacjd/home.html.* An interesting site that contains a crime statistics tutorial is *www.crime.org.*

that, if accepted, would cause that public official to act in such a way as to violate the public trust. Today there is also commercial bribery. **Perjury** involves knowingly making a false statement while under oath. Finally, treason consists of either attempting to overthrow the government or betraying the government to a foreign power.

2. Elements of a Crime

In order for a crime to take place, someone with a "guilty intent" (**mens rea**) must commit a "guilty act" (**actus rea**) that causes specified harmful results. The guilty act part of the formula consists of an action such as taking someone's life or property (such as homicide or theft) or making an improper physical contact with someone (such as battery or rape). The classification of what crime has been committed often depends on the results of the act. For example, if one person shoots another with intent to kill that person, the actual damage done by the shooting (that is, did the victim live or die?) will determine whether the person has committed homicide or only attempted homicide.

In order for an act to be considered a crime, the person who commits the guilty act must also have the appropriate mens rea. The difference between innocently bumping into someone on a crowded street and the commission of the crime of battery depends for the most part on the state of mind of the person who initiated the contact. In order for the act to be considered a crime, there has to be evidence of a "guilty mind."

Although it is difficult to prove what was going on in someone's mind when a crime was committed, the courts allow judges and juries to infer the defendant's state of mind from both statements made and actions undertaken at that time. Furthermore, the law assumes that people know the probable consequences of their acts. A person who strikes another may be presumed to have intended the infliction of harm in that such a result naturally flows from hitting another.

The mens rea is also important in distinguishing one crime from another. The same act and the same result can constitute different crimes based on the intent of the criminal. For example, murder, voluntary manslaughter, involuntary manslaughter, and reckless homicide all involve the taking of a human life. They differ primarily in terms of the intent of the person responsible for the

killing. Compare the ways in which these offenses are defined in the Illinois criminal code:

720 Ill. Comp. Stat. 5/9-1 First Degree Murder

(a) A person who kills an individual without lawful justification commits murder if, in performing the acts which cause the death:

(1) he either intends to kill or do great bodily harm to that individual or another, or knows that such acts will cause death to that individual or another; or

(2) he knows that such acts create a strong probability of death or great bodily harm to that individual or another; or

(3) he is attempting or committing a forcible felony other than second degree murder.

720 Ill. Comp. Stat. 5/9-2 Second Degree Murder

(a) A person commits the offense of second degree murder when he commits the offense of first degree murders as defined in paragraphs (1) and (2) [above] and . . .

(1) At the time of the killing he is acting under a sudden and intense passion resulting from serious provocation by the individual killed. . . .

(b) Serious provocation is conduct sufficient to excite an intense passion in a reasonable person.

720 Ill. Comp. Stat. 5/9-3 Involuntary Manslaughter and Reckless Homicide

(a) A person who unintentionally kills an individual without lawful justification commits involuntary manslaughter if his acts whether lawful or unlawful which cause the death are such as are likely to cause death or great bodily harm to some individual, and he performs them recklessly, except in cases in which the cause of the death consists of the driving of a motor vehicle or operating a snowmobile, all-terrain vehicle, or watercraft, in which case the person commits reckless homicide.

Notice how first degree murder requires a mens rea of either the intention to kill or knowledge that the act in question will cause death or that there is a strong probability of death. For example, a hired assassin would have the intent to kill. Someone who as a matter of political protest throws a bomb into a crowd, may have the intent to make a statement and not to kill. However, if someone is killed because the person who threw the bomb would have known that such an action would result in death or at least in the strong probability of death, that person would also be guilty of first degree murder. The third provision, while "attempting or committing a forcible felony" applies to those situations where the defendant's intent was to do some other unlawful act, such as burn down a warehouse, but the actions caused death. Second degree murder consists of the same acts as murder but the person doing the killing was provoked by the person killed and acted under a sudden and intense passion. The classic example is the husband who comes home early to find his wife in bed with his best friend. Finally, involuntary manslaughter and reckless homicide involve an unintentional killing that results from reckless behavior. Examples would include driving while intoxicated, resulting in an accident that causes the death of

Legal Reasoning Exercise

1. Apply the Illinois first degree murder, second degree murder, and involuntary manslaughter and reckless homicide statutes to each of the following situations. What crimes, if any, have been committed?

a. Sam, a hired assassin, pulls out a gun and points it at Mary's head. He pulls the trigger, the bullet strikes Mary in the temple, and she is killed instantly.

b. Janet, to protest what she views as the increasing decadence of modern society, leaves a bomb in an empty adult movie theater. Later that night the bomb goes off and kills the janitor, who was there cleaning the theater.

c. Rita accompanies John while he robs a store owner at gunpoint. The gun goes off, and the owner is killed by the gunshot.

d. Five boys are playing a game of "chicken" in which they pass a partially loaded gun (one of the six chambers contains a live bullet) around the circle. Each player takes a turn spinning the cylinder, pointing the gun at his head, and pulling the trigger. When Dan takes his turn, the gun goes off, and he dies instantly.

e. After leaving a bar, Ralph and Sam started arguing in the parking lot. Both had been drinking, and they began to fight. Ralph threw the first punch but Sam soon retaliated, by pulling out a gun and pistol-whipping him on his head. Ralph was overcome by rage, grabbed Sam around the neck, and flung him to the pavement. As a result of his injuries Sam died.

your passenger, and shooting a gun into the air while walking through a park, resulting in the death of an elderly gentleman sitting on a park bench.

Every state defines murder and manslaughter in slightly different ways. That is why it is always essential to research the law in your own state. For example, in California murder is defined as an unlawful killing with malice aforethought.[1] Malice can be shown through a deliberate intention to kill (similar to the Illinois definition) or can be implied when "the circumstances attending the killing show an abandoned and malignant heart."[2] In contrast, voluntary manslaughter occurs when the actions that cause the death occur because of the failure to use "due caution and circumspection."[3]

A controversial application of these statutes occurred in the 2002 California conviction of Marjorie Knoller. The jury surprised many legal commentators by finding the defendant guilty of second degree murder after her two dogs killed a neighbor in the hallway of their San Francisco apartment building.[4] The jury concluded that Ms. Knoller had acted recklessly in not properly restraining the dogs when she knew them to be vicious and dangerous. In gaining its conviction, the

---

[1] Cal. Pen. Code § 187 (2006).

[2] Cal. Pen. Code § 188 (2006).

[3] Cal. Pen. Code § 192 (2006).

[4] "Dogs' keepers guilty in mauling," USA Today, Friday, March 22, 2002, p. 3A.

state had presented evidence that the dogs had been bred to fight and that they had not been properly trained to be around people. Through witness testimony the state established that Ms. Knoller had failed to restrain the dogs properly even though there had been more than thirty prior incidents in which the dogs had lunged at or otherwise shown overly aggressive behavior toward other people. Do you think Ms. Knoller's actions warranted a finding of murder, or only of voluntary manslaughter? If you are unsure, you are in good company. The events following the jury's verdict illustrate just how difficult it is to determine what level of mens rea is required for a murder conviction.

On the day Knoller was sentenced, the trial court judge reversed the jury's verdict. Although the judge thought Knoller's actions were "despicable," he did not think that her mental state was sufficient to satisfy the murder statute's requirement for malice. The judge stated, "I cannot say as a matter of law that she subjectively knew on January 26 that her conduct would cause death."[5]

Three years later, a California appeals court reinstated her second-degree murder conviction, stating that the question "was not whether Knoller knew her conduct was likely to result in the death of someone but whether Knoller knew her conduct endangered the life of another and acted in conscious disregard for life or in wanton disregard for life"[6] As this text is going to print, the *Knoller* case is on appeal to California's Supreme Court. The question facing that court is whether the trial court or the appellate court applied the correct legal standard as to the mental state required for implied malice—i.e., to prove the malice required for a murder conviction, does the prosecution have to prove only that Knoller exhibited a conscious disregard for human life, or must it prove she was aware that her actions created a likelihood of great bodily injury.[7] No matter how the *Knoller* case is resolved, as noted above, keep in mind that criminal law is state law, and each state controls its own definition of what constitutes murder.

3. Parties to the Crime

When more than one person commits a crime, the perpetrators may be classified as principals, accomplices, or accessories. The person who commits a criminal act is a **principal** in the first degree. A principal in the second degree, sometimes also referred to as an accomplice, assists the principal in the first degree during the commission of the crime, for example, by driving the getaway car. An **accessory before the fact** is someone who assisted in the preparation of the crime, but was not present during the crime. Finally, an **accessory after the fact** is someone who aided the principal after the commission of the crime. When it comes to punishment, principals of any degree and accessories are generally all treated the same, although in the past accessories after the fact have not been punished as severely as principals and accessories before the fact.

4. Defenses

In some circumstances the law excuses a person from criminal responsibility if he or she has what the law considers to be a valid excuse for their actions. The alibi

---

[5] "Dog-Mauling Murder Conviction Overturned," abcNews.com, June 17, 2002.

[6] People v. Noel, 128 Cal. App. 4th 1391, 1446 (2005).

[7] People v. Noel, 116 P.3d 475 (Cal. 2005).

P R A C T I C E T I P

Depending on your jurisdiction, the defendant may have the burden of raising defenses and proving them. Check to determine who has the burdens of production and proof. In many jurisdictions, defenses must be alleged prior to the start of the trial.

---

and insanity defenses are perhaps the best known. Other criminal defenses include ignorance or mistake, intoxication, duress, necessity, and entrapment.

An **alibi defense** is one in which the defense attempts to show that the defendant could not have committed the crime because the defendant was in a specified place at a specific time that would make it impossible for him or her to have committed the crime. For example, if four witnesses testify that they were playing poker with the defendant at a home on the east side of town, then the defendant could not have been the person who robbed a liquor store on the west side of town at that time.

We have all heard that ignorance of the law is no excuse. Generally, that is true. On the other hand, ignorance or mistake as to facts can form the basis for a defense if it can be shown that the defendant's ignorance or mistake negated the requisite mens rea. For example, if you left a classroom with a classmate's textbook, thinking it was your own, you would be mistaken as to the fact of ownership. Therefore, you could not be prosecuted for theft, as you did not have the required mens rea, the intent to steal the property of another.

Infancy, insanity, and intoxication are referred to as status defenses. They all involve excusing people from the criminal consequences of their actions because their status or condition renders them incapable of formulating the required element of mens rea.

Under the common law, children under the age of seven were conclusively presumed to be incapable of forming criminal intent, while there was a rebuttable presumption that those between the ages of seven and fourteen were not capable of forming such intent. The juvenile court system was created to provide a noncriminal alternative for processing juveniles who are accused of acts that are considered crimes if they are committed by adults. In recent years, however, especially with the increase in violent, gang-related crimes, there has been a movement to waive juvenile court jurisdiction and apply adult standards to the prosecution of these juvenile offenders.

The **insanity defense** is based on the assertion that the defendant is incapable of forming the requisite mens rea. While most jurisdictions have the insanity defense available to criminal defendants, there is disagreement among the states and the federal circuits about the standard that should be used to determine insanity. The three most common alternatives are the M'Naghten test, the irresistible impulse test, and the Model Penal Code Substantial capacity test. These tests are summarized in Figure 10-2, on page 224.

When the **M'Naghten** test is used, a defendant is not considered guilty of the crime if, at the time of committing the actus reus, the defendant was suffering from a defect or disease of the mind and could not understand whether the act was right or wrong.

Insanity defense
A defense requiring proof that the defendant was not mentally responsible.

M'Naghten test
A test that provides that the defendant is not guilty due to insanity if, at the time of the killing, the defendant suffered from a defect or disease of the mind and could not understand whether the act was right or wrong.

M'Naghten or "Right from Wrong" Test

"[T]o establish insanity sufficient to relieve the defendant of guilt, it must be proved that, at the time of the commission of the act, the defendant was laboring under such a defect of reason, from disease of the mind as not to know the nature and quality of the act he was doing, or if he did know it, that he did not know that what he was doing was wrong." *M'Naghten's Case,* 8 Eng. Rep. 718, 722 (1843).

Irresistible Impulse Test

One is not guilty by reason of insanity if it is determined that the defendant has a mental disease that kept the defendant from controlling his or her conduct.

Substantial Capacity Test (Model Penal Code)

(1) A person is not responsible for criminal conduct if at the time of such conduct, as a result of mental disease or defect, he or she lacks substantial capacity to appreciate the criminality (wrongfulness) of his or her conduct or to conform that conduct to the requirements of law.

(2) The terms *mental disease* and *mental defect* do not include an abnormality manifested only by repeated criminal or otherwise antisocial conduct.

Figure 10-2   Insanity Tests

Irresistible impulse test
A test that provides that the defendant is not guilty due to insanity if, at the time of the killing, the defendant could not control his or her actions.

Under the M'Naghten test a defendant will be found sane if he or she knew that a certain action was wrong but could not stop from taking that action. Therefore, some jurisdictions have both the M'Naghten standard and a variation of what is commonly known as the **irresistible impulse test**. With this test, the focus is on the defendant's ability to control his or her own actions. If a mental disease robs the individual of control over his or her conduct, the person is not guilty by reason of insanity.

The drafters of the American Law Institute's Model Penal Code, developed a third test, which combines elements of the other two. This test is known as the **substantial capacity test**. It requires that the defendant "appreciate," rather than "know," the wrongfulness of his or her actions. Under the two options provided in this test defendants can lack either the ability to understand that their acts were wrong or the ability to control their behavior. Although the complete Model Penal Code has not been widely adopted, this section has been accepted as the test for insanity in a majority of jurisdictions.

Substantial capacity test
Part of the Model Penal Code; a test that provides that the defendant is not guilty due to insanity if, at the time of the killing, the defendant lacked either the ability to understand that the act was wrong or the ability to control the behavior.

P R A C T I C E   T I P

Jurisdictions differ greatly on how children should be treated when they commit acts that would be crimes if committed by adults. Carefully check a young person's age at the time the offense was committed, and do the research necessary to determine when a child perpetrator can be treated as an adult.

The insanity defense is rarely used, and when it is used, it is difficult to prove as illustrated by the highly publicized Andrea Yates case. Yates confessed to having drowned her five young children in the bathtub because she heard voices telling her to kill her children in order to "save them from Satan."[8] The case was tried in Texas, a state that still follows the M'Naghten "Right from Wrong" test. Therefore, to prove insanity, the defense had to show not just that Yates was mentally ill, about which there was no dispute, but also that she was not aware what she had done was wrong. In a three-week-long trial, the defense called as witnesses psychiatrists, relatives, and friends to testify that Yates suffered from severe post-partum depression. The prosecution countered by arguing that Yates's prompt action in reporting the drowning to the police established that she did know what she had done was wrong. The jury apparently agreed with the prosecution that Yates was not legally insane and convicted her of murder. She was sentenced to life in prison and sent to a prison psychiatric ward to receive treatment for her mental illness.[9]

It is also possible that the jury found her guilty not because they thought she was sane when she drowned her children, but because they were afraid that a not guilty by reason of insanity verdict would have resulted in her being released from state custody. What the jury did not know, because by Texas statute[10] they could not be told, is that even a not guilty by reason of insanity verdict would most likely have resulted in her immediate involuntary commitment to a mental institution. When a trial ends in a verdict of "not guilty" by reason of insanity, the defendant is absolved of any criminal responsibility but is often civilly committed to a mental health facility for treatment. According to the American Psychiatric Association, "studies show that persons found not guilty by reason of insanity, on average, are held at least as long as—and often longer than—persons found guilty and sent to prison for similar crimes."[11]

Even if a defendant was sane at the time the crime was committed, he or she can be considered legally incompetent at the time of trial. If a defendant cannot understand the legal process or assist in his or her own defense by, for example, talking about the case with the attorney or testifying meaningfully at trial, the defendant may not be tried until the court determines the defendant is mentally competent.

In some jurisdictions and under some circumstances, being under the influence of drugs or alcohol is considered a valid defense. This is referred to as an **intoxication defense**. The theory is that the intoxicating substance interfered with the defendant's ability to form the required mens rea. Although intoxication cannot be used as a defense for charges involving reckless behavior (such as drunk driving or criminal damage to property), it can generally be used as a defense for crimes requiring a specific intent, such as murder.

---

[8] "Jury to Decide Yates' Sentence," USA Today, March 14, 2002, p. 3A.

[9] Later a Texas appeals court reversed Yates conviction based on improper expert testimony and ordered a retrial. As of this writing, she remains in a Texas prison psychiatric ward waiting for her new trial.

[10] Tex. Code Crim. Proc. art. 46.03(1)(e) ("The court, the attorney for the state, or the attorney for the defendant may not inform a juror . . . of the consequences to the defendant if a verdict of not guilty by reason of insanity is returned.").

[11] American Psychiatric Association, The Insanity Defense, *www.healthyminds.org/insanitydefense.cfm.*

PRACTICE TIP

The most important part of using or disproving a defense is to research the elements of the defense carefully. It is especially important to look at past cases where the defense has already been asserted. Then you will know which defenses are available in your jurisdiction and which defenses the courts tend to favor.

Duress
A defense requiring proof that force or a threat of force was used to cause a person to commit a criminal act.

Necessity
A defense requiring proof that the defendant was forced to take an action to avoid a greater harm.

Entrapment
A defense requiring proof that the defendant would not have committed the crime but for police trickery.

Self-defense
The justified use of force to protect oneself or others.

Because one of the fundamental principles of criminal law is that criminal behavior must be the result of a voluntary act, the law recognizes both duress and necessity as legitimate defenses. If a defendant can establish that the criminal act was committed because he or she was forced to carry it out, that individual is not held accountable for the criminal act. This is called a **duress defense**.

Section 2.09 of the Model Penal Code defines duress as coercion through "the use of, or a threat to use, unlawful force against his person or the person of another, which a person of reasonable firmness in his situation would have been unable to resist." To assert this defense, you must prove that you reasonably believed that you were threatened with your death, the death of another person, or serious injury to yourself or others unless you committed the crime.

The **necessity defense** is similar to the duress defense except the force is exerted by nature rather than by another person. For example, you may be forced to trespass across a neighbor's yard to escape a fire in your home. In addition, this defense may be used in a more general way to exonerate otherwise criminal conduct when a person believes that such conduct is necessary to avoid a greater injury. An example would be where a motorist chooses to crash an automobile into a building in order to avoid hitting a child who runs into the street.

The defense of **entrapment** arises when a defendant believes that he or she was tricked or led to commit a crime by a law enforcement agency when the defendant would not have committed the crime without the government's enticement. It is not entrapment if the government agents provide a person with the opportunity to commit a crime that he or she was already contemplating. The key is whether the defendant had a predisposition to commit the crime before the government agents contacted the person.

Reactive defenses include self-defense and the use of force in law enforcement. As to **self-defense**, individuals are allowed to use force in defending themselves or others and in defending their dwellings and other property. There is significant variation among the states as to the amount of force that can be used and the circumstances under which one is required to retreat when that is a viable option. Generally, however, this right to use force is valid only as long as the following conditions are met. First, the person claiming self-defense must not have been the initiator of the violence. Second, the threat of bodily harm must be immediate. Third, once the threatening party ceases the threatening behavior, the right to self-defense disappears. Fourth, the amount of force used must be no more than is reasonably necessary to repel the attack. Deadly force, a force that would cause serious bodily injury or death, can be used only when the danger faced includes fear of serious bodily injury or death.

PRACTICE TIP

Not all jurisdictions accept the battered woman's syndrome as a defense. Research your jurisdiction's law to determine whether this defense is available to defendants or whether the time is right in your jurisdiction for a new defense to be tested.

This right to defend oneself does not extend to all people at all times. In fact, it does not even extend to all people who find themselves in dangerous positions. Most jurisdictions include a **retreat exception** to the right to self-defense. This doctrine of retreat generally requires a person in danger to get away from the danger, or give up possessions, before resorting to the use of deadly force. If the victim can avoid danger but chooses instead to use deadly force, that victim may be prosecuted for any crime committed. Potential victims need not retreat if they are in their own homes or if retreating would create additional danger for them. Potential victims using nondeadly force need not retreat.

Retreat exception
The rule that in order to claim self-defense there must have been no possibility of retreat.

In most jurisdictions the rights and requirements of self-defense can also be applied to a person's right to protect another person. The defense of others permits you to use reasonable force to protect another person if you believe that the threat of bodily harm is immediate and that the amount of force used is reasonable.

You may also act against another person in defense of property. Rarely can deadly force be applied to protect property. Generally, we value human life over property even when the human life in question is trying to steal property. However, the right to self-defense extends inside of the home, and deadly force is still permitted if the home intruder is attempting to do great bodily harm.

The so-called **battered spouse's syndrome** is a variation on self-defense that does not require the defendant to have been in immediate danger at the moment of the attack if it can be established that the defendant had been the victim of repeated attacks and did not believe escape from future attacks was possible. However, not all states have been willing to accept this defense, as the defendant's actions usually are not taken in the face of "imminent" death or great bodily harm. The effects of the battered spouse syndrome may be used, however, to reduce the charge from murder to manslaughter.

Battered woman's or spouse's syndrome
Being the victim of repeated attacks, self-defense is sometimes allowed to the victim, even when the victim is not in immediate danger.

It should be noted that law enforcement and military personnel are given special exemptions from the law to take actions that are required as part of their official duties. Soldiers killing enemy soldiers in battle and police officers killing an escaping felon fall under the category of justifiable homicide.

Finally, defendants may raise a constitutional defense that the statute they are being accused of violating is unconstitutional. The most common constitutional grounds for challenging criminal statutes are that they are vague or overbroad or that they violate the First Amendment protections of freedom of speech and religion. For example, Gregory Johnson's conviction for burning an American flag was reversed when the U.S. Supreme Court ruled that the Texas flag desecration law violated the First Amendment freedom of speech clause.[12]

---

[12] Texas v. Johnson, 491 U.S. 397 (1989).

Legal Reasoning Exercise

2. Working as a member of the defense team, apply each of the three tests for insanity to determine whether this defendant might succeed with an insanity defense.

Emanuel Jones had been on medication for several years to stop the voices he heard in his head. He recently stopped taking his medication because it made him feel sleepy. Five days ago, during a visit with his best friend, Sam, Emanuel became angry and confused. He attacked Sam with a golf club and chased him from room to room as he tried to escape. He hit Sam several times with the golf club, and Sam died as the result of the wounds he sustained.

a. Emanuel walked out of the house and stopped at a nearby restaurant for a hamburger. When the waiter asked him how Sam was, Emanuel replied that he thought Sam was at home sleeping.

b. Before leaving the house Emanuel put the golf club and his bloody clothes in the bath tub and filled the tub with water. He changed his clothes and ran home.

c. When the police questioned Emanuel the next day and asked him about Sam, he replied, "I killed him. He'll be back tomorrow."

d. When the police questioned Emanuel the next day and asked him about Sam, he replied, "I killed him. I tried to stop, but he just kept laughing at me."

e. Several weeks after the incident and his return to his medication Emanuel expressed great grief and guilt over the death of Sam.

Consider the same facts as a member of the prosecution team. Do you come to the same conclusions?

Void for vagueness
A reason for invalidating a statute where a reasonable person could not determine a statute's meaning.

Overbreadth
A reason for invalidating a statute where it covers both protected and criminal activity.

Double jeopardy
A constitutional protection against being tried twice for the same crime.

The due process clauses of the Fifth and Fourteen Amendments can form the basis for a **void for vagueness** or **overbreadth** argument. For example, the Texas stalking statute made it illegal to engage in conduct that is "reasonably likely to harass, annoy, alarm, abuse, torment, or embarrass" someone. The highest Texas criminal appellate court found the statute to be unconstitutionally vague on its face.[13] Recently the overbreadth argument has been used to challenge city ordinances aimed at stopping gang activity. Such ordinances empower the police to order groups of loiterers to disperse if an officer reasonably believes one of the loiterers is a gang member. Obviously, such ordinances have the potential for abuse and for interfering with lawful activities. Therefore, because they cover both criminal activity and protected activity, these ordinances can be challenged as overbroad.

In cases involving the Fifth Amendment **double jeopardy clause**, defendants challenge the constitutionality of their prosecutions rather than that of the criminal laws under which they are being charged. They argue that they cannot be prosecuted because they have previously been tried for the same offense. Once jeopardy attaches, a defendant cannot be tried for the same offense again.

[13] Long v. State, 931 S.W.2d 285 (Tex. 1996).

Generally, jeopardy attaches once a jury has been selected. However, the same action can sometimes constitute two different criminal offenses. An act that is prosecuted as a homicide in state court may also be prosecuted as a violation of civil rights in federal court. Furthermore, double jeopardy does not prevent a civil action for damages that arose from the criminal action. Finally, if the defendant appeals a conviction and wins the appeal, the appellate court may remand the case for a new trial.

5. The Practice of Criminal Law

Because a criminal offense is viewed as an offense against the people, the attorneys who prosecute criminal cases are government employees. Most of these prosecutors are based in local **district attorneys'** or **states' attorneys'** offices. At the federal level they work in one of the **United States Attorneys'** offices spread around the country or for the Department of Justice.

Many defense attorneys are also employed by the government in **public defenders'** offices. The U.S. Supreme Court has interpreted the Sixth Amendment Aright to counsel" as requiring the government to provides attorneys for defendants who cannot afford to hire one on their own.[14] While the government can meet this burden by appointing private attorneys, many find it more cost effective to hire attorneys and paralegals specifically for the purposes of defending indigent defendants.

Private attorneys involved in the practice of criminal law often got their start as either prosecutors or public defenders. While some of the private attorneys who practice in the criminal law area specialize in criminal law, it is not uncommon for general practitioners to occasionally handle a criminal law case, especially if it deals with a relatively minor infraction.

Paralegals working on criminal cases often assist with the interviewing of witnesses and other investigative functions. Some prosecutor's offices have special victim assistance units. They also assist attorneys by preparing summaries of arrest reports and statements made to the police, doing legal research for pretrial motions, and preparing exhibits for trials. If appeals are involved they order and abstract copies of the record and do legal research on the issues that are involved in the appeal.

Paralegals may also work as research and writing assistants to judges, participate in victim/witness advocate programs, and in some jurisdictions

Many prosecutors use paralegals to work with crime victims. Paralegals may assist victims with investigations, preparation for trial, and impact statements. While paralegals may act as a type of advocate, paralegals may not dispense legal advice to the victims and should be supervised by an attorney.

---

[14] Gideon v. Wainwright, 372 U.S. 335 (1963).

even be assigned as court-appointed special advocates for children and others involved in criminal proceedings as victims or as defendants.

Paralegals should not ignore the possibilities for nontraditional roles within the criminal justice system. Law enforcement agencies hire paralegals as researchers, investigators, interpreters, and enforcement officers. Newspapers and magazines consider paralegals for positions as court liaisons who investigate and report on court proceedings. Paralegals are sometimes employed within the penal system as prison librarians. They may also serve as probation or parole officers and may work in prerelease or day-reporting programs, which help inmates make the transition from incarceration to the outside world.

DISCUSSION QUESTIONS

1. What does the Latin maxim *nullum crimen, null poena sine lege* mean, and why is it important for our understanding of criminal law?

2. What criteria should be used in determining when something should be considered a crime? For example, what, if any, "victimless crimes" should be decriminalized?

3. Some states, such as Illinois, distinguish between first and second degree murder. Study the Illinois statute on p. 220. How does that statute differentiate between first and second degree murder? What to you think was the legislators' rationale for making that distinction?

4. Which of the three major insanity defenses do you think is the most appropriate? Do you support the concept of "guilty but insane" verdict? Why or why not?

5. Why is the entrapment defense so controversial? Where do you think the line should be drawn with respect to what constitutes entrapment?

6. Do you support the "battered spouse's syndrome" defense? Why or why not?

B. CRIMINAL PROCEDURE

Civil and criminal procedure share many similarities, especially at the trial stage. However, there are significant differences as well. For example, whereas civil lawsuits begin with the official filing of the complaint, criminal cases begin with the arrest of the accused. Figure 10-3, on page 231, provides an overview of the stages in a criminal prosecution.

Be warned that the details of criminal procedure vary greatly among jurisdictions. For example, only about half the states have a grand jury system. Also, especially for misdemeanors, the stages may be accelerated or even combined.

PRACTICE TIP

To fully evaluate a file for procedural errors, the paralegal should read *every word* of the file. Do not overlook dates, times, and locations. Even a wrong date on a traffic ticket could make a difference!

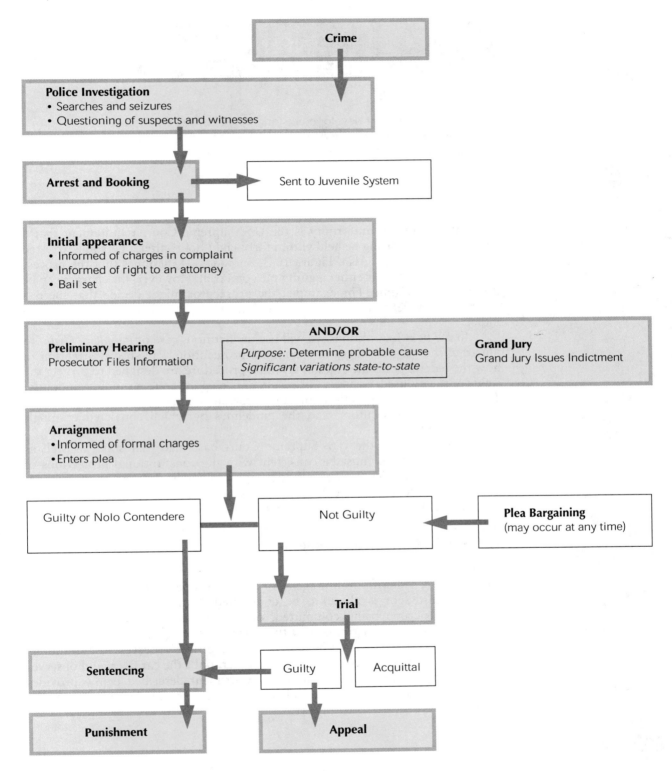

Figure 10-3   Stages in Criminal Procedure

NETNOTE

To read about recent developments and issues involving criminal justice, go to the home page of the American Civil Liberties Union at *http://aclu.org/issues/criminal/hmcj.html*.

The only mandated uniformity is the U.S. Supreme Court requirement that a probable cause hearing be held within forty-eight hours after a person is arrested without a warrant.[15] Also, Figure 10-3, on page 231, assumes that the process continues until there is either a guilty plea or a trial. However, the charges can be dropped at any time. For example, the prosecutor might decide that there is insufficient evidence to file an information, or the grand jury might refuse to indict.

In the next few sections we will use the fictitious case of *People v. Grant* to illustrate the various stages in a criminal prosecution. Pay special attention to how the federal and state rules of criminal procedure are designed to protect the rights of the accused, ensure a just result, and keep the system running smoothly. These rules cover the actions of law enforcement, the court system, defense attorneys and prosecutors, and the guidelines by which convicted criminals are sentenced.

Also note that the U.S. Supreme Court has ruled that state, as well as federal, prosecutions must be consistent with the constitutional protections of the Bill of Rights. Therefore, although approximately 95 percent of criminal prosecutions occur in state courts, the U.S. Constitution has a significant impact on how these prosecutions are conducted.

1. Investigation of the Crime

The criminal process usually begins when a law enforcement officer (such as a police officer, a sheriff, an FBI agent, or a state trooper) learns that a crime has been committed or is about to be committed. Either the officer personally observes the crime being committed, or the officer is sent to investigate a crime that either the victim or a witness has reported. A good example of the former would be a situation in which a police officer observes an automobile being driven in a dangerous and erratic manner, pulls the car over, and observes that the driver appears to be drunk. The incident described below provides an example of the situation in which the police learn of the crime from the victim.

---

[15] County of Riverside v. McLaughlin, 500 U.S. 44 (1991).

The Case of People v. Grant

When Stephen Joseph returned home about 10:00 P.M. on April 30, he discovered that the window of his porch door was broken and someone had taken his stereo, VCR, and television. Mr. Joseph called the police.

The police took information from Mr. Joseph, and they searched the scene for additional clues. The next door neighbor, Pat Baker, remembered seeing a van parked in Mr. Joseph's driveway earlier in the evening. According to the neighbor, the van had Grant's Audiovisual Equipment written on the side. She saw two men in dark clothes standing at the end of the driveway. When the police finished at the scene, they left the Joseph home.

At this stage the police are trying to determine if a crime was committed and, if so, who committed the crime. When police investigate a crime and search a crime scene, they are gathering the first, and sometimes the most important, information needed to solve the case. They typically interview any possible witnesses and collect physical evidence that might be linked to the perpetrator.

a. Search and Seizure

As part of their investigation the police will typically search the crime scene and seize evidence. For the results of those searches and seizures to be admissible in court, the police must comply with the requirements of the Fourth Amendment.

Amendment IV

The right of the people to be secure in their persons, houses, papers, and effects, against unreasonable searches and seizures, shall not be violated, and no Warrants shall issue, but upon probable cause, supported by Oath or affirmation, and particularly describing the place to be searched, and the persons or things to be seized.

As you can see, the Fourth Amendment requires that all searches and seizures be "reasonable." There are literally thousands of cases in which the courts have interpreted whether certain types of searches or seizures were "reasonable."

(1) Stop and frisk

The police are entitled to stop (detain) an individual for a brief period of time, to ask a few questions, and to frisk (pat down the outside of a suspect's clothes). The origin of this right dates back to 1963, when an Ohio police officer thought that a group of individuals was hanging around a street corner to plan a "stick-up." The officer asked the men to identify themselves. Then the officer patted down the men's clothing. The officer uncovered two guns. After one of the men was convicted of carrying a concealed weapon, he appealed to the U.S. Supreme Court. In *Terry v. Ohio*[16] the Supreme Court declared that the officer's stop and frisk was a search and seizure covered by the Fourth Amendment of the Constitution, giving the people the right "to be secure in their persons, houses, papers and effects, against unreasonable searches and seizures." However, because the intrusion into the person's privacy was slight, there was no Fourth Amendment violation.

Stop and frisk
The right of the police to detain an individual for a brief period of time and to search the outside of the person's clothing if the police have a reasonable suspicion that the individual has committed or is about to commit a crime.

---

[16] 392 U.S. 1 (1968).

Reasonable suspicion
A suspicion based on specific facts; less than probable cause.

But the police cannot stop and frisk any individual they want at any time they want. An individual, even a motorist, may be stopped only when the officer has a **reasonable suspicion** that the individual has committed, is in the process of committing, or is about to commit a crime. According to *Terry,* that reasonable suspicion must be based on "specific and articulable facts which, taken together with rational inferences from those facts, reasonably warrant that intrusion."[17] Therefore, an officer cannot simply guess that an individual is a suspect. The officer must be able to tell the court about the facts that led to the suspicion.

But what if the person stopped refuses to identify himself to the police officer? In *Hiibel v. Nevada,*[18] a Nevada police officer was responding to a call reporting that a man had assaulted a woman. When the officer found a man standing outside a parked truck that matched the description Court the police had been given and observed a woman inside the truck, the U.S. Supreme concluded that the officer had reasonable suspicion to stop the defendant and to ask him to identify himself. When the defendant did not do so, the police were justified in arresting him. So in states with "stop and identify" statutes, police officers may detain persons under suspicious circumstances, ask them to identify themselves, and arrest them if they refuse to do so. The Court also noted that asking an individual to reveal his or her name does not violate the Fifth Amendment privilege against self-incrimination.[19]

Consider what happened next in *People v. Grant.*

The Case of People v. Grant (continued)

As the police were returning to the station to file a report, they noticed two men in dark clothes walking about ten blocks from the Joseph home. The police turned on their cruiser lights and pulled up behind the men. After briefly questioning the men and patting down their clothes to make sure that they did not carry any weapons, the police determined that these men were late-night joggers and not related to the crime.

Based on the information the police gathered, they could argue there was reasonable suspicion that the men were involved in the crime.

- The neighbor's description of the men matched their appearances.
- They were two in number.
- They wore dark clothes.
- They were in the neighborhood of the crime late at night.

The court will also look at the circumstances of the stop. The length of time that the officers detain the suspect cannot be long. The longer the period of time is, the closer the court will look at the intrusiveness of the search. The court will also look at the number and the type of questions the police ask. If the questions

---

[17] Id. at 21.
[18] 542 U.S. 177 (2004).
[19] Id. at 191.

become detailed or the officers begin to accuse the suspect of committing a crime, then the court may consider the stop too intrusive.

The court will also look carefully at the circumstances of a frisk. Because the purpose of the frisk is to protect the officers and to aid in the detection and prevention of crime, the officers may frisk the suspect only if the officers, in their experience, believe that the suspect is carrying a weapon. The frisk may take place outside the suspect's clothes. The officers are not allowed to search the inside clothing or pockets of the suspect. If a motorist is stopped, the officer may pat down the areas within the suspect's immediate control, such as the car's seat.

(2) Arrest

Persons are under **arrest** when their freedom is restrained by law enforcement officers and they are charged with a crime. If the officers want to arrest or completely search a suspect, they must either have an **arrest warrant** or be able to prove independently that there is **probable cause**, a higher standard than "reasonable suspicion." To determine probable cause, the police can rely on their knowledge of the suspect and information provided by witnesses and victims. In the above example a stop and frisk was probably justified. There was not enough evidence, however, to establish probable cause for a full body search or an arrest.

Police can arrest a suspect with or without a warrant so long as there is probable cause to believe the suspect committed the crime. If, however, the arrest is to be made at a person's home, then generally an arrest warrant must first be obtained unless an exception exists, as when the police are in "hot pursuit" of a suspect.

(3) Searches and seizures of evidence

Searches of a suspect's home, business, or automobile and seizures of property from those locations are crucial law enforcement tools. Through legal searches and seizures officers may uncover items that are illegal on their face, such as illegal drugs or weapons. Officers may also locate the fruits of crime, such as stolen property, or the instruments of crime, such as burglary tools, weapons, and plans.

Because the Fourth Amendment protects only against unreasonable searches, the court must first determine whether the police activity constituted a search. To determine whether a search has taken place, the court evaluates the defendant's expectation of privacy. Some areas, such as a suspect's bedroom closet and the inside of a suspect's refrigerator, are private places where the

Arrest
Occurs when the police restrain a person's freedom and charge the person with a crime.

Probable cause
Not susceptible to a precise definition; a belief based on specific facts that a crime has been or is about to be committed; more than a reasonable suspicion.

PRACTICE TIP

Copies of all requests for warrants, the warrants themselves, and the officers' warrant receipts (also called returns) usually may be obtained from the clerk of court. These documents should be carefully compared to make sure that the warrants were properly requested, executed, and documented. If a flaw exists, a search might not be valid.

suspect expects people will enter only by the suspect's invitation. Other areas, such as the license plate of a suspect's automobile and the outside stairs of a suspect's home, are less private. The suspect expects that these areas will be seen by anyone passing by. Therefore, it is not a "search" to write down a speeding car's license plate number. Entering the private places in the suspect's life, however, constitutes a search for which the police must show probable cause.

Warrant
A court's prior permission for the police to search and seize.

Searches and seizures, if supported by probable cause, may be conducted with or without warrants. A **warrant** is the court's prior permission for the officers to search and seize. However, because the suspect's right to privacy is so important, the courts prefer that officers search with a warrant. The officers must show probable cause to the court that the items they seek are located where the officers intend to search. Here is what happened next in *People v. Grant*.

The Case of People v. Grant (continued)

After some investigation the officers determined that Bruce Grant is the owner of Grant's Audiovisual Equipment. By checking with the motor vehicle department the police also discovered that the vehicle was registered to Bruce Grant, age forty-two. The business is located at 17 Hastings Street. When they checked Mr. Grant's record, they discovered that he had twice been convicted of stealing audiovisual equipment and selling the stolen goods.

The officers wanted to search the business premises to look for Mr. Joseph's missing goods. They wanted to be able to take those goods, and any other stolen goods, from Mr. Grant's place of business to be used against him at a trial.

The officers went to court and told the judge what their investigation has produced. They told the judge exactly what they wanted to search (Grant's place of business and the inside of the van), and they told the judge exactly what they expected to find there (Mr. Joseph's stolen items). The judge determined that there was probable cause and issued the warrant to search.

The officers must show that they are looking for specific items and are not just going on a hunt to find something incriminating. The officers must show probable cause to believe that the items they seek are connected to criminal activity. In our case it would probably not be appropriate for the officers to simply ask the court for a warrant to search for TV sets because the business could have several TVs for sale that are not the products of the crime. The officers should list the specific brands, models, model numbers if they are known, and any other specific characteristics of the stolen items. Where the police are looking for illegal drugs, however, they need not be as specific. They can indicate on the warrant that they are looking for heroin because there is no legal heroin that can be found by mistake. The officers should also be as specific as possible about the location, noting street address, apartment number, or level. This not only makes the officers' probable cause stronger but also assists the officers who execute the warrant.

Execute
To perform.

The search warrant must be **executed**—that is, the search must actually be carried out—within a specific period of time. The officers must announce them-

selves as police officers and execute the warrant during the daytime unless the warrant specifically allows other arrangements. They must inventory and describe in writing all the items they seize, and usually they must give the suspect a receipt.

Under special conditions the courts will sometimes issue **no-knock warrants**, which allow the police to enter at night without announcing their presence in advance. In order to receive one of these special search warrants, the police must convince the judge that evidence is likely to be destroyed or that the police administering the warrant will be in danger.

One exception to the warrant requirement is the **plain view doctrine**. Because the Fourth Amendment is designed to protect one's privacy, it is reasoned that police have the right to seize contraband items or evidence of a crime when they see such items "in plain view." Therefore, when an officer looks in the driver's window of a car that has been stopped for a minor traffic offense, that police officer can seize a partially filled beer can that she observes sitting on the automobile's front seat.

In addition to the "plain view" circumstances discussed above, there are several other situations in which the police are not required to obtain a warrant prior to conducting a search. Figure 10-4, on page 238, lists the various **exigent circumstances** that allow for warrantless searches, the rationales behind them, and how they would affect the search in our case.

If one of the exigent circumstances applies to our case, then the officers may enter and search for or seize items from Grant's Audiovisual Equipment without a warrant. If the defendant objects to the search, the court will look carefully at the search by considering the totality of the circumstances—that is, all the facts that the officers and the defendant believe are true. The court will then decide whether the search was valid and whether the information found because of the search can be used against the defendant.

No-knock warrant
A warrant that allows the police to enter without announcing their presence in advance.

Plain view doctrine
Without the need for a warrant, the police may seize objects that are openly visible.

Exigent circumstances
Generally, an emergency situation that allows a search to proceed without a warrant.

DISCUSSION QUESTIONS

7. Which of the following areas do you think should be considered "private" and therefore require a warrant to be searched?
   a. your bedroom in your parents' home
   b. your garage
   c. your office at work
   d. your school locker
   e. your garbage that you have placed at your roadside curb

8. For each of the following, determine if you believe marijuana could be lawfully seized if its discovery was based on the following:
   a. Using a helicopter, the police fly over your fenced backyard and see it growing in pots on your back patio.
   b. Standing across the street from your house, the police use binoculars and see it growing inside your sunroom.
   c. Aiming a thermal-imaging device at your house, the police find suspicious "hot spots," indicating the probable presence of marijuana growing within your home.
   d. Using a police dog that has been specially trained to smell marijuana and other illegal drugs, the dog "points" to your briefcase, when
      i. you are walking down the street.
      ii. you are walking through an airport.

Exigent Circumstance	Rationale	Impact on Our Case
Plain view	The suspect leaves the item where it can be seen. The officers may not touch or move the item for a better view.	If the officers can see the Joseph equipment by looking into the windows of the shop, they may enter and seize it.
Consent	The suspect voluntarily invites the officers into the premises or lets the officers search his or her person. The suspect consents to the scope of the search, and the officers cannot exceed the scope.	If Mr. Grant allows the officers to search, they can seize anything they have probable cause to believe is related to the crime. Mr. Grant can limit their search to an area of any size and can demand that they stop searching at any time.
Third-party consent	If a person shares access and control of a location with the suspect, that person may give consent for the suspect.	If Mr. Grant has a partner who shares access to and control of the business, the partner can consent to the search.
Emergency (plain view items only)	The officers enter a premises to answer a call for help or to assist an emergency vehicle, such as an ambulance.	If Mr. Grant calls for help or suffers another emergency, the police cannot be expected to ignore illegal items in plain view.
Preservation of evidence	When evidence might be destroyed if the officers wait for the court to issue a warrant, they may act without one.	If the officers see Mr. Grant taking the Joseph equipment apart or otherwise destroying it, they can seize it.
Hot pursuit	When officers are chasing a suspect, they do not have to stop the chase when the suspect enters a building. They should enter, secure the location, and then get a warrant before searching.	If Mr. Grant runs from the scene of the crime with the police chasing him, the police can follow him into the store and arrest him but should not search until they get a warrant.
Incident to lawful arrest (vehicles and persons)	When a suspect is arrested, the officers need not get a warrant before searching the suspect's person or impounding and doing an inventory of the suspect's vehicle so that evidence is not destroyed or lost and the officers' lives are not endangered. The officers probably cannot search a locked glove box or trunk without a warrant.	If Mr. Grant is arrested and booked for a crime, the officers do not have to get a warrant before emptying his pockets.
Prisoners	Safety and security outweigh the privacy interests of prisoners. The Fourth Amendment does not apply to prisoners.	If Mr. Grant is in prison, his person and his room can be searched and items can be seized.

Figure 10-4   Exigent Circumstances Justifying Warrantless Searches

iii. your briefcase is located in the locked trunk of your car, and you have been stopped for speeding 6 miles per hour over the limit on a major highway.

b. Questioning Suspects

As previously noted, police officers usually investigate criminal activity by questioning victims and witnesses. As is well illustrated on TV shows, the interrogation of the leading suspects is one of the most glamorous parts of the investigation. In many cases the suspects will reveal information that can then be used against them in a trial. In some cases they even confess. If the suspects did not commit the crime, they may be able to help the officers refocus their investigation.

The Case of People v. Grant (continued)

When the search warrant was executed, the police found the stolen items in an unlocked cabinet in the rear of the store. The officers seized the equipment, gave Mr. Grant a receipt for the items they seized, and filed a report with the court. The police officers then asked Mr. Grant to come to the station to talk to them about the equipment. Mr. Grant rode along with them in the back seat of one of the patrol cars.

On the ride to the station one of the officers asked Mr. Grant where he had been on the evening of April 30. He replied that he and his cousin had gone to a movie. The officer then asked him what movie they had seen and what time it had started. Mr. Grant said they had gone to an 8 o'clock showing of Star Wars. Next the officer asked him where he had gotten the electronic equipment that they had seized from his store. He replied that he had taken it as a trade-in as part of a sale of a big-screen TV.

When they arrived at the police station, the officers took Mr. Grant into an interrogation room and read him his Miranda rights. He responded that he did not want to talk to them unless he had an attorney present. When they gave him a telephone so he could call his attorney, he told them he wanted a court-appointed attorney because he could not afford to hire one on his own.

Both the Fifth and Sixth Amendments to the Constitution are relevant to interrogation situations. The Fifth Amendment prohibits law enforcement agents from forcing defendants to give testimonial evidence that would tend to incriminate them. Note that this applies only to testimonial evidence and does not protect a suspect from having to take a breathalizer test, to be fingerprinted, or to provide a handwriting sample. The Sixth Amendment guarantees a right to be represented by an attorney.

Amendment V

No person shall . . . be compelled in any criminal case to be a witness against himself. . . .

Amendment VI

In all criminal prosecutions, the accused shall enjoy the right to . . . have the assistance of counsel for his defense.

In the landmark cases of *Escobedo v. Illinois*[20] and *Miranda v. Arizona*[21] the U.S. Supreme Court ruled that the privilege against self-incrimination and the right to assistance of counsel apply to the interrogation stage, as well as to the trial. The Court reasoned that the right to counsel at trial would not benefit the defendant if the defendant had already confessed before meeting with an attorney and that the presence of an attorney during an interrogation would help to ensure that any statements given would be truly voluntary rather than coerced. The famous **Miranda warnings** are designed to notify defendants of their rights and to explain those rights in language they will understand.

Miranda warnings
The requirement that defendants be notified of their rights to remain silent and to have an attorney present prior to being questioned by the police.

Miranda Warnings

Prior to custodial interrogation, the suspect must be told of these rights:

1. The right to remain silent.
2. That anything said can be used against the suspect in a court of law.
3. The right to the presence of an attorney.
4. That if the suspect cannot afford an attorney, one will be appointed prior to any questioning.[22]

Once these *Miranda* warnings are given, the police cannot interrogate the suspect further unless he or she waives these rights.

Although the *Miranda* warnings are now firmly entrenched in our criminal justice system, at the time it was announced the *Miranda* decision was quite controversial. Prior to *Miranda* courts had judged the admissibility of a suspect's confession under a voluntariness test. Under that approach, the voluntary nature of a confession and hence its admissibility as evidence of guilt was judged based on all of the circumstances, rather than being subject to exclusion solely because the suspect was not advised of his or her rights. Two years after *Miranda* was decided, Congress enacted a law that was intended to nullify the *Miranda* decision and to return the requirement to the voluntariness test that prevailed prior to *Miranda*. This federal statute was largely ignored until the late 1990s when the United States Court of Appeals for the Fourth Circuit held that *Miranda* was not required by the Constitution. Thus Congress had the power by statute to have the final say on the question of the admissibility of confessions. According to the Fourth Circuit, the totality-of-the-circumstances test outlined in the statute and not the *Miranda* warnings were to be used by courts to determine the

---

[20] 378 U.S. 478 (1964).
[21] 384 U.S. 436 (1966).
[22] Id. at 479.

voluntary nature and hence admissibility of confessions. The Supreme Court disagreed. In *Dickerson v. United States*, the Court held that "*Miranda*, being a constitutional decision of this Court, may not be in effect overruled by an Act of Congress."[23] Therefore, *Miranda* and not the federal statute continues to govern the admissibility of statements made during custodial interrogations in both state and federal courts.

In the *People v. Grant* case we have been discussing, the police read Mr. Grant his *Miranda* rights before they began questioning him at the police station. However, they questioned him in the car about his activities on the night of the burglary before they informed him of his *Miranda* rights. Did this questioning in the car constitute an interrogation, and were the police required to have read the *Miranda* rights before they questioned him in the car?

The answer depends on the definition of a custodial interrogation. Suspects are in police custody when they feel that their freedom has been deprived in a significant way. It does not matter whether the suspects have been arrested (formally charged with a crime), although an arrest might indicate that the suspects are not free to leave. When suspects are in police custody and are questioned by the police, it is difficult, and maybe even frightening, for them to say, "No, thank you," to police questions. Therefore, before beginning this custodial interrogation (questioning of suspects when they feel that their liberty has been deprived), the police are required to tell the suspects about their rights.

However, what constitutes "interrogation" is not always clear. In *Rhode Island v. Innis*,[24] the U.S. Supreme Court had to determine whether a back-and-forth conversation between two patrolmen constituted an interrogation. The patrolmen had arrested the defendant on suspicion of murder and robbery. After advising him of his *Miranda* rights, they began to drive him to the station house. The shotgun that had been used in both crimes was missing, and the two patrolmen began a conversation in which they noted how terrible it would be if a child should find the gun. After "overhearing" this conversation, the defendant interrupted the patrolmen, told them to turn the car around, and led them to the gun's location. The issue before the Court was whether the conversation was an improper interrogation. If it was, then the gun should not have been used at trial as evidence against the defendant. The Court, however, ruled that the officer's expression of concern about innocent children being hurt did not constitute the type of interrogation that required *Miranda* warnings. Therefore, the gun was admissible.

Although suspects have the right not to answer questions during custodial interrogation, this does not mean that they have to remain silent. Suspects may waive their *Miranda* rights as long as they do so voluntarily, knowingly, and intelligently. To determine whether a suspect waived his or her rights, the court will look carefully at all the circumstances. The court will consider the educational level of the suspect, language barriers, the existence of a mental condition or impairments, addictions to alcohol or illegal substances, the suspect's prior court experiences, the duration and intensity of the questioning period, and any other facts brought to the court's attention. The prosecution has the burden of proving that the defendant made a proper waiver.

---

[23] Dickerson v. U.S., 530 U.S. 428 (2000).

[24] 446 U.S. 291 (1980).

A signed *Miranda* card and evidence of the defendant's waiver of rights should be part of the defendant's file. The defense team should have access to these records so that motions to suppress can be considered. Police departments can be compelled to give this information to the defense team.

To avoid confusion about whether a suspect received *Miranda* warnings or about whether there were proper waivers of the suspect's rights, law enforcement agencies usually require defendants to sign a card that lists the suspect's rights and asks the defendant questions, such as these:

1. Do you understand these rights as they have been explained to you?
2. Understanding these rights, do you wish to speak to me now?
3. Please sign this card indicating that you understand the above information.

In addition to the *Miranda* cards, many police departments videotape or tape-record the suspects as they receive their rights and consider waiving their rights. Then if the suspects later claim that they did not receive their rights or that they did not understand the waiver of their rights, the police have documentation to show to the court.

Once a suspect decides to remain silent, the police cannot continue the questioning and must give the suspect an opportunity to communicate with an attorney. The police cannot try to continue questioning at a later time unless an attorney is present. A suspect can waive his or her *Miranda* rights at a later interrogation.

Juvenile suspects are also entitled to be given their *Miranda* rights. In addition to a right to speak to an attorney, juvenile suspects are given the right to talk to an interested adult, such as a parent or guardian, before deciding to waive their rights. Because of their age or in some circumstances because of their lack of experience with the criminal justice system, juveniles may need extra help making such important decisions. Just as parents or guardians may help juveniles with other life decisions, the court recognizes that a juvenile needs the extra protection that talking to a trusted adult may provide.

PRACTICE TIP

Many police stations now videotape the booking process. This protects the police from allegations of abuse and protects defendants from the misuse of police powers at booking. These tapes may also provide evidence of a defendant's physical or mental condition at booking. Defense teams and prosecutors must carefully review all booking materials. There may be sanctions against the prosecutors if they fail to provide these materials to the defense.

Because Mr. Grant told police that he did not wish to be questioned without his lawyer being present and because he indicated that he could not afford to hire a lawyer, the police must withhold any further questioning until they can arrange to have a public defender present or have the court appoint counsel.

Legal Reasoning Exercises

3. Using the standard discussed in this chapter, did custodial interrogation take place during the following incidents?

a. A suspect ran up to the police officer and cried, "Help! I killed him. I killed him. I didn't mean to do it!"

b. An officer walked up to a group of boys hanging around a street corner and said, "Hey, guys. What are you doing here?"

c. While at the police station the suspect explained how he stole the car from the parking lot down the street.

d. As an officer asked questions, the suspect wrote answers on a piece of paper.

e. In the case scenario being used in this chapter the police questioned Bruce Grant on the ride to the police station.

2. The Court System

A suspect's involvement with the court system begins with the initial appearance and then continues through a series of stages, eventually leading to either a guilty or a not guilty plea. If a guilty plea is entered, the case moves into the sentencing phase. If a not guilty plea is entered, the case is scheduled for trial. Finally, in some situations either the defendant or the prosecution may appeal the results of a court proceeding.

a. Formal Charges, Initial Appearances, and Bail

The formal process of charging someone with a crime begins by notifying the person that he or she is being placed under arrest. How a defendant actually discovers that he or she must answer to criminal charges depends on the circumstances of the case. In some cases, especially when the crime is a misdemeanor, the defendant may be notified by mail to appear at court to answer criminal charges. When the defendant is caught in the act or shortly thereafter, he or she may be arrested on the spot without a warrant. Otherwise, officers must obtain a warrant for arrest.

Normally a defendant who is arrested is brought to the police facility and booked. The **booking process** usually includes taking the defendant's personal information, giving the defendant an opportunity to read and sign a *Miranda* card, and allowing the defendant the opportunity to use a telephone. Additionally, the police may take photographs, or "mug shots," of the defendant for identification purposes. The police may also require the defendant to be fingerprinted. Fingerprints may then be compared to fingerprints found at the scene of the crime or saved to be compared to prints found at future crime scenes.

Booking
The process after arrest that includes taking the defendant's personal information, giving the defendant an opportunity to read and sign a *Miranda* card, and allowing the defendant the opportunity to use a telephone.

The defendant is then searched, and his or her belongings are inventoried and stored by the police.

Some defendants are released by the police after the booking process is completed. They are usually given the date of their first court appearances and instructed that they must appear at court or risk a court default. Other defendants may give the police a fee and promise to appear as instructed to face criminal charges. The process of giving money and promising to appear as instructed is called **posting bail**. Usually, when the case is over, the court will return the bail money to the defendants. Persons can also be released prior to the trial date on a **personal recognizance bond**, by which defendants personally promise to appear in court when instructed to do so. These defendants are indebted to pay a specified amount if they fail to fulfill the conditions of the bond. In many states one's driver's license is accepted in lieu of a cash bail for most traffic offenses. Other defendants may be held in the police facility until the next possible court session, when they are delivered by the police into the custody of the court.

Bail
Money or something else of value that is held by the government to ensure the defendant's appearance in court.

Personal recognizance bond
A defendant's personal promise to appear in court.

The Case of People v. Grant (continued)

On the basis of the witness's testimony about seeing the Grant's Audiovisual Equipment van and the evidence seized from Mr. Grant's store, the police were convinced that Mr. Grant had burglarized Stephen Joseph's home. They therefore informed him that he was under arrest and began the process of fingerprinting and booking him.

The following morning he was taken to court to have bail set and to determine if he was qualified to have a public defender appointed. At this initial appearance the judge told Mr. Grant of the charges being brought against him, set bail at $5,000, and denied his request for a public defender because he appeared to have enough assets in his business to be able to afford to hire his own attorney.

His case was then bound over to the grand jury to determine if there was sufficient evidence to proceed to trial.

After an individual has been placed in custody, the law requires that he or she be brought before a judge or magistrate without unnecessary delay. At this initial appearance the defendant must be told of the charges being brought against him or her, be advised of the right to counsel, and have bail set. In some states the amount of bail is preset for minor offenses, and the accused can post bail at the police station prior to this initial appearance.

At the initial appearance a defendant who cannot afford the services of a private attorney will usually have either a public defender or a member of the private bar appointed to provide representation. Most courts have developed local guidelines that take into consideration the income and assets of the defendant, as well as the nature of the offense. In *Scott v. Illinois*[25] the U.S. Supreme Court ruled that attorneys do not have to be provided in all misdemeanor cases

---

[25] 440 U.S. 367 (1979).

but that indigent defendants cannot be given jail sentences unless they either were provided with counsel or waived their right to such representation.

b. Preliminary Hearings and Grand Juries

A defendant in a felony case cannot be put through the ordeal of a trial solely on the authority of the prosecutor. The evidence must be tested independently to determine whether sufficient probable cause exists to justify placing the individual on trial. This independent testing of the evidence often occurs through a preliminary hearing or the use of the grand jury.

The Fifth Amendment to the U.S. Constitution requires that "[n]o person shall be held to answer for a capital, or otherwise infamous crime, unless on a presentment or indictment of a Grand Jury. . . . " Although this applies only to federal cases, about half the states require the use of a **grand jury.** Other states allow the prosecutor the option of using or not using a grand jury; some do not use grand juries at all.

Historically, grand juries were seen as a protection against arbitrary governmental prosecutions. Today, however, there are many who advocate abolition of the grand jury system. Critics point out that the government, in the form of the prosecutors, has too much control over the proceedings. It is the prosecutor who presents witnesses and evidence. The defendant is not even allowed to attend, and the proceedings are kept secret. Generally, the use of grand juries does appear to be declining. The federal government and most states that do use grand juries follow the common-law format of having twenty-three persons serve during a term and requiring at least twelve votes for an **indictment.**

As an aside, the grand jury also can serve as an investigative arm of the government and can be especially useful when it comes to investigating organized crime or corruption in the government's own bureaucracy. The Watergate grand jury is probably the most famous example of a grand jury used for such investigations. The ability to subpoena and give immunity to key witnesses makes the grand jury an effective weapon in the hands of a well-trained prosecutor. When the grand jury takes on this type of investigative role, its investigations frequently include people who are not yet under arrest. If the grand jury decides that those people should be brought to trial, arrest warrants are issued on the basis of the grand jury's indictment. Defendants arrested in this manner go directly from the initial appearance stage to the arraignment.

In sum, the main function of a preliminary hearing or a grand jury proceeding is to review the government's case to determine whether there is enough evidence to justify holding the defendant for trial. If a grand jury is used and the decision is to proceed, an indictment is issued. If the same decision is reached after a preliminary hearing, the prosecutor files an **information.**

Grand jury
A group of people, usually twenty-three, whose function is to determine if probable cause exists to believe that a crime has been committed and that the defendant committed it.

Indictment
A grand jury's written accusation that a given individual has committed a crime.

Information
A prosecutor's written accusation that a given individual has committed a crime.

The Case of People v. Grant (continued)

Two weeks later the grand jury heard testimony from the police officers who had taken the report of what had been stolen from Mr. Joseph's home and had interviewed the witness about seeing the Grant's Audiovisual Equipment truck there. It also heard from the officer who was involved in executing the search warrant and had heard Mr. Grant

say that he had been watching Star Wars at the local theater that night. In addition to describing the goods they had seized, the officer reported that when he checked with the local theaters, he discovered that none had been showing Star Wars on April 30.

The grand jury never heard any testimony from Mr. Grant.

The grand jury then followed the prosecuting attorney's suggestion and indicted Bruce Grant for possession of stolen property, selling stolen property, and larceny.

Finally, not all states require either a preliminary hearing or a grand jury indictment. In some instances, especially for misdemeanors, after the initial court appearance the prosecutor can simply file the information.

c. Arraignments, the Exclusionary Rule, and Pretrial Motions

Arraignment
A criminal proceeding at which the court informs the defendant of the charges being brought against him or her and the defendant enters a plea.

At the **arraignment** the court informs the defendant of the charges contained in the indictment or the information. The judge then asks the defendant to answer the charges by pleading guilty or not guilty. If the defendant wishes to plead guilty, the judge must speak with the defendant to be sure that he or she understands the nature of the charge, the minimum and maximum sentences prescribed by law, and that by entering a guilty plea he or she waives the right to have a trial and to confront and cross-examine witnesses. The prosecution usually reads the facts of the case, and the defendant agrees that the facts are true. If the court determines that the defendant is aware of the guilty plea and is voluntarily pleading guilty, usually the court will ask the prosecution to recommend the sentence. The judge may either pronounce the sentence at that time or set a specific time for a sentencing hearing at some later date.

Plea bargaining
A process whereby the prosecutor and the defendant's attorney agree for the defendant to plead guilty in exchange for the prosecutor's promise to charge him or her with a lesser offense, drop some additional charges, or request a lesser sentence.

Sometimes the prosecution and the defense negotiate the defendant's punishment. This negotiation is called **plea bargaining**. In plea bargaining the defendant may agree to plead guilty to the crime, or to a lesser included offense of the crime, in exchange for the prosecution's recommendation for a lighter sentence. The judge may consider the results of the plea bargain but is not required to accept it. If the defendant enters a not guilty plea, a tentative date is set for the trial based on whether the defendant requests a jury trial or a bench trial.

Nolo contendere
A defendant's plea meaning that the defendant neither admits nor denies the charges.

Defendants usually have a third option at arraignment. They may plead **nolo contendere**. This Latin phrase means "no contest." A defendant neither admits nor denies the charges. He or she simply agrees that if the case went to trial, the prosecution would have sufficient evidence to prove its case beyond a reasonable doubt. This plea is not considered an admission of guilt and so cannot be used later against the defendant at a civil trial. However, for purposes of the arraignment the case proceeds as though the defendant had pleaded guilty.

The Case of People v. Grant (continued)

Mr. Grant was released from custody after posting his bond, and he arrived at his arraignment with a private attorney he had hired. The judge informed him that he had been charged with possessing

stolen property, selling stolen property, and committing larceny. Following his attorney's advice Mr. Grant pleaded not guilty and demanded a jury trial. The judge accepted his plea and assigned the case to the next jury calendar.

At this point Mr. Grant's attorney filed a motion to require the state to turn over police notes regarding interviews with witnesses. She also moved to suppress the statements her client had made in the back of the police car about his activities on the night of the crime.

As in civil proceedings, the parties in a criminal case have an opportunity to use various discovery devices to avoid "trial by ambush." Although the particulars vary from one jurisdiction to another, the defense generally has a right to discover all the evidence that the prosecution intends to use at trial, including such things as the names, addresses, and statements of persons that the prosecution intends to call as witnesses; transcripts of any electronic surveillance; and physical evidence, such as a gun, a knife, illegal drugs, or the results of scientific tests. In addition to turning over **inculpatory evidence**, which suggests the defendant's guilt, the prosecution is required to produce **exculpatory evidence,** which suggests that the defendant did not commit the crime. If the prosecution refuses to provide discovery to the defense, the defense team may file motions to compel the evidence and ask the court to force the prosecution to supply the evidence. The prosecution, in turn, has a right to have the defendant appear in line-ups, give handwriting samples, provide names and addresses of people who will be called as defense witnesses, and provide results of laboratory and medical reports to be used as evidence.

The most common pretrial motions relate to facilitating the discovery process and preventing certain types of evidence from being used at the trial. Figure 10-5, on pages 248–249, lists the motions you are most likely to encounter. Note, however, that not all of these are available in every jurisdiction. You need to check local court rules to determine the availability and format of specific motions. The federal and state rules of criminal procedure typically require that motions be accompanied by a memorandum of law, analyzing how the courts have decided similar motions in past cases and arguing how the motions should be decided in this case.

Because criteria for presenting and proving each motion depend on the jurisdiction, not all of these motions are available to every defendant and prosecutor in every jurisdiction. Other pretrial motions may also be available. The format and requirements for each motion, such as the requirement to file a memorandum of law to accompany the motion, will also depend on the jurisdiction. Remember, nothing in the table of typical motions, or in this chapter, takes the place of your research in your own jurisdiction.

Inculpatory evidence
Evidence that suggests the defendant's guilt.

Exculpatory evidence
Evidence that suggests the defendant's innocence.

P R A C T I C E T I P

Many prosecutors and defense teams create checklists of possible pretrial motions and attach them to each case. Using a checklist helps the parties evaluate all the possible motions. By including the criteria for each motion on the checklist, the parties can save valuable time during strategy meetings.

The plea is the defendant's decision, *not* the attorney's decision. Helping the defendant determine the proper plea is an important defense team task, especially if plea bargaining is involved. It is the defense team's responsibility to ensure that the defendant is aware of all plea options and has an opportunity to discuss those options with an attorney.

Ethics Alert

Type of Motion	Goal	Rationale
Motion to suppress	To eliminate all or some of the evidence against the defendant	Without evidence, the state cannot meet its burden of proof. Evidence obtained during an illegal search and seizure, or other improper behavior, may be suppressed.
Motion to dismiss	To dismiss all or some of the charges against the defendant	The best way for the defense team to win is to get the case (or at least a few charges) dismissed before subjecting the defendant to the dangers of trial.
Motion to compel	To force the opposition to provide evidence that has been refused	There is no more trial by ambush. The prosecution must disclose inculpatory *and* exculpatory evidence.
Motion to server	To try multiple defendants at separate trials	If several defendants are tried together, they may be deprived of certain defenses that point to another defendant as more culpable, and the jury may be overwhelmed and confused about what evidence pertains to each defendant. Through this motion the court attempts to eliminate undue prejudice.
Motion to bifurcate	To isolate the charges against a defendant and try each charge at a separate trial	If the jury would be misled by alternative charges, the defendant would benefit by defending against one charge at a time. Prejudice and unfairness are considered proper grounds under most circumstances.
Motion for a bill of particulars	To force the prosecution to provide specific information regarding the case	The defense team is entitled to know the details of the case with as much specificity as possible.
Motion to sequester witnesses	To keep witnesses out of the courtroom until after they testify	The testimony of one witness or the questioning tactics used by the attorneys may influence the testimony of witnesses yet to testify. Keeping witnesses outside the courtroom may help keep their testimony pure.

Figure 10-5   Typical Pretrial Motions

Type of Motion	Goal	Rationale
Motion to recuse	To remove a particular judge from a case	If a judge knows a victim or defendant in a case, publicly voices an opinion about the outcome of the case, or otherwise has a conflict of interest, the judge should step down, and another judge should proceed.
Motion for funds	To allow indigent defendants access to funds from the state	An indirect defendent has the same legal needs for trial preparation as a wealthy defendant. Money may be made available through the court for expert witnesses, scientific tests, or other investigatory needs.
Motion for change of venue	To achieve an impartial jury panel through a request for a change of the location for trial	Sometimes a defendant cannot get a fair trial in the location where the crime was committed. Pretrial publicity or local prejudice may inhibit justice.
Motion to continue	To change the date of trial, usually to postpone to a later date	The parties may require more time to prepare or to allow witnesses to travel to the trial. Attorneys, witnesses, or the defendant could fall ill. When the trial cannot proceed as scheduled, this motion should be filed. Motions of this type, if not abused, are usually allowed.
Motion in limine	To make evidentiary and trial decisions prior to the beginning of trial	Some decisions, such as the order of witnesses, the scope of examination or cross-examination, and the admission of certain documents, may be decided by the parties prior to the start of trial. This speeds up the trial process and avoids bickering in front of the jury.
Motion for a view	To let the jury visit the scene of the crime	A viewing can give the jury members a better understanding of the crime scene than they could otherwise gain from witness testimony alone.

Figure 10-5   (continued)

Because these pretrial motions are designed to significantly influence the course of the case, defending against pretrial motions is a crucial job. Carefully dissect the factual analysis, legal research, and legal reasoning of your opponent's motion and, if applicable, the supporting memoranda of law. Do not take any detail or citation for granted.

DISCUSSION QUESTION

9. How do you reconcile the purpose behind a motion for a view with the traditional belief that jurors are supposed to base their decision solely on what they hear and see in the courtroom?

Motion to suppress
A request that the court prohibit the use of certain evidence at the trial.

Exclusionary rule
A rule that states that evidence obtained in violation of an individual's constitutional rights cannot be used against that individual in a criminal trial.

A **motion to suppress,** the first type of motion listed in Figure 10-5, on page 248, is a request to have the court prohibit the use of certain evidence at the trial. Motions to suppress are based on what is known as the exclusionary rule. Under the terms of the **exclusionary rule,** evidence that has been obtained in violation of an individual's constitutional rights cannot be used against that individual in a criminal trial. For example, if police interrogate a suspect without first informing him of his *Miranda* rights, then the confession cannot be used in court. The exclusionary rule applies to both state and federal prosecutions. The rationale for this rule was explained by the U.S. Supreme Court in the landmark case of *Mapp v. Ohio.*[26] Not only does the rule deter police from using illegal means to catch criminals, but also the integrity of the judicial system itself would be compromised by the admission of evidence gathered in violation of constitutional requirements.

Fruit of the poisonous tree doctrine
Evidence that is derived from an illegal search or interrogation is inadmissible.

The exclusionary rule applies to evidence that is illegally obtained, such as the confession mentioned above. If that evidence in turn leads to the discovery of other evidence (such as the location of stolen property), that evidence is likewise inadmissible under the doctrine known as the **fruit of the poisonous tree.** Any evidence that is spawned by or directly derived from an illegal search or illegal interrogation is inadmissible against the defendant by virtue of being tainted by original illegality. If the tree (the primary evidence) has been poisoned from the illegal search, then all the fruit (collateral or additional evidence) must also be suppressed.

The application of the exclusionary rule does not invalidate the arrest or prevent the defendant from being convicted on the basis of independent evi-

Ethics Alert

It may be considered legal malpractice *not* to file a motion to suppress evidence when that motion has a probability for success. Any time there is a search, the file should be carefully evaluated to determine whether these motions are required.

---

[26] 367 U.S. 643 (1961).

Legal Reasoning Exercise

4. Suppose someone fired a bullet through the floor of an apartment into the apartment below. The police entered the shooter's apartment looking for the shooter, for other weapons, and possibly for victims. While they were in the apartment, the police discovered weapons and a stocking cap. The police also noticed stereo equipment and, suspecting it was stolen, recorded the serial numbers. In order to read all the numbers, the police moved some of the equipment. When the police headquarters notified the police that the equipment was stolen, the police officers seized it.

a. If you worked as a paralegal for the defense team, what arguments would you make to convince the court to suppress the evidence?

b. If you worked for the prosecution, what arguments would you make to convince the court that the search was legal?

c. Which side has the most persuasive arguments?

dence. Nor does it prohibit officers from later conducting legal searches and gathering additional evidence as long as that evidence was gathered without the aid of knowledge gained from the tainted evidence that was suppressed. Nevertheless, the exclusionary rule does make law enforcement's job more difficult, and police may not be able to gather enough evidence to obtain a conviction. In these cases the application of the exclusionary rule does in fact result in guilty persons going free.

d. Plea Bargaining

The Case of People v. Grant (continued)

After several continuances had pushed back the original court date, the judge announced that he would tolerate no further delays in the case and that both attorneys needed to be ready to begin the trial on January 10. Shortly before Christmas Mr. Grant's attorney called the assistant prosecutor that had been assigned to the case to discuss the terms of a possible plea bargain.

The prosecutor offered to drop the larceny charges if Mr. Grant would plead guilty to possession of stolen property. Mr. Grant's attorney then proceeded to inquire as to what the prosecutor would recommend for jail time if her client accepted this offer. When the prosecutor said five years, she countered with one year. The prosecutor then laughed and said that his absolute minimum offer was four years. She responded that she would discuss the offer with her client but that she doubted he would accept. When she discussed the matter with Mr. Grant, he told her he would rather take his chances with a trial.

Plea bargaining was mentioned briefly above in the context of arraignment. However, a plea bargain can happen at any time in the process. Ninety percent of criminal cases never reach trial, as they are settled through a plea bargain. The defendant agrees to plead guilty to a criminal charge in exchange for a reduction in the charges or the sentence. The incentives offered by the government can include reducing the severity of the charge (for example, the prosecutor can settle for a guilty plea on a robbery charge where the original charge was for the more serious offense of armed robbery), dropping related counts (for example, an original indictment may include three counts of burglary, but the prosecutor may agree to drop two of them in return for a guilty plea to the third), and recommending the minimum sentence or even a suspended sentence rather than going for the maximum authorized by the law.

Prosecutors are willing to make these types of bargains for a variety of reasons. Because most prosecutors' offices are understaffed and overworked, plea bargaining provides a way to more efficiently manage their workloads and produce high conviction rates. Many prosecutors are willing to settle for a sure conviction on the record with at least some jail time for the defendant rather than risking an uncertain conviction for the sake of longer jail time. In *Santobello v. New York*[27] the U.S. Supreme Court spoke of the benefits of encouraging plea bargaining in a case in which the government tried to change the terms of a bargain after the defendant had entered a guilty plea. The Court stated that this was improper. Once a deal has been struck and the defendant has entered a guilty plea, the state cannot change the terms of the agreement.

e. The Right to a Jury Trial

The Sixth Amendment to the U.S. Constitution creates a right to trial by an impartial jury in federal criminal cases. The due process clause of the Fourteenth Amendment applies the right to a trial by jury to defendants in state criminal actions who face possible incarceration of six months or more.[28]

The U.S. Constitution requires that criminal juries at the federal level consist of twelve members and that their verdicts be unanimous. The U.S. Supreme Court has ruled that six-member juries are permissible at the state level,[29] as are less-than-unanimous verdicts.[30] It is left to the states to select which of these options they wish to use.

One of the most frequently misunderstood principles of the jury system is the concept of being tried before a jury of one's peers. This does not mean that the jury must consist of a group of people who are similar to the defendant. Rather the jury simply must be broadly representative of the community in which the trial takes place.

If the defendant waives the right to a jury trial, a bench trial is held, in which the judge serves as the fact finder, as well as the presiding officer.

PRACTICE TIP

Many prosecutors and defense teams hire jury specialists who can create "perfect" juror profiles to assist with jury selection.

[27] 404 U.S. 257 (1971).
[28] Baldwin v. New York, 399 U.S. 66 (1970).
[29] Williams v. Florida, 399 U.S. 78 (1970).
[30] Apodaca v. Oregon, 406 U.S. 404 (1972).

f. Trial Procedures

There are few, but very important, differences between civil and criminal trials. The major difference is that the prosecutor in a criminal case must bear the burden of a higher standard of proof, beyond a reasonable doubt, as opposed to preponderance of the evidence. The defense is not required to put the defendant, or any other witnesses, on the stand. If the defendant chooses not to testify, the prosecution cannot comment or otherwise draw attention to it during any part of the trial.

The prosecution goes first, presenting all the information necessary to meet its burden of proof beyond a reasonable doubt. Through witnesses and the introduction of evidence the prosecution attempts to prove each element of each charge. With cross-examination of the prosecution's witnesses, the defense attempts to discredit their testimony.

When the prosecution has completed its case, it "rests." At that time, in most jurisdictions, the defense may make a **motion to require a finding of not guilty** for some or all of the charges. Outside of the hearing of the jury the defense may argue

Motion to require a finding of not guilty
The defense's request that the court find the prosecution failed to meet its burden and that it remove the case from the jury by finding the defendant not guilty.

PRACTICE TIP

Prepare Your Case for Trial

Every legal team, whether prosecution or defense, has a slightly different way of preparing for trial. Some attorneys carefully craft in advance every word they plan to speak at trial, including both their opening and their closing arguments. They also draft every question they anticipate asking during examination and cross-examination of witnesses. Other teams take a more open approach, knowing in advance what material they need to present during opening and closing arguments and having goals to reach with each witness but leaving the actual construction of questions to the moment at trial. And, yes, some attorneys do not appear to prepare for their performance in any meaningful way. So, in the role of trial support, the paralegal should adopt the technique of the attorneys but concentrate on preparing as much as possible in advance of trial to avoid last-minute confusion and to reduce last-minute stress.

Organize materials: Many attorneys and paralegals find it helpful to prepare a trial notebook that contains all the documents they may need during the trial. Include reports, statements, documents to be entered into evidence, the names and addresses of potential witnesses, some sample questions, and clean copies of all statutes and court opinions used to support motions and memoranda of law. Organize them for easy access.

Subpoena all witnesses: Even witnesses you believe are anxious to testify should be summonsed and required to attend. Remember, today's friend might be tomorrow's disinterested acquaintance or, even worse, tomorrow's enemy. Do not count on good will alone to get witnesses to court. If witnesses who were not subpoenaed fail to appear, the attorney tries the case without them. If subpoenaed witnesses fail to appear, they may be brought to court by the police or sheriff.

Prepare the defendant and witnesses for trial: Never assume that the potential witnesses will be as comfortable testifying in court as they were

discussing the case in your office or at home. Reviewing potential questions and preparing your witnesses for the stress of cross-examination are crucial. Remember, however, that you may not supply the answers, and witnesses should testify only to their own personal knowledge. You may also want to review documents, such as police reports and witness or defendant statements, so that the witnesses can remember what they might have said or done at earlier stages of the proceedings.

Prepare Yourself for Trial

Read the case file from start to finish, including all motions and all supporting law.

Make a list or a file of all motions filed by each party and the outcomes of the motions. The attorneys or the judge may forget what was actually decided as the result of any motion.

Make a list of all potential witnesses, their addresses, and their telephone numbers. Keep one copy of the list in the file, and keep one copy with you in case you must contact witnesses in a hurry.

Prepare explicit directions to the courthouse for potential witnesses, and carry them with you in case witnesses get lost on the way. Decide with the attorneys before trial whether to provide taxi assistance for expected witnesses.

Bring coins or the office telephone calling card number with you so that you can use pay telephones in an emergency. There is no feeling like the one of needing to make a call and having to beg for help.

Wear clothes that reflect your important position at trial. Conform to local customs and habits, but remember that you may have to move in a hurry and should not encumber yourself with unnecessarily complicated clothes, shoes, and accessories. Do not bring a purse or briefcase unless you can guard the contents, especially your trial information, at all times.

Remember that the jury can see you as easily as you can see them. And they can hear you, too. Avoid impatient or disappointed gestures, comments, or facial expressions, and even avoid expressions of delight or gloating. The jury members, who are not acquainted with the law, may look to you to determine how much importance to attach to particular statements or rulings. Avoid moving about the courtroom during crucial moments of testimony or argument. You do not want anything you do to detract from proceedings so important to the outcome of the trial. Remember, also, that the judge and the jurors may be in the courthouse halls or on the courthouse steps prior to trial and could even be in the same parking garage. Be aware of them at all times, and consider yourself to be "in trial" from the minute you leave for court.

Work with your attorney to define your role at trial. Listen carefully to the trial. Do not be simply a body in a chair. By acting as another set of eyes and ears you might be able to pick up information that the attorney missed. Check carefully with your attorney prior to trial to determine whether you should converse with the attorney during trial or whether you should make notes of your impressions.

> *Never talk to the press or to anyone about the trial, your client, or even your own role at trial. Do not talk to your client in the presence of strangers. Do not respond to the comments of others.*

that the prosecution failed to meet its burden and that the court should remove the case from the jury by finding the defendant not guilty. The judge looks at the evidence presented and evaluates it in the light most favorable to the prosecution. If the judge grants this defense motion, the defendant can be found not guilty of the individual charges or the entire case. There is no penalty if the judge does not allow this motion. The jury returns and simply resumes hearing the case.

As mentioned above, the defense is not required to put witnesses on the stand. If the defense calls witnesses, the defense examines and the prosecution cross-examines each witness, again with an eye toward credibility.

Once the defense has rested its case, the defense may renew the motion for a required finding of not guilty. This time the judge looks at the motion in the light most favorable to the defendant. If the motion is allowed, the case never goes to the jury for a verdict. If the motion is denied, the court process begins again. The attorneys deliver their closing arguments to the jury, and the judge informs the jurors of the law that they need to know to make their decision, which is called **charging the jury**. Once they are charged and sworn to do their duty, the jury members are released from the courtroom to deliberate. They may bring any items entered into evidence into the jury room with them to help them decide, and they can come back into the courtroom to ask questions.

Charging the jury
The judge informs the jurors of the law they need to know to make their decision.

Nothing can describe the waiting period while the jury is deliberating. It is too late to change anything, too soon to know whether your strategy worked. Many attorneys spend this time discussing possible outcomes with their clients or evaluating their trial performances. There is no set length of time that a jury can deliberate and no special process that a jury must follow. If the defendant is found not guilty, the case is over. If the defendant is found guilty, then the case moves into the sentencing phase.

DISCUSSION QUESTION

10. Criminals are guaranteed a jury of their peers. If you were on trial for a criminal offense, what factors would you consider when trying to select a jury of your peers? Is there really such a thing?

PRACTICE TIP

The opening statements and closing arguments are not considered evidence. But they are the first and last statements that the jury hears. Therefore, they may be the most effective method the attorneys have to present their case.

3. Sentencing

With the exception of capital punishment cases, in which statutes frequently give the defendant the option of having the jury decide if the death penalty should be imposed, the jury usually has no role to play in the sentencing process. Once the jury has found the defendant guilty of a specified crime, the judge is responsible for determining what the sentence will be. Because criminal codes usually provide a broad range of options between a minimum and a maximum sentence, judges are given a great deal of discretion to fashion a penalty that best fits the particular facts of the case. Under the Model Penal Code, for example, the sentence for murder can range from one year to life imprisonment. Furthermore, judges often have the power to sentence defendants to **probation**, to give them a conditional discharge, or to suspend their sentences altogether.

After a guilty verdict has been returned, the judge usually holds a special sentencing hearing, in which evidence can be presented "in aggravation and mitigation." At such a hearing both the prosecution and the defense have an opportunity to present evidence was not relevant to whether the defendant committed the crime but is relevant to the nature of the punishment that is to be imposed. The judge also receives a presentence report, which reviews the defendant's criminal record, work record, family background, and other factors considered relevant in determining the appropriate punishment. In some states, "victims' rights laws' provide for "victim impact statements," in which the victim of the crime describes how it negatively affected his or her life and the lives of family members.

While the broad ranges between minimum and maximum sentences give judges discretion to personalize the sentence, they sometimes lead to very great disparities in the sentences received by individuals who had committed similar crimes. Such disparities raise equity and potential discrimination concerns and have led the federal government and some state governments to create sentencing guidelines. These guidelines reduce the discretion given to trial judges by specifying narrower ranges of prison terms based on factors such as prior criminal record, the amount of illegal drugs sold or possessed, and the degree of harm to the victim.

The U.S. Supreme Court first addressed the constitutionality of these types of sentencing guidelines in 2004. Ralph Blakely had pled guilty to kidnapping his estranged wife. Washington's statutory maximum sentence for second-degree kidnapping is ten years, but the state's statutory sentencing guidelines set a presumptive range of 49 to 53 months. At sentencing, the judge imposed a 90-month sentence after finding that Blakely had acted with deliberate cruelty. The Court held that Blakely's sentence was imposed in a manner inconsistent with the Sixth Amendment right to a jury trial because the guidelines allowed the judge to increase the length of the sentence based on facts the defendant had not admitted and that had not been proven beyond a reasonable doubt to a jury.[31]

Although the *Blakely* decision involved state sentencing guidelines, the rationale for the Court's decision cast doubt upon the validity of the **Federal Sentencing Guidelines**. One year later, in *United States v. Booker*,[32] the Court ruled the Federal Sentencing Guidelines were unconstitutional to the extent that they forced judges to increase prison time based on facts that had not been determined by the jury. Although the Guidelines are no longer mandatory, judges are supposed to consult them so as to impose sentences that "reflect the seriousness

Federal Sentencing Guidelines
Government guidelines that specify an appropriate range of sentences for each class of convicted persons based on factors related to the offense and the offender.

---

[31] Blakely v. Washington, S42 U.S. 296 (2004).
[32] 543 U.S 220 (2005).

of the offense, promote respect for the law, provide just punishment, afford adequate deterrence, protect the public, and effectively provide the defendant with needed educational or vocational training and medical care.[33]

In 2006, an official federal study on the impact of *Booker* reported a wide variation in the way that district court judges modified their sentencing practices after the decision was announced. For example, some judges began to consider only those facts that had been proved beyond a reasonable doubt, while others continued to apply the pre-*Booker* preponderance of the evidence standard.[34] The study found that while a majority of federal defendants continue to be sentenced in conformity with the sentencing guidelines, the average length of the sentences being given increased after *Booker*.[35] One of the most troubling findings was that black offenders are associated with sentences that are 4.9% higher than those of white offenders.[36]

Constitutional challenges have also been brought against so called "three strikes" or habitual offender statutes. Aimed at **recidivists** (criminals who continue to commit crimes after their first offense), these laws mandate required prison sentences for third-time offenders. As was true of the sentencing guidelines, these statutes reduce the amount of discretion given to judges, and many believe they create unfair results in individual cases. For example, a man in California was sentenced to twenty-five years to life under the state's three-strikes law for attempting to steal three golf clubs. He argued that his twenty-five-year sentence violated the Eighth Amendment's prohibition against cruel and unusual punishment because of the disproportionality between the crime and the punishment. However, in a 5 to 4 decision, the U.S. Supreme Court upheld the sentence and ruled that such three-strikes provisions do not violate the Eighth Amendment.[37]

Finally, we end this discussion of sentencing with a note about the death penalty, found in the federal system as well as in the majority of states. Such capital punishment raises one of the most controversial issues in our criminal justice system. In recent years, the U.S. Supreme Court has placed some limits on who may be subjected to the death penalty. In 2002, the Court held that mental

Recidivist
A repeat offender; one who continues to commit more crimes.

NETNOTE

The Southern Center for Human Rights represents defendants facing the death penalty. To read about their work in that and other areas of criminal law, go to *www.schr.org*.

---

[33] Id. at 260.

[34] United States Sentencing Commission, Final Report on the Impact of United States v. Booker on Federal Sentencing iv (Mar. 2006).

[35] Id. at vi.

[36] Id. at viii.

[37] Ewing v. California, 538 U.S. 11 (2003).

retardation diminishes personal culpability. It also noted that the impairments of mentally retarded offenders make it less defensible to impose the death penalty as retribution and less likely that the death penalty will have a real deterrent effect.[38] Stating that a national consensus had formed against executing the mentally retarded, the Court held that such executions are excessive and violate the Eighth Amendment's prohibition against cruel and unusual punishment.[39] Three years later, when it was confronted with a case involving a seventeen-year-old convicted murderer, the Court reaffirmed its reliance on the concept of an evolving standard of decency to guide its decisions as to which punishments are so disproportionate as to be cruel and unusual. As it had found in respect to the mentally retarded, the Court determined that the death penalty as applied to juveniles does not serve either purpose of retribution or of deterrence. This reasoning led the Court to hold that the Constitution forbids the imposition of the death penalty on offenders who are under the age of 18 when their crimes are committed.[40]

Discussion Questions

11. How might you respond to your neighbor who says the judicial system is "falling apart" because of plea bargaining?

12. "It is better that ten guilty men go free than one innocent man be convicted" is an often-quoted legal expression. Do you agree or disagree?

13. How much discretion should the judge have in sentencing? How should judges balance the individual circumstances of each defendant with the needs for equity throughout the system?

14. On November 4, Leandro Andrade stole five videotapes worth $84.70 from a Kmart store. Fourteen days later, Andrade entered a different Kmart store and placed four videotapes worth $68.84 in the rear waistband of his pants. (The tapes included "Batman Forever" and "Cinderella.") The police arrested Andrade for these crimes. At trial, Andrade was found guilty of two counts of petty theft. The jury also made a special finding that he had previously been convicted of three counts of first-degree residential burglary. (One case involved his attempt to steal a bicycle.) Each of his petty theft convictions for stealing the videotapes triggered a separate application of the three-strikes law. Therefore, the judge sentenced him to two consecutive terms of twenty-five years to life, with no chance for parole. Does it seem as though his punishment was proportionate to his crime? How would you argue that his case is similar to or different from the *Ewing* case, discussed above?

15. The Eighth Amendment prohibits cruel and unusual punishment. What does the term "cruel and unusual" mean to you? Should it have to be cruel *and* unusual or can it be either cruel or unusual? Can the death penalty ever be carried out in a manner that is not cruel?

---

[38] Atkins v. Virginia, 536 U.S. 304, 318-320 (2002).

[39] Id. at 321.

[40] Roper v. Simmons, 543 U.S. 551 (2005).

4. Appel

As with parties who want to pursue civil appeals, a criminal defendant who wishes to appeal a conviction must file the appropriate post-trial motions, usually accompanied by a notice of appeal. There is a specified time during which an appeal may be filed. The Fifth Amendment protection against double jeopardy prohibits the state from trying a defendant more than once for the same crime and prevents the government from appealing an acquittal. It does not prevent a prosecutor from appealing the dismissal of a case on technical grounds or from appealing a lower appellate court ruling to a higher court.

After the appeal period has expired, the only avenue for relief is through a **writ of habeas corpus,** a request that the court review the legality of the incarceration. The convicted defendant argues that the incarceration is illegal because of a defect in the case. It is uncommon for this tactic to be successful.

Writ of habeas corpus
A request that the court release the defendant because of the illegality of the incarceration.

SUMMARY

Criminal law defines what behaviors are illegal and what punishments convicted defendants are to receive. Criminal procedure governs how the criminal process works.

Crimes can generally be divided into felonies, crimes that usually involve punishment by incarceration for a year or more, and misdemeanors. For any crime the government must prove that the defendant had the requisite mens rea while committing the actus reus. Common defenses include alibi, ignorance or mistake, infancy, insanity, intoxication, duress, necessity, entrapment, self-defense, and defense of others. In addition, a defendant may challenge a prosecution on the basis of a statute of limitations or the Constitution.

The rules governing criminal procedure begin with the criminal investigation and continue in force thorough trial and any possible appeal. The Fourth Amendment requires that all searches and seizures be reasonable. The court-crafted exclusionary rule provides that any evidence unlawfully seized may not be used in court against the defendant. The Fifth Amendment protects defendants against self-incrimination, and the Sixth Amendment guarantees a right to an attorney. While every defendant has a right to a trial, most cases end through a negotiated plea bargain.

If a trial does occur, the prosecution bears the burden of proving guilt beyond a reasonable doubt. The defense attorney is not required to put the defendant, or any other witnesses, on the stand. If the defendant chooses not to testify, the prosecution cannot comment or otherwise draw attention to the defendant's silence.

If the jury finds the defendant guilty, the judge is usually responsible for determining what the sentence will be. Most state statutes give the judge a broad range of discretion between a minimum and a maximum sentence for the crime. Many states, as well as the federal government, adopted sentencing guidelines in the hopes of creating more consistency and equity in sentencing. Recent U.S. Supreme Court decisions, however, have called into question the constitutionality of such guidelines.

If a criminal defendant wishes to appeal a conviction, he or she may do so. The Fifth Amendment protection against double jeopardy prohibits the state from trying a defendant twice for the same crime and prevents the government from appealing an acquittal. It does not, however, prevent a prosecutor from appealing the dismissal of a case on technical grounds or from appealing a lower appellate court ruling to a higher court.

REVIEW QUESTIONS

Pages 215 through 222

1. Why is "[n]o behavior a crime unless the law makes it a crime"?
2. What are the differences between felonies and misdemeanors?
3. What is the actus reus of a crime? What is the mens rea of a crime?
4. Who is the principal of a crime? What is the difference between the principal and the accessory to a crime?

Pages 222 through 230

5. What defense(s) might be available to the following individuals?
   a. The Elliots complained to the police that the son of their next-door neighbor broke their garage windows with rocks. They wanted him arrested. The police went next door to arrest the boy, and they discovered that he is seven years old. They arrested him and brought him to the police station. He was charged with destroying the Elliots' property.
   b. Marcus was arrested for the murder of his cousin Michael. At the time that Michael was killed Marcus claimed that he was on a business trip 300 miles away.
   c. Every day on the way to school Rosa pushed Carmen to the ground and stole her lunch. On Tuesday Carmen hid behind a car on the way to school, and when she saw Rosa walking toward her, she jumped out and hit her. Rosa pushed Carmen to the ground and walked away without taking her lunch.
   d. As Paula walked toward her car after work, she was confronted by Terry, who pointed a realistic toy gun at Paula and demanded that Paula hand over her wallet. Paula took a gun out of her purse and shot and killed Terry.
   e. After his car was forced off the road, Patrick tried to stop the bleeding on his wife's face. When she passed out, Patrick ran to a nearby home, jumped over the fence, and banged on the front door. When the occupants would not let him in, Patrick broke a window of the house, climbed through, and ran toward the telephone. The homeowner grabbed a rifle and shot Patrick in the back.
   f. During a grocery store robbery a thief held a gun to a customer's head and demanded that he put all the money from the store safe into a bag, which he did. When the police arrived, they arrested the customer for robbery.
   g. During the last five years of their marriage David beat his wife, Mary, so severely that she was hospitalized four times. About six months after the last beating Mary stabbed David to death while he was sleeping. She was arrested for murder.
   h. Officer Kaplan responded to an emergency call for a store robbery in progress. When the masked thief shot at the officer, Officer Kaplan shot and killed the thief. The man's family wanted Officer Kaplan charged with murder.
6. Describe the various tests that have been developed to determine whether a defendant was insane at the time he or she committed the crime.
7. What are the possible results of successfully proving an insanity defense?
8. What is the difference between the duress and the necessity defenses?
9. What does a defendant have to show to prove entrapment?
10. When can a potential victim use deadly force to protect himself or herself?
11. What is the retreat exception to the self-defense doctrine?
12. What protections are afforded by the double jeopardy clause?
13. When might a statute be challenged for vagueness? For overbreadth?

Pages 230 through 243

14. What is a stop-and-frisk search?
15. What is the difference between reasonable suspicion and probable cause? Why does it matter?

16. Why does the court consider the suspect's expectation of privacy when evaluating a search?
17. What is a warrant?
18. List some specific facts that must be included when police officers apply for a warrant to search a suspect's home.
19. What is a no-knock warrant?
20. What exigent circumstances may allow the police to search without a warrant?
21. What are the *Miranda* warnings, when are the police required to give them, and under what circumstances might a defendant waive them?
22. What extra protection do juveniles usually get when they are given their *Miranda* rights?

Pages 243 through 253

23. What might a defendant expect to occur during booking?
24. What is the exclusionary rule?
25. How do motions to suppress affect the prosecution's case against defendants?
26. What are the differences between a guilty plea and a plea of nolo contendere?
27. If you worked for the prosecution, would you consider the following items to be potentially inculpatory or exculpatory? Could this evidence be potentially inculpatory *and* exculpatory?;
    a. the fingerprints of a second person on the murder weapon
    b. a statement that the defendant gave to the police shortly after the arrest disclosing the location of the mising body
    c. samples of hair and skin found at the scene of the crime
28. If the following facts are true, what pretrial motions might you file on behalf of the defendants?
    a. All the local papers have reported that the judge on the case used to be married to the victim.
    b. Each of the two defendants claims that the other defendant was the sole assassin.
    c. The defendant, who was represented by a public defender, needs to conduct an independent drug evaluation, especially since the defendant alleged the green, leafy substance was oregano bought to add spice to spaghetti sauce.
    d. Four of the seven witnesses prepared to testify at trial are related by blood or marriage.
    e. The police stopped the defendant for speeding and then proceeded to search the glove compartment, in which they found a bag of heroin.

Pages 253 through 259

29. Describe the basic steps that occur in a criminal trial.
30. What is there no requirement that the defendant take the stand?
31. What is the purpose of charging the jury?
32. What are the Federal Sentencing Guidelines, and why are they controversial?
33. Why is it not double jeopardy for the prosecutor to appeal an intermediate-appellate-level decision?

Chapter 11

Legal Ethics

A lawyer should avoid even the appearance of professional impropriety.
ABA Model Code of Professional Responsibility
Canon 9

INTRODUCTION

Paralegals hold positions of responsibility and trust. Their actions directly and indirectly affect the well-being of the firm's clients, the public's interest, and the public's perception of the legal system. In this chapter we will introduce you to some of the ethical dilemmas faced by legal professionals and provide you with an overview of the existing statutes and ethical rules regulating attorneys and paralegals. There are three main ethical areas about which paralegals must be particularly knowledgeable: the unauthorized practice of law, client confidentiality, and conflict of interest. In addition, we will be discussing the proper procedures for handling client funds, the limits to zealous representation, and liability for legal malpractice.

An attorney is bound by the set of ethical guidelines that has been adopted in that attorney's state. Most states have chosen to follow the newer **Model Rules of Professional Conduct,** but a few states still follow the older **Model Code of Professional Responsibility**. As employees of attorneys, paralegals are expected to abide by those guidelines. To date, however, there is no comparable code of ethics that paralegals are required to follow. In addition, as we saw in Chapter 2, no state has taken the step of requiring that paralegals be licensed or fulfill a particular educational requirement. If such legislation is passed, those licensing statutes will undoubtedly place specific obligations or restrictions on those who

Model Rules of Professional Conduct
A set of ethical rules developed by the American Bar Association in the 1980s. The Model Rules have been adopted by more than half the states.

Model Code of Professional Responsibility
An older set of standards governing attorney ethics developed by the American Bar Association.

receive such a license. Meanwhile, most states have laws regarding liability for negligent acts and an unauthorized practice of law statute. Therefore, paralegals currently are regulated in three ways:

1. indirectly by the bar's regulation of lawyers through ethical codes,
2. directly by laws on the unauthorized practice of law, and
3. directly by the tort law of negligence.

As you read the chapter, see if you can pinpoint all the possible ethical violations raised in the following fact scenario:

The Case of the Ethically Challenged Paralegal

One day attorney John Bloom asked paralegal Sally Green to sit in on an initial client interview. Attorney Bloom introduced Ms. Green to the client, Sara Smith, and to Mrs. Smith's friend, Bertha. Mrs. Smith was very nervous about going to a lawyer and so had brought her friend Bertha for support. Attorney Bloom explained to them that Ms. Green is a paralegal. Mrs. Smith told them the following story.

She recently served a pot roast to her family. That night her entire family developed severe stomach cramps and diarrhea. The doctors in the hospital emergency room told them that they were suffering from food poisoning. Mrs. Smith wanted to know if she could sue the grocery store that sold her the meat. Attorney Bloom told Mrs. Smith they would be happy to accept her as a client and that they handled cases such as hers on a contingency basis. He explained that meant she would owe them one-third of whatever they recovered for her. He then told her they would get back to her as soon as they completed some preliminary research. After the interview, attorney Bloom asked Ms. Green to conduct a factual investigation, research the issue, and draft the complaint.

As part of her research Ms. Green called the grocery store. Saying she was from the Department of Health, she asked the store manager how many customer complaints they had in the past month regarding spoiled meat purchased from the store.

Later that afternoon, attorney Bloom asked Ms. Green to write the paychecks for herself and the firm receptionist. Because the firm was temporarily a little short of cash, attorney Bloom told her to take the money from the client escrow account. He assured her that he would replace the money before the end of the week and that no clients would be harmed. Ms. Green did as attorney Bloom requested.

The next day Mrs. Smith called the office. As attorney Bloom was in court, Ms. Green took the call. Mrs. Smith said that she was confused about some of the terminology that attorney Bloom had used the day before. First, she asked Ms. Green to explain to her what a complaint is. Ms. Green did so. Then Mrs. Smith asked her what sorts of information would be put in the complaint. Ms. Green pulled out the complaint that she had just drafted (but had not yet shown to attorney Bloom) and read it to Mrs. Smith. Finally, Mrs. Smith asked whether Ms. Green thought she would win her negligence claim. Ms. Green told Mrs. Smith that she was not an attorney and could not give legal advice. However, her personal opinion was that Mrs. Smith had a very good chance of winning her case.

Right after Ms. Green got off the phone with Mrs. Smith, Joan, the firm's receptionist, brought a letter into her office. The letter had just been faxed to them from another attorney's office. The letterhead indicated that the letter was from the firm Smith and Smith, was signed by attorney Sam Smith, and was addressed to Mr. Defendant. Attorney Smith was representing Mr. Defendant in a lawsuit that attorney Bloom had initiated on behalf of Ms. Plaintiff, one of attorney

Bloom's clients. Ms. Green assumed that someone in attorney Smith's office had mistakenly sent the letter to her firm as it was obvious Mr. Defendant was the intended recipient. Quickly reading through the letter, she saw it contained information that could be very helpful to attorney Bloom. The fax cover sheet stated that the enclosed material contained information protected by the attorney-client privilege.

Later that evening, while unwinding over a leisurely dinner with her husband, Sally Green told him of the day's events. She discussed various client cases but was always very careful never to reveal any names. She also told her husband that another law firm had offered her a job. It would entail a significant increase in pay. However, she said it made her feel a bit sad to know that the new firm might ask her to work on the opposite side of some cases that she was currently working on with attorney Bloom.

A. REGULATION OF ATTORNEYS

Historically, state supreme courts have claimed the power to regulate attorneys and to determine who can or cannot "practice law." Typically, they establish specialized boards or agencies to administer bar exams, investigate the character and fitness of applicants, review complaints against attorneys, and discipline those who violate their rules of professional conduct.

While each state is responsible for establishing its own rules of professional conduct, the content of these rules generally follows model rules promulgated by the American Bar Association (ABA). In 1908, the ABA adopted the first set of rules dealing directly with attorney behavior. Entitled the Canons of Ethics, this document contained suggestions for what attorneys should do. It was over sixty years (1969) before the ABA produced a more detailed document, the **Model Code of Professional Responsibility**, that for the first time told lawyers what they must do or be in danger of being disciplined through reprimand, suspension, or loss of their license to practice law. Then came a series of incidents, including the Watergate scandal of the Nixon presidency, that increased the public's sensitivity to the issue of attorneys and ethics. Working quickly, it took the ABA only a little more than eleven years to produce an entirely new set of rules, the **Model Rules of Professional Conduct**. Adopted in 1983, these rules have been amended many times, most recently in 2003 as a result of an ABA initiative known as Ethics 2000.

While most states have adopted some version of the Model Rules of Professional Conduct, a few states still follow the Model Code of Professional Responsibility. Therefore, as you read this text, keep in mind that in any given state attorneys in that state may be subject to any one of the following:

1. The Model Code of Professional Responsibility;
2. The Model Rules of Professional Conduct (pre-2003 version);
3. The Model Rules of Professional Conduct (as revised in 2003); or
4. A state's individual variation on any of the above three.

NETNOTE

You can locate the ABA Model Rules of Professional Conduct at *www.abanet. org/cpr/mrpc/mrpc_toc.html.*

With so many different approaches in existence, you may well ask how can any of these sets of rules claim to guide attorneys as to ethical behavior? One answer is that neither the Code nor the Rules are actually ethical codes based on moral values; rather, they are simply rules to govern attorney behavior. This explanation is supported by the change in name from the Canon of *Ethics* to the Rules of Professional *Conduct*. That is, arguably these rules are not meant to offer attorneys moral guidance but rather to set forth a strict set of rules that attorneys must follow at the peril of losing their license to practice law. Therefore, when they study these rules in law school, law students are not really studying a code of ethics but rather a series of rules governing behavior, violation of which could result in disbarment. Hence, when confronted with what might be seen as an ethical dilemma, attorneys may not immediately ask, "what is right?" but rather "what does the rule say I have to do?"[1]

In summary, when studying these rules, keep in mind that although the ABA was responsible for drafting both the older Model Code of Professional Responsibility and the newer Model Rules of Professional Conduct, it is a voluntary association. Lawyers are not required to become ABA members, and the ABA has no authority to require attorneys to abide by either the Model Code of Professional Responsibility or the Model Code of Professional Conduct. States, however, through their licensing power, do have the power to require attorneys to abide by a code of ethics. It is the version of the code that a particular state has adopted that is binding on the attorneys in that state. If an attorney is found to have violated an ethical rule, he or she can be subjected to sanctions, including suspension and disbarment.

DISCUSSION QUESTIONS

1. On a basic level, do you think attorneys have to face ethical dilemmas that are fundamentally different from those faced by other professionals, such as physicians or accountants?

2. In the popular media, attorneys are often referred to as "hired guns." We have also all heard the lawyer jokes: "How do you know when a lawyer is lying? His lips are moving." Why do you think there is this negative perception of lawyers and what they do? Do you think it is a fair characterization?

3. What do you think of the statement: "At times following the rules may not lead to the best moral response and indeed may produce an amoral or even immoral response"?

---

[1] American Bar Association, Section on Tort Trial & Insurance Practice, Leonard Bucklin, Ethics in a Time of Historical Change, available at *www.edicta.org/NeoethicsBucklin/O4A_history.htm* (last visited May 16, 2005).

NETNOTE

Both NALA and NFPA have placed their codes of ethics on their web sites. To find NALA's Code of Ethics and Professional Responsibility go to *www.nala.org/98model.htm*. To find NFPA's Model Code of Ethics, go to the NFPA home page, *www.paralegals.org*, and click on "Professional Development." To view the ABA Model Guidelines go to *www.abanet.org/legalservices/paralegals/*.

B. REGULATION OF PARALEGALS

As we indicated earlier, no state has yet adopted a code of ethics that directly governs the ethical behavior of paralegals. However, both major national paralegal organizations, the National Association of Legal Assistants (NALA) and the National Federation of Paralegal Associations (NFPA) have adopted model codes. The ABA has also developed standards to guide attorneys in their ethical employment of paralegals. Excerpts from the NALA Code of Ethics and Professional Responsibility and the NFPA Model Code of Ethics and Professional Responsibility are set out in Appendix D.

The NALA Code of Ethics and Professional Responsibility was drafted in 1975 and most recently revised in 1995. The code consists of nine canons. The first five canons focus on a legal assistant's avoiding the unauthorized practice of law. Canon 6 stresses the importance of maintaining competency through continuing education, and Canon 7 deals with protecting client confidences. Canons 8 and 9 both emphasize the need to follow rules of ethics as defined by statute, court rule, or bar association.

Adopted in 1993, NFPA's Model Code of Ethics and Responsibility contains eight canons, as well as ethical considerations. While this code also has provisions regarding the unauthorized practice of law (Canons 5 and 6) and client confidences (Canon 7), it goes beyond NALA's code in that it specifically deals with conflicts of interest (Canon 8). In its first four canons NFPA's code also emphasizes that paralegals should maintain a high level of competence, integrity, and professional conduct. An expansionist document, NFPA's code encourages paralegals to dedicate themselves "to the improvement of the legal system and [to expanding] the paralegal role in the delivery of legal services."

As the name implies, the ABA Model Guidelines for the Utilization of Paralegal Services are directed to lawyers employing paralegals rather than to paralegals themselves. For example, Guideline 6 states: "A lawyer is responsible for taking reasonable measures to ensure that all client confidences are preserved by a paralegal." The ABA Standing Committee on Paralegals developed these guidelines hoping that they would encourage attorneys to make better use of paralegal skills. The committee also hoped that these model guidelines would encourage states to develop their own rules regarding paralegal employment.

The Model Rules of Professional Conduct also contain a provision relating directly to the responsibilities of attorneys who supervise or employ paralegals.

Rule 5.3 Responsibilities Regarding Nonlawyer Assistants

With respect to a nonlawyer employed or retained by or associated with a lawyer:

(a) a partner in a law firm shall make reasonable efforts to ensure that the firm has in effect measures giving reasonable assurance that the person's conduct is compatible with the professional obligations of the lawyer;

(b) a lawyer having direct supervisory authority over the non lawyer shall make reasonable efforts to ensure that the person's conduct is compatible with the professional obligations of the lawyer; and

(c) a lawyer shall be responsible for conduct of such a person that would be a violation of the Rules of Professional Conduct if engaged in by a lawyer if:

(1) the lawyer orders or, with the knowledge of the specific conduct, ratifies the conduct involved; or

(2) the lawyer is a partner in the law firm in which the person is employed, or has direct supervisory authority over the person, and knows of the conduct at a time when its consequences can be avoided or mitigated but fails to take reasonable remedial action.

Finally, some states have prepared reports that contain guidelines for paralegal behavior, but no state has as yet developed a set of ethical standards to which paralegals must adhere. Kentucky was the first state to develop guidelines to inform *attorneys* of proper paralegal conduct.

Legal Reasoning Exercise

1. Read the following excerpts from the Kentucky Paralegal Code, Rule 3.700, Provisions Relating to Paralegals (1980):

Sub-Rule 1

A lawyer shall ensure that a paralegal in his employment does not engage in the unauthorized practice of law.

Sub-Rule 2

For purposes of this rule, the unauthorized practice of law shall not include any service rendered involving legal knowledge or legal advice, whether representation, counsel or advocacy, in or out of court, rendered in respect to the acts, duties, obligations, liabilities or business relations of the one requiring services where:

A. The client understands that the paralegal is not a lawyer;

B. The lawyer supervises the paralegal in the performance of his duties; and

C. The lawyer remains fully responsible for such representation, including all actions taken or not taken in connection therewith by the paralegal to the same extent as if such representation had been furnished entirely by the lawyer and all such actions had been taken or not taken directly by the lawyer.

Using your skills of statutory interpretation, take a careful look at Sub-Rule 2 of the Kentucky Paralegal Code. Does it mean a paralegal can do anything, including representing a client in court, if the three conditions are met? Do you think that is what the legislature intended?

C. THE BIG THREE: CONFIDENTIALITY, CONFLICT OF INTEREST, AND THE UNAUTHORIZED PRACTICE OF LAW

Three areas covered by most of the ethical codes mentioned above are of particular concern to paralegals. They are the rules regarding client confidentiality, conflict of interest, and the unauthorized practice of law. In addition, paralegals should be aware of the proper procedures for managing client funds and the limits on zealous representation.

1. Client Confidentiality

A lawyer cannot effectively serve a client without knowing all the facts of a particular case. Without the assurance of **confidentiality** many clients would be reluctant to reveal potentially embarrassing or incriminating information to their attorneys.

Confidentiality
The ethical rule prohibiting attorneys and paralegals from disclosing information regarding a client or a client's case.

The rule against revealing client confidences applies to potential clients, clients, and prior clients. Without the protection of confidentiality clients would hesitate to be as open and frank with their attorneys as is necessary for full representation. It is crucial that paralegals realize that they can never mention any aspect of a client's case to those outside the law firm. In fact, the very presence of the client in the firm should be kept confidential.

The ethical codes of the paralegal associations and the ABA Guidelines on the Utilization of Legal Assistants all emphasize the importance of maintaining confidentiality. The ABA Model Code of Professional Responsibility provides the following.

ABA Canon 4

A lawyer should preserve the confidences and secrets of his client.

DR 4-101(A) "Confidence" refers to information protected by the attorney-client privilege under applicable law, and "secret" refers to other information gained in the professional relationship that the client has requested be held inviolate or the disclosure of which would be embarrassing or would be likely to be detrimental to the client.

DR 4-101(C) A lawyer may reveal:
(1) Confidences or secrets with the consent of the client or clients affected, but only after a full disclosure to them. . . .
(3) The intention of his client to commit a crime and the information necessary to prevent the crime. . . .

DR 4-101(D) A lawyer shall exercise reasonable care to prevent his employees . . . from disclosing or using confidences or secrets of a client. . . .

> **PRACTICE TIP**
>
> Make sure your computer has a screen saver that you can use to hide from view any confidential information you may have on the screen.

The Model Code is broader in its protection than are the Model Rules. While the Model Code protects both a client's confidences and a client's secrets, no matter their source, the Model Rules speak of "information relating to representation of a client."

Model Rule 1.6

(a) A lawyer shall not reveal information relating to representation of a client unless the client consents after consultation, except for disclosures that are impliedly authorized in order to carry out the representation, and except as stated in paragraph (b).

(b) A lawyer may reveal such information to the extent the lawyer reasonably believes necessary:

(1) to prevent the client from committing a criminal act that the lawyer believes is likely to result in imminent death or substantial bodily harm; or

(2) to establish a claim or defense on behalf of the lawyer in a controversy between the lawyer and the client, to establish a defense to a criminal charge or civil claim against the lawyer based upon conduct in which the client was involved, or to respond to allegations in any proceeding concerning the lawyer's representation of the client.

As you can see, both the Model Code and the Model Rules create exceptions to the confidentiality rule. One of the most controversial exceptions is the one regarding situations in which the attorney has knowledge that the client plans a criminal act. While the Model Code simply speaks of "a crime," the Model Rules specify a criminal act "that the lawyer believes is likely to result in the imminent death or substantial bodily harm." In either case the exemption applies only to *future* crimes. The area of disagreement relates primarily to the nature of the crime that would warrant revealing a client confidence. The safest course for any paralegal who becomes aware of situations involving any of these exceptions is to notify the supervising attorney so that the attorney can determine the proper course of action.

In sum, according to the ethical rules, confidences can be revealed only if

1. the client consents after full disclosure or
2. it is necessary to prevent a serious crime or
3. it is necessary in order for an attorney to collect a fee or defend himself or herself.

DISCUSSION QUESTIONS

4. The common justification for having such strict limits on when an attorney may reveal client confidences is that without such restrictions, clients would be afraid to give their attorneys the complete story. Do you think this is really true? Given the complexities of the legal system and hence the need for an attorney to help people through it, do you think a client would risk not getting adequate representation by not being forthcoming to the attorney?

5. What do you make of the fact that in every jurisdiction the confidentiality rules do not apply when the litigation is between a lawyer and the client and the issue is the attorney's fees?

6. As discussed in the text there is substantial disagreement as to when an attorney should be required or even allowed to report a client's future crime. Do you think there are any instances when such reporting should be required? Allowed? Classify each of the following according to whether you think an attorney should be required to report the future crime, allowed to do so at his or her discretion, or prohibited from disclosing it at all. You should also consider

whether the test should be a subjective one, based on what the attorney actually thought was likely to happen, or an objective test, based on what a reasonable person would think would happen.

    a. A deliberately wrongful act
    b. Harm to a financial or property interest
    c. Substantial harm to a financial or property interest
    d. Any crime
    e. A serious violent crime
    f. Bodily harm
    g. Substantial bodily harm
    h. Death
    i. Imminent death

In addition to the exceptions to client confidentiality contained in the ethical codes, under certain circumstances a court may order an attorney or a paralegal to testify, thereby forcing the revelation of confidential information. Rather than testifying, the attorney or paralegal may object on the grounds of **attorney-client privilege**. The attorney-client privilege is not part of the ethical codes. Rather it is contained within the rules of evidence.

> **Attorney-client privilege**
> A rule of evidence that prevents an attorney or a paralegal from being compelled to testify about confidential client information.

    In state and federal courts, rules of evidence govern what testimony and documentary evidence can be used at trial. Some evidence is not allowed because it is considered privileged. That is, in some instances it is more important to protect the communication than it is to allow the evidence to be heard. An example is the privilege that prohibits the use of a spouse's statement against the other spouse. Similarly, the attorney-client privilege protects an attorney or a paralegal from being compelled to supply information when called as a witness. In addition, the attorney's work product cannot be subpoenaed. This protected work product includes private memoranda, written statements of witnesses, and mental impressions, conclusions, or legal strategies related to litigation. It is particularly important to note that this privilege also covers paralegal employees. The paralegal cannot be compelled to reveal confidential information that an attorney could not be compelled to reveal. The paralegal's notes are also part of the protected work product.

    For the attorney-client privilege to apply, the client, while seeking legal advice, must speak directly to an attorney or his or her employee, with no unnecessary third parties present. This is more restrictive than the ethical rule protecting client confidences. The ethical rule applies no matter how the attorney or paralegal acquired the confidential information. Figure 11-1, on page 272, summarizes the differences between the attorney-client privilege and the ethical rules regarding confidentiality.

    As you can see from Figure 11-1, the attorney-client privilege does not cover as many situations as do the ethical rules regarding confidentiality. The ethical rules generally cover any confidence regarding the client no matter the source. Therefore, a paralegal cannot voluntarily repeat that information without the client's consent. However, a court could require the paralegal to testify regarding that information unless it also meets the four-part test for satisfying the attorney-client privilege:

1. The *client* made a statement
2. to the paralegal or attorney
3. while seeking legal advice and
4. no unnecessary persons were present.

> **PRACTICE TIP**
>
> End all conversations in the office. Do not carry them on out into the reception area.

Ethical Rule Regarding Confidentiality	Attorney-Client Privilege
Under the Model Code applies to ■ confidences and secrets ■ learned from any source ■ regarding anything and ■ made anywhere	*Applies to* ■ a client statement ■ to an attorney or a paralegal ■ made while seeking legal advice and ■ given in confidence (no unnecessary persons present)
Under the Model Rules applies to ■ information ■ relating to representation of the client	
Result: If all of the conditions are present, the attorney or paralegal may not voluntarily reveal the information (but may be compelled to testify unless statements also satisfy criteria for the attorney-client privilege).	*Result:* If any of these four conditions is missing, the attorney can be compelled to testify.

Figure 11-1   A Comparison of the Ethical Rule Regarding Confidentiality and the Attorney-Client Privilege

Figure 11-2   Attorney-Client Privilege: A Subset of Confidentiality

Therefore, you can think of information covered by the attorney-client privilege as a subset of all confidential information. See Figure 11-2.

The attorney-client privilege can be breached if law office personnel fail to recognize the requirements for establishing the privilege. Consider the case of *People v. Mitchell.*[2] The defendant, John Mitchell, had been indicted for the stabbing death of his girlfriend. Attorney Lapin was representing him in that case. On January 5 a prostitute died of eleven stab wounds. The next morning the defendant went to attorney Lapine's office. Attorney Lapine was not in, and the defendant spoke to a legal secretary who was stationed in the reception area. He told her that "he had been out drinking and met a girl and then he woke up in the morning and she was dead." While he was talking to the first secretary, a second secretary entered the reception area. He then muttered something about a knife. Finally, a paralegal entered the room. She asked Mr. Mitchell what was wrong. He told her "that there was a dead body and he felt that he had done it and that the person was dead, that she was dead because of being stabbed." The prosecution found out about these conversations and subpoenaed the two secretaries and the paralegal to testify at Mr. Mitchell's trial. Naturally Mr. Mitchell's attorney tried to have this testimony kept out of the trial as violating the attorney-client privilege. Review the criteria for establishing an attorney-client privilege. Do you think the secretaries and paralegal were required to testify?

[2] 448 N.Y.S.2d 332 (1982).

What additional facts do you think you would want to know before making that decision?

The trial court ordered the secretaries and paralegal to testify, stating that their testimony was not protected by the attorney-client privilege. The appellate court agreed. The conversation had happened in a reception area, where "unnecessary persons" might have been present. Also, while attorney Lapin was representing the defendant regarding a prior murder, as attorney Lapin was away from the office, he had had no opportunity to accept the defendant as his client in regards to this second murder. Therefore, the court ruled that the communication could not have been "for the purposes of securing legal advice or assistance."[3]

Closely related to the concept of attorney-client privilege is the doctrine of attorney work product. If materials can be categorized as attorney-work product, then they are protected from discovery requests and need not be disclosed even during trial. Generally, to be protected, the materials must be prepared by an attorney or an agent of the attorney, such as a paralegal, contain thoughts, strategy, or opinions of the attorney or paralegal, and be prepared in anticipation of litigation or for trial. Examples include notes outlining trial strategy or evaluation of the effectiveness of a witness's testimony. Items that would not be included are those that are prepared routinely but not in anticipation of litigation. While the attorney-client privilege in effect belongs to the client and can only be waived by the client, the doctrine of attorney-work product is meant to protect the mental impressions and creativity of the attorney.

An interesting issue arises when an attorney or paralegal accidentally sends privileged information to the opposing law firm. Especially in this day of fax machines and e-mails, it is all too easy to pick the wrong fax number off of a list or the wrong address from a computerized address book. In 1992, the ABA issued an ethics opinion in which it stated that the correct course was to refrain from reading the inadvertently received confidential documents. Instead, the attorney should notify the other lawyer and comply with any request, such as to return the unread documents.[4] However, many commentators and state bar associations disagreed with that approach. For example, the Massachusetts Bar Association's Committee on Professional Ethics advised that a lawyer's primary ethical duty is to zealously advocate his client's interests, and therefore the documents do not have to be returned. In 2005, the ABA reversed its position. It withdrew its 1992 opinion and amended Rule 4.4 to require that the attorney who receives the materials must do no more than notify the lawyer who inadvertently sent them. There is no longer an obligation to comply with the other attorney's request as to how to dispose of the materials.

Of course, when an attorney or paralegal receives privileged material, not through the mistake of the opponent but through some other means, the appropriate response is to notify the opponent and dispose of or return the material. In a recent decision from Washington,[5] a paralegal, Mr. Haegele, reviewed a disk he had received from one of the firm's clients, Mr. Richards. Mr. Richards was the corporate vice president for Infospace, Inc., the defendant. The disk

---

[3] Id. at 333.

[4] ABA, formal ethics opinion No. 92-368.

[5] *Richards v. Jain*, 168 F. Supp. 1195 (2001).

contained approximately 100,000 e-mails from and to Mr. Richards and various other company personnel, including the defendant's attorneys. Many of the e-mails were clearly marked "Attorney-Client Privileged." Mr. Haegele stated that he had seen the notation but had chosen to ignore it. The defendant moved to have the plaintiff's firm disqualified.

The court found that a portion of the e-mails that Mr. Haegele had read were relevant to the case and were protected by attorney-client privilege. The plaintiff's firm tried to argue that no *attorney* knew of the privileged information. However, the court held that the rules regarding confidential information apply equally to paralegals as to attorneys and that the conduct and knowledge of the paralegal must be imputed to the law firm. "Mr. Haegele's review of privileged material was an ethical violation regardless of his status as a paralegal."[6] Finally, the court found that the paralegal's review of the documents had tainted the proceedings so severely that the only remedy was to disqualify the firm from its continuing representation of the plaintiff.

DISCUSSION QUESTIONS

7. When an attorney receives information that the opposing side has sent accidentally, that attorney has four options:
   a. to refrain from reading the information, and then to contact the opposing attorney and return the document unread;
   b. to read the information, contact the opposing attorney, and return the document;
   c. to read the information, contact the opposing attorney, and refuse to return the document; or
   d. to read the information and use it.

Given our adversarial system and your own sense of justice, which approach do you think is best?

8. Attorney White represents a plaintiff who was injured in an automobile accident. She and her client have decided to settle the case if they can obtain at least $200,000. The settlement talks are set to begin tomorrow, and her strategy is to start by asking for $300,000, hoping to end up at $200,000. As attorney White is reviewing the files in preparation for the settlement talks, she discovers a one-page fax that she had not noticed before. It is from the defendant's insurer and was obviously intended to reach the defendant's attorney. It contains just one line: "Offer $100,000, but you have authority to settle for up to $500,000."

   a. What should attorney White do?
   b. Do you think that it should matter that the fax was intermixed with other documents?
   c. What if attorney White was wandering by the fax machine as it came in? As she pulled it out, she saw the cover sheet that contained the following language:

---

[6] Id. at 1200.

Privileged and Confidential—All information transmitted hereby is intended only for the use of the addressee(s) named above. If the reader of this message is not the intended recipient or the employee or agent responsible for delivering the message to the intended recipient(s), please note that any distribution or copying of this communication is strictly prohibited. Anyone who receives this communication in error should notify us immediately by telephone and return the original to us at the above address via the U.S. mail.

The cover sheet showed that the fax was to be sent to the opposing attorney but the fax number was for Ms. White's office. What should she do?

2. Conflict of Interest

Our legal system is classified as adversarial because it places lawyers in an adversarial relationship and then relies on them to present all the relevant facts and arguments needed for a neutral judge or jury to reach a proper decision. In this type of adversarial system attorneys may not represent parties with conflicting interests. For example, by representing both the plaintiff and the defendant in a negligence action, an attorney creates a **conflict of interest**. An attorney's duty to the client is impaired when the attorney cannot consider and recommend a particular action because it may adversely affect the interests of another client.

Conflict of interest
The ethical rule prohibiting attorneys and paralegals from working for opposing sides in a case.

Paralegals must be careful how they respond to situations that present possible conflicts of interest. A serious problem could develop if the law firm for which a paralegal works takes a case that involves a friend, relative, former employer, former client, or business interest of the paralegal. Problems can also arise when a paralegal changes jobs if the new employer represents clients on the opposite side of cases handled by the paralegal's previous employer. It is therefore very important that paralegals understand the prevailing interpretations as to what constitutes a conflict and that they inform their supervising attorney of any interest that could result in such a conflict—or even the appearance of such a conflict.

There are two basic types of conflicts of interest. The first occurs when lawyers or paralegals have a personal or business interest that suggests they cannot give their undivided loyalty to a client. The second involves either present or past client representation that presents a conflict with the representation of a new client.

Conflicts of the first type can occur when a lawyer is related to another lawyer or paralegal who represents the opposite side of a case. Other examples include entering into certain types of business relationships with clients, preparing instruments for a client that give some benefit to the lawyer or a family member of the lawyer (such as a bequest in a will), providing financial assistance to a client in connection with pending litigation, and accepting compensation from third parties. Each of these situations poses either a real or a potential conflict of interest.

As an example of this first type of conflict, assume Mrs. Abbot is an attorney working for a defendants' firm. Her husband is an attorney who works for a plaintiffs' firm. One of Mr. Abbot's clients is suing the local grocery store for allegedly selling tainted meat. Mrs. Abbot represents the grocery store. See

Figure 11-3. Mr. and Mrs. Abbot had been hoping for some time to get away from the pressures of work for a week or so, but their lack of finances was standing in their way. If Mr. Abbot wins his case against the grocery store (through either a settlement or a court judgment), he will earn 33 percent of the amount awarded to his client. This is quite ethical and a common practice for plaintiffs' attorneys. Defendants' attorneys, however, usually receive a fee that does not vary based on whether their clients win. Can you see any potential conflict of interest? Would anyone knowing all the facts think that perhaps Mrs. Abbot might not be quite as diligent in her representation of the grocery store as she would be if another attorney were representing the plaintiff? In addition, do you think anyone might be concerned that in a careless moment either Mr. or Mrs. Abbot might let some confidential information slip?

The second type of conflict of interest occurs when the attorney or paralegal has information about the client on the opposite side of the case and therefore may know information that will be detrimental to that person. For example, assume attorney Smith and paralegal Jones worked for Mr. Brown when he was getting a divorce. During the divorce proceedings attorney Smith and paralegal Jones naturally became quite informed on Mr. Brown's financial state, including his partnership interest in a local gymnasium. It is now two years later, and one of Mr. Brown's partners has approached the firm seeking representation in a case he wants to bring against Mr. Brown. If attorney Smith is allowed to take the case, his knowledge of Mr. Brown's finances that he gained while he represented him in his divorce might put Mr. Brown at an unfair disadvantage.

As you can see, client confidentiality and conflicts of interest are very closely related. In the case of Mr. and Mrs. Abbot there is the fear that confidentiality might be breached because of the close relationship between the attorneys representing the two sides. In the second case the fear is more real, as attorney Smith actually knows confidential information and the only issue is whether he might use it against his former client. Because of this possibility the ethics codes require that attorney Smith either obtain Mr. Brown's consent to proceed as the attorney representing the partner or resign from the case. In addition, all other attorneys at attorney Smith's firm would be barred from representing Mr. Brown's partner.

Conflicts of interest that involve representing two potentially adverse clients can be classified as **concurrent** (representing both clients simultaneously) or

Concurrent conflict of interest
Simultaneously representing adverse clients.

Figure 11-3 Personal Conflict

Example: Husband and wife represent opposing sides at litigation.

π Store customer ⟶ Δ Grocery store
(Attorney, Mr. Abbot)   (Attorney, Mrs. Abbot)
Receives 33 percent   Receives fee no matter the outcome.
if he wins   Might the store question Mrs. Abbot's
                               zealous representation?

---

successive (representing one client and then later representing the second client). The conflicts can also be classified as actual or potential.

a. Concurrent Representation/Actual Conflict

The Model Rules of Professional Conduct provide the following:

Rule 1.7(a) A lawyer shall not represent a client if the representation of that client will be directly adverse to another client, unless:

(1) the lawyer reasonably believes the representation will not adversely affect the relationship with the other client; and
(2) each client consents after consultation.

Notice that there are two parts to this test. First, the attorney must reasonably believe that the other client will not be adversely affected, and second, each client must consent.

Assume attorney Baker is representing Deb Driver against Tracy Trucker. If Tracy asks attorney Baker to also represent her, this is an obvious conflict of interest. If attorney Baker is to fully represent Deb, she must try to get the maximum settlement from Tracy. However, to fully represent Tracy, she would have to try to minimize any settlement that Tracy would have to pay. Attorney Baker may not represent both Deb Driver and Tracy Trucker. See Figure 11-4.

b. Concurrent Representation/Potential Conflict

Now assume Patti Passenger, who was in Deb's car, also wants to sue Tracy Trucker. Can attorney Baker represent Patti? It appears that there is no conflict, as both Patti and Deb want to sue Tracy. But let's stop for a moment and think about what could happen. Assume Tracy decides to countersue Deb, claiming the accident was really Deb's fault. If the jury awards Patti damages by finding Deb 50 percent at fault and Tracy 50 percent at fault, attorney Baker is put in an untenable position. Attorney Baker will have to decide whether to appeal the decision (to the detriment of Patti, who would have to wait for her damages award or who might lose it entirely) or not appeal the decision (to the detriment of Deb). Figure 11-5, on page 278, illustrates the problems inherent in this type of situation. In such cases of a **potential conflict**, attorney Baker probably should decline to represent both the driver and the passenger. If the clients are insistent about wanting joint representation, the attorney must completely explain the situation to the potential clients and obtain their consent. In addition, it must be

> **Successive conflict of interest**
> Representing someone who is in a position adverse to a prior client.

> **Potential conflict**
> A situation in which a conflict of interest may arise in the future—for example, representing business partners.

Figure 11-4 Concurrent Representation/Actual Conflict

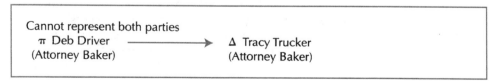

Cannot represent both parties
π Deb Driver ⟶ Δ Tracy Trucker
(Attorney Baker)   (Attorney Baker)

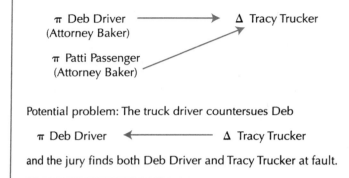

Probably should decline the representation. Before an attorney can represent both clients, the attorney must give both clients full disclosure, she or he must obtain client consent, and it must be obvious that the attorney can adequately represent the interests of each.

π Deb Driver ⟶ Δ Tracy Trucker
(Attorney Baker)

π Patti Passenger
(Attorney Baker)

Potential problem: The truck driver countersues Deb

π Deb Driver ⟵ Δ Tracy Trucker

and the jury finds both Deb Driver and Tracy Trucker at fault.

Figure 11-5   Concurrent Representation/Potential Conflict

obvious to the attorney that he or she can adequately represent the interests of each. Similar situations arise when two potential partners ask an attorney to draft a partnership agreement for them, when spouses assume that an attorney can represent both of them in a no-fault divorce, and when two criminal defendants want the same lawyer to represent them.

c. Successive Representation

Usually, once an attorney has represented someone, that attorney cannot represent another client who wishes to sue one of the attorney's former clients. Courts generally disallow such representation if the new matter is substantially related to the subject matter of the prior representation. As you can imagine, frequently there is disagreement as to whether the two matters are "substantially related." Consider the example we cited earlier, where attorney Smith represented Mr. Brown when he was getting his divorce. Two years later one of Mr. Brown's partners approached attorney Smith seeking representation in a case he wants to bring against Mr. Brown. These two matters are certainly different. However, there is the possibility that attorney Smith's knowledge of Mr. Brown's business dealings that he acquired during the divorce proceedings may give her an unfair advantage in representing the business partner. Therefore, attorney Smith should decline the representation of the business partner. See Figure 11-6, on page 279.

To summarize, in cases of actual conflict an attorney can never represent both sides. In those situations involving potential conflict or successive representation a court might allow the representation so long as the client consented after being fully informed of the potential problems. However, the court could still disallow the representation if the court thought that there was in fact an actual conflict or that the client had not been fully informed.

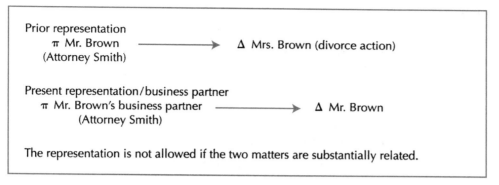

Figure 11-6   Successive Representation

d. Vicarious Representation

Under the Model Rules of Professional Conduct, if one lawyer in a firm is disqualified from representing a client, then all of the lawyers are disqualified.

Rule 1.10(a) While lawyers are associated in a firm, none of them shall knowingly represent a client when any one of them practicing alone would be prohibited from doing so. . . .

(c) A disqualification prescribed by this rule may be waived by the affected client under the conditions stated in Rule 1.7.

This is known as **vicarious representation,** whereby all members of a law firm are treated as though they had represented the client. Therefore, the disqualification of one attorney means that everyone in the firm is disqualified.

This rule creates problems when a lawyer leaves one firm to join another. Assume a lawyer is representing Mary in the case of Mary versus Tom. Clearly, he cannot also represent Tom. Then assume the lawyer switches firms to the firm representing Tom. May that firm continue in its representation of Tom? The rules indicate that it may not. This is because this scenario is really no different from the prior example. An attorney in the firm has confidential information about the opposing party. On the other hand, if every time an attorney switches firms it means that no one in the new firm can ever take a case against one of that attorney's former clients, then it is very difficult for attorneys to make necessary career moves. Whether the same applies to a paralegal changing firms is currently one of the most hotly debated ethical issues.

Finally, assume it is not the attorney representing Mary who switches firms but rather an attorney who has had no dealings with Mary's case. Now may the second firm continue its representation of Tom? Absent client consent, some courts say no. Even though the attorney did not work directly on the case, there is still the appearance of impropriety, that is, that confidences may have been breached. Other courts follow a more flexible approach. They give the attorneys an opportunity to prove either that they did not receive any confidential information or that, if they did, the information was not substantially material and they have been totally screened from the case. See Figure 11-7, on page 280.

Vicarious representation
The rule whereby all members of a law firm are treated as though they had represented the former client.

Figure 11-7   Vicarious Representation

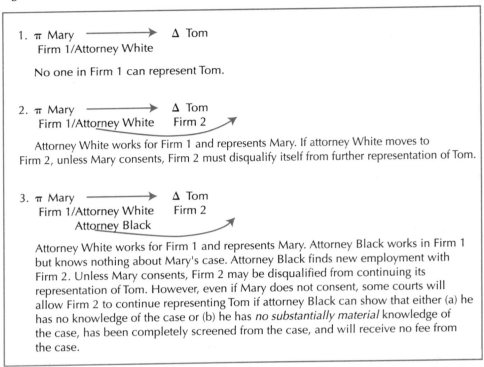

1. π Mary ————————➤ Δ Tom
   Firm 1/Attorney White

   No one in Firm 1 can represent Tom.

2. π Mary ————————➤ Δ Tom
   Firm 1/Attorney White   Firm 2 ↗

   Attorney White works for Firm 1 and represents Mary. If attorney White moves to
   Firm 2, unless Mary consents, Firm 2 must disqualify itself from further representation of Tom.

3. π Mary ————————➤ Δ Tom
   Firm 1/Attorney White   Firm 2
   Attorney Black   ↗

   Attorney White works for Firm 1 and represents Mary. Attorney Black works in Firm 1
   but knows nothing about Mary's case. Attorney Black finds new employment with
   Firm 2. Unless Mary consents, Firm 2 may be disqualified from continuing its
   representation of Tom. However, even if Mary does not consent, some courts will
   allow Firm 2 to continue representing Tom if attorney Black can show that either (a) he
   has no knowledge of the case or (b) he has *no substantially material* knowledge of
   the case, has been completely screened from the case, and will receive no fee from
   the case.

The rule that a firm must refuse new clients when one of its attorneys has had
prior involvement with the opposing side becomes particularly oppressive when
applied to paralegals. A firm might be willing to hire an attorney, knowing that it
might mean declining to take any case where the attorney has worked on the other
side. Many firms would not be willing to make this sacrifice to hire a paralegal.

And yet because paralegals have access to confidential information
about a firm's clients, the movement of a paralegal from one law firm to
another presents the same types of conflict of interest problems as when a
lawyer moves from one firm to another. In 1988 an ABA Standing
Committee on Ethics and Professional Responsibility informal opinion concluded that a law firm should not automatically be disqualified from a case
simply because a paralegal employee used to work for another attorney who
represents someone who is suing one of the firm's clients. The nonlawyer
must be cautioned

PRACTICE TIP

Use a computerized conflict-checking program. Years after the fact, you do
not want to be relying on your memory as to the names of all the clients with
whom you have had significant contact.

1. not to disclose any information relating to the representation of a client of the former employer and
2. not to work on any matter on which the employee worked for the prior employer or about which the employee has information relating to the representation of the client of the former employer.

The key requirement in such a situation is that the new law firm and the paralegal must strictly adhere to a screening process. Establishing such a screening process is known as erecting an **ethical wall or screen** or a **cone of silence**. With an ethical wall an attorney or a paralegal can be shielded from a case so that the law firm cannot use the attorney's or paralegal's confidential information to the detriment of the former client. To create an effective wall, the firm must undertake the following steps:

Ethical wall or screen or cone of silence
A system developed to shield an attorney or a paralegal from a case that otherwise would create a conflict of interest.

1. Develop an educational program for employees that includes warning all employees of the firm about the importance of not sharing information. Have firmwide meetings to discuss the importance of confidentiality and why ethical walls must be built.
2. Specifically prohibit those with confidential information from discussing the case or the client with others in the firm.
3. Restrict access to files. This can be done by "flagging" the files so they are easily identifiable at a distance and by physically removing them from areas where the person with the conflict can have access to them.
4. Write a memorandum to all personnel instructing them not to discuss the conflict matter with the conflict person.
5. Separate those working on the file from those with the information.
6. Circulate a policy statement concerning the specific wall, and announce the methods for enforcement, including sanctions.
7. Notify the client. The client's consent may be necessary to avoid disqualification.

3. The Unauthorized Practice of Law

As you know, lawyers are licensed to practice law; paralegals are not. This difference has important consequences for paralegals. Many of the issues regarding the **unauthorized practice of law** by nonlawyers are bound to change if the licensing of paralegals becomes a reality. Meanwhile, however, you need to be aware that most states have statutes that prohibit nonlawyers from practicing law. Take a moment to read the following excerpts from two Massachusetts statutes.

Unauthorized practice of law
When nonlawyers do things that only lawyers are allowed to do. In most states this is a crime.

Penalties on Disbarred or Unauthorized Attorneys and for Soliciting Law Business
[W]hoever, not having been lawfully admitted to practice as an attorney at law, represents himself to be an attorney . . . by means of a sign, business card, letter head or otherwise, or holds himself out or represents or advertises himself as having authority or power in behalf of persons who have claims for damages to procure settlements of such claims for damages either to person or property, . . . shall be punished for a first offence by a fine of not more than one hundred dollars or by imprisonment for not more than six

months, and for a subsequent offence by a fine of not more than five hundred dollars or by imprisonment for not more than one year.[7]

Only Member of Bar in Good Standing to Practice Law
No individual, other than a member, in good standing, of the bar of this commonwealth shall practice law, or, by word, sign, letter, advertisement or otherwise, hold himself out as authorized, entitled, competent, qualified or able to practice law. . . .[8]

Practice of law
An activity that requires professional judgment, or the educated ability to relate law to a specific legal problem.

Professional judgment
The educated ability to apply law to specific facts.

First, notice that the unauthorized practice of law is a crime punishable by fine or imprisonment. Those sanctions have been rarely used. Second, while the statutes prohibit nonlawyers from practicing law, they do not give any guidance as to what it is. The Model Code defines the **practice of law** as an activity that calls for the exercise of professional judgment. **Professional judgment** is further defined in EC 3-5 as the "educated ability to relate the general body and philosophy of law to a specific legal problem of a client." Contrast this definition of professional judgment with the definition of what a paralegal or legal assistant does developed by NALA in its Code of Ethics and Professional Responsibility.

Legal assistants, also known as paralegals, are a distinguishable group of persons who assist attorneys in the delivery of legal services. Through formal education, training and experience, legal assistants have *knowledge and expertise regarding the legal system and substantive and procedural law* which qualify them to do work of a legal nature under the supervision of an attorney. (*Emphasis added.*)

In this course you have been acquiring knowledge "regarding the legal system and substantive and procedural law." But you have also been gaining an "educated ability to relate the general body and philosophy of law to a specific legal problem of a client." Does this mean that once you are working as a paralegal, you can rely on your knowledge of the law but you cannot use your ability to apply that knowledge to a specific situation? The short answer is no, if your work is done under the supervision of an attorney and you avoid doing any of the following:

1. establishing the attorney-client relationship or setting the legal fee,
2. giving legal advice to clients to inform them of their rights and obligations,
3. preparing for clients (as opposed to your supervising attorney) documents that require knowledge of legal principles not possessed by ordinary lay people, and
4. appearing for clients in court.

This does not mean that paralegals cannot meet with clients. They can, if they refrain from establishing the attorney-client relationship, setting the fee, and giving legal advice. They can also draft documents if a supervising attorney reviews those documents and takes full responsibility for their content.

---

[7] Mass. Gen. L. ch. 221, § 41 (2006).
[8] Mass. Gen. L. ch. 221, § 46A (2006).

Finally, paralegals can be present in court to assist an attorney.

a. Justifications for Restrictions

Some argue that unauthorized practice of law statutes have historically been used to protect lawyers from competition with lay persons seeking to perform similar services for less money. Others defend unauthorized practice of law statutes based on the "public interest." The following statement from *West Virginia State Bar v. Earley* is typical of the manner in which courts have justified these restrictions:

> The justification for excluding from the practice of law persons who are not admitted to the bar and for limiting and restricting such practice to licensed members of the legal profession is not the protection of the members of the bar from competition or the creation of a monopoly for the members of the legal profession, but is instead the protection of the public from being advised and represented in legal matters by unqualified and undisciplined persons over whom the judicial department of the government could exercise slight or no control.[9]

However, as Deborah Rhode pointed out in a Stanford Law Review article:

> Courts have not required any factual showing that unqualified restraints on lay practice are necessary—or even closely related—to the states' interest in preventing incompetent assistance. Nor have courts inquired whether that interest could be realized through less restrictive means. Existing research in the most active areas of unauthorized practice enforcement suggests that states would have considerable difficulty making either demonstration.[10]

One major empirical study found that only 2 percent of the 1,188 cases concerning lay advocates originated from complaints by dissatisfied customers, and few of those involved claims of incompetence.[11]

This appears to make little difference to the courts. For example, in State exrel. *Johnson v. Childe* the court conceded that Childe, a nonlawyer, may have been more knowledgeable about one specialized area of the law than most lawyers; however,

> [t]his is not a defense. We do not doubt that respondent possesses high qualifications in the transportation rate field. But the fact that he can qualify as an expert in a particular field will not permit his engaging lawfully in the profession of the law without a license to do so.[12]

A key factor in the courts' justification of unauthorized practice statutes is that lawyers are governed by ethical restraints that do not apply to their lay competitors. In response to this argument, advocates of the legal technician

---

[9] 109 S.E.2d 420, 435 (W. Va. 1959).

[10] Deborah Rhode, Policing the Professional Monopoly: A Constitutional and Empirical Analysis of Unauthorized Practice of Law Prohibitions, 34 Stan. L. Rev. 1, 85 (1991).

[11] Id.

[12] 295 N.W. 381, 382 (Neb. 1941).

movement and other legal reformers point out that the limited licensing approaches we discussed in Chapter 2 would also impose these types of fiduciary duties and provide a mechanism for enforcing them. Thus, they argue, non lawyers could be licensed to practice in limited designated areas of the law without endangering the public interest.

b. Defining the Practice of Law

Beyond stating that the practice of law involves professional judgment, no ethical code defines the practice of law. In fact, EC 3-5 in the Model Code begins with the declaration that "[i]t is neither necessary nor desirable to attempt the formulation of a single, specific definition of what constitutes the practice of law."

The ABA's Model Guidelines for the Utilization of Legal Assistant Services provide limited guidance as to what constitutes the unauthorized practice of law. Guideline 3 declares:

> A lawyer may not delegate to a legal assistant:
> (a) Responsibility for establishing an attorney-client relationship.
> (b) Responsibility for establishing the amount of a fee to be charged for a legal service.
> (c) Responsibility for a legal opinion rendered to a client.

These activities are forbidden because they are considered to be an essential part of the practice of law.

In seeking to apply the concept of unauthorized practice of law to specific situations, the courts have frequently sought to define the practice of law by listing the activities that lawyers usually perform. Besides involving circular reasoning, it is difficult to defend a proposition that asserts that a nonlawyer can be prohibited from doing a task simply because traditionally lawyers have performed it. Also, this approach is simply not accurate. Just because a lawyer does a task does not make the task the practice of law. For example, if an attorney were to type a letter, that the attorney was the one typing would not transform a clerical task into a legal one.

The U.S. Supreme Court impliedly rejected this approach in *Missouri v. Jenkins*,[13] the case that dealt with assessing fees for paralegal work. In that decision the Court suggested that it would not allow a lawyer to recover legal fees for clerical work done by a lawyer.

A second, seemingly more productive approach to the problem of defining unauthorized practice is to focus on whether the activity in question requires legal skills and knowledge beyond that of the average lay person. One problem with this standard is that accountants, real estate brokers, insurance agents, bankers, and other lay persons also exercise professional judgment on matters affected by the law. Some of these professionals may know more about recent legal developments in their specialty than does the average lawyer. Some courts have created exceptions to the general unauthorized practice standard for activities that lay persons frequently perform as incidental to another business or transaction. For example, in Arizona the voters approved a constitutional amendment giving real estate brokers the right to perform certain legal tasks.

---

[13] 491 U.S. 274, 288 (1989).

c. Prohibited Tasks

Nonetheless, certain tasks traditionally have been considered tasks that only lawyers could perform. They include making courtroom appearances, preparing legal documents, and giving legal advice. As you will see, while it is still true that nonlawyers are limited in what they can do in each of these areas, there is room for paralegal involvement.

(1) Courtroom and administrative agency representation

The application of unauthorized practice statutes is least ambiguous in the area of courtroom representation. With very few exceptions only licensed attorneys are allowed to present motions and argue cases in court. Although the courts have recognized a constitutional right to self-representation, they have rejected interpreting the Sixth Amendment right to counsel to require the courts to allow a defendant who so wishes to be represented by a nonlawyer.

However, nonlawyers are sometimes allowed to act in a representative capacity at administrative hearings. At the federal level the Administrative Procedure Act states:

> A person compelled to appear in person before an agency or representative thereof is entitled to be accompanied, represented, and advised by counsel or, if permitted by the agency, by other qualified representatives.[14]

More than thirty federal agencies provide for lay representation, including the Bureau of Indian Affairs, the Departments of Agriculture, Justice, Labor, and Veterans Affairs, the Environmental Protection Agency, the Food and Drug Administration, the Immigration and Naturalization Service, the Internal Revenue Service, the Patent and Trademark Office, and the Social Security Administration.

NETNOTE

For a complete list of federal agencies that provide for lay representation, along with the Code of Federal Regulation references, go to *www.paralegals.org*.

Sometimes state unauthorized practice of law statutes may conflict with federal statutes allowing for lay representation. For example, in *Sperry v. State of Florida*,[15] the U.S. Supreme Court upheld the right of the Patent Office to

---

[14] 5 U.S.C. § 555(b) (2006) (emphasis added).
[15] 373 U.S. 379 (1963).

authorize nonlawyers to practice before it. The Court ruled that this congressional authorization superseded conflicting provisions of Florida's attorney licensing act. Thus, although the preparation and prosecution of patent applications for others constitutes the practice of law under Florida statutes, these statutes cannot be applied to the practices of a federal agency.

At the state level some statutes and administrative regulations also permit lay representation in many agencies. Workers' compensation boards, unemployment compensation boards, and public utility commissions are most apt to have made such allowances.

(2) Preparation of legal documents

In *Davies v. Unauthorized Practice Committee* the Texas Supreme Court noted that

> the practice of law is not confined to cases conducted in court. In fact, the major portion of the practice of any capable lawyer consists of work done outside of the courts . . . and includes the giving of advice or the rendering of any service requiring the use of legal skill or knowledge, such as preparing a will, contract or other instrument. . . .[16]

Court cases regarding this type of activity have generally arisen in the areas of real estate, divorce, workers' compensation, and estate planning.

In the real estate area some courts have applied the principle that it is permissible for lay persons to prepare standard business forms when such preparation is incidental to their business. Thus, as noted above, in several states real estate agents and brokers have been allowed to draft sales contracts and leases. This is especially true when they are merely filling in the blanks on standardized forms drafted by attorneys.

In recent years a growing number of nonlawyers (using titles such as legal technician, lay advocate, legal scrivener, forms practitioner, forms preparer, and legal information specialist) have been engaged in the business of filling out standardized legal forms. One of the most famous pioneers in this area was Rosemary Furman, whose battle with the Florida State Bar Association over her divorce forms preparation service attracted a great deal of media attention. Furman was a former court stenographer and legal secretary who opened her own secretarial service. For a $50 fee she would provide clients with the court documents they needed to file for an uncontested divorce. She also sold kits for adoptions, name changes, powers of attorney, wills, and bankruptcies. She is said to have handled as many as twenty divorces a week and serviced over 10,000 clients.[17] She informed her clients orally and in writing that she was not an attorney and did not have any attorneys working in her office.[18]

In 1977 the state bar started legal actions against her for the unauthorized practice of law. Two years later the Florida Supreme Court held that she could sell preprinted court forms and general instructions on do-it-yourself divorces but that she could not advise clients on the various remedies that were available. Although she could type her client's answers in the blanks, the client had to

---

[16] 431 S.W.2d 590, 593 (Tex. 1968).

[17] Murray, Slugging It Out for Justice, 1 Legal Assistant Today 20, 22 (Summer 1984).

[18] Id.

independently decide what those answers should be, and she was not allowed to modify their responses.[19] She could not even correct their spelling errors.

When Furman continued her business after this decision, the bar association again took her to court. It alleged that she was violating the terms of the court's injunction, which ordered her to refrain from doing more than merely selling the forms and typing her client's answers. In April 1984 the Florida Supreme Court held that she was in contempt of court, sentenced her to 120 days in jail, and ordered her to pay $7,802 in court costs. Ninety days of this sentence was to be suspended if she did not violate the injunction during the next two years.[20] The governor (with the unanimous concurrence of his cabinet) suspended her sentence and reduced the court costs owed to $5,000 when she agreed to close her business.[21]

Although a lay person is not allowed to give a particular individual personal legal advice on a specific problem, some court decisions have allowed publications to offer general legal advice. *New York County Lawyers Association v. Dacey*[22] was one of several cases considering Norman F. Dacey's book How to Avoid Probate!, which consists of about 300 pages of forms for inter vivos trusts, wills, and other related documents. The book also has fifty-five pages of textual material with advice as to how the forms should be completed. In rejecting the conclusion that the publication of this book constituted the unauthorized practice of law, the New York court found that the publication of a text that purports to tell what the law says does not constitute the practice of law because there is no personal contact that involves the establishment of a relationship of confidence and trust. There is no express or implied contract to perform a service. Finally, because every individual has a right to self-representation, the court reasoned that such do-it-yourself material cannot be suppressed. The individual who chooses to rely on this information has to assume the risks that accompany a reliance on this type of information.

The development and marketing of do-it-yourself legal software has made the preparation of legal documents by lay persons considerably easier. While some of these computer programs are sold primarily to legal technicians and scriveners, others are marketed to the public. Programs such as Hyatt Legal Services' HOME LAWYER and Parson's IT'S LEGAL make it relatively easy for the average lay person to complete, for example, a promissory note, a contract for the sale of a car, an apartment lease, or a will.

(3) Giving legal advice

As the *Furman* case illustrates, a lay person can type a client's answers onto a standardized legal form but cannot advise the client as to which form to use or how to word the answers. While paralegals can meet with clients and gather information necessary to draft legal documents, as illustrated by the case of *In re Hessinger & Associates*,[23] the key is supervision. Hessinger & Associates was a

---

[19] Florida Bar Assn. v. Furman, 376 So. 2d 378 (Fla. 1979).

[20] Murray, supra note 12, at 23.

[21] Pearson, Update, 2 Legal Assistant Today 7 (1985).

[22] 234 N.E.2d 459 (N.Y. 1967).

[23] 171 B.R. 366 (Bankr. N.D. Cal. 1994), aff'd in part & rev'd in part by In re Hessinger & Assocs, 192 B.R. 211 (N.D. Cal 1996).

bankruptcy firm that hired paralegals to meet with new clients, to get the clients to sign a contract agreeing to retain the firm, and then to prepare the bankruptcy papers. The paralegals worked in an office where no attorney was present. Once a number of bankruptcy petitions had been completed, a courier picked them up and took them to another office where an attorney signed and filed them. Typically a lawyer saw the client debtor for the first time at the bankruptcy hearing. The court noted that merely reviewing the paperwork was insufficient supervision as the attorney could not possibly know what advice the paralegal had given nor whether that advice was correct. "The incidental availability of a lawyer does not make the practice legal where the attorney exercised no actual and significant supervision of the nonlawyers."[24] The court concluded that the firm had violated the Rules of Professional Conduct by assisting the paralegals in engaging in the unauthorized practice of law.

d. Appropriate Paralegal Tasks

The cases discussed in the previous section all involved the activities of nonlawyers who were working independently or who were working without adequate attorney supervision. The situation changes when the lay person is working under the proper supervision of a licensed attorney: Such a lay person is allowed to perform various legal tasks that otherwise would be considered the unauthorized practice of law. While these tasks may still be considered part of the practice of law, they are no longer unauthorized.

The Model Code, in EC 3-6, provides that delegation to lay persons is proper "if the lawyer maintains a direct relationship with his client, supervises the delegated work, and has complete professional responsibility for the work product."

(1) Contact with clients and people outside the office

As long as paralegals clearly identify their lay status, they can deal directly with clients, attorneys, witnesses, and other relevant people. The major limitations are that they cannot commit an attorney to represent a client or negotiate fee arrangements for the attorney's services and that they cannot give legal advice.

Paralegals can gather and summarize information from clients and can keep clients informed as to developments in their cases. However, they are limited to being information conduits; that is, they can relay instructions from attorneys to clients but cannot provide their own opinions.

Paralegals can make telephone calls, send out correspondence, and in other ways interact with third parties on behalf of the client as long as they identify their status with the law firm and act only within the bounds of their delegated authority. In most states paralegals may be listed on a firm's letterhead and may have their own business cards as long as the listing makes it clear that they are not lawyers.

[24] Id. at 372.

(2) Participation in legal proceedings

A lay person working under the supervision of an attorney can, of course, directly represent clients in those situations discussed above in which lay representation is authorized (as it is in some administrative agencies and inferior courts). Thus legal aid agencies frequently assign paralegals to handle government benefits cases involving administrative hearings.

States differ on such things as whether a paralegal can supervise will executions and represent clients at real estate closings. Although paralegals can apparently attend and observe depositions, they are not allowed to question the deponent on the record.

A few states allow paralegals to answer calendar calls and make purely ministerial motions for such things as uncontested continuances. When working under the supervision of an attorney, a lay person can, of course, perform various "second chair" duties by assisting an attorney during a trial.

(3) Drafting legal documents

Lay personnel who are working under the supervision of an attorney can draft a wide range of legal documents from contracts to pleadings and briefs. However, the supervising attorney is responsible for approving the final draft. An attorney must sign all court documents, and they can be filed only with the attorney's approval.

e. Nature of the Supervision

The ABA Model Guidelines for the Utilization of Legal Assistants clearly hold attorneys responsible for reviewing and supervising the work done by legal assistants who are either employed or retained by them. Guideline 1 instructs the lawyer to "take reasonable measures to ensure that the legal assistant's conduct is consistent with the ABA Model Rules of Professional Conduct." The other guidelines contain phrases such as "provided the lawyer maintains responsibility" and "it is the responsibility of a lawyer to. . . ."

But what does it really mean to be "under the supervision of an attorney"? Is it enough that the paralegal receives general instructions from an attorney? Must the attorney review everything the paralegal does or just the final work product? To completely eliminate the danger of substituting the paralegal's independent legal judgment for that of the attorney, the attorney would have to completely redo the paralegal's work. If that is the case, why should an attorney bother to delegate any tasks? These are questions that, for the most part, have been left to the judgment of individual attorneys. Because the attorney is ultimately responsible for the paralegal's actions, it is generally thought that the attorney should decide how much supervision is needed based on the complexity of the task and the experience of the paralegal.

However, on November 15, 1990, the New Jersey Bar Association's Committee on the Unauthorized Practice of Law issued a controversial advisory opinion that challenged many of the prevailing assumptions about what it meant to act "under the supervision of an attorney." The opinion was the outgrowth of complaints the committee had received from attorneys. In one case the complaining attorney had received a written solicitation from a free-

NETNOTE

There are two excellent web sites that track developments in legal ethics and provide links to the states' Rules of Professional Conduct or Code of Professional Responsibility and to ethics opinions. You can find them at:

www.law.cornell.edu/ethics and www.legalethics.com

lance paralegal containing an offer to prepare real estate closings. Another complaint was made by an attorney who had received a settlement offer from a firm of paralegals. The committee held a hearing at which the independent paralegals as well as attorneys testified. Many aspects of that testimony concerned the committee, including a fear that attorneys were hiring paralegals to work in areas in which they themselves were unfamiliar and that at least some paralegals were sending out letters on firm stationery without prior attorney review. In Opinion No. 24 the committee concluded that freelance paralegals were engaged in the unauthorized practice of law. By working on a contractual basis (rather than as employees), they did not receive adequate supervision from a licensed attorney.

In a 1992 opinion[25] the New Jersey Supreme Court reviewed the committee's decision. The court cited with approval the 1989 United States Supreme Court opinion *Missouri v. Jenkins*, 491 U.S. 274 (1989), agreeing that the use of paralegals represents a means for achieving the goal of providing legal services to the public at an affordable cost while maintaining the quality of legal services.[26]

The court also noted that "[t]here is no question that paralegals' work constitutes the practice of law.... However, paralegals who are supervised by attorneys do not engage in the unauthorized practice of law."[27] Therefore, any lack of supervision is a problem. However, the court held that there is no logical reason to distinguish between the degree of supervision required in regard to freelance as opposed to employed paralegals. "The key is supervision, and that supervision must occur regardless of whether the paralegal is employed by the attorney or retained by the attorney."[28] Of special note to all paralegals was the court's admonition that

> [a]lthough fulfilling the ethical requirements of RPC 5.3 is primarily the attorney's obligation and responsibility, a paralegal is not relieved from an independent obligation to refrain from illegal conduct and to work directly under the supervision of the attorney. A paralegal who recognizes that the attorney is not directly supervising his or her work or that such supervision is illusory because the attorney knows nothing about the field in which the paralegal is working must understand that he or she is engaged in the unauthorized practice of law. In such a situation an independent paralegal must withdraw from representation of the client.[29]

---

[25] In re Opinion No. 24 of the Committee on the Unauthorized Practice of Law, 128 N.J. 114, 607 A.2d 962 (1992).

[26] Id. at 123, 607 A.2d at 966.

[27] Id. at 122-123, 607 A.2d at 966.

[28] Id. at 127, 607 A.2d at 969.

[29] Id.

Finally, the court pointed out that no standards have been set down by any regulatory authority regarding paralegal activities. Therefore, the court stated that it would establish a standing committee to make recommendations regarding paralegal education and regulation. "Any such regulations or guidelines should encourage the use of paralegals while providing both attorneys and paralegals with a set of principles that together with the Rules of Professional Conduct can guide their practices. The guidelines drafted will not be static but subject to modification as new issues arise."[30] In July of 1998 the Committee's report was published. It contained nine recommendations, including that rules for licensing the practice of paralegals be developed. To be eligible for plenary licensure, a paralegal would have to earn a certificate of completion at an American Bar Association–approved paralegal program, complete a minimum of 60 college credits, and pass an ethics examination to be administered by the Office of Paralegal Licensure. After a period of public comment the New Jersey Supreme Court decided not to follow any of the committee's recommendation. The court determined that the best method for overseeing paralegal activity is through attorney supervision, rather than through a new court-directed licensing system.

DISCUSSION QUESTION

9. John has worked as a paralegal for ten years. Over the years he has gained a great deal of expertise, especially in the area of personal injury work. Recently his boss, attorney Amanda Butler, asked him to draft a complaint alleging fraud and negligence as alternate claims. He drafted the complaint, and Amanda read it and then signed it. As was customary practice in the firm, John then sent a copy of the complaint to the client with the following cover letter. Discuss each of John's activities, beginning with his drafting of the complaint, and decide whether he has or has not committed the unauthorized practice of law.

LAW OFFICES OF
PROCTOR & WHITNEY

Jonathan Proctor, Esq.   Cynthia Shore, Esq.
William Whitney, Esq.   John Jake, Paralegal
Rebecca Whalen, Esq.   Janet Smith, Esq.
Amanda Butler, Esq.

May 7, 2006

Dear Ms. Brown:

Enclosed please find a copy of the complaint that this law firm has filed on your behalf. Do not be confused by the seemingly inconsistent claims of fraud and negligence. Although fraud requires an intent to deceive, while negligence only requires unreasonable conduct, we do not yet have enough facts to know which is the most appropriate theory. However, based on the facts as you presented them, we will probably end up proceeding under the fraud theory.

Sincerely,
John Jake
John Jake, Legal Aide

---

[30] Id. at 135, 607 A.2d at 974.

C. MONEY MATTERS

P R A C T I C E
T I P

Color code your checks
so that there can be no
danger of your acci-
dentally using a client
account check when
you mean to use a
general office account
check.

Four issues dealing with money are particularly important for you to know about. First, the firm's money and the client's money must be kept in separate accounts with no possible commingling. Second, attorneys may charge clients for the time paralegals spend working on a case, but it is unethical to charge paralegal fees for clerical work or to charge attorney time for work a paralegal actually accomplished. Third, usually attorneys are forbidden from forming partnerships and sharing profits with nonattorneys. Finally, attorneys may not pay paralegals for bringing new clients into the firm.

1. Client Funds

Client trust account

A bank account used to hold money belonging to the client or to a third party.

Generally, attorneys maintain two types of accounts: a general office account out of which they pay their daily operating expenses and **client trust accounts** into which they deposit client funds. For example, when the firm receives a retainer fee from a client, the fee is deposited in the client trust account, and sums are withdrawn from that account only as the firm earns them. All moneys in client trust accounts belong to the clients, and the attorney managing the accounts must be scrupulous in making sure that there is no commingling of funds; that is, money the attorney has earned must always be kept entirely separate from the client funds.

A particularly sad case of an attorney being caught borrowing client funds is *In re Warhtig*.[31] Attorney Warhtig found himself in financial straits created by his wife's having to undergo cancer treatment and his son's need for extensive psychiatric counseling. Mr. Warhtig was a real estate attorney, and he routinely deposited large sums of money into a trust account in anticipation of a real estate closing. Periodically, prior to the closing, he would advance himself his fee that was due at the closing. He always made the proper disbursements at the closing, and no clients ever lost any money. The New Jersey Disciplinary Review Board recommended a public reprimand. The N.J. Supreme Court refused to accept that recommendation and instead ordered Mr. Warhtig disbarred.

Even when attorneys do not actually take or "borrow" client funds, their mishandling of such funds can lead to serious sanctions. In reviewing the case of an attorney, who had also been charged with assisting in the unauthorized practice of law, the court noted that

> Edwins clearly violated DR 9-102 by failing to deposit his client's funds in a separate trust account, by failing to notify the client of the receipt of his funds, by failing to account to the client properly with respect to the distribution of the funds, by failing to maintain complete records of the client's funds, and by failing to pay the client the funds he was entitled to receive.[32]

---

[31] 524 A.2d 398 (N.J. 1987).

[32] Louisiana State Bar Assn. v. Edwins, 540 So. 2d 294, 301 (La. 1989).

These actions contributed to the decision to order attorney Edwin's disbarment.

2. Charging Clients for Paralegal Time

Since the case of *Missouri v. Jenkins*[33] it has been widely accepted that attorneys may bill the client for paralegal time. However, they still must ensure that the hourly amount being charged is fair, must ensure that the work the paralegal did was paralegal work and not clerical work, and must document the actual hours spent. Because many firms have a target number of hours that they expect their attorneys and paralegals to bill, there is often a temptation to pad the hours actually spent or to double-bill. Double-billing occurs when, for example, an attorney waiting in court for a case to begin works on another client's file. Occasionally, paralegals may even see attorneys billing out time at the attorney rate for work done by the paralegal. Obviously, these practices are unethical and illegal, as they result in the attorney's unlawfully taking money from the client.

3. Fee-Splitting

When lawyers use lay assistants, traditionally they have not been allowed to share fees with them or to form a partnership, an association, or a professional corporation with a nonlawyer if any of the activities of the partnership, association, or corporation involve the practice of law. The rule prohibiting lawyers from forming partnerships with nonlawyers has recently come under attack, and the practice is now allowed, at least on a limited basis, in some states.

Model Utilization Guideline 8 authorizes lawyers to charge separately for work performed by a legal assistant. However, Guideline 9 prohibits the lawyer from splitting legal fees with a legal assistant or paying a legal assistant for the referral of legal business. A lawyer may compensate a legal assistant based on the quantity and quality of his or her work and the value of that work to the law practice. The compensation cannot, by advance agreement, be contingent on the profitability of the lawyer's practice. The commentary accompanying Guideline 9 states:

> The linchpin of the prohibition seems to be the advance agreement of the lawyer to "split" a fee based on a preexisting contingent arrangement. There is no general prohibition against a lawyer who enjoys a particularly profitable period recognizing the contribution of the legal assistant to that profitability with a discretionary bonus.

4. Avoiding Solicitation

The new Model Rules specifically allow attorneys to advertise through telephone directories, newspapers, periodicals, billboards, radio, and television. However, although lawyers may pay for advertising, they cannot pay another person for sending them clients. Thus paralegals cannot go out and solicit clients on behalf of their employers.

D. OVERZEALOUS REPRESENTATION

Attorneys are expected to be zealous advocates for their clients. As an attorney's assistant, a paralegal is also expected to actively support the client's cause.

---

[33] 491 U.S. 274 (1989).

However, there are limits to how far either an attorney or a paralegal can go in that zealous representation. Specifically, paralegals must be aware that they usually may not talk to an adverse party who is represented by an attorney and that they must always avoid any form of deception when dealing with persons outside the law firm.

1. Talking to the Opposing Party or Jurors

A lawyer may not communicate directly with the opposing party if the lawyer knows that the other party is represented by a lawyer. Therefore, a paralegal cannot interview the opposing party in a civil case or a co-defendant in a criminal case without first receiving the permission of that party's attorney. In addition, in a few states there are very specific prohibitions, such as one limiting the right of an attorney or a paralegal to talk to jurors during or after a case is concluded. To be on the safe side, be sure to check your local rules.

2. Avoiding Deception

Model Rule 8.4 provides that it is "professional misconduct for a lawyer to . . . engage in conduct involving dishonesty, fraud, deceit or misrepresentation." Attorneys must be candid when dealing with the court, opposing counsel, and third parties. Usually, there is no affirmative duty to inform an opposing party of relevant facts. But misrepresentation can occur if you affirm a statement made by someone else when you know it is false.

Also, attorneys must not make statements or present evidence they know is false. Model Rule 4.1(a) states that when an attorney is dealing with others on the client's behalf, the attorney may not make a false statement of material fact. Because paralegals act as agents for their supervising attorneys, they must live by the same restrictions.

Model Rule 4.4 is of special importance to paralegals who do investigative or collections work. It states:

> In representing a client, a lawyer shall not use means that have no substantial purpose other than to embarrass, delay, or burden a third person, or use methods of obtaining evidence that violate the legal rights of such a person.

These restrictions mean that paralegals cannot misrepresent their identity or make other false statements in order to gain the confidence of a reluctant witness. Nor can any compensation beyond ordinary witness fees be offered to a lay witness as an inducement to testify.

Another restriction imposed on attorneys and paralegals, but not applicable to police or private investigators, is the requirement that a conversation not be recorded without the consent of all parties.

E. ENFORCEMENT

The legal and ethical restrictions mentioned above are enforced through a variety of sanctions. Acts of fraud, bribery, obstruction of justice, and so forth can result

in felony convictions and imprisonment. In most states violation of the unauthorized practice of law statutes can result in a misdemeanor conviction; however, the courts usually respond to unauthorized practice of law charges with injunctions and the threat of contempt charges.

Attorneys who breach ethical requirements can be reprimanded, suspended, or disbarred. A **reprimand or censure** is an announcement that the attorney's conduct violated the code of ethics. A **suspension** means that the attorney may not practice law for a specified time, and a **disbarment** means that the attorney's license to practice is revoked. The specific mechanisms for imposing these sanctions vary from one state to another, but it is ultimately up to the state's judiciary to impose a suspension or a disbarment.

Because paralegals are not licensed, they cannot be suspended or sanctioned as attorneys can. Attorneys can, however, be sanctioned for the misdeeds of their employees because the codes of ethics hold them responsible for adequately supervising their lay employees. This gives attorneys a vested interest in sanctioning their own employees. Any breach of their ethical duties means that the employees will probably lose their jobs and have difficulty finding new ones.

F. TORT LAW OF NEGLIGENCE

In general, the law of **negligence** requires that all of us act reasonably given the circumstances. For paralegals this means that they must perform their job duties in a reasonable manner or they may find themselves being sued for negligence. In addition, a supervising attorney might be liable in a negligence suit if the plaintiff shows that the attorney was negligent. Negligence can occur in the supervision of the paralegal, in the proper delegation of duties to the paralegal, or originally in the hiring of the paralegal.

Generally, to prove a **legal malpractice** case, it must be shown that

1. an attorney-client relationship existed (the duty element),
2. the duty was breached by the attorney's negligence,
3. the negligence caused
4. harm, and
5. the client's original claim would have succeeded but for the negligence.

This last element is known as having to **prove a case within a case.**

In determining whether a professional is liable for negligence, the courts look to see whether the defendant exercised the skill and knowledge normally possessed by members of that profession. Furthermore, some courts have held that any violation of prescribed standards (such as codes of ethics or licensing statutes) constitutes negligence per se. Finally, breach of a confidential or fiduciary relationship constitutes an intentional tort.

After a comprehensive analysis of these principles as applied to paralegals, John Wade, in a Vanderbilt Law Review article, concluded that, in civil cases where the plaintiff is claiming some sort of injury or harm because of actions

Reprimand or censure A public or private statement that an attorney's conduct violated the code of ethics.

Suspension A determination that an attorney may not practice law for a set period of time.

Disbarment The revocation of an attorney's license.

Negligence The failure to act reasonably under the circumstances.

Legal malpractice The failure of an attorney to act reasonably.

Proving a case within a case The requirement in a legal malpractice case that the plaintiff-client prove that but for the attorney's negligence, the client would have won.

taken by a paralegal, the paralegal will not be judged by the standard of care expected of a lawyer

> as long as he (1) holds himself out only as a paralegal, (2) does not attempt to perform services outside the scope of that customary for paralegal personnel, and (3) conforms to the standard of care, skill, and knowledge normal for the paralegal. On the other hand, if he fails to make clear that he is only acting as a paralegal, or if he undertakes to render legal services outside the scope of his competency, he will be held to the higher standard applicable to the normal attorney.[34]

DISCUSSION QUESTIONS

10. Attorney Janice Brown has an extremely busy practice. A few months ago she began complaining of stress headaches and chest pain. Her paralegal Susan Smith became concerned that if attorney Brown did not slow down her practice, she would become ill. Trying to help, paralegal Smith started screening all of attorney Brown's telephone calls, only telling her about the ones that paralegal Smith felt it was essential for attorney Brown to deal with herself. In her effort to be helpful, what problems may paralegal Smith be creating for her boss?

11. Paralegal Graham misplaces a client's file. By the time it is found, the statute of limitations has run out. The client wants to sue the firm for malpractice. An objective evaluator would say that the client had very little chance of winning his original claim. What problems will the client have in succeeding in a malpractice claim?

Legal Reasoning Exercise

2. Reread the situation presented at the beginning of the chapter. Write a legal analysis discussing any ethical issues raised by each of paralegal Green's activities. As part of your answer be sure to include the generally accepted definition for the unauthorized practice of law and to explain why paralegal Green, a nonlawyer, must nonetheless worry about abiding by the attorney's code of ethics.

SUMMARY

As members of the legal team, paralegals must abide by the attorneys' code of ethics adopted in their state. While both paralegal associations, NFPA and NALA, have devel-

---

[34] Wade, Tort Liability of Paralegals and Lawyers Who Utilize Their Services, 24 Vand. L. Rev. 1133, 1140 (1971).

oped ethical codes specifically designed to cover paralegal behavior, to date no state has adopted such a code.

The three main ethical areas of concern for paralegals are the unauthorized practice of law, client confidentiality, and conflicts of interest. In addition, paralegals must be aware of the need to keep client and office funds separate and of the limits to zealous representation. Finally, the tort law of negligence can come into play if a paralegal does not perform his or her job duties in a reasonable manner.

REVIEW QUESTIONS

Pages 263 through 268

1. Attorneys are governed by either the Code of Professional Responsibility or the Rules of Professional Conduct. How do they differ from each other?
2. Are attorneys in your state bound by the Code of Professional Responsibility or the Rules of Professional Conduct?
3. Explain the following statement: Although paralegals are not yet licensed, they are still bound by ethical standards.
4. What steps have NFPA, NALA, the ABA, and various states taken toward the development of a set of ethical standards for paralegals?

Pages 269 through 274

5. How does the attorney-client privilege differ from the ethical rules regarding confidentiality?
6. Mrs. Smith, who is seeking a divorce, entered attorney Black's office for her first interview. Because she was very disturbed over the prospect of a divorce, Mrs. Smith brought her best friend along with her to the interview. Should attorney Black let Mrs. Smith's best friend sit in on the interview? Why?
7. At a cocktail party paralegal Sims sees one of his firm's clients kissing someone not the client's wife. At the client's divorce hearing could paralegal Sims be required to testify about what he saw at the party? Could paralegal Sims ethically tell his wife about what he saw at the party? Why?
8. What does the attorney-client work product doctrine protect?
9. What should attorneys or paralegals do if they receive confidential information from the other side? Should it matter how they receive the information, that is, whether the opposing side accidentally sent it to them or whether they acquired it by some other means?

Pages 275 through 281

10. What are the two major causes of conflict of interest?
11. In each of the following situations determine whether you see any potential conflict of interest problems.
    a. Sam was injured in an automobile accident when the car he was riding in was struck in an intersection by a pickup truck. Both Sam and the driver of the car want attorney Black to represent them against the driver of the pickup truck.
    b. Sara and Emily were arrested for the attempted robbery of United Bank. They would like attorney Jones to represent both of them.
    c. Attorney Lacy is the prosecuting attorney for the murder trial of Tom Black. Jim White represents the defendant. Halfway through the murder trial, attorney Lacy and attorney White start dating.

12. What should a paralegal do if she suspects that she has confidential information pertaining to the opposite side of a case?
13. What is the function of an ethical wall (or cone of silence), and how do you erect one?

Pages 281 through 291

14. Give the generally accepted definition of the practice of law. What are the problems with applying it to paralegals working under the supervision of an attorney?
15. What tasks can an attorney perform that a paralegal cannot?
16. What is the major justification for enforcing unauthorized practice of law statutes?
17. What should paralegals do to avoid the unauthorized practice of law?

Pages 291 through 295

18. Why do attorneys keep two separate types of bank accounts?
19. What are the limitations on an attorney's billing for paralegal time?
20. Each year at Christmas, if the Goodman firm has had a particularly profitable year, it rewards its employees by giving them bonuses based on the quality of their work throughout the year. Is this an ethical practice? Why?
21. Mary, a paralegal with the Goodman firm, is taking classes at a local paralegal school. In her family law class, classmates who are going through a divorce frequently complain about how uncaring their attorneys are. Mary thinks the Goodman attorneys would be much more supportive. Would there be anything wrong in Mary's handing out her firm's card to her fellow students?
22. What limitations on zealous representation are of particular importance to paralegals?
23. Describe the various sanctions that can be applied to an attorney who violates the ethical codes.

Pages 295 through 296

24. What elements must a plaintiff prove to win a legal malpractice case?
25. In a legal malpractice case what does it mean to say that the plaintiff must prove a case within a case?

PART 3

Legal Analysis
and Research

Chapter 12

Finding and Interpreting Statutory Law

A word is not a crystal, transparent and unchanged, it is the skin of a living thought and may vary greatly in color and content according to the circumstances and the time in which it is used.
Justice Oliver Wendell Holmes

INTRODUCTION

In Chapter 1 we gave a brief overview of the process involved in legal reasoning. You begin with an analysis of the client's facts and the identification of the legal rules applicable to that set of facts. You then apply those rules to the facts in order to predict the likely outcome, analyzing both the weaknesses and the strengths of the client's case. In this and the next chapter we look at how to find the law and the methods you can use to interpret the law.

Recall that the two main sources of law are

1. court-made law (common law) and
2. enacted law.

Enacted law can be further subdivided into constitutional, statutory, and administrative law. In this chapter we will explore the methods you use to analyze enacted law. While the emphasis will be on analyzing statutes, you can apply the same principles to constitutional provisions and agency regulations.

Although all four areas of the law—common, constitutional, statutory, and administrative law—must be considered in any legal situation, most attorneys begin their legal analysis of a specific legal problem with a review of statutes. They initially focus on statutes because statutes supersede the common law. In addition, reading an annotated statute will alert the attorney to administrative agencies and regulations that may also be relevant. (In annotated statutes, in addition to finding the text of the statute, you will find summaries of court decisions that have interpreted the statute, citations to administrative regulations, and cross-references to secondary sources that will help explain or summarize the law.) Thus if a client has been arrested for murder, an attorney will start by locating and then analyzing the state statutes on homicide. If a client is seeking a divorce, alimony, and child support, the attorney will locate and then analyze the state's domestic relations statutes.

Citation
A statutory citation is a formalized method for referring to a statute's chapter (or title) and section numbers.

A. LOCATING THE APPROPRIATE STATUTE

Before you can interpret a statute, you have to have a copy of what it is you are being asked to interpret. In this section we will discuss the ways in which you can locate a statute if you have its "popular name" or its official **citation**. A statutory citation is a formalized method for referring to a statute's chapter (or title) and section numbers. In Chapter 14 we will discuss other methods for locating relevant statutes.

State and federal statutes are usually published in three primary forms:

Slip laws
A form in which statutes are published; they are printed individually at the time they are first enacted.

1. individual slip laws,
2. periodic compilations of new laws passed within a certain time period, and
3. unified codes.

Statutes at large or session laws
The chronological publication of statutes at the end of a legislative session.

When laws are first officially enacted, they are usually published individually as **slip laws**. At the end of a legislative term the federal and most state governments publish the laws passed during that term as one or more volumes in a continuing set. They are usually arranged in chronological order by date of passage and are referred to as either **statutes at large** or **session laws**.

Code
A compilation of federal or state statutes in which the statutes are organized by subject matter rather than by year of enactment.

The above publications are arranged chronologically by date of passage and contain only those laws passed during a particular time period. **Codes**, on the other hand, arrange the laws by subject matter and contain all public laws currently in force in a particular area. The United States Code is the official codification of federal statutes and is printed and distributed by the U.S. Government Printing Office. The United States Code Annotated and the United States Code Service are published by West and Lexis Law Publishing, respectively. In addition to the text of the laws themselves, these two **annotated** versions of the code have information about the legislative history and references to court decisions that have interpreted the statutes. Some state statutes are also

Annotated statutes
A privately published statutory code that includes editorial features, such as summaries of court opinions that have interpreted the statutes.

Publication	Abbreviation	Coverage
United States Code	U.S.C.	Official codification of federal statutes arranged by subject matter.
United States Code Annotated	U.S.C.A.	West's unofficial codification of federal statutes arranged by subject matter with annotations.
United States Code Service	U.S.C.S.	Lexis Law Publishing's unofficial codification of federal statutes arranged by subject matter with annotations.
Alabama Code	Ala. Code	Official codification of Alabama statutes arranged by subject matter.
West's Annotated California Code, Business and Professions	Cal. Bus. & Prof. Code	West's unofficial codification of California statutes relating to business and the professions with annotations.
General Laws of the Commonwealth of Massachusetts	Mass. Gen. L.	Official codification of Massachusetts statutes arranged by subject matter.
Massachusetts General Laws Annotated	Mass. Gen. Laws Ann.	West's unofficial codification of Massachusetts statutes arranged by subject matter with annotations.

Figure 12-1 Common Publications Containing the Texts of Federal and State Statutes

published by West and other private publishers in annotated form. Figure 12-1 lists the most common publications and abbreviations for federal statutes and gives a few examples for state statutes. These abbreviations, as well as those for any statutory compilation, can be found in citation manuals such as The Bluebook, A Uniform System of Citation and the ALWD Citation Manual.

PRACTICE TIP

Always check the annotated version of your statutes so that with one resource you can locate not only the relevant statute but also the cases that have interpreted the statute.

NETNOTE

At the Cornell Law School site you can find an "Introduction to Basic Legal Citation," an on-line tutorial designed to teach the Bluebook rules. Go to *www.law.cornell.edu/citation/citation.table.html.*

A reference to a specific statute should include enough informationso that others can easily locate and check the source. This is known as giving the statute's **citation**. A complete statutory citation includes the name of the book in which the statute is found, the statute's chapter number (sometimes referred to as its title number), and its section number. Sometimes the citation will also include the name of the statute. For example, you might see

Administrative Procedure Act, 5 U.S.C. § 552(b)(3) (1994)
Cannabis Control Act, Ill. Rev. Stat. ch. 56[42], § 701 (1994)

The first citation is to a federal statute. You can tell it is a federal statute because of the abbreviation U.S.C., which stands for United States Code. The number 5 preceding the U.S.C. designation indicates that the statute is part of Title 5; 552 (*b*)(3) is the section number (the symbol § stands for section). The second citation is to an Illinois state statute (*ch*. stands for chapter). In each the date in parentheses refers to the date the book in which the statute is published was last updated. It does not refer to the date when the statute was enacted.

As you can see, the citation gives you the information you need to locate a specific statute. If you have only the name of a statute (e.g., the Freedom of Information Act), you can use the table of names index found in most state and federal codes to find the citation.

B. THE FORMAT OF STATUTES

Statutes can be quite lengthy, containing many subsections and cross-references to other statutes. For example, the Illinois Criminal Code is more than 200 pages long. There are separate sections defining key terms, spelling out the jurisdiction of the state criminal courts, listing requirements for different mental states, determining who can be considered parties to a crime, and listing affirmative defenses. All these are separated from the section that actually lists specific crimes, and to find the punishments that go with the crimes, you have to turn to a separate one-hundred-page Code of Corrections. To find sections of the law relevant to juvenile offenses and domestic violence, you must consult other Illinois statutes.

Statutes are usually subdivided into subsections, sometimes called articles. Note in Exhibit 12-1, on page 305, how the Illinois Domestic Violence Act of 1986 is organized into four articles: General Provisions, Orders of Protection, Law Enforcement Responsibilities, and Health Care Services. Notice also how the General Provisions article is subdivided into Short title, Purposes—Rules of construction, and Definitions. This last subsection contains definitions of key words used in the statute.

CHAPTER 750

FAMILIES

Act
60. Illinois Domestic Violence Act of 1986.
70. Parental Notice of Abortion Act of 1995.

ACT 60. ILLINOIS DOMESTIC VIOLENCE ACT OF 1986

Article
  I   General Provisions.
  II Orders of Protection.
  III Law Enforcement Responsibilities.
  IV. [Health Care Services].

ARTICLE I—GENERAL PROVISIONS

Section
60/101. Short title.
60/102. Purposes—Rules of construction.
60/103. Definitions.

60/101. Short title
§ 101. Short Title. This Act shall be known and may be cited as the "Illinois Domestic Violence Act of 1986".
P.A. 84-1305, Art. I, § 101, eff. Aug. 21, 1986.
Formerly Ill.Rev.Stat.1991, ch. 40, ¶ 2311-1.

Title of Act:
An Act concerning domestic violence, amending and repealing certain Acts and parts of Acts herein named. P.A. 84-1305, approved and eff. Aug. 21, 1986.

60/102. Purposes—Rules of construction
§ 102. Purposes; rules of construction. This Act shall be liberally construed and applied to promote its underlying purposes, which are to:
(1) Recognize domestic violence as a serious crime against the individual and society which produces family disharmony in thousands of Illinois families, promotes a pattern of escalating violence which frequently culminates in intra-family homicide, and creates an emotional atmosphere that is not conducive to healthy childhood development;
(2) Recognize domestic violence against high risk adults with disabilities, who are particularly vulnerable due to impairments in ability to seek or obtain protection, as a serious problem which takes on many forms, including physical abuse, sexual abuse, neglect, and exploitation, and facilitate accessibility of remedies under the Act in order to provide immediate and effective assistance and protection;
(3) Recognize that the legal system has ineffectively dealt with family violence in the past, allowing abusers to escape effective prosecution or financial liability, and has not adequately acknowledged the criminal nature of domestic violence; that, although many laws have changed, in practice there is still widespread failure to appropriately protect and assist victims;
(4) Support the efforts of victims of domestic violence to avoid further abuse by promptly entering and diligently enforcing court orders which prohibit abuse and, when necessary, reduce the abuser's access to the victim and address any related issues of child custody and economic support, so that victims are not trapped in abusive situations by fear of retaliation, loss of a child, financial dependence, or loss of accessible housing or services;
(5) Clarify the responsibilities and support the efforts of law enforcement officers to provide immediate, effective assistance and protection for victims of domestic violence, recognizing that law enforcement officers often become the secondary victims of domestic violence, as evidenced by the high rates of police injuries and deaths that occur in response to domestic violence calls; and
(6) Expand the civil and criminal remedies for victims of domestic violence; including, when necessary, the remedies which effect physical separation of the parties to prevent further abuse.
P.A. 84-1305, Art. I, § 102, eff. Aug. 21, 1986. Amended by P.A. 86-542, § 1, eff. Jan. 1, 1990; P.A. 87-1186, § 3, eff. Jan. 1, 1993.
Formerly Ill.Rev.Stat.1991, ch. 40, ¶ 2311-2.

60/103. Definitions
§ 103. Definitions. For the purposes of this Act, the following terms shall have the following meanings:
(1) "Abuse" means physical abuse, harassment, intimidation of a dependent, interference with personal liberty or willful deprivation but does not include reasonable direction of a minor child by a parent or person in loco parentis.
(2) "Adult with disabilities" means an elder adult with disabilities or a high-risk adult with disabilities. A person may be an adult with disabilities for purposes of this Act even though he or she has never been adjudicated an incompetent adult. However, no court proceeding may be initiated or continued on behalf of an adult with disabilities over that adult's objection, unless such proceeding is approved by his or her legal guardian, if any.
(3) "Domestic violence" means abuse as defined in paragraph (1).
(4) "Elder adult with disabilities" means an adult prevented by advanced age from taking appropriate action to protect himself or herself from abuse by a family or household member.
(5) "Exploitation" means the illegal, including tortious, use of a high-risk adult with disabilities or of the assets or resources of a high-risk adult with disabilities. Exploitation includes, but is not limited to, the misappropriation of assets or resources of a high-risk adult with disabilities by undue influence, by breach of a fiduciary relationship, by fraud, deception, or extortion, or the use of such assets or resources in a manner contrary to law.
(6) "Family or household members" include spouses, former spouses, parents, children, stepchildren and other persons related by blood or by present or prior marriage, persons who share or formerly shared a common dwelling, persons who have or allegedly have a child in common,

718

Exhibit 12-1   Illinois Domestic Violence Act of 1986

Therefore, the first step in reading and understanding a statute is to pay attention to its overall organizational layout. Here
    Chapter 750 deals with families
        Act 60 is the Illinois Domestic Violence Act
            Article I contains General Provisions of that act
                § 103 gives definitions
                    (1) defines the word *abuse*

When reading specific sections, pay close attention to the use of punctuation and indentation. Both give you further clues as to the statute's organizational scheme. Finally, be sure to notice the use of "or" and "and." For example, in the definition of *abuse* notice the use of the word "or." This means that any of those items listed could by itself constitute abuse.

In an annotated set the statutes will be followed by editorial information, including summaries of the court opinions that have interpreted the statute. To see an example of an annotated statute, look at Exhibit 14-7 in Chapter 14.

C. AMBIGUITY IN STATUTES

Before we begin our discussion of how to analyze a statutory problem, we need to remember that when a legislative body formulates a statute, it is setting down general rules that will be applied to a variety of future situations. Trying to lay down rules today for situations that will arise in the future is a difficult task, as illustrated by the following classic example.

Assume a town council passed the following ordinance:

> It shall be unlawful to operate any vehicle on town park paths. Violators will be subject to a $100 fine for the first offense and up to a $500 fine for each additional offense.

The council passed the ordinance in response to citizen complaints about a group of teenagers who had been riding their motorcycles on the paths of the town's parks. Not only are motorcycles noisy, but also the citizens were afraid that one day an accident would occur and a child walking down one of the paths would be injured.

Following the passage of this ordinance the following four events took place in a town park:

1. For a "lark," two teenagers drove a Jeep Cherokee down one of the park paths.
2. Once a week the garbage collector backs his truck approximately six feet down one of the park paths to pick up garbage from one of the trash receptacles.
3. A child pushed her doll's baby carriage along a park path.
4. An ambulance drove down one of the park paths to pick up a man who had collapsed in the middle of the park.

Based on a literal reading of the town's new ordinance, all four of these situations are violations of the law. All four involve a "vehicle" being on a park path. However, while the town council undoubtedly wished to ban joyriding Jeep Cherokee drivers as much as it wanted to ban joyriding motorcycle riders, it is highly unlikely that it actually wished to prohibit situations 2, 3, and 4. The problem is that the town council members chose language that was more inclusive than they really intended, and now all four parties are technically guilty of violating the ordinance.

This example illustrates how slippery language can be and how difficult it is to draft a law that encompasses only what you are trying to prohibit. It also illustrates how ambiguities in a statute may not appear until you apply it to

STEPS TO STATUTORY INTERPRETATION

1. Get the facts.
2. Locate a relevant statute.
3. Analyze the statute.
   - Determine if it applies to the client's facts.
   - Divide the statute into its elements.
   - Determine the issues raised by the statute's language or the client's facts, and develop arguments for each side.
4. Conclude.

individual factual situations. Therefore, even though on its face statutory interpretation may seem straightforward, always remember that even the most seemingly clear language can appear ambiguous when applied to a new factual situation.

Sometimes statutory ambiguities result from sloppy draftsmanship. More often, however, ambiguities arise when the statute is applied to unanticipated circumstances. There are also times when the drafters purposely write the ambiguity into the statute in order to provide a basis for compromise by glossing over conflicts among the legislators.

D. THE FOUR BASIC STEPS TO STATUTORY INTERPRETATION

There are four steps involved in finding and applying a statute to a client's situation. First, the attorney or paralegal must obtain the facts from the client or other sources. Second, he or she must determine whether any statute governs the situation and locate that statute. Third, he or she must analyze the statute by first reading it carefully to make sure that it does apply to the client's case. Then he or she must determine its requirements. This is known as dividing the statute into its elements. If there is any ambiguity as to whether the client's facts satisfy any of the elements, those ambiguities must be resolved. This will involve legal analysis—that is, applying the statutory elements to the client's facts to develop arguments on each side of each issue. Finally, the attorney or paralegal must conclude by deciding which arguments are most persuasive, thereby determining the most likely outcome for the client. In this section we will look at each of these four steps in more detail.

1. Get the Facts

The first step is to get as many of the relevant facts as possible. Often this is accomplished through a combination of interviewing the client, talking to witnesses, and obtaining information through other sources, such as police or doctor reports. Assume Mary Smith met with attorney Pat Harper and related the following events.

The Case of the Clearance Sale

Last week Mary, a cellist with the local symphony orchestra, was doing some shopping at Ajax's Country Hardware Store. Mary had gone to Ajax's specifically in response to an ad announcing a clearance sale. When she got to the store, most of the clearance items were gone, but she did spot one last 50-foot tape measure. Just as she was about to pick it up, another customer grabbed it. Outraged, Mary picked up a hammer that had been lying on the counter and told the other customer to hand over the tape measure.

The other customer quickly did so, and Mary put the hammer back on the counter. At home the next day Mary answered the door to find herself confronted by a police officer who had a warrant for her arrest. Based on the incident in the store, Mary had been charged with the crime of carrying a dangerous weapon. That statute reads:

> It is unlawful for anyone, other than a police officer, to carry a dangerous weapon.

2. Locate a Relevant Statute

The next step is to locate statutes that appear to be applicable to the client's facts. Sometimes the initial research will already be done for you. For example, as in Mary's case, when representing a criminal defendant, you will frequently know the statute that the client has been charged with violating. However, there will be other times when you have to go out and find relevant statutes on your own. We will discuss some of the methods you can use to locate such statutes in Chapter 14.

After finding an arguably relevant statute, you must take a close look at its language and purpose to make sure it does apply to your client's facts. For example, assume your client has a problem with his apartment lease, a type of contract. There is a statute, the Uniform Commercial Code, that sets out uniform rules governing business relationships. Article Two deals specifically with contracts. You might wonder if Article Two applies to your client's problem with his lease. While Article Two does deal with contracts, it applies only to those contracts that involve "transactions in goods." Therefore, the statute would apply to your client's lease only if an apartment lease qualifies as a "transaction in goods." To find the answer to that question, you would consult the section in Article Two that defines the most important terms used within the statute. That section defines "goods" as "all things . . . which are moveable." Because an apartment is not moveable, you would conclude that Article Two does not apply to your client's case.

In addition to analyzing whether the statute's language was intended to cover your client's situation, be sure to check the statute's effective date. Usually, the events of your client's case must have occurred after the statute's effective date for the statute to govern the outcome of your client's case. Occasionally, the legislature will give a statute a retroactive effect, but that is very rare. You must also check to be sure the statute has not been superseded by a more recent statute.

NETNOTE

To find an on-line copy of the United States Code, the Code of Federal Regulations, and state statutes, start at *www.findlaw.com*. Click on the tab "For Legal Professionals." Then click on the link to "Cases & Codes."

3. Analyze the Statute

Once you have located a statute that appears to be relevant, you must decide how it will affect your client's case. This involves a two-step process. First, you must break the statute down into separable parts, known as elements, each of which must be satisfied for the statute to apply. Then you must apply those elements to your client's facts.

a. Divide the Statute into Its Elements

The first step in statutory interpretation is to break the relevant statute down into its elements. **A statutory element** can be defined as a separable part of the statute that must be satisfied for the statute to apply. Another way of stating this is to say that an element is a precondition to the application of the statute. In Mary's case the statute contains three elements. For Mary to be found guilty,

Statutory element
A separatable part of a statute that must be statisfied for the statute to apply

1. she must not be a police officer and
2. she must have "carried"
3. a "dangerous weapon."

b. Determine the Issues and Develop Arguments for Each Side

Next you must apply the statutory elements to your client's facts. Sometimes this will be a straightforward process. For example, because the facts state that Mary is not a police officer, the first element of the crime is satisfied. However, sometimes ambiguities will be created either by the statutory language or by the client's facts. For example, it is not clear that Mary "carried" a "dangerous weapon." While she did pick up the hammer, most people think of carrying something as more than just picking it up and then setting it back down in the same place. Similarly, while a hammer could be used to harm someone, most people think of a hammer as a common household tool rather than as a weapon. Therefore, the facts in Mary's case, when combined with the statutory language of two of the elements, create issues. An **issue** arises whenever an element applied to the specific facts fails to give you a clear-cut answer.

When trying to determine whether an element will create an issue, first ask yourself whether you detect any ambiguity in the statute's words. Sometimes the words will seem to have only one possible meaning. However,

Issue
When the law is applied to the client's facts and the result is not obvious, an issue is created.

as we just demonstrated in Mary's case, when you try to apply statutory language to a specific factual situation, often you will find that the language is ambiguous and that it can be interpreted in more than one way.

Ask yourself which of the possible interpretations makes the most sense. That is, which interpretation do you think would best further the purposes for which the statute was enacted? As we will see in a moment, courts have devised several methods to assist them when they are asked to interpret statutory language. These methods can assist you as well. However, before resorting to any of those methods, focus on the statutory language, and use your common sense to try to ferret out a sensible legislative purpose.

(1) Think creatively

One of the most powerful legal reasoning skills that you can acquire is the ability to think creatively about a problem. The best way to develop that skill is to try to work with a statute on its own terms before turning to other sources, such as court opinions and legislative history, for guidance. Take the time to develop arguments that you think would best convince a court that the language should or should not be applied to your client's case. Ask yourself, What was the legislature trying to accomplish with the statute, and will that purpose be better fulfilled by saying that an element is or is not satisfied given the client's particular set of facts?

To help you brainstorm the statute, develop a chart. List the elements, and then under each element list the facts that you would use to make arguments both for and against satisfying the element. Figure 12-2 is a sample chart that you might develop for Mary's case.

At this stage do not worry about finding the "right" answer. Let yourself feel free to explore all the possible arguments on both sides of each issue. This process of looking at the language of the statute and at the facts of your client's case is an ongoing one. Each time you look at the statute, you may see new ambiguities, and each time you look at your client's facts, you may see new arguments about whether or not the statute's language applies to your client's facts.

Figure 12-2   Sample Chart of Statutory Elements

Element 1—"to carry"
Element satisfied—moved hammer from counter.

Element not satisfied—did not move it from the building; legislature used specific term of "carry" rather than a broader term, such as "possess."

Element 2—"dangerous weapon"
Element satisfied—a hammer is a heavy, hard object capable of causing physical harm; purpose of legislation is to protect people from physical harm.

Element not satisfied—hammers are normally viewed as tools, not weapons.

Legal Reasoning Exercise

1. Before the enactment of the following statute, under the common law a married woman was not allowed to sue in her own name. Instead the lawsuit was brought in her husband's name. Assume you have a client who wishes to sue her spouse for negligence. Read the statute. Do you think she will be able to sue her husband? Why?

Mass. Gen. L. ch. 209, § 6
> A married woman may sue and be sued in the same manner as if she were sole; but this section shall not authorize suits between husband and wife.

(2) Methods for finding legislative intent

After dealing with a statute on its own terms, you should use the same methods that the courts have developed to help them interpret statutes. These methods include looking at the "plain meaning" of the statute, using the canons of construction, referring to other parts of the statute, and considering evidence external to the statute. These methods may be used separately or in combination. The judges' own views as to the role of the courts relative to the legislature will also have an impact on how they interpret a statute. No matter which method or combination of methods is used, the court's goal is to ascertain the **legislature's intent** when it enacted the statute. As Charles Evans Hughes, former Chief Justice of the U.S. Supreme Court, once put it:

> In the interpretation of statutes, the function of the courts is easily stated. It is to construe the language so as to give effect to the intent of Congress.[1]

Legislative intent
The purpose of the legislature at the time it enacted the statute.

The court's objective is to interpret the statute in such a way as to frustrate whatever evil the legislature wanted to prevent or to further whatever positive goals the legislature wanted to achieve.

(a) Plain meaning Courts usually begin the process of statutory interpretation by using the **plain meaning** approach. In fact, courts will frequently say that if the language's meaning is clear, then there is no need for the court to search further for the legislature's intent. Based on a literal reading of the statute's language, this plain meaning approach assumes that

Plain meaning
A method for interpreting statutes in which the ordinary meaning of the statute's language is examined.

1. the words used reflect the true intentions of the legislature (i.e., they meant what they said); and
2. the legislature intended that the words used would be interpreted in light of their common, ordinary meanings.

---

[1] United States v. American Trucking Assn., 310 U.S. 534, 542 (1940).

The plain meaning approach is a commonsense, logical approach to statutory interpretation. It is essentially the same method we suggested you use when you first approach a statutory interpretation problem. One place to search for the plain meaning of statutory language is in definitions contained within the statute itself. Many statutes begin with a list of key terms to clarify the meaning of the most important terms used in the statute. However, many times either the legislative body did not choose to define the word in question or the definition is itself ambiguous.

The plain meaning approach fails to resolve statutory ambiguity when its use causes portions of the statute to stand in apparent contradiction to each other. For example, assume the phrase "every wife and mother" is used in a statute. Should you interpret this phrase as applying to all wives and also to all mothers or just to everyone who is both a wife and a mother?

Another problem arises when there is more than one commonly accepted, ordinary meaning for a term. Return for a moment to the problem we discussed earlier with regard to the interpretation of "carrying" when Mary lifted the hammer from the counter. The American Heritage Dictionary lists thirty-two different meanings for the word *carry*. One definition involves conveying something from one place to another, while another definition speaks in terms of simply holding something. Mary's criminal liability will thus depend on which of these two competing definitions the court decides is the common, ordinary meaning.

Occasionally a court will openly reject the plain meaning approach and ignore the literal meaning of the words in a statute. This occurs when the court is convinced that such a reading does not properly reflect the "true intent" of the legislature. For example, a court might decide to reject a literal interpretation of the town ordinance prohibiting vehicles on park paths if it were being applied to the little girl pushing her doll carriage or to the ambulance picking up the injured man.

Canons of construction
General principles that guide the courts in their interpretation of statutes.

Ejusdem generis
A canon of construction meaning "of the same class."

(b) Canons of construction   Another method courts use to deal with ambiguity in statutes is to apply what are known as the **canons of construction**. For example, when a series of specific items is followed by a catchall phrase, such as "and others," the courts may assume that the legislature intended to limit the statute to matters that are like the ones specifically listed. This is known as the principle of **ejusdem generis** (of the same class). Assume a statute prohibited the outdoor sale of perishables, such as food, drink, beverages, and the like. Does it apply to flowers? You could argue that the legislature did not intend for the statute to cover the sale of flowers, as all items on the list are edible and flowers are not.

A major problem in relying on a canon of construction is that most canons can be negated by yet other canons. For example, when looking at a list, another rule of statutory construction states that the members of that list are only examples and are not meant to be exclusive. Because all the items on the list are examples of perishable items and because flowers are perishable, you could argue that they were not meant to be excluded.

In the 1917 case of *Caminetti v. United States*,[2] two U.S. Supreme Court justices illustrated how the use of the same canon, in this instance ejusdem

---

[2] 242 U.S. 470 (1917).

generis, could lead them to reach entirely different conclusions. In that case Caminetti was convicted of violating the Mann Act after he transported a woman from Sacramento, California, to Reno, Nevada, where she was to become his mistress. At the time of the *Caminetti* decision, the Mann Act stated that

> any person who shall knowingly transport . . . in interstate or foreign commerce . . . any woman or girl for the purpose of prostitution or debauchery, or for any other immoral purpose . . . shall be punished by a fine not exceeding five thousand dollars, or by imprisonment of not more than five years, or by both. . . .

Relying on the doctrine of ejusdem generis, Justice Day quoted an earlier Supreme Court opinion in which the Court had stated:

> "Now the addition in the last statute of the words, 'or for any other immoral purpose,' after the word 'prostitution,' must have been made for some practical object. . . . In accordance with the familiar rule of ejusdem generis, the immoral purpose referred to by the words 'any other immoral purpose' must be one of the same general class or kind as the particular purpose of 'prostitution' specified in the same clause of the statute. . . . The immoral purpose charged in the indictment is of the same general class or kind as the one that controls in the importation of an alien woman for the purpose strictly of prostitution. The prostitute may, in the popular sense, be more degraded in character than the concubine, but the latter nonetheless must be held to lead an immoral life, if any regard whatever be had to the views that are almost universally held in this country as to the relations which may rightfully, from the standpoint of morality, exist between man and woman in the matter of sexual intercourse. . . ."[3]

Therefore, Justice Day, along with the majority of the Court, concluded that Caminetti had violated the statute. The dissenters disagreed.

> Our present concern is with the words "any other immoral practice," . . . . "Immoral" is a very comprehensive word. It means a dereliction of morals. In such sense it covers every form of vice, every form of conduct that is contrary to good order. It will hardly be contended that in this sweeping sense it is used in the statute. . . .
>
> [I]t is vice as a business at which the law is directed, using interstate commerce as a facility to procure or distribute its victims. . . .[4]

Therefore, the dissenters concluded that because Caminetti's case did not involve commercial prostitution, the statute did not apply, and he should not be convicted under it.

Two general rules of statutory construction are particularly important. First, normally courts **strictly construe** criminal statutes and **statutes in derogation of the common law**—that is, those that change the common law. When courts strictly construe a statute, they narrow the scope of its coverage. For example, a court interpreting the phrase "dangerous weapon" in the statute dealing with "carrying a dangerous weapon" would say that it does not include hammers. Courts strictly construe criminal statutes because of the severe penalties that defendants face. It is thought to be unfair to make someone suffer

Strict construction
An approach whereby the courts give a statute a narrow interpretation.

Statute in derogation of the common law
A statute that changes the common law.

[3] Id. at 487 (quoting United States v. Bitty, 208 U.S. 393, 401-402 (1908)).
[4] Id. at 496-497, 498.

Remedial statute
A statute enacted to correct a defect in prior law or to provide a remedy where none existed.

Liberal construction
An approach whereby the courts give a statute a broad interpretation.

criminal sanctions if the legislature did not clearly intend to include that particular behavior within the statute. Similarly, courts strictly construe statutes in derogation of the common law because they assume the legislature meant to change the common law no more than was necessary to achieve its purpose.

On the other hand, courts normally give **remedial statutes** a **liberal construction**. When the courts give a statute a liberal construction, they broaden the scope of its coverage. The courts presume that when the legislature is trying to remedy a situation, it does not want its intent thwarted by too narrow an interpretation. An example of a remedial statute is Title VII, the federal statute outlawing discrimination in employment. As we saw earlier, the court liberally construed the term *sex discrimination* to include sexual harassment.

Legal Reasoning Exercises

2. Assume you represent a client who shipped obscene phonograph records from Massachusetts to California. He has been charged with violating a federal criminal statute that prohibits interstate shipment of any obscene "book, pamphlet, picture, motion-picture film, paper, letter, writing, print or other matter of indecent character." Has he violated the statute?

3. Assume you represent a client who knowingly transported a stolen airplane from Illinois to Oklahoma. He is charged with violating the following federal statute:

National Motor Vehicle Theft Act, 18 U.S.C. § 408
Sec. 2. That when used in this Act: (a) The term "motor vehicle" shall include an automobile, automobile truck, automobile wagon, motor cycle, or any other selfpropelled vehicle not designed for running on rails;
Sec. 3. That whoever shall transport or cause to be transported in interstate or foreign commerce a motor vehicle, knowing the same to have been stolen, shall be punished by a fine of not more than $5,000, or by imprisonment of no more than five years, or both.

Do you think your client should be found guilty? Why?

4. On the basis of the U.S. Supreme Court's decision in the *Caminetti* case, which, if any, of the following situations would be a violation of the Mann Act?

    a. A man drives a woman whom he knows to be a prostitute from Los Angeles to Las Vegas. The man receives no compensation for providing this transportation, nor does he receive any share of any money she makes as a prostitute. He took her as a favor to a friend and to have someone to talk to on the trip.

    b. A man drives his girlfriend from Newark, New Jersey, to New York City so that she can perform a striptease at a stag party.

    c. A man picks up his girlfriend in Sacramento, California, and drives her to Seattle, Washington, where they cohabit without getting married.

However, even these two basic rules of construction can conflict. For example, what should a court do when interpreting a statute such as one creating a workers' compensation system? Under the common law if a worker was hurt on the job, the worker's only recourse was to sue the employer under tort law. State legislatures created workers' compensation laws so that employers would automatically be required to compensate injured employees. Therefore, it is a statute that both serves a remedial purpose and is in derogation of the common law.

(c) Reference to other parts of the statute   Judges often look for clues to the meaning of a particular statutory section by focusing on the context in which the disputed clause occurs. This contextual analysis involves looking at the overall structure of the larger legislative package. For example, under the discussion of the plain meaning approach we mentioned that one place courts sometimes look for guidance is a definitions section. A contextual analysis requires you to think about the following questions:

- What title did the legislature give the act? (It is usually assumed that the name chosen for the act is significant.)
- Are relevant subheadings provided?
- Does the statute contain a definitions section?
- Even if there is no definitions section, is the same term used elsewhere in the statute or in a related statute? (One can assume that any given clause is intended to be read as part of a larger, more comprehensive regulatory scheme and that the legislature intended to be consistent in its approaches to the problem.)

As with the canons of construction, reference to other parts of the statute (even the statute's title) can lead to contradictory results. In *Caminetti*, the dissenting justices used the official title of the statute to support their interpretation of the statute.

> [O]f the purpose of the statute Congress itself has given us illumination. It devotes a section to the declaration that the "act shall be known and referred to as the 'White Slave Traffic Act.'" And its prominence gives it prevalence in the construction of the statute. It cannot be pushed aside or subordinated by indefinite words in other sentences, limited even there by the context. It is a peremptory rule of construction that all parts of a statute must be taken into account in ascertaining its meaning, and it cannot be said that § 8 has no object. Even if it gives only a title to the act, it has especial weight. . . . But it gives more than a title; it makes distinctive the purpose of the statute. The designation "white slave traffic" has the sufficiency of an axiom. If apprehended, there is no uncertainty as to the conduct it describes. It is commercialized vice, immoralities having a mercenary purpose, and this is confirmed by other circumstances.[5]

Justice Day, for the majority, disagreed with the dissent's reliance on the statute's title.

> It is true that § 8 of the act provides that it shall be known and referred to as the "White Slave Traffic Act," . . . . Still, the name given to an act by way of designation or description . . . cannot change the plain import of its words. If the words are plain, they give

---

[5] Id. at 497.

meaning to the act, and it is neither the duty nor the privilege of the courts to enter speculative fields in search of a different meaning.[6]

(d) Evidence external to the statute   Finally, in their search for legislative intent courts frequently look for evidence of legislative intent that they can find outside the statute itself. This type of evidence includes decisions by other courts, the act's legislative history, current events at the time the statute was enacted, a comparison of this statute with similar statutes from the same or other jurisdictions, administrative agency interpretations, and scholarly works.

(1) *Other court opinions* Following the doctrine of stare decisis courts will normally consider the manner in which other courts have interpreted the same words. In addition to looking to decisions from their own state, courts will frequently look to judicial interpretations of similar statutes in other states.

(2) *Legislative history* The term **legislative history** refers to the background documents created during the process of a bill becoming a statute. These documents can include alternative versions of the legislation, proceedings of committee hearings and reports, and transcripts of floor debates. The exact nature of the materials that exist for a particular statute will vary depending on the importance of the statute and the type of legislative body involved. For example, generally there is more recorded legislative history for federal statutes than there is for state statutes.

To understand why certain documents form a statute's legislative history, you need to recall the steps that the legislature follows to create a statute. Statutes begin as bills. A legislator introduces a draft of what the proposed law should look like. Before passage there may be amendments that change various sections of the bill. The pattern that emerges from examining multiple bills and amendments can sometimes provide insight into the legislative intent of the final act. The court, for example, would probably not read the act as applying to a particular situation if the legislative history shows that an amendment that would have applied to that situation was defeated.

Before bills are presented on the floor of the legislative body, they are usually sent to a committee. Committees often hold public hearings where interested parties can testify about the proposed law. The proceedings of these committee hearings are published, and the transcript becomes a part of the statute's legislative history. A committee sometimes will issue an official report discussing the nature of the proposed legislation and what it is expected to accomplish. The committee report also becomes part of the legislative history.

When the bill is debated on the floor of the legislative body, proponents and opponents often make statements about what they expect the bill to do or not do. The transcripts of these floor debates are another source of information about legislative intent. In determining legislative intent courts may quote from any of these sources.

When you see a court relying on legislative history or when you are thinking of relying on it yourself, keep in mind that legislative history should be viewed with an open mind. First, it is frequently incomplete, especially at the state level. Second, it is usually based on what just one or a few of the legislators said. There is no way of knowing if the other legislators agreed or even knew of the statements. Ultimately

Legislative history
The background documents created during the process of a bill becoming a statute. These documents can include alternative versions of the legislation, proceedings of committee hearings and reports, and transcripts of floor debates.

---

[6] Id. at 489.

PRACTICE TIP

A legislature often enacts legislation as a reaction to a specific event. Therefore, to gain insight into the legislative thinking at the time, search through archived newspaper reports for major events around the time the legislation was enacted.

---

it was not what the other legislators said, but what the statute says that got enacted. Third, legislative history is similar to the canons of construction in that you can usually find history to support opposing points of view.

For example, in the 1975 case of *United States v. Powell*,[7] both the majority and the dissenting justices attempted to use the legislative history of a federal gun control statute to justify their differing interpretations. Powell was convicted of violating a federal statute, 18 U.S.C. § 1715, when he mailed a sawed-off shotgun. The statute prohibits the mailing of "pistols, revolvers, and other firearms capable of being concealed on the person." The issue was whether sawed-off shotguns qualify as "other firearms capable of being concealed on the person." In the Court's opinion, Justice Rehnquist stated:

> The legislative history of this particular provision is sparse, but the House report indicates that the purpose of the bill upon which § 1715 is based was to avoid having the Post Office serve as an instrumentality for the violation of local laws which prohibited the purchase and possession of weapons. H.R. Rep. No. 610, 69th Cong., 1st Sess. (1926). It would seem that sawed-off shotguns would be even more likely to be prohibited by local laws than would pistols and revolvers. A statement by the author of the bill, Representative Miller of Washington, on the floor of the House indicates that the purpose of the bill was to make it more difficult for criminals to obtain concealable weapons. 66 Cong. Rec. 726 (1924). To narrow the meaning of the language Congress used so as to limit it to only those weapons which could be concealed as readily as pistols or revolvers would not comport with that purpose.[8]

In dissent, Justice Stewart stated:

> The legislative history of the bill on which § 1715 was based contains persuasive indications that it was not intended to apply to firearms larger than the largest pistols or revolvers. Representative Miller, the bill's author, made it clear that the legislative concern was not with the "shotgun, the rifle, or any firearm used in hunting or by the sportsman." 66 Cong. Rec. 727. As a supporter of the legislation stated: "The purpose . . . is to prevent the shipment of pistols and revolvers through the mails." 67 Cong. Rec. 12,041. The only reference to sawed-off shotguns came in a question posed by Representative McKeown: "Is there anything in this bill that will prevent the citizens of Oklahoma from buying sawed-off shotguns to defend themselves against these bank-robbing bandits?" Representative Blanton, an opponent of the bill, responded: "That may come next. Sometimes a revolver is more necessary than a sawed-off shotgun." 66 Cong. Rec. 729. In the absence of more concrete indicia of

---

[7] 423 U.S. 87 (1975).

[8] Id. at 91.

legislative intent, the pregnant silence that followed Representative Blanton's response can surely be taken as an indication that Congress intended the law to reach only weapons of the same general size as pistols and revolvers.[9]

Sometimes the legislative history can include the failure of the legislative body to react to administrative or judicial interpretations. This aspect of the judicial reasoning process is well illustrated in the continuing controversy over the antitrust status of professional sports. In *Federal Baseball Club v. National League*[10] and *Toolson v. New York Yankees, Inc.*,[11] the Supreme Court held that professional baseball was not covered by federal antitrust laws. In subsequent cases the Court ruled that other professional sports, such as football, hockey, and boxing, were covered. In 1972 in a decision involving baseball the Court was faced with having to justify this inconsistency.[12] The majority asserted that because Congress, knowing of the Court's position on baseball, had not passed a specific law to include it under the antitrust laws, Congress must have approved the Court's earlier position excluding it.

Of course, it is always dangerous to make assumptions about why some group or individual did not act. In the case of Congress and baseball, Congress may have remained silent not because it agreed with the Supreme Court ruling, but because it was simply too hazardous politically to attack America's favorite pastime.

(3) *Other external sources of evidence* In addition to legislative history, courts will sometimes take into account events that occurred at the time the statute was enacted. They may also compare the statute in question to similar statutes from the same or other jurisdictions. If the legislature has empowered an administrative agency to write regulations interpreting the statute, the court will defer to the administrative agency's interpretation unless the court thinks it does not support the intent of the legislation. Finally, the courts will occasionally rely on scholarly works for gaining insight into the legislative intent.

(e) Judicial philosophy Ultimately how a particular court interprets a statute will also be influenced by the judicial philosophy of the judge hearing the case. Some judges are strong believers in **judicial restraint** and will tend to rely on the plain meaning of the statute, giving it the narrowest construction possible. They do not view their role as one of second-guessing the legislature. Even if they think something beyond the strict language of the statute would produce a better result, they will not so interpret the statute. It is not their role to correct legislative omissions. Finally, they tend to think that legislative intent is static. That is, the courts should give the statute the meaning that the original drafters of the legislation intended. The meaning of the statute should not change as the needs of society change.

Judges who believe in **judicial activism** see the issue of statutory construction a little differently. While they, too, will search for legislative intent, they are more willing to see the need for the meaning of a statute to change over time as society changes. They are also more likely to search for a more general purpose behind the statute as opposed to a specific intent in the minds of the legislators. For example, in the situation regarding the prohibition against vehicles in public

Judicial restraint
A judicial philosophy that supports a limited role for the judiciary in changing the law, including deference to the legislative branch.

Judicial activism
A judicial philosophy that supports an active role for the judiciary in changing the law.

[9] Id. at 95.
[10] 259 U.S. 200 (1922).
[11] 346 U.S. 356 (1953).
[12] Flood v. Kuhn, 407 U.S. 258 (1972).

parks, while the immediate concern and intent of the city council were to ban motorcycles, the broader purpose of the ordinance was to protect life. With that in mind a judicial activist would have no problem saying that the prohibition against vehicles would not apply to an ambulance driving through the park for the very purpose of saving a human life.

(f) Summary of interpretation methods   When courts are asked to interpret the meaning of statutes, they can use several techniques. For example, they can use a dictionary and a grammar book to give a literal interpretation, or they can study committee hearings and floor debates from the legislature to try to ascertain the legislative intent. The following list summarizes the major principles of statutory interpretation:

1. Statutes should be interpreted to be consistent with the intent of the legislators who enacted them.
2. Statutes should be read literally and their words given meanings that were commonly used at the time the statutes were written.
3. Individual parts of a statute should be interpreted so that they will be consistent with the other parts of the statute.
4. Unless the legislative intent is clearly to the contrary, statutes should be interpreted to be consistent with other statutes and with the common law.
5. Statutes should be interpreted to be consistent with committee reports, floor debates, and other aspects of the legislative history.
6. Ultimately a judge's view of the role of courts in interpreting statutes will have some influence on which method of statutory interpretation is used.

The legislative intent is often unclear, and sometimes the application of these principles can lead to contradictory results. When the legal advocate is attempting to persuade a court to interpret a statute in a way favorable to a client, that advocate urges the court to adopt the method of interpretation that favors the client. Paralegals therefore need to develop the ability to work comfortably with each approach to finding legislative intent.

4. Conclude

You should consider each of the methods that we discussed when you analyze a statute. There will be times when you find that these alternative methods suggest contradictory interpretations. At some point, however, you will have to reach a conclusion on each issue. Based on those individual conclusions, you will decide about the question as a whole.

Returning to the case of Mary and the hammer, assume you conclude that Mary did possess a "dangerous weapon" but that she did not "carry" it. Therefore, one of the statute's elements is not satisfied. Because we have defined an element as a precondition to the applicability of the rule and because one element has not been met, the statute would not apply to Mary's case. She would not be convicted of carrying a dangerous weapon. Of course, a court might not agree with your analysis and might instead find that both elements had been satisfied. If that were to happen, Mary would be convicted.

Keep in mind that often there is no one right answer. At this stage of learning legal reasoning, developing sound arguments in support of your conclusions is more important than the conclusions you reach.

In summary, the process of analyzing a statute and applying it to your client's facts is as follows:

1. Find the main facts of the client's case.
2. Research the law.
3. Analyze the statutory language.
   a. Determine if there is a statute applicable to your client's situation.
   b. Break the statute down into its elements, specifically noting any ambiguous language.
   c. State the issues raised by the specific language of the statute and the specific facts of the client's case. Analyze the problem.
      ■ Determine how each element applies to the facts of your client's case, striving to see the arguments that hurt as well as those that help your client. (*Hint*: Based on our definition of an issue, if you cannot find two sides to the argument, you are probably not dealing with an issue.)
      ■ Think about why the legislature enacted the statute. Thinking about the purpose behind the statute will help you determine how best to interpret ambiguous statutory language.
4. Given the statute's language and the likely purpose behind the statute, conclude as to the statute's effect on your client's facts.

E. THE CASE OF THE UNHAPPY CUSTOMER

To reinforce the four steps of legal analysis, we will examine how that process applies to a situation involving a civil statute. The steps are the same. All that varies is that now you will be dealing with a civil rather than a criminal statute.

Assume you and your supervising attorney met with Sarah Howard. During the initial interview she related the facts as outlined in The Case of the Unhappy Customer.

The Case of the Unhappy Customer

Last week Sarah and a friend were enjoying a delightful dinner at the Westly Inn. Everything had gone well until it was time for dessert. The waiter offered Sarah's companion the dessert menu. When Sarah asked for one for herself, the waiter replied, "Absolutely not. The last thing you need is more calories, you fat cow." Naturally Sarah was outraged. She jumped up, threw $50 on the table, and proceeded toward the doorway.

Unfortunately her napkin hid the money, and the waiter thought she was trying to leave the restaurant without paying. He grabbed her by the arm and in front of all the customers accused her of trying to leave without paying.

When the waiter grabbed her arm, the strap to her purse broke. The purse fell to the floor, spilling its contents.

Sarah began to search under the tables and chairs, looking for her valuables. Five minutes later the waiter discovered the $50 Sarah had left on the table and told her she was free to go. However, it took Sarah nearly twenty more minutes to collect all of her purse's contents. She then left the restaurant.

Sarah is understandably upset over what occurred at the restaurant and wants to know whether or not she has grounds for a lawsuit, based on the waiter's actions.

E. The Case of the Unhappy Customer

The first step is to determine if there is any immediate need to gather additional facts beyond those you obtained through the client interview. For now, we will assume the supervising attorney decided that you have sufficient facts to proceed with the next step.

Based on the facts from the interview the supervising attorney could decide that Sarah might have a good claim for **false imprisonment**. False imprisonment is an intentional tort. It occurs whenever one person unlawfully detains another person against his or her will. In your search to determine if there are any statutes that might govern the situation, you find the following state statute:

> In an action for false imprisonment by reason of having been detained for questioning on or in the immediate premises of a merchant, if such person was detained in a reasonable manner and for not more than a reasonable length of time by the merchant or his servant and if there were reasonable grounds to believe that the person so detained was committing or attempting to commit larceny of goods for sale on such premises, it shall be a defense to such action.[13]

Because this statute provides a defense to a charge of false imprisonment in some situations, it may help the restaurant avoid liability in Sarah's case.

Step three involves deciding whether the statute even applies to Sarah's situation. Is a restaurant a "merchant"? If it is not, the statute will not apply. Assume the statute does not define the term *merchant*. How would you argue that a restaurant should be considered a merchant? That it should not? Besides using your common sense about the plain meaning of the term, remember to think about why the legislature enacted such a statute. Who were the legislators trying to protect and why? Should that protection be extended to restaurant owners?

If you are unsure about whether the statute would apply to the restaurant, the safest course is to assume that it would and to continue with your analysis. Never analyze only part of a problem and then stop. Why? Because you might be wrong. For example, assume you decided a restaurant is not a "merchant" and stopped your analysis there. If a court were later to decide otherwise and asked your boss his thoughts on the remaining issues and if he relied solely on your work, he would be unprepared to answer.[14] Therefore, you should continue with your analysis of the statute. To do that, you must break the statute down into the following elements:

It will be a defense to false imprisonment if the person was

1. detained for questioning on or in the immediate premises of a merchant,
2. if such person was detained in a reasonable manner and
3. for not more than a reasonable length of time
4. by the merchant or his servant and

---

[13] Based on Mass. Gen. L. ch. 231, § 94B (2006).

[14] This advice is also applicable to exam taking. Assume your instructor hands out a test question worth one hundred points. If your instructor thinks the question involves four issues, she may develop a grading sheet whereby she will award up to twenty-five points for the discussion on each of the four issues. If you decide that your analysis of one issue answers the problem and therefore do not write about the other three issues, you will have just made it impossible to earn more than twenty-five points for your answer.

5. if there were reasonable grounds to believe
6. that the person so detained was committing or attempting to commit larceny of goods for sale on such premises.

When reading statutes, you must pay careful attention to every word. Some words are especially important. For example, always take note of whether the legislature used a mandatory word, such as *shall*, or a discretionary word, such as *may*. Double-check to see whether the elements of the statute are connected with "and" or "or." If the statute uses "and," each part connected by "and" must be satisfied. If the statute uses "or," the parts are alternatives to each other. Note how many times "and" and "or" are used in this statute.

Now, based on your client's facts, you need to determine which, if any, of these elements create an issue—that is, an argument for or against the applicability of that particular element to the client's case. Under different facts the first element, "detained for questioning on or in the immediate premises of a merchant," could give rise to an issue. Assume the questioning had taken place in the restaurant's parking lot. Would that qualify as being "in the immediate premises"? However, given the facts of our case, it does not appear that the first element raises any issues.

The second element, however, "if such person was detained in a reasonable manner," raises a host of issues. Was it reasonable for the waiter to grab Sarah with such force as to break the strap on her purse? Should he have done so in front of other customers? The answers to these and similar questions suggest that there could be at least some argument that the manner was not reasonable.

There is also an issue as to whether the detention was for a reasonable length of time. While the questioning itself took only a few minutes, it took Sarah another twenty minutes to collect the contents of her purse.

The fourth element, "by the merchant or his servant," may seem to raise an issue but does not. While a waiter would probably not appreciate being called a servant, the law sometimes uses such antiquated terms. For example, children are often called infants. Similarly, employers are sometimes called masters.

The fifth and sixth elements also present issues: Did the waiter have "reasonable grounds" to believe Sarah was attempting to leave without paying her bill? Do food and drink served in a restaurant qualify as "goods for sale"?

In developing your arguments on each side of every issue, you should, of course, use any of the methods of statutory interpretation available to you. However, focus first on the language of the statute, the facts of your client's case, and your commonsense reasoning as to which interpretations would best satisfy the legislation's intent. Then you can look to other sources, such as prior court opinions interpreting the statute and legislative history, for assistance.

In the final step you conclude whether or not the restaurant could use the statute to defend itself against Sarah's charge of false imprisonment.

Legal Reasoning Exercises

5. For Sarah's case develop a chart listing each element and the arguments you could make under each for Sarah and for the restaurant. For each issue reach a conclusion. Finally, decide whether you think the restaurant has a valid defense to detaining Sarah.

6. Assume your firm represents Carl Clay. He has been charged with burglary. Briefly the facts are as follows:

> Last Friday Carl was watching As the Word Turns, his favorite soap opera, when suddenly the TV screen went blank. Nothing he could do would cause it to work. Unfortunately Carl did not have enough money to buy a new set. He decided to help himself to someone else's.
>
> He drove to the nearby Sleep Well Motel because he knew that the owners had recently purchased new nineteen-inch TVs. When he got to the motel around 5:00 p.m., he waited in his car until he saw a lady leave her room, ice bucket in hand. She had left the door to her room slightly ajar. Carl quickly ran to the door, opened it, and saw the TV. He went over to the TV, unplugged it, and picked it up. He was about to leave when the woman unexpectedly returned. Knowing karate, she felled him on the spot and then called the office manager, who, in turn, called the police. The TV, which was purchased for $600 and had a resale price of approximately $400, was returned to its rightful place in the room.

Carl has been charged with violating the following statutes:

General Laws ch. 228, $ 1
Burglary is defined as the breaking and entering of a dwelling at nighttime with the intent to commit a felony therein.

General Laws ch. 228, $ 2
Theft of personal property over the value of $500 is a felony.
Theft of personal property of a value less than $500 is a misdemeanor.

   a. Develop a chart listing the elements of each statute.
   b. For each element determine whether the facts raise an issue.
   c. For each issue list arguments that both Carl's attorney and the prosecution would raise. Reach a conclusion on each issue.
   d. Do you think Carl can be convicted of burglary?

F. WRITTEN ANALYSIS—THE USE OF IRAC

The results of your legal analysis should be put in writing so that they are preserved for future reference by you or by others with an interest in the legal problem. In addition, writing your analysis will force you to rethink the assumptions you have made. Your written analysis will mirror your thought process thus far. That is, you will discuss each issue raised by the statute's elements and the client's facts.

Legal readers do not appreciate reading something that simply reproduces your stream of consciousness thinking. An attorney or judge wants to know four things:

1. what your client's problem (the issue) is,
2. what the law (the rule) is,
3. how that law will affect your client's case (the analysis), and
4. what your answer as to the likely result (the conclusion) is.

One widely accepted method for conveying your thoughts in a logical order is known as **IRAC**. IRAC is an acronym for Issue-Rule-Analysis-Conclusion. The IRAC approach is not the only or necessarily always the best approach for every legal issue, but it is an excellent starting point. If you consciously try to write using IRAC, you will find that you will be forced to think about what you are writing and you will be less likely to leave out important information. The result will be better-organized and clearer paragraphs. Figure 12-3 describes each of the IRAC elements.

To see a practical application of the use of the IRAC technique, consider the following problem.

The Case of the Book Battery

Your client Mark Brown was at home one night. He had been studying in bed when he fell asleep. He was awakened when he heard and then saw a stranger in his darkened bedroom. He shouted, and the stranger moved toward the door. Frightened of what the stranger might do next, Mark took one of his heavy law books and threw it at the man's departing back. Unfortunately the man's spine was broken. Assume your boss wants you to analyze whether Mark is guilty of committing a criminal battery.

Mark has been charged with violating a criminal statute:

Any person committing an intentional, harmful, unprivileged touching of another shall be guilty of battery.

Figure 12-3   Elements of an IRAC Analysis

Issue:	Have a topic sentence that states the issue you will be discussing in that paragraph.
Rule:	State the rule of law that arguably governs the particular issue in question.
Analysis:	Explain how the statutory language and policy behind the statute determine the outcome given your client's specific facts.
Conclusion:	Conclude. State what you think the result will be. Do not leave your reader to decide what the bottom line is. That is why your supervisor asked you to analyze the problem.
Transition:	Use a short transition sentence to lead to the next issue that you want to discuss.

From our earlier discussions we know that one of the first steps in analyzing this statute is to break it down into its elements.

Battery is

1. the intentional,
2. harmful,
3. unprivileged
4. touching
5. of another.

The following is a brief description of each of the IRAC elements with an example of how each would be used to analyze Mark's problem.

1. Issue

Have a topic sentence that states the issue you will be discussing in that paragraph. This sentence should be brief and clear. It should also contain only one idea: the one to be discussed in that particular paragraph. If there is more than one issue, devote a separate IRAC paragraph to each one.

> The issue is whether Mark Brown can be found guilty of battery.

2. Rule

State the rule of law that arguably governs the particular issue in question. Quote the exact statutory language. If the statute is quite long, quote only the relevant language. Use ellipses[15] to show any omissions. Make sure your omissions do not change the statute's meaning.

> Battery requires "an intentional . . . unprivileged touching of another."

3. Analysis

Explain how the statutory language and policy behind the statute determine the outcome given your client's specific facts. Note the strengths as well as the weaknesses in your client's case. You will be doing your client a great disservice if you only point out the helpful arguments and leave out the harmful ones.

---

[15] Note the use of three dots. Each is separated by a space. If you omit the end of a sentence, use four dots: three to show the omission and one for the period.

> Because Mark threw a book at a stranger he found in his bedroom, there was a touching. The touching, however, was privileged. The stranger was a trespasser in Mark's house. He awoke Mark from his sleep, thereby frightening him. Mark had a right to defend himself. Although the man had his back turned to Mark and was possibly leaving the room when Mark threw the book at him, it was quite dark in the room. In his half-awake state Mark could not be held responsible for making a necessary and quick decision to defend himself.

4. Conclusion

Conclude. Do not leave your reader to decide what the bottom line is. That is why you were asked to analyze the problem.

> Therefore, while Mark did touch the stranger, the touching was privileged. Mark should not be found guilty of battery.

If you are discussing more than one issue, use a short transition sentence to lead to the next element you want to discuss. When you put all of the IRAC elements together, the final discussion would look like this.

> The issue is whether Mark Brown can be found guilty of battery. Battery requires "an intentional . . . unprivileged touching of another." Because Mark threw a book at a stranger he found in his bedroom, there was a touching. The touching, however, was privileged. The stranger was a trespasser in Mark's house. He awoke Mark from his sleep, thereby frightening him. Mark had a right to defend himself. Although the man had his back turned to Mark and was possibly leaving the room when Mark threw the book at him, it was quite dark in the room. In his half-awake state Mark could not be held responsible for making a necessary and quick decision to defend himself. Therefore, while Mark did touch the stranger, the touching was privileged. Mark should not be found guilty of battery.

Some attorneys prefer the CRAC as opposed to the IRAC method. With CRAC you start with the conclusion. If that is what your boss wants, that is, of course, what you will do. But for now, it is better to use IRAC. IRAC forces you to support your conclusion with a well-developed analysis. When you start your writing with a conclusion, the answer may seem so self-evident that you will not see any need to justify it with an analysis. However, when you start your paragraph with a statement of the issue and end it with a conclusion, there is all that space in between just crying out to be filled with an explanation that will convince your reader of how you logically moved from your issue to your conclusion. This will help prevent the most common error in legal writing: stating the rule and simply jumping to the conclusion with no supporting reasoning. Look at the following paragraph. What is missing?

The issue is whether Mark Brown can be found guilty of battery. Battery requires both that there be an intentional touching of another and that the touching be "unprivileged." While Mark did touch the stranger, the touching was privileged. Mark should not be found guilty of battery.

After reading this you would be left wondering:But why? Why was the touching privileged? The writer gave an answer but not the reasons for that answer. Always double-check your writing to make sure you are not leaving your reader with any questions about how you reached your conclusion.

If the statute you are analyzing contains more than one issue, start with an introductory paragraph, also known as a **road map paragraph**, that tells your reader where you will be going. In that paragraph very briefly outline the facts, the rule, and the issues you will be discussing. This is not the place to completely retell the client's story. Give just enough of the facts to set the stage. Follow that paragraph with an IRAC analysis of each major issue, using the rest of the facts to make arguments based on the statute's elements.

Road map paragraph
An introductory paragraph listing issues to be discussed in the order they are to be discussed.

Sometimes an issue will be simple enough that you can put all the IRAC elements into a single paragraph. At other times you may want to divide the IRAC elements into more than one paragraph. For example, you might wish to set out the issue and the rule of law in one paragraph. Then in the next paragraph you could include the arguments for one side of the issue. You could follow this with a third paragraph outlining the arguments for the other side and your conclusion on that issue, along with a transitional phrase or sentence to lead into the next issue.

You need to use **transitions** between your issues to help lead your reader from one issue to the next. A transition can be as simple as "The next issue is. . . ." Finally, wrap up your discussion with a **concluding paragraph** that summarizes your analysis.

Transition
In writing, a technique used to help your reader move from one thought to the next and to see the connections between them.

When using IRAC remember that each paragraph should contain one and only one idea. A paragraph, indeed any written work, is a structure. It should build, grow, and develop toward a denouement. If you cannot discern such a progression in your own work, go back and rework it until you do.

Concluding paragraph
The final paragraph in a written legal analysis that summarizes the writer's conclusions.

Finally, do not view IRAC as a straightjacket. It is meant not to limit your creative abilities but simply to provide a structure for your writing.

Exhibit 12-2, on page 329, is a sample analysis using the IRAC format for the problem of Mary and the hammer, introduced earlier in the chapter. We have added the marginal notes to help you locate each of the IRAC elements. When writing a legal analysis yourself, do not include these marginal notations.

G. LOCATING AND INTERPRETING ADMINISTRATIVE REGULATIONS

Legislatures often delegate considerable lawmaking authority to administrative agencies. Therefore, frequently you must look beyond the statutes to administrative regulations that interpret the statute. For example, you may recall from Chapter 3 that Congress enacted a statute prohibiting discrimination in employment on the basis of sex. In that same statute Congress also created an administrative agency, the Equal Employment Opportunity Commission (EEOC), and

gave that agency the power to write regulations interpreting the statute. One such regulation defines sex discrimination to include sexual harassment.

> Unwelcome sexual advances, requests for sexual favors, and other verbal or physical conduct of a sexual nature constitute sexual harassment when (1) submission to such conduct is made either explicitly or implicitly a term or condition of an individual's employment, (2) submission to or rejection of such conduct by an individual is used as the basis for employment decisions affecting such individual, or (3) such conduct has the purpose or effect of unreasonably interfering with an individual's work performance or creating an intimidating, hostile, or offensive working environment.[16]

Code of Federal Regulations (C.F.R.) A compilation of federal administrative regulations arranged by agency.

As you can see, administrative regulations are published in formats that resemble those used for statutes. Federal regulations are published in the **Code of Federal Regulations (C.F.R.)**. The C.F.R. is analogous to the United States Code in that it contains only those regulations that are of a general, permanent nature and are currently in force. The regulations are arranged by agency.

Some states publish codes of regulations that correspond to the Code of Federal Regulations in that they contain all the current state regulations and are organized by subject matter. In other states you must obtain the regulations from each individual agency. At both the state and the federal levels some private publishers issue loose-leaf reporters that contain administrative regulations in specialized areas such as taxes and labor law.

Citations for administrative regulations follow a form that is analogous to that for statutes. For example:

49 C.F.R. § 6.1 (1997)
Ill. Admin. Code tit. 5, § 4430 (1995)

In the first citation *C.F.R.* tells you that it is a reference to the Code of Federal Regulations. The number 49 stands for title 49, while § 6.1 refers to section 6.1 of title 49. As with statutes, the date in parentheses refers to the last publication date for the book in which the regulation appears, not the date the regulation was promulgated. The second citation is to an Illinois regulation.

Administrative regulations have the same basic features as statutes, and they are similarly future oriented. However, they tend to be more detailed than statutes, as their function is to spell out the specifics of the statute. Nonetheless, the basic approaches you use when interpreting statutes can also be used to interpret regulations. In addition, keep in mind that the courts will seek an interpretation that is consistent with the intent of the statute that established and controls the agency in question.

---

[16] 29 C.F.R. § 1604.11 (2000).

Road map paragraph	Mary is concerned about whether she can be convicted of carrying a dangerous weapon. During an argument with another customer in a local store Mary briefly picked up a hammer from the counter. The statute under which she has been charged makes it unlawful for "anyone, other than a police officer, to carry a dangerous weapon." Because Mary is not a police officer, the first element of the statute is satisfied. However, as Mary only picked up the hammer, there is an issue as to whether she "carried" it. Second, there is an issue as to whether a hammer can be considered a "dangerous weapon."	
Issue 1 **Rule** **Analysis** **Conclusion on issue 1**	As to the first issue of whether her lifting of the hammer constituted "carrying," the statute simply reads that it is unlawful "to carry" a dangerous weapon. While in the hardware store Mary did move the hammer from the counter into the air. However, she did not take it from one location to another, such as from the store out into the street. Therefore, while she may have "possessed" the hammer, she cannot be said to have "carried" the hammer. The second issue, however, is not as clear-cut.	**Transition**
Issue 2 **Rule** **Analysis** **Conclusion on issue 2**	The second issue is whether the hammer should be viewed as a "dangerous weapon." The statute does not define "dangerous weapon." A hammer is normally viewed as a tool and not as a weapon. However, being a large, hard object, a hammer certainly has the capacity to become a dangerous weapon. Also, it was only when Mary lifted the hammer and told the other customer to hand over the item that Mary wanted that the other customer did as Mary wished. Because the legislature was probably more concerned about the potential harm that a dangerous weapon could cause than about the specific identity of any particular weapon, the hammer should be seen as a dangerous weapon.	

(continued)

Exhibit 12-2   Sample IRAC Analysis

> In conclusion, both elements must be satisfied to find Mary guilty. The hammer could be seen as a dangerous weapon, but Mary did not take it from one place to another. Therefore, she did not "carry" it. Because both elements are not satisfied, Mary cannot be found guilty of carrying a dangerous weapon.

Concluding paragraph

Exhibit 12-2 Sample IRAC Analysis (*concluded*)

Legal Reasoning Exercises

7. Use the IRAC approach to write an analysis of one of the issues you outlined for Exercise 5 regarding Sarah and the defenses to her possible false imprisonment claim.

8. Apply the principles we have been discussing to Carl's situation, described in Exercise 6, and write an IRAC analysis of his problem.

H. LOCATING AND INTERPRETING CONSTITUTIONS

Constitutions set out the structure of the government itself, as well as the limitations on the government's power. Therefore, you would turn to a constitutional provision to challenge an objectionable statute or the manner in which government agents conducted themselves (as in a Fourth Amendment challenge to an allegedly unreasonable search).

State and federal constitutions are usually included in the corresponding statutory compilation. For example, the U.S. Constitution can be found in the United States Code, the United States Code Annotated, and the United States Code Service. Similarly, a state statute compilation usually includes a copy of its state constitution, and a few even feature a copy of the U.S. Constitution with annotations to decisions from their own state courts.

Sections of constitutions are cited as follows:

U.S. Const. art. I, § 8, cl. 3
U.S. Const. amend. XX, § 3
Ill. Const. art. IV, § 2(b)

Just as you will see ambiguity in statutes and administrative regulations, you will see it in constitutions. Indeed, the broader and more general the

document, the greater the likelihood that ambiguity will occur. Consider, for example, the following clauses contained in the U.S. Constitution:

The Congress shall have Power . . .

To regulate *Commerce* with foreign Nations, and among the several States, and with the Indian Tribes. . . .

To make all Laws which shall be *necessary and proper* for carrying into Execution the foregoing Powers, and all other Powers vested by this Constitution in the Government of the United States, or in any Department or Officer thereof. (art. I, § 8) (emphasis added) Congress shall make no law respecting an establishment of religion, or prohibiting the free exercise thereof; or abridging the freedom of speech, or of the press, or the right of the people peaceably to assemble, and to petition the Government for a redress of grievances. (amend. I) (emphasis added)

The right of the people to be secure in their persons, houses, papers, and effects, against unreasonable searches and seizures, shall not be violated. . . . (amend. IV) (emphasis added)

We added the italics to emphasize the ambiguity of various words and phrases. Note that these provisions are broadly written and hence contain a great deal of ambiguity.

Over the years the courts have interpreted these and other parts of the Constitution. To do so, the courts generally use the same approaches discussed in the section on statutory construction. They attempt a literal reading of the words themselves (plain meaning), consider the relationship of the clause in question to similar clauses located elsewhere in the document (contextual analysis), and go back to the minutes of the Constitutional Convention and to the legislative history of amendments (external analysis).

Once a court has formally interpreted the meaning of a particular clause of the Constitution, that court decision takes on precedential value and becomes case law on the meaning of the Constitution. Therefore, rather than going back to begin the interpretive process over again, succeeding courts follow the lead of previous decisions, and gradually a series of cases develops that explains, for example, that the words *no law* as they are used in the First Amendment really mean that the government can pass laws restricting obscene materials or punishing libelous statements. As the case law expands, it becomes clearer as to when something might be considered obscene and when it might not or as to when a search is a reasonable search and when it is not.

It is important to realize that it is in the area of constitutional law that the courts (particularly the U.S. Supreme Court) have the greatest freedom to exercise discretion. This is not only because the meaning of the Constitution is sometimes ambiguous but also because the Constitution is a "living" document. The Supreme Court is thus legitimately able to change its interpretations of constitutional law to meet the needs of a changing society.

SUMMARY

Once you have located a relevant statute, you must analyze it by breaking it down into its elements and then applying those elements to your client's facts. In analyzing the statute you should look at the plain meaning of the statutory language and try to ascertain the legislative intent in enacting the statute. You can use several strategies to assist you in this process, including relying on the canons of construction, reading legislative history, and seeing how the courts have interpreted the statute. Once you have analyzed the statute, you may be asked to summarize your thinking in writing. One form of written analysis is known as IRAC (Issue-Rule-Analysis-Conclusion).

As we suggested in the first chapter, many view studying law as a skill that simply requires the memorization of rules: If you know the right rule, you will know the right answer. By now we hope you more fully understand why that is not true. While a lot of memorization is involved in learning about the law, applying the law is a process. You do need to know the rules, but that is only the beginning and not the end of the process. Furthermore, the rules change as we apply them to new situations. It is only when the rules are applied to facts that we are forced to give a clearer definition to otherwise ambiguous language.

REVIEW QUESTIONS

Pages 301 through 323

1. Why do statutes often contain ambiguous language?
2. What is meant by looking for the plain meaning of a statute?
3. What are the canons of construction? How do courts use them in interpreting statutes?
4. What types of statutes are courts most likely to strictly construe? To liberally construe?
5. What types of documents could make up a statute's legislative history?
6. What are the dangers in relying on legislative history?
7. What type of judge would be more likely to interpret Title VII's prohibition against employment discrimination based on sex to include discrimination based on sexual preference: one who believes in judicial restraint or judicial activism? Why?
8. What are the main steps in analyzing a statutory problem?
9. What is a statutory element?
10. How does an issue differ from an element?
11. When reading a statute, why is it important to pay attention to the use of "and" and "or"?

Pages 323 through 331

12. What does IRAC stand for, and why does it provide a useful structure for your legal writing?
13. What is the function of a road map paragraph? Of a concluding paragraph?
14. Why is it important to use transitions?
15. We asked you this question at the end of Chapter 1, but we want to ask it again. Why does the study of law involve more than the mere memorization of rules?

Chapter 13

Finding and Interpreting Court Opinions

The picture of the bewildered litigant lured into a course of action by the false light of a decision, only to meet ruin when the light is extinguished and the decision is overruled, is for the most part a figment of excited brains.
Justice Benjamin Cardozo

INTRODUCTION

In Chapter 12 we discussed how to locate and interpret statutes, administrative regulations, and constitutions. In this chapter we will discuss how to locate and interpret court opinions. The terms *court opinion*, *case*, and *decision* are synonymous.

As you will recall from Chapter 5, there are two basic types of courts: trial and appellate courts. While trial courts determine the facts and apply the law to those facts, appellate courts act as the final interpreters of the law. As the final interpretation of the law, appellate court opinions serve as precedent for future court decisions. For that reason it is principally appellate decisions that you will be studying and briefing. **Case briefing** is a stylized method that you will use to summarize those court opinions.

A. TYPES OF COURT OPINIONS

Court opinions generally fall in one of four categories:

1. those interpreting and applying enacted law, such as statutes;
2. those deciding the constitutionality of a law;
3. those applying established common-law principles; and
4. those creating new common-law principles.

The first type of opinion, which interprets and applies enacted law, consumes a great deal of the courts' time. As we said in Chapter 12, statutes, administrative regulations, and constitutional provisions often contain ambiguous words and phrases. When interpreting enacted law and attempting to determine legislative intent, the courts rely on the same methods we have discussed: looking at the plain meaning, relying on the canons of construction, examining other parts of the statute, and searching for external evidence, such as legislative history and prior court decisions. Under the doctrine of stare decisis, if previous courts have already interpreted the same or similar language, a court will generally try to reach a decision that is consistent with those earlier interpretations.

Judicial review
The court's power to review statutes to decide whether they conform to the Constitution.

A second type of case involves challenges to the constitutionality of a law. Under the power of **judicial review** the courts are responsible for ensuring that all laws comport with the Constitution's requirements. In this type of decision the court's focus is on the intent of the Constitution's framers and the purpose the constitutional provision was meant to fulfill. Then the court determines whether the law in question is consistent with the Constitution's intended purpose.

The third and fourth types of cases involve the common law rather than enacted law. Despite the tremendous growth in statutory law, there are times when no statute covers a litigant's situation. Then the courts rely on the common law, or court-made law. Usually, the court will be faced with a group of prior cases and will use them to form an opinion on the current case. Those cases will be seen as either mandatory or persuasive authority.

Mandatory authority
Court decisions from a higher court in the same jurisdiction.

A decision is **mandatory authority** when it comes from

1. a higher court
2. in the same jurisdiction.

For state cases, that means higher courts within that state's own court system. Federal courts deciding a case involving state law must follow the interpretations given by that state's courts. Within the federal court system it means cases from within that circuit and the U.S. Supreme Court.

Persuasive authority
Court decisions from an equal or a lower court from the same jurisdiction or from a higher court in a different jurisdiction; also includes secondary authority.

Persuasive authority consists of the decisions of courts that do not constitute mandatory authority and the writings of legal scholars. It may therefore include primary authority, such as decisions of other state courts, and secondary authority, such as legal treatises or law review articles.

Figure 13-1, on page 335, shows the hierarchical nature of mandatory authority. A decision handed down by a court is mandatory authority for those courts below it connected by an arrow. For example, a federal district court in the First Circuit is required to follow the decisions of the federal court of appeals for the First Circuit. But the decisions of the Second Circuit

court of appeals are only persuasive authority for the First Circuit district courts. Likewise, the decisions of state A's highest appellate court are mandatory authority for state A's intermediate appellate and trial courts but are only persuasive authority for state B's courts.

When looking to mandatory authority, unless there is a good reason not to do so, a court will decide a new case based on how courts have held in prior **analogous cases**—that is, cases that involved similar facts and rules of law. If the court decides that the prior cases and the present one are dissimilar, on either the facts or the law, the court will **distinguish** the prior cases and reach a contrary decision in the case before it. As you will recall, this process of looking to **precedent**, prior cases, for guidance is known as following the doctrine of **stare decisis**.

However, there will be times when a court will create new common law. This can occur either because there is no law governing the situation or because the court decides to overrule its own prior decisions. When there is no law covering a situation, the court is faced with an **issue of first impression**. If there are decisions from other jurisdictions, the court may look to those decisions for guidance. In addition, the court may look to secondary authority, such as law reviews and treatises. In cases of first impression the court has the option of creating new common-law rules to cover the situation or refusing to do so and deferring to the legislature. If the court defers to the legislature, it does so because

Analogous cases
Cases that involve similar facts and rules of law.

Distinguishable cases
Cases that involve different facts and/or rules of law.

Issue of first impression
An issue that the court has never faced before.

Figure 13-1   Mandatory Authority

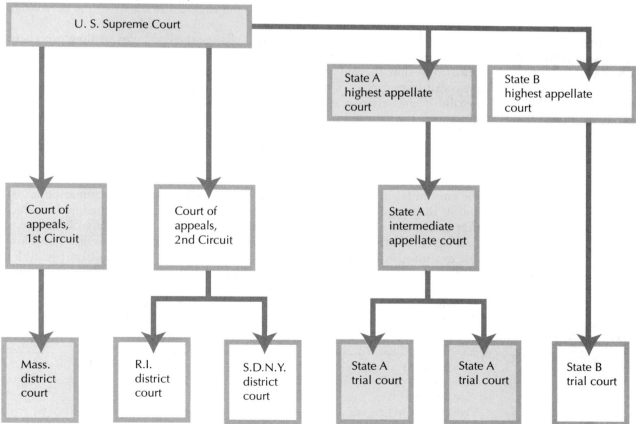

it thinks the case involves an area of law that an elected body can handle better than the courts.

Landmark decision
A court opinion that establishes new law in an important area.

A leading example of a court deciding to change the current law, thereby creating a new common-law rule, occurred in the 1968 **landmark decision** of *Dillon v. Legg*.[1] Prior to that decision bystanders could not recover for the emotional distress they suffered when witnessing an accident. Then in *Dillon v. Legg* the California Supreme Court created new law. The court stated that a mother could recover for the emotional injury she suffered when she saw her child injured. When deciding this type of case, the courts are literally making new law, and at times this can create quite dramatic and swift changes in the law. This can be contrasted with cases that revolve around the application of established legal principles to a set of facts. Then the law slowly evolves as the courts evaluate new fact patterns. For example, once the California Supreme Court had established that a mother could recover for seeing a child injured, questions were raised as to whether the mother actually had to see the accident or whether hearing it was enough, whether other family members could recover, and so on. The courts were then flooded with cases in which the issue was no longer whether a bystander could recover but rather under what circumstances.

Returning for a moment to our earlier discussion regarding mandatory versus persuasive authority, note that the California Supreme Court's decision in *Dillon v. Legg* became mandatory authority for all lower California state courts. However, it is only persuasive authority in the federal courts and in other state courts. Each of those courts is free to decide whether to follow the standards set out in *Dillon* based solely on each court's view of the persuasiveness of the *Dillon* court's arguments.

Overrule
A decision is overruled when a court in a later case changes the law so that the decision in the earlier case is no longer good law.

Finally, in rare cases the court will change the law by **overruling** precedent. This usually occurs when the court decides that society's needs have changed so drastically that the old rules should no longer apply. This illustrates the true power of stare decisis. While it normally is a force for stability, it also allows for flexibility and change when the times require it. Figure 13-2, on page 337, illustrates the various possibilities that a court can pursue when confronted with an issue governed by the common law.

Sometimes a court implies but does not explicitly state that it is overruling a prior decision. When that occurs, it is hard to determine whether the court has overruled the prior decision or merely distinguished it. For an understanding of the continuing validity of the prior court decision, such a determination is crucial. If the court overruled the prior decision, then the legal principle for which that case stood is no longer the law. However, if the court merely distinguished that case from the current one, the prior case's legal principle is still good law. For example, in 1896, in *Plessy v. Ferguson*,[2] the U.S. Supreme Court held that providing separate railway cars for white and black passengers was constitutional under the principle of separate but equal. Fifty-eight years later, in 1954, in *Brown v. Board of Education*,[3] a case involving segregation of public schools, the Supreme Court stated: "We conclude that in the field of public education the doctrine of 'separate but equal' has no place."[4] Did the Court in *Brown* overrule

---

[1] 441 P.2d 912 (Cal. 1968).
[2] 163 U.S. 537 (1896).
[3] 347 U.S. 483 (1954).
[4] 347 U.S. 483, 495 (1954).

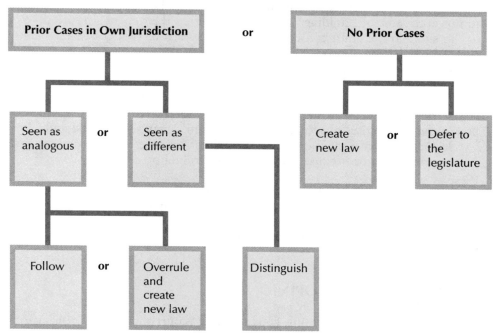

Figure 13-2   Four Routes Open to a Court Faced with a Common-Law Problem

Plessy? If so, then the doctrine of separate but equal could no longer be applied in any situation. Or did the Court merely distinguish *Plessy?* If it merely distinguished *Plessy*, then while the principle of separate but equal could not be applied to educational facilities, it could still be applied in other situations, such as transportation.

While it could be argued that the Court had merely distinguished *Plessy*, in reality the Court did not have to utter the precise words "We hereby overrule *Plessy v. Ferguson*" for that to be the effect of the decision. All subsequent courts faced with cases involving separate facilities assumed the *Brown* decision had overruled Plessy. In fact, two years after the *Brown* decision a federal court in a case involving transportation (city buses) stated: "[W]e think that *Plessy v. Ferguson* has been impliedly, though not explicitly, overruled, and that... there is now no rational basis upon which the separate but equal doctrine can be validly applied to public carrier transportation."[5]

As you can see, on a theoretical level it can be difficult to decide if a court has overruled or merely distinguished a prior case. However, because of the nature of our legal system this problem basically disappears in practice. Attorneys are hired to present their client's point of view and therefore will argue that a prior case has been overruled or distinguished based upon the needs of their client's position. To some this may seem disingenuous, reinforcing the popular notion that attorneys are nothing more than hired guns. However, if there is no one, "true" holding of a case, then attorneys, who are required to

---

[5] *Browder v. Gayle*, 142 F. Supp. 707, 717 (M.D. Ala. 1956).

zealously advocate their client's point of view, would be less than ethical if they did not argue for the "holding" that best supported their client's position.

In summary, a court can be faced with one of four types of cases:

1. a question regarding the interpretation of enacted law, such as a statute, a constitutional provision, or an administrative regulation;
2. a question regarding the constitutionality of a statute or an administrative regulation;
3. the application of settled common law to a new set of facts; and
4. the creation of new common law, either because this is a case of first impression or because the court is overruling precedent.

In this chapter you will read an example of each type of case. Notice that in all of the cases the judges are looking for and evaluating precedential cases. But also note how they have some latitude in the way they handle the precedent; at times they are able to ignore or even overrule it.

B. LOCATING COURT OPINIONS

Case reporters
Books that contain appellate court decisions. There are both official and unofficial reporters.

Official reporter
Governmental publication of court opinions.

Unofficial reporter
Private publication of court opinions—for example, the regional reporters, such as N.E.2d, published by West.

Case citation
Information that tells the reader the name of the case, where it can be located, the court that decided it, and the year it was decided. The Bluebook gives precise rules as to how case citations are to be written.

In this chapter we will describe how you can locate a court opinion once you have its citation. A **citation** is a formalized method for giving information about (1) the name of the case, (2) where it can be located, (3) the court that decided the case, and (4) the year in which it was decided. In Chapter 12 we will discuss various ways in which you can locate relevant court cases without this information.

Case reporters are sets of books, consisting of hundreds of volumes, that contain copies of appellate court opinions. They are usually arranged in chronological order and divided into volumes named for the court that rendered the opinions. Thus opinions of the Massachusetts Supreme Judicial Court, the highest appellate court in Massachusetts, are found in the Massachusetts Reports. Likewise, those of the highest appellate court in Illinois are reported in the Illinois Reports. The federal government publishes U.S. Supreme Court cases in the United States Reports.

West is the major publisher of case reporters, and the West National Reporter System covers all appellate court decisions in the fifty states.

Reporters are generally divided into two categories—**official** and **unofficial**. They are official when published at the direction of state or federal statutes. All others are unofficial. The texts of the opinions published in the unofficial reporters are the same as those in the official ones. What differs are the editorial features, such as case summaries, that the publishers add at the beginning of the unofficial reports.

At a minimum a **case citation** to a court opinion will include the names of the parties, the volume and page number of the reporter(s) in which the opinion is published, and the date of the case. Here is a typical citation for a state court case:

Callow v. Thomas, 322 Mass. 550, 78 N.E.2d 637 (1948)

Each part of the citation is explained in Figure 13-3, on page 339. Starting at the left the parties' last names are listed. Notice that their names are underlined, as is

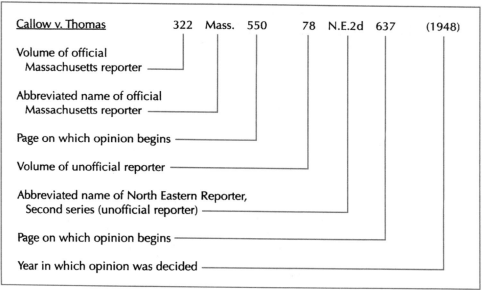

Figure 13-3   Case Citation

the *small v. The v.* stands for "versus." The party bringing the appeal (the **appellant** or **petitioner**) is usually listed first, and the opposing side (the **appellee** or **respondent**) is listed second. However, some states follow the practice of listing the name of the original plaintiff first, no matter which party brought the appeal.

 When there is more than one party on any side of a dispute or when several cases have been consolidated, the citation uses only the names of the first parties listed on each side or the first case listed. When the state is a party to a case in its own courts, it is usually listed as *People v. or State v.* On the other hand, if a state is a party to a suit in federal court, the case name would include the state name—for example, *Illinois v. Smith.*

 After the parties' names, the reporters where the case can be found are listed. Some state court opinions are published in two reporters, the official state reporter and a West unofficial regional reporter. Some state opinions are only published in the West unofficial reporter.

 State reporters use abbreviated versions of the state name—for example, Mass. for Massachusetts and Cal. for California. West regional reporters are abbreviated as follows:

 P. or P.2d for the Pacific region
 N.W. or N.W.2d for the North Western region
 S.W. or S.W.2d for the South Western region
 So. or So. 2d for the Southern region
 S.E. or S.E.2d for the South Eastern region
 N.E. or N.E.2d for the North Eastern region
 A. or A.2d for the Atlantic region

Appellant or petitioner
A person who initiates an appeal.

Appellee or respondent
The party in a lawsuit against whom an appeal has been filed.

NETNOTE

The courts are beginning to post their appellate opinions on-line. In fact, you can find U.S. Supreme Court opinions dating back to the 1800s at Findlaw: *www.findlaw.com.* On Findlaw's home page under "Laws: Cases & Codes" click on "US Sup Ct." However, do not expect to find most other federal and state opinions older than the early 1990s.

To locate appellate court opinions on-line for your circuit, start by going to *www.findlaw.com.* Click on the tab "For Legal Professionals." Then click on the link to "Cases & Codes." Under "US Courts of Appeals—Opinions & Web Sites" select your circuit. Follow the same approach to locate court opinions for your state, except go under "US State Laws—Cases, Codes, Statutes and Regulations" to select your state.

The number immediately in front of the reporter abbreviation indicates the volume in which the case is found. The number immediately after the reporter abbreviation is the page number on which the case begins. Thus you could find *Callow v. Thomas* either on page 550 of volume 322 of the Massachusetts Reports or on page 637 of volume 78 of the North Eastern Reporter, Second Series.

Following the volume and page numbers of the reporters, the year of the decision appears in parentheses. *Callow v. Thomas* was decided in 1948.

In those cases where the identification of the court is not obvious from the name of the reporter, there will be additional information about the court in parentheses. In the *Callow v. Thomas* citation, you can tell that the Massachusetts Supreme Judicial Court wrote the decision because only Massachusetts Supreme Judicial Court decisions are published in the Massachusetts Reports. However, if the citation had been only to N.E.2d, then the abbreviation for the state would have to be included in the parentheses:

Callow v. Thomas, 78 N.E.2d 637 (Mass. 1948)

Whenever you see a citation to a federal district court or court of appeals case, you will see the name of the district or the circuit in the parentheses:

Chambers v. Maroney, 409 F.2d 1186 (3d Cir. 1969)
Brown v. Merkel, 355 F. Supp. 90 (D. Mass. 1990)

Pinpoint cite
The reference to a particular page within an opinion.

Sometimes a writer will refer to a specific part of the court decision where a particular quote appears or where an issue is discussed. This reference to a particular page within an opinion is sometimes referred to as a **pinpoint cite**. In those instances a second page number will appear after the page number on which the case begins. For example, a quotation taken from page 1189 of the *Chambers v. Maroney* decision would be cited as follows:

<u>Chambers v. Maroney</u>, 409 F.2d 1186, 1189 (3d Cir. 1969)

Finally, while citations will never include **prior case history**, sometimes they include information about the **subsequent history** of the case. For example:

<u>Telex Corp. v. International Business Machines Corp.</u>, 367 F. Supp. 258 (N.D. Okla. 1973), <u>rev'd</u>, 510 F.2d 894 (10th Cir.), <u>cert. denied</u>, 423 U.S. 802 (1975)

This citation indicates that the case was first decided by the U.S. District Court for the Northern District of Oklahoma and can be found on page 258 of volume 367 of the Federal Supplement. The case was then appealed to the Tenth Circuit, where the decision was reversed and reported on page 894 of volume 510 of the Federal Reporter, Second Series. The U.S. Supreme Court's decision not to grant certiorari is reported on page 802 of volume 423 of the United States Reports.

Prior case history
Information about what happened procedurally to the cited case before it was heard by the cited court. Do not include this information in a citation.

Subsequent case history
Information about what happened procedurally to the litigation after the case cited. Include this information in a citation.

C. THE ELEMENTS OF A COURT OPINION

All court opinions contain some preliminary information, such as the names of the parties, followed by the decision itself. The decision usually contains a statement of the facts on which the case is based; a discussion of the law and how that law, combined with the facts, created legal issues; the court's decision; and an explanation why the decision was reached. If the opinion is one printed by West, there will also be the additional editorial features added by West.

1. Preliminary Material and West Editorial Features

The court opinion in *Callow v. Thomas* is reprinted for you beginning on page 370. It is reprinted exactly as it appears in West's North Eastern Reporter. We have added explanatory material in the right and left margins in order to help you identify the various editorial features that West adds to the opinion.

First, notice that West uses its trademarked key number symbol to separate the cases. Following that are the names of the parties, the name of the court that rendered the decision, and the dates the case was argued and decided. This, in turn, is followed by the **headnotes** and the **syllabus**. The headnotes are short summaries of each of the legal issues decided by the court in this decision as West has identified them. The headnote title and key number (e.g., Husband and Wife, key 205(2)) are cross-references to the West Digest System, which are explained in Chapter 14. The syllabus is a summary of the facts and the court's decision.

Below that is a listing of the judges who decided the case and the attorneys involved in the case. The actual opinion itself begins with the name of the judge who drafted the majority opinion.

Headnote
Summary of one legal point in a court opinion; written by the editors at West.

Syllabus
A summary of a court opinion that appears at the beginning of the case.

2. Facts of the Case

Because court decisions are based on the facts of the case, you must have a thorough knowledge of these facts in order to understand the true meaning and impact of a case. Facts can be divided into two groups: substantive and procedural.

Substantive facts

In a case brief, facts that deal with what happened to the parties before the litigation began.

The **substantive facts** deal with what happened to the parties before the litigation began—that is, why one party is suing the other. Under the principle of **standing**, courts cannot decide abstract issues or render advisory opinions. Rather they are limited to deciding cases that involve litigants who are personally affected by their decisions. The facts must therefore establish that a true adversarial relationship exists and that the legal requirement of a "case or controversy" is met.

In approaching a civil case ask yourself the following questions:

Who was the original plaintiff (the person who first brought the matter to court)?
Who was the original defendant?
What was the nature of the injury?
What was the plaintiff asking the trial court to do about it?

In criminal cases your questions should include

Who is the defendant?
What is the nature of the alleged criminal activity?
Did the police use any questionable methods in obtaining the evidence used against the defendant?
Was the trial conducted in accordance with the requirements of the due process clause?

Procedural facts

In a case brief, facts that relate to what happened procedurally in the lower courts or administrative agencies before the case reached the court issuing the opinion.

Procedural facts refer to what happened in the lower courts or administrative agencies as well as the action taken by the appellate court issuing the opinion. For example, in the trial court did the plaintiff win after a jury verdict, or did the plaintiff lose on a motion to dismiss? These procedural facts are sometimes referred to as the **judicial history** of the case.

Look again at the *Callow v. Thomas* case, beginning on page 370, and you will see that Justice Spalding began his opinion with a brief discussion of the substantive facts. The parties were married at the time they were involved in an automobile accident. Several months later the wife sought and received an annulment. The wife then sued her former husband for negligence in causing the accident. At that time the law in Massachusetts was that spouses could not sue each other for negligence. Therefore, this case raised the interesting question of whether or not she could sue her former husband for something that happened before the annulment. The trial court, obviously at a loss as to how it should decide the case, agreed to the parties' request to send the case to the Massachusetts Supreme Judicial Court for a determination. The parties stipulated (agreed on) the amount of damages should the Supreme Judicial Court decide as a matter of law that the defendant could be held liable for his negligence.

In *Callow v. Thomas*, Justice Spalding followed his discussion of the substantive facts with a review of that procedural history. Justice Spalding stated: "The judge at the request of the parties reported the case to this court without decision... 'upon the stipulation that if the plaintiff is entitled to recover, judgment shall be entered for the plaintiff in the sum of $3,000, otherwise judgment for the defendant."

3. Law Analyzed

A trial court must base its decision on the law as it exists when the litigants arrive in court. The court's statement of the current law may involve a quotation from the relevant statute or a discussion of a series of prior cases. In *Callow v. Thomas* the court stated that the rule that prohibited spouses from suing each other was "too well settled to require citation of authority."

4. Issues Raised

A trial court applies the law to what it determines are the facts of the case. When that case is appealed, the appellate court can either approve or disapprove of the manner in which the trial was conducted and either accept or reject the way in which the lower court interpreted and applied the law. A single appellate case may involve several issues. In *Callow v. Thomas*, immediately following the facts, Justice Spalding gave his view of the issue as follows: "The question for decision is whether a wife after the marriage has been annulled can maintain an action against her former husband for a tort committed during coverture."

5. Decisions Reached

In its decision the court will reach a result not only for these particular litigants but also for future litigants faced with a similar situation. The result reached in this particular case is known as the **disposition**. The result reached not only for these particular litigants but also for future litigants is known as the **holding**.

The disposition usually consists of **affirming** (approving) or **reversing** (disapproving) the judgment of the lower court. If the case is affirmed, the matter is considered settled unless a higher-level appellate court decides to review it. If the lower court's decision is reversed, the appellate court either sends the case back to the lower court for review or substitutes its own judgment for that of the lower court. If the appellate court sends the case back to the lower court, it is with the understanding that the lower court must act consistently with the principles of law the higher court laid down in its decision.

As mentioned above, the new rule of law created by this case that will apply to future litigants is known as the **holding**. The holding is the court's answer to the issue and will be looked to by future courts and litigants for assistance in deciding similar cases. Therefore, the court decision should be analyzed at two different levels: How was the issue settled in this particular case? What general principle of law has been enunciated by the way in which the court resolved this issue?

In *Callow v. Thomas* the court combined its holding with the disposition for these particular litigants:

> The better rule, we think, is that in the case of voidable marriage transactions which have been concluded and things which have been done during the period of the supposed

Disposition
The result reached in a particular case.

Affirm
A decision is affirmed when the litigants appeal the trial court decision and the higher court agrees with what the lower court has done.

Reverse
A decision is reversed when the litigants appeal the trial court decision and the higher court disagrees with the decision of a lower court.

Holding
The new legal principle established by a court opinion.

marriage ought not to be undone or reopened after the decree of annulment. Applying that principle here, the plaintiff is not entitled to recover.

Finally, do not confuse **reversing** a decision with **overruling** a case. An appellate court reverses a decision when it concludes that a lower court failed to properly apply the law. An appellate court overrules a prior appellate court decision when it determines that the law needs to be changed.

6. The Reasoning

Most written court opinions devote considerable space to justifying the court's decision. In the reasoning section of an opinion the court reviews the relevant provisions of the constitutions, statutes, and case law and then specifies the logical reasoning process used to arrive at the court's judgment.

Dictum
A statement in a judicial opinion not necessary for the decision of the case.

In reviewing the reasoning section it is important to distinguish between the **ratio decidendi** and the **obiter dictum**. The ratio decidendi is a decision on the legal issues raised in that specific case, whereas obiter dictum refers to a comment the judge makes that is not necessary to the resolution of the issues of the case and that is in effect a discussion of a hypothetical situation. For example, it is dictum when a judge talks about what might have been if the facts had been different from the ones presented. Even though courts have power to decide only the precise case with which they are faced, human nature being what it is, judges often cannot resist discussing issues that were not really presented to them. While that part of the opinion will have no effect on the litigants, it could give you a very good clue as to how the court might decide a different case in the future.

7. Concurring and Dissenting Opinions

Concurring opinion
An opinion that agrees with the majority's result but disagrees with the reasoning.

Following the court's opinion, there may also be one or more **concurring** or **dissenting opinions**. Judges write concurring opinions when they agree with the disposition of the case but disagree with respect to the reasoning. Judges write dissenting opinions when they disagree with the holding.

Dissenting opinion
An opinion that disagrees with the majority's decision and reasoning.

D. CASE BRIEFING

The word *brief* has several meanings. In this chapter we use the term *briefing a case* to mean using your own words to make a brief written summary of a court opinion. This is to be contrasted with an **appellate brief**, which is a formal written argument to an appellate court, in which a lawyer argues why that court should affirm or reverse a lower court's decision.

1. An Overview of Case Briefing

Briefing court opinions serves two purposes. First, and most important, it makes you read the case thoroughly. You have to go back and dig out the essentials, organize them, and state them in your own words. This is necessary for an adequate understanding of the court opinion. Second, it gives you a permanent condensed record of each case. You can use your case briefs later to refresh your memory about the cases without having to go back and reread whole opinions.

Be warned: There are almost as many different briefing styles as there are attorneys and paralegals writing briefs. Everyone develops his or her own favorite method for summarizing a court opinion. Therefore, if you are not writing a brief just for yourself, you should always ask the person for whom you are writing the brief about his or her preferred method. Also keep in mind the purpose for which you are writing the brief. For this course the principal reason is so that you can learn to analyze and criticize court opinions. Therefore, we will ask you to follow a very structured method, designed to teach you that process. Later when you are working, your boss may have a very different purpose for asking you to brief cases. For example, your boss may want a factual comparison among a series of cases and so ask you to summarize (brief) only the facts of each case. The bottom line: Follow a briefing style that accomplishes your purpose.

2. Format for a Case Brief

The case briefing method we will be using in this chapter breaks the case down into the following elements: (1) case citation, (2) facts—both procedural and substantive, (3) rule, (4) issue, (5) holding, (6) reasoning, and (7) criticism. After you read the opinion once, put the case citation at the top of your paper, and list the next six items on the left side of the paper, leaving enough room opposite each for the appropriate information. Reread the opinion and fill in the various items.

Although you list the items in a specific order, you may find yourself filling them in out of order. That is fine. Case briefing is a circuitous process. You will often rewrite one part of your brief as your understanding of that part changes based on your work on other parts. As with any type of writing, thinking and writing are intertwined.

To illustrate how a case brief is done, we will start by using a simplified fictional case of Jim Jones and Sam Smith.

Jim Jones v. Sam Smith
440 Mass. 99, 548 N.E.2d 50
Decided June 4, 1990

The defendant appeals from a judgment for the plaintiff in the amount of $30,000. The plaintiff, Jim Jones, who is blind, was walking on the sidewalk in front of his house, located on Lily Street. He had just returned from classes he was taking at the local community college. A group of youths approached him. One of the youths, sixteen-year-old Sam Smith, said, "Hey, man, what a cool cane." He then knocked Jim's cane from his hand. In knocking the cane from his hand, the defendant never touched the plaintiff's body. Jim began to search for his cane. While searching, Jim fell over the curb and broke his ankle. We hereby affirm the trial court's decision.

We have long held that an intentional, offensive contact to a person's body constitutes battery. Here the sixteen-year-old defendant intended to knock the cane from the plaintiff's hand. While the defendant did not actually touch the plaintiff's body, the plaintiff was holding the cane at the time it was knocked away from him. Because the plaintiff was able to go about on his own only with the use of the cane, it was as though the cane were a part of his body. The cane was so closely connected to his person that touching it was tantamount to touching the plaintiff himself. We also note the increased awareness that the legislature has exhibited in recent years for the needs of the disabled.

Affirmed.

a. Case Citation

At the top of a sheet of paper write the **case citation**. If this is a case that you are reading for class, you may also want to indicate its page number in your textbook. As we discussed earlier, the citation contains enough information to let the reader know (1) the name of the case, (2) the court that decided it, (3) where the reader can locate it, and (4) the year of decision. For example, this case was between Jim Jones and Sam Smith. The Massachusetts Supreme Judicial Court decided the case in 1990. You can find it on page 99 of volume 440 of the Massachusetts Reports. You can also find it on page 50 of volume 548 of the North Eastern Reporter, Second Series. Therefore, you cite this case in the following manner.

> Jones v. Smith, 440 Mass. 99, 548 N.E.2d 50 (1990).

Notice that there is more information supplied with the case, such as the parties' first names, than you actually need to provide for a complete citation. Also notice that in the citation, but not in the case, there is a comma after the case name.

b. Facts

Include a summary of both kinds of facts: substantive and procedural. Recall that the **substantive facts** deal with what happened to the parties before the litigation began; that is, why are they suing each other? These are the facts that caused the lawsuit. Be sure to state the relevant facts in your own words rather than copying them directly from the opinion. Omit any facts that you think did not form the basis of the court's decision, but be sure to include all facts that the court relied on in reaching its decision.

When giving the facts, it is always best to be as precise as possible. For example, if the case involves an eight-year-old girl, say so. Do not say that it involves simply a girl or a child. If you give specific details, you can always generalize later. If you start with a generalization, such as that the plaintiff was a child, later you may have difficulties remembering the specifics.

For the **procedural facts** be sure to include what happened in the lower court or courts. For example, in the trial court did the plaintiff or the defendant win? Did the lower court proceedings conclude after a motion or a jury verdict? You should conclude the procedural facts with a statement as to how this court responded by way of disposition; that is, did it reverse, reverse and remand, or affirm the lower court's decision? You will usually find the court's disposition near the end of the opinion, stated in a few words, such as reversed or vacated and remanded. Some legal writers prefer to put the court's disposition in a separate section rather than including it with the other procedural facts. If you include the disposition with the procedural facts, however, then the reader can see the "whole story" right at the beginning of the brief. Study the following example of a facts section.

Facts: The plaintiff, Jim Jones, is blind. A group of youths approached him. One of the youths, sixteen-year-old Sam Smith, knocked Jim's cane from his hand. In knocking the cane from the plaintiff's hand the defendant never touched the plaintiff's body. In searching for his cane, Jim fell, breaking his ankle. Judgment for plaintiff; affirmed.

First are the substantive facts: who did what to whom. Notice how specific facts that could have changed the outcome of the case are included: Jim is blind. Sam is sixteen years old. However, facts that would not influence the outcome, such as the name of the street down which Jim was walking, are not included. The last sentence gives the procedural facts. "Judgment for plaintiff" means the plaintiff won at the trial court level. "Affirmed" means this court, the court that issued the opinion you are reading, agreed with that result. The amount of the trial court award is not included because it was not an issue in this case. If the parties were disagreeing about the amount of the award, as opposed to whether there should have been an award at all, then it would be appropriate to include it.

c. Rule

The **rule** is a general legal principle in existence *before* the case began. The court might base it either on prior court decisions or on a statute.

First, explicitly state the area of law, such as burglary. Then give a precise definition of the law in that area: For example, burglary occurs when there is a breaking and entering of the dwelling of another at nighttime with the intention of committing a felony therein. You do not always need to give the complete definition of a rule. For example, if the only issue in the case is whether breaking into a house at 5 P.M. qualifies as nighttime, you would state only the relevant part of

> **Rule**
> In a case brief, the general legal principle in existence before the case began.

Rule: A battery occurs when there is an intentional, offensive contact to a person's body.

the rule: Burglary occurs when there is a breaking and entering at nighttime.

Our sample brief would contain the following statement of the rule. Notice how the general area of law, battery, is given first. We will call that the *label*. The label is followed by a definition of what constitutes battery.

d. Issue

Phrase this as a "whether" question. The **issue** has two components: first, the rule of law that the court used to resolve the current dispute (section c above) and, second, the specific facts of the case to which the rule of law is being applied (section b above). This is the hardest part of briefing a case. In one sentence you want to let your reader know exactly why the parties are in court. Include facts that make it clear why the issue is an issue; that is, let the reader see what the fight is all about. Modeling your issue after the following formula will assist you in making sure that you have included both the rule and the specific facts in your issue statement.

> **Issue**
> In a case brief, the rule of law applied to the case's specific facts.

Whether the defendant is [guilty of or liable for]
(name the general area of law involved—e.g., battery or murder),
which requires that
(give the specific part of the rule at issue—e.g., intended contact or willful intent)
when
(give the specific facts—e.g., the defendant accidentally bumped into the plaintiff).

Keep in mind that this is just a model. There are times when you will need to vary the pattern. Learning to state the issue precisely is a skill you will be working on throughout your legal career; therefore, do not feel discouraged if it seems difficult now.

If a court opinion deals with more than one issue, brief each issue separately.

> Issue: Whether the defendant is liable for battery, which requires that there be an intentional, offensive contact to a person's body, when the sixteen-year-old defendant did not touch the blind plaintiff but did knock his cane from his hand.

Notice how the issue contains both the rule and the specific facts involved in the case. Given the rule of law in existence prior to these parties going to court and given the specific facts of the case, what problem must the court resolve? That is the issue.

Never state your issue as follows: whether or not the trial court erred. Although technically that would be correct, it is not very helpful, as it would be true of all cases; that is, no one would have appealed unless there was an allegation that the court made an error. Remember to include the specific rule of law and the facts involved so that your reader, hearing only your statement of the issue, will know exactly why the litigants were in court.

Finally, be sure to state the issue in an unbiased manner. Do not slant the issue by giving conclusions. Stick to the facts. For example, the following issue is too biased.

> **Example of a biased statement of the issue:**
> Whether the defendant was negligent, which requires failing to act as a reasonable person, when he got drunk, sped down the highway, and crashed into the plaintiff's car.

To keep it unbiased, you must state the facts underlying your conclusions. And you must include facts that show both sides of the issue.

> **Example of an unbiased statement of the issue:**
> Whether the defendant was negligent, which requires failing to act as a reasonable person, when he drank one beer, drove 55 mph in a 50-mph zone, and hit the plaintiff's car as he ran a red light.

e. Holding

The **holding** is the court's answer to the issue. The holding is the new version of the rule, a rule that future courts will look to for assistance in deciding similar cases.

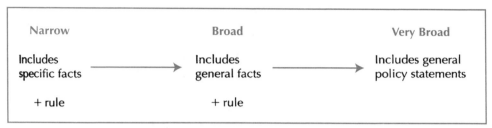

Figure 13-4   Possible Holdings for a Case

If you have given a complete issue statement, technically the holding could be a simple yes or no answer. However, it is always best to give the holding as a complete sentence. Therefore, include the same elements as you did for the issue statement except state them as a positive sentence. That is, make sure the holding contains both the rule of law the court was relying on to resolve the dispute and the specific facts of the case.

One of the most difficult aspects of developing the holding is determining how narrow or broad it should be. A **narrow holding** contains many of the case's specific facts, thereby limiting its future applicability to a narrow range of cases. A **broad holding** states the facts in very general terms so that the holding will apply to a wider range of cases. See Figure 13-4.

To be useful, a holding should be broad enough to help courts resolve similar cases. But a holding should not be so broad that it stands for no more than a general legal principle. Learning how to state a holding either very narrowly, by including very specific facts, or very broadly, by stating the facts as generalizations only, is a skill you will acquire over time. For now, state your holdings narrowly. As with the facts portion of the brief you will find it easier to amend a narrow holding to make it broader than you will to amend a broad holding to make it narrower. However, even with a narrow holding, include only those facts that you think truly affected the court's decision.

Holding: Yes, the defendant should be liable for battery, which requires that there be an intentional, offensive contact to a person's body, when the sixteen-year-old defendant did not touch the blind plaintiff but did knock his cane from his hand. (Narrow)

Yes, the defendant should be liable for battery, which requires that there be an intentional, offensive contact to a person's body, when something closely connected to the plaintiff's body was touched. (Broad)

A battery occurs whenever a person's sense of bodily integrity is threatened. (Probably too broad; really a policy statement)

Holding
In a case brief, the court's answer to the issue presented to it; the new legal principle established by a court opinion.

Narrow holding
A statement of the court's decision that contains many of the case's specific facts, thereby limiting its future applicability to a narrow range of cases.

Broad holding
A statement of the court's decision in which the facts are either omitted or given in very general terms so that it will apply to a wider range of cases.

Also be sure to include any possible limitations to the holding. If the court specifically states that its decision covers only a certain set of circumstances, let your reader know that. For example, in a case dealing with a social host's liability for serving alcohol to a minor, a court might relieve the social host of any responsibility but limit its holding to situations where alcohol is not being served for a profit.

Finally, note that the court's procedural answer—reversed, remanded, affirmed, and so on—can never be the holding. The holding is always a statement of the new rule that results from the court's decision.

f. Reasoning

This is an explanation of *why* the court ruled as it did, stated in your own words. The court's reasoning gives you your best clue as to how the court may act in the future in a different but similar situation.

Pinpoint as far as is possible the explicit and implicit reasons that the court gave to justify its holding. But do not quote the court's exact language unless the precise phrasing is critical. It will be easier for the reader to understand your summary if it is primarily in your own words.

In this section you may want to note reasoning that is really dictum. As we mentioned earlier, dictum (the plural is *dicta*) is language unnecessary to the decision of the case. For example, if the court talks about how it might decide a future case based on different facts, that is dictum. Courts have power to decide only the precise case with which they are faced. By definition the court's dicta are not relevant to the case's litigants, but they do give you an idea of how the court might be predisposed to rule in a future case. Therefore, dicta are often worth noting in your brief.

Reasoning:	While the defendant did not touch the plaintiff's body, the cane was so closely connected to his person that touching it was tantamount to touching the plaintiff himself. (In dicta the court noted the increased awareness in recent years of the needs of persons with disabilities.)

g. Criticism

Take a few minutes to think critically about the case. Do you agree with the result? Even if you agree with the result, do you think the court gave the best or only reasons for reaching that result? If the court included a limitation in the holding, what problems do you think that will cause for future litigants?

PRACTICE TIP

Do not be afraid to use the power of a word processor. Once you have entered the important facts and the rule, you have essentially written the issue and the holding. Just copy the important facts and the rule from the prior sections, and insert the appropriate connective phrases.

If there were **concurring** or **dissenting opinions**, include a discussion of their reasoning. Remember that a concurring decision is one in which the judge agrees with the majority's result but not with the reasoning. A dissenting opinion is one in which the judge disagrees with both the majority's result and its reasoning. While only the majority opinion represents the court's view, what individual concurring and dissenting judges have to say can influence later courts.

The reason for including a criticism section is to accustom you to thinking critically about court decisions. There will be times when an opinion will harm your client's case and you will need to argue either that the decision was incorrectly decided or that the reasoning does not apply to your client's case. Practice in thinking critically about court decisions now will prepare you to assist your clients later.

> **P R A C T I C E   T I P**
>
> Do not overlook the power of a dissent. It may help you predict the path the court may take in the next case.

> Criticism: The court left open the question of what constitutes an object so closely connected to a person's body as to be considered a part of it. Because the case involved a blind person, it is unclear whether the court meant to limit future cases to objects used by persons with disabilities, such as canes, hearing aids, and the like, or whether the court meant to include anything closely connected to a person's body, such as clothing.

Do not be discouraged if you find the criticism section one of the most difficult parts of the brief to write. It is the court's job to convince you that it has reached the right result for the right reasons. Therefore, your first reaction may be to simply agree with everything it says. Resist that inclination. Remember that the case would not have been appealed unless someone thought there were two sides to the issue.

Once put together, the entire brief should look similar to the sample brief in Exhibit 13-1, on page 352. You can find a summary of case briefing in Exhibit 13-2, on page 353.

3. Six Hints for Better Brief Writing

Here are six hints to help you with your brief writing.

a. Read the Case First, Then Brief

Do not try to brief the case as you read it for the first time. Read it through, underlining if you wish and making notes in the margin, before you start your brief. When you are reading more than one case on a particular topic, it may save time to first read all of the cases and then begin briefing.

b. Develop a Workable Style

Develop a briefing style that works best for you. As mentioned above, there is no right or wrong method. However, if your brief is to serve its intended purpose, you must write it in such a way that you can return to it later and easily find the information for which you are looking.

c. Write Based on the Needs of Your Reader

If you will be using the brief just as a reference for yourself, abbreviate commonly used terms. For example, use π or P. for plaintiff and Δ or D. for

---

<u>Jones v. Smith</u>, 440 Mass. 99, 548 N.E.2d 50 (1990).

The plaintiff, Jim Jones, is blind. A group of youths approached him. One of the youths, sixteen-year-old Sam Smith, knocked Jim's cane from his hand. In knocking the cane from the plaintiff's hand the defendant never touched the plaintiff's body. In searching for his cane, Jim fell, breaking his ankle. Judgment for plaintiff; affirmed.

Rule: A battery occurs when there is an intentional, offensive contact to a person's body.

Issue: Whether the defendant is liable for battery, which requires that there be an intentional, offensive contact to a person's body, when the sixteen-year-old defendant did not touch the blind plaintiff but did knock his cane from his hand.

Holding: Yes, the defendant should be liable for battery, which requires that there be an intentional, offensive contact to a person's body, when the sixteen-year-old defendant did not touch the blind plaintiff but did knock his cane from his hand.

Reasoning: While the defendant did not touch the plaintiff's body, the cane was so closely connected to his person that touching it was tantamount to touching the plaintiff himself. (In dicta the court noted the increased awareness in recent years of the needs of persons with disabilities.)

Criticism: The court left open the question of what constitutes an object so closely connected to a person's body as to be considered a part of it. Because the case involved a blind person, it is unclear whether the court meant to limit future cases to objects used by persons with disabilities, such as canes, hearing aids, and the like, or whether the court meant to include anything closely connected to a person's body, such as clothing.

Exhibit 13-1 Sample Brief

defendant. You may also want to write in phrases rather than complete sentences. However, if you are writing the brief for another person, whether it is your instructor now or your boss later on, make sure to ask whether that person wants you to use abbreviations and phrases or prefers that you use complete words and sentences.

d. Cross-Reference

Develop a cross-reference system that will allow you to find the court's full discussion of the points you summarized in your brief. For example, you could place numbers in the margin of the case to correspond to the points you discuss in your brief.

e. Paraphrase

Write the brief in your own words. A brief should not be a long series of quotations, so do not copy large parts of the opinion. A brief is your summary of the case, not merely a listing of quotations from it.

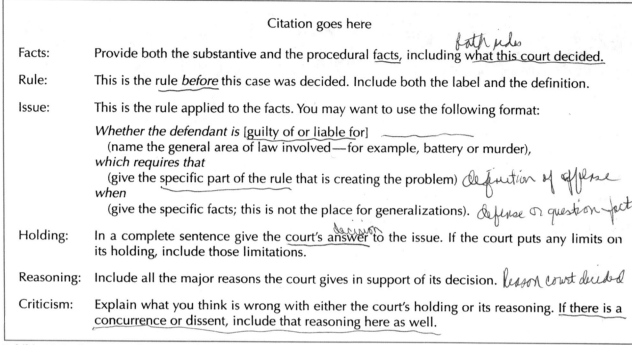

Citation goes here

Facts: Provide both the substantive and the procedural <u>facts</u>, including *both rules* what this court decided.

Rule: This is the rule *before* this case was decided. Include both the label and the definition.

Issue: This is the rule applied to the facts. You may want to use the following format:

Whether the defendant is [guilty of or liable for] _____
   (name the general area of law involved—for example, battery or murder),
which requires that
   (give the specific part of the rule that is creating the problem) *definition of offense*
when
   (give the specific facts; this is not the place for generalizations). *defense or question of fact*

Holding: In a complete sentence give the court's *decision* answer to the issue. If the court puts any limits on its holding, include those limitations.

Reasoning: Include all the major reasons the court gives in support of its decision. *reason court decided*

Criticism: Explain what you think is wrong with either the court's holding or its reasoning. If there is a concurrence or dissent, include that reasoning here as well.

Exhibit 13-2 Summary of Case Briefing

f. Use a Dictionary

Make sure you understand every unfamiliar legal term. Initially, you will find the courts using many unfamiliar terms. Do not hesitate to turn to a legal dictionary for help.

4. A Sample Case Brief

Before we tackle a real court opinion, we would like to give you some practice in case briefing. On the next page, you will find a hypothetical court opinion based on the case of *People v. Blair*.[6]

Once you have read *People v. Blair*, try your hand at briefing it. We have included a sample brief in Exhibit 13-3, on page 355. It will be tempting to turn to the sample brief before trying it yourself, but resist the temptation. Now is the time to experiment with briefing. Write the case citation at the top of a sheet of paper. Then write each of the six parts of a standard brief in the left-hand margin. Fill in each part of the case brief as best you can. Finally, when you can no longer stand it, turn to the sample brief. Remember that the sample brief is only a sample. Your approach may be different and yet be just as valid.

Remember that everyone has his or her own style for briefing, and the court may not follow the definitions we have given you for the different elements of the brief. A court may not even include every element of a case brief in its decision.

---

[6] 288 N.E.2d 443 (Ill.1972).

People v. Blair
52 Ill. 2d 371, 288 N.E.2d 443 (1972)

UNDERWOOD, Chief Justice.

In February 1969, defendant Gary Blair was convicted in superior court of burglary for actions that took place in a carwash. He was sentenced to imprisonment for two to four years. The defendant appealed his conviction, and the intermediate appellate court vacated the judgment of conviction, finding that the carwash structure here involved was not a building as that word is used in the burglary statute. We granted leave to appeal. The statute in part provides:

> A person commits burglary when without authority he knowingly breaks into and enters a building or house trailer with intent to commit a felony or theft therein.

The carwash in question consists of wash bays or stalls completely open at each end (there are no doors), a roof, concrete side walls and floor; attached to the side walls are the wash-ing apparatus and a coin box. The defendant allegedly drove into one of the stalls, washed his car, and then forced open the coin box, took the coins, and fled.

The burglary statute contains no definition of the word "building," and, in the absence of a statutory definition indicating a different legislative intention, the courts will assume that statutory words have their ordinary and popularly understood meanings. In the past, this court has defined a building to be any structure designed for the habitation of men or animals or for the shelter of property. The carwash comes within this definition. It is a structure designed for the shelter and protection of the carwash equipment and the fact that it is not completely enclosed does not necessitate a contrary conclusion.

The judgment of the appellate court is reversed, and the trial court's judgment of conviction for burglary is affirmed.

Also, courts do not always explicitly label the parts of their opinion that contain the issue, holding, reasoning, and so on. Nor do they tell you which of the facts or reasons they give are the most important. Therefore, while the language of the court often provides helpful clues, do not be surprised if you do not always find every part of the brief in every case. Also do not be surprised if the court appears to be "mislabeling" various parts of the case. For example, in *People v. Blair* assume the court had stated:

> The legislature did not see fit to include a definition of "building" within the statute. Over the years, this court has had to decide whether other structures such as barns and garages were meant to fit the statutory meaning of a "building." Likewise, in this case there is no need for us to wait until the legislature decides to act and amend the statute so as to include a definition that might or might not encompass carwashes. We hold that we have the power to include a partially enclosed carwash within the definition of "building."

It would not be correct to give the last sentence in the holding section of your brief. We have defined a holding as the current rule applied to the case's specific facts. This statement by the court therefore is not a holding but rather is reasoning. That is, the reason the court thinks it can hold that a carwash comes within the definition of a "building" is that the court has the power to do so.

People v. Blair
52 Ill. 2d 371, 288 N.E.2d 443 (1972)

Facts: Inside a carwash the defendant forced open a coin box and took the coins. The carwash had concrete walls and floor but was completely open at each end and covered the washing apparatus and a coin box. Convicted; vacated; reversed, affirming trial court's judgment.

Rule: "A person commits burglary when without authority he knowingly breaks into and enters a building or house trailer with intent to commit a felony or theft therein."

Issue: Whether the defendant committed burglary, which requires entering a building or house trailer, when he entered a partially enclosed carwash.

Holding: Yes, burglary, which requires the entering of a building or house trailer, is committed when someone enters a partially enclosed carwash.

Reasoning: The statute did not contain a definition for "building." Therefore, the court followed the ordinary meaning of the word and looked to past decisions, where a building was defined as a structure meant to protect people or property. Here the carwash protected property and so should be considered a building.

Criticism: In the statute the word "building" is coupled with the words "house trailer." This suggests that the legislature intended to limit the statute to dwellings. Also, the carwash was not entirely enclosed. Therefore, although the defendant definitely "entered" the carwash, it is difficult to see how he could have been charged with "breaking" into the carwash.

Exhibit 13-3 Sample Brief

Words can have more than one meaning, and this is just one example of how the courts may use words differently from the way we have been using them.

5. Briefing Cases Involving Statutes

Now that you have experience with the purpose of case briefing, it is time to try your hand with real court opinions. In this section we will look at two court opinions that illustrate the first two types of cases that courts face: interpreting statutes and ruling on their constitutionality.

a. Interpreting a Statute

Recall the situation from a legal reasoning question in Chapter 12 in which you were asked to apply a federal statute to a situation where a client had been charged with illegally transporting an airplane across state lines. This was the very situation that the Supreme Court had to face in the following case, *McBoyle v. United States*. We have reprinted the *McBoyle* opinion exactly as it appears in the official United States Reports in Exhibit 13-4, beginning on page 356. The U.S. government pays for the printing and publishing of all U.S. Supreme Court decisions in a series of books called the United States Reports. The opinions are printed and published in chronological order as they are decided. In the margins we have added labels to describe the different parts of a typical court opinion.

Read and then brief *McBoyle v. United States*, paying special attention to the methods of statutory analysis that the Court relied on in reaching its decision. There is a sample brief following the opinion. See Exhibit 13-5, on page 359.

The case name; McBoyle was the petitioner and the U.S. government was the respondent.

MᴄBOYLE *v.* UNITED STATES.   **25**

15   Opinion of the Court.

Page in volume 283 of the United States Report where the case begins.

U. S. 192; *Jacob Ruppert* v. *Caffey*, 251 U. S. 264; *Lambert* v. *Yellowley*, 272 U. S. 581.   *Affirmed.*

End of a different decision.

MᴄBOYLE *v.* UNITED STATES.

This lets you know the court is hearing a case from the Tenth Circuit.

CERTIORARI TO THE CIRCUIT COURT OF APPEALS FOR THE TENTH CIRCUIT.

Docket number and dates the case was argued and decided.

No. 552.   Argued February 26, 27, 1931.—Decided March 9, 1931.

Known as the syllabus, this is a summary of the court's opinion.

The National Motor Vehicle Theft Act, U. S. C., Title 18, § 408, which punishes whoever transports, or causes to be transported, in interstate or foreign commerce a motor vehicle knowing it to have been stolen, and which defines "motor vehicle" as including "an automobile, automobile truck, automobile wagon, motor cycle, or any other self-propelled vehicle not designed for running on rails," does not apply to aircraft. P. 26.
43 F. (2d) 273, reversed.

Where it is reported that cert, was granted.*

CERTIORARI, 282 U. S. 835, to review a judgment affirming a conviction under the Motor Vehicle Theft Act.

Mr. Harry F. Brown for petitioner.

Petitioner's attorney.

Mr. Claude R. Branch, Special Assistant to the Attorney General, with whom *Solicitor General Thacher, Assistant Attorney General Dodds* and *Messrs. Harry S. Ridgely* and *W. Marvin Smith* were on the brief, for the United States.

Responder's attorneys.

Mʀ. Jᴜsᴛɪᴄᴇ Hᴏʟᴍᴇs delivered the opinion of the Court.

This is where the opinion begins.

The petitioner was convicted of transporting from Ottawa, Illinois, to Guymon, Oklahoma, an airplane that he knew to have been stolen, and was sentenced to serve three years' imprisonment and to pay a fine of $2,000. The judgment was affirmed by the Circuit Court of Appeals for the Tenth Circuit. 43 F. (2d) 273. A writ of certiorari was granted by this Court on the question whether the National Motor Vehicle Theft Act applies to aircraft.

This is where the Tenth Circuit court's decision is reported.

*This one sentence contains a lot of information. Combined with what you already know about the structure of the federal court system, it gives you the complete procedural history of the case. Start at the end of the sentence and work your way forward. First, we read that McBoyle was convicted. As he was tried in the federal system, his trial and conviction would have occurred in a federal district court. Next the conviction was affirmed. This would have occurred in a court of appeals. In fact, right under the case name we see that the Tenth Circuit court of appeals decided this case. Finally, the U.S. Supreme Court agreed to hear the case by granting certiorari.

Exhibit 13-4 *McBoyle v. United States*   *(continues)*

Act of October 29, 1919, c. 89; 41 Stat. 324; U. S. Code, Title 18, § 408. That Act provides: " Sec. 2. That when used in this Act: (a) The term ' motor vehicle ' shall include an automobile, automobile truck, automobile wagon, motor cycle, or any other self-propelled vehicle not designed for running on rails; . . . Sec. 3. That whoever shall transport or cause to be transported in interstate or foreign commerce a motor vehicle, knowing the same to have been stolen, shall be punished by a fine of not more than $5,000, or by imprisonment of not more than five years, or both."

Section 2 defines the motor vehicles of which the transportation in interstate commerce is punished in § 3. The question is the meaning of the word ' vehicle ' in the phrase " any other self-propelled vehicle not designed for running on rails." No doubt etymologically it is possible to use the word to signify a conveyance working on land, water or air, and sometimes legislation extends the use in that direction, e. g., land and air, water being separately provided for, in the Tariff Act, September 22, 1922, c. 356, § 401 (b), 42 Stat. 858, 948. But in everyday speech ' vehicle ' calls up the picture of a thing moving on land. Thus in Rev. Stats. § 4, intended, the Government suggests, rather to enlarge than to restrict the definition, vehicle includes every contrivance capable of being used " as a means of transportation on land." And this is repeated, expressly excluding aircraft, in the Tariff Act, June 17, 1930, c. 997, § 401 (b); 46 Stat. 590, 708. So here, the phrase under discussion calls up the popular picture. For after including automobile truck, automobile wagon and motor cycle, the words " any other self-propelled vehicle not designed for running on rails " still indicate that a vehicle in the popular sense, that is a vehicle running on land, is the theme. It is a vehicle that runs, not something, not commonly called a vehicle, that flies. Airplanes were well known in 1919, when this statute was passed; but it is admitted that they were not mentioned in the reports or in the debates in Congress.

Exhibit 13-4 *McBoyle v. United States*   (continues)

CARBICE CORP. *v.* AM. PATENTS CORP.   27

25   Syllabus.

It is impossible to read words that so carefully enumerate the different forms of motor vehicles and have no reference of any kind to aircraft, as including airplanes under a term that usage more and more precisely confines to a different class.   The counsel for the petitioner have shown that the phraseology of the statute as to motor vehicles follows that of earlier statutes of Connecticut, Delaware, Ohio, Michigan and Missouri, not to mention the late Regulations of Traffic for the District of Columbia, Title 6, c. 9, § 242, none of which can be supposed to leave the earth.

Although it is not likely that a criminal will carefully consider the text of the law before he murders or steals, it is reasonable that a fair warning should be given to the world in language that the common world will understand, of what the law intends to do if a certain line is passed. To make the warning fair, so far as possible the line should be clear.   When a rule of conduct is laid down in words that evoke in the common mind only the picture of vehicles moving on land, the statute should not be extended to aircraft, simply because it may seem to us that a similar policy applies, or upon the speculation that, if the legislature had thought of it, very likely broader words would have been used. *United States* v. *Thind,* 261 U. S. 204, 209.

Judgment reversed.

The court's decision

CARBICE CORPORATION OF AMERICA *v.* AMERICAN PATENTS DEVELOPMENT CORPORATION ET AL.

The beginning of the next case

CERTIORARI TO THE CIRCUIT COURT OF APPEALS FOR THE SECOND CIRCUIT.

No. 54. Argued January 16, 19, 1931.—Decided March 9, 1931.

1. A patentee can not lawfully exact, as the condition of a license, that unpatented materials used in connection with the invention shall be purchased only from himself. P. 31.

Exhibit 13-4 *McBoyle v. United States (concluded)*

However, as you did with *People v. Blair*, wait to look at the sample until after you have briefed the opinion yourself. That way you will have a better idea as to whether you are on the right track with your case briefing. Also, as with the *People v. Blair* sample brief, the sample brief for *McBoyle* is just that, a sample. Do not worry if yours does not match the sample exactly. However, if yours is significantly different, reread the prior section on the functions of each part of the brief.

Now that you have read *McBoyle v. United States*, take a close look at how the procedural facts are given in the sample brief shown in Exhibit 13-5. Ask your instructor about his or her preferred method for including the procedural facts. What is given here is a shorthand way of saying that the defendant was convicted. His conviction was affirmed by the U.S. Court of Appeals for the

---

McBoyle v. United States, 283 U.S. 25 (1931)

Facts: The defendant transported across state lines an airplane that he knew was stolen. He was convicted; aff'd; cert. granted; rev'd.

Rule: National Motor Vehicle Theft Act, Section 3
Whoever transports in interstate commerce a motor vehicle, knowing it to be stolen, shall be punished.

Section 2
A motor vehicle shall include "any other self-propelled vehicle not designed for running on rails."

Issue: Whether the defendant violated the National Motor Vehicle Theft Act, which requires that the defendant transport across state lines a stolen motor vehicle, defined as "any other self-propelled vehicle not designed for running on rails," when he transported a stolen plane across state lines.

Holding: No, the defendant did not violate the National Motor Vehicle Theft Act, which requires that the defendant transport across state lines a stolen motor vehicle, defined as "any other self-propelled vehicle not designed for running on rails," when he flew a stolen plane across state lines.

Reasoning: The Court based its decision on what it saw as the plain meaning of the statute. In support of this view the Court also looked to other statutes and to other portions of this statute. The legislative history also favored this interpretation, as airplanes were in existence when the statute was enacted and yet no mention was made of them. Also, because this is a criminal statute, the Court said that it should be construed narrowly so as to give any potential defendant fair warning of what was not allowed. Finally, the Court showed great deference to the legislature. The Court stated that it would not extend the statute simply because it might seem to the justices that "a similar policy applies, or upon the speculation that, if the legislature had thought of it, very likely broader words would have been used" (p. 27).

Criticism: The plain meaning approach could also be used to argue that the statute uses the word "including" but does not say "excluding." Therefore, presumably it would cover other "self-propelled vehicles," such as airplanes. Also, it does not stand to reason that the defendant would not have suspected that it was a crime to transport a stolen airplane across state lines.

Exhibit 13-5 Sample Brief

Tenth Circuit. The Supreme Court granted certiorari and then reversed the decision of the court of appeals. For someone versed in the structure of the court system, the method used in the sample brief is quick and to the point. However, when you first start briefing, you may feel more comfortable avoiding abbreviations and writing out each of the procedural steps.

Also notice that the entire procedural story is given, including the final resolution by the U.S. Supreme Court—that is, that it reversed the lower appellate court.

In the reasoning section, notice the use of the verbs *saw*, *said*, and *stated*. Never use language that suggests that the court was emotional about the case. For example, do not say the court "felt" something was so. Say the court *thought, explained, discussed*, and the like.

DISCUSSION QUESTIONS

1. Do you agree with the Court's reasoning and holding in *McBoyle*? Why?
2. Did you notice the similarities between the Court's approach to analyzing a statute and those discussed in Chapter 12? List the methods of statutory interpretation that the *McBoyle* Court used.
3. Why would each of the following not be a correct issue for *McBoyle*?
   a. whether the defendant knew the airplane was stolen
   b. whether the defendant stole the airplane
   c. whether the defendant was guilty
   d. whether the trial court erred

The role of the courts in interpreting ambiguous language is to strive to find the meaning that the legislature intended. In this they are engaged in something of a guessing game, and if they guess wrong, the legislature has the power to amend the statute. For example, sometime after the Supreme Court decided *McBoyle* the legislature amended the statute to include airplanes within the definition of motor vehicles.

b. Ruling on a Statute's Constitutionality

As you will recall from Chapter 5, most cases decided by state courts cannot be appealed to the U.S. Supreme Court. The major exception is if a federal law is involved. In the following case, because the constitutionality of the state statute was in doubt, the U.S. Supreme Court had jurisdiction to hear it.

As you read the U.S. Supreme Court's decision in *Texas v. Johnson*, decide whether you agree with the majority, the concurrence, or the dissent. Recall that the majority opinion represents the final decision of a court and is binding. In a concurrence the judge agrees with the result but not with the reasoning or simply wants to add his or her own thoughts. The judge who writes the dissent disagrees with the majority opinion, but the dissent is not binding and does not represent the law in that jurisdiction.

Because a dissent has no effect in the present case, you might wonder why judges bother writing dissents. There are at least three reasons to do so.[7] First, it

---

[7] For a fascinating discussion of this topic view the PBS documentary, This Honorable Court.

keeps the majority honest. Because a dissent is being written, the majority knows that what they write can be contradicted. Second, a dissent limits the precedential effect of the opinion. An opinion with a strong dissent does not carry the same weight with future courts as does a unanimous opinion. Finally, there is always the hope that someday a later court will see the wisdom of the dissent and decide to follow that path. Although that hope is not always realized, it can be the motivating force behind continued dissents on such issues as capital punishment. One Supreme Court justice dissented in every capital punishment case, arguing that it always represented cruel and unusual punishment. To date, the Court has not accepted that argument.

We have omitted the footnotes and most of the citations to the cases the Court cites. Also we have greatly condensed the opinion for you. The original was over thirty pages long. The numbers in brackets, such as [*399], refer to the page numbers in the United States Reports.

Texas v. Johnson
491 U.S. 397 (1989)

[*399] Justice BRENNAN delivered the opinion of the Court.

After publicly burning an American flag as a means of political protest, Gregory Lee Johnson was convicted of desecrating a flag in violation of Texas law. This case presents the question whether his conviction is consistent with the First Amendment. We hold that it is not.

I

While the Republican National Convention was taking place in Dallas in 1984, respondent Johnson participated in a political demonstration dubbed the "Republican War Chest Tour."... [T]he purpose of this event was to protest the policies of the Reagan administration and of certain Dallas-based corporations....

The demonstration ended in front of Dallas City Hall, where Johnson unfurled the American flag, doused it with kerosene, and set it on fire. While the flag burned, the protestors chanted: "America, the red, white, and blue, we spit on you."...[*400] Of the approximately 100 demonstrators, Johnson alone was charged with a crime. The only criminal offense with which he was charged was the desecration of a venerated object in violation of Tex. Penal Code Ann. § 42.09(a)(3)

(1989). After a trial, he was convicted, sentenced to one year in prison, and fined $2,000. The Court of Appeals for the Fifth District of Texas at Dallas affirmed Johnson's conviction, 706 S.W.2d 120 (1986), but the Texas Court of Criminal Appeals reversed, 755 S.W.2d 92 (1988), holding that the State could not, consistent with the First Amendment, punish Johnson for burning the flag in these circumstances....

We granted certiorari, 488 U.S. 907 (1988), and now affirm.

II ...

[*404] The First Amendment literally forbids the abridgment only of "speech," but we have long recognized that its protection does not end at the spoken or written word. While we have rejected "the view that an apparently limitless variety of conduct can be labeled 'speech' whenever the person engaging in the conduct intends thereby to express an idea," *United States v. O'Brien*, supra, at 376, we have acknowledged that conduct may be "sufficiently imbued with elements of communication to fall within the scope of the First and Fourteenth Amendments," [*Spence v. Washington*, 418 U.S. 405, 409 (1974) (reversing the conviction of a college

student who displayed the flag with a peace symbol affixed to it by removable black tape)]. . . .

The State of Texas conceded for purposes of its oral argument in this case that Johnson's conduct was expressive conduct, . . . and this concession seems to us as [*406] prudent. . . . Johnson burned an American flag as part—indeed, as the culmination—of a political demonstration that coincided with the convening of the Republican Party and its renomination of Ronald Reagan for President. The expressive, overtly political nature of this conduct was both intentional and overwhelmingly apparent. At his trial, Johnson explained his reasons for burning the flag as follows: "The American Flag was burned as Ronald Reagan was being renominated as President. And a more powerful statement of symbolic speech, whether you agree with it or not, couldn't have been made at that time. It's quite a just position [juxtaposition]. We had new patriotism and no patriotism." 5 Record 656. In these circumstances, Johnson's burning of the flag was conduct "sufficiently imbued with elements of communication," *Spence,* 418 U.S., at 409, to implicate the First Amendment.

III . . .

The State offers two separate interests to justify this conviction: preventing breaches of the peace and preserving the flag as a symbol of nationhood and national unity. We hold that the first interest is not implicated on this record and that the second is related to the suppression of expression.

A

Texas claims that its interest in preventing breaches of the peace justifies Johnson's conviction for flag desecration. [*408] However, no disturbance of the peace actually occurred or threatened to occur because of Johnson's burning of the flag. . . .

The State's position, therefore, amounts to a claim that an audience that takes serious offense at particular expression is necessarily likely to disturb the peace and that the expression may be prohibited on this basis. Our precedents do not countenance such a presumption. On the contrary, they recognize that a principal "function of free speech under our system of government is to invite dispute. It may indeed best serve its high purpose when it induces a condition of unrest, creates dissatisfaction with conditions as they are, or [*409] even stirs people to anger." . . .

Nor does Johnson's expressive conduct fall within that small class of "fighting words" that are "likely to provoke the average person to retaliation, and thereby cause a breach of the peace." *Chaplinsky v. New Hampshire,* 315 U.S. 568, 574 (1942). No reasonable onlooker would have regarded Johnson's generalized expression of dissatisfaction with the policies of the Federal Government as a direct personal insult or an invitation to exchange fisticuffs. . . .

[*410] We thus conclude that the State's interest in maintaining order is not implicated on these facts. The State need not worry that our holding will disable it from preserving the peace. We do not suggest that the First Amendment forbids a State to prevent "imminent lawless action." *Brandenburg,* supra, at 447. And, in fact, Texas already has a statute specifically prohibiting breaches of the peace, Tex. Penal Code Ann. § 42.01 (1989), which tends to confirm that Texas need not punish this flag desecration in order to keep the peace. See *Boos v. Barry,* 485 U.S., at 327-329.

B

[T]he State's claim is that it has an interest in preserving the flag as a symbol of nationhood and national unity, a symbol with a determinate range of meanings. Brief for Petitioner 20-24. According to Texas, if one physically treats the flag in a way that would tend to cast doubt on either the idea that nationhood and national unity are the flag's referents or that national unity actually exists, the message conveyed thereby is a harmful one and therefore may be prohibited. . . .

If there is a bedrock principle underlying the First Amendment, it is that the government may not prohibit the expression of an idea simply because society finds the idea itself offensive or disagreeable. . . .

To conclude that the government may permit designated symbols to be used to communicate only a limited set of messages would be to enter territory having no discernible or defensible boundaries. Could the government, on this theory, prohibit the burning of state flags? Of copies of the Presidential seal? Of the Constitution? In evaluating these choices under the First Amendment, how

would we decide which symbols were sufficiently special to warrant this unique status? To do so, we would be forced to consult our own political preferences, and impose them on the citizenry, in the very way that the First Amendment forbids us to do. See *Carey v. Brown,* 447 U.S., at 466-467. . . .

We are fortified in today's conclusion by our conviction that forbidding criminal punishment for conduct such as Johnson's will not endanger the special role played by our flag or the feelings it inspires. To paraphrase Justice Holmes, we submit that nobody can suppose that this one gesture of an unknown [*419] man will change our Nation's attitude towards its flag. See *Abrams v. United States,* 250 U.S. 616, 628 (1919) (Holmes, J., dissenting). . . .

We are tempted to say, in fact, that the flag's deservedly cherished place in our community will be strengthened, not weakened, by our holding today. Our decision is a reaffirmation of the principles of freedom and inclusiveness that the flag best reflects, and of the conviction that our toleration of criticism such as Johnson's is a sign and source of our strength. Indeed, one of the proudest images of our flag, the one immortalized in our own national anthem, is of the bombardment it survived at Fort McHenry. It is the Nation's resilience, not its rigidity, that Texas sees reflected in the flag—and it is that resilience that we reassert today.

The way to preserve the flag's special role is not to punish those who feel differently about these matters. It is to persuade them that they are wrong. . . . And, precisely because it is our flag that is involved, one's response to the flag [*420] burner may exploit the uniquely persuasive power of the flag itself. We can imagine no more appropriate response to burning a flag than waving one's own, no better way to counter a flag burner's message than by saluting the flag that burns, no surer means of preserving the dignity even of the flag that burned than by—as one witness here did—according its remains a respectful burial. We do not consecrate the flag by punishing its desecration, for in doing so we dilute the freedom that this cherished emblem represents.

V

Johnson was convicted for engaging in expressive conduct. The State's interest in preventing breaches of the peace does not support his conviction because Johnson's conduct did not threaten to disturb the peace. Nor does the State's interest in preserving the flag as a symbol of nationhood and national unity justify his criminal conviction for engaging in political expression. The judgment of the Texas Court of Criminal Appeals is therefore

Affirmed.

Justice KENNEDY, concurring.

I write not to qualify the words Justice Brennan chooses so well, for he says with power all that is necessary to explain our ruling. I join his opinion without reservation, but with a keen sense that this case, like others before us from time to time, exacts its personal toll. This prompts me to add to our pages these few remarks.

The case before us illustrates better than most that the judicial power is often difficult in its exercise. We cannot here ask another Branch to share responsibility, as when the argument is made that a statute is flawed or incomplete. For we are presented with a clear and simple statute to be judged against a pure command of the Constitution. The outcome can be laid at no door but ours.

The hard fact is that sometimes we must make decisions we do not like. We make them because they are right, right [*421] in the sense that the law and the Constitution, as we see them, compel the result. And so great is our commitment to the process that, except in the rare case, we do not pause to express distaste for the result, perhaps for fear of undermining a valued principle that dictates the decision. This is one of those rare cases. . . .

Though symbols often are what we ourselves make of them, the flag is constant in expressing beliefs Americans share, beliefs in law and peace and that freedom which sustains the human spirit. The case here today forces recognition of the costs to which those beliefs commit us. It is poignant but fundamental that the flag protects those who hold it in contempt.

For all the record shows, this respondent was not a philosopher and perhaps did not even possess the ability to comprehend how repellent his statements must be to the Republic itself. But whether or not he could appreciate the enormity of the offense he gave, the fact remains that his acts were speech, in both the technical and the fundamental meaning of the Constitution. So I agree with the Court that he must go free.

Chief Justice REHNQUIST, with whom Justice WHITE and Justice O'CONNOR join, dissenting.

In holding this Texas statute unconstitutional, the Court ignores Justice Holmes' familiar aphorism that "a page of history is worth a volume of logic." *New York Trust Co. v.* [*422] *Eisner,* 256 U.S. 345, 349 (1921). For more than 200 years, the American flag has occupied a unique position as the symbol of our Nation, a uniqueness that justifies a governmental prohibition against flag burning in the way respondent Johnson did here. . . .

[T]he Court insists that the Texas statute prohibiting the public burning of the American flag infringes on respondent Johnson's freedom of expression. Such freedom, of course, is not absolute. . . . In *Chaplinsky v. New Hampshire,* 315 U.S. 568 (1942), a unanimous Court said: "Allowing the broadest scope to the language and purpose of the Fourteenth Amendment, it is well understood that the right of free speech is not absolute at all times and under all circumstances. There are certain well-defined and narrowly limited classes of speech, the prevention and punishment of which have never been thought to raise any Constitutional problem. These include the lewd and obscene, the profane, the libelous, and the insulting or 'fighting' words— those which by their very utterance inflict injury or tend to incite an immediate breach of the peace. It has been well observed that such utterances are no essential part of any exposition of ideas, and are of such slight social value as a step to truth that any benefit that may be derived from them is clearly outweighed by the social interest in order and morality." Id., at 571-572 (footnotes omitted). The Court upheld Chaplinsy's conviction under a state statute that made it unlawful to "address any offensive, derisive or annoying word to any person who is lawfully in any street or other public place." Id., at 569. Chaplinsky had told a local marshal, "'"You are a God damned racketeer" and a "damned Fascist and the whole government of Rochester are Fascists or agents of Fascists."'" Ibid.

Here it may equally well be said that the public burning of the American flag by Johnson was no essential part of any exposition of ideas, and at the same time it had a tendency to incite a breach of the peace. Johnson was free to make any verbal denunciation of the flag that he wished; indeed, he was [*431] free to burn the flag in private. He could

publicly burn other symbols of the Government or effigies of political leaders. He did lead a march through the streets of Dallas, and conducted a rally in front of the Dallas City Hall. He engaged in a "die-in" to protest nuclear weapons. He shouted out various slogans during the march, including: "Reagan, Mondale which will it be? Either one means World War III"; "Ronald Reagan, killer of the hour, Perfect example of U.S. power"; and "red, white and blue, we spit on you, you stand for plunder, you will go under." Brief for Respondent 3. For none of these acts was he arrested or prosecuted; it was only when he proceeded to burn publicly an American flag stolen from its rightful owner that he violated the Texas statute. . . .

[*432] The result of the Texas statute is obviously to deny one in Johnson's frame of mind one of many means of "symbolic speech." Far from being a case of "one picture being worth a thousand words," flag burning is the equivalent of an inarticulate grunt or roar that, it seems fair to say, is most likely to be indulged in not to express any particular idea, but to antagonize others. . . . It was Johnson's use of this particular symbol, and not the idea that he sought to convey by it or by his many other expressions, for which he was punished. . . .

The Court concludes its opinion with a regrettably patronizing civics lecture, presumably addressed to the Members of both Houses of Congress, the members of the 48 state legislatures that enacted prohibitions against flag burning, and the troops fighting under that flag in Vietnam who objected to its [*435] being burned: "The way to preserve the flag's special role is not to punish those who feel differently about these matters. It is to persuade them that they are wrong." Ante, at 419. The Court's role as the final expositor of the Constitution is well established, but its role as a Platonic guardian admonishing those responsible to public opinion as if they were truant schoolchildren has no similar place in our system of government. The cry of "no taxation without representation" animated those who revolted against the English Crown to found our Nation—the idea that those who submitted to government should have some say as to what kind of laws would be passed. Surely one of the high purposes of a democratic society is to legislate against conduct that is

regarded as evil and profoundly offensive to the majority of people—whether it be murder, embezzlement, pollution, or flag burning. . . .

I would uphold the Texas statute as applied in this case.

DISCUSSION QUESTIONS

4. Did you notice that more and slightly different facts were brought out by the dissenting justices? This frequently happens. Why do you think the majority did not include all the facts?

5. Were you surprised by the tone of the opinion, especially the way in which the dissent was written? Do you think it is appropriate for U.S. Supreme Court justices to criticize each other? Each other's opinions?

6. In the past few years many U.S. Supreme Court decisions have been decided by a divided court. It is not uncommon to find five/four splits. What do you think this does to the public's perception of the power and role of the Court?

6. Briefing Cases Involving the Common Law

So far in this chapter, in addition to learning the basics of case briefing, we have explored the responsibility of courts to interpret statutes and to strike down unconstitutional statutes. In areas where there are no statutory or constitutional issues involved, the courts are free to develop the common law. In dealing with common-law issues much of what the courts do involves areas where the law is well settled. What is not so settled is whether a particular litigant's facts fit within the law. Occasionally, however, the court is faced not with applying the established law to new facts, but with deciding what the common-law rule should be.

To make the process of reading cases more interesting and practical, we will introduce you to a new client and ask you to assist in the evaluation of her case by briefing three court opinions. In the first opinion, *Keller*, the court relies on a long and well-established line of cases to decide liability in a negligence action. In the other two opinions, *Callow* and *Lewis*, the court has the much more difficult task of deciding whether to create a new rule of law to meet society's changing values.

For these final three cases assume paralegal Chris Kendall has just received the following memorandum from senior partner Pat Harper. The firm is located in Springfield, Massachusetts.

a. Applying Established Law

Memorandum

TO: Chris Kendall
FROM: Pat Harper
RE: Miller Intake Interview; Possible Negligence Claim
DATE: March 25

Last week Ms. Janice Miller came to our office seeking advice about whether she could sue Mr. George Booth for the injuries that she received

due to his alleged negligence. She initially presented the facts to me as follows: She and Mr. Booth were cutting firewood. Mr. Booth was using a chain saw, and Ms. Miller was stacking the pieces of wood as Mr. Booth cut them. Neither was wearing safety glasses although each owned a pair. Ms. Miller explained the omission by saying that they had both thought that they would only be cutting wood for a short time and neither wanted to be bothered by putting on the glasses.

As it turned out, the wood-cutting session took longer than anticipated. After about an hour, both Mr. Booth and Ms. Miller were getting tired. In particular, Mr. Booth complained that he was feeling fatigued and that it was getting harder and harder to hold the saw sufficiently perpendicular to the wood to cut a straight line. Ms. Miller suggested that they quit for the day, but Mr. Booth wanted to cut just a few more pieces. One his next attempt, probably due to his tired condition, he allowed the chain saw to slip slightly so that it hit the log at a slant, slicing off a piece of bark that flew into Ms. Miller's right eye. Unfortunately the accident has left Ms. Miller totally blind in that eye. Neither she nor Mr. Booth has medical or homeowners' insurance to cover her medical bills, which currently amount to almost $50,000. In addition, Ms. Miller would like to be compensated for her loss of sight, as well as her pain and suffering. I have tentatively attached a value of $400,000 for the former and $150,000 for the latter, for a total possible claim of $600,000.

Attorney Harper first wants to address the issue of whether Mr. Booth can be held liable for negligence. Because the injury occurred in Massachusetts, the ideal situation would be to find cases from Massachusetts that have dealt with a similar situation. The only authorities that are binding on a state court are statutes and court opinions from higher courts within that same state. Similarly, in the federal system the courts are bound only by federal statutes and court opinions from higher federal courts. This constitutes **mandatory authority**—authority from a higher court within the same jurisdiction. All else is **persuasive authority**, and the courts need not follow it. But if the court finds an argument in nonbinding authority persuasive, it may choose to follow it. Researchers usually rely on such persuasive authority when they cannot find any useful mandatory authority because the cases are too old, they go against the client's position, or the facts are not sufficiently similar to the client's facts or when there simply are no prior court opinions dealing with that area of the law.

As it happens, neither attorney Harper nor paralegal Kendall could find any Massachusetts cases dealing with a similar issue of negligence. They did, however, find the following New Hampshire court opinion. The bracketed numbers refer to the pages within the Atlantic Reporter, Second Series. As is true in most states, New Hampshire Supreme Court decisions are published in both an official reporter, New Hampshire Reports, and an unofficial reporter, Atlantic Reporter.

Read and brief *Keller v. DeLong*. Because negligence is a well-established area of the law, most negligence cases, such as this one, involve applying settled principles to new factual situations. Therefore, make sure throughout your brief that you are very specific about which facts seemed to matter to the litigants and the court.

Keller v. DeLong
108 N.H. 212, 231 A.2d 633 (1967)

Case, for wrongful death. Trial was by the Court (Grimes, J.), without a jury. The Court made findings and rulings in writing and returned a verdict for the defendant. Reserved and transferred by the Presiding Justice upon the plaintiff's exceptions. Exceptions sustained; new trial.

Westcott, Millham & Dyer (Mr. Harold E. Westcott orally), for the plaintiff.

[*634] Wiggin, Nourie, Sundeen, Nassikas & Pingree and Dort S. Bigg (Mr. Bigg orally), for the defendant.

DUNCAN, Justice.

The plaintiff's intestate, a registered nurse who was twenty-eight years of age, died in consequence of injuries suffered at Tyngsboro, Massachusetts at approximately 11:40 P.M. on April 14, 1963, when her automobile, operated by the defendant, collided with a utility pole at the side of the highway. She and the defendant had left Laconia late in the afternoon of the same day. Until shortly before the accident, the decedent had done the driving. A stop had been made at Bow, at which time both parties had some beer to drink. Thereafter they had sandwiches at a restaurant in Concord, and then proceeded toward Lowell, Massachusetts with the decedent at the wheel. At some place near the Massachusetts line, the defendant took the wheel at the decedent's request, and the decedent went to sleep. The accident occurred a few miles from where the defendant commenced to drive.

The Trial Court found "that the sole cause of the accident was the fact that the defendant dozed off to sleep and did not awaken in time to avoid collision with the pole." It further found: "While the defendant had been drinking, the evidence does not convince me that he was unable properly to control the vehicle while awake or that he had difficulty in doing so before dozing off. Neither is it found that after he took the wheel he had any warning that he was going to fall asleep." The Court granted the defendant's request as follows: "After taking over the wheel, Carl DeLong had no advance warning that he was about to doze, but suddenly and unexpectedly dozed at the time of the occurrence of the accident." After reasoning that dozing as a passenger "does not mean that a person cannot keep awake when charged with the responsibility of driving," the Trial Court was "not convinced . . . that in taking over the wheel . . . under all the circumstances was anything different than the ordinary man of average prudence would have done and I therefore do not find the defendant was negligent in doing so."

Under principles which receive general recognition an operator of a motor vehicle who permits himself to fall asleep while driving is guilty of ordinary negligence if he has continued to drive without taking reasonable precautions against sleeping after premonitory symptoms of drowsiness or fatigue. Annot. 28 A.L.R.2d 12, 44 et seq; *Bushnell v. Bushnell*, 103 Conn. 583; *Bernosky v. Greff*, 350 Pa. 59; *Carvalho v. Oliveria*, 305 Mass. 304. Cf. *Theisen v. Milwaukee Automobile Mut. Ins. Co.*, 18 Wis. 2d 91 . . . .

[*635] We are of the opinion that in the case before us, the Trial Court erred in the application of the law to the evidence. The error is best illustrated by the finding made at the defendant's request: "After taking over the wheel, Carl DeLong had no advance warning that he was about to doze, but suddenly and unexpectedly dozed at the time of occurrence of the accident." The effect of this finding, and of the like finding made by the Court of its own motion, was to isolate selected portions of the evidence, in disregard of the evidence upon which the Court found that the defendant had dozed on a "couple of occasions" before he undertook to drive, and was "drowsy just before taking the wheel."

This evidence disclosed ample warning to the defendant that he might fall asleep. It was not disputed that when he took the wheel, the windows of the automobile were closed, and the heater turned on. There was no evidence that he took any precaution to arouse himself before proceeding, whether

by walking around the vehicle, opening windows, or reducing the heat. See *Sater v. Owens,* 67 Wash. 2d 699. On the contrary, it appeared that it was the decedent who left the vehicle and walked to the opposite side, to permit the defendant to slide under the wheel without leaving the seat.

Under these circumstances, a finding that "after taking over the wheel" the defendant had "suddenly and unexpectedly dozed at the time of . . . the accident" cannot be sustained. Such an occurrence could not be unexpected in the absence of precaution to prevent it. Thus it was error to judge the defendant's care solely with reference to what occurred after he took the wheel, in disregard of the evidence of "advance warning" which he had just prior thereto. See *Shine v. Wujick,* 89 R.I. 22, 27-28. The plaintiff was entitled to have the defendant's care determined upon a basis of all of the evidence, rather than just what occurred after he took the wheel. See *Murray v. Boston & Maine R.R.,* 107 N.H. 367, 373-374; *Lynch v. Sprague,* 95 N.H. 485, 490. The verdict for the defendant must therefore be set aside.

Exceptions sustained; new trial.

GRIMES, J., did not sit; the others concurred.

Once you have finished briefing a case, the next step is to use that opinion to help you predict how a court will rule in your client's case. If you think the opinion and your client's situation share many similarities, you can assume that a court will decide your client's case as courts have done in the past. If, however, you find many dissimilarities, that could lead you to believe that the court might rule differently than it has in the past. In Chapter 15 we will spend more time on this process of applying court opinions to our client's facts. For now, however, it is important to realize that once you are in the workforce, you will rarely have the luxury of reading cases just for the enjoyment of reading them. You will be reading them to gain insight into how courts have handled similar situations and hence how they might rule in your client's case.

One method for finding similarities and differences between a court decision and your client's case is to make a chart. First, list all the key facts from the court decision. Then list all the key facts from your client's case. For each fact, note whether it is similar to or different from one of the facts in the prior court decision. Most important, decide if any similarities and differences matter. Then based on your chart make an educated guess as to what a court would do.

Legal Reasoning Exercise

1.   Your boss has asked you to analyze whether, based on the same reasoning used by the *Keller* court, a court would find George negligent. (*Note:* The question is not, Was Janice contributorily negligent? At this stage your boss wants you to think only about George's potential liability.) Recall from Chapter 4 our discussion regarding the importance of distinguishing between a prima facie case and the defenses. Here you are being asked to focus exclusively on the prima facie case of negligence.

Make a chart in which you list all the ways in which you think *Keller* and George's situation are analogous and all the ways in which you think they are distinguishable. (*Hint:* To argue that two situations are analogous, think in general terms. For example, both situations involved a dangerous activity. To argue that two situations are distinguishable, think specifically. For example, *Keller* involved a motor vehicle, while George's case involved a chain saw.) Then ask yourself whether the similarities or the differences are more important. If you think the similarities are more important, then you will assume the court will find George negligent. If you think the differences are more important, then you will assume the court will not find George negligent.

b. Creating New Law

Memorandum

TO: Chris Kendall
FROM: Pat Harper
RE: Miller Intake Interview; Possible Spousal Immunity Defense
DATE: April 15

There is a development in the Miller situation. It seems that Ms. Miller and Mr. Booth are married. Since the accident they have been living apart, but they are not legally separated or divorced. This may create a problem for us because to the best of my recollection I do not believe spouses can sue each other. However, it has been quite a while since I researched that area of the law. Would you please do so for me and report on your findings?[8]

We have reproduced the two cases in Exhibits 13-6 and 13-7 exactly as you would find them in the North Eastern Reporter. We have added the marginal notes to help explain some of the editorial features that West adds.

After reading *Callow* (Exhibit 13-6) try writing a brief. In the procedural history, note that there was no trial in this case. The case was sent from the trial court directly to the Supreme Judicial Court. (This usually happens when the

---

[8] All research materials are contained in your readings. *Do not* do any additional research.

West key symbol

These are headnotes, so called because they appear at the head of the case. They are written by the editors at West, not by the court. Do not quote them, and do not rely on them.

CALLOW v. THOMAS
Cite as 78 N.E.2d 637   Mass.   637

N.E.2d 729, 731. Consequently, no error of fact or of law being made to appear, we cannot modify this provision of the decree.

The matter of allowance of attorney's fees, briefs and expenses in this court will be settled by a separate order of a single justice upon presentation of an itemized list of the expenses.

Decree affirmed.

CALLOW v. THOMAS.

Supreme Judicial Court of Massachusetts.
Middlesex.

April 1, 1948.

1. Husband and wife ⬥205(2)

No cause of action arises in favor of either spouse for a tort committed by the other during coverture.

2. Husband and wife ⬥205(2)

Where either spouse commits a tort upon the other during coverture recovery is denied, not merely because of the disability of one spouse to sue the other during coverture, but because of the marital relationship, no cause of action ever came into existence.

3. Divorce ⬥313

After divorce, no action can be maintained by either spouse for a tort committed by the other during coverture.

4. Marriage ⬥57, 67

Generally an "annulment" is distinguished from a "divorce" in that annulment is not a dissolution of the marriage but is a judicial declaration that no marriage has ever existed, and decree of annulment makes the marriage void ab initio even though the marriage be voidable only at the instance of the injured party. G.L.(Ter.Ed.) c. 207, § 14.

See Words and Phrases, Permanent Edition, for all other definitions of "Annulment" and "Divorce".

5. Marriage ⬥67

Where marriage was voidable and not void and so was valid until set aside by decree of nullity, wife could not after annulment, recover for a tort committed upon her by husband during coverture because of his gross negligence in operation of automobile in which wife was a guest passenger. G.L.(Ter.Ed.) c. 207, § 14.

6. Marriage ⬥67

Where a voidable marriage has been annulled things which have been done during the period of the supposed marriage ought not be undone or reopened after the decree of annulment. G.L.(Ter.Ed.) c. 207, § 14.

———————

Report from Superior Court, Middlesex County.

Action by Muriel Callow against Frederick Thomas for injuries sustained when plaintiff was riding as a gratuitous passenger in an automobile owned and operated by defendant. The case was reported to Supreme Judicial Court without decision.

Judgment for defendant.

Before QUA, C. J., and LUMMUS, DOLAN, WILKINS, and SPALDING, JJ.

M. Harry Goldburgh and J. Finks, both of Boston, for plaintiff.

K. C. Parker, of Boston, for defendant.

SPALDING, Justice.

The plaintiff and the defendant were married in this Commonwealth on August 6, 1944, and thereafter lived together here as husband and wife. On November 9, 1944, while riding as a "gratuitous passenger" in an automobile owned and operated by the defendant, the plaintiff was injured when the automobile, due to the gross negligence of the defendant, ran into a tree. The plaintiff was in the exercise of due care. The accident occurred on a public way in this Commonwealth and the defendant's automobile was registered in accordance with the laws thereof. On June 28, 1945, upon the petition of the plaintiff to annul the marriage because of the defendant's fraud, the Probate Court decreed that the marriage was "null and

1–6 headnotes

The bold word or phrase is called a West topic. There are 414 West topics. The number preceded by a key symbol is called a key number.

Syllabus

Judges hearing the case.

Attorneys of the parties.

This is where the opinion begins.

Each headnote summarizes one legal point. You can find those points in the opinion by locating the bracketed numbers corresponding to the headnote numbers. For example, you can find the points summarized in headnotes 1-3 in one long paragraph beginning at the bottom of the left-hand column on the next page. Headnote 4 is covered in five paragraphs beginning on page 639 of the opinion.

Exhibit 13-6   *Callow v. Thomas*

(continues)

638   Mass.   78 NORTH EASTERN REPORTER, 2d SERIES

void." [1] Two months later the plaintiff commenced this action of tort to recover compensation for her injuries.

The foregoing facts were submitted to a judge of the Superior Court upon a case stated in which it was agreed that no inferences should be drawn. See G.L.(Ter.Ed.) c. 231, § 126. The judge at the request of the parties reported the case to this court without decision. G.L.(Ter.Ed.) c. 231, § 111; Scaccia v. Boston Elevated Railway Co., 317 Mass. 245, 248, 249, 57 N.E.2d 761, "upon the stipulation that if the plaintiff is entitled to recover, judgment shall be entered for the plaintiff in the sum of $3,000, otherwise judgment for the defendant."

The question for decision is whether a wife after the marriage has been annulled can maintain an action against her former husband for a tort committed during coverture. The question is one of first impression in this Commonwealth. Indeed no case in any other jurisdiction has been brought to our attention, and we have found none, in which this question has been presented.

[1-3]   That no cause of action arises in favor of either husband or wife for a tort committed by the other during coverture is too well settled to require citation of authority. Recovery is denied in such a case not merely because of the disability of one spouse to sue the other during coverture, but for the more fundamental reason that because of the marital relationship no cause of action ever came into existence.[2] That this is so is revealed by the fact that it has uniformly been held that even after divorce no action can be maintained by either spouse for a tort committed by the other during coverture. Phillips v. Barnet, 1 Q.B.D. 436; Abbott v. Abbott, 67 Me. 304, 24 Am.Rep. 27; Bandfield v. Bandfield, 117 Mich. 80, 75 N.W. 287, 40 L.R.A. 757, 72 Am.St.Rep. 550; Strom v. Strom, 98 Minn. 427, 107 N.W. 1047, 6 L.R.A.,N.S., 191, 116 Am.St.Rep. 387; Lillienkamp v. Rippetoe, 133 Tenn. 57, 179 S.W. 628, L.R.A.1916B, 881, Ann.Cas. 1917C, 901; Schultz v. Christopher, 65 Wash. 496, 118 P. 629, 38 L.R.A.,N.S., 780. There is nothing in our statutes enlarging the rights of married women that can be construed as altering this rule.[3] See Lubowitz v. Taines, 293 Mass. 39, 198 N.E. 320; Luster v. Luster, 299 Mass. 480, 482, 483,

---

[1] The material portions of the decree are as follows: "On the libel of Muriel Gladys Thomas, of Sudbury, in said county of Middlesex, representing that she and Frederick A. Thomas, now of Lexington, in said county, were joined in marriage lawfully solemnized at Boston, in the county of Suffolk, on August 6, 1944; and that they last lived together in this Commonwealth at said Sudbury; that she now doubts the validity of said marriage for the reason that at the time of said marriage said libellee fraudulently concealed from her the fact that he was afflicted with a contagious disease, thereby practicing a fraud upon her; and praying that said marriage between the said libellant and libellee be annulled and declared void: Said Frederick A. Thomas having had due notice of said libel, objection being made, and after hearing, it appearing to the court that said libellant entered into said marriage in good faith but that said libellee practiced a fraud upon her: It is decreed that said marriage between the said libellant and libellee be and the same hereby is declared to be null and void."

[2] There are, to be sure, instances where one spouse may have a cause of action against the other but cannot enforce it because of the rule prohibiting, with certain exceptions, legal proceedings between husband and wife. See G.L. (Ter.Ed.) c. 209, § 6. Thus in Giles v. Giles, 279 Mass. 284, 181 N.E. 176, it was held that a wife could not maintain a suit in equity against her husband to recover money lent to him before the marriage. But after the parties had been divorced it was held that the suit could be maintained. Giles v. Giles, 293 Mass. 495, 200 N.E. 378. The right to sue was merely suspended during coverture. In Charney v. Charney, 316 Mass. 580, 55 N.E.2d 917, it was held that a wife who, without the intervention of a trustee, had entered into a separation agreement with her husband in New York could not, although the contract was valid by the law of that State, enforce the agreement in the courts of this Commonwealth. Compare Whitney v. Whitney, 316 Mass. 367, 55 N.E.2d 601. See Lubowitz v. Taines, 293 Mass. 39, 198 N.E. 320; Mertz v. Mertz, 271 N.Y. 466, 3 N.E.2d 597, 108 A.L.R. 1120.

[3] In other jurisdictions it has usually been held that statutes removing the common law disabilities of the wife do not

---

Footnotes can be very important. They are part of the opinion. Always read them.

Exhibit 13-6   *Callow v. Thomas*

(continues)

CALLOW v. THOMAS   Mass.   639
Cite as 78 N.E.2d 637

13 N.E.2d 438. Recognizing the common law rule and the fact that it has not been changed by statute, the plaintiff argues that the decree of nullity "effaced the marriage between the plaintiff and defendant ab initio, and, therefore, at the time of the accident the relationship of husband and wife did not exist."

[4] General Laws (Ter.Ed.) c. 207, § 14, which governs proceedings for annulment, so far as material, reads as follows: "If the validity of a marriage is doubted, either party may file a libel for annulling such marriage. * * * Upon proof of validity or nullity of the marriage, it shall be affirmed or declared void by a decree of the court." In general it may be said that an annulment is to be distinguished from a divorce in that it is not a dissolution of the marriage but is a judicial declaration that no marriage has ever existed. In other words, the decree of annulment makes the marriage void ab initio. Restatement: Conflict of Laws, § 115(1), comment b; Clarke v. Menzies, [1922] 2 Ch. 298; Dodworth v. Dale, [1936] 2 K.B. 503, 511; Mason v. Mason, [1944] N.I. 134; Millar v. Millar, 175 Cal. 797, 804, 805, 167 P. 394, L.R.A.1918B, 415, Ann.Cas.1918E, 184; McDonald v. McDonald, 6 Cal.2d 457, 461, 58 P.2d 163, 104 A.L.R. 1290; Griffin v. Griffin, 130 Ga. 527, 61 S.E. 16, 16 L.R.A.,N.S., 937, 14 Ann.Cas. 866; Henneger v. Lomas, 145 Ind. 287, 298, 44 N.E. 462, 32 L.R.A. 848; Ridgely v. Ridgely, 79 Md. 298, 305,

29 A. 597, 25 L.R.A. 800; Steerman v. Snow, 94 N.J.Eq. 9, 13, 14, 118 A. 696; Jones v. Brinsmade, 183 N.Y. 258, 76 N.E. 22, 3 L.R.A.,N.S., 192, 111 Am.St.Rep. 746, 5 Ann.Cas. 378; Leventhal v. Liberman, 262 N.Y. 209, 211, 186 N.E. 675, 88 A.L.R. 782. See Loker v. Gerald, 157 Mass. 42, 45, 31 N.E. 709, 16 L.R.A. 497, 34 Am.St. Rep. 252; Hanson v. Hanson, 287 Mass. 154, 157, 191 N.E. 673, 93 A.L.R. 701. And this is true even though, as here, the marriage be only voidable at the instance of the injured party. Dodworth v. Dale, [1936] 2 K.B. 503, 511–512; Mason v. Mason, [1944] N.I. 134; McDonald v. McDonald, 6 Cal.2d 457, 461, 58 P.2d 163, 104 A.L.R. 1290; Matter of Moncrief's Will, 235 N.Y. 390, 139 N.E. 550, 27 A.L.R. 1117; Sleicher v. Sleicher, 251 N.Y. 366, 369, 167 N.E. 501, 502.

But the doctrine that such a decree makes the marriage void ab initio has not always been applied unqualifiedly. See Sleicher v. Sleicher, 251 N.Y. 366, 369, 167 N.E. 501, 502.[4] In England, where the question of the effect of a decree of annulment seems to have been considered to a greater extent than in this country, the rule is that such a decree is void for most purposes but not for all. In discussing the effect of such a decree in Mason v. Mason, [1944] N.I. 134, it was said by Lord Chief Justice Andrews, "It is further to be observed that the marriage, after such decree absolute, is void for almost every purpose;

permit her to maintain an action against her husband for a tort committed during coverture. Libby v. Berry, 74 Me. 286, 43 Am.Rep. 589; Bandfield v. Bandfield, 117 Mich. 80, 75 N.W. 287, 40 L. R.A. 757, 72 Am.St.Rep. 550; Strom v. Strom, 98 Minn. 427, 107 N.W. 1047, 6 L.R.A.,N.S., 191, 116 Am.St.Rep. 387; Longendyke v. Longendyke, 44 Barb., N. Y., 366; Lillienkamp v. Rippetoe, 133 Tenn. 57, 179 S.W. 628, L.R.A.1916B, 881, Ann.Cas.1917C, 901; Thompson v. Thompson, 218 U.S. 611, 31 S.Ct. 111, 54 L.Ed. 1180, 30 L.R.A.,N.S., 1153, 21 Ann. Cas. 921. But some statutes have been construed to permit actions in such cases. Johnson v. Johnson, 201 Ala. 41, 77 So. 335, 6 A.L.R. 1031; Brown v. Brown, 88 Conn. 42, 89 A. 889, 52 L.R.A.,N.S., 185, Ann.Cas.1915D, 70; Gilman v. Gilman, 78 N.H. 4, 95 A. 657, L.R.A.1916B, 907. See note in 38 Harv.L.Rev. 383.

4 In that case the defendant was directed by a decree of divorce to pay alimony to the plaintiff "so long as she remains unmarried." Thereafter the plaintiff remarried but the marriage was subsequently annulled on the ground of fraud. Alimony payments ceased at the time of the second marriage. In an action to recover unpaid instalments of alimony it was held that the plaintiff could recover instalments of alimony falling due from the time of the annulment but not for the period during which the second marriage was in force. The court refused to give retroactive effect to the decree of annulment, saying, "The retroactive effect of rescission from the beginning is not, however, without limits, prescribed by policy and justice."

Exhibit 13-6   *Callow v. Thomas*   (continues)

and, speaking in general terms, the only exception to the rule—an exception founded on general equitable principles—may be said to be such transactions as have been concluded and such things as have been done during the period of the supposed marriage. These cannot be undone or reopened after the marriage has been declared null and void" (page 163).

This exception has been recognized in several decisions. Thus in Anstey v. Manners, Gow. 10, the plaintiff, after a sentence of nullity had been pronounced by the Ecclesiastical Court, brought suit against the former husband to recover for necessaries which he (the plaintiff) had supplied to the wife. Some of the necessaries were supplied during the supposed marriage and some were supplied afterwards. In a very brief opinion which is somewhat obscure it was held that the defendant was not liable for debts contracted after the date of the decree. The case has been considered as impliedly holding that the defendant was liable for necessaries furnished prior to that date. See Dodworth v. Dale, [1936] 2 K.B. 503, 512.

In Dunbar v. Dunbar, [1909] 2 Ch. 639, it was held that a completed and executed transaction, namely, an advancement, effected while the plaintiff and the defendant were living together as man and wife, was unaffected by a subsequent decree annulling a marriage which was voidable but not void.

In Dodworth v. Dale, [1936] 2 K.B. 503, it was held that a husband who had obtained an annulment of his marriage on the ground of his wife's impotency and who during the period of his purported marriage had filed tax returns as a married man, could not be compelled to pay additional taxes for that period on the ground that the deductions which he had taken for the support of his wife were improper. The court stated "that what has been done during the continuance of the de facto marriage cannot be undone—cannot be overturned by the operation of law" (page 519).

In Fowke v. Fowke, [1938] Ch. 774, it was held that a decree of nullity granted on the ground of the wife's impotency did not affect a previous deed of separation whereby the husband convenanted to pay the wife an annuity so long as she continued to lead a chaste life. See also P. v. P. [1916] 2 Ir.R. 400; De Reneville v. De Reneville, [1947] A.C.[5]

[5, 6] We are of opinion that the exception recognized in these cases is sound and that the present case falls within it. At the time of the accident the parties were husband and wife for all intents and purposes. Had no proceedings been brought to annul the marriage, this status would have endured until the marriage was terminated by death or divorce. In other words, the marriage here was voidable and not void and was valid until it was set aside by the decree of nullity. 1 Bish.Mar. Div. & Sep. §§ 258, 259, 271, 281; Anders v. Anders, 224 Mass. 438, 441, 113 N.E. 203, L.R.A.1916E, 1273; Sleicher v. Sleicher, 251 N.Y. 366, 369, 167 N.E. 501, 502. It is to be observed that this is not a case of a marriage prohibited by law such as a bigamous marriage or one prohibited by reason of consanguinity or affinity between the parties. G.L.(Ter.Ed.) c. 207, §§ 1, 2, 4. Such a marriage is no marriage at all and is "void without a decree of divorce or other legal process." G.L.(Ter. Ed.) c. 207, § 8. While it doubtless is true that a decree of nullity ordinarily has the effect of making a marriage, even one which is voidable, void ab initio, this is a legal fiction which ought not to be pressed too far. To say that for all purposes the marriage never existed is unrealistic. Logic must yield to realities. Public policy requires that there must be some limits to the retroactive effects of a decree of annulment. It was said by Cardozo, C. J., in American Surety Co. v. Conner, 251 N.Y. 1, 9, 166 N.E. 783, 786, 65 A.L.R. 244, "The decree of annulment destroyed the marriage from the beginning as a source of rights and duties * * * but it could not obliterate the past and make events unreal." The better rule, we think, is that in the case of a voidable marriage transactions which have been concluded and things which have been done during

5 64 T. L. R. 82.

Exhibit 13-6   *Callow v. Thomas*

(continues)

JOYCE v. DEVANEY
Cite as 78 N.E.2d 641
Mass. **641**

the period of the supposed marriage ought not to be undone or reopened after the decree of annulment. Applying that principle here, the plaintiff is not entitled to recover. On the day after the accident if the plaintiff had brought suit against the defendant it could not have been maintained, for the marriage at that time had not been declared invalid. The situation was unaffected by the subsequent decree of annulment.

It follows that in accordance with the stipulation judgment is to be entered for the defendant.

So ordered.

JOYCE et al. v. DEVANEY et al.

Supreme Judicial Court of Massachusetts.
Middlesex.

April 1, 1948.

1. Easements ⟜16

The owner of realty may make use of one part of his realty for the benefit of another part in such a way that, on severance of the title, an easement, which is not expressed in the deed, may arise, which corresponds to the use which was previously made of the realty while it was under common ownership.

2. Easements ⟜15

Implied easements, whether by grant or by reservation, do not arise out of necessity alone, and their origin must be found in presumed intention of parties, to be gathered from language of instruments when read in the light of circumstances attending their execution, physical condition of premises, and knowledge which parties had or with which they are chargeable.

3. Easements ⟜15

The creation in deeds of express easements that were unambiguous and definite negatived any intention to create easements by implication, since the expression of one thing is the exclusion of another.

78 N.E.2d—41
Mass.Dec.76–79 N.E.2d—23

4. Easements ⟜17(1)

Where deeds of adjoining lots at time of severance created specific easements shown by plan providing for an 8-foot wide driveway 4 feet of which was to be on each lot, but 10-foot wide driveway was constructed, 8½ feet of which was on defendant's lot, and 1½ feet of which was on plaintiff's lot, there was no implied easement entitling plaintiff to use driveway as constructed, and plaintiff was entitled only to easement expressly set forth in deeds.

———◆———

Appeal from Superior Court, Middlesex County; Goldberg, Judge.

Bill in equity by John J. Joyce and another against John T. Devaney and another to restrain defendants from interfering with plaintiff's use of a common driveway, and for a determination of plaintiff's rights in the driveway, wherein the defendants filed a counterclaim to restrain plaintiffs from trespassing on defendant's land. From an adverse decree, plaintiffs appeal.

Interlocutory decree affirmed and final decree affirmed.

Before QUA, C. J., and LUMMUS, DOLAN, WILKINS, and SPALDING, JJ.

R. B. Brooks, of Boston, for plaintiffs.

M. E. Gallagher, Jr., of Boston, and A. J. Kirwan, of Medford, for defendants.

SPALDING, Justice.

The plaintiffs by this bill in equity seek to restrain the defendants from interfering with their use of a common driveway; they also ask that their rights in the driveway be determined. The answer of the defendants included a counterclaim in which they ask that the plaintiffs be restrained from trespassing on their land. The case was referred to a master whose report, to which there were no objections, was confirmed by an interlocutory decree. The case comes here on the plaintiffs' appeal from a final decree.

We summarize the findings of the master as follows: On April 30, 1931, MacNeil Bros. Corporation, hereinafter called the corporation, acquired for development purposes a parcel of vacant land in West Med-

The beginning of the next case.

Exhibit 13-6   *Callow v. Thomas (concluded)*

parties agree as to what happened but disagree as to what the law should be.) In your holding be particularly careful to note any limitations the court places on its holding. View a limitation as a red flag. A limitation is an indication that the court has left some area open that can be resolved only through future litigation.

DISCUSSION QUESTIONS

7. In Chapter 12 (Legal Reasoning Exercise 1) we looked at the following statute, which would seem to govern Janice's case. What does the *Callow* court say about it?

> A married woman may sue and be sued in the same manner as if she were sole; but this section shall not authorize suits between husband and wife.

8. What is the difference between a void and a voidable marriage? Do you think the court would have ruled the same way if the marriage had been void? Should such technicalities matter?

9. The result here was the finding that Muriel Callow could not sue her ex-husband. This does not mean that the court thought he was not negligent. Because the court said she could not sue, the court never heard any evidence regarding his behavior that caused his car to run into a tree. Do you think that there should be such absolute bars to even having a case heard? If so, can you think of other situations where the courts should not allow potential litigants to sue each other?

Legal Reasoning Exercise

2. Based on *Callow* analyze whether you think the doctrine of spousal immunity will bar Janice's claim.

In 1975 the Massachusetts Supreme Judicial Court was asked to change the law regarding parental immunity. A child was hurt when his father allegedly caused an automobile accident. After considering the two major arguments against allowing such suits, the possibility of disrupting the family's peace and harmony and the tendency to promote fraud, the court allowed the child to sue his father. One year later, and twenty-eight years after the Supreme Judicial Court decided *Callow*, the court revisited the issue of spousal immunity in *Lewis*, reprinted here in Exhibit 13-7, beginning on page 376.

As you read and brief this opinion, ask yourself why the court went to such lengths to explain itself and whether you agree with its reasoning. Pay particular attention to why the court said this was not a matter in which they should defer to the legislature. In the holding section, again be particularly careful to note any limitations the court puts on its holding.

As in *Callow*, there was no trial in *Lewis*. The court granted Mr. Lewis's summary judgment motion. The case then went to the Supreme Judicial Court by way of *direct appellate review*. This occurs when the courts think a case is so significant that the highest appellate court will eventually hear it, no matter

526   Mass.   **351 NORTH EASTERN REPORTER, 2d SERIES**

Headnotes

Court is not barred by the principle of double jeopardy. Accordingly the defendant's motion is to be denied, and the indictments are to stand for trial in the Superior Court.

So ordered.

Blanche LEWIS

v.

Larry C. LEWIS.

Supreme Judicial Court of Massachusetts, Hampden.

Argued Jan. 8, 1976.

Decided July 9, 1976.

Syllabus

Action was brought by wife against husband for personal injuries sustained in automobile accident. The Superior Court, Moriarty, J., granted defendant's motion for summary judgment, and plaintiff's motion for direct appellate review was allowed. The Supreme Judicial Court, Reardon, J., held that it was open to the Supreme Judicial Court to reconsider common-law rule of interspousal immunity, and that such rule no longer barred wife's action against husband for injuries sustained in automobile accident.

Judgment vacated.

1. **Husband and Wife** ⬅205(2)

Arguments that tort actions between husband and wife would tend to disrupt peace and harmony of family and that such actions would tend to promote fraud and collusion on part of husband and wife for purpose of reaping undeserved financial reward at expense of family's liability insurer are insufficient to justify common-law rule of interspousal immunity.

2. **Constitutional Law** ⬅70.1(11)

Statute which provides that a married woman may sue and be sued in same manner as if she were sole but provides that such statute does not authorize suit between husband and wife except in connection with certain contracts left interspousal immunity rule in its common-law status susceptible to reexamination and alteration by Supreme Judicial Court. M.G.L.A. c. 209 § 6.

3. **Courts** ⬅90(6)

It is within power and authority of court to abrogate judicially created rule and mere longevity of rule does not by itself provide cause for Supreme Judicial Court to stay its hand if to perpetuate rule would be to perpetuate inequity.

4. **Courts** ⬅90(6)

When rationales which gave meaning and coherence to judicially created rule are no longer vital, and rule itself is not consonant with needs of contemporary society, court not only has authority but also duty to reexamine its predecents rather than to apply by rote an antiquated formula.

5. **Constitutional Law** ⬅70.1(11)

Where legislature recognized rule of interspousal immunity but left rule in its common-law form, expressing preference, at least implicitly, that Supreme Judicial Court continue to evaluate usefulness and propriety of rule, it was open to Supreme Judicial Court to reconsider common-law rule of interspousal immunity. M.G.L.A. c. 209 § 6.

6. **Husband and Wife** ⬅205(2)

Wife's action against her husband for personal injuries sustained in automobile accident was not barred by common-law rule of interspousal immunity.

7. **Torts** ⬅5

If there is tortious injury there should be recovery, and only strong arguments of public policy can justify judicially created

Exhibit 13-7   *Lewis v. Lewis*   *(continues)*

LEWIS v. LEWIS   Mass. **527**

Cite as, Mass., 351 N.E.2d 526

immunity for tort-feasors and bar recovery for injured victims.

———◆———

Morton J. Sweeney, Springfield (Patricia A. Bobba, Springfield, with him), for the plaintiff.

George J. Shagory, Boston (Edward J. Shagory, Boston, with him), for defendant.

Robert M. Fuster, Pittsfield, for Juliette G. Pevoski, amicus curiae, submitted a brief.

J. Norman O'Connor and John D. Lanoue, Adams, for Joseph J. Pevoski, amicus curiae, submitted a brief.

Before HENNESSEY, C. J., and REARDON, BRAUCHER, KAPLAN and WILKINS, JJ.

REARDON, Justice.

This matter raises the question of the continuance in Massachusetts of the doctrine of interspousal immunity. The case originated as a civil action of tort for personal injuries brought by the plaintiff Blanche Lewis against her husband, the defendant Larry Lewis. The defendant's motion for summary judgment was granted, and we allowed the plaintiff's motion for direct appellate review. Blanche Lewis was a passenger in a car owned and driven by her husband on July 27, 1973, when about 9 P.M., on a public highway in the town of Agawam, the car slid on a wet pavement, struck a light pole and rolled over on its side, causing injury to the plaintiff. The motion for summary judgment which was allowed was based on the common law doctrine of interspousal immunity and on the provisions of G.L. c. 209, § 6, as amended by St.1963, c. 765, § 2. In addition to briefs filed by the parties we also reviewed briefs filed by counsel in a case raising a similar question commenced in the Superior Court for Berkshire County. We are thus led to a discussion of the current status of the doctrine of inter-

spousal immunity and our opinion relative to the argument here presented by the plaintiff.

The fundamental basis for the common law rule of interspousal immunity was the special unity of husband and wife within the marital relationship. For most purposes the common law treated husband and wife as "a single person, represented by the husband." *Nolin v. Pearson*, 191 Mass. 283, 284, 77 N.E. 890, (1906). See *Butler v. Ives*, 139 Mass. 202, 203, 29 N.E. 654 (1885). This merger of legal identities has been described in the following terms: "By marriage, the husband and wife are one person in law: . . . that is, the very being or legal existence of the woman is suspended during the marriage, or at least is incorporated and consolidated into that of the husband; under whose wing, protection, and *cover*, she performs everything . . . . Upon this principle, of a union of a person in husband and wife, depend almost all the legal rights, duties, and disabilities, that either of them acquire by the marriage." 1 W. Blackstone, Commentaries *442.

Among the many disabilities visited upon a woman once she took her marriage vows was an inability to sue or be sued in her own name. To enforce any right of action for tortious injury to her person her husband had to be joined as a plaintiff; and, furthermore, he was entitled to the proceeds of any judgment obtained. Conversely, to enforce an action against a married woman it was necessary to join the husband as a defendant, and a judgment, if obtained during coverture, became the obligation of the husband. McCurdy, Personal Injury Torts Between Spouses, 4 Vill.L.Rev. 303, 304 (1959). 1 F. Harper & F. James, Torts § 8.10 at 643 (1956).

Within this framework a rule prohibiting suits between husband and wife made some sense. Not only was there the conceptual problem of the single marital entity suing itself but, as a practical matter, the rules of liability would have rendered such suits

---

Exhibit 13-7 *Lewis v. Lewis*

(continues)

528   Mass.   **351 NORTH EASTERN REPORTER, 2d SERIES**

idle exercises. As Dean Prosser pointed out: "If the man were the tort-feasor, the woman's right would be a chose in action which the husband would have the right to reduce to possession, and he must be joined as a plaintiff against himself and the proceeds recovered must be paid to him . . . . If the wife committed the tort, the husband would be liable to himself for it, and must be joined as a defendant in his own action." W. Prosser, Torts § 122 at 860 (4th ed. 1971).

These antediluvian assumptions concerning the role and status of women in marriage and in society which animated and gave support to the common law rule of interspousal immunity were soon perceived as inconsistent with the principles and realities of a progressing American society. Beginning in the middle of the nineteenth century, women's emancipation acts were passed in all American jurisdictions in order to secure to married women their own independent legal identities. See W. Prosser, Torts § 122 at 861 (4th ed. 1971); McCurdy, Torts Between Persons in Domestic Relation, 43 Harv.L.Rev. 1030, 1036–1037 (1930). In Massachusetts, beginning with St.1845, c. 208, the Legislature through a series of enactments now found in G.L. c. 209, §§ 1–13, has moved to recognize and invigorate the legal identity of the married woman. Most of the disabilities which rendered women second class citizens under the common law were removed by these statutes in Massachusetts. They provide inter alia that a married woman may hold and dispose of both real and personal property (G.L. c. 209, § 1), may enter into contracts in her own name (G.L. c. 209, § 2), and may sue and be sued in her own name without joinder of her husband, and without her husband's

being liable for judgments against her (G. L. c. 209, §§ 6, 8). As we recognized as early as 1906 in *Nolin v. Pearson, supra*, 191 Mass. at 285, 77 N.E. at 890, "This remedial legislation has resulted in very largely impairing the unity of husband and wife as it existed at common law." The old order has been changing and the doctrine of the legal unity of husband and wife is no longer a satisfactory foundation on which to base a rule of interspousal tort immunity.[1]

Despite the demise of the unity theory of husband and wife and the enactment of married women's acts, the rule of interspousal tort immunity has survived in Massachusetts and in many other jurisdictions. This court could say in 1948 in very broad and dogmatic terms, "That no cause of action arises in favor of either husband or wife for a tort committed by the other during coverture is too well settled to require citation of authority. Recovery is denied in such a case not merely because of the disability of one spouse to sue the other during coverture, but for the more fundamental reason that because of the marital relationship no cause of action ever came into existence." *Callow v. Thomas*, 322 Mass. 550, 551–552, 78 N.E.2d 637, 638 (1948). Indeed at that time interspousal immunity was the rule in a substantial majority of jurisdictions. However, in the interim there has been a significant trend in other jurisdictions toward abrogating the doctrine. Currently, State jurisdictions are about evenly divided between those which have abandoned and those which have maintained the interspousal immunity rule. Furthermore, among commentators who have considered the topic, criticism of the rule is pratically universal. See, e. g., 1 F. Harper & F. James, *supra* at 643–647;

1. What we have said is not to be interpreted as a derogation of the spiritual and emotional unity that many hold as an ideal in marriage. As the Supreme Court of Washington pointed out, "The 'supposed unity' of husband and wife, which serves as the traditional basis of interspousal disability, is not a reference to the common nature or loving oneness

achieved in a marriage of two free individuals. Rather, this traditional premise had reference to a situation, coming on from antiquity, in which a woman's marriage for most purposes rendered her a chattel of her husband." *Freehe v. Freehe*, 81 Wash.2d 183, 186, 500 P.2d 771, 773 (1972).

Exhibit 13-7   *Lewis v. Lewis*   *(continues)*

LEWIS v. LEWIS
Cite as, Mass., 351 N.E.2d 526   **Mass. 529**

W. Prosser, *supra* at 859–864; McCurdy, Torts Between Persons in Domestic Relation, 43 Harv.L.Rev. 1030 (1930); McCurdy, Personal Injury Torts Between Spouses, 4 Vill.L.Rev. 303 (1959); Comment Tort Liability Between Husband and Wife: The Interspousal Immunity Doctrine, 21 U.Miami L.Rev. 423 (1966); Note, Interspousal Immunity—Time for a Reappraisal, 27 Ohio St.L.J. 550 (1966).

[1] While most jurisdictions recognize that the theory of the legal identity of husband and wife can no longer support the interspousal immunity rule, those courts which have upheld the rule have generally done so on grounds of public policy. The two arguments most frequently advanced in favor of the rule are, first, that tort actions between husband and wife would tend to disrupt the peace and harmony of the family, and, second, that such actions would tend to promote fraud and collusion on the part of husband and wife for the purpose of reaping an undeserved financial reward at the expense of the family's liability insurer. Both of this arguments were considered and rejected in the analogous context of parental immunity in the recent case of *Sorensen v. Sorensen,* —— Mass. —— [a], 339 N.E.2d 907 (1975), decided this term. We refer to our discussion and resolution of these issues in that case. *Id.* at —— – —— [b], 339 N.E.2d 907. Suffice it to say that just as we did not find the arguments concerning the preservation of family harmony and the avoidance of family fraud sufficient to justify a rule barring tort suits for personal injuries by a

child against a parent, we are similarly unconvinced by these arguments in the present context of interspousal immunity. We further note that most of the jurisdictions which have rejected the rule of interspousal immunity have considered these very same arguments and found them wanting. See *Self v. Self,* 58 Cal.2d 683, 689–691, 26 Cal.Rptr. 97, 376 P.2d 65 (1962) (intentional torts); *Klein v. Klein,* 58 Cal.2d 692, 694–696, 26 Cal.Rptr. 102, 376 P.2d 70 (1962) (negligent torts); *Brooks v. Robinson,* 259 Ind. 16, 20–22, 284 N.E.2d 794 (1972); *Rupert v. Stienne,* 90 Nev. 397, 401–402, 528 P.2d 1013 (1974); *Immer v. Risko,* 56 N.J. 482, 488–495, 267 A.2d 481 (1970); *Flores v. Flores,* 84 N. M. 601, 603, 506 P.2d 345 (Ct.App.1973) (intentional torts); *Maestas v. Overton,* 87 N.M. 213, 531 P.2d 947 (1975) (negligent torts); *Surratt v. Thompson,* 212 Va. 191, 192, 183 S.E.2d 200 (1971); *Freehe v. Freehe,* 81 Wash.2d 193, 187–189, 500 P.2d 771 (1972).

However, the defendant argues that, unlike the situation prevailing in most other jurisdictions, the rule of interspousal immunity has taken on statutory dimensions in Massachusetts. The argument is based on G.L. c. 209, § 6, as appearing in St. 1963, c. 765, § 2, which provides: "A married woman may sue and be sued in the manner as if she were sole; *but this section shall not authorize suits between husband and wife* except in connection with contracts entered into pursuant to the authority contained in section two" (emphasis supplied).[2] By including the italicized lan-

---

a. Mass.Adv.Sh. (1975) 3662.

b. Mass.Adv.Sh. (1975) at 3674–3683.

2. As to the historical development of G.L. c. 209, § 6, briefly, married women were first given a limited right to sue and be sued in their own names in St.1845, c. 208, which provided for the separate ownership of property by married women and authorized suits by and against married women "in respect to such property." The first mention of tort actions appears in St.1871, c. 312, which

351 N.E.2d—34

provided that a married woman could sue and be sued in tort in the same manner as if she were unmarried but contained no reference to suits by or against her husband. In 1874 the interspousal language we are concerned with in this case was added in substantially the same form as it appears today in G.L. c. 209, § 6. Statute 1874, c. 184, § 3, read: "A married woman may sue and be sued in the same manner and to the same extent as if she were sole, but nothing herein contained shall authorize suits between hus-

---

Exhibit 13-7   *Lewis v. Lewis*   *(continues)*

530 Mass.   351 NORTH EASTERN REPORTER, 2d SERIES

guage in the statute, the Legislature, according to the defendant's argument, has chosen to incorporate the rule of interspousal immunity into the statutory law of the Commonwealth and, therefore, this court is without power to abrogate the rule. With this contention we do not agree. The Supreme Court of New Jersey was faced with similar statutory language when called on to reëxamine the doctrine of interspousal immunity in *Immer v. Risko*, 56 N.J. 482, 267 A.2d 481 (1970). New Jersey's Married Persons' Act included the following provision: "Nothing in this chapter contained shall enable a husband or wife to contract with or to sue each other, except as heretofore, and except as authorized by this chapter." N.J.Stat.Ann. tit. 37:2–5 (1968). The court held that this provision did not incorporate the doctrine of interspousal immunity but merely left the common law undisturbed and " 'intact with its inherent capacity for later judicial alteration.' " *Id.* 56 N.J. at 486, 267 A.2d at 483. The court went on to scrutinze the reasons behind the rule of interspousal immunity and abrogated the rule at least with respect to automobile negligence torts.

The Supreme Court of Indiana in abrogating interspousal immunity in the case of *Brooks v. Robinson*, 259 Ind. 16, 284 N.E.

2d 794 (1972), construed a similar statutory limitation to the same effect, holding that the Legislature was not barring tort actions between husband and wife but was preserving the rule of interspousal immunity in its common law form "subject to amendment, modification, or abrogation by this Court." *Id.* at 24, 284 N.E.2d at 798.[3]

[2] With respect to G.L. c. 209, § 6, it was open to the Legislature to take the position that while it did not wish to abolish the common law rule of interspousal immunity neither did it wish to convert the common law rule into a mandate of statutory law. In G.L. c. 209, § 6, it chose apt language to express such an intention. The Legislature apparently recognized the broad scope of the language, "A married woman may sue and be sued in the same manner as if she were sole," and realized that unless some limiting provision were included the statute itself could be construed as authorizing suits between spouses. By making clear that the statute itself does not alter the rule of interspousal immunity, the Legislature closed the path taken by many courts in other jurisdictions in interpreting the broad, general provisions of their married women's acts as in and of themselves removing the barrier of interspousal immunity. See, e. g., *Katzenberg v. Katzenberg*,

band and wife." This statutory language was adopted with minor changes in subsequent consolidations and revisions of the laws of the Commonwealth. See Pub.Sts. (1882), c. 147, § 7; R.L. (1902), c. 153, § 6. Finally, in St.1963, c. 765, § 2, the Legislature added the language authorizing interspousal suits on contracts entered into pursuant to G.L. c. 209, § 2, which section was simultaneously amended to authorize such contracts (St. 1963, c. 765, § 1) and now reads, "A married woman may make contracts, oral and written, sealed and unsealed, in the same manner as if she were sole, and may make such contracts with her husband."

3. The court in the *Brooks* case was concerned with the following statutory language of TR. 17(D) of the Indiana Rules of Procedure: "*Sex, marital and parental status.* For the purposes of suing or being sued there shall

be *no distinction* between men and women or between men and women because of marital or parental status; *provided, however, that this subsection (D) shall not apply to actions in tort.*" The court held that this language should not be construed as "anything more than *legislative awareness* of the judicially created doctrine of the common law. The proviso in TR. 17(D) does not purport to abolish tort actions between husband and wife. Rather it merely provides that if any distinction between husband and wife exists in tort actions, such distinction is not removed by the rule as adopted. The 'distinction' which has existed up to the present is, of course, the common law doctrine of interspousal immunity which is, and always has been, subject to amendment, modification, or abrogation by this Court." *Brooks v. Robinson, supra* at 23–24, 284 N.E.2d at 798 (emphasis in the quoted opinion).

Exhibit 13-7 *Lewis v. Lewis*   (continues)

LEWIS v. LEWIS
Cite as, Mass., 351 N.E.2d 526   Mass. **531**

183 Ark. 626, 37 S.W.2d 696 (1931); *Lorang v. Hays,* 69 Idaho 440, 209 P.2d 733 (1949); *Brown v. Gosser,* 262 S.W.2d 480 (Ky.1953); *Gilman v. Gilman,* 78 N.H. 4, 95 A. 657 (1915); *Wait v. Pierce,* 191 Wis. 202, 209 N.W. 475 (1926). On the other hand, G.L. c. 209, § 6, does not directly forbid tort suits between husband and wife. The Legislature could have used language more prohibitory in nature had it been its intention to bar such suits; and its choice of the words, "shall not authorize" cannot be considered inadvertent or accidental. Compare with G.L. c. 209, § 6, the Married Women's Property Act of the English Parliament, 45 & 46 Vict., c. 75, § 12 (1882), which provides that "no husband or wife shall be entitled to sue the other for a tort," and Ill.Rev.Stat. c. 68, § 1 (1973), which provides: "A married woman may, in all cases, sue and be sued without joining her husband with her, to the same extent as if she were unmarried; *provided, that neither husband nor wife may sue the other for a tort to the person committed during coverture"* (emphasis supplied).

In *Frankel v. Frankel,* 173 Mass. 214, 53 N.E. 398 (1899), holding that the enactment of the statutory language now contained in G.L. c. 209, § 6, did not abolish the equitable remedies previously available between husband and wife, this court noted that "[t]he section referred to above does not forbid suits between husband and wife, but simply provides that it shall not be construed to authorize them." *Id.* at 215, 53 N.E. at 398. See *Zwick v. Goldberg,* 304 Mass. 66, 70, 22 N.E.2d 661 (1939). In addition, in *Gahm v. Gahm,* 243 Mass. 374, 375, 137 N.E. 876 (1923), a case decided prior to the amendments to G.L. c. 209, §§ 2, 6, contained in St.1963, c. 765, §§ 1, 2, which authorize contracts between husband and wife and suits on those contracts, the court observed that "[t]he common-law disabilities of married women as to the making of contracts have been removed by statute so that they now can contract and

sue and be sued in the same manner as if single, subject, however, to the limitation that contracts and suits between husband and wife are not permissible but *stand on the same footing as heretofore"* (emphasis supplied). The "footing" which was the basis of the prohibition of suits between husband and wife "heretofore" was the *common law rule* of interspousal immunity. See *Fowle v. Torrey,* 135 Mass. 87, 89–90 (1883). The "shall not authorize" language of G.L. c. 209, § 6, would appear then to be a reference to, not an incorporation of, the common law rule of interspousal immunity. We conclude that the statute has left the rule in its common law status susceptible to reëxamination and alteration by this court.

[3, 4] The defendant further argues that even if interspousal immunity is not mandated by statute, a common law rule of such long standing should be abolished, if at all, by legislative and not judicial action. The defendant concedes, as he must, that it is within the power and authority of the court to abrogate this judicially created rule; and the mere longevity of the rule does not by itself provide cause for us to stay our hand if to perpetuate the rule would be to perpetuate inequity. When the rationales which gave meaning and coherence to a judicially created rule are no longer vital, and the rule itself is not consonant with the needs of contemporary society, a court not only has the authority but also the duty to reëxamine its precedents rather than to apply by rote an antiquated formula. Chief Justice Vanderbilt described this interaction between the judiciary and the evolving common law in an oft cited passage from *State v. Culver,* 23 N.J. 495, 505, 129 A.2d 715, 721, cert. denied, 354 U.S. 925, 77 S.Ct. 1387, 1 L.Ed.2d 1441 (1957): "One of the great virtues of the common law is its dynamic nature that makes it adaptable to the requirements of society at the time of its application in court. There is not a rule of the common

Exhibit 13-7 *Lewis v. Lewis*   *(continues)*

532 Mass.   **351 NORTH EASTERN REPORTER, 2d SERIES**

law in force today that has not evolved from some earlier rule of common law, gradually in some instances, more suddenly in others, leaving the common law of today when compared with the common law of centuries ago as different as day is from night. The nature of the common law requires that each time a rule of law is applied it be carefully scrutinized to make sure that the conditions and needs of the times have not so changed as to make further application of it the instrument of injustice. Dean Pound posed the problem admirably in his *Interpretations of Legal History* (1922) when he stated, 'Law must be stable, and yet it cannot stand still.' "

This court has frequently had occasion to effect through its decisions not insignificant changes in the field of tort law. See, e. g., *Sorensen v. Sorensen*, —— Mass. —— [c], 339 N.E.2d 907 (1975); *Mone v. Greyhound Lines, Inc.*, —— Mass. —— [d], 331 N. E.2d 916 (1975); *Diaz v. Eli Lilly & Co.*, 364 Mass. 153, 302 N.E.2d 555 (1973), and cases cited at 166 n. 43, 302 N.E.2d 555. In the *Diaz* case, in rejecting the argument that the court should defer to the Legislature on the question of recovery for loss of consortium, we noted that "the Legislature may rationally prefer to act, if it acts at all, after rather than before the common law has fulfilled itself in its own way." *Id.* at 166, 302 N.E.2d at 563. We are of opinion that this is an especially appropriate comment in the context of this case where the Legislature in G.L. c. 209, § 6, has recognized the rule of interspousal immunity but has left the rule in its common law form, expressing the preference, at least implicitly, that this court continue to evaluate the usefulness and propriety of the rule. We further note that the argument that any change in the doctrine of interspousal immunity should come from the Legislature, not the judiciary, has been considered and rejected in many decisions

abrogating the common law rule. See, e. g., *Brooks v. Robinson*, 259 Ind. 16, 22–23, 284 N.E.2d 794 (1972); *Beaudette v. Frana*, 285 Minn. 366, 370–371, 173 N.W.2d 416 (1969); *Rupert v. Stienne*, 90 Nev. 397, 399–401, 528 P.2d 1013 (1974); *Immer v. Risko*, 56 N.J. 482, 487, 267 A.2d 481 (1970); *Flores v. Flores*, 84 N.M. 601, 603–604, 506 P.2d 345 (Ct.App.1973); *Freche v. Freche*, 81 Wash.2d 183, 189, 500 P.2d 771 (1972).

[5–7] We conclude therefore that it is open to this court to reconsider the common law rule of interspousal immunity and, having done so, we are of opinion that it should no longer bar an action by one spouse against another in a case such as the present one. We believe this result is consistent with the general principle that if there is tortious injury there should be recovery, and only strong arguments of public policy should justify a judicially created immunity for tortfeasors and bar to recovery for injured victims. See *Morash & Sons, Inc. v. Commonwealth*, 363 Mass. 612, 621, 296 N.E.2d 461 (1973); *Freehe v. Freehe, supra*, 81 Wash.2d at 192, 500 P.2d 771. We have examined the reasons offered in support of the common law immunity doctrine and, whatever their vitality in the social context of generations past, we find them inadequate today to support a general rule of interspousal tort immunity. In arriving at this conclusion we are mindful that the rights and privileges of husbands and wives with respect to one another are not unaffected by the marriage they have voluntarily undertaken together. Conduct, tortious between two strangers, may not be tortious between spouses because of the mutual concessions implied in the marital relationship. For this reason we limit our holding today to claims arising out of motor vehicle accidents. Further definition of the scope of

c. Mass.Adv.Sh. (1975) 3662.

d. Mass.Adv.Sh. (1975) 2326.

Exhibit 13-7 *Lewis v. Lewis*   (continues)

COMMONWEALTH v. LODER   Mass. 533
Cite as, Mass.App., 351 N.E.2d 533

the new rule of interspousal tort liability will await development in future cases.[4]

It follows that the motion for summary judgment should not have been allowed and that the judgment is to be vacated.

So ordered.

COMMONWEALTH
v.
Robert D. LODER.

Appeals Court of Massachusetts, Middlesex.

Argued May 10, 1976.

Decided July 27, 1976.

Defendant was convicted in Superior Court, Middlesex County, of rape, armed robbery, burglary and the commission of an unnatural and lascivious act, and he appealed. The Appeals Court held that the trial court acted correctly in denying in part defendant's motion to suppress in-court and out-of-court identifications by the victims.

Affirmed.

Criminal Law ⚌ 339.7(1), 339.8(1)

In prosecution for rape and related offenses, trial court acted properly in refusing to suppress photographic and other pretrial identifications of defendant by victims.

Daniel F. Toomey, Boston, for defendant.

Bonnie H. MacLeod-Griffin, Asst. Dist. Atty., for the Commonwealth.

Before HALE, C. J., and KEVILLE and GOODMAN, JJ.

RESCRIPT.

The defendant appeals under G.L. c. 278, §§ 33A–33G from convictions, after a jury trial, of rape, armed robbery and burglary, and the commission of an unnatural and lascivious act. He claims error in the denial in part, after a voir dire, of his motion to suppress in-court and out-of-court identifications by the victims, a young man and woman. At the time of the crimes the victims were occupying the bedroom of an apartment of the young woman. Two men entered and assaulted them during a period of one and one-half to two hours. The only light in the room came from a street light opposite the window and lights from the park across the street. These dimly illuminated the room. In the course of the episode the young man, despite being nearsighted, was able to view both assailants for a total period of ten minutes. For one minute, the face of the individual, later identified by the victims as the defendant, was only several inches distant from his eyes. The young woman was assaulted by the defendant for approximately thirty minutes. During that time her face was within inches of his face. Later that day the young man selected the defendant's photograph from an array of more than one hundred photographs shown him by the police and the young woman separately selected the defendant's photograph from six to ten

4. In *Sorensen v. Sorensen*, —— Mass. ——, ——, 339 N.E.2d 907 (1975) (Mass.Adv.Sh. [1975] 3662, 3665), in abrogating parental immunity in automobile tort cases we limited the liability to the extent of the parent's automobile liability insurance coverage. In the present case there is nothing in the record concerning the availability or the amount of the defendant's liability insurance, and we do not refer to insurance as a limiting factor in our holding. We do not interpret the logic (as opposed to the precise holding) of *Sorensen* as turning on the availability of insurance in each case, and we decline to limit liability in interspousal tort actions in such a fashion.

Do not overlook this footnote. It is part of the *Lewis* decision.

Exhibit 13-7 *Lewis v. Lewis (concluded)*

how the intermediate court decides. Therefore, to save time, the middle step of going through the intermediate appellate court on the way to the highest court is simply omitted.

DISCUSSION QUESTIONS

10. Compare the court's view in *Lewis* regarding the need to defer to the legislative branch with that of the court in *McBoyle*. Those cases, as well as the dissent in *Johnson*, illustrate a constant tension in our system between the elected legislature and the appointed judiciary. While the court will often defer to the legislative branch, there are times when it will not, especially in areas of law not yet touched by legislation. It is then that you will probably see a phrase similar to the one used by the *Lewis* court: "[T]he court not only has the authority but also the duty to reexamine its precedents." Do you think it is appropriate in a democratic society for a court to wield such power?

11. What exactly did Mrs. Lewis win?

12. On page 529 of the opinion, the court cites *Sorensen v. Sorensen*, a case in which a child wanted to sue his father for negligent driving. By citing this case the court seems to suggest that the same principles that apply to children suing their parents should apply to spouses suing each other. Do you agree?

Legal Reasoning Exercise

3. Based on *Lewis* analyze whether you think the doctrine of spousal immunity will bar Janice's claim.

E. THE POWER OF THE COURTS TO MAKE NEW LAW

In this chapter we have examined how to interpret the four major types of court opinions. In *McBoyle* the Court thought it was bound to narrowly interpret the statute. In another, *Johnson*, the Court struck down a state statute as unconstitutional. In *Callow* the court clung to stare decisis, whereas in *Lewis* the same court chose to remake the law.

How can you know whether a court will take a more liberal or a more conservative view of its role in changing the law? You can never know for sure, but here are some general guidelines. First, remember that all courts, even the U.S. Supreme Court, are bound to follow the Constitution. Therefore, the first question to ask is whether the issue involves a constitutional provision. If it does, then the court has the power to invalidate any statute or common law principle that is not in conformity with the Constitution.

If there is no constitutional provision involved, then the court's only role in statutory cases is to interpret the statute. The court is not free to rewrite the statute to reach a result that it thinks is more just. This is the type of case where the court has the least amount of freedom. (Of course, a determined court can often find ambiguity in the seemingly clearest of language and thereby "rewrite" the statute.) If there is no constitutional provision and no statute involved,

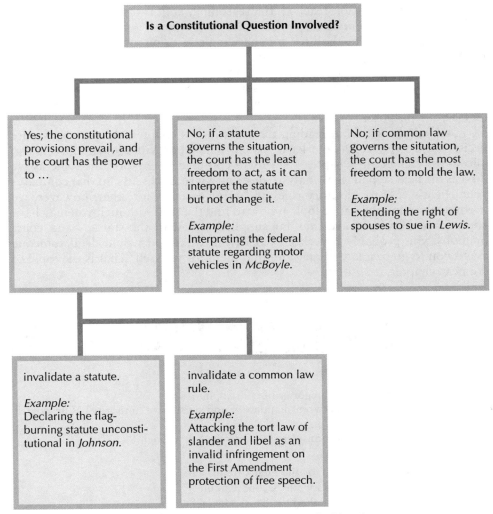

Figure 13-5   Factors Affecting the Power of a Court to Make New Law

then the court has the most freedom to shape the common law as it deems best to meet the needs of justice. See Figure 13-5, on page 385.

SUMMARY

When interpreting a court opinion you must first determine if it is mandatory or persuasive authority. Mandatory authority comes from a higher court in the same jurisdiction. Second, you should be aware of the standard elements of any court opinion: the headnotes (in West editions) and the syllabus (prepared by the court or by West), the facts of the case, the statement of existing law, the

issues raised, the decision reached, the reasoning, and, if they exist, concurring and/or dissenting opinions.

The traditional method for summarizing court opinions is known as case briefing. In this chapter we have examined one approach to case briefing that emphasizes the analytical skills that are the focus of this book. Depending on your purpose, however, you or your supervising attorney may wish to follow another method. There is no one right way to brief. Use the method that best serves your purpose.

As you can see from reading the cases in this chapter, the theory of stare decisis plays a vital role in our legal system: While it provides for stability, it also allows for change. In Chapter 15 we will continue to explore this topic as we discuss the next step in legal analysis: drafting a written discussion that compares your client's case to statutory rules and prior cases. Before that, however, we need to take a more detailed look at how to find the law. Although you may have appreciated how we have thus far supplied you with the statutes and court opinions, you probably have been wondering what you would do if someone asked you to go to a law library and find them for yourself. That is the topic of the next chapter.

REVIEW QUESTIONS

Pages 333 through 344
1. What are the four basic categories of court opinions?
2. What is the difference between mandatory and persuasive authority? Why does it matter?

Listed below are the possible answers for Questions 3 through 8.

a. U.S. Supreme Court
b. U.S. Court of Appeals for the First Circuit
c. U.S. Court of Appeals for the Second Circuit
d. U.S. District Court for the District of Massachusetts
e. Massachusetts Supreme Judicial Court
f. New Hampshire Supreme Court
g. Massachusetts Appeals Court
h. Massachusetts Superior Court
i. New Hampshire trial court

3. If the U.S. District Court for the District of Massachusetts heard a case regarding a federal statutory issue, which of the courts listed above could issue decisions that the district court would have to follow? Why?
4. If the U.S. Court of Appeals for the First Circuit heard a case regarding a federal statutory issue, which of the courts listed above could issue decisions that the court of appeals would have to follow? Why?
5. If the U.S. Supreme Court heard a case regarding a federal statutory issue, which of the courts listed above could issue decisions that the U.S. Supreme Court would have to follow? Why?
6. If a Massachusetts superior court (a trial court) heard a case regarding a Massachusetts state law issue, which of the courts listed above could issue decisions that the superior court would have to follow? Why?

7. If the Massachusetts Appeals Court (an intermediate-level appellate court) heard a case regarding a Massachusetts state law issue, which of the courts listed above could issue decisions that the appeals court would have to follow? Why?

8. If the Massachusetts Supreme Judicial Court (the highest appellate court in Massachusetts) heard a case regarding a Massachusetts state law issue, which of the courts listed above could issue decisions that the Supreme Judicial Court would have to follow? Why?

9. For each of the situations listed in Questions 3-8, indicate which of the following would be seen as mandatory authority by the court hearing the case. Give a short explanation for each of your answers. (Assume all constitutional provisions and statutes deal with the same issue that the court is facing.)

    a. U.S. constitutional provision

    b. U.S. statute

    c. Massachusetts statute

    d. Massachusetts constitutional provision

    e. New Hampshire constitutional provision

    f. New Hampshire statute

10. What is the difference between analogizing a case and distinguishing a case?

11. Give an example of when a court decided to overrule precedent and thereby dramatically changed the current law.

12. Why does court-made law generally evolve slowly?

13. Explain the difference between overruling a decision and reversing a decision.

Pages 344 through 384

14. List each part of a brief, and describe the function of each.

15. Look at each of the following potential case holdings for the *Blair* case. Which one do you think best represents a holding as it should appear in a case brief? Why? What is wrong with the others? Which is the broadest holding? The narrowest?

    a. Yes. *too brief*

    b. Yes, burglary is committed when someone enters a partially enclosed *- rules missing* carwash.

    c. Yes, it is unlawful to enter a partially enclosed carwash. *- rule is missing*

    d. Yes, the defendant should be found guilty. *guilty of what ?*

    e. Yes, burglary, which requires the entering of a building or house trailer, is committed when someone enters any partially enclosed building designed to protect people or property. *too broad*

    f. Yes, burglary, which requires the entering of a building or house trailer, is committed when someone enters a partially enclosed carwash. *- good - not too broad or narrow*

    g. Reversed. *- only procedural info .*

    h. The trial court's decision was correct.

16. Why is it sometimes important to include the reasoning of concurring and/or dissenting opinions in a case brief?

Chapter 14

Finding the Law

I have found that a great part of the information I have was acquired by looking for something and finding something else on the way.
Franklin P. Adams

INTRODUCTION

In Chapters 12 and 13 we described how you can locate statutory materials and court cases when you have a formal citation. In this chapter we will introduce you to some of the basic researching aids that will help you find and better understand both primary and secondary legal materials.

This chapter begins with a research strategy that assumes the researcher knows very little about the particular area involved. A paralegal who comes to a legal problem with a more complete background can eliminate some of the preliminary stages of the researching process. One caution: If you feel overwhelmed by the amount of material in this chapter, do not despair. It takes years of experience to become a truly competent legal researcher, but it can be done.

In this chapter we will follow the process that a paralegal might use to research the issue of spousal immunity. Recall the situation of Janice Miller, who was injured while working in her backyard with her husband, George. Because the problem of Janice and George occurred in Springfield, Massachusetts, we will focus our research on Massachusetts law. However, the principles that we will be discussing can be applied to research in any state. Because the purpose of this chapter is to introduce you to the many researching resources, our journey will be more all-inclusive than would be typical of a normal researching session.

A. OVERVIEW OF THE RESEARCHING PROCESS

Primary authority
The law itself, such as statutes and court opinions.

Your main goal in conducting legal research is to look for and find **primary authority**—that is, court opinions and enacted law (such as statutes and regulations) governing the situation. Your starting point for your research will depend on what you already know about the facts of the case and the law in that general area.

If, for example, your boss hands you the citation for a statute or court opinion, you can go directly to the appropriate volume of the code or reporter and proceed to read the cited document. Even if you do not have a citation, if you are fairly familiar with the area of law, you might go directly to primary sources. For example, if you knew that a statute governed the situation but did not know its citation, you could go directly to the statutes and search the index for the relevant citation. If you knew that the problem was governed by case law but did not have a citation, you could not go directly to the court reporters. Unlike statutes, which are organized by subject matter and contain their own indexes, court opinions are organized chronologically, being published in the order in which they are decided. To solve the problem of locating a court opinion by subject matter, West Group has provided us with a master index to all court opinions, the **digests**. These are organized by subject matter and will help you find relevant court opinions.

Digest
A book that contains court opinion headnotes arranged by subject matter.

If, on the other hand, your boss gives you no information other than the client's facts, you may have absolutely no idea if the situation will be covered by statutes or court opinions or both. Your best approach then might be to begin your work in the **secondary sources** and read general background information on your topic. Secondary sources tell you about the law. Secondary sources, such as legal encyclopedias, are a great resource because they have done much of the preliminary research for you. While your goal is to find primary sources,

Secondary authority
Information about the law, such as that contained in encyclopedias and law review articles.

Figure 14-1 Primary and Secondary Authority

Books That Contain the Law (Primary Authority)	Books about the Law (Secondary Authority)	Books That Index (Help You Locate) the Law (Secondary Authority)
Statutory codes	Encyclopedias *General* Am. Jr 2d C.J.S. *State Specific* Ex.: Mass. Practice	Digests
Case reporters	Scholarly publications Law school journals Ex.: Harvard Law Review Bar Association Journals Ex.: ABA Journal	American Law Reports
Regulations	Newspapers *National* Ex.: National Law Journal *State Specific* Ex.: Mass. Lawyer's Weekly	Shepard's

secondary sources are a great beginning point. Not only will they give you general background information, but also they will often include references to relevant primary authority. Figure 14-1, page 390, gives you a listing of the types of books you will encounter in your library.

B. THE FIVE STEPS OF LEGAL RESEARCH

Legal research involves five basic steps:

1. Identify your search terms.
2. Go to secondary authority (optional).
3. Go to primary authority.
4. Update your research.
5. Decide when to stop researching.

Step two is labeled optional because, for example, a paralegal already familiar with spousal immunity law would know that issues of spousal immunity involve state tort law and, after identifying the relevant search terms, could proceed directly to finding state statutes and court opinions. A paralegal not familiar with the law in this area might first turn to secondary sources in order to learn some of the basic principles of spousal immunity law and decide where to begin researching in primary authority.

1. Identify Your Search Terms

Because much of your research will begin with indexes, you need to develop a list of words to describe your client's facts and the legal issues. These will be the words that you will look for in the indexes. Several techniques have been developed to help you think of words to look for. They include TAPP—Thing, Acts, Person, or Place (developed by Lawyers Co-operative)—and TARP—Thing, Cause of Action, Relief, Parties (developed by Jacobstein & Mersky). The function of these acronyms is simply to suggest words that you could look for in an index. Once you have thought of words that fit these categories, you should try to enlarge your search possibilities by thinking of synonyms, antonyms, broader words, and narrower words. For example, in a case involving possible malpractice by a pediatrician, for Person or Parties you would certainly think of *physician*. Synonyms would include *doctor* and perhaps *surgeon*. A broader term might be *medical professional* or *practitioner*, while narrower terms would include *pediatrician* and *pediatric neurologist*.

In analyzing Janice's situation we can see that the central research issue concerns her ability to sue her husband. We begin by developing a list of words that indexers might use to categorize this problem. In this case Cause of Action (as well as defenses) and Person or Parties seem to be the most likely categories. Possible words to look for in indexes include

> **PRACTICE TIP**
>
> Always think through your proposed researching project before entering the library or going on-line.

Cause of Action or Defenses:	Tort, Negligence, Action, Interspousal Immunity, Immunity, Spousal Immunity
Person or Parties:	Spouses, Marriage, Husband, Wife

Can you think of other words?

It is always best to enter the library with too many rather than too few possibilities. There is a strange library fog that settles on many researchers that prevents them from thinking. If you have thought of only a few words before entering the library and then you do not find them in an index, be assured that this mysterious fog will settle in and prevent you from thinking of any alternative approaches. Therefore, do your brainstorming *before* entering the library. Assume you will not be able to find any of your initial words in an index. To handle that eventuality, come to the library armed with a long list of possible words. Also think of several synonyms for each word. Alternatively, if you can find nothing in one source, try a different one. Different indexers use different words to categorize the same topic.

As an example, let's assume you wished to start your research in a general legal encyclopedia, such as Am. Jur. 2d. (We discuss legal encyclopedias more fully below.) To locate the appropriate sections to research, you would begin by consulting the index. The index is printed in separate volumes at the end of the series. The procedure is similar to that used in reading any normal index. The key is to determine the correct words to locate. Exhibit 14-1, on page 393, demonstrates that if you look up the word Spouse in the Am. Jur. 2d index, you will find that this is not the correct word. However, the indexers for Am. Jur. 2d anticipated that this is a word you might use and direct you to the topic Husband and Wife in the index, reproduced here as Exhibit 14-2 on page 394.

As this index entry shows, you may find what appear to be too many listings. Should you write down all of them or try to be selective? At this stage of your research your best approach is to write down all the possibilities and check them all. It is better to include too many possibilities than to eliminate a potentially relevant section. If you have no luck finding index entries in one source, you can switch to another source, and you may have more success.

Although indexes can be very frustrating to use, once you have found relevant information in one source, you will rarely have to start from scratch with a new resource. This is because many resources cross-reference each other. If you are lucky enough to have a cross-reference from another source, simply go to the proper section in that source, and read about your topic.

2. Go to Secondary Authority (Optional)

Secondary authority is helpful because it contains general overviews of various areas of the law, as well as citations to primary authority. You can find general overviews of various areas of the law in encyclopedias, treatises, articles in periodicals, and annotations.

Treatises, periodical articles, and annotations usually focus on a specific topic. Encyclopedias provide a broader overview of the general language and principles of the law.

a. National Legal Encyclopedias

There are two major national encyclopedias: **American Jurisprudence Second**, most commonly referred to and cited as **Am. Jur. 2d**, and **Corpus Juris Secundum**, referred to as **C.J.S.** Each encyclopedia is divided into hundreds of separate topics, ranging from abandoned property to zoning and planning.

AMERICAN JURISPRUDENCE 2d

SPLITTING CAUSES OF ACTION —Cont'd
Wages, claims for payment, **Actions** § 120
Waiver of rule against splitting, **Actions** § 113
Wrongful death actions. Death and death actions, above

SPLITTING CLAIMS
Courts, effect on amount in controversy, **Courts** § 127
Trusts, **Trusts** § 659

SPLITTING COMMISSIONS OR FEES
Notaries public, **Notaries** § 25
Partnerships, **Partn** § 234
Physicians and surgeons, **Phys & S** § 82, 157
Profit Sharing (this index)

SPLITTING OF CORPORATE STOCK
Corporations (this index)

SPLITTING OF MOTIONS
Generally, **Motions** § 6

SPLITTING PROFITS
Profit Sharing (this index)

SPLIT TRIAL
Joint or Separate Action or Trial (this index)

SPLIT WEEK PLANS, OVERTIME, Labor § 4341

SPOILAGE OF GOODS
Contamination (this index)

SPOLIATION
Alteration of Instruments (this index)
Evidence, **Evid** § 244
Property. **Destruction of Property** (this index)

SPONATSKI RULE
Workers' compensation, **Work C** § 344

SPONGES
Malpractice By Medical Profession (this index)

SPONSORS
Cooperative Apartments (this index)
Supplemental Security Income (SSI) (this index)

SPONSORS OR SPONSORED AFFAIRS
Aliens and Citizens (this index)
Copyright and literary property, **Copy & Lit P** § 199
Penal and correctional institutions, religious services sponsor, **Penal Inst** § 37, 41

SPONSORS OR SPONSORED AFFAIRS—Cont'd
Pensions and Retirement (this index)
Recall election or petition, **Pub Off** § 214
Statutes, statements by sponsors of bill as aid to construction, **Stat** § 177
Workers' compensation, sponsorship of recreational activities, **Work C** § 287, 288

SPONTANEITY
Homicide, res gestae, **Homi** § 325

SPONTANEOUS COMBUSTION
Insurance, **Ins** § 685
Ships and shipping, **Ins** § 685; **Ship** § 841

SPONTANEOUS DECLARATIONS
Res Gestae (this index)

SPONTANEOUS REMARKS OF AGENTS, Labor § 998

SPONTANEOUS RESCUE
Generally. **Negl** § 1089

SPONTANEOUS UTTERANCES
Carriers. personal injuries, **Carriers** § 1183

SPORADIC ACTS
Casual or Occasional Acts or Matters (this index)

SPORADIC PURSUITS
Social security. **Soc Sec** § 555

SPORTS
Entertainment and Sports Law (this index)

SPORTS AND ATHLETICS
Gambling on sports events. **Gambl** § 79
Highways, Streets, and Bridges (this index)
Hotels and motels, premises liability, **Hotels** § 116

SPORTS ARENAS
Civil rights, **Civ R** § 260

SPORTSHIRTS
Contempt, **Contempt** § 73

SPOT REMOVER
Expert and opinion evidence, spot remover causing hepatitis. **Expert** § 252

SPOTS AND STAINS
Bloodstains (this index)
Expert and opinion evidence. **Expert** § 293. 294

SPOT ZONING
Generally, **Zoning** § 146-159
For detailed treatment, see index topic **Zoning and Planning** (this index)

SPOUSAL SUPPORT
Divorce and Separation (this index)

SPOUSE
Husband and wife (this index)

SPOUT
Downspout (this index)

SPRAINS
Damages (this index)

SPRAY OR SPRAYING
Adjoining landowners. **Adj L** § 38
Aerosol Containers (this index)
Aviation generally, **Avi** § 169
Dusting Crops or Vegetation (this index)
Premises liability, **Prem Liab** § 558
Zoning and planning. **Zoning** § 493

SPRAY TRUSTS
Trusts. **Trusts** § 11

SPREADING VEGETATION
Adjoining landowners. **Adj L** § 30

SPRING GUN
Nuisances. **Nuis** § 222
Premises liability, generally, **Prem Liab** § 195, 196

SPRING GUNS
Homicide. **Homi** § 76

SPRINGING AND SHIFTING USES
Trusts (this index)

SPRINGS
Water Pollution (this index)

SPRINGS-WATERS
Waters (this index)

SPRINKLER SYSTEMS
Building regulations, **Bldgs** § 28
Fixtures, **Fixt** § 106, 107

SPRINKLING AND SPRINKLER DEVICES OR SYSTEMS
Automatic Sprinkler System or Fire Extinguisher (this index)
Expert and opinion evidence. **Expert** § 344
Highways, Streets. and Bridges (this index)
Insurance, **Ins** § 479, 521, 1198, 1244, 1245
Telecommunications. **Telecom** § 200
Warehouses (this index)

SPRINKLING TRUSTS
Trusts, **Trusts** § 11

SPURIOUS CLASS ACTION
Class Actions or Proceedings (this index)

512   For assistance using this index, call 1-800-328-4880

Exhibit 14-1   American Jurisprudence Second, Index

Each topic is broken down into numerous subtopics. Each subtopic contains a narrative description of the general rules in that area. Wherever different states follow conflicting rules, the encyclopedia points out the conflict and briefly explains both positions. In addition to this type of general narrative discussion, Am. Jur. 2d provides various cross-references with citations to specific court cases, selected law review articles, other sections of Am. Jur. 2d, and annotations in American Law Reports Annotated. This latter reference is

Once you look under the topic **Husband and Wife** and then the subtopic **Immunity from suit, Interspousal,** you will find several likely entries.

To find the first entry, you would go to the main volume (not the index) that contains the topic Husband & Wife and look for Section 291. (§ stands for section.)

In an index you may notice the use of the words infra, supra, and et seq. In this index, the word below is used instead of infra and the word above is used instead of supra. Et seq. simply means "and following."

AMERICAN JURISPRUDENCE 2d

HUSBAND AND WIFE—Cont'd
Governing law, **Marr § 63**
Governing law. Conflict of Laws (this index)
Grandchildren or Grandparents (this index)
Grounds. Alimony, support, or maintenance without divorce, suit for, above
Guardian and ward
   mental incompetent, marriage of, **Marr § 23**
   minor, consent to marriage of, **Marr § 17**
Guardian and Ward (this index)
Guilt or innocence, adultery and fornication, innocent spouse. **Adult § 8, 9**
Habeas corpus, restraint without judicial order, **Hab Corp § 89**
Harboring criminals, **Harb § 2**
Head of family, rights of husband as, **Husb & W § 10**
Health
   Annulment of Marriage (this index)
   Breach of Promise (this index)
Heart Balm Statutes (this index)
Home, obligation to provide, **Husb & W § 171**
Homestead (this index)
Homicide (this index)
Husband and Wife (this index)
Husband's duty to support. Support, duty of, below
Idiots or imbeciles. Insane or other incompetent persons, below
Illegality. Unlawful or irregular marriages, below
Illegitimate Children (this index)
Illicit sexual relations, interference with family relationships by soliciting another's wife for sexual intercourse. **Torts § 33**
Immunity from suit, interspousal
   generally. **Husb & W § 291-302**
   abrogation or modification of doctrine generally, **Husb & W § 292-294**
   statute, by, **Husb & W § 293**
   annulment of marriage, separation, or divorce, effect of, **Husb & W § 297**
   application of rule in particular circumstances, **Husb & W § 296-302**
   community property, abrogation in jurisdictions following doctrine of, **Husb & W § 294**
   employer's liability for married employee's tort, **Husb & W § 300**
   estate of tortfeasor, action against, **Husb & W § 299**
   insurer's liability, **Husb & W § 301**
   intentional torts, **Husb & W § 302**
   law governing existence of interspousal immunity, **Husb & W § 295**
   motor vehicle, action for negligent operation of, **Husb & W § 302**
   negligence, immunity abolished, **Negl § 1800**
   statute, abrogation or modification of doctrine by, **Husb & W § 293**
   tort committed prior to marriage, **Husb & W § 296**
   trials. **Trial § 503**

594

HUSBAND AND WIFE—Cont'd
Immunity from suit, interspousal—Cont'd
   wrongful death, action for. **Husb & W § 298**
Impairment of Contracts (this index)
Impediments to lawful marriage
   capacity to marry, above
Impediments to marriage
   generally, **Marr § 47-61**
   common law marriage. **Marr § 44**
   divorce, waiting period after. **Marr § 47**
   family relationship of parties. **Incest** (this index)
   incarceration, **Marr § 48**
   same sex of parties, **Marr § 49, 50**
   sex change surgery, **Marr § 50**
   waiting period after divorce, **Marr § 47**
Implied contractual liability for goods and services, **Husb & W § 181**
Impotence, **Marr § 25**
Impotency (this index)
Imprisonment for debt, **Const L § 631**
Improper relations, alienation of affections and criminal conversation. **Husb & W § 274**
Improvements
   agency, improvements to property. **Husb & W § 156**
   community property, liability for debts of other spouse, **Husb & W § 166**
   separately held property, improvement of or service to property of other spouse, **Husb & W § 110**
Imputed negligence
   generally. **Negl § 1773, 1799-1802**
   agency, **Negl § 1799**
   community property, **Negl § 1813**
   instructions to jury, **Negl § 1758**
   joint interest in recovery, **Negl § 1802**
   joint venture or enterprise. **Negl § 1775, 1801**
   loss of consortium, imputation of impaired spouse's negligence to spouse seeking recovery for, **Husb & W § 261**
   nominal plaintiff, **Negl § 1780**
   questions of law and fact, **Negl § 1757**
   statutory abolition, **Negl § 1800**
Incarceration, **Marr § 48**
Incest, husband or wife as witness against spouse, **Incest § 21**
Incest (this index)
Incidental relief. Alimony, support, or maintenance without divorce, suit for, above
Incidental rights and liabilities, partnership, **Husb & W § 163**
Incompetency. Insane or incompetent persons, below
Incompetents. Insane or incompetent persons, below
Indemnity, validity of contract for indemnification of husband for support of wife and children, **Support Per § 7**
Index of conveyance, inclusion of names in. **Records § 94**
Indians, **Marr § 77, 78**
Inducement of marriage
   generally, **Marr § 93-97**

For assistance using this index, call 1-800-328-4880

HUSBAND AND WIFE—Cont'd
Inducement of marriage—Cont'd
   criminal liability, **Marr § 97**
   damages, **Marr § 96**
   third person, liability of. **Marr § 95**
In equity, suit for alimony, support, or maintenance without divorce. **Husb & W § 212**
Infants. Children, above
Inferences. Presumptions, inferences, and burden of proof, below
Injunctions, **Inj § 90**
   transactions with third persons, **Husb & W § 90**
Insane or incompetent persons
   adjudication of insanity
     capacity to marry, **Marr § 23**
   Annulment of Marriage (this index)
   capacity to marry, above
   effect of, duty of support, **Husb & W § 177**
   necessaries, **Husb & W § 337, 338, 368; Incom P § 99 (Special Pamphlet)**
Insolvency (this index)
Insurance (this index)
Intent
   alienation of affections and criminal conversation, **Husb & W § 276**
   common law marriage, **Marr § 37, 43**
   interspousal immunity from suit, intentional torts, **Husb & W § 302**
Interracial marriages. Miscegenation, below
Interspousal debts and liabilities, generally, **Husb & W § 17**
Interspousal immunity from suit. Immunity from suit, interspousal, above
Intoxicating Liquors (this index)
Intoxication. **Marr § 21**
Invalidity. Validity, below
Irregular marriages. Unlawful or irregular marriages, below
Issuance of licenses. Marriage licenses, below
Jest or mock marriage
   annulment of marriage, lack of intent to enter into binding marriage as grounds for, **Annul § 3**
Job Discrimination (this index)
Joinder of parties to action
   husband, **Husb & W § 76**
   loss of consortium, **Husb & W § 269**
   wife, **Husb & W § 77-79**
Joint deposits and accounts, **Banks § 685**
Joint enterprise. **Negl § 1775, 1801**
Joint interest in recovery, negligence, **Negl § 1802**
Jointly committed torts, liability for, right of action against husband or wife or both, **Husb & W § 242**
Joint ownership. Cotenancy and joint ownership, above
Joint Ventures (this index)
Jones Act, **Husb & W § 258**
Judges (this index)
Judgments and decrees
   alimony, support, or maintenance without divorce, suit for, above
   assignment of judgments, **Judgm § 482**

Exhibit 14-2 American Jurisprudence Second, Index

abbreviated as A.L.R. and is discussed in greater detail beginning on page 402. C.J.S. includes cross-references to the key number system used in West's digests. (Beginning on page 414 there is an explanation of key numbers and the digest system.)

Am. Jur. 2d tends to take a fairly selective approach to case inclusion. C.J.S. attempts to be more all-inclusive. You will notice the difference when you compare the amount of textual material with the amount of footnote material. Because C.J.S. includes more case citations, the footnote material tends to dominate its pages.

Our work in the Am. Jur. 2d index (Exhibit 14-2) indicated we should go to the volume containing the topic Husband and Wife and look under sections 291-302. Exhibit 14-3, on page 396, takes you to volume 41 of Am. Jur. 2d and the topic of Husband and Wife. Section 290 begins on page 192 of Am. Jur. 2d. Look at the way in which Am. Jur. 2d begins its discussion of the right of spouses to sue each other. Notice that the footnotes are full of citations to court opinions that support the textual narrative. They are arranged in alphabetical order by state. However, one of the disadvantages of the way Am. Jur. 2d cites cases is that no date is included.

On page 193 of Am. Jur. 2d note the references to A.L.R. annotations. A.L.R. stands for American Law Reports. We discuss it beginning on page 402 in this chapter. Notice the reference to *Lewis v. Lewis* in footnote 89.

Exhibit 14-4, on page 398, shows how C.J.S. discusses the same issue of the right of one spouse to sue the other. Each section begins with bold text. This is the **black letter law** in the area, that is, the generally accepted legal principles. Also locate the references to the digest topic and key numbers. Finally, notice that the number of footnotes exceeds what you would find in Am. Jur. 2d because C.J.S. claims to be all-inclusive. As with Am. Jur. 2d, all cases in the footnotes are listed in alphabetical order by state. Also, once again the dates of the decisions are omitted.

Like most secondary legal reference books, Am. Jur. 2d and C.J.S. are kept current with the publication of **pocket part** supplements. New material is organized to correspond with the section, page, and footnote numbers used in the bound volume. It is then inserted in a special pocket at the back of the volume. When these pocket supplements get too thick and unwieldy, the publisher issues a replacement volume.

Black letter law
Generally accepted legal principles.

Pocket part
A pamphlet inserted into the back of a book containing information new since the volume was published.

b. State-Specific Encyclopedias

Am. Jur. 2d and C.J.S. cover cases from all fifty states. This is useful when you want to compare and contrast the differences between the laws of various states. Usually, however, you will find that only the laws of your state are relevant. In those situations you should use a local encyclopedia specifically geared to your state.

These local encyclopedias carry names such as California Jurisprudence 2d, Michigan Law and Practice, and Pennsylvania Law Encyclopedia. They are usually arranged by topics that parallel those in the national encyclopedias. They have subject analysis sections, indexes, and supplements that also closely resemble those in Am. Jur. 2d and C.J.S. Unfortunately, such local encyclopedias are not published in some states, while other states have two publishers vying for your business. For example, Massachusetts has both the Massachusetts Practice Series and Massachusetts Jurisprudence.

Exhibit 14-5, on page 399, shows the type of discussion that can occur in a state encyclopedia. Notice the cross-references to Westlaw, West's on-line database containing court opinions and statutes from around the country. References

§ 288   HUSBAND AND WIFE   41 Am Jur 2d

criminal conversation, to show the motives, feelings, emotions, and relations of the parties with respect to the loss of affection or consortium or the desertion of the plaintiff by his or her spouse,[80] and in an action for alienation of affections to show affection or lack of affection between the spouses at the time of the alienation.[81]

§ 289. Competence of spouse as witness; maritally privileged communications

The plaintiff in an action for alienation of affection or criminal conversation is generally competent to testify as to the conduct of his or her spouse. A statute which provides that one spouse is not competent to give evidence for or against the other spouse in an action in consequence of adultery or criminal conversation does not bar a spouse's testimony where the other spouse is not a party to the action.[82] A communication between a husband and wife may, however, be privileged under applicable rules of evidence pertaining to marital privilege.[83]

XIII. INTERSPOUSAL IMMUNITY FROM SUIT [§§ 290–301]

A. IN GENERAL [§§ 290–294]

Research References
ALR Digest: Husband and Wife §§ 148-154
ALR Index: Husband and Wife; Privileges and Immunities; Torts

---

§ 290. Generally

The common law established interspousal tort immunity as a consequence of the legal identity of husband and wife: the husband and wife were one person, and that person was the husband, so it was both morally and conceptually objectionable to permit a tort suit between spouses.[84] The doctrine has been justified on the grounds that immunity is necessary to preserve marital harmony

SW2d 470; Turner v PV International Corp. (Tex App Dallas) 765 SW2d 455, writ den (Tex) 778 SW2d 865, rehg of writ of error overr on other grounds (Nov 22, 1989).
Practice References: 1 Am Jur Proof of Facts 237, Adultery.

80. Blaylock v Strecker, 291 Ark 340, 724 SW2d 470.

81. Giltner v Stark (Iowa) 219 NW2d 700; Shaw v Stringer, 101 NC App 513, 400 SE2d 101.

82. Scott v Kiker, 59 NC App 458, 297 SE2d 142 (criticized on other grounds by Cannon v Miller, 71 NC App 460, 322 SE2d 780).

83. Scott v Kiker, 59 NC App 458, 297 SE2d 142 (criticized on other grounds by Cannon v Miller, 71 NC App 460, 322 SE2d 780) (defendant waived privilege by failing to object to

testimony by plaintiff husband concerning conversation he had with his wife).
As to marital privilege, generally, see 81 Am Jur 2d, Witnesses §§ 296-336.

84. Hamilton v Hamilton, 255 Ala 284, 51 So 2d 13 (noting that under statute, actions at law between spouses may be maintained); Rains v Rains, 97 Colo 19, 46 P2d 740; Saunders v Hill (Sup) 57 Del 519, 202 A2d 807 (criticized on other grounds as stated in Hudson v Hudson (Del Super) 532 A2d 620) and (ovrld in part on other grounds by Beattie v Beattie (Del Sup) 630 A2d 1096); Taylor v Vezzani, 109 Ga App 167, 135 SE2d 522; Perkins v Blethen, 107 Me 443, 78 A 574 (ovrld in part on other grounds by Moulton v Moulton (Me) 309 A2d 224); Ex parte Badger, 286 Mo 139, 226 SW 936, 14 ALR 286; Mertz v Mertz, 271 NY 466, 3 NE2d 597, 108 ALR 1120; Shaw v Lee, 258 NC 609, 129 SE2d 288 (superseded by statute on other grounds as stated in Henry v Henry, 291 NC

192

Exhibit 14-3   American Jurisprudence Second, Volume 41   *(continues)*

41 Am Jur 2d   HUSBAND AND WIFE   § 291

by shutting off interspousal disputes[85] and to prevent fraud and collusion between parties to an interspousal suit.[86]

Common-law interspousal tort immunity has withstood a variety of constitutional challenges relating to due process, equal protection, and the availability of remedies generally.[87]

▌▌▌▌ *Practice guide:* The defense of interspousal tort immunity must be affirmatively pleaded and may be waived by failure to include it in the answer.[88]

§ 291.   Abrogation or modification of doctrine; generally

In some jurisdictions, the common law relating to interspousal immunity has been judicially abrogated or modified.[89] Other authority, however, holds that such change is outside the sphere of proper judicial action and that any change in the common-law rule is a matter for the legislature.[90] Courts willing to abrogate the doctrine have done so on the grounds that interspousal immunity

156, 229 SE2d 158) (by statute, spouses may sue each other); Lillienkamp v Rippetoe, 133 Tenn 57, 179 SW 628; Vigilant Ins. Co. v Bennett, 197 Va 216, 89 SE2d 69 (ovrld in part on other grounds by Surratt v Thompson, 212 Va 191, 183 SE2d 200) (statute permits suits between spouses).

The common-law immunity of a husband from action by his wife was based on the conception of husband and wife as one, and the disqualification of the wife from owning property and maintaining actions independently of the husband. Welch v Davis, 410 Ill 130, 101 NE2d 547, 28 ALR2d 656.

Annotations: Modern status of interspousal tort immunity in personal injury and wrongful death actions, 92 ALR3d 901 § 8.

85. Burns v Burns, 111 Ariz 178, 526 P2d 717 (ovrld in part on other grounds by Fernandez v Romo, 132 Ariz 447, 646 P2d 878); Sturiano v Brooks (Fla) 523 So 2d 1126, 13 FLW 224; Shoemake v Shoemake, 200 Ga App 182, 407 SE2d 134, 102-136 Fulton County D R 14B; Counts v Counts, 221 Va 151, 266 SE2d 895.

Annotations: 92 ALR3d 901 § 9.

86. Burns v Burns, 111 Ariz 178, 526 P2d 717 (ovrld in part on other grounds by Fernandez v Romo, 132 Ariz 447, 646 P2d 878); Sturiano v Brooks (Fla) 523 So 2d 1126, 13 FLW 224.

Annotations: 92 ALR3d 901 § 10.

87. Paiewonsky v Paiewonsky (CA3 VI) 446 F2d 178, cert den 405 US 919, 30 L Ed 2d 788, 92 S Ct 944 (applying Virgin Islands law); Harris v Harris, 252 Ga 387, 313 SE2d 88; Heckendorn v First Nat'l Bank, 19 Ill 2d 190, 166 NE2d 571, cert den 364 US 882, 5 L Ed 2d 104, 81 S Ct 172 and (ovrld on other grounds as stated in Farmers Ins. Group v Nudi (1st Dist) 108 Ill

App 3d 151, 63 Ill Dec 897, 438 NE2d 1260); Williams v Williams (3d Dist) 108 Ill App 3d 936, 64 Ill Dec 390, 439 NE2d 1055, mod 98 Ill 2d 128, 74 Ill Dec 495, 455 NE2d 1388.

88. De Guido v De Guido (Fla App D3) 308 So 2d 609.

The defense of interspousal immunity can be waived, because it does not involve subject-matter jurisdiction. Policino v Ehrlich, 478 Pa 5, 385 A2d 968.

89. Brooks v Robinson, 259 Ind 16, 284 NE2d 794; Ebert v Ebert, 232 Kan 502, 656 P2d 766; Boblitz v Boblitz, 296 Md 242, 462 A2d 506; Lewis v Lewis, 370 Mass 619, 351 NE2d 526, 92 ALR3d 890; Beaudette v Frana, 285 Minn 366, 173 NW2d 416; Rupert v Stienne, 90 Nev 397, 528 P2d 1013; Maestas v Overton, 87 NM 213, 531 P2d 947; Shearer v Shearer, 18 Ohio St 3d 94, 18 Ohio BR 129, 480 NE2d 388 (ovrld on other grounds as stated in Petrie v Nationwide Mut. Ins. Co. (Ohio App, Franklin Co) 1994 Ohio App LEXIS 6072); Digby v Digby, 120 RI 299, 388 A2d 1; Davis v Davis (Tenn) 657 SW2d 753; Freehe v Freehe, 81 Wash 2d 183, 500 P2d 771 (ovrld in part on other grounds by Brown v Brown, 100 Wash 2d 729, 675 P2d 1207).

Annotations: Modern status of interspousal tort immunity in personal injury and wrongful death actions, 92 ALR3d 901 § 18.

90. Paiewonsky v Paiewonsky (CA3 VI) 446 F2d 178, cert den 405 US 919, 30 L Ed 2d 788, 92 S Ct 944 (applying Virgin Islands law); Burns v Burns, 111 Ariz 178, 526 P2d 717 (ovrld in part on other grounds by Fernandez v Romo, 132 Ariz 447, 646 P2d 878); Luna v Clayton (Tenn) 655 SW2d 893.

Annotations: 92 ALR3d 901 § 6.

Exhibit 14-3   American Jurisprudence Second, Volume 41 *(concluded)*

---

longer entitled to such presumption.[74]

Thus, when a wife is coerced by her husband to perpetrate an illegal act, she remains exempt from punishment, just as would anyone who

could demonstrate that the crime was committed under duress,[75] and the same rules of proof are applied to duress or coercion by a husband as are applied to duress or coercion by anyone else.[76]

VI. ACTIONS

§ 111. In General

A married woman may sue and be sued in her own name as if she were unmarried.

Library References
Husband and Wife ⬤203, 203½.

The rule at early common law that a married woman could not sue or be sued as a feme sole,[77] is no longer adhered to.[78]

It is now the rule that a married woman may sue and be sued,[79] in her own name,[80] as if she were unmarried.[81]

What law governs.

A number of different choice of law rules or tests have been used to determine whether one spouse has the capacity to sue the other in tort, or is instead barred from doing so by interspous-

al tort immunity, including the most significant relationship test,[82] the government interest analysis,[83] and the place-of-the wrong rule.[84] Where the most significant relationship test is employed, the applicable law will usually be the local law of the state of the married couple's domicile.[85]

Depending on the applicable choice of law rule, whether one spouse has a right of action for loss of consortium or loss of care, consideration and society, has been determined to be governed by the lex loci delicti,[86] or by the law of the married couple's domicile.[87]

§ 112.   Right of Action Between Husband and Wife

Except where prohibited by statute or by the doctrine of interspousal tort immunity, suit may be brought by one spouse against the other.

---

74. N.C.—State v. Smith, 235 S.E.2d 860, 33 N.C.App. 511, certiorari denied Smith v. North Carolina. 98 S.Ct. 1267, 434 U.S. 1076, 55 L.Ed.2d 782.

Doctrine outdated

Independence of women in political, social, and economic matters renders the doctrine of coercion outdated and inapplicable to modern society.
Pa.—Commonwealth v. Santiago, 340 A.2d 440, 462 Pa. 216.

75. N.C.—State v. Smith, 235 S.E.2d 860, 33 N.C.App. 511, certiorari denied Smith v. North Carolina, 98 S.Ct. 1267, 434 U.S. 1076, 55 L.Ed.2d 782.
Pa.—Commonwealth v. Santiago, 340 A.2d 440, 462 Pa. 216.

76. Mass.—Commonwealth v. Barnes, 340 N.E.2d 863, 369 Mass. 462.

77. Fla.—McGill v. Cockrell, 88 So. 268, 81 Fla. 463.
Ga.—Heyman v. Heyman, 92 S.E. 25, 19 Ga.App. 634.
N.J.—Klinger v. Steffens, 6 A.2d 217, 17 N.J.Misc. 118.

78. Alaska—Cramer v. Cramer, 379 P.2d 95.
Ark.—Leach v. Leach, 300 S.W.2d 15, 227 Ark. 599.
Cal.—Self v. Self, 26 Cal.Rptr. 97, 376 P.2d 65, 58 C.2d 683.
Hawaii—Peters v. Peters, 634 P.2d 586, 63 Haw. 653.
Ohio—Kobe v. Kobe, 399 N.E.2d 124, 61 Ohio App.2d 67, 15 O.O.3d 86.
Tex.—Broadway Drug Store of Galveston, Inc. v. Trowbridge, 435 S.W.2d 268.

79. Alaska—Cramer v. Cramer, 379 P.2d 95.
Ark.—Leach v. Leach, 300 S.W.2d 15, 227 Ark. 599.
Mich.—Hosko v. Hosko, 187 N.W.2d 236, 385 Mich. 39.
Neb.—Imig v. March, 279 N.W.2d 382, 203 Neb. 537.

Ohio—Shearer v. Shearer, 480 N.E.2d 388, 18 Ohio St.3d 94, 18 O.B.R. 129.
W.Va.—Coffindaffer v. Coffindaffer, 244 S.E.2d 338, 161 W.Va. 557.

80. Cal.—Self v. Self, 26 Cal.Rptr. 97, 376 P.2d 65, 58 C.2d 683.
W.Va.—Coffindaffer v. Coffindaffer, 244 S.E.2d 338, 161 W.Va. 557.

81. Alaska—Cramer v. Cramer, 379 P.2d 95.
Ark.—Leach v. Leach, 300 S.W.2d 15, 227 Ark. 599.
Mich.—Hosko v. Hosko, 187 N.W.2d 236, 385 Mich. 39.
Neb.—Imig v. March, 279 N.W.2d 382, 203 Neb. 537.
Ohio—Shearer v. Shearer, 480 N.E.2d 388, 18 Ohio St.3d 94, 18 O.B.R. 129.
W.Va.—Coffindaffer v. Coffindaffer, 244 S.E.2d 338, 161 W.Va. 557.

82. Ill.—Nelson v. Hix, 522 N.E.2d 1214, 119 Ill.Dec. 355, 122 Ill.2d 343, certiorari denied 109 S.Ct. 309, 488 U.S. 925, 102 L.Ed.2d 328.
Mo.—Huff v. LaSieur, App., 571 S.W.2d 654.
Tex.—Robertson v. McKnight's Estate, 609 S.W.2d 534.

83. N.J.—Veazey v. Doremus, 510 A.2d 1187, 103 N.J. 244.

84. N.C.—Henry v. Henry, 229 S.E.2d 158, 291 N.C. 156.
Va.—McMillan v. McMillan, 253 S.E.2d 662, 219 Va. 1127.

85. Ill.—Nelson v. Hix, 522 N.E.2d 1214, 119 Ill.Dec. 355, 122 Ill.2d 343, certiorari denied 109 S.Ct. 309, 488 U.S. 925, 102 L.Ed.2d 328.
Mo.—Huff v. LaSieur, App., 571 S.W.2d 654.
Tex.—Robertson v. McKnight's Estate, 609 S.W.2d 534.

86. U.S.—Madison v. Deseret Livestock Co., C.A.Utah, 514 F.2d 1027.
Miller v. Holiday Inn's, Inc., D.C.Va., 436 F.Supp. 460.

87. U.S.—Linnell v. Sloan, C.A.Va., 636 F.2d 65.

407

Exhibit 14-4   Corpus Juris Secundum, Volume 41

to Massachusetts General Laws Annotated are also included. As with national encyclopedias, the textual material is supported by references to case law, here with the focus on Massachusetts state law. Also, as with national encyclopedias, most state encyclopedias are supplemented with pocket parts.

Review the sample pages from a Massachusetts encyclopedia in Exhibit 14-5, on page 399. Note the footnoted references to M.G.L.A. c. 209 §§ 2, 6 (a common but incorrect way of citing to Mass. Gen. Laws Ann.), to *Callow*, and

Ch. 9   **DOMESTIC RELATIONS**   **§ 151**

contract with each other and may bring an action against each other on the contract.[5]

Actions by and between the spouses founded on negligence, once outlawed on the grounds of public policy, even after divorce or annulment,[6] are now maintainable.[7] Courts with equitable jurisdiction will entertain actions between husband and wife (1) to secure her separate property; (2) to prevent fraud; (3) to relieve from coercion; (4) to enforce trusts; (5) to establish other conflicting interests.[8]

Interspousal immunity was diminished in Brown v. Brown,[9] where the wife fell on property owned by her and her husband as tenants by the entirety. The court could find no reason to bar the wife's claim where it was argued that the husband had control of the premises and was responsible for maintaining it after a snowstorm and where the court was persuaded by the argument that

order has health insurance on a group plan available to him through an employer or organization that may be extended to cover the spouse for whom support is ordered. When said court has determined that the obligor has such insurance, said court shall include in the support order a requirement that the obligor exercise the option of additional coverage in favor of such spouse.

See also, M.G.L.A. c. 208 § 1. Cf. Bianco v. Bianco, 371 Mass. 420, 358 N.E.2d 243 (1976).

5. M.G.L.A. c. 209 §§ 2, 6 provide:

§ 2. Married Woman; Power to Contract

A married woman may make contracts, oral and written, sealed and unsealed, in the same manner as if she were sole, and may make such contracts with her husband.

§ 6. Married Woman; Power to Sue and Be Sued

A married woman may sue and be sued in the same manner as if she were sole; but this section shall not authorize suits between husband and wife except in connection with contracts entered into pursuant to the authority contained in section two.

Gahm v. Gahm, 243 Mass. 374, 375, 137 N.E. 876 (1922).

6. Callow v. Thomas, 322 Mass. 550, 78 N.E.2d 637 (1948).

As to immunities, see Restatement, Second, Torts § 895F.

7. Lewis v. Lewis, 370 Mass. 619, 629–630, 351 N.E.2d 526, 532–533 (1976).

Restatement, Second, Torts § 895F provides:

§ 895F. Husband and Wife

(1) A husband or wife is not immune from tort liability to the other solely by reason of that relationship.

(2) Repudiation of general tort immunity does not establish liability for an act or omission that, because of the marital relationship, is otherwise privileged or is not tortious.

8. Gahm v. Gahm, 243 Mass. 374, 376, 137 N.E. 876 (1922).

9. 381 Mass. 231, 232–233, 409 N.E.2d 717, 718–719 (1980).

37 Mass.Tort Law 2d Ed. (Nolan & Sartorio)—10   259

Exhibit 14-5 Massachusetts Practice, Chapter 9   *(continues)*

§ 151   INTENTIONAL TORTS   Ch. 9

the tortious conduct did not invade the more private aspects of married life.

The Court has not changed the traditional immunity as to intentional torts. The spouses are not permitted to maintain actions for personal torts against each other such as assault and battery, false imprisonment, malicious prosecution, defamation and the like.[10]

The Restatement recognizes a cause of action for a fraudulent nondisclosure of physical conditions making marital relations dangerous to the other's health [11] and for fraud in inducing the plaintiff to contract marriage when the defendant is not free to marry.[12]

Spouses have always been criminally liable for offenses against each other.

> **Library References:**
> C.J.S. Husband and Wife § 163.
> West's Key No. Digests, Husband and Wife ⊕≈53.

10. Thompson v. Thompson, 218 U.S. 611, 31 S.Ct. 111, 54 L.Ed. 1180 (1910).

Nogueira v. Nogueira, 388 Mass. 79, 80–82, 444 N.E.2d 940, 941–942 (1983) (However, the doctrine of interspousal immunity was inapplicable to a spouse's claim for libel and intentional infliction of emotional distress once the marriage was terminated by divorce and even upon the entry of the judgment of divorce nisi).

Garrity v. Garrity, 399 Mass. 367, 370–372 & n. 9, 504 N.E.2d 617, 619–620 (1987) (Interspousal immunity inapplicable to wife's claim against husband for violation of fiduciary duties with respect to their close corporation and for fraudulently conveying property in which plaintiff had an interest).

→ 11. Restatement, Second, Torts

§ 554. Fraudulent Nondisclosure of Physical Conditions Making Marital Relation Dangerous

A husband or wife who fraudulently conceals from the other a physical condition that makes cohabitation dangerous to the health of the other spouse is subject to liability to the other spouse for the harm suffered as a result.

12. Restatement, Second, Torts

§ 555. Fraudulent Misrepresentation or Nondisclosure Inducing Recipient to Enter Into Meretricious Relations With the Maker or Third Person

One who by fraudulent misrepresentation that he or she is free to contract a lawful marriage or by a failure to disclose a bar to the marriage induces another to cohabit as husband and wife is subject to liability to the other for any harm suffered as a result of the cohabitation.

Restatement, Second, Torts

§ 556. Fraudulent Misrepresentation of a Third Person's Fitness for or Freedom to Marry

One who by fraudulent misrepresentation that a third person is physically fit and legally free to marry intentionally induces another to enter into a marriage with the third person is subject to liability to the other for any harm caused to the other by the misrepresentation.

260

Exhibit 14-5   Massachusetts Practice, Chapter 9   *(concluded)*

to *Lewis*. You will also find references to other publications: C.J.S. and the digest system, as well as the Restatement of the Law of Torts.

Legal Reasoning Exercise

1. Read the paragraph in Exhibit 14-5 that begins, "The Court has not changed. . . . "Given what the court said about negligence actions in *Lewis*, do you agree with the analysis, which states that "spouses are not permitted to maintain actions for personal torts against each other such as assault"? If the court no longer thinks spousal immunity is a bar in negligence cases, do you think that the court would keep it as a bar when one spouse intentionally hurts the other?

c. Special Subject Encyclopedias, Treatises, and Restatements

In addition to the types of encyclopedias discussed above, other sources of general background information include special subject encyclopedias, treatises, and restatements. Special subject encyclopedias focus on a single topic, such as contracts or evidence. They bear names like Fletcher's Cyclopedia of the Law of Private Corporations.

A **treatise** summarizes, interprets, and evaluates the law. This differentiates a treatise from an encyclopedia, which simply summarizes the law. Although some treatises are published as multivolume sets, most look just like standard library books. In addition to the usual table of contents, text, and index, legal treatises usually contain a table of cases, and many are also supplemented with pocket parts. They are given regular library call numbers and can be found in the standard library card catalog. Two well-known treatises are Corbin on Contracts and Wigmore on Evidence.

Restatements represent still another source of general background information. In 1923 a group of prominent law professors, judges, and lawyers founded the American Law Institute (ALI) and began a series of books—the Restatements of the Law—to summarize the basic principles of the common law in several major areas. Recognizing that there was disagreement among the courts on the meaning of some of these principles, the ALI sought to present what its experts thought were the best rules. These are printed in the Restatements in boldface type as relatively short statements. Each principle is then followed by an explanation of the situations in which it should be applied. Restatements have been published in the areas of agency, conflict of laws, foreign relations, torts, and trusts.

d. Legal Periodicals and Newspapers

Law reviews and other types of legal periodicals are still another source for researching the meaning of the law. Law reviews, published by law schools and edited by law students, contain a wealth of thoroughly researched information about specific areas of the law. The lead articles are usually expansive pieces,

often written by law professors. A comments or notes section contains contributions of the student editors. Because the law review staffs are traditionally made up of the brightest students, their work has earned a high reputation. Other periodicals are often more specialized and practitioner oriented and also can contain articles of great value.

There are also weekly newspapers devoted to legal topics. Two that are national in scope are the National Law Journal and Lawyers Weekly USA. Many states also have state-specific newspapers. For example, the same publisher that prints Lawyers Weekly USA prints Massachusetts Lawyers Weekly. Not only will these newspapers keep you up to date on current developments in the legal field, but also they will frequently provide background information on specific topics. Finally, you should be aware of Legal Assistant Today, a monthly publication that contains articles about the law, as well as about the paralegal profession.

e. American Law Reports Annotated

American Law Reports Annotated is similar to an encyclopedia in that it provides you with information from around the country on selected topics. It differs from an encyclopedia, however, in that only selected topics are covered. In addition, those topics are covered in much more depth than you will find in an encyclopedia. The approach of the A.L.R. is to select a timely topic, reprint a leading case in that area, and then follow it with a discussion of related cases and an analysis of any trends that appear to be developing. If you find a pertinent A.L.R. annotation, you will have a good overview of the law in that given area. However, because the coverage of the A.L.R. is not encyclopedic, there may not be an A.L.R. annotation covering your area.

Many other publications contain cross-references to one of the A.L.R. series. If you do not have such a reference, begin your research with the A.L.R. Quick Index.

f. Citing Secondary Authority

In terms of citation value all secondary sources are not created equal. Unless you have absolutely nothing else on which to rely, you should never cite to an encyclopedia. Encyclopedias give you valuable background information, but once you have that, you should then proceed with your research into primary authority. It is appropriate to cite to other types of secondary authority, especially if they evaluate and analyze the law rather than simply describe it. Of the secondary sources that we have discussed the most authoritative and hence the most valuable to cite are Restatements, law review articles written by known authorities in the field, and treatises. Generally, you should not cite to A.L.R. annotations except when giving general information, such as the number of states that have held a certain way on a particular legal issue. Finally, you can cite to newspaper articles if you cannot find that information in any other source.

> ## PRACTICE TIP
>
> Be warned: Secondary sources provide only descriptions of the author's view of the law. Never rely only on a secondary source. Always read and analyze the primary authority yourself.

g. Ending Your Secondary Research and Relying on Secondary Sources

How do you know when you have done enough background researching and you are ready to move on to primary sources? There is no magic litmus test, but generally it will be time to move on when you start finding references to the same court decisions in each of the secondary sources you consult.

3. Go to Primary Authority

Your ultimate goal in conducting research is to find statutes, administrative regulations, and court opinions. Secondary sources are designed to help you find and understand this primary authority. As mentioned earlier, there will be times when you will dispense altogether with these secondary sources.

As we discussed in Chapter 3, there are three basic sources of law: legislatures, administrative agencies, and courts. Legislatures enact statutes, administrative agencies enact and enforce regulations, and courts write court opinions. Figure 14-2 summarizes the sources of primary authority for Massachusetts. Most states follow a similar approach.

Figure 14-2   Sources of Law: Massachusetts Primary Authority

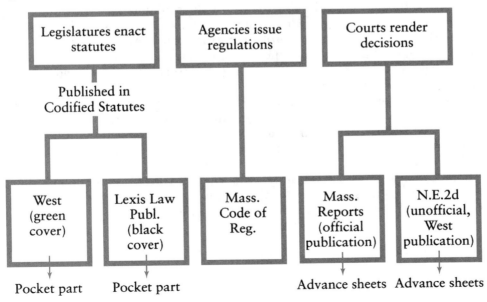

NETNOTE

You can find the text of most state and federal statutes and regulations on government web sites. A good place to start your search is at the home page of Findlaw: *www.findlaw.com*. Click on the tab "For Legal Professionals." Then click on "Cases & Codes." For federal materials, click on "US Code" or "Code of Federal Regulations." For state statutes and regulations, under "US State Laws— Cases, Codes, Statutes and Regulations," select your state.

When litigants ask a trial court to rule on a legal issue, the trial court will look to statutes and prior appellate court decisions from its own state for guidance. For example, in Massachusetts on a Massachusetts state law issue, appellate court decisions from the Massachusetts Appeals Court and the Massachusetts Supreme Judicial Court are binding on all Massachusetts trial courts. This is known as mandatory authority—that is, a statute or court opinion from a higher court in the same state (jurisdiction). Appellate decisions from other states and the federal system can be influential, but they are not binding on Massachusetts trial courts and hence are known as persuasive authority. Therefore, if you are working in a Massachusetts law firm and are assigned to research the question of whether or not a wife can sue her husband, you will begin with the realization that the trial court assigned to decide your case will be looking primarily to Massachusetts statutes and appellate decisions for guidance.

When beginning research into primary resources, statutes and court opinions, first think about whether the facts of your client's case suggest that the situation will be governed by a statute or by the common law. For example, if your client has been charged with a crime, you know that for something to be a crime, there must be a statute prohibiting that behavior. Therefore, you will begin with the statutes. On the other hand, if your client wants to sue someone for negligence, you know that most of tort law is still common law, and you will want to start with the court opinions.

If you are unsure as to whether to start your research with statutes or court decisions, you will usually begin your research with the statutes. The reason for starting with statutes is that if a statute governs your problem, the courts must follow it. The courts may, of course, interpret the statute, but they cannot ignore it. (This assumes there is no problem with the constitutionality of the statute.) After locating any applicable statutes, you will next read any court opinions that have interpreted those statutes. Finally, you will update your research to make sure the statutes and court opinions you found are still valid.

> # PRACTICE TIP
>
> Recall that in our federal system of government state courts and federal courts are co-equal partners. Except in matters of federal law, federal court decisions are not mandatory on state courts. Therefore, when a federal court decides a matter of state law because it has jurisdiction based on diversity of citizenship, its decision is *not* mandatory on state trial courts. The federal court is merely guessing as to how state appellate courts would have handled the issue if it had been presented to them.

a. A Note on Lawbook Publishers

Traditionally, two commercial publishers have published most of the materials you use when doing legal research: West Publishing Company and Lawyers Co-operative. Generally, they published the same materials but added their own specialized editorial features and did not cross-reference each other's publications. In most states, the state statutes were published by one or both of these companies. Then, in 1996, Thomson Legal Publishing Company became the owner of both West and Lawyers Co-operative. As a result, most of the titles that were published by either West Publishing Company or Lawyers Co-operative are now owned and published by a subsidiary of Thomson, known as West Group. However, because of possible antitrust problems, West Group has and is still in the process of divesting itself of some of its publications, such as the United States Code Service, now owned by The Michie Company, a subsidiary of Lexis Law Publishing.

These changes in the publishing industry should not greatly impact the way in which you conduct your research. However, it may mean that you will see more cross-referencing between the various books. Also, as individual volumes need to be replaced, on the replacement book's spine you will see the designation for the new publisher.

Many states also publish an official version of their statutes. As a researching tool, the main disadvantage to using the official statutes is that they usually do not contain any editorial features, such as summaries of court opinions that have interpreted the statutes.

When researching a state that has annotated statutes published by more than one publisher, feel free to begin your research with either version. Before proceeding to read court decisions, however, you should always consult the case summaries located in both versions. You will usually find summaries of the same court decisions in each publication—but not always. That is because the editors at the different publishing companies decide which opinions to summarize and to include after the statute.

To begin your research into the question of spousal immunity, you could start with one of the two privately published versions of the Massachusetts statutes annotated. You could also begin your research in the official Massachusetts General Laws, but then you would not receive the benefit of the annotations provided by the private publishers.

b. Finding Statutes

Each year as legislatures enact new laws, they are compiled and published in statutory codes. The codes are generally arranged by subject matter, and if the code is annotated, it will also include such editorial features as historical notes and summaries of court opinions that have interpreted the statute.

NETNOTE

For current information on federal legislation a good source is http://thomas.loc.gov provided by the Library of Congress. You can also find information on the legislative branch at *http://fedlaw.gsa.gov*.

(1) Starting with the citation

The simplest way to begin statutory research is with a citation to a relevant statute. For example, your boss might know that Mass. Gen. L. ch. 209 § 6 governs suits between spouses and might merely want you to check whether the legislature has recently amended the statute. Or if you were lucky during your background research, as we were with the information we found in Massachusetts Practice, you may have found a statutory reference in one of those secondary sources.

If you have the citation for a statute, you know its chapter and section number. You can simply go to the appropriate volume and locate the statute. Remember that the citation gives chapter numbers, not volume numbers. The chapter numbers are printed on the spine of the statutory code volumes.

(2) Starting with an index

If you do not know the citation, you will have to use a subject matter index. Both the Massachusetts General Laws Annotated and the Annotated Laws of Massachusetts have subject matter indexes, called the General Index, which can be used to find the citation for any statute that might govern our problem.

As with indexes for secondary sources, before consulting a statutory index you should always try to think of several words or phrases that might pertain to your problem. Sometimes the indexes will help you out by trying to second-guess the words you might use. For example, if you look under the word Spouse in the Massachusetts General Laws Annotated index, it will send you to Husband and Wife. Exhibit 14-6, on page 407, shows what you will find in the index, once you go to the topic Husband and Wife. Under the subtopic Actions and proceedings, notice the reference to "Between husband and wife, 209 § 6." You should follow the same process of working with the index to find the statute's citation in the index for the Annotated Laws of Massachusetts.

HUNTER

HUNTER EDUCATION
Generally, 131 § 14
Fish and game licenses, compliance, 131 § 11

HUNTING
Fish and Game, generally, this index

HUNTINGTON
See, also, Cities and Towns, generally, this index
Congressional districts, 57 § 1
District court, 218 § 1
Senatorial districts, 57 § 3

HUNTINGTON AVENUE
Railroad station, mileage tickets, distances, computation, 160 § 189

HUNTINGTON'S CHOREA
Advisory committee, genetically handicapped persons, 111 § 6D

HURRICANES
Bids, public contracts, 30 § 39M
Homeowners insurance, market assistance plans, 175C § 9
Municipal finance, incurring liabilities in excess of appropriation, 44 § 31
Restraining use of water, 40 § 41A

HUSBAND AND WIFE
See, also, Marriage, generally, this index
Generally, 209 § 1 et seq.
Abandonment. Desertion, generally, this index
Abuse Between Family and Household Members, generally, this index
Accessory after the fact, 274 § 4
Accident and health insurance, 175 § 108
Aged persons, group policy, 175 § 110C
Continuation of coverage, divorce or separation, 175 § 110I
Deductibles, 175 § 111G
Limited extension of benefits, 175 § 110G
Account, work and labor performed by wife, 209 § 4
Acknowledgment by married woman, 183 § 31
Actions and proceedings,
Between husband and wife, 209 § 6
Cause against wife prior to marriage, 209 § 8
Emergency treatment, consent, 112 § 12F
Mortgage or sale, real estate, mentally ill spouse, venue, 209 § 24
Privileged communications, 233 § 20
Wife prosecuting and defending, 209 § 6
Acts of husband, wife acting as fiduciary, 209 § 5
Administration granted to surviving spouse, 193 § 1
Administratrix, wife acting as, 209 § 5
Adoption of Children, generally, this index
Adultery, generally, this index
Adults, adoption, consent, 210 § 3
Aged persons, assault and battery, 265 § 13K

HUSBAND AND WIFE—Cont'd
Agreements, work and labor performed by wife, 209 § 4
Alcoholic beverages license, pharmacists, 138 § 30B
Alcoholics and intoxicated persons, commitment, petitions, 123 § 35
Alienation of affection, actions and proceedings, 207 § 47B
Alimony, generally. Divorce, this index
Allowances, surviving spouse and children, 196 §§ 1, 2
Anatomical gifts, 113 § 7 et seq.
Antenuptial Contracts, generally, this index
Application of law,
Jurisdiction of probate court children of parents living apart, 209 § 37
Marriage contracts, 209 § 13
Appointment, guardian, mentally deficient and mentally ill persons, notice, 201 § 7
Assault and battery. Abuse Between Family and Household Members, generally, this index
Assent of husband, wife acting as fiduciary, 209 § 5
Assessments, real property, aged persons, exemption, 59 § 5
Time for application, 59 § 59; 60 § 3A
Assignment of Wages, generally, this index
Attachment, husbands property, 209 § 33
Bail and Recognizance, this index
Bonds (officers and fiduciaries), visitation, child return, 209 § 38; 209A § 3
Business, contracts of wife, liability, 209 § 9
Capacity to sue and be sued, 209 § 6
Cause against wife prior to marriage, husband liability, 209 § 8
Cemeteries, interment rights, 114 §§ 32, 33
Certified copies, orders and decrees involving real estate, mentally deficient or mentally ill spouse, 209 § 24
Chemically dependent persons, commitment petitions, 123 § 35
Cohabitation, generally, this index
Complaints,
Abandoned spouse, sale of property for support, 209 § 30
Desertion by spouse or living apart, 209 § 36
Desertion or failure to support, 209 § 32
Parents living apart, care, custody and education of children, 209 § 37
Confidential or privileged information, 233 § 20
Abuse between family and household members, 233 § 20K
Programs, location, address, disclosure, 233 § 20L
Desertion, nonsupport, 273 § 7
Support, interstate enforcement, 209D § 3–316
Consent,
Adoption of adults, 210 § 3
Adoption of children, 210 § 2
Assignment of wages, 154 §§ 2, 3

1470

Exhibit 14-6   Index to Massachusetts General Laws Annotated

PRACTICE TIP

Different publishers may use different words to describe the same concept (for example, car instead of motor vehicle). Therefore, if you cannot find what you are looking for in one index, look in a competitor's index.

(3) Reading an annotated statute

Exhibit 14-7, on pages 409-410, shows you what you will find once you locate chapter 209, section 6. Under the statute you will see the heading Historical Note. This contains information about when the statute was amended. The years, such as 1845 and 1902, refer to the years in which the statute was amended. The other numbers, such as c. 208 § 5, refer to the chapter numbers of the statute as it was enacted by the legislature before it was **codified**—that is, placed in the statute books with other statutes dealing with similar subject matter. At the bottom of the page are references to law review articles.

Codification
The process of organizing statutes by subject matter.

Also notice the references on the second page to other resources: the relevant digest topic and key number, C.J.S., M.P.S. (Massachusetts Practice Series), and Westlaw. Finally, at the bottom of the second page notice the index to the case summaries, called Notes of Decisions.

Many cases are summarized following the statute. One such case is *Lewis*. In Exhibit 14-8 on page 411 notice how the citation following the summary for *Lewis* lists the North Eastern Reporter citation first. Remember that when you cite, you should always give the official citation (in this case Massachusetts Reports) first.

You could also have conducted your research in the Annotated Laws of Massachusetts. The statutory language is identical to what you found in the Massachusetts General Laws Annotated. However, the cross-references differ. Also occasionally you will find a case listed in one source but not the other. Therefore, before leaving the annotated statutes, it is worthwhile to take the time to check both sets for case summaries.

(4) Checking the pocket part

Any changes to the statute that have occurred since the time the hardbound volume was printed will be found in the pocket part. Always check the pocket part. In addition to any statutory changes, the pocket part will include any recent court opinions that have interpreted the statute. Exhibit 14-9, on page 412, shows the changes to chapter 209 contained in the pocket part for West's Massachusetts General Laws Annotated. As you can see, there has been a change to the statutory language in section 1A. There has been no change to the language of section 6, but two new court decisions have been added since the main volume was printed.

PRACTICE TIP

Always check the pocket part!

c. Finding State Agency Regulations

Once you have located a state statute, you should check to see whether any state agency has issued regulations interpreting that statute. Unfortunately, research into state regulations is often a hit-or-miss affair. Some states have compiled their agency regulations into codes, similar to the statutory codes,

HUSBAND AND WIFE   209 § 6

Who may be appointed trustee, competency, see M.P.S. vol. 22, Lombard, § 1346.

WESTLAW Electronic Research

See WESTLAW guide following the Foreword of this volume.

Notes of Decisions

In general 2
Prior law 1

_____

1. Prior law

Under St.1783, c. 24, § 19, the marriage of a single woman, who was sole administratrix, did not terminate her authority, but made her husband joint administrator with her. Barber v. Bush (1812) 7 Mass. 510.

2. In general

Where A., a married woman, during the lifetime of her husband and before the passage of St.1855, c. 304, deposited in a savings bank a sum of money in her name as "trustee for B," and A., until her death, retained possession of the deposit book, and at times drew out portions of the money, and A.'s executor took possession of the deposit book, charged himself with the amount of the deposit in his inventory, and about two years after her death paid it over to B., who until then had no knowledge of the deposit, the deposit was a part of A.'s estate and was improperly paid to B. Jewett v. Shattuck (1878) 124 Mass. 590.

---

§ 6. Married woman; power to sue and be sued

A married woman may sue and be sued in the same manner as if she were sole; but this section shall not authorize suits between husband and wife except in connection with contracts entered into pursuant to the authority contained in section two.

Amended by St.1963, c. 765, § 2.

Historical Note

St.1845, c. 208, § 5.   G.S.1860, c. 108, § 8.   P.S.1882, c. 147, § 7.
St.1855, c. 304, §§ 2, 4.   St.1871, c. 312.   R.L.1902, c. 153, § 6.
St.1857, c. 249, § 3.   St.1874, c. 184, § 3.

St.1963, c. 765, § 2, approved Oct. 22, 1963, added the exception.

Cross References

Recovery of money or goods lost at gaming; limitations, see c. 137, § 1.

Law Review Commentaries

Collateral-source rule. William Schwartz (1961) 41 Boston U.L.Rev. 348.

Consortium damages in Massachusetts. John E. Hannigan 21 Boston U.L.Rev. 452 (1941).

Contracts between husband and wife. Frederick M. Hart, 10 Annual Survey of Mass. Law, Boston College, p. 57 (1963).

Equity jurisdiction in Massachusetts, the wife's equity in money advanced to the husband. Frank W. Grinnell (1946) 31 Mass.L.Q. No. 2, p. 47.

Domestic relations, foreign decrees. William J. Greenler, Jr., 6 Annual Survey of Mass. Law, Boston College, p. 74 (1959).

Husband and wife, contract for married woman's services. William J. Greenler, Jr., 3 Ann.Surv.Mass.L. 81 (1956).

Husband and wife tort actions. Monroe L. Inker, 11 Annual Survey of Mass. Law, Boston College, p. 76 (1964).

Interspousal contracts. (1974) 9 Suffolk U.L. Rev. 185.

Interspousal immunity: Application of domiciliary law. Francis J. Nicholson. 13 Annual

351

Exhibit 14-7 Massachusetts General Laws Annotated ch. 209, § 6   *(continues)*

209 § 6 DOMESTIC RELATIONS

Survey of Mass. Law, Boston College, p. 136 (1966).

Interspousal immunity, conflict of laws. Francis J. Nicholson, S. J., 15 Annual Survey of Mass. Law, Boston College, p. 122 (1968).

Law affecting interspousal immunity. Francis J. Nicholson, 11 Annual Survey of Mass. Law, Boston College, p. 91 (1964).

Right of husband to recover for expenses of future medical care of wife. 43 Harvard L.Rev. 661 (1930).

Suits between husband and wife. Harry Zarrow (1957) 4 Ann.Surv.Mass.L. 109.

Wife's liability as husband's surety, disability to sue spouse. Bernard A. Riemer and William E. Hogan, 2 Ann.Surv.Mass.L. 81, 82 (1955).

Written contracts between husband and wife. (1945) 30 Mass.L.Q. No. 4, p. 20.

Library References

Husband and Wife ☞203, 204.
C.J.S. Husband and Wife § 389 et seq.

Comments.

Actions between husband and wife, marshalling of assets, see M.P.S. vol. 31, Nolan, § 316.

Antenuptial agreements and contracts, probate, see M.P.S. vol. 23, Lombard, § 1626.

Capacity, husband and wife, defendant's case, the obligation in tort, see M.P.S. vol. 17, Bishop, § 465.

Capacity of parties to contract, see M.P.S. vol. 14, Simpson and Alperin, § 301 et seq.

Capacity to be party, proceedings involving husband and wife, see M.P.S. vol. 9, Nolan, § 155.

Capacity to contract, husband and wife, the plaintiff's case, see M.P.S. vol. 17, Bishop, § 11.

Contracts and suits directly between husband and wife, see M.P.S. vol. 2, Lombard, § 1256.

Contracts between husband and wife, see M.P.S. vol. 3, Lombard, § 2161.

Contracts between husband and wife and trustees, separation agreements, see M.P.S. vol. 2, Lombard, § 1255.

Married women, capacity, contracts, see M.P.S. vol. 14, Simpson and Alperin, § 308.

Married women, capacity, torts, see M.P.S. vol. 14A, Simpson and Alperin, § 1711.

Property and property rights, see M.P.S. vol. 3, Lombard, § 2141 et seq.

Spouse vs. Spouse, actionable tort, see M.P.S. vol. 11, Martin and Hennessey, § 93.

Suits between husband and wife, particular relationships, see M.P.S. vol. 14, Simpson and Alperin, § 771.

Torts between the spouses, see M.P.S. vol. 37, Nolan, § 121.

Forms.

Action by husband against wife to recover savings bank deposit, complaints, pleadings and motions, see M.P.S. vol. 10, Rodman, § 1699.

Agreement between husband and wife, effect of reconciliation, form, see M.P.S. vol. 2, Lombard, § 1306.

WESTLAW Electronic Research

See WESTLAW guide following the Foreword of this volume.

Notes of Decisions

In general 1
Abortions, actions between husband and wife 30
Accounting, equitable proceedings between husband and wife 40
Actions between husband and wife 28–37
  In general 28
  Abortions 30
  Foreign judgments 37
  Marriage settlements 31
  Prior law 29
  Probate proceedings 32
  Professional services 33
  Torts, generally 34

Actions between husband and wife—Cont'd
  Trusts 36
  Vehicular torts, generally 35
Agency, liability of wife 17
Alienation of affections, right of action by wife 9
Burden of proof 55
Clean hands doctrine, equitable proceedings between husband and wife 41
Common law 3
Consortium
  Generally 51
  Right of action by wife 10
Contracts, right of action by wife 6

352

Exhibit 14-7 Massachusetts General Laws Annotated ch. 209, § 6 *(concluded)*

rectly, without intervention of a trustee. Charney v. Charney (1944) 55 N.E.2d 917, 316 Mass. 580.

Where, if final and absolute decree of divorce had been entered, remedy of wife to sue at law for alimony awarded would be complete; in action to recover alimony under interlocutory order entered in foreign state, law of forum governed, where laws of foreign state did not appear and under R.L.1902, c. 153, § 6, and St.1910, c. 576, wife could not sue husband in Massachusetts for alimony awarded by interlocutory order. Golder v. Golder (1920) 126 N.E. 382, 235 Mass. 261.

A foreign sister state which by statute conferred jurisdiction upon its courts over nonresidents by service upon them in respective places of their residence within sister states, for causes of action which arose from business transactions within the enacting state, enabled courts of that state to render a judgment against a non-resident husband who entered into and breached a marriage settlement agreement with his wife while they were both domiciled there and where she was still domiciled. Spitz v. Spitz (1965) 31 Mass.App.Dec. 124.

3. Common law

This section which provides that a married woman may sue and be sued in same manner as if she were sole, but provides that this section does not authorize suit between husband and wife except in connection with certain contracts, left interspousal immunity rule in its common-law status susceptible to reexamination and alteration by Supreme Judicial Court. Lewis v. Lewis (1976) 351 N.E.2d 526, 370 Mass. 619.

At common law, one spouse could not sue the other in an action at law. Zwick v. Goldberg (1939) 22 N.E.2d 661, 304 Mass. 66.

At common law, husband, by one action, might recover for wife's personal injuries and expenses and other damage resulting to husband therefrom. Thibeault v. Poole (1933) 186 N.E. 632, 283 Mass. 480.

In the case of Fowle v. Torrey (1883) 135 Mass. 87, the court said: "While the Legislature has removed from a wife many of the disabilities she was under at common law, and has authorized her to hold property as a feme sole, to deal with it as such, and to sue and be sued in relation thereto, it has carefully provided always, in the acts by which this has been done, that nothing therein contained shall be construed as authorizing contracts between husband and wife, conveyances or gifts to each other (except by the husband to a limited amount), or as giving the right to either to sue or be sued by the other. Gen.Sts. c. 108, § 1. Sts.1874, c. 184; 1879, c. 133. Whatever rights

they had in these respects remain as they stood at common law before this legislation commences."

4. Retroactive effect

St.1871, c. 312, providing that any married woman could be sued in an action of tort as if she were sole, and her husband should not be liable to pay the judgment against her in any such suit, did not apply to actions against husband and wife for the wife's tort, begun before the passing of the statute. Hill v. Duncan (1872) 110 Mass. 238.

5. Right of action by wife—In general

By divorce, the marriage was so far suspended that the wife could maintain her rights by suit upon causes which arose after the divorce, and she was to the same extent liable to be sued alone. Chase v. Chase (1856) 72 Mass. 157, 6 Gray 157; Dean v. Richmond (1827) 22 Mass. 461, 5 Pick. 461.

Wife's right to sue "in the same manner as if she were sole" refers both to extent of rights to be established and mode of ascertaining and declaring those rights. Cassidy v. Constantine (1929) 168 N.E. 169, 269 Mass. 56.

In the case of MacKeown v. Lacey (1909) 86 N.E. 799, 200 Mass. 437, 21 L.R.A.,N.S., 683, 16 Ann.Cas. 220, the court said: "The indorsements operated as assignments of the notes to the plaintiff (Hill v. Lewis, 1 Salk. 132; 2 Ames' Cases on Bills and Notes, 100, note 1), and under St.1897, p. 378, c. 402 (Rev.Laws, c. 173, § 4), which was in force at the time of the transfer and of the bringing of the action, the assignee could sue in her own name."

Where a man and woman living in another state came into this commonwealth for the purpose of being married, and were married here, and a few days afterwards, while they were living here at an inn, she wrote to a broker in that state, with whom before the marriage she had deposited property earned by her, to send her a sum of money by an expressman, which the broker did and instructed the expressman to deliver it to her upon her personal receipt; but the expressman delivered it to the husband, who absconded with it, under St.1855, c. 304, she could maintain an action in her own name against the expressman for the money, if she had not authorized her husband to receive it, or held him out as her agent to collect money. Read v. Earle (1859) 78 Mass. 423, 12 Gray 423.

The desertion of a wife by her husband which would enable her to sue, and render her liable to be sued, as a feme sole, should be an absolute and complete desertion by his continued absence from the commonwealth, and a voluntary separation from and abandonment

Exhibit 14-8   Massachusetts General Laws Annotated ch. 209, § 6

＊   ＊   ＊

→ **§ 1A.   Tenants by entirety under older deed; electing treatment of tenancy**

Tenants by the entirety holding under a deed dated prior to February eleventh, nineteen hundred and eighty may elect to have their tenancy treated as being subject to the provisions of chapter seven hundred and twenty-seven of the acts of nineteen hundred and seventy-nine; provided, however, that such election is made in writing, identifying the real estate with reference to the book and page of the registry of deeds wherein such deed is filed. Such election shall be executed by the grantees named as tenants by the entirety on the deed who are electing to be subject to this section, duly notarized, and recorded in said registry.

Added by St.1989, c. 283.

Historical and Statutory Notes

1989 Legislation

St.1989, c. 283, was approved July 25, 1989.

＊   ＊   ＊

→ **§ 6.   Married woman; power to sue and be sued**

Library References

Comments.

Actions between husband and wife, marshalling of assets, see M.P.S. vol. 31, Nolan and Sartorio, §§ 316, 317.

Capacity, husband and wife, defendant's case, the obligation in tort, see M.P.S. vol. 17, Bishop, § 546.

Capacity to contract, husband and wife, the plaintiff's case, see M.P.S. vol. 17, Bishop, § 22.

Consequential damages, see M.P.S. vol. 17, Bishop, § 589.

Domestic immunities, see M.P.S. vol. 37A, Nolan and Sartorio, § 553.

Notes of Decisions

34. —— Torts, generally, actions between husband and wife

Wife was not prohibited by this section from bringing suit against her husband to recover damages for bodily injuries sustained incident to an assault and battery allegedly committed by the husband. Knobel-Aronova v. Knobel (App. Div. 1987) 1987 Mass.App.Div. 75.

35. —— Vehicular torts, generally, actions between husband and wife

Coster v. Coster, 1943, 46 N.E.2d 509, 289 N.Y. 438, [main volume] motion denied 49 N.E.2d 621, 290 N.Y. 662.

Exhibit 14-9   Pocket Part, Massachusetts General Laws Annotated ch. 209, § 6

---

complete with a subject matter index. Some states, however, make no attempt to publish all their state regulations in one location. Finally, some states, such as Massachusetts, are somewhere in between. Massachusetts publishes a Code of Massachusetts Regulations. However, it is organized by agency rather than by subject matter, and there is no index for the series. Instead, the researcher must know the name of the agency involved, find the volume of the code that covers that agency, and then search through the table of contents for that agency to find the desired information.

For state administrative regulation questions you are often best advised to consult directly with the agency on the most convenient source for this type of information. In Massachusetts there are no state agency regulations governing the topic of spousal immunity.

d. Finding Court Opinions

Court opinions are published in court reporters. If the reporter is published by a private publishing company, such as West, it will also include editorial features, such as the **headnotes** added by West at the beginning of each case.

Most state court decisions are published in both an official government-published reporter and an unofficial regional reporter, published by West.

For example, the North Eastern Reporter contains court decisions from Illinois, Indiana, New York, and Ohio, as well as Massachusetts. Because many attorneys are not interested in purchasing out-of-state court decisions, West also publishes condensed versions of its regional reporters, containing the decisions from just one state. For example, West offers an abbreviated version of N.E.2d that contains just Massachusetts decisions, called, appropriately enough, Massachusetts Decisions. This can be a confusing book to use. First, because the decisions from the other states are missing, West is able to combine three to four volumes of the North Eastern Reporter into each volume of Massachusetts Decisions. When trying to locate decisions in a combined reporter, such as the Massachusetts Decisions, first make sure that you are in the correct portion of the volume. Second, because the out-of-state cases are missing, there are also missing pages in the condensed volumes.

The wording of the court decisions found in West's North Eastern Reporter and the Massachusetts Reports is identical. Their differences lie in the editorial features. The most useful West editorial feature is the headnotes located at the beginning of each decision. These headnotes summarize the court opinion. Never forget that these are a West editorial feature written by West. They are not part of the court decision. The decision itself begins with the justice's name who wrote the opinion.

If you have the full citation to a case, it is relatively easy to locate the text of that case in a reporter. If you do not have the citation, but you do have other information, there are three different approaches you can use. First, if you have only a name, you can use a table of cases to find the full citation. Second, if you know a case interprets a specific statute, you can look up the statute in an annotated version of the statutes and get the citation from that source. Third, you can use a digest to locate relevant cases by their subject matter.

> **Headnote**
> A summary of one legal point in a court opinion; written by the editors at West.

(1) Starting with a citation or name

If you are given a citation by your boss or a co-worker or if you find it through your own research in secondary sources, it is relatively easy to find the case.

A typical Massachusetts Supreme Judicial Court decision cite would be as follows:

<u>Mounsey v. Ellard</u>, 363 Mass. 693, 297 N.E.2d 43 (1973).

It tells us that the name of the case is *Mounsey v. Ellard* and that it can be found either on page 693 of volume 363 of the Massachusetts Reports or on page 43 of volume 297 of the North Eastern Reporter, Second Series.

More often, however, you will know the name but not the citation. For example, now that you have worked with the problem of spousal immunity, you will

probably remember that one decision dealing with this problem is *Callow v. Thomas*. You will probably not remember its citation. Because this is a common problem, West has come up with a solution. West publishes a series of books called the Massachusetts Digest, summarizing all Massachusetts court decisions decided before 1933, and the Massachusetts Digest 2d, summarizing all Massachusetts court decisions from 1933 to date. Contained in each of those series is a volume entitled Table of Cases.

Exhibit 14-10, on page 415, shows a page from the Massachusetts Digest 2d Table of Cases listing *Callow v. Thomas*. In addition to the citation, you will see a listing of the West topics that are discussed in that opinion. These are the same topics listed at the beginning of the headnotes to *Callow v. Thomas*. This can be very helpful in locating the right case. For example, assume you are looking for a negligence case called *Callahan v. Somebody*. The Massachusetts Digest Table of Cases lists many Callahan cases but only one with the topic of libel. Notice that once again a publisher has given you an incomplete citation by omitting the date.

If you remember the defendant's name but not the plaintiff's name, West has a solution for that, too. In the volume following the Table of Cases is a Defendant-Plaintiff Table, listing all the cases with defendant's name first.

Exhibit 14-11, on page 416, shows the first page of *Callow*. Take a look at the headnote topics at the beginning of *Callow*, and compare them to those listed in the Table of Cases. For example, the first topic listed in the Table of Cases for *Callow* is Divorce 313. That corresponds to headnote 3.

Finally, if you do not have the name for the opinion, but you do have the citation to one reporter, and your library only contains the other reporter, you can use a book called Shepard's Citations to help you find the parallel citation.

Take a look at a page from Shepard's in Exhibit 14-12 on page 417. Assume you have the North Eastern Reporter citation for *Callow v. Thomas*, 78 N.E.2d 637, but are missing the Massachusetts Reports citation. You would look in the Shepard's volume that contains information on cases reported in volume 78 of the North Eastern Reporter, Second Series, for the North Eastern Reporter cite 78 N.E.2d 637. Look in the first column for the reference to page 637, listed as —637—. Immediately under the —637— you will see the name of the case—*Callow v. Thomas*— and then (322Mas550). That is the Massachusetts Reports citation for Callow. Shepard's indicates this is the parallel citation by including it in parentheses. Do not be put off by the seemingly endless list of numbers on the Shepard's page. These are simply case citations in a very abbreviated format. We will talk about the purpose of these other citations later in the chapter when we discuss updating your research.

(2) Using a summary following a statute

As you have already seen, if you have found a statute governing your problem, an annotated version of those statutes will contain a summary of court opinions interpreting it. This summary will include a citation so that you can locate it in the case reporters.

(3) Using a digest

Court opinions are published in chronological order, not by subject matter. Therefore, if there is no statute governing your problem and if you do not know the citation for any court decision relevant to your problem, absent a better way

30 Mass D 2d—233

See Guidelines for Arrangement at the beginning of this Volume

CAMBEX

Callahan; Nelson v., CA1 (Mass), 721 F2d 397.—Crim Law 273.1(1), 273.1(4); Hab Corp 85.1(2), 85.2(1), 85.5(4), 90.3(5).

Callahan; Nguyen v., DMass, 997 FSupp 179.—Social S 175.25, 175.30.

Callahan; N.O. v., DMass, 110 FRD 637.—Fed Civ Proc 1559, 1598, 1600(4), 1623, 1653; Mental H 51.5, 486, 487, 490; Witn 184(1), 212.

Callahan; O. v., DMass, 110 FRD 637. See N.O. v. Callahan.

Callahan; Reddick v., DMass, 587 FSupp 880.—Crim Law 1030(1), 1178; Hab Corp 45.3(1.30), 45.3(4).

Callahan; Ricci v., DMass, 646 FSupp 378.—Fed Civ Proc 2397.6.

Callahan; Ricci v., DMass, 576 FSupp 415.—Inj 210.

Callahan; Ricci v., DMass, 97 FRD 737.—Fed Civ Proc 219.

Callahan; Richard v., CA1 (Mass), 723 F2d 1028.—Crim Law 273(4), 273.1(1); Hab Corp 113(12); Homic 234(5), 354.

Callahan; Richard v., DMass, 564 FSupp 511, aff 723 F2d 1028.—Const Law 270(1); Fed Cts 386; Hab Corp 45.1(4).

Callahan; Robinson v., CA1 (Mass), 694 F2d 6.—Crim Law 778(5), 789(13).

Callahan; Setian v., DMass, 973 FSupp 16.—Social S 140.85, 148.1.

Callahan; Sheffield v., DMass, 9 FSupp2d 75.—Social S 140.10, 143.60, 148.15.

Callahan; Shoobridge v., Mass, 39 NE2d 429, 310 Mass 632.—App & E 989; Autos 242(8); Evid 589; Refer 99(4), 99(6).

Callahan; Subilosky v., CA1 (Mass), 689 F2d 7, cert den 103 SCt 1788, 460 US 1090, 76 LEd2d 356.—Const Law 269; Crim Law 938(1); Hab Corp 45.2(4), 45.2(7), 85.2(1).

Callahan v. Superior Court, Mass, 570 NE2d 1003, 410 Mass 1001.—Mand 1, 3(1), 4(4), 31, 176.

Callahan v. Town of Athol, Mass, 188 NE2d 371, 345 Mass 572.—Towns 29.

Callahan v. U.S. I.R.S., BkrtcyDMass, 168 BR 272. See Callahan, In re.

Callahan; Watkins v., CA1 (Mass), 724 F2d 1038.—Crim Law 412.1(4), 667(1); Hab Corp 45.3(1.40), 90.2(6); Homic 8; Witn 2(1).

Callahan v. Westinghouse Broadcasting Co., Inc., Mass, 363 NE2d 240, 372 Mass 582.—Libel 112(2), 124(2); Trial 295(5).

Callahan; Woods v., CA1 (Mass), 172 F2d 179.—Fed Civ Proc 2505; Land & Ten 149; War 210, 220.

Callahan; Young v., CA1 (Mass), 700 F2d 32, cert den 104 SCt 194, 464 US 863, 78 LEd2d 170.—Crim Law 637, 1166.8.

Callahan; Zeigler v., CA1 (Mass), 659 F2d 254.—Const Law 268(5); Crim Law 553, 627.8(6), 627.9(2.1), 1171.8(1); Hab Corp 25.1(8).

Callahan & Sons, Inc. v. Board of Appeals of Lenox, MassAppCt, 565 NE2d 813, 30 MassAppCt 36. See Maurice Callahan & Sons, Inc. v. Board of Appeals of Lenox.

Callan v. Winters, Mass, 534 NE2d 298, 404 Mass 198.—Const Law 93(1); Statut 174; Wills 498.

Callanan, In re, BkrtcyDMass, 190 BR 137.—Bankr 2702.1.

Callanan v. International Fidelity Ins. Co., BkrtcyDMass, 190 BR 137. See Callanan, In re.

Callanan v. Personnel Adm'r for Com., Mass, 511 NE2d 525, 400 Mass 597.—Inj 231; Mun Corp 197; Offic 11.7, 11.8.

Calledare v. Sawyer, Mass, 225 NE2d 367, 352 Mass 769.—Theaters 6(19).

Callen; Com. v., MassAppCt, 524 NE2d 861, 26 MassAppCt 920, review den 531 NE2d 1274, 403 Mass 1105.—Autos 144.2(8).

Callender; Com. v., Mass, 673 NE2d 22, 423 Mass 771. See Mendonza v. Com.

Calligaris' Case, Mass, 198 NE 607, 292 Mass 397.—App & E 843(2); Work Comp 2215.

Callinan v. Larsen, MassAppDiv, 1979 MassAppDiv 186. —Judgm 97.

Callow v. Thomas, Mass, 78 NE2d 637, 322 Mass 550, 2 ALR2d 632.—Divorce 313; Hus & W 205(2); Marriage 57, 67.

Callum; Liberty Leather Corp. v., CA1 (Mass), 653 F2d 694.—Fed Civ Proc 839.1, 2146, 2152; Fed Cts 615, 907; Fraud 12, 20, 50, 58(2), 58(3), 58(4); Torts 10(1), 28.

Callum; Liberty Leather Corp. v., DMass, 86 FRD 550. —Fed Civ Proc 2736, 2738.

Calnan; Becker v., Mass, 48 NE2d 668, 313 Mass 625.— App & E 870(5); Equity 417; Labor 107, 109, 114, 122, 127, 763, 769; Plead 8(1), 34(3); Stip 14(3).

Calnan; Weeks v., MassAppCt, 658 NE2d 173, 39 Mass-AppCt 933.—Damag 23; Land & Ten 164(1).

Calore Exp. Co. v. U. S., CA1 (Mass), 351 F2d 596.— Autos 128.

Calore Exp. Co., Inc., In re, DMass, 226 BR 727, opinion after grant of writ 228 BR 338, opinion after grant of writ 228 BR 338.—Atty & C 54; Mand 1, 29, 51, 53.

Calore Exp. Co., Inc., In re, BkrtcyDMass, 199 BR 424. —Bankr 2156, 2671, 2674, 2675, 2679, 2680; Sec Tran 138, 147.

Calvanese v. A. S. W. Taxi Corp., MassAppCt, 405 NE2d 1001, 10 MassAppCt 817.—Autos 244(36.1), 246(1); Pretrial Proc 3; Refer 91, 99(6); Witn 379(10).

Calvanese v. W. W. Babcock Co., Inc., MassAppCt, 412 NE2d 895, 10 MassAppCt 726.—App & E 1067; Damag 166(1); Evid 150, 350, 547, 547.5; Pretrial Proc 383; Prod Liab 54, 83, 97; Sales 1.5; Witn 347.

Calvary Holdings, Inc. v. Chandler, CA1 (Mass), 948 F2d 59.—Fed Civ Proc 2553; Fed Cts 643; Sec Reg 53.15.

Calvert-Distillers Corp.; Jackman v., Mass, 28 NE2d 130, 306 Mass 423.—Courts 91(1); Trade Reg 93, 97, 98, 99, 251, 257, 485, 736.

Calvine Mills, Inc.; Prudhomme v., Mass, 225 NE2d 592, 352 Mass 767.—Neglig 1130, 1173, 1177.

Calvin Hosmer, Stolte Co. v. Paramount Cone Co., Mass, 189 NE 192, 285 Mass 278.—App & E 992, 1050, 1110(10); Contracts 352(1); Damag 78(6), 175; Evid 213(1), 213(4); Sales 177, 371, 383; Trial 260(9).

Calvo; Com. v., MassAppCt, 668 NE2d 846, 41 MassApp-Ct 903.—Crim Law 982.9(5).

Camacho v. Board of Selectmen of Stoughton, Mass-AppCt, 535 NE2d 1290, 27 MassAppCt 178.—Towns 18, 49.

Camaioni, Case of, MassAppCt, 389 NE2d 1028, 7 Mass-AppCt 927.—Work Comp 1738, 1950.

Camara v. Board of Appeals of Tewksbury, MassAppCt, 662 NE2d 719, 40 MassAppCt 209.—Evid 43(4).

Camara v. Capeto, MassAppCt, 446 NE2d 91, 15 Mass-AppCt 955.—Mun Corp 710.

Camara; Smola v., MassAppCt, 449 NE2d 678, 16 Mass-AppCt 908.—Int Rev 4790; Receivers 29(1).

Camara; U.S. v., CA1 (Mass), 451 F2d 1122, cert den 92 SCt 1513, 405 US 1074, 31 LEd2d 808.—Armed S 20.1(2), 20.8(1), 40.1(7); Crim Law 1031(3), 1115(1), 1186.1; Gr Jury 8.

Camar Corp. v. Preston Trucking Co., Inc., DMass, 18 FSupp2d 112.—Carr 111, 133, 134, 135, 147, 153, 155, 158(1); Evid 351.

Camarra; Bowie v., MassAppDiv, 36 MassAppDec 105.— App & E 192(1); Damag 118; New Tr 74.

Cambara; U.S. v., CA1 (Mass), 902 F2d 144.—Consp 33(1), 47(6); Crim Law 742(1), 1159.2(7), 1166.18.

Cambex Corp.; Greenstone v., CA1 (Mass), 975 F2d 22.— Fed Civ Proc 636.

Cambex Corp.; Greenstone v., DMass, 777 FSupp 88, aff 975 F2d 22.—Fed Civ Proc 636; Sec Reg 60.28(2.1), 60.28(4), 60.28(13).

For Later Case History Information, see KeyCite on WESTLAW

Exhibit 14-10 Massachusetts Digest, Table of Cases

CALLOW v. THOMAS
Cite as 78 N.E.2d 637
Mass.   637

N.E.2d 729, 731. Consequently, no error of fact or of law being made to appear, we cannot modify this provision of the decree.

The matter of allowance of attorney's fees, briefs and expenses in this court will be settled by a separate order of a single justice upon presentation of an itemized list of the expenses.

Decree affirmed.

CALLOW v. THOMAS.

Supreme Judicial Court of Massachusetts. Middlesex.

April 1, 1948.

1. Husband and wife ⚷205(2)

No cause of action arises in favor of either spouse for a tort committed by the other during coverture.

2. Husband and wife ⚷205(2)

Where either spouse commits a tort upon the other during coverture recovery is denied, not merely because of the disability of one spouse to sue the other during coverture, but because of the marital relationship, no cause of action ever came into existence.

3. Divorce ⚷313

After divorce, no action can be maintained by either spouse for a tort committed by the other during coverture.

4. Marriage ⚷57, 67

Generally an "annulment" is distinguished from a "divorce" in that annulment is not a dissolution of the marriage but is a judicial declaration that no marriage has ever existed, and decree of annulment makes the marriage void ab initio even though the marriage be voidable only at the instance of the injured party. G.L.(Ter.Ed.) c. 207, § 14.

See Words and Phrases, Permanent Edition, for all other definitions of "Annulment" and "Divorce".

5. Marriage ⚷67

Where marriage was voidable and not void and so was valid until set aside by decree of nullity, wife could not after annulment, recover for a tort committed upon her by husband during coverture because of his gross negligence in operation of automobile in which wife was a guest passenger. G.L.(Ter.Ed.) c. 207, § 14.

6. Marriage ⚷67

Where a voidable marriage has been annulled things which have been done during the period of the supposed marriage ought not to be undone or reopened after the decree of annulment. G.L.(Ter.Ed.) c. 207, § 14.

———◆———

Report from Superior Court, Middlesex County.

Action by Muriel Callow against Frederick Thomas for injuries sustained when plaintiff was riding as a gratuitous passenger in an automobile owned and operated by defendant. The case was reported to Supreme Judicial Court without decision.

Judgment for defendant.

Before QUA, C. J., and LUMMUS, DOLAN, WILKINS, and SPALDING, JJ.

M. Harry Goldburgh and J. Finks, both of Boston, for plaintiff.

K. C. Parker, of Boston, for defendant.

SPALDING, Justice.

The plaintiff and the defendant were married in this Commonwealth on August 6, 1944, and thereafter lived together here as husband and wife. On November 9, 1944, while riding as a "gratuitous passenger" in an automobile owned and operated by the defendant, the plaintiff was injured when the automobile, due to the gross negligence of the defendant, ran into a tree. The plaintiff was in the exercise of due care. The accident occurred on a public way in this Commonwealth and the defendant's automobile was registered in accordance with the laws thereof. On June 28, 1945, upon the petition of the plaintiff to annul the marriage because of the defendant's fraud, the Probate Court decreed that the marriage was "null and

Exhibit 14-11 *Callow v. Thomas* (First Page)

Vol. 78   NORTHEASTERN REPORTER, 2d SERIES (Massachusetts Cases)

Column 1

—629—
Wright v
Health
Commissioner
of Boston
1948

(322Mas535)
107NE[1]775
157NE228
360NE[9]1060
387NE188

—633—
Watson's Case
1948

(322Mas581)
d 85NE[8]75
88NE[5]639
102NE[4]415
116NE[4]128
120NE[4]756
127NE[4]193
d 138NE[4]288
138NE[3]633
138NE[7]751
148NE[4]373
154NE[4]605
155NE[4]790
f 173NE[4]644
232NE[4]927
258NE[1]927
363NE[4]1336
373NE[71]1178
408NE[8]894
Cir. 5
186F2d277

—637—
Callow v
Thomas
1948

(322Mas550)
173NE[4]269
178NE[4]283
178NE[8]283
236NE[4]201
351NE[2]528
373NE[3]358
373NE[8]358
489NE[8]673
574NE[4]405
Cir. 1
504FS[4]654

—641—
Joyce v
Devaney
1948

(322Mas544)
95NE[1]175
103NE[1]322

Column 2

115NE[1]495
116NE[2]155
141NE[1]516
142NE[1]405
146NE[2]514
165NE[1]116
224NE[1]224
372NE[1]283
372NE[4]283

—644—
Massachusetts
v Hall
1948

(322Mas523)
82NE[3]10
87NE[6]202
178NE[3]267
317NE[3]831
334NE[2]616
366NE[2]726
421NE[2]761
421NE[1]764
440NE[5]769
d 595NE[1]777
58USLW4925

—649—
Franklin
Square House
v Siskind
1948

(322Mas556)
124NE[5]231
183NE[5]291
226NE[5]196

—651—
Provost's Case
1948

(322Mas604)

—652—
Rosenthal
v Maletz
1948

(322Mas586)
80NE[5]15
84NE552
97NE[17]171
99NE[1]927
d 103NE[4]251
105NE[1]248
126NE[1]531
129NE[19]906
140NE[18]646
163NE[10]160
170NE[4]839
170NE[19]840
247NE[1]393
q 342NE[13]717

Column 3

d 374NE[10]350
Cir. 1
331F2d33
97FS[17]777

—697—
Massachusetts
v Farrell
1948

(322Mas606)
85NE[2]451
95NE[18]541
109NE[18]174
126NE[18]808
132NE[20]303
142NE[10]389
182NE[1]128
201NE[18]832
216NE[18]426
226NE[14]210
235NE[14]800
265NE[4]382
314NE[4]450
326NE[6]714
334NE[1]648
337NE711
344NE[16]927
348NE[19]820
355NE478
363NE[7]1316
370NE[7]1026
370NE[14]1026
373NE[14]1126
383NE[20]1121
387NE[7]164
389NE[10]762
402NE[6]1056
402NE[5]1057
f 402NE[12]1060
406NE[4]419
406NE[4]421
417NE[6]980
422NE[4]452
436NE[6]1217
436NE[6]1223
457NE[12]624
471NE[7]1358
487NE[8]1370
504NE[13]615
509NE[7]304
522NE[6]6
547NE944
564NE[5]378
574NE[7]344
576NE[12]711
594NE[14]868
23MJ325

Column 4

Vol. 79

—1—
King v
Tewksbury
1948

(322Mas668)
cc 81NE737

—2—
Morin v
Trailways
of New
England Inc.
1948

(322Mas744)

—3—
Wagstaff v
Director of the
Division of
Employment
Security
1948

(322Mas664)
82NE[1]2
84NE[1]544
85NE[1]780
86NE[1]57
89NE[1]782
92NE[1]253
96NE[2]862
97NE640
98NE[1]362
99NE[1]59
106NE[3]422
117NE[1]165
118NE[1]774
197NE[4]597
344NE[2]895
382NE[2]201
454NE[4]95

—5—
Kubilius
v Hawes
Unitarian
Congregational
Church
1948

(322Mas638)
87NE[1]214
154NE[8]601
244NE[4]279
244NE[6]279
Cir. 1
735FS[6]1097

Column 5

—10—
Royal v Royal
1948

(322Mas662)
s 87NE850
j 133NE[1]240

—11—
Seltmann v
Seltmann
1948

(322Mas650)
85NE[3]442
q 146NE[2]499
294NE[1]557
316NE[1]763

—13—
Herald v Rich
1948

(322Mas659)

—15—
Goff v Hickson
1948

(322Mas655)
88NE[1]337
89NE[3]1
91NE[4]235
91NE[4]927
104NE[1]495

—17—
Ryder v Ryder
1948

(322Mas645)
269NE[8]94
412NE[7]917

—185—
Delgreco v
Delgreco
1948

(322Mas706)
145NE[2]688
215NE[3]670

—187—
General v
Woburn
1948

(322Mas634)
85NE[1]230
86NE[1]645
99NE[1]43
111NE[2]671

Column 6

e 115NE[5]149
129NE[1]895
175NE[2]916
208NE[1]234
214NE[1]43
252NE[1]213
252NE[1]896
269NE[1]233
438NE[5]91
461NE771
556NE[4]117

—189—
Connolly v
John Hancock
Mutual Life
Insurance Co.
1948

(322Mas678)
116NE[4]678
129NE[1]619
141NE[4]513
141NE[4]726
d 174NE[1]138
258NE[1]20
Cir. 1
201F2d[4]422
282FS[4]376

—192—
McCartin
v School
Committee
of Lowell
1948

(322Mas624)
111NE[3]750
q 184NE[3]343
217NE[1]769
294NE211
d 294NE[3]212
d 310NE[2]336
335NE[2]655
336NE752
356NE[3]263
378NE[21]1376
378NE[31]1376
384NE[2]230
384NE[3]230
417NE[2]461
486NE46
486NE[3]47

—195—
Owens-Illinois
Glass Co. v
Bresnahan
1948

(322Mas629)
d 110NE[2]125
142NE[2]762

318

Exhibit 14-12   Massachusetts Shepard's

to find relevant court decisions, you would simply have to begin reading court decisions until you stumbled on one that related to your problem. Fortunately, West developed its digest system to help us locate cases more efficiently. A digest is a collection of court decision summaries arranged by subject matter. These summaries are in reality the headnotes located at the beginning of cases "cut and pasted" into the right digest locations.

West has organized the law into hundreds of legal topics. Each topic is then subdivided into key numbers, or sections. The job of the West editor who is reading a new decision is to categorize each aspect of the decision by labeling it with a West topic name and key number. If a given case involves five different points of law, it will be listed in five different parts of the digest. If it contains ten different points of law, it will be listed in ten different parts of the digest, and so on. Take another look at the headnotes to *Callow v. Thomas* in Exhibit 14-11 on page 416. Each headnote summarizes one aspect of that decision. Each headnote is also labeled with a legal topic, such as Divorce; a key symbol; and then a number (known as the key number). For example, when reading Callow, the editor thought that the second legal point raised in the case dealt with the topic of Husband and Wife.

There are 354 separate subtopics under Husband and Wife. The editor thought this particular point belonged under key number 205(2). To find out what all the possible subtopics under Husband and Wife are, you could consult the Analysis section, located at the beginning of the Husband and Wife topic in the Massachusetts Digest.

Exhibit 14-13, on page 419, shows a copy of that Analysis page. Note that key number 205(2) comes under the general heading VI. ACTIONS. Following the Analysis is a further breakdown, showing the subject matter of each key number.

Once the West editor has finished labeling the headnotes and writing the one-paragraph headnote summaries, they are placed at the beginning of the decision, and the decision is published in the appropriate regional reporter. For Massachusetts cases that would be the North Eastern Reporter. In addition, each headnote is published in a state digest along with the headnotes from all other decisions from that state relating to the same topic. In state digests West lists the summaries as follows: (1) Federal cases that originated in that jurisdiction (if there are any) are listed before state cases; (2) the highest courts are listed before the intermediate appellate courts; and (3) the cases are listed in reverse chronological order, with the newest cases listed first.

Exhibit 14-14, on page 420, shows a page from the Massachusetts Digest 2d on the topic Husband and Wife, key number 205(2). Find the summaries of *Callow v. Thomas*. Then compare them to headnotes 1 and 2 of the Callow decision in Exhibit 14-11, on page 416. They are identical. Similarly, you could read an exact duplicate of headnote 3 in the Massachusetts Digest by looking under the topic Divorce and the key number 313.

The beauty of the digest system is this: Once you know that the West editors think your problem is categorized under the topic Husband and Wife, key number 205(2), you can go to the Massachusetts Digest and look under that topic and key number to find every other Massachusetts case that West thinks has dealt with that topic. Look again at the digest page, Exhibit 14-14. What other decision do you see summarized there? *Lewis*! If you compare those summaries with headnotes 1 and 6 in *Lewis*, located in exhibit 13-7 on page 376, you will see that once again the digest summaries and headnotes are identical.

HUSBAND AND WIFE

SUBJECTS INCLUDED

The marital relation; rights, powers, duties and liabilities of married persons as between themselves and as to others, incident to the existence of the relation or arising from conveyances or agreements in consideration or in consequence of marriage

Disabilities and privileges of married women by reason of their coverture, and protection of their persons and property

Legal proceedings affecting husbands and wives and their property

Abandonment, community property and separate maintenance

Tort liability for interference with the marriage relation, as by enticing and alienating or by criminal conversation

SUBJECTS EXCLUDED AND COVERED BY OTHER TOPICS

Adultery and bigamy as criminal offenses, see ADULTERY, BIGAMY

Contracts to marry, see BREACH OF MARRIAGE PROMISE

Contracts to procure marriage or in restraint of marriage, see CONTRACTS

Divorce and judicial separation, see DIVORCE

Marriage and annulment thereof, see MARRIAGE

Surviving spouse's property rights, see DOWER AND CURTESY, HOME-STEAD, DESCENT AND DISTRIBUTION, WILLS

Testamentary capacity of married women, see WILLS

Witnesses, competency of husband and wife for or against each other and privileged communications, see WITNESSES

For detailed references to other topics, see Descriptive-Word Index

---

Analysis

I. MUTUAL RIGHTS, DUTIES, AND LIABILITIES, ☞1–25(6).

II. MARRIAGE SETTLEMENTS, ☞26–35.

*   *   *

VI. ACTIONS.—Continued.

      205. Rights of action between husband and wife.
         (1). Nature and form of remedy.
         (2). Rights of action in general.
         (3). Actions on contract in general.
         (4). Actions in respect to wife's separate property.
         (5). Intervention of prochein ami or next friend.
         (6). Allowance to wife to maintain action.
      206. Rights of action by husband or wife or both.
      207. —— In general.
      208. —— On contracts.
      209. —— For torts.

Exhibit 14-13   Analysis Page from Massachusetts Digest

HUSBAND & WIFE ☞205(2)

For references to other topics, see Descriptive-Word Index

that statute shall not authorize suits between husband and wife. M.G.L.A. c. 209, § 6.
Patuleia v. Patuleia, 127 F.Supp. 60.

Mass. 1980. Common–law rule of interspousal immunity did not bar action in which it was alleged that husband was in control of premises and responsible for sanding, salting or shoveling after snowstorm, that his failure to do so caused wife to fall, and that she suffered fractures and incurred medical expenses in excess of $2,500.
Brown v. Brown, 409 N.E.2d 717, 381 Mass. 231.

Mass. 1978. Common–law doctrine of interspousal immunity did not protect husband as host driver from liability to his wife as passenger for injuries sustained in collision and, hence, did not preclude owner and operator of other vehicle, named as defendants in main action by wife, from seeking to recover in third-party action against husband for contribution as a joint tort-feasor. M.G.L.A. c. 231B § 1 et seq.
Hayon v. Coca Cola Bottling Co. of New England, 378 N.E.2d 442, 375 Mass. 644.

Mass. 1976. Arguments that tort actions between husband and wife would tend to disrupt peace and harmony of family and that such actions would tend to promote fraud and collusion on part of husband and wife for purpose of reaping undeserved financial reward at expense of family's liability insurer are insufficient to justify common-law rule of interspousal immunity.
Lewis v. Lewis, 351 N.E.2d 526, 370 Mass. 619, 92 A.L.R.3d 890.

Wife's action against her husband for personal injuries sustained in automobile accident was not barred by common-law rule of interspousal immunity.
Lewis v. Lewis, 351 N.E.2d 526, 370 Mass. 619, 92 A.L.R.3d 890.

Mass. 1974. Supreme Judicial Court had jurisdiction over suit by estranged husband seeking declaratory and injunctive relief against his pregnant wife, who intended to procure an abortion over his objection, as against contention of wife that there was no jurisdiction because of statute relating to suits between husband and wife. M.G.L.A. c. 209 § 6.
Doe v. Doe, 314 N.E.2d 128, 365 Mass. 556, 62 A.L.R.3d 1082.

Mass. 1959. Purpose of statute to effect that probate court shall have jurisdiction to enforce foreign judgments for support of wife against husband who is resident or inhabitant of commonwealth was to enable wife to enforce in commonwealth a foreign judgment for support against husband, provided he resides in or was an inhabitant of commonwealth but

right to enforce such judgment must be exercised solely in probate court. M.G.L.A. c. 209 § 6; c. 215 § 6.
Adams v. Adams, 157 N.E.2d 405, 338 Mass. 776.

Mass. 1958. Where bank books and bonds had stood in joint names of husband and wife and husband evidenced intent to give his wife a one half interest in deposits and bonds if she returned to live with him by saying "that they would belong to both equally", wife's interest in deposits and bonds upon return to live with husband was that of a tenant in common, and as such wife could maintain a suit in equity against husband who had converted the property held in common to his own use and by his appropriation of it had finally precluded her from any future enjoyment of it.
Arsenault v. Arsenault, 148 N.E.2d 662, 337 Mass. 189.

Mass. 1952. A wife had no cause of action against husband for past nonsupport which could be the subject of set-off in proceeding by husband for accounting of his property and business which wife took over upon husband's commitment to hospital as mental patient.
Peteros v. Peteros, 104 N.E.2d 149, 328 Mass. 416.

Husband was entitled to recover his property or its value and was entitled to an accounting of profits derived therefrom by wife during period husband was committed to hospital as a mental patient, but wife was entitled to credit for her services in operating the business during such period.
Peteros v. Peteros, 104 N.E.2d 149, 328 Mass. 416.

Mass. 1948. No cause of action arises in favor of either spouse for a tort committed by the other during coverture.
Callow v. Thomas, 78 N.E.2d 637, 322 Mass. 550, 2 A.L.R.2d 632.

Where either spouse commits a tort upon the other during coverture recovery is denied, not merely because of the disability of one spouse to sue the other during coverture, but because of the marital relationship, no cause of action ever came into existence.
Callow v. Thomas, 78 N.E.2d 637, 322 Mass. 550, 2 A.L.R.2d 632.

Mass. 1947. Jurisdiction in equity exists to adjudicate conflicting rights of husband and wife concerning property.
Yurkanis v. Yurkanis, 73 N.E.2d 598, 321 Mass. 375.

Mass. 1945. The fact that parties are husband and wife does not in general enable them to maintain against each other in equity equiv-

see **Massachusetts General Laws Annotated**

13 Mass.Dig.2d—21

Exhibit 14-14 Massachusetts Digest Case Summaries

PRACTICE TIP

Use headnotes and digest summaries to help you locate relevant opinions. But never quote from or rely on the headnote or digest language. Always read the case for yourself.

As you can see by looking at the digest page, there have also been more recent decisions on your topic. If you were researching this problem in the real world, you would want to read those decisions also. As with the secondary sources, digests are kept current with annual pocket parts and six-month interim supplements. Always check the pocket parts and interim supplements.

If you already know the topic and key number that you are interested in (for example, by having read *Callow v. Thomas* and thereby knowing that the topic Husband and Wife governs your issue), you can access a digest by looking up that key number topic. If you do not already know the topic or key number, you need to consult the subject matter index, just as you did with the statutes.

West places headnotes on *all* cases, federal and state. West then organizes these headnotes by subject matter in several different digests, including the American digest system (all cases, federal and state, from 1658 to the present time), regional digests (cases from a particular region), state digests (federal and state cases from a particular state), and federal digests (all federal cases). The topic and key number system is the same in all these digests. As we have seen, if you look under Husband and Wife, key number 205(2), in the Massachusetts Digest, you will find Massachusetts cases dealing with whether spouses can sue each other. If you want to know how another state handles that same problem, you simply go to the state digest for that state and look under the topic Husband and Wife, key number 205(2). If you want to find recent cases from around the country, you go to the most recent general digest.

When seeking court opinions through the West digest system, you first have to decide what types of cases you want and what time period you want to cover. The first question to ask yourself is whether you want federal or state cases. If you want federal, do you want all federal cases or only Supreme Court cases and cases from your circuit and district? If you want state cases, do you want them from only your state, your region, a mixture of states, or all states? Second, do you want cases from the beginning of time or only the most recent cases? Depending on your answers you will select one or more of the available digests. See Figure 14-3, on page 422.

e. Summary of the Steps for Locating Primary Authority

Figure 14-4, on page 423, presents a checklist summarizing the main approaches that we have been discussing for locating statutes and court opinions.

If you want	Use
only U.S. Supreme Court decisions	the U.S. Supreme Court Digest.
recent federal cases	the Federal Practice Digest 4th.
older federal cases	the Federal Digest, the Modern Federal Practice Digest, or the Federal Practice Digest 2d or 3d.
individual states cases, along with federal cases that originated in federal courts in that state or that were appealed from state court to the federal courts	the state digest (available for all states except Delaware, Nevada, and Utah). State digests may also be organized by date. For example, the Massachusetts Digest covers decisions before 1933, while the Massachusetts Digest 2d includes cases from 1933 to date.
a group of state and the federal cases that originated in federal courts in that region or that were appealed from a state court in that region to the federal courts	a number of individual state digests or a regional digest (available for all regions except the Northeast, South, and Southwest). Regional digests may also be organized by date. For example, the Atlantic Digest covers decisions up to 1938, and the Atlantic Digest 2d covers cases from 1938 to date.
all cases, both federal and state	the Decennials and General Digest.

Figure 14-3   Summary of Available Digests

4. Update Your Research

In order to feel confident about your researching results, you must do everything you can to make sure your results are as up to date as possible. If you do not do this, there will always be the possibility that one of the cases you are relying on has been **reversed** or overruled. Recall that we say a case is reversed when the litigants appeal the decision and a higher court overturns or negates the decision of the lower court. A case is **overruled** when the court in a later case changes the law as it was found in a prior appellate decision. Finally, even if the case has not been reversed or overruled, a later court decision may explain the earlier case in such a way as to change its meaning. It is hard to imagine any more terrible researching nightmare than to turn over the results of your research to someone else and then to have that someone else rely on those results, only to find out that a recent case you did not find invalidates your conclusions. Making sure that your researching results are complete and up to date is vital.

The following is a discussion of two of the main methods to update your researching results: checking the regional reporter "mini-digests" and using Shepard's Citations. In the last section of this chapter we will discuss a third method, conducting on-line research. Computerized on-line databases, such as Westlaw and Lexis, are definitely much more current than any printed materials used for updating. In fact, both Westlaw and Lexis claim to have most court

Reverse
A decision is reversed when an appellate court overturns or negates the decision of a lower court.

Overrule
A decision is overruled when a court in a later case changes the law so that its prior decision is no longer good law.

1. Look for Relevant Statutes
   A. Locate the statutes.
      ■ If you have the citation, go immediately to the correct chapter and section number.
      ■ If you do not have a citation, locate it by
           —using the subject matter index,
           —finding it in a secondary source, or
           —seeing it in a case decision.
   B. Update the statutes by checking the pocket parts.
   C. Read the case annotations.
      ■ If your state has more than one set of annotated statutes, check them both.
      ■ Check the pocket part.

2. Look for Relevant Court Opinions
   A. If you have the citation, go immediately to the correct volume and page number.
   B. If you do not have a citation, locate it by
      ■ looking up one of the party's names in the Digest Table of Cases or Defendant/Plaintiff's Table,
      ■ using Shepard's to locate a parallel citation if you have only one of the citations,
      ■ searching the summaries following a relevant statute,
      ■ doing background research in a secondary source, or
      ■ looking in a digest under the appropriate topic and key number.
   Locate the appropriate topic and key number either
           —by using the same topic and key number as found in another relevant case or
           —by searching in the subject matter index for your issue.

Figure 14-4   Summary of Steps for Locating Primary Authority

decisions in their computers, and hence accessible to researchers, within twenty-four to forty-eight hours after they are decided. National law journals and newspapers, such as Lawyers Weekly USA, and state-specific newspapers, such as Massachusetts Lawyers Weekly, are also good resources for keeping current with legal changes.

a. Using the Digest Topics and Key Numbers

This method will help you find all recent court opinions that have been digested under the particular topic and key number that you have been using when doing your research. Recall that West reviews all new court decisions in order to summarize the key legal points in headnotes. The headnotes are then arranged by subject matter in the digest. Headnotes from older cases are found in the hardbound volumes of the digest. Headnotes from more recent cases are found in the pocket parts of the digest. Therefore, when doing research, once you have found a pertinent case, you must read the headnotes to determine which ones are relevant to the issues you are researching. Those headnotes will be labeled with topics and key numbers. You then go to the digest's hardbound volume *and* pocket part under those topics and key numbers and check for additional cases.

Pocket parts are published only once a year. These are supplemented halfway through the publication year with a paperback supplement. Check to see whether your library contains the interim supplement. If there is such a supplement, check it for cases that have been published since the pocket parts were printed.

In order to bring your research up to date, you must take one further step: You must check for cases that have been decided since the pocket part or supplement was published. To do that, you check the first page of the digest pocket part or supplement. On that page is a list that states when this particular pocket part was printed and which volumes of which reporters are included. We will be referring to this list as the closing table.

For example, if you checked the first page of the pocket part of the Massachusetts Digest 2d volume covering Husband and Wife, you would find a list similar to the following:

Closing with Cases Reported in

North Eastern Reporter, Second Series 828 N.E.2d

Supreme Court Reporter . . . . 125 S. Ct. 2316

Federal Reporter, Second Series 407 F.3d 1219

Federal Supplement . . . . 367 F. Supp. 2d

This listing tells you that when this particular pocket part was printed, the North Eastern Reporter, Second Series, was current through volume 828. This means that all court decisions that have been printed through that volume are summarized in the digest. The cases published in volume 829 and later, however, have not been summarized, as they did not exist at the time the pocket part was printed.

Unfortunately for you, a case published in volume 829 or later might be just the one you need. One method to bring the research up to date would be to read through every court decision that has been published in those volumes from volume 829 on. There is a better method, however.

In every hardbound volume of court decisions West includes a minidigest. That mini-digest includes headnotes from only those cases published in that hardbound volume. Therefore, instead of having to read through each case that has been published since the digest pocket part was printed, you can scan through the mini-digests in the recently published hardbound volumes for your topic and key number and then note only the relevant cases for further study. In addition, prior to publishing cases in the hardbound volumes West issues a few opinions at a time in pamphlets called advance sheets. These pamphlets also contain mini-digests of just the cases in those pamphlets. Therefore, to complete your updating, you will want to search in these advance sheet mini-digests as well.

Exhibit 14-15, on page 425, shows what such a mini-digest looks like. Notice that in this particular advance sheet there are two cases on the topic Husband and Wife but none for our specific key number.

Figure 14-5, on page 426, summarizes the steps that you need to take when updating your research using the digest topic and key number method.

INDEMNITY ☞27

Commonwealth was purchasing the entire road, the deeds were very similarly worded, and the Commonwealth recorded the two deeds on the same day within minutes of each other.—Id.

☞**89. Use of highway for other purposes by abutting owner.**

Mass.App.Ct. 2005. Road which Commonwealth purchased from prior owners subject to easements was a private way and thus landowner who had easement over road lots had right to lay utilities "in, on, along, under and upon" the lots; road was a private way when lots were sold to Commonwealth, and there had been no changes in road's use. M.G.L.A. c. 187, § 5.—Haugh v. Simms, 835 N.E.2d 1131, 64 Mass.App.Ct. 781.

Easement allowing lot owner to lay utilities on road lots deeded to Commonwealth did not violate doctrine of prior public use; easements were created at time lots were transferred, and statute allowing owner to lay utilities applied retroactively. M.G.L.A. Const.Amend. Art. 49, § 179; M.G.L.A. c. 187, § 5.—Id.

Easement over road lots extended from road to state forest and did not allow easement holder to lay utilities upon whole of state forest. M.G.L.A. c. 187, § 5.—Id.

HOMICIDE

II. MURDER.

☞**540. —— In general.**

Mass. 2005. To determine whether a murder was committed with extreme atrocity or cruelty, jury may consider: (1) indifference to and taking pleasure in the victim's suffering; (2) consciousness and degree of suffering of the victim; (3) extent of physical injuries to the victim; (4) the number of blows delivered by the defendant to the victim; (5) the manner and degree of force with which the blows were delivered; (6) the instrument or weapon employed by the defendant; and (7) the disproportion between the means needed to cause death and those employed.—Com. v. Anderson, 834 N.E.2d 1159, 445 Mass. 195.

Fact that victim apparently died instantaneously from single gunshot, with no evidence of defensive wounds, did not preclude finding that murder was committed with extreme atrocity or cruelty; encounter between defendant and victim lasted several minutes, victim was likely kneeling and pleading prior to being shot, and gun was fired point blank into victim's face.—Id.

XII. INSTRUCTIONS.

(B) SUFFICIENCY.

☞**1391. —— In general.**

Mass. 2005. Instruction on malice, in prosecution for murder, correctly stated elements required. —Com. v. Anderson, 834 N.E.2d 1159, 445 Mass. 195.

HUSBAND AND WIFE

I. MUTUAL RIGHTS, DUTIES, AND LIABILITIES.

☞**14.11. —— Rights of creditors as to estate in entirety or in common.**

Mass.App.Ct. 2005. Husband and wife, who held residential property under common law tenancy by the entireties at time of sheriff's sales arising from claims of husband's creditor, did not,

through any retroactive effect of subsequent election to have their ownership interests treated as a statutory tenancy, increase rights of creditor, which purchased only a survivorship interest in the property and acquired no interest as against wife. M.G.L.A. c. 209, § 1A.—Maynard Realty Corp. v. Testa, 835 N.E.2d 262, 64 Mass.App.Ct. 909.

VIII. SEPARATION AND SEPARATE MAINTENANCE.

☞**279(6). Performance or breach.**

Mass.App.Ct. 2005. Former husband, who was obligated under separation agreement incorporated into divorce judgment to establish an estate plan leaving one-third of his estate in trust to former wife, did not breach the agreement or implied covenant of good faith and fair dealing when setting up his estate plan, though former husband had moved to Japan and remarried, and former wife claimed he had invested, divested, and diminished his assets in such ways it was unlikely one-third of estate would be available for her; former husband executed will literally complying with separation agreement, former husband's handling of his assets did not violate separation agreement, and former wife had not experienced a diminution in benefits. —Abeggan v. Abeggan, 834 N.E.2d 764, 64 Mass. App.Ct. 590.

Former husband, who was obligated under separation agreement incorporated into divorce judgment to establish an estate plan leaving one-third of his estate in trust to former wife, did not breach any fiduciary duty when setting up his estate plan, though former wife claimed he had invested, divested, and diminished his assets in such ways it was unlikely one-third of estate would be available for her; with the exception of the estate plan provision, there was no question former husband had complied with all other requirements of separation agreement, and former husband complied with letter of separation agreement by including the required one-third provision in his will.—Id.

IMPLIED AND CONSTRUCTIVE CONTRACTS

I. NATURE AND GROUNDS OF OBLIGATION.

(D) EFFECT OF EXPRESS CONTRACT.

☞**60.1. —— In general.**

Mass.App.Ct. 2005. Where a valid contract covers the subject matter of dispute, the law need not create a quantum meruit right to receive compensation for services rendered.—Palriwala v. Palriwala Corp., 834 N.E.2d 1241, 64 Mass.App.Ct. 663, review denied 838 N.E.2d 577, 445 Mass. 1107.

INDEMNITY

II. CONTRACTUAL INDEMNITY.

☞**27. —— In general.**

Mass.App.Ct. 2005. Indemnity provision in resin seller's invoices materially altered terms set forth in buyer's purchase order and thus did not become part of contract between seller and buyer; purchase order provided that seller warranted that resin was merchantable and that acceptance of resin was not waiver of that warranty or of buyer's rights and remedies for losses stemming from resin. M.G.L.A. c. 106, § 2-207(2)(b).—Borden Chemical, Inc. v. Jahn Foundry Corp., 834 N.E.2d

(31)

Exhibit 14-15   Example of a Digest Page Located in Regional Reporters and Their Advance Sheets

1. **Check the Digest's Main Volume, Supplement, and Pocket Part.**
   Use the relevant topics and key numbers to check the pocket part (and supplement if it exists) for recent decisions.

2. **Check the Closing Table.**
   Check the listing on the first page of the most recent digest pocket part or supplement to determine the last volume of your regional reporter covered in that pocket part.

3. **Check Recent Hardbound Reporter Volumes.**
   Check the mini-digest located in each hardbound volume of your regional reporter published since the digest pocket part or most recent supplement was printed (as determined by the digest closing table).

4. **Check the Pamphlets Containing the Advance Sheets.**
   Check the mini-digest located in each advance sheet of your regional reporter published since the digest pocket part or most recent supplement was printed (as determined by the digest closing table).

Figure 14-5   Summary of Steps for Updating through the Digest Topic and Key Number Method

Subsequent case history
Information about what happened procedurally to the litigation after the case cited. Include this information in a citation. There is no entry for the topic Husband and Wife.

Treatment
How subsequent cases have affected the case you are Shepardizing. It is sometimes indicated by a one-letter abbreviation before the Shepard's citation.

Sheparding
The process of using Shepard's citations to check a court citation to see whether there has been any subsequent history or treatment by other court decisions.

b. Using Shepard's

Researchers use Shepard's Citations for several purposes. First, as we explained earlier, it is a source of parallel citations. For example, if you have only the Massachusetts citation for a court opinion, Shepard's will give you the North Eastern Reporter citation. It also works in the opposite direction; that is, if you have only the North Eastern Reporter citation, Shepard's will provide you with the Massachusetts citation.

The second major reason for using Shepard's is to find **subsequent history** for your case. Subsequent history includes such actions as an appellate court modifying, affirming, or reversing your case. For example, assume you find a Massachusetts intermediate appellate court decision that harms your client. You will be delighted if the Massachusetts Supreme Judicial Court (Massachusetts's highest appellate court) reversed that decision. That is an example of how you can use subsequent history, and Shepard's will give you that information.

The third reason for using Shepard's is to find out what later courts, deciding cases involving different litigants, have had to say about your case. In Shepard's this is called the **treatment** of your case. Assume you **Sheparized** a Massachusetts appellate court decision that harms your client, and it was affirmed by the Massachusetts Supreme Judicial Court. Things look bleak for your client. But there is always the possibility that the Massachusetts Supreme Judicial Court changed its mind regarding the legal issue involved and in a later decision, involving other litigants, overruled that earlier opinion. While this will not affect the outcome of the original case (as subsequent history does), it will have an effect on the precedential value of that case for future cases. Shepard's will also give you that information. (In addition to using Shepard's for updating case law, you can use it to determine whether a statutory provision is still in force.)

Shepard's is comprised of several red hardbound volumes, supplemented with red, gold, and white paper pamphlets. Using Shepard's is a very straightforward process, but it requires that you be absolutely precise. When Shepardizing, there is no room for even the slightest mistake in writing the citation because all of Shepard's is based on numbers: the numbers that make up the case citation.

To see how Shepard's works, assume that in the course of your research you located *Callow v. Thomas*, 322 Mass. 550, 78 N.E.2d 637 (1948), and that you would like to find additional cases that have discussed the topic of spousal immunity. Using Shepard's would be a good approach because, having read *Callow*, you would assume recent decisions that have discussed spousal immunity would mention *Callow* somewhere in the course of their discussion. Shepard's will give you the citation for every case (known as the **citing case**) that mentions the case you are Shepardizing (known as the **cited case**).

Citing case
A case listed in Shepard's that cites your case.

As the first step in Shepardizing, you would write down the citation for *Callow*. It is essential that you write down the correct volume number, page number, and reporter. It is also important to include the date so you will know with which Shepard's you need to begin your research.

Shepard's will inform you of whether a later case has dealt with your case as a whole or whether it has treated only specific issues. Therefore, the second step is to review the headnotes at the beginning of the case you want to Shepardize. In order to avoid finding cases that have cited your case but for irrelevant points, you need to write down the relevant headnote numbers from your case. For example, turn to Exhibit 14-11 on page 416. The *Callow* headnotes that relate to the topic of spousal immunity are headnotes 1, 2, and 3. You do not want to find every case that has cited *Callow*. For example, you do not want to find cases that have cited *Callow* for what the court said regarding annulment. That topic is discussed in headnotes 4, 5, and 6. Therefore, you would write down just those headnote numbers that relate to your issue of whether spouses can sue each other: headnotes 1, 2, and 3. Your notes would now look like the following:

Callow v. Thomas, 322 Mass. 550, 78 N.E.2d[1,2,3] 637 (1948)

The third step is to select the appropriate Shepard's volumes. There is a Shepard's for each state, for each region covered by West's regional reporters, and for each level in the federal court system. Which volumes you select will depend on your goal in Shepardizing. The state Shepard's will give you references to that state's state and federal court decisions that have cited your case. A regional Shepard's will give you references to *all* state and federal court decisions that have cited your case. Therefore, in Shepardizing *Callow*, if you want to find recent Massachusetts court decisions, the appropriate Shepard's would be the Massachusetts Shepard's volumes. If you want to find court decisions from around the country, the appropriate Shepard's would be the North Eastern Shepard's.

Once you have determined which Shepard's set to use, you must find the most recent paper supplement updating the hardbound Shepard's volumes for that set. On the front cover of that supplement you will see a box indicating how many hardbound volumes and supplements you will have to consult. A new paper supplement is issued each month. Depending on the month you may find anywhere from one to three paper supplements to the hardbound volumes.

These could include an annual or a semiannual supplement, a cumulative supplement, and a white advance sheet. In September of 2006, the "What Your Library Should Contain" box on the latest Massachusetts Shepard's supplement contained the following information:

WHAT YOUR LIBRARY SHOULD CONTAIN

1993 Bound Volume, Cases (Parts 1-4)*

1993 Bound Volume, Statutes (Parts 1 and 2)*

*Supplemented with
—September 2006 Cumulative Supplement Vol. 98 No.9

DISCARD ALL OTHER ISSUES

Of course, as of the time you are reading this text, the information in the "What Your Library Should Contain" box will have changed to reflect the current status of the Shepard's supplements.

Now you are finally ready to begin the process of Sheparding. Look for your citation in either the first Shepard's that could contain references to your case or the most recent Shepard's. Usually, you will want to start with the most recent Shepard's to save yourself from unnecessary work. For example, if you are Sheparding a case that was overruled six months ago, you could find that information fairly quickly by starting in the most recent Shepard's supplement. If you had started in the hardbound volume, you would have noted many citations that would no longer be relevant given the recent decision.

You can use either the North Eastern Reporter citation or the Massachusetts Reports citation. If you use the North Eastern Reporter citation, you will get North Eastern Reporter citations. If you use the Massachusetts Reports citation, you will get Massachusetts Reports citations. You will also get citations to some additional sources, such as law reviews, if you use the Massachusetts Reports citation. However, if you are relying on headnote numbers from the case as printed in the North Eastern Reporter to focus your search, be sure to use the North Eastern Reporter citations. Otherwise, the raised numbers you see in Shepard's will not match the numbers on the North Eastern Reporter headnotes.

For our example problem first we will use the N.E.2d cite, and we will start with the first Shepard's that could contain references to Callow. Because Callow is a 1948 decision, that would be the 1993 hardbound volume of Shepard's. Take a look at the page from the hardbound volume of Shepard's reproduced as Exhibit 14-16 on page 429.

First, notice that we are in the right part of Shepard's, as the words NORTHEASTERN REPORTER, 2d SERIES (Massachusetts Cases) appear centered at the top of the page. Second, find the reference to Vol. 78 in the

| Vol. 78 | NORTHEASTERN REPORTER, 2d SERIES (Massachusetts Cases) | | | | |

Vol. 78

—629—

Wright v
Health
Commissioner
of Boston
1948

(322Mas535)
107NE[1]775
157NE228
360NE[9]1060
387NE188

—633—

Watson's Case
1948

(322Mas581)
d 85NE[6]75
88NE[3]639
102NE[4]415
116NE[4]128
120NE[4]756
127NE[4]193
d 138NE[4]288
138NE[3]633
138NE[7]51
148NE[4]373
154NE[4]605
155NE[4]790
f 173NE[4]644
232NE[4]927
258NE[4]927
363NE[4]1336
373NE[7]1178
408NE[6]894
Cir. 5
186F2d277

—637—

Callow v
Thomas
1948

(322Mas550)
173NE[4]269
178NE[4]283
178NE[6]283
236NE[4]201
351NE[2]528
373NE[4]358
373NE[6]358
489NE[4]673
574NE[4]405
Cir. 1
504FS[4]654

—641—

Joyce v
Devaney
1948

(322Mas544)
95NE[1]175
103NE[1]322

115NE[2]495
116NE[2]155
141NE[3]516
142NE[4]405
146NE[2]514
165NE[3]116
224NE[2]224
372NE[1]283
372NE[4]283

—644—

Massachusetts
v Hall
1948

(322Mas523)
82NE[3]10
87NE[6]202
178NE[3]267
317NE[1]831
334NE[2]616
366NE[2]726
421NE[2]761
421NE[7]764
440NE[6]769
d 595NE[1]777
58USLW4925

—649—

Franklin
Square House
v Siskind
1948

(322Mas556)
124NE[6]231
183NE[6]291
226NE[6]196

—651—

Provost's Case
1948

(322Mas604)

—652—

Rosenthal
v Maletz
1948

(322Mas586)
80NE[6]15
84NE552
97NE[17]171
99NE[1]927
d 103NE[4]251
105NE[1]248
126NE[1]531
129NE[16]906
140NE[16]646
163NE[10]160
170NE[4]839
170NE[19]840
247NE[1]393
q 342NE[13]717

---

d 374NE[10]350
Cir. 1
331F2d33
97FS[17]777

—697—

Massachusetts
v Farrell
1948

(322Mas606)
85NE[2]451
95NE[16]541
109NE[16]174
126NE[16]808
132NE[20]303
142NE[10]389
182NE[1]128
201NE[16]832
216NE[16]426
226NE[14]210
235NE[14]800
265NE[4]382
314NE[6]450
326NE[6]714
334NE[1]648
337NE711
344NE[16]927
348NE[16]820
355NE[2]478
363NE[7]1316
370NE[7]1026
370NE[14]1026
373NE[14]1126
383NE[20]1121
387NE[7]164
389NE[10]762
402NE[6]1056
402NE[6]1057
f 402NE[12]1060
406NE[6]419
406NE[6]421
417NE[6]980
422NE[6]452
436NE[6]1217
436NE[6]1223
457NE[12]624
471NE[7]1358
487NE[6]1370
504NE[13]615
509NE[7]304
522NE[6]6
547NE944
564NE[6]378
574NE[7]344
576NE[17]711
594NE[14]868
23MJ325

Vol. 79

—1—

King v
Tewksbury
1948

(322Mas668)
cc 81NE737

—2—

Morin v
Trailways
of New
England Inc.
1948

(322Mas744)

—3—

Wagstaff v
Director of the
Division of
Employment
Security
1948

(322Mas664)
82NE[1]2
84NE[1]544
85NE[1]780
86NE[1]57
89NE[1]782
92NE[1]253
96NE[2]862
97NE646
98NE[1]362
99NE[1]59
106NE[3]422
117NE[1]165
118NE[1]774
197NE[4]597
344NE[2]895
382NE[2]201
454NE[4]95

—5—

Kubilius
v Hawes
Unitarian
Congregational
Church
1948

(322Mas638)
87NE[1]214
154NE[6]601
244NE[4]279
244NE[6]279
Cir. 1
735FS[6]1097

—10—

Royal v Royal
1948

(322Mas662)
s 87NE850
j 133NE[1]240

—11—

Seltmann v
Seltmann
1948

(322Mas650)
85NE[3]442
q 146NE[2]499
294NE[1]557
316NE[1]763

—13—

Herald v Rich
1948

(322Mas659)

—15—

Goff v Hickson
1948

(322Mas655)
88NE[1]337
89NE[3]1
91NE[4]235
91NE[4]927
104NE[1]495

—17—

Ryder v Ryder
1948

(322Mas645)
269NE[2]94
412NE[7]917

—185—

Delgreco v
Delgreco
1948

(322Mas706)
145NE[2]688
215NE[3]670

—187—

General v
Woburn
1948

(322Mas634)
85NE[1]230
86NE[1]645
99NE[1]43
111NE[2]671

---

e 115NE[5]149
129NE[1]895
175NE[2]916
208NE[1]234
214NE[1]43
252NE[1]213
252NE[1]896
269NE[1]233
438NE[6]91
461NE771
556NE[4]117

—189—

Connolly v
John Hancock
Mutual Life
Insurance Co.
1948

(322Mas678)
116NE[4]678
129NE[1]619
141NE[4]513
141NE[4]726
d 174NE[4]138
258NE[1]20
Cir. 1
201F2d[4]422
282FS[4]376

—192—

McCartin
v School
Committee
of Lowell
1948

(322Mas624)
111NE[3]750
q 184NE[3]43
217NE[1]769
294NE211
d 294NE[3]212
d 310NE[2]336
335NE[2]655
336NE752
356NE[3]263
378NE[2]1376
378NE[3]1376
384NE[2]230
384NE[3]230
417NE[1]461
486NE46
486NE[3]47

—195—

Owens-Illinois
Glass Co. v
Bresnahan
1948

(322Mas629)
d 110NE[2]125
142NE[2]762

318

Exhibit 14-16   Massachusetts Shepard's

History of a Case

a (affirmed on appeal)

D (appeal dismissed)

m (modified on appeal)

r (reversed on appeal)

s (same case)

US cert den (Certiorari denied by U.S. Supreme Court)

Treatment of a Case

c (criticized)

d (case distinguished from cited case)

e (case explains cited case)

f (case follows cited case)

j (dissenting judge refers to cited case)

l (limited)

o (case expressly over-rules cited case)

q (soundness of deci-sion or reasoning questioned)

Figure 14-6 Shepard's Analysis Abbreviations

left-hand corner. This means we have located the right volume number. Next look in the first column for —637—, our page number.

The first citation following —637— is (322Mas550). This is the parallel citation for *Callow*. The parallel citation will always be the first reference, and it will always be surrounded by parentheses. Shepard's will give you this citation only once: in the first Shepard's that contains references to your case. Because *Callow* is a 1948 case, the parallel citation is found in the hardbound volume. For cases decided after 1993, the parallel citation will be in the first paper pamphlet to contain references to that case.

Following the parallel citation Shepard's always gives references to case history *if there* is any, and it will *always* be preceded by a letter. There is none for *Callow*. If you had seen a listing, such as D335US849, that would be a reference to case history. The D means that the appeal of the case was dismissed by the U.S. Supreme Court.

Look once again at the citations for *Callow* under —637—. Following the parallel citation are nine citations. Notice the raised numbers that follow some of the N.E.2d abbreviations. These numbers refer to the headnotes in our cited case, *Callow*. Again, this is Shepard's way of helping you narrow your research so that you can search for cases that cited your case on a specific topic as referenced in a particular headnote. Based on this information we see that only one of the listed cases, $351NE2d^2528$, pertains to our issue.

Finally, under *Callow* you will see one reference to a federal case. FS stands for Federal Supplement. A state Shepard's, such as the one for Massachusetts, will tell you about federal cases that originated in that state.

Notice that some of the citations on the Shepard's page are *preceded* by a letter. For example, the first citation under 78 N.E.2d 633 is preceded by the letter *d*. A listing of the letters used and what they mean can be found at the beginning of each Shepard's volume. For example, *d* means distinguished and *f* means followed. Three letters are of particular concern: *r* for reversed, *o* for overruled, and *q* for questioned. Figure 14-6 summarizes the one-letter abbreviations most commonly seen in Shepard's.

Before leaving this page of Shepard's, you should write down any citations that meet the requirements listed above—that is, any decision that is preceded by a letter, that contains a raised number corresponding to one of your decision's relevant headnote numbers, or that contains no raised headnote numbers. For our example there is only one citation that meets those requirements, and that is $351N.E.2d^2528$.

Next you need to repeat this process for each of the other supplements and hardbound volumes in the Shepard's set you are using. Once this is done, the last step is to find the cases for which you have found citations. To find the case that corresponds to the citation $351N.E.2d^2528$, take a look in your text at Exhibit 13-7, on page 378. This is where we have reproduced page 528 from *Lewis*. Can you find the reference to *Callow*? Notice that Shepard's takes you right to the page on which the citing case cites the decision that you are Shepardizing. To correctly cite the citing case, in this instance *Lewis*, remember that you need to include the beginning page number.

If you had Shepardized using the official state citation, all the citing case references would also have used the official Massachusetts citations. You would also have found references to law review articles and American Law Reports

Annotated. You can find ALR annotations and law review articles only if you Shepardize using the official state citation.

In addition to state Shepard's, there are also regional Shepard's. The advantage to using regional Shepard's is that they include references to cases from around the country. Exhibit 14-17, on page 432, shows what such a regional listing looks like. This North Eastern Reporter edition of Shepard's shows citations to Callow from several states, including California and Wisconsin.

In conclusion, Shepard's is an invaluable resource. However, to be successful in using Shepard's, you must pay attention to every detail, such as the number of volumes and supplements to check. Use Figure 14-7, on page 433, to assist you with this process. It summarizes the steps you must take when using Shepard's to update your research.

c. Using Both Digests and Shepard's

Finally, you may be wondering why a researcher would use both methods of updating: the digest topic/key number method and Shepard's. The reason is that you may find different cases using the different methods. The digest method will only help you find cases that West thinks should be categorized as your case has been categorized. For example, the digest method will not work if you are researching spousal immunity cases under the topic Husband and Wife, key number 205(2), and a West editor categorizes a newer and relevant case as Torts, key number 168. On the other hand, Shepardizing will help you find all recent court opinions that have *cited* your decision whether or not they are digested under the same topic and key number. To be found through Shepard's, however, the more recent opinion must have cited your opinion. If the opinion simply discusses the same topic without citing your case, you will not find out about that more recent case using Shepard's.

5. Decide When to Stop Researching

This can often be one of the most difficult parts of a researching assignment. How can you know when to stop? Usually, you will know it is time to stop when you keep finding the same references in different resources. For example, you may find the same court opinion mentioned in an encyclopedia, a state digest, and an annotated code. When looking at more resources no longer gives you new citations to add to your list, stop.

C. RESEARCH INVOLVING FEDERAL STATUTES AND REGULATIONS

Up to this point we have been discussing how you perform state law research. Research into federal law follows a similar pattern. Assume you are representing Diane, the waitress whom we met in Chapter 3 whose boss fired her when he discovered she was pregnant. If she wants to sue for sex discrimination, which is prohibited by federal law, you will want to begin your research in the federal statutes.

The official publication for the federal statutes is the United States Code (U.S.C.). It is organized by subject matter into fifty titles. Like its official state

| Vol. 78 | | NORTHEASTERN REPORTER, 2nd Series | | | |

—611—

Case 3

Anchor Trading Corp. v Ryerson & Son Inc. 1948

(297NY817)
s 69 NYS2d844
83 NYS2d876
Cir. 5
119FS817
Calif
225 P2d960

—612—

Case 1

Spinelli v Arthur Tickle Engineering Works Inc. 1948

(297NY818)
s 67 NYS2d713
s 74 NYS2d11
261 NYS2d625

—612—

Case 2

New York Central Railroad Co. v New York and Harlem Railroad Co. 1948

(297NY820)
s 56 NYS2d712
s 72 NYS2d404
s 72 NYS2d830
s 85 NYS2d112
s 90 NYS2d309
cc 93 NE451
h 85 NYS2d270
132 NYS2d24
Cir. 2
203F2d707
Cir. 3
d 354FS741
354FS769
f 354FS772
Cir. 5
403F2d550
Md
86 A2d488

—613—

Eisemann v Fidelity & Deposit Company of Maryland 1948

(297NY822)
s 71 NYS2d186
s 87 NYS2d333

—614—

Case 1

Ruina v Commercial Travelers Mutual Accident Association of America 1948

(297NY824)
s 73 NYS2d641
182 NYS2d921
208 NYS2d325
j 467 NYS2d651

—614—

Case 2

New York State ex rel Whitney v Chambers 1948

(297NY826)
s 69 NYS2d360

—614—

Case 3

Ginsberg v Horvath 1948

(297NY827)
s 66 NYS2d631
s 67 NYS2d701
s 74 NYS2d409

—616—

Broman v Byrne 1948

(322Mas578)
82 NE[5]882
95 NE[4]186
j 107 NE[6]26
q 156 NE[6]805

j 314 NE[6]137
344 NE[2]907
555 NE[3]875
Ill
125 NE[4]648
N H
82 A2d603
Wyo
276 P2d466
35 A2d681n
47 A2d848n

—618—

Sullivan v Municipal Court of the Roxbury District 1948

(322Mas566)
85 NE[2]217
87 NE[2]21
89 NE[4]782
97 NE[11]183
101 NE[1]890
103 NE[3]697
130 NE[7]692
131 NE[6]748
142 NE[10]344
171 NE[1]276
171 NE[2]282
174 NE[10]448
174 NE[4]659
174 NE[3]660
205 NE[4]709
d 205 NE[1]710
214 NE[2]736
243 NE[2]925
247 NE[4]381
f 268 NE[1]348
f 268 NE[2]348
f 268 NE[3]348
f 269 NE[2]451
f 269 NE[3]451
271 NE[2]591
303 NE129
309 NE[10]890
332 NE[1]904
332 NE[2]904
332 NE[3]904
337 NE[2]685
337 NE[3]685
338 NE[2]833
343 NE[2]368
375 NE[11]343
389 NE[2]434
f 396 NE[2]995
396 NE[7]995
407 NE[10]368
451 NE445
d 471 NE[1]66
502 NE[3]958
Mont
530 P2d465
Tex
422 SW147

—623—

Broussard v Melong 1948

(322Mas560)
92 NE255
384 NE205
389 NE438
402 NE[2]1020

—624—

National Shawmut Bank of Boston v Hallett 1948

(322Mas596)
f 143 NE[8]535
149 NE[7]370
212 NE[7]560
292 NE[4]32
298 NE839
345 NE[3]924
Cir. 1
808FS[7]64

—629—

Wright v Health Commissioner of Boston 1948

(322Mas535)
107 NE[1]775
157 NE228
360 NE[9]1060
387 NE188

—633—

Watson's Case 1948

(322Mas581)
d 85 NE[8]75
88 NE[3]639
102 NE[4]415
116 NE[4]128
120 NE[4]756
127 NE[4]193
d 138 NE[4]288
138 NE[3]633
138 NE[7]751
148 NE[4]373
154 NE[4]605
155 NE[4]790
f 173 NE[4]644
232 NE[4]927
258 NE[2]927
363 NE[4]1336
373 NE[7]1178
408 NE[8]894

Cir. 5
186F2d277
N M
237 P2d355

—637—

Callow v Thomas 1948

(322Mas550)
(2 A2632)
173 NE[4]269
178 NE[4]283
178 NE[5]283
236 NE[4]201
351 NE[2]528
373 NE[4]358
373 NE[6]358
489 NE[4]673
574 NE[4]405
Cir. 1
504FS[4]654
Calif
240 P2d1006
283 P2d347
Conn
137 A2d355
142 A2d528
Kan
239 P2d934
Me
216 A2d32
Mo
331 SW656
478 SW337
N H
156 A2d133
193 A2d439
216 A2d782
241 A2d373
260 A2d98
279 A2d586
N M
269 P2d750
N D
68 NW665
Tenn
336 SW26
Utah
384 P2d391
Wis
95 NW823
43 A2637n
43 A2653n
92 A3945n

—641—

Joyçe v Devaney 1948

(322Mas544)
95 NE[1]175
103 NE[1]322

115 NE[1]495
116 NE[2]155
141 NE[1]516
142 NE[1]405
146 NE[2]514
165 NE[1]116
224 NE[1]224
372 NE[1]283
372 NE[4]283
N Y
137 NYS2d327
Conn
109 A2d589
Md
142 A2d819

—644—

Massachusetts v Hall 1948

(322Mas523)
82 NE[3]10
87 NE[6]202
178 NE[3]267
317 NE[3]831
334 NE[2]616
366 NE[2]726
421 NE[2]761
421 NE[1]764
440 NE[5]769
d 595 NE[1]777
617 NE[1]613
111 LE254
N Y
462 NYS2d116
Calif
140 CaR289
140 CaR293
Iowa
124 NW721
Md
596 A2d661
Mich
208 NW660
S D
134 NW109
Utah
585 P2d63
Va
141 SE714
61 A31210n
61 A31217n

—649—

Franklin Square House v Siskind 1948

(322Mas556)
124 NE[5]231
183 NE[5]291
226 NE[5]196

Exhibit 14-17   Northeastern Shepard's

1. **Start with the Full Citation.**
   Write down the full citation of the decision you want to Shepardize.

2. **Note the Relevant Headnotes.**
   Write down the relevant headnote numbers of the decision you want to Shepardize.

3. **Locate the Appropriate Shepard's.**
   Select the appropriate Shepard's volumes.

4. **Find the Most Recent Shepard's.**
   Find the most recent paper supplement updating the hardbound Shepard's volumes for that set. Then look on the front cover of that supplement to see how many hardbound volumes and supplements you will have to consult.

5. **Using the Most Recent Supplement, Find Your Citation.**
   Look for your citation in the most recent Shepard's.
   a. Make sure you are in the *right part* of Shepard's for your reporter; for example, looking in the N.E. section for an N.E.2d cite is fatal.
   b. Make sure you have the *right volume number.*
   c. Make sure you have the *right page number.*
   d. Write down the citation for any decision that is preceded by a letter, that contains a raised number corresponding to one of your decision's relevant headnote numbers, or that contains no raised headnote numbers.

6. **If Necessary, Repeat Step 5.**
   Repeat this process for each of the other supplements and hardbound volumes in the Shepard's set you are using.

7. **Locate Your Citations.**
   Remember that Shepard's will take you to the page on which your case is mentioned.

Figure 14-7   Summary of Steps for Updating Using Shepard's

counterparts it does not contain summaries of court decisions. Therefore, most researchers will begin with one of the two private publications: the United States Code Annotated (U.S.C.A.), published by West Group, or the United States Code Service (U.S.C.S.), published by Lexis Law Publishing.

As with state law research, you first need to think of words to describe your client's situation. Next you should consult an index.

In addition to using an index, you might be able to find a citation by looking in a popular name table. Some statutes are commonly referred to by the names of the sponsors (the Taft-Hartley Act) or a descriptive title (the Truth in Lending Act). All three publications—U.S.C., U.S.C.A., and U.S.C.S.—contain **popular name tables**, which give the formal citations for these acts. In addition, Shepard's Acts and Cases by Popular Names, Federal and State provides a convenient source for both federal and state legislation. The U.S. Supreme

Popular name table
Located in most codified statutes, this table lists

Court Reports Digest also contains a popular name table. In Diane's situation the statute that governs unlawful employment practices was enacted as part of the Civil Rights Act of 1964. It is codified in the United States Code in title 42, beginning at section 2000.

A few pages of 42 U.S.C.S. § 2000e-2, the part of the statute that outlaws certain employment practices, are reproduced in Exhibit 14-18, on page 435. As with annotated state codes, in the federal annotated codes following each statute there is some basic information about the law's legislative history. The United States Code Service also includes cross-references to the Code of Federal Regulations, as well as to other publications, such as Am. Jur. 2d. Finally, the annotated codes also include summaries of court decisions.

Just as when doing state-based research, once you have located and analyzed a federal statute, you must determine whether an administrative agency has interpreted the statute through regulations. Like the United States Code, the Code of Federal Regulations is organized by subject matter into fifty titles. Unfortunately, however, those fifty titles are not the same as those used in the United States Code. Therefore, your first step is to find the correct citation for any applicable regulation. To assist you, the Code of Federal Regulations contains a table of all those sections of the C.F.R. that have been promulgated under the authority of a particular statute.

You can also begin your research with the subject index to C.F.R., using it in the same way you would use the subject index of a statutory code. Exhibit 14-19, on page 436, presents a portion of the text of the Code of Federal Regulations covering sexual harassment. Notice the reference to 42 U.S.C. 2000e, the enabling statute that gives the Equal Employment Opportunity Commission authority to issue regulations setting out what constitutes sexual harassment.

In order to be as up to date as possible, you should also check the latest issues of the Federal Register. The Federal Register is published on a daily basis and contains any newly proposed regulations, as well as any proposed amendments to old regulations.

Unfortunately, there is no clear pattern for the publication of agency rulings (as opposed to agency regulations). Some loose-leaf services provide administrative regulations and rulings in such special-interest areas as employment, axation, and commerce. When available, they are a particularly useful source.

D. COMPUTER-ASSISTED RESEARCH

Two great advantages of computers are their abilities to store large amounts of information and to rapidly sort through and retrieve this information. These characteristics make computers valuable tools for legal researchers. Through the Internet and direct connections to Lexis, Westlaw, or Loislaw, law offices and libraries can access legal research materials that are stored on large mainframe computers. When connected to an on-line legal database, your computer can provide you with instant access to legal information that goes far beyond what the normal law firm can maintain in the form of traditional books and journals.

EQUAL EMPLOYMENT OPPORTUNITIES   **42 USCS § 2000e-2**

∗   ∗   ∗

§ 2000e-2. Unlawful employment practices

(a) Employer practices. It shall be an unlawful employment practice for an employer—

(1) to fail or refuse to hire or to discharge any individual, or otherwise to discriminate against any individual with respect to his compensation, terms, conditions, or privileges of employment, because of such individual's race, color, religion, sex, or national origin; or

(2) to limit, segregate, or classify his employees or applicants for employment in any way which would deprive or tend to deprive any individual of employment opportunities or otherwise adversely affect his status as an employee, because of such individual's race, color, religion, sex, or national origin.

∗   ∗   ∗

(July 2, 1964, P. L. 88-352, Title VII, § 703, 78 Stat. 255; Mar. 24, 1972, P. L. 92-261, § 8(a), (b), 86 Stat. 109.)

HISTORY; ANCILLARY LAWS AND DIRECTIVES

References in text:

"The Subversive Activities Control Act of 1950", referred to in subsec. (f) of this section, is Act Sept. 23, 1950, c. 1024, Title I, and appears as 18 USCS §§ 792 note, 793, note prec. 1501, 1507; 22 USCS § 618; 50 USCS §§ 781 et seq., 788 et seq.

Effective date of section:

Section 716(a) and (b) of Act July 2, 1964, provided: "(a) This title [42 USCS §§ 2000e et seq.] shall become effective one year after the date of its enactment.

"(b) Notwithstanding subsection (a), sections of this title other than sections 703, 704, 706, and 707 [42 USCS §§ 2000e-2, 2000e-3, 2000e-5, 2000e-6] shall become effective immediately.".

Amendments:

1972. Act Mar. 24, 1972, in subsec. (a), in paragraph (2), inserted "or applicants for employment"; and, in subsec. (c), in paragraph (2), inserted "or applicants for membership".

CODE OF FEDERAL REGULATIONS

Nondiscrimination requirements, 12 CFR Part 528.

Bureau of Indian Affairs, Department of the Interior; roads of the Bureau of Indian Affairs, 25 CFR Part 170.

Pennsylvania Avenue Development Corporation, Affirmative Action policy and procedure, 36 CFR Part 906.

RESEARCH GUIDE

Federal Procedure L Ed:

12 Fed Proc, L Ed, Evidence, § 33:66.

21 Fed Proc, L Ed, Job Discrimination, §§ 50:1, 16, 85, 127, 144, 176, 270, 275, 480, 488, 558, 576.

33 Fed Proc, L Ed, Trial, § 77:256.

Am Jur:

3A Am Jur 2d, Aliens and Citizens § 2001.

452

Exhibit 14-18   United States Code Service tit. 42, § 2000e-2

§ 1604.11   Sexual harassment.

(a) Harassment on the basis of sex is a violation of section 703 of title VII.[1] Unwelcome sexual advances, requests for sexual favors, and other verbal or physical conduct of a sexual nature constitute sexual harassment when (1) submission to such conduct is made either explicitly or implicitly a term or condition of an individual's employment, (2) submission to or rejection of such conduct by an individual is used as the basis for employment decisions affecting such individual, or (3) such conduct has the purpose or effect of unreasonably interfering with an individual's work performance or creating an intimidating, hostile, or offensive working environment.

(b) In determining whether alleged conduct constitutes sexual harassment, the Commission will look at the record as a whole and at the totality of the circumstances, such as the nature of the sexual advances and the context in which the alleged incidents occurred. The determination of the legality of a particular action will be made from the facts, on a case by case basis.

(c) Applying general title VII principles, an employer, employment agency, joint apprenticeship committee or labor organization (hereinafter collectively referred to as "employer") is responsible for its acts and those of its agents and supervisory employees with respect to sexual harassment regardless of whether the specific acts complained of were authorized or even forbidden by the employer and regardless of whether the employer knew or should have known of their occurrence. The Commission will examine the circumstances of the particular employment relationship and the job junctions performed by the individual in determining whether an individual acts in either a supervisory or agency capacity.

(d) With respect to conduct between fellow employees, an employer is responsible for acts of sexual harassment in the workplace where the employer (or its agents or supervisory employees) knows or should have known of the conduct, unless it can show that it took immediate and appropriate corrective action.

(e) An employer may also be responsible for the acts of non-employees, with respect to sexual harassment of employees in the workplace, where the employer (or its agents or supervisory employees) knows or should have known of the conduct and fails to take immediate and appropriate corrective action. In reviewing these cases the Commission will consider the extent of the employer's control and any other legal responsibility which the employer may have with respect to the conduct of such non-employees.

(f) Prevention is the best tool for the elimination of sexual harassment. An employer should take all steps necessary to prevent sexual harassment from occurring, such as affirmatively raising the subject, expressing strong disapproval, developing appropriate sanctions, informing employees of their right to raise and how to raise the issue of harassment under title VII, and developing methods to sensitize all concerned.

(g) Other related practices: Where employment opportunities or benefits are granted because of an individual's submission to the employer's sexual advances or requests for sexual favors, the employer may be held liable for unlawful sex discrimination against other persons who were qualified for but denied that employment opportunity or benefit.

(Title VII, Pub. L. 88–352, 78 Stat. 253 (42 U.S.C. 2000e et seq.))

[45 FR 74677, Nov. 10, 1980]

APPENDIX TO PART 1604—QUESTIONS AND ANSWERS ON THE PREGNANCY DISCRIMINATION ACT, PUBLIC LAW 95–555, 92 STAT. 2076 (1978)

INTRODUCTION

On October 31, 1978, President Carter signed into law the *Pregnancy Discrimination Act* (Pub. L. 95–955). The Act is an amendment to title VII of the Civil Rights Act of 1964 which prohibits, among other things, discrimination in employment on the basis of sex. The *Pregnancy Discrimination Act* makes it clear that "because of sex" or "on

---

[1] The principles involved here continue to apply to race, color, religion or national origin.

Exhibit 14-19   Code of Federal Regulations tit. 29, § 1604.11

1. Major On-Line Providers

On-line research via the Internet is rapidly becoming the principal, if not the primary, type of legal and factual research. Internet-based research shares many of the advantages of research using CD-ROMs. First, with an Internet connection and a laptop computer the law library becomes instantly portable. Second, the researcher can search for information by citation or by conducting a full-text search. Third, Internet-based research is becoming increasingly cost-effective, and sometimes, aside from the cost of the Internet connection itself, it is free.

The major law-related Internet-based research providers fall into two general categories. The first are commercial operations that charge a fee for their services, such as Lexis, Westlaw, and Loislaw. The second includes various governmental agencies, educational institutions, and private enterprises that provide both primary and secondary resources at minimal or even no cost.

a. The Major Commercial Databases: Lexis, Westlaw, and Loislaw

Until recently, Lexis and Westlaw were the only two major competing sources for on-line legal information. In 1996, Loislaw joined them as a lower-cost Internet-based alternative. All three services are accessed through their Internet sites. To use any one of the three, a law firm must pay a subscription fee.

(1) Lexis

The **Lexis** database includes the full text of federal and state court cases, statutes, and administrative regulations and of various specialized legal publications. The inclusion of Shepard's citations makes Lexis particularly useful to a researcher. Shepard's in FULL format provides the same information that can be obtained from the print volumes. You use Shepard's in KWIC format to check the accuracy of your case citation and to locate cases that directly affect your case's validity as precedent.

(2) Westlaw

Westlaw covers the same types of materials contained in the Lexis database. Perhaps the most significant difference is that in addition to the full text of appellate court cases, Westlaw contains the headnotes and key numbers that appear in West's National Reporter System. This feature can simplify the search process for some users and makes it easier to coordinate the results with materials gathered from West's regular publications.

To verify the continuing validity of court decisions, Westlaw also includes KeyCite, a service similar to Shepard's. In Westlaw you can also search for additional cases on the basis of West key numbers.

(3) Loislaw

Loislaw is the newest entrant into on-line delivery of legal researching materials. While the materials contained in its database are not nearly as extensive as those you can find in Lexis and Westlaw, the service is also considerably

Lexis
An on-line legal database containing court decisions and statutes from the entire country, as well as secondary authority; a competitor to Westlaw.

Westlaw
An on-line legal database containing court decisions and statutes from the entire country, as well as secondary authority; a competitor to Lexis.

Loislaw
An on-line legal database containing court decisions and statutes from the entire country. While its coverage of other legal materials is not as extensive as that of Westlaw and Lexis, it is also less expensive.

less expensive. Loislaw does contain all of the primary research material from the federal and state systems and is constantly adding new sources of information, such as treatises and news sources.

Loislaw includes GlobalCite as its citation verification service. Once you have completed a search, you click on the GlobalCite button and Loislaw produces a list of all primary and secondary materials in its database that contain a reference to your search result.

b. Other Internet-Based Resources

Within the last five years, there has been an explosion of legal materials on the Internet. The **Internet** is a worldwide network of networks—that is, a number of smaller regional networks all linked together. The Internet has been likened to the superhighways that connect large cities. From these large cities smaller freeways link smaller towns, where travelers move on slower, narrower side streets.

Many Internet sites contain legal materials, such as federal statutes, regulations, and Supreme Court opinions. The federal government, as well as many state and local governments, now maintains **web sites**, where they publish official documents on their **web pages**. In addition to combining text, pictures, and sometimes even sound, these web pages often contain **hypertext links** to other web pages with related information.

The major newspapers and television networks have web sites that cover law-related news. In the future we expect to see even more materials available through the Internet. However, while most of the information on the Internet is now free, it is not always as reliable or complete as the materials accessed through commerial providers such as Lexis, Westlaw, and Loislaw.

2. Computer Search Techniques

Fortunately, the same general principles apply to all computer searches, whether they are done using a commercial service such as Lexis or Westlaw, or other Internet-based sources. The most difficult part of computerized research is learning how to define and limit the nature of the search. You would not begin traditional legal research by going to the law library and simply paging through the books in the order that they appear on the shelf. You would first think of key terms to look for in the appropriate legal indexes. Similarly, when you approach the computer terminal, you should already have carefully thought out the nature of the issues and have identified key words or phrases that will become the basis of your computer search. Although the computer can process information at dazzling speeds, computerized research can still be expensive. Also, the old computer adage "garbage in, garbage out" is particularly applicable to computerized legal research. Because commercial on-line services often charge by the minute or by the search, you should develop your research strategy before you actually sign on.

Internet
A worldwide network of computer networks.

Web site
A location on the Interner that contains a series of web pages that are linked to a home page.

Web page
A computer page, accessible on the Internet, that contains links to other page.

Hypertext links
Computer codes that, when clicked on with a mouse, connect the user to other web pages with related information.

a. Determining Which Database to Use

If you have access to Lexis, Westlaw, or Loislaw, you will probably utilize one of these commercial services because they are generally more reliable and up-to-date than web sites on the Internet. However, once you have decided to use one of these service providers, you need to determine which of their many databases you wish to search. For example, if you are searching for court cases, you can search a particular district or circuit court in a specific state, all courts within a particular state, or all state courts in all fifty states. Then you have to decide if you also want to search federal court decisions and, if so, in which states or circuits.

When you first sign on to one of the commercial databases, you will be asked to designate which database you wish to use. Although the list of databases or "libraries" you can choose from will be shown on the computer screen, it is a good idea to make your decision before you go on-line.

You should limit your search to the smallest database that will accomplish your goal. Searching in too large a database—for example, by selecting all state cases when you are only looking for Florida case law—can result in extra on-line charges and may cause you to retrieve a very sizeable and therefore unmanageable list of cases.

If you are using other sources on the Internet, you can "surf the web" to locate legal databases. This surfing is done through a web browser, such as Netscape or Microsoft Explorer. These browsers give you access to many popular **search engines**. However, while all search engines are intended to perform the same task, each goes about it in a slightly different way, and they often produce very different results.

Search engine
A computer program that allows the user to retrieve web documents that match the key words entered by the searcher.

b. Searching within a Database

One of the main advantages of using a computerized database is that you are not limited to indexes. Instead, you can search the full-text of statutes, court opinions, and other materials contained in the on-line database. There are two main methods for conducting **full-text searches** in a computerized database. The first is known as terms and connectors. To use that method you must first think of terms to describe your legal issues and then connect those terms with Boolean operators, such as *or* and *and*, or proximity connectors. The second method is known as natural language. When you use that method, you simply tell the computer what you want it to find using a normal English sentence.

Full-text searches
A computer search that identifies every place in which the search term appears in the actual text of the document being searched.

(1) Terms and connectors

There are two basic steps in using the terms and connectors approach. First, you must determine which words best describe the legal issue you are researching. Then you must connect those words. The most critical step in this process is the first one: entering key words and phrases that tell the computer for what it is to search. Because the cost of computer research is sometimes based on the

number of searches conducted, there is a clear incentive to be as prepared as possible before the meter starts running.

The two most common errors in conducting computerized research are making your search request too general, resulting in hundreds of cases, or making it too narrow, potentially eliminating the very case you want. For example, if you instruct the computer to search for a single key word, frequently you will get back an overwhelming number of cases, with many of them not even relevant to your legal issue. For example, a list of all cases that includes a term as general as *negligence* is not helpful. One solution is to substitute narrower terms, such a *legal malpractice*. Also you can search for combinations of terms appearing together within a specifically defined space, such as *assumption* and *risk* appearing together or *store, wet, floor*, and *negligent* all appearing within the same paragraph.

The second problem, finding too few cases, usually occurs when too specific a term is used. For example, if you are searching for cases dealing with malpractice by a pediatric oncologist for failure to diagnose leukemia, you could certainly search by typing in *pediatric oncologist*. However, if there were a case directly on point but the court referred to the defendant simply as a pediatrician, then you would not find it. Therefore, you should always enter synonyms. In this example your search might be for *pediatrician* or *pediatric oncologist* or *physician* or *doctor* or *surgeon*.

In addition to using synonyms, in most computer databases you can also broaden your search by asking the computer to locate any word with a specific root, such as *pediatric*. In Westlaw and Lexis you do this by using the root expander: !. If you typed in *pediatric!* in either Lexis or Westlaw, you would get cases referring to *pediatric* or *pediatrician*. Other services, such as Loislaw, use the asterisk (*) as the root expander. Therefore, in Loislaw you would type pediatric*. Be careful with root expanders. Entering the search *child!* (or *child** in Loislaw) would get you references to *child* and *children*, but it would also retrieve *childish, childhood, childlike*, and so on.

Once you have determined the words to use, you must select your connectors. There are two types of connectors, Boolean (or logical) and proximity. The two most common Boolean connectors are *or* and *and*. You use or to find alternatives, such as in the example given above of *pediatrician* or *pediatric oncologist* or *physician*. You use *and* to require that both terms appear somewhere within the opinion: *pediatrician and negligence*.

Please note that in all three main commercial providers you can use the word *or* to indicate alternatives. However, in Westlaw a space also equals *or*. Therefore, in Lexis or Loislaw the search *pediatric oncologist* would find the phrase "*pediatric oncologist.*" In Westlaw the same search would find cases that contained either the word "*pediatric*" or the word "*oncologist.*" In any of the three systems you can ensure that you are searching for a phrase by including the words in quotation marks: "*pediatric oncologist.*"

P R A C T I C E   T I P

When using the terms and connectors method of searching, you will often find yourself with either too few or too many cases.

If you find too few or no cases:

■ If you found no cases, the first thing to do is to check your spelling. If you typed *grandfater* when you meant *grandfather*, you will get no search results.

■ Run your search in a larger database. For example, if you were searching in the database that covered cases from only the state's highest court, expand your search to cases from all of the courts of that state.

■ Either eliminate some terms or use less-restrictive terms. Instead of *poodle*, search for *dog*. Instead of *dog*, search for *pet*.

■ Use less-restrictive connectors. Instead of w/10, use w/25. Instead of w/p, use "and."

■ Use more synonyms. Instead of doctor, use "*doctor* or *physician* or *surgeon* or *medical*."

If you find too many cases:

■ Run the search in a smaller database. If you were looking at all state courts, change to the highest state courts or to all courts in a specific state.

■ Add additional terms or use more restrictive terms. For example, change *negligence* to *malpractice* and add the term *legal*.

■ Use more restrictive connectors. Change a w/p to a w/s.

■ Add a date restriction to find just the most recent cases.

As indicated above, the use of *and* will require that both terms occur somewhere within the opinion. However, to ensure that the terms are related to each other, you should use a proximity connector, such as w/s or w/p for within the same sentence or paragraph. For the "s" or "p" you can also substitute a precise number, such as w/10 to find two terms that occur within ten words of each other. Some Internet services, including Loislaw, use the proximity connector "near." Depending on the service, "near" may mean anything between ten and fifty words. In Loislaw "near" by itself means within twenty words. You can also specify an exact number. For example, "near2" requires the terms to be within two words of each other.

Finally, the computer will allow you to limit your search so that you retrieve only cases decided before or after a certain date or opinions authored

by a particular judge. This power to limit your request means that you can perform searches that would be far too time consuming if using conventional means. Imagine trying to use the hardbound reporters to find all cases decided by a particular judge, such as Justice Scalia, and involving a specific issue, such as freedom of religion. A task that would take hours using books only can be done in seconds using a computerized on-line service.

Once you have entered a terms and connectors search, you will be presented with a list of cases, arranged by most recent case first, that match your search criteria. Keep in mind that the computer can only work with the information you give it. As noted above, the use of synonyms is crucial if you want to retrieve all cases that deal with a similar fact pattern.

(2) Natural language

Both Lexis and Westlaw also include a "natural language query" method. You can phrase your search request as a normal English sentence, and the computer program will translate it into the type of search request the computer can understand. For example, for the problem discussed above you could type:

> When can a pediatric oncologist be sued for malpractice because of a failure to diagnose leukemia?

Unlike a terms and connectors search, in a natural language search, there is no requirement that every term (not connected with *or*) be found in every case. Rather, the computer first evaluates the search, looking for the most unique terms, and then lists those cases that have the greatest number of those terms. Finally, it ranks the results by relevance, that is, the first case listed will be the case the computer determines will most likely answer the question you asked.

(3) Variation among services

One of the challenges in conducting on-line research is that the various on-line researching services have not developed a uniform method for conducting a search. For example, as noted above, in both Westlaw and Lexis, the exclamation point is used as a root expander. However, Loislaw uses the asterisk for the same purpose. As another example, in AltaVista, a popular general search engine, simple searches are essentially treated like natural language searches, and the results are listed with those documents contained the most unique terms listed first. To make a term mandatory, you insert a "+" mark before the word. When in doubt about how to conduct a search, read the help section for that service.

3. Updating with Lexis, Westlaw, and Loislaw

Another major advantage of using computer programs is the ease with which you can update your research. Using the electronic version of Shepard's is much simpler than using the books and supplemental pamphlets. You simply type in the citation, and the results from all volumes of Shepard's, including the pamphlet updates, are automatically displayed for you. You can also limit the displayed results to cases that negatively treated the cited opinion or that deal with topics from specific headnotes in the cited case. In Westlaw, KeyCite performs a similar function, while Loislaw use GlobalCite.

If your law firm has access to a commercial service, such as Lexis, Westlaw, or Loislaw, and you do not use it to update your research, that may be grounds for a malpractice action.

Ethics Alert

NETNOTE

There are various search engines that can assist you with your Internet legal research. Two that have been designed specifically for legal research include *www.lawcrawler.com* and *http://gsulaw.gsu.edu/metaindex*.

4. Beyond Researching Primary Authority

Westlaw and Lexis are becoming increasingly useful because of the types of information they store in addition to federal and state statutes and court decisions. For example, in the Nexis part of Lexis a researcher can find full-text versions of news articles from major newspapers, jury verdicts, secretary of state filings, and asset information. While legal researchers have traditionally relied on primary law sources, these other sources are becoming increasingly important. Because most cases settle, and hence never make it to a trial court, let alone an appellate court, you may not be able to find a published court opinion discussing the product that harmed your client. However, by searching news articles you may find that the product manufacturer recently settled a similar case.

Legal Reasoning Exercise

2. You are working as a paralegal in Pennsylvania. One of your firm's clients, Melba Street, had a pet poodle, Suzie, whom she dearly loved. She left the poodle one weekend at the local kennel. On Saturday a new kennel worker accidentally let Suzie loose in the fenced-in yard with Butch, a vicious German shepard. Unfortunately, that was the end of Suzie. Melba would like to sue the kennel for the emotional distress she suffered in having her pet killed.

a. What terms and connectors search would you construct to try to find cases that would indicate whether she can recover for her emotional distress?
b. What natural language search would you construct?

PRACTICE TIP

When deciding whether to research state or federal case law, remember that even state law issues can end up in federal court under diversity jurisdiction.

1. Identify Search Terms.

2. Check Secondary Authority (Optional).
   - ■ Look for references to relevant statutes and court opinions.

3. Decide Whether to Research State or Federal Law or Both.

4. Check Statutes and Their Pocket Parts.
   - ■ Look for cases that have interpreted the statute.
   - ■ Look for references to administrative regulations.

5. Check Court Opinions.
   - ■ Check for any references to relevant statutes and other court opinions.
   - ■ Note the relevant headnote topics and key numbers.
     - – Use them to find more cases in the digests.
     - – Use them to find more cases in Shepard's.

6. Update Your Research.
   - ■ Check the pocket parts.
   - ■ Use Shepard's.
   - ■ Check the digest interim supplement and recent hardbound volumes and the advance sheets of regional reporters for recent cases.
   - ■ Use on-line services, such as Lexis, Westlaw, and Loislaw.

Figure 14-8 Summary Checklist for Legal Research

E. THE INTERRELATIONSHIP OF RESEARCHING MATERIALS

It may seem that there is a lot to learning how to conduct legal research—and there is. However, the more researching you do, the more comfortable you will become with the process. Also always keep in mind one of the major tricks of legal researching: Once you have found *one* relevant authority, you can proceed from there just by following up on the leads that your first authority gives you. For example, if you find a relevant section in Am. Jur. 2d, the footnotes will give you references to the A.L.R. and to cases. Even if none of the cases is from your jurisdiction, look one of them up in a regional reporter. Read the headnotes, and write down the appropriate key numbers. You can then go to your state's digest to find cases from your state. Figure 14-8 contains a summary checklist for conducting legal research.

SUMMARY

The goal of legal research is to find relevant primary authority, court opinions, and enacted law, such as statutes and regulations. Secondary sources, such as legal encyclopedias and law review articles, can provide valuable background information.

The first step in legal research is to identify search terms. If you are unfamiliar with the area of law, you may next want to consult secondary sources. However, you can also go directly to primary authority. Never forget to update your research by consulting pocket parts and supplements, by checking Shepard's, and, if available, by using on-line resources, such as the commercial providers and other Internet-based sources.

Computer-assisted research programs are becoming more sophisticated, and the number of decided cases continues to increase. Thus, the need for legal researchers to become proficient in computer-assisted research also continues to grow.

REVIEW QUESTIONS

Pages 389 through 392
1. What is your main goal when conducting legal research?
2. In what type of books can you read general background information on a particular legal topic?
3. What is the difference between primary and secondary authority?
4. What are TAPP and TARP, and how do they aid a legal researcher?

Pages 392 through 403
5. What are the two major legal encyclopedias? In what ways are they the same, and how do they differ?
6. Why should you never end your research with an encyclopedia?
7. What is a law review, and what types of articles does it contain?
8. How do you locate relevant law review articles?
9. How does the A.L.R. differ from an encyclopedia?
10. Why do you think the general rule is that it is appropriate to cite to a law review article but not to an encyclopedia?

Pages 403 through 422
11. When researching primary authority, should you generally begin your research with statutes or court opinions? Why?
12. What makes an annotated statutory code "annotated"?
13. How are digest summaries and headnotes similar? What is the function of each?
14. Assume you are researching the topic of whether minors can get out of their contractual obligations and that you have found a New Hampshire case directly on point. That case's third headnote lists the topic as Contracts 211. How would you go about locating a Kansas case dealing with that same issue?

Pages 422 through 434
15. What is the difference between saying a case has been reversed and saying it has been overruled?
16. When using the digest topic method, what steps do you need to take to make sure your research is up to date?
17. What are the three main reasons for using Shepard's?
18. In Shepard's what is subsequent history, and what is the treatment of a case?
19. In Shepard's, to what do the terms *citing case* and *cited case* refer?
20. Your boss has asked you to Shepardize 89 N.E. 542.
    a. What is your first step? What do you do next?
    b. In Shepardizing you found the following information. What does it mean? Is there any history of the case? How do you know?

—542—
(203Mas364)
f90NE²864
94NE¹691
129NE718

21. Your boss has asked you to Shepardize a case giving you only the official citation. Describe the steps you would take to Shepardize the case.

22. Your boss knows of a California case, *Tarasoff v. The Regents of the University of California*, 551 P.2d 334 (Cal. 1976), that stands for the proposition that if a psychiatrist knows a patient is a threat to another person, the psychiatrist must warn that person. If you want to find out whether any New York cases have followed the *Tarasoff* decision, which Shepard's would you use and why? (*Note:* California is in the Pacific region, and New York is in the Northeast region.)

23. Last month the police saw your client Bill Johnson exchange money for a packet of white powder. Without a warrant the police placed an electronic tracking device on your client's car. The police then followed him to an alley where he handed the packet to a woman who gave him money in return. They arrested your client for selling illegal drugs. Your boss would like to make a motion to have the evidence excluded by arguing that it was unlawful for the police to put the electronic tracking device on your client's car without a warrant.

Assume that in the course of your research you have found *Commonwealth v. Boven*, 413 Mass. 755, 306 N.E.2d 222 (1986). The headnotes in the North Eastern Reporter, Second Series, appear as follows:

1. Searches and Seizures Key 7(26)
   Defendant did not have standing to challenge X-ray search of suitcase, where the suitcase belonged to his co-defendant.
2. Searches and Seizures Key 7(10)
   Utilization of electronic tracking device, without prior court approval, may be justified by probable cause and exigent circumstances.
3. Criminal Law Key 1144.13
   On appeal from jury conviction, Court must view evidence, both direct and circumstantial, and all reasonable inferences to be drawn therefrom.
4. Criminal Law Key 696(1)
   Trial court did not err in failing to grant defense motion to strike testimony of agent, although all of agent's investigatory notes had been destroyed.

Using the information *from the headnotes*, describe how you would go about finding out whether there are any other court opinions in Massachusetts dealing with the subject of when police officers can place electronic surveillance devices on cars without first obtaining a warrant. Describe the steps you would take in as much detail as possible. Include a description of how you would bring your research up to date, using both the digest and the Shepard's approaches.

24. In updating your research what is the advantage of using the digest method over Shepardizing? In using Shepard's over the digests?

25. Your boss asks you to Shepardize *Brown v. Smith*, 322 Mass. 89, 78 N.E.2d 640 (1946). You determine that headnotes 4 and 8 are most relevant to your client's problem. In Shepard's you find the following information:

—640—
99 N.E.2d^3 888
99 N.E.2d 904
q101 N.E.2d 44
102 N.E.2d^8 99
102 N.E.2d^1 301

Explain which citations you would look up, in what order, and why.

Pages 434 through 444

• 26. How does the use of on-line research differ from traditional book research?

• 27. What are the two main methods for conducting full-text research in an on-line database, and how do those two methods differ from each other?

28. You need to find cases dealing with free speech, and using the terms and connectors method, you type in the following search: *free speech*. How do you think Westlaw, Lexis, and Loislaw would differ in the ways they would interpret that search request?

29. Your boss represents a client who was injured when his Handy Hardy riding tractor tipped over. You searched through the on-line sources that contained primary authority but did not find any appellate decisions involving the Handy Hardy riding tractor. In what other types of on-line databases might you want to search and why?

Chapter 15

Applying the Law

If you do not know where you are going, it is damnably hard to get there. It is even harder for the instructor to see how you got there.
Karl Llewellyn

INTRODUCTION

Written analysis based on court opinions is similar to what we discussed in Chapter 12 on statutory interpretation. Now, however, instead of gleaning the rule from the statutory language and presumed legislative intent, the rule comes from the holding of a court decision or a series of court decisions. Also, your analysis section will now be very fact based as you compare and contrast your client's facts with those of the cases you cite.

A. PREDICTING THE OUTCOME IN YOUR CLIENT'S CASE

As a practical matter few people (lawyers and paralegals included) read cases in a vacuum just for the fun it. Usually, they read cases because they are striving to keep current in their area of expertise or because they have a client and need to see whether prior cases will help or hurt the client's situation.

1. Looking for Analogies and Distinctions

In determing the extent to which a court opinion applies to a client's facts, you engage in a process of comparing the facts involved in the prior cases with those of the client's situation. As we have discussed, this process of looking at two

decisions and deciding that they are similar is called analogizing. If you find that the two cases are similar, then the doctrine of **stare decisis** will suggest that they should be decided the same way. If they are different in important respects, the prior case is distinguishable and is not applicable to the client's problem.

Therefore, after case briefing, the next step is to use the opinions that you have briefed as a basis for predicting the likely outcome in your client's situation. To do that, you must find both the factual similarities (analogies) and the factual differences (distinctions) between your client's situation and that of the prior decision.

The steps that are necessary to evaluate whether a prior decision and a client's case will be seen as essentially similar or dissimilar follow.

a. Determine Whether the Governing Rules of Law and Issues Are the Same in Both Cases

Obviously, you should not rely on a case dealing with wills to decide a situation involving an intentional tort. However, if yours is one of those situations when there is no established law in the area, you will need to rely on cases in closely related, though not identical, areas of the law, where a logical extension can be made. For example, if there are no cases in your jurisdiction on parental immunity, you might look to cases on spousal immunity for guidance. Because the rules and issues are not identical, however, you will have to work at convincing the court why the same policies that applied in the prior cases should apply to your case.

b. Decide Which Facts Are the Key Facts in the Prior Case

Key facts are those facts that, if changed, might have caused the court to reach a different result.

c. Decide How Those Facts Are Similar to or Different from the Facts of Your Client's Case

To find similarities between the prior decision and the client's situation, think in general terms. For example, both the prior case and your client's situation might involve children who were injured in the daytime. To find distinctions between the prior case and your client's situation, be as specific as possible, within reason. For example, you might find the following differences between your case and the prior case: In your case the child was a six-year-old, but in the prior case the child was thirteen years old. In both cases the accident happened in the daytime; however, in the prior case it was at noon on a bright sunny day, and in your case it was at 4:30 in the afternoon on a cold wintery overcast day. All these differences might matter. On the other hand, it probably is irrelevant that the child's name in the prior case was Mark and your client's name is Bill.

Generally, whenever you have a precedent that you like and that you would like the court to apply to your client's situation, you should search for as many similarities as possible between your facts and the key facts in the prior case. For any facts that do differ you must find ways to convince the court that those differences are so insignificant that they do not matter. On the other hand, if you have a precedent that you do not like, try to find as many differences as possible between the facts in your client's situation and those in the precedent. It is only by

thus distinguishing the two situations that you can convince the court it should not apply the precedent to your client's situation. If there are any similar facts, you must argue that they are insignificant and should not affect the court's view that the two situations are fundamentally different. (*Note:* There are times, however, when a difference between two cases actually supports an argument that they should be decided the same way. For example, assume a court found that a store owner who had detained a suspected shoplifter for one hour had acted unreasonably. If in the next case the shopkeeper detained a suspected shoplifter for two hours, the facts in the two cases would differ. However, rather than helping the shopkeeper in the second case, the difference actually reinforces the argument that he, too, acted unreasonably.)

As a tool to help you find similarities and differences, it is often a good idea to draw a chart. In the chart explicitly label specific facts as facts that tend to show how the two situations are analogous or distinguishable. This is the most important step in legal analysis. If you take the time to note as many analogies and distinctions as possible, most of your work will be done.

d. Explain Why Those Similarities or Differences Matter

A mere listing of the factual similarities and differences is not enough. You must explain to your reader why particular similarities or differences should affect the outcome of your client's case. In the example given above assume our six-year-old client accidentally shot a neighbor child with his father's hunting rifle. The issue is whether or not he should be tried for manslaughter. If in the prior case under similar facts a thirteen-year-old child was tried for manslaughter, we would, of course, point to the differences in the children's ages. But do not assume that pointing to differences, even obvious differences, is enough. Explain why a six-year-old should be treated differently from a thirteen-year-old.

2. Selecting among Precedents

Once you have completed your initial thinking about the similarities and differences between your case and those cases that you found through your research, you must decide which of the cases to emphasize and which to mention only briefly or not at all.

Naturally you will rely on **primary authority** over **secondary authority** and **mandatory authority** over **persuasive authority**. Among mandatory authority you will usually rely more on cases from the highest appellate court in your jurisdiction than on those from an intermediate-level appellate court. Other factors that will influence your choice include the age of the case and how close the facts are to your client's facts. Two similar cases are said to be **on point** with each other. If the facts of the two cases are almost identical, they are said to be **on all fours**. You would also rather rely on a unanimous decision or one written by a well-known jurist. Therefore, all things being equal, you would prefer to use

1. a case from the highest appellate court in your jurisdiction
2. that was decided recently
3. with facts similar to your own and
4. decided by a unanimous court and
5. written by a well-known and respected judge.

On point
A term used to describe a case that is similar to another case.

On all fours
A term used to describe two cases that are almost identical, with similar facts and legal issues.

In addition to following these rules for deciding on which precedents to rely, you must develop an ability to analyze the cases in the light most favorable to your client.

It will be your job, as well as that of someone working on the opposing side, to develop a list of what you believe are the most relevant cases and statements of what you believe the holdings of those cases to be. You will frequently find that you disagree with your colleagues, as well as with those representing the opposing side, as to which cases belong on that list and what those cases stand for. In fact, not even courts are immune from this ability to, in effect, see "both sides of a case." A good example of this was illustrated in a U.S. Supreme Court decision, *Texas v. White*.[1] In that case Mr. White was arrested at 1:30 in the afternoon. The police had his car towed to the police station, where they conducted a warrantless search. Based on the evidence found in the case Mr. White was convicted. Both Mr. White's attorneys and the attorneys for the state argued that the holding in the prior U.S. Supreme Court decision of *Chambers v. Maroney* supported their point of view. Take a few minutes to read the following excerpts from *Chambers v. Maroney*, and decide whether you think the holding in *Chambers* should have helped or hurt Mr. White.

Chambers v. Maroney
399 U.S. 42 (1970)

Mr. Justice WHITE delivered the opinion of the Court.

The principal question in this case concerns the admissibility of evidence seized from an automobile, in which petitioner was riding at the time of his arrest, after the automobile was taken to a police station and was there thoroughly searched without a warrant. The Court of Appeals for the Third Circuit found no violation of petitioner's Fourth Amendment rights. We affirm.

I

During the night of May 20, 1963, a Gulf service station in North Braddock, Pennsylvania, was robbed by two men, each of whom carried and displayed a gun. . . . Two teenagers, who had earlier noticed a blue compact station wagon circling the block in the vicinity of the Gulf station, then saw the station wagon speed away from a parking lot close to the Gulf station. About the same time, they learned that the Gulf station had been robbed. They reported to police, who arrived immediately, that four men were in the station wagon and one was wearing a green sweater. Kovacich told the police that one of the men who robbed him was wearing a green sweater and the other was wearing a trench coat. A description of the car and the two robbers was broadcast over the police radio. Within an hour, a light blue compact station wagon answering the description and carrying four men was stopped by the police about two miles from the Gulf station. Petitioner was one of the men in the station wagon. He was wearing a green sweater and there was a trench coat in the car. The occupants were arrested and the car was driven to the police station. In the course of a thorough search of the car at the station, the police found concealed in a compartment under the dashboard two .38-caliber revolvers (one loaded with dumdum bullets), a right-hand

glove containing small change, and certain cards bearing the name of Raymond Havicon, the attendant at a Boron service station in McKeesport, Pennsylvania, who had been robbed at gun-point on May 13, 1963. . . .

II

We pass quickly to the claim that the search of the automobile was the fruit of an unlawful arrest. Both the courts below thought the arresting officers had probable cause to make the arrest. We agree. . . .

In terms of the circumstances justifying a warrantless search, the Court has long distinguished between an automobile and a home or office. In *Carroll v. United States,* 267 U.S. 132 (1925), the issue was the admissibility in evidence of contraband liquor seized in a warrantless search of a car on the highway. After surveying the law from the time of the adoption of the Fourth Amendment onward, the Court held that automobiles and other conveyances may be searched without a warrant in circumstances that would not justify the search without a warrant of a house or an office, provided that there is probable cause to believe that the car contains articles that the officers are entitled to seize. . . .

On the facts before us, the blue station wagon could have been searched on the spot when it was stopped since there was probable cause to search and it was a fleeting target for a search. The probable-cause factor still obtained at the station house and so did the mobility of the car unless the Fourth Amendment permits a warrantless seizure of the car and the denial of its use to anyone until a warrant is secured. In that event there is little to choose in terms of practical consequences between an immediate search without a warrant and the car's immobilization until a warrant is obtained. [It was not unreasonable in this case to take the car to the station house. All occupants in the car were arrested in a dark parking lot in the middle of the night. A careful search at that point was impractical and perhaps not safe for the officers, and it would serve the owner's convenience and the safety of his car to have the vehicle and the keys together at the station house.] The same consequences may not follow where there is unforeseeable cause to search a house. Compare *Vale v. Louisiana,* ante, 399 U.S. 30. But as *Carroll,* supra, held, for the purpose of the Fourth Amendment there is a constitutional difference between houses and cars. . . .

Affirmed.

What do you think the Court's holding in *Chambers* was? Certainly the Court ruled that the police did have probable cause to stop the automobile and arrest the occupants. The Court also ruled that the police had a legal right to search the car at the station without first obtaining a search warrant. But what is the significance of this decision for future defendants? What general principles of law emerged that were likely to be applied to future cases?

More specifically, do you think the Court held that the police have the right to search any vehicle at the police station if they had probable cause to search it at the scene of the arrest? Or do you think the police can conduct warrantless searches of vehicles at the police station only when they stopped the automobile in a dark parking lot at night, the facts that existed in *Chambers?* Justice White's opinion specifically mentioned that the arrests took place "in a dark parking lot in the middle of the night" and that a "careful search at the point was impractical and perhaps not safe for the officers."

In *Texas v. White*[2] lawyers for the state of Texas argued that Chambers stood for the principle that whenever the police had the right to conduct a warrantless search of an automobile at the scene of the arrest, they also had the right to conduct such a warrantless search at the police station.

---

[2] 423 U.S. 67 (1975).

White's lawyers disagreed. They argued that *Chambers* stood for the principle that police could conduct a warrantless search of an automobile at the station only when conditions at the scene of the arrest made it unsafe to conduct a search there. White's lawyers argued that because the police could have safely searched White's car in daylight, the *Chambers* decision did not apply to White's situation.

In a per curiam decision the U.S. Supreme Court agreed with the state, declaring that

> [i]n Chambers v. Maroney we held that police officers with probable cause to search an automobile on the scene where it was stopped could constitutionally do so later at the station house without first obtaining a warrant.[3]

Justices Marshall and Brennan, writing for the dissent, argued that Mr. White's conviction should be reversed and that the majority had misstated the true holding of the *Chambers* case:

> Only by misstating the holding of *Chambers v. Maroney*, can the Court make that case appear dispositive of this one. The court in its brief *per curiam* opinion today extends *Chambers* to a clearly distinguishable factual setting. . . .
>
> *Chambers* did not hold as the court suggests, "that police officers with probable cause to search an automobile on the scene where it was stopped could constitutionally do so later at the station house without first obtaining a warrant.". . . *Chambers* simply held that to be the rule when it is reasonable to take the car to the station house in the first place.[4]

This discussion regarding more than one possible "right" holding for a case should remind you of the one we had in Chapter 13. In that discussion we observed that in briefing a case you can state a holding either broadly so that it is not limited by the specific facts of the case or quite narrowly so that it is limited to those facts. When you are faced with a case that is harmful to your client, develop a narrow statement of the holding so that it is limited to the facts of the prior case. That is what the attorneys for White attempted to do by pointing out that the arrest in the prior case had occurred "in a dark parking lot in the middle of the night," whereas their client had been arrested in the middle of the day. If you have a case that is beneficial to your client, state the holding in broad enough terms so that it will cover both the facts of the prior case and those of your client's case. That is what the attorneys for the government did in *Texas v. White*.

B. A NOTE ON LOGIC

As we have seen, legal reasoning requires that we identify and evaluate arguments. This is a form of deductive logic. While learning about logic will not teach you all there is to know about legal reasoning, an understanding of deductive reasoning will help you understand the basic structure of legal thinking.

---

[3] Id. at 68.
[4] Id. at 69.

All arguments involve evidence, assumptions, and the conclusion the speaker wants you to reach. Politicians make arguments so that you will conclude you should vote for them, car salespersons make arguments so that you will conclude you should buy your next car from them, and lawyers make arguments so that courts or opponents will conclude that the law should be interpreted in favor of their clients.

The strength of an argument's conclusion ultimately rests on the strength of the **evidence** in support of it. Strong evidence strengthens an argument, while weak evidence dilutes the strength of the conclusions. A car salesperson will be more persuasive if the evidence includes a Consumer Reports article highly rating the particular model that dealership sells. In a criminal trial the prosecutor has to present compelling evidence that a crime was committed and that the defendant was the person who did it.

Assumptions serve as a bridge between the evidence and the conclusion. An assumption is often an unstated belief that justifies the author in arguing his conclusion on the basis of the evidence presented. To take an example from daily life, a mother may note that her three-year-old child is crying and generally cranky. The conclusion she reaches is that he needs a nap. Her unstated assumption is that the crying and crankiness are due to a lack of sleep.

In legal reasoning it is important to know what your assumptions are. An argument is only **valid** if the assumptions that underlie it are valid. To take the prior example one step further, if the child is crying not because he needs sleep but because a dog just bit him, then the mother's conclusion, or solution, to the problem—putting the child to bed—is invalid.

Most legal arguments are presented in the form of **deductive reasoning**. Deductive reasoning involves a major premise, a minor premise, and a conclusion. The major and minor premises are assumptions. The most famous example of deductive reasoning is the following:

MAJOR PREMISE	All men are mortal.
MINOR PREMISE	Socrates is a man.
CONCLUSION	Therefore, Socrates is mortal.

In legal reasoning, the **major premise** is a statement of a legal rule that you can find in a statute or a court opinion. The **minor premise** consists of the client's facts. The conclusion is the answer you reach when you apply the law to the facts.

MAJOR PREMISE	Anyone intentionally taking the life of another human being is guilty of murder.
MINOR PREMISE	John intentionally shot Bill, taking his life.
CONCLUSION	Therefore, John is guilty of murder.

It is important to understand that "logic is concerned with form and not with truth. Perfectly ridiculous arguments can be logically correct."[5] Take the following example:

MAJOR PREMISE	All men are twenty feet tall.
MINOR PREMISE	George is a man.
CONCLUSION	Therefore, George is twenty feet tall.

---

[5] Landau, Logic for Lawyers, 13 Pac. L.J. 59, 62 (1981).

Evidence
The way in which a question of fact is established. Evidence can consist of witness testimony or documents and exhibits. It is the proof presented at a trial.

Assumption
In logic, a belief that justifies one in arguing a conclusion.

Valid
In logic, an argument is considered to be valid or sound if the assumptions underlying the argument are true.

Deductive reasoning
A form of logical reasoning based on a major premise, a minor premise, and a conclusion.

Major premise
In deductive reasoning, the statement of a broad proposition that forms the starting point; in law, the statement of a legal rule that you can find in a statute or court opinion.

Minor premise
In deductive reasoning, the second proposition, which along with the major premise leads to the conclusion; in law, the minor premise consists of the client's facts.

Because the major premise is false, the conclusion is false. Nonetheless, because the form follows the deductive model, the conclusion is logically correct. It is just not true. Take a more serious example:

MAJOR PREMISE	Anyone intentionally taking the life of another human being is guilty of murder.
MINOR PREMISE	As required by his job, Sam, the state executioner, intentionally takes the life of prisoners sentenced to die in the electric chair.
CONCLUSION	Therefore, Sam is guilty of murder.

Again the conclusion is false because the major premise is not true. It is not true that *anyone* taking the life of another is guilty of murder. Clearly there are exceptions.

Therefore, while the deductive model provides the structure for legal argument, logic can never tell us whether our conclusions are right. The conclusions we reach depend on us using the correct law for the major premise and accurately reflecting the facts in the minor premise. In the first example given above assume John shot Bill as they were struggling with a gun that Bill had aimed at John's head. These additional facts suggest that the minor premise as stated is false because it does not contain all the relevant information. With that additional information, we might conclude that John did not "intentionally" shoot Bill.

When you are presented with a deductive argument, there are two ways to attack it. First, you can argue that there is something wrong with the major premise. Perhaps it has been stated too broadly, as in the second example. Second, you can try to find flaws with the minor premise. Examine whether the writer has omitted or distorted the facts.

When creating deductive arguments yourself, you must ensure not only that the facts that make up the minor premise are accurate but also that you portray them in the light most favorable to your client. For example, it is not only permissible but also necessary to interpret ambiguous facts in the best way to help your client. However, be aware that there is a definite line between interpreting facts and changing facts. You must interpret the facts. You must not distort them.

This leads us to our last reason for including this short lesson on logic. The deductive model requires three things: a major premise, a minor premise, and a conclusion. As we have mentioned before, one of the most common and fatal flaws in legal analysis is the omission of the reasoning. Keeping the three components of the deductive model in mind will remind you that legal analysis is more than the statement of a major premise (the law) and a conclusion. It also requires that you discuss the minor premise (the facts) that provide the logical link between the major premise and the conclusion and that you supply your reasoning, justifying your conclusion.

In a famous quotation Justice Oliver Wendell Holmes said that "the life of the law has not been logic: it has been experience."[6] Justice Holmes was right: The process of legal analysis is a very human, creative process. However, logic still plays an important role in legal analysis. Logic provides the structure of legal

---

[6] Oliver Wendell Holmes, Jr., The Common Law 1 (1881).

reasoning even when judges and lawyers appeal to other factors to justify their conclusions.

C. THE FORMAT FOR A WRITTEN ANALYSIS

In Chapter 12 we discussed how the IRAC (Issue-Rule-Analysis-Conclusion) format can help you organize your arguments when you write a statutory analysis. Likewise, when writing an analysis based on court opinions, following the IRAC format will help ensure that your writing follows a logical pattern. In addition, you should develop a style that allows you to synthesize the points raised by a group of cases rather than a style whereby you simply report the cases one by one.

1. Using IRAC

The breakdown of each of the IRAC elements, when writing an analysis based on court opinions, is as follows:

ISSUE	Have a topic sentence that states the issue you will be discussing in that paragraph. This sentence should be brief and clear. It should also contain only one idea: the one to be discussed in that particular paragraph.
RULE	State the rule of law that arguably governs the particular issue in question.
ANALYSIS	Explain how prior court opinions determine the outcome for your client's case. When citing a court opinion, briefly give the facts, holding, and reasoning to demonstrate how and why that case relates to the facts and issues of your own situation. Note the strong parallels (analogies) and the critical differences (distinctions) between the cited opinion and your own situation. Be very specific both when refer ring to facts from the cited court opinions and when referring to facts from your client's situation. Be sure to explain *why* you think those similarities or differences matter. Remember that the reasoning in the court's opinion will determine whether a court will see your case and the precedent as fundamentally similar or different.
CONCLUSION	Conclude! Do not leave your reader to decide what the bottom line is. That is why your supervisor asked you to analyze the problem.
TRANSITION	Use a short transition sentence to lead to the next issue that you want to discuss.

When faced with a fairly simple legal problem, all the IRAC elements may fit into a single paragraph. At other times you may want to divide the IRAC elements. For example, you might wish to set out the issue and the rule of law in one paragraph, the analysis for the plaintiff in a second paragraph, the analysis for the defendant and your conclusion in a third paragraph, and the transitional phrase or sentence in the first sentence of yet a fourth paragraph.

The amount of emphasis that you place on the factual comparisons between your case and the cited cases will vary, however, depending on whether you are working for a change in the law or are dealing with well-established legal principles that require you to analogize and distinguish your client's case relative to existing case law. If you are engaging in the first type of analysis, arguing for a change in the law, then your analysis section will be more policy based. For example, recall the case of Janice Miller, the woman who was injured when she was working with her husband cutting and stacking wood. If you were representing Janice in 1977, shortly after the Massachusetts Supreme Judicial Court decided that spouses could sue each other but limited their holding to motor vehicle accidents, you would be arguing for a change in the law that would allow suits in any negligence claim. Your analysis would be primarily based not on the factual issues, but on the policy reasons for extending the holding in Lewis. Such an analysis might look similar to the following:

Our client Janice Miller would like to sue her husband for injuries that she received when they were working together in their backyard cutting wood. The current law in Massachusetts is that spouses can sue each other only for injuries sustained in motor vehicle accidents. *Lewis v. Lewis*, 351 N.E.2d 526 (Mass. 1976). In the *Lewis* decision the court changed the longstanding rule that spouses could never sue each other for injuries sustained during their marriage. While recognizing the spiritual unity of marriage, *id.* at 528, n.1, the court stated that the doctrine of the legal unity of marriage was no longer a sufficient reason to bar such suits. Id. at 528. The principal motivating force behind this decision was the "general principle that if there is tortious injury there should be recovery." *Id.* at 532. Similarly, in our case the wife was injured by the negligence of her husband, and spousal immunity should not shield her husband from suit.

The court did, however, limit its holding to motor vehicle accidents. Id. While recognizing that injured parties should be able to pursue their claims, the court was mindful that "[c]onduct, tortious between two strangers, may not be tortious because of the mutual concessions implied in the marital

relationship." Id. This is such a case. The spouses were working together on a joint project. This was not the situation where one spouse was solely responsible for the enterprise as is true when driving a car. If the court were to allow suit in this case, it would open the court system to every injury that occurs when spouses are working together on household chores. For example, if one winter morning a husband were to forget to salt the front steps and his wife were to slip on them, expanding the holding in Lewis would allow such suits into the courthouse. Therefore, in acknowledgment of the special unity of marriage, suits between spouses should be limited to situations such as motor vehicle accidents, where one party is solely responsible for the safety of the undertaking. In conclusion, Janice Miller should not be allowed to sue her husband for a non-motor vehicle accident.

The purpose of an analysis is to present the arguments that each side will make and to predict how a court will resolve the issue. In the analysis you should candidly evaluate both the strengths and the weaknesses of the client's case. An analysis that tells only about the strengths of a client's case will do little good, as a supervising attorney needs to know not only what arguments to make but also how to combat the arguments that the opposing side will make. As one well-known authority on legal writing has said, the purpose of an analysis

> is to explore and evaluate candidly the strength and weakness of the client's case. It should therefore be as much concerned with the weaknesses of the case as with the favorable aspects, and should devote at least as much attention to precedents and other authorities against the client's position as to those that are for him. The cases and authorities contra should, of course, be carefully analyzed too so if they can be distinguished or otherwise minimized, but this too should be done with complete willingness to face the situation realistically.
>
> . . . Try to put yourself in the position of your opposite number. Ask yourself: If I were he, how would I answer the analysis or argument just made? How would I rebut or distinguish the cases cited? What countervailing arguments could I offer? Minimizing or covering up what may prove to be fatal weaknesses is the worst thing you can do. It is your responsibility to point out where the dangers lie, where the decisive battles are going to be fought.[7]

While it is always nice to turn out to be right in your prediction of how the court will ultimately resolve the issue, it is more important that you fairly present both sides of the issue than that you select the correct result. Remember, until a court resolves the issue, there is no correct result, just better or worse arguments. As it turns out, the Massachusetts Supreme Judicial Court did not think it was so ridiculous to let a wife sue her husband for failing to salt the front steps. In 1980, in *Brown v. Brown*,[8] a case involving that very fact scenario, the court expanded the Lewis decision to allow spouses to sue each other in all types of negligence cases. As in Lewis, the trial court had dismissed the case at the pretrial stage. Therefore, the appellate court was not in a position to determine whether the husband should be found negligent. All the appellate court decided was that the wife had the right to take her case to court and to let a jury hear the facts in order to determine whether her husband should be found liable for negligence.

---

[7] Henry Weihofen, Legal Writing Style 230 (2d ed. 1980).
[8] 409 N.E.2d 717 (Mass. 1980).

Legal Reasoning Exercise

1. Read the following article that appeared in the Boston Globe shortly after the Massachusetts Supreme Judicial Court decided *Brown v. Brown*. What do you think of the author's comments? Why is the statement "the Superior Court agreed, more or less, with defendant Bill that the wife would have hauled ashes" misleading?

By Mike Barnicle

Spouse suits, a new wave of Americana

Here, in the middle of summer, comes the perfect story to put your mind on vacation. It is the story of Brown vs. Brown.

It begins in Wakefield at 8 o'clock in the morning on the 21st day of December, 1978. It is a miserable day with snow and sleet drawing a gray shade over the dawn.

A husband gets out of bed to go to work. He leaves the house about 7 o'clock. A wife gets out of bed. She leaves the house about 8 o'clock.

The wife walks from the front door to the driveway. She slips and falls on the ice. She lands on her pelvis. Shortly, you will think she landed on her head.

She goes to the hospital. Two pelvic bones are broken.

Guess where she goes later? Figure it out: This is America. What is the absolutely most American thing to do when anything bothers you?

Right: The wife goes to court. She sues the husband. For $35,000: says the husband should have shoveled the walk before he went to work.

The couple used to be known as William and Shirley Brown. Since December of 1978, they have been affectionately called the plaintiff and the defendant.

"Do they still live together?" the wife's lawyer Charles Blumstack was asked.

"They live together and they love each other," the lawyer said.

"Can they settle out of court?" the husband's lawyer, Anil Madan was asked.

"The question you want to ask is will they?" Madan answered. "And I can't answer that."

You are nothing in this country today unless you go to court. It is a badge of honor: proof that you are alive.

Plaintiff Shirley took her damage suit to the courts in 1979. Then, the Superior Court agreed, more or less, with defendant Bill that the wife could have hauled ashes to sprinkle on the ice that infamous morning. Case dismissed.

However, worse than not going to court is going and giving up at the first level. Naturally, Shirley Brown went forward to the Supreme Judicial Court.

Wednesday, Justice Robert Braucher knocked the Superior Court ruling over and said that Mrs. Brown should have the right to sue her husband. The Browns now go back to the lower court to fight the thing out.

There will be a discovery motion. This is the process where both parties are asked written questions and come up with written lies for answers. Lies are the things that keep courts in business, especially in anything involving a husband and wife.

Then there will be a trial. This will be the most fun of all.

The defense, the lawyers for Plaintiff Bill, could call Bella Abzug as a witness. They could ask her if a woman should not be given the right to handle a snow blower or a shovel.

As a matter of fact, this whole bizarre case raises the question: Where is the women's movement? Why isn't Bill Brown being praised by the feminists?

A snowstorm is an equal opportunity employer. Ice can be chipped by both women and men. Salt can be spread by a construction worker or a housewife. You don't need special muscles to put ashes on a sidewalk.

Instead of settling the thing in the kitchen though, we might now have the spectacle of a jury being asked to decide whether the husband was guilty for not scraping the walk clean before he went to work. You do not have to be a genius to figure out the ramifications of such a trial.

Imagine what the courts would be flooded with next.

Broken garbage disposal, bookshelves that fall down, clogged toilets, stuck windows, ripped screens, carpets with holes and walls with cracks . . . all of it could become the potential property of the judicial system. Unless a husband uses common sense and makes sure the wife knows he is totally irresponsible and thus, judgment proof, Brown vs. Brown is just the beginning.

"I even make my wife go out and start the car on cold mornings," Joe Buccieri of the East Boston Buccieris was saying. "It's only fair.

"She's grown to like it, too. It gives her a chance to get out of the house once in awhile. She goes out, takes the paper and a cup of coffee with her and sits there and reads until the car and the seat are both warm."

"Sounds to me like they should give the husband a saliva test," my friend Albert Baranello was saying. "His old lady sues him for something like that and he's still in the house with her. That's crazy."

"What would you do?" he was asked.

"Do what I've done four times already," Baranello answered. "Get divorced. You don't even need a trial for that."

Mike Barnicle was a Globe columnist.[9]

If your client's case requires you to work not at changing the law but rather at analogizing or distinguishing the case from existing law, then your analysis will be much more fact based. However, not all factual distinctions and similarities are equally important. Therefore, you will still need to turn to policy arguments to explain why some facts are more important than others. For example, if Janice were to overcome the hurdle of spousal immunity, then the next issue should be whether her husband would be found negligent. Look at the following two possible approaches to analyzing this problem. In the margins of each approach label each of the IRAC elements. Then decide which approach is better and why.

---

[9] Barnicle, Spouse Suits, A New Wave of Americana, Boston Globe, Aug. 1, 1980.

Approach 1

I

R

The issue is whether Mr. Booth can be found negligent because of the injuries his wife suffered when Mr. Booth allowed the chain saw he was using to slip, slicing off a piece of bark that flew into Ms. Miller's eye. The general rule is that to avoid negligence a person should take precautions once warned of drowsiness or fatigue. *Keller v. DeLong*, 231 A.2d 633, 634 (N.H. 1967). In *Keller* the defendant, while a passenger, felt sleepy. Before taking over at the wheel he did not take any precautions against falling asleep, such as rolling down the windows or turning on the radio. Soon after that he fell asleep and hit a utility pole, killing his passenger. The court held that the defendant was negligent because

A

he had felt sleepy as a passenger but had taken no precautions before taking over at the wheel. Id. at 635. The court reasoned that because the defendant did not take any precautions to avoid the accident, the accident was foreseeable. Id.

Unlike the *Keller* case, Mr. Booth would argue that the harm to Ms. Miller was not foreseeable. There are significant differences between driving a car and operating a chain saw. If someone drives a car negligently, the passengers are just as likely as the driver to be injured. But when using a chainsaw, the person most likely to be hurt is the one using it, in this case Mr. Booth, not Ms. Miller.

However, while the person most likely to be hurt may be the operator of the chain saw, any dangerous instrument, if used carelessly, can easily inflict injury on others. Indeed, that is what happened in this case. As in *Keller*, the defendant was warned of the impending danger. In *Keller* the driver felt drowsy as a passenger and yet took no precautions before taking over at the wheel. In Mr. Booth's case, he told his wife that he was feeling fatigued just before the accident occurred. If anything, the negligence in Mr. Booth's case is greater because the defendant felt tired while operating the chain saw and yet continued to operate it. It would have been a simple matter to have taken a break, but Mr. Booth chose to continue with a dangerous activity even while knowing he was fatigued. As in *Keller*, once the defendant is warned of his fatigue, an

C

injury is foreseeable. Therefore, Mr. Booth should be found negligent.

Approach 2

Mr. Booth's wife suffered injuries when they were working together in their backyard sawing wood. Mr. Booth had told his wife that he was feeling fatigued just before the accident happened. In Keller the defendant, while a passenger, felt sleepy. Before taking over at the wheel he did not take any precautions against falling asleep, such as rolling down the windows or turning on the radio. Soon thereafter he fell asleep and hit a utility pole, killing his passenger. On its face that case is easily distinguishable from our own. There are significant differences between driving a car and operating a chain saw. However, both a chain saw and an automobile can cause injuries.

In Approach 1 the writer uses the IRAC format. The paragraph starts with a statement of the issue, followed by the rule that will be applied. The analysis section gives both the holding and the reasoning of a prior court decision, *Keller*. This is followed by two paragraphs comparing and contrasting the facts of the client's case with those of *Keller*. Finally, the writer concludes that Mr. Booth should be found negligent. In Approach 2 the writer begins with a statement of the facts without first putting those facts into context by starting with an issue statement. Next the writer begins a discussion of a prior case without first explaining what the general rule of law is or why the writer is discussing that particular case. For an analysis the writer simply states that the facts are similar or different without explaining why the similarities or differences matter. Finally, the writer forgets to conclude. Therefore, Approach 2 fails in its mission to start off with a clear issue statement, explain the current state of the law, apply that law to the client's facts, and conclude.

In sum, when writing an analysis you may be trying to argue for a change in the law, or you may be working to show how your client's case fits into a pattern of well-established case law. In this latter type of case, however, you should be aware that you are still asking the court to "change the law," even if only in an evolutionary sense, in that after your case we will know more about exactly what the law means than we knew before the case was decided. Finally, besides analyzing cases there will be times when, as we discussed in Chapter 12, a statute will govern your problem. In that situation you will begin with an analysis of the statute itself, but then you will probably add an analysis of any cases that have interpreted the statute. The three legal reasoning exercises at the end of this section will give you practice with each of these three types of analysis.

2. Synthesizing Cases

When you are doing research, you read cases one at a time and summarize them one at a time. If that is then how you report them to your reader, you have done little more than hand over your case briefs. What you need to do is to synthesize them so that the reader understands what principles of law arise out of reading the series of cases as a unit. The following is an example taken from Writing and Analysis in the Law by Helene S. Shapo, Marilyn R. Walter, and Elizabeth Fajans.[10] Read each approach and then decide which you like better and why.

PRACTICE TIP

Here are some hints for a successful analysis:

- Tell enough about each case so that the reader will not have to read the cases.
- Give both sides of the argument.
- Work with the facts.
- Explain *why* the court should care that the facts are the same or that the facts are different.

---

[10] Helen S. Shapo, Marilyn R. Walter & Elizabeth Fajans, Writing and Analysis in the Law 51 (3d ed. 1995).

Approach 1

Two factors determine parental immunity for a tort suit in Kent: the type of tort involved and the age of the child. First, immunity extends to suits for negligence only. Parents are not immune from suits for intentional torts. The Kent Supreme Court has held that parents are not immune from their child's suit for assault, *Brown v. Brown*, and for battery, *White v. White*. But the court has held that parents are immune from a negligence suit brought by their child. *Abbott v. Abbott.* Second, parental immunity extends only to a suit brought by a minor child. Id. (immunity against twelve-year-old child's suit for negligence); *Black v. Black* (no immunity against twenty-four-year-old's suit for negligence).

Approach 2

The Kent Supreme Court has decided four cases on parental immunity from tort suits by their children. In the first case in 1965, the court decided that a parent was immune from suit for negligence brought by his twelve-year-old son. *Abbott v. Abbott* (1965). However, in the next suit, in 1968, the court held that a parent was not immune from suit for battery brought by a ten-year-old son. *White v. White* (1968). Only a year later in *Brown v. Brown* (1969), the court affirmed that a parent is not immune from suit for assault brought by a twenty-four-year-old daughter. The most recent case on this topic is *Black v. Black*, decided in 1982. In Black, the court decided another suit by a twenty-four-year-old against his parent, this time for negligence. The court still decided that the parent is not immune.

Hopefully, you found the first example much easier to understand. The author starts by giving you a frame of reference: There will be two factors determining parental immunity. The author then goes on to discuss each of these factors. In the second example the author simply lists the cases in chronological order. The first approach does a much better job of explaining to the reader the principles for which these cases stand.

Legal Reasoning Exercise

2. In this problem you need to argue for a change in the law.

Your firm represents Amanda and Sam Baker, grandparents of two-year-old Brian Baker. Brian was recently injured in a home accident. The two-year-old stuck a hairpin into an electrical outlet and was severely burned. The parents had not installed safety plugs in the outlets because they felt the plugs gave a false sense of security. The plugs are easily removed and were not present in many of their friends' homes. The grandparents want to bring a negligence suit on the child's behalf against the parents.

Assume the Massachusetts Supreme Judicial Court has decided the following cases:

- *Sorensen v. Sorensen*, 399 N.E.2d. 907 (Mass. 1975)—A child was injured when his father negligently caused an automobile accident. The court held that children could sue their parents but limited the holding to motor vehicle cases and limited the recovery to the amount of available insurance. For its reasoning the court stated that neither the argument that such suits would disrupt the peace and harmony of the family nor the argument that such actions would tend to promote fraud and collusion was valid.

- *Lewis v. Lewis*, 351 N.E.2d 526 (Mass. 1976)—A wife was injured when her husband negligently caused an automobile accident. The court held that the wife could sue her husband but limited the holding to motor vehicle cases. The court did not limit the recovery to the amount of insurance, stating: "In the present case there is nothing in the record concerning the availability or the amount of the defendant's liability insurance, and we do not refer to insurance as a limiting factor in our holding. We do not interpret the logic (as opposed to the precise holding) of *Sorenson* as turning on the availability of insurance in each case, and we decline to limit liability in interspousal tort actions in such a fashion." The court cited *Sorenson* with approval as standing for the proposition that such suits would not disrupt the peace and harmony of the family or tend to promote fraud and collusion. Finally, while acknowledging that some actions that would constitute torts between strangers might not constitute torts if committed between spouses, the court based its decision on the general principle that normally there should be recovery for tortious injury.

- *Brown v. Brown*, 409 N.E. 717 (Mass. 1980)—A wife was injured when she slipped on the front steps that her husband had forgotten to salt. The court held that the wife could sue her husband. The court reasoned that while certain behavior between spouses might not be tortious, that was for a trial court to determine at trial, and the case should not be dismissed as a matter of immunity.

Based on the prior case law develop arguments both for and against the child's being able to sue his parents for negligence.

3. In this problem you need to show how your case fits with established law.

Your firm represents the Gilberts. Last week the Gilberts went out to dinner at a fashionable lakeshore restaurant. After dinner they decided to take a stroll down a boardwalk that leads from the restaurant out onto a pier. The walkway was not lighted. About halfway down the pier Ms. Gilbert stepped on a board that gave way due to dry rot. She fell and was seriously injured. About five years ago the restaurant, which owns the pier, decided it was too expensive to keep up with the necessary repairs and had done nothing to maintain the pier since. The restaurant owners posted a sign near the entry to the pier that said "Danger."
Assume the Nebraska Supreme Court decided the following case:

- *Weiss v. Autumn Hills*, 395 N.W.2d 481 (Neb. 1986) —One night the plaintiff, a tenant in the defendant landlord's apartment building, was

walking across the unlighted grassy area adjoining the patio of her street-level apartment. Although there was a sidewalk leading to the parking lot, taking the sidewalk took longer than cutting across the grass, and many people chose this shorter route. The area was eroded due to water falling from a defective rain gutter. The plaintiff stepped in a rut covered by weeds and fell. The landlord was found negligent.

Based on the *Weiss* decision, will your client be able to show that the restaurant was negligent? List all the factual similarities that make you think the restaurant might be negligent. Then list all the factual differences that make you think the restaurant might not be negligent. Decide which of the factual differences or similarities are most important and why.

4. In this last problem you need to base your analysis on a statute and a case interpreting that statute.

Assume you have a client, Jack Brilliant, who has been charged with violating the National Motor Vehicle Theft Act. Last weekend a friend of his, Sam Slick, told your client that he had just acquired a new motorboat but that he did not know how to run it. He asked your client if he would go out for a ride with him on the Connecticut River and show him how to drive the boat. Your client agreed. They left from a marina in Massachusetts and headed south with your client at the wheel. Soon after they crossed the Connecticut border, they were flagged down by the marine patrol and arrested. Apparently Sam had stolen the motorboat.

Based on the language of the statute and the *McBoyle* decision (page 355), what are the arguments that your client should be convicted of violating the National Motor Vehicle Theft Act? What are the arguments that he should not be convicted?

D. INTERNAL OFFICE MEMORANDA

We have been focusing on how to analyze prior court opinions in order to predict how a court will decide your client's case. In a law office setting your supervisor may ask you to include this analysis within a law office memorandum. A law office memorandum is made up of various sections. The most important section is the Discussion section. It is in that section that you include your analysis.

You write a law office memorandum to inform the person to whom it is addressed (usually an attorney or a paralegal supervisor) of what you have discovered. But you will also be creating a concise, permanent record that can be used by you, your supervisor, or someone else working on the same or a similar problem in the future. Such memoranda are usually placed in a permanent file. Later, when the firm has a similar case, attorneys and paralegals can take advantage of the work that has already been done and avoid needless duplication of effort. As we have discussed, to fully understand the issues, the analysis section should fairly evaluate both sides. Another reason for this two-sided approach is that someone in your firm representing a client on the other side of a similar issue may later use your memorandum.

As the quotation at the beginning of this chapter suggests, before you start to write, you must have thoroughly thought through the problem. It may be tempting to just sit down and hope the good thoughts will come to you as you write your memo. Do not fool yourself. It usually does not work that way. Legal analysis is complicated enough in its own right without being further complicated by stream of consciousness writing.

First, think about the problem. Then write an outline. The purpose of the outline is to force you to think through everything you want to say and the order in which you want to say it. To do that, you have to organize your ideas into issues and subissues, with some logical progression between issues. Be clear in your own mind why you are citing a particular case or including a specific argument. Ask yourself, How does this idea fit into the general structure of my argument? As you write your outline, many new thoughts probably will come to you. That is the time to organize them into a logical order—not as you write.

1. Format and Content

The degree of detail and the precise elements of a legal memorandum vary from one law office to another (or even from one lawyer within an office to another), but a law office memorandum usually consists of a heading, a listing of the issues raised (called the questions presented), brief answers to those issues, a statement of the facts, a discussion of the law and how it applies to the client's case, and a conclusion. The following outlines how a law office memorandum is ordinarily organized.

a. Heading

Use a traditional To:, From:, Re:, Date: format. Identify the person to whom you are directing the memo; yourself; the client's name, the office file number, and the memo's subject matter; and the date on which you prepared the memo.

b. Question Presented (Issue)

State the legal issues raised by the facts of the problem in as concrete a fashion as possible; that is, the legal issues should be related to the specific facts of the case. A general legal proposition or abstract question of law will do little to inform your reader of the specific facts and issues involved in your client's specific problem. The issue identification process is similar to that used in case briefs. It contains a general statement of the law and the specific facts to which that law will be applied.

You should carefully identify your issues before you begin your research because in writing the memorandum you should organize the analysis section around these issues.

Here are some general guidelines you should follow in formulating the Question Presented section:

1. State the question in terms of the *facts* of the case.
2. Identify the specific narrow legal question raised by the problem's facts.
3. Make sure the reader can understand the question on the first reading.
4. Eliminate all unnecessary verbiage.
5. Only include issues—that is, questions for which there are more than one possible answer.

Following these guidelines serves two purposes: (1) It will ensure that the question informs the reader of the content of this specific memorandum, and (2) it will aid you in your analysis by requiring you to focus on the specific issues of your client's problem. To arrive at such a precise statement, you may have to rewrite the question several times. Do not let that discourage you. If you can write a clear, simple statement of the issue, you will have gone a long way toward understanding how to analyze your client's problem.

c. Brief Answer

The brief answer should be brief. Write a short, specific answer to the question presented. First, give a definite answer. Follow that with a brief statement of the reasons that led you to that conclusion. A good check is to see if you have included a "because" in your answer. Generally, this section should not include restatements of the facts, citations, or argumentation. If you have researched more than one issue, you should write separate Question Presented and Brief Answer sections.

d. Facts

State the relevant facts of the legal problem you researched. Begin with a short summary of the general nature of the case and continue with a review of the key events in chronological order. As with case briefing be very specific about the facts. For example, rather than saying that a car was new, give the car's model year; instead of merely stating that a day was cold, provide the day's actual temperature. Do not omit facts that might influence the analysis of the problem. One good practice is to be sure that every fact you refer to in the Discussion section is set out in the statement of facts. Conversely, a fact you do not need for analysis is an irrelevant fact and should be omitted. Of course, you may also need to include some facts that are not strictly relevant to the issue to give the reader necessary background information. If you are unsure about how much to include, err on the side of including too many rather than too few facts.

e. Applicable Statutes

If the problem is controlled by a statute, a constitution, or an administrative regulation, quote the relevant language in this section. However, if it is only tangentially related to your main analysis, you may omit this section and quote the necessary language in the Discussion section.

f. Discussion

Start your discussion with an introductory paragraph that sets out the issues you will be discussing. Often this can be simply an expanded version of your question presented. The function of this paragraph is to tell the reader what issues you will be discussing and in what order you will be discussing them. This paragraph can also contain background information if your problem involves an area of the law that would not be familiar to most attorneys.

Following your introductory paragraph, use IRAC to help you frame your analysis for each issue. For each case that you cite, decide how much you want to say about it. At one extreme you can list a bare ruling of law followed by one or more case citations. This is known as a naked cite and

PRACTICE TIP

Busy people are most likely to read the first and last sentences of a paragraph. Therefore, to make sure you are conveying your main points, go through your analysis reading only the first and last sentences of each paragraph.

should be avoided unless you are citing a case only for a nondisputed rule of law. At a minimum always tell the reader why you are citing the case, what its facts were, what it stands for, and how it relates to your case. At the other extreme you do not have to convince your reader that you read the case by setting forth all the facts. The trick, of course, is to be selective in your statement of the facts of a particular case so that you include only those that show the case's relevance. The discussion of the holding should be similarly limited. Therefore, for each major case you cite you should tell the reader why you are citing the case (it is the most recent case, the leading case, etc.) and then briefly state the facts, the nature of the case, the holding, and how it applies to your case.

Whatever you do, do not simply give a series of case descriptions. As discussed earlier under the section Synthesizing Cases, if your supervisor had merely wanted to know what the cases said, she could have read them for herself. Your job is much more difficult. You must analyze those cases and apply them to your client's problem. Your discussion should constantly be shifting back and forth between a discussion of your client's facts and a discussion of how the cases you read relate to those facts.

Similarly, do not give long quotations. Again, if your supervisor had wanted to read the cases, she would not have asked you to do it. Generally, it is better to restate the court's holding in your own words and then to apply that holding to the facts of your case. In that way you are not simply parroting the court but fulfilling your job of translating the court's language for your reader. The only exception to this rule is if it is important for the reader to see the exact language of the court to understand your analysis.

Finally, remember that your basic job in writing a memorandum of law is to relate the law to the facts of your case. Keep in mind the famous observation of Justice Oliver Wendell Holmes that "general propositions do not decide concrete cases." Do not engage in extended abstract discussions of the law; devote your energy to applying the law to your facts. One quick method to ascertain the effectiveness of your Discussion section is to review it with an eye toward learning the facts of the case. A successful discussion will continually refer to the facts and thus paint a picture, as well as analyze.

In sum, in this section you should analyze relevant constitutional provisions, statutes, administrative regulations, and court cases. Quote from the key provisions of statutory materials. With cases, state the holdings of relevant cases. Also discuss the similarities and differences between the facts of the case being cited and the facts involved in the problem being researched. All references to legal authorities should include proper citations. Be sure to report the extent to

which intervening court cases have modified any statutes or earlier court opinions. In assessing the strengths and the weaknesses of the client's case be as objective as possible. Specify which courses of action appear most promising, and when relevant also identify facts that need to be clarified or additional legal materials that need to be examined.

g. Conclusion

Give a brief review of the most significant conclusions. Do not introduce new ideas or authorities in this paragraph. This final section of the memo should provide a brief and concise summary that points out the strengths and weaknesses of the client's position. It also may include the writer's recommendations for further action, including additional factual investigation and further legal research on specific points.

2. Sample Law Office Memorandum

TO: Janice Brown, Senior Partner

FROM: Chris Parker

RE: Janice Miller; File No. 06-1234

             Possibility of Proving Mr. Booth's Negligence

DATE: April 5, 2006

Questions Presented

Issue 1: Whether Mr. Booth can be found negligent, for failing to take precautions once warned of his fatigue, when Mr. Booth stated to Ms. Miller that he was tired, he continued to use a chain saw to cut wood, and the chain saw slipped, slicing off a piece of bark that flew into Ms. Miller's eye, blinding her.

Issue 2: Whether Ms. Miller will be barred from recovering for Mr. Booth's negligence if the jury determines that she was negligent in failing to wear a pair of safety goggles.

Brief Answers

Issue 1: Yes, Mr. Booth will be found negligent. If someone is fatigued while using a chain saw, it is foreseeable that an injury will occur. Mr. Booth was warned of his fatigue but continued to use the chain saw. Therefore, Ms. Miller's injury was foreseeable, and Mr. Booth was negligent in failing to heed the warning.
Issue 2: Ms. Miller will not be barred from recovering for Mr. Booth's negligence so long as she was not more than 50 percent responsible for her injuries. However, based on Massachusetts statutory law the amount that she can recover will be decreased by the percentage of her negligence.

Facts

Last March our client, Janice Miller, was injured in an accident that occurred in her backyard. She and her husband, George Booth, were cutting firewood. Mr. Booth was using a chain saw, and Ms. Miller was stacking the pieces of wood as Mr. Booth cut them. Neither was wearing safety glasses although each owned a pair. Ms. Miller explained the omission by saying that they had both thought they would be cutting wood only for a short time and neither wanted to be bothered by putting on the glasses.

As it turned out, the wood-cutting session took longer than anticipated. After about an hour both Mr. Booth and Ms. Miller were getting tired. In particular, Mr. Booth complained that he was feeling fatigued and that it was getting harder and harder to hold the saw sufficiently perpendicular to the wood to cut a straight line. Ms. Miller suggested that they quit for the day, but Mr. Booth wanted to cut just a few more pieces. On his next attempt, probably due to his tired condition, he allowed the chain saw to slip slightly so that it hit the log at a slant, slicing off a piece of bark that flew into Ms. Miller's right eye. Unfortunately the accident has left Ms. Miller totally blind in that eye.

Applicable Statutes

Issue 1: There are no statutes that apply.

Issue 2:

Contributory negligence shall not bar recovery in any action by any person . . . to recover damages for negligence . . . if such negligence was not greater than the total amount of negligence attributable to the person . . . against whom recovery is sought, but any damages allowed shall be diminished in proportion to the amount of negligence attributable to the person for whose injury . . . recovery is made.

Mass. Gen. L. ch. 231, § 85 (2006).

Discussion

The resolution of two issues will determine whether Mr. Booth will be found liable for the injuries Ms. Miller sustained. The first relates to whether Mr. Booth was negligent for continuing to use his chain saw after he acknowledged that he was feeling fatigued. The second is whether Ms. Miller will be barred from recovery because of her failure to wear safety goggles.

Issue 1—Mr. Booth's Actions Constitute Negligence

Mr. Booth will be found liable for negligently causing his wife's injuries if the injury was foreseeable and Mr. Booth did nothing to prevent it. To avoid negligence, a person should take precautions once warned of drowsiness or fatigue. *Keller v. DeLong*, 231 A.2d 633, 634 (N.H. 1967). In *Keller* the defendant, while a passenger, felt sleepy. Before taking over at the wheel he did not take any precautions against falling asleep, such as rolling down the windows or turning on the radio. Soon after that he fell asleep and hit a utility pole, killing his passenger. The court held that the defendant was negligent because he had felt sleepy as a passenger but had taken no precautions before taking over at the

wheel. *Id.* at 635. The court reasoned that because the defendant did not take any precautions to avoid the accident, the accident was foreseeable. *Id.*

Unlike the *Keller* case, Mr. Booth would argue that the harm to Ms. Miller was not foreseeable. There are significant differences between driving a car and operating a chain saw. If someone drives a car negligently, the passengers are just as likely as the driver to be injured. But when using a chain saw, the person most likely to be hurt is the one using it, in this case Mr. Booth, not Ms. Miller.

However, while the person most likely to be hurt may be the operator of the chain saw, any dangerous instrument if used carelessly can easily inflict injury on others. Indeed, that is what happened in this case. As in *Keller*, the defendant was warned of the impending danger. In *Keller* the driver felt drowsy as a passenger and yet took no precautions before taking over at the wheel. In Mr. Booth's case, he told his wife that he was feeling fatigued just before the accident occurred. If anything, the negligence in Mr. Booth's, case is greater because the defendant felt tired while operating the chain saw and yet continued to operate it. It would have been a simple matter to have taken a break, but Mr. Booth chose to continue with a dangerous activity even while knowing he was fatigued. As in *Keller*, once the defendant is warned of his fatigue, an injury is foreseeable. Therefore, Mr. Booth should be found negligent.

Issue 2—Ms. Miller's Contributory Negligence Will Reduce Her Damages

The second issue is whether a jury, finding that Ms. Miller failed to use reasonable care by not protecting her eyes with safety glasses, would bar her from recovering. A jury finding of contributory negligence will not bar a plaintiff from recovery so long as her negligence "was not greater than" the defendant's negligence. Mass. Gen. L. ch. 231, § 85 (2006). Therefore, so long as the jury finds that Mr. Booth's negligence was at least 50 percent of the reason for Ms. Miller's injury, she will not be barred from recovery. However, the statute also provides that "any damages allowed shall be diminished in proportion to the amount of negligence attributable" to Ms. Miller's actions. For example, if the jury were to decide that Ms. Miller's own actions contributed 25 percent to her injuries and that her damages are $400,000, she would be able to recover $300,000. Therefore, so long as the jury finds that Ms. Miller's actions contributed 50 percent or less to her injuries, she will be allowed to recover for her injuries, with the total damages reduced by the amount of her contributory negligence.

Conclusion

On the first issue, regarding Mr. Booth's failure to stop using the chain saw after experiencing warning symptoms of fatigue, he will be found negligent. Once he felt tired, an accident was foreseeable, and Mr. Booth was negligent in continuing to use a dangerous tool, such as a chain saw. On the second issue, regarding Ms. Miller's failure to use safety goggles, if the jury determines that her contributory negligence did not cause more than 50 percent of the harm, then she will still be allowed to recover, but her damages will be reduced by the amount of her negligence.

SUMMARY

The purpose of analyzing court opinions is to try to predict the outcome of your client's case. The process involves searching for analogies and distinctions between prior court opinions and the facts of your client's situation. Generally, to find analogies, you will think in general terms, while to find distinctions, you will think as specifically as possible about the facts. Legal analysis also involves selecting among available precedents based on such factors as the court that decided the case, the age of the case, and the number of factual similarities or differences between that case and your own.

In writing an analysis, the deductive model—major premise (rule of law), minor premise (facts), and conclusion—can provide a structure for your argument. Another method is to rely on IRAC (Issue-Rule-Analysis-Conclusion). Finally, whenever you are analyzing more than one case, you are engaging in synthesis, the process of integrating the concepts you find in the cases so that the reader can appreciate the principles of law that arise from seeing the series of cases as a unit.

REVIEW QUESTIONS

—ALL—

1. Why is it important to find both analogies and distinctions between your client's facts and the facts of prior cases?
2. Why is it not enough simply to list the similarities and differences between your client's facts and the facts of prior cases?
3. What factors help determine whether you should use a particular case in support of your client's position?
4. Assume you have been asked to write an analysis of whether a client is guilty of murder. The case occurred and will be tried in California. List the following in order from most to least authoritative. Explain your choices.
   a. 1995 Illinois Supreme Court decision, with facts similar to your client's facts, in which the defendant was found not guilty of murder.
   b. A 1989 law review article that surveys all of the murder statutes in the fifty states.
   c. A 1980 California Supreme Court decision, with facts similar to your client's facts, in which the defendant was found guilty of murder.
   d. A 1990 California intermediate court decision, with facts similar to your client's facts, in which the defendant was found guilty of manslaughter.
   e. A California state statute defining murder and manslaughter.
   f. A section from Am. Jur. 2d explaining the differences between murder and manslaughter.
   g. A 1995 California Supreme Court decision on breach of warranty in automobile sales.
5. What does it mean to say a case is on all fours?
6. What is the relationship between deductive reasoning and legal reasoning?

PART 4

Paralegals and the
Work World

Chapter 16

Interviewing

Life is not so short but that there is always time enough for courtesy.
Ralph Waldo Emerson

INTRODUCTION

Resolving legal conflicts involves applying general principles of law to a specific set of facts. Therefore, an attorney needs to know not only the law but also the factual details of the client's situation in order to be able to advise the client on a specific course of action. These facts begin to emerge in the initial client interview and then are developed further as part of the case preparation process. In this chapter we will look at how paralegals gather facts through client and witness interviews. In the next chapter we will take a closer look at gathering facts through documentary evidence (such as police reports, hospital and doctor records, employment records, contracts, and photographs) and from personal observation (by visiting an accident scene or examining the condition of a defective piece of machinery).

Depending on the procedures established in the office in which they work, paralegals may be involved in several types of interview situations. These situations can include the initial client interview, follow-up interviews with the client (either in the office or in the field), and field interviews with both friendly and hostile witnesses. In this chapter we will use the case of Donald Drake, which we introduced in Chapter 1, to illustrate interviewing techniques. You will recall that Mr. Drake witnessed the death of his grandson, Philip, when Philip was struck by the car Wilma Small was driving. Here's the case again for your review.

The Case of the Distressed Grandfather

Approximately one year ago Mr. Drake and his six-year-old grandson, Philip, were walking down a residential road on their way home from visiting one of Philip's friends. Philip was walking on the sidewalk approximately 30 feet in front of Mr. Drake. Suddenly a car sped past Mr. Drake, seemingly went out of control, jumped the curb, and hit Philip. Mr. Drake ran to Philip's side, but it was too late. Philip had been killed instantly. The driver of the car, Mrs. Wilma Small, was unhurt.

At the time of the accident Mr. Drake's only concern was for the welfare of his grandson because he himself was clear of the danger. Naturally, Mr. Drake suffered a great deal of mental pain and shock because of seeing his grandson killed. While being driven home from the accident, he suffered a heart attack that necessitated a lengthy hospital stay.

One year later he still does not feel completely recovered and often suffers from nightmares, reliving the accident and his grandson's death. Mr. Drake would like to sue Mrs. Small to recover for his hospital bills and for his pain and suffering.

A. COMMUNICATION SKILLS

To be a good interviewer, you must have strong verbal communication skills. You must be able to relate well to other people, be able to "read" their reactions, and be able to adjust to their situations and their moods. Perhaps most important of all, you must be able to put others at ease and be able to win their confidence.

1. Communication as a Two-Way Street

It is quite possible for two people to receive different messages from the same set of words and gestures. The authors of a book on communication problems report having seen the following sign in a lawyer's office:

> I know you believe you understand what you think I said, but I am not sure you realize that what you heard is not what I meant.[1]

This sign points out a common communication problem—the listener is not getting the message that the speaker has intended to convey.

Communication is a two-way street: You have an obligation to make sure that you understand what the other person is saying. But you also must ensure that the other person understands what you are saying. Be very conscious of the words, expressions, and gestures you use, as well as the reactions they evoke.

To as great a degree as possible, keep legal jargon out of the conversation. Think back to when you first started your legal studies. If you were like most students, you assumed burglary meant stealing. (Of course, now you know it means breaking and entering a building at nighttime with the intent to commit a crime, which could be but does not necessarily have to be theft.) Law is a foreign

---

[1] G. Nierenberg and H. Calero, Meta-talk 16 (1975).

language that you are rapidly mastering. But remember that your clients may have an entirely different understanding of the legal terms you use. Therefore, whenever possible, avoid all legal terminology. Another reason for avoiding legal jargon is that its use can unintentionally lead you into the unauthorized practice of law: The more you use it, the more the client will ask you to explain what it means, and the more likely it is that you will eventually pass over that forbidden line into the unauthorized practice of law.

Finally, watch for signals that other people do not understand what you are saying. They may not let you know that their understanding of what you are saying differs from what you mean. This may occur because they do not realize there is a difference between what you said and what they understood or because they are too embarrassed to tell you they did not understand the terminology you used. In those cases go back and restate the message in different terms.

When first meeting a client, it is also important to avoid the trap of allowing previous experiences to color your perception. For example, after you have interviewed dozens of clients with landlord-tenant disputes, you may start to think in terms of stereotyped categories. You may then begin to assume that simply because something happened one way in a similar case, it happened the same way in the present case. Having categorized the current case, you may fail to hear what the interviewee really says. Experience with similar cases may also have created some bias on your part. For example, if you have interviewed a series of "deadbeat" dads, that is, fathers who are unwilling to support their children, you may unconsciously begin to view all noncustodial fathers as "deadbeats." However, the person you are interviewing may be willing but simply unable to provide support.

2. Nonverbal Communication

Good listening skills involve more than simply hearing what is being said. It is essential to watch, as well as listen. As Alfred Benjamin has written in an excellent book on interviewing skills:

> Listening requires, first of all, that we not be preoccupied, for if we are we cannot fully attend. Secondly, listening involves hearing the way things are being said, the tone used, the expressions and gestures employed. In addition, listening includes the effort to hear what is not being said, what is only hinted at, what is perhaps being held back, what lies beneath or beyond the surface. We hear with our ears, but we listen with our eyes and mind and heart and skin and guts as well.[2]

Pay attention to nonverbal communication. Nonverbal messages can be either conscious or unconscious and either intentional or unintentional. A smile is both intentional and conscious. A quivering voice is usually conscious yet unintentional.[3]

Nonverbal behavior plays an important role in the feedback process. Just as the client sends nonverbal cues to the interviewer, so, too, the interviewer sends nonverbal cues to the client. The paralegal therefore must remain conscious of

---

[2] A. Benjamin, The Helping Interview 46 (3d ed. 1981).

[3] Id. at 67.

nonverbal behavior and the effect it has on the client. For example, crossing your arms, leaning back, or frowning might convey hostility. On the other hand, a relaxed posture while leaning forward generally conveys a positive attitude.

3. Active Listening

Active Listening
The process of signaling that you are really listening, accomplished by using verbal and nonverbal clues, paraphrasing, and reflecting the client's feelings.

Active listening involves the process of signaling that you are really listening. This is accomplished by

1. using verbal and nonverbal clues,
2. paraphrasing, and
3. reflecting the client's feelings.

Active listening is so named because the interviewer is actively engaged in the conversation. Not only does active listening show the person being interviewed that you are listening, but also it conveys a sense of empathy, that you not only hear but also understand what the other person is trying to convey. It also gives the interviewee an opportunity to correct you if you did not correctly interpret what the interviewee said.

You can use a number of verbal and nonverbal clues to convey that you are listening and that the person interviewed should continue with his or her story. These include head nods and short, nonintrusive expressions such as "And?," "Could you tell me a bit more about that?," and even "Um-hm."

Paraphrasing is simply the process of repeating, in a shortened form, what the interviewee has just finished saying. It serves three basic functions:

1. to convey to the client that you are with him, that you are trying to understand what he is saying;
2. to crystallize a client's comments by repeating what he has said in a more concise manner; and
3. to check the interviewer's own perceptions to make sure he really does understand what the client is describing.[4]

For example, if a client relates a rather involved conversation with a bill collector, the interviewer might respond: "So the bill collector threatened to get you fired if you didn't pay by Tuesday. Is that right?" Be careful with this, however. Shortening an involved conversation to one sentence might leave the client viewing you as brusque and unfeeling.

In addition to using paraphrasing to reflect the interviewer's perception of the facts, you should use it to acknowledge the client's emotions. A reflection of feelings demonstrates that you have been listening closely and understand the feelings the client has expressed.[5] The goal is to communicate an understanding of how the client feels—a sense of empathy. It is not necessary to show acceptance for the person's feelings—just that those feelings are respected.

Thus, after listening to a client describe an incident in which her husband made derogatory remarks about her at a party, the interviewer might comment,

[4] A. Ivey, Microcounseling: Innovations in Interviewing Training 35, 156 (1971).
[5] Id. at 154.

"My goodness, that must have been difficult for you." However, do not become so overcome by the client's plight that you lose your professional distance. There is a fine balance required to show acceptance while keeping your objectivity.

When using either the paraphrasing or the reflection of feelings technique, deliver the feedback in a tentative tone of voice. This offers the interviewee a chance to respond by (1) affirming that the stated understanding is correct, (2) correcting what was a false understanding on the interviewer's part, (3) elaborating further on the topic, or (4) using some combination of the first three. These techniques show the interviewee that you are listening and encourages him or her to correct any misunderstandings.

4. The Influence of Ethnic, Racial, and Gender Differences

Because the interviewer's ability to establish rapport and trust with the person being interviewed is critical to the success of the interview, cultural and gender difference can present special challenges. For example, it is often suggested that one facilitator to good communication is the use of direct eye contact. Yet in some cultures direct eye contact between strangers is interpreted as rudeness.

The more you can educate yourself about racial, cultural, and gender differences, the better off you will be. However, it is also important that you not treat people on the basis of stereotypes. The best approach to interviewing is to be yourself and to let your own personality come through. Be especially careful, however, not to appear condescending or patronizing. Listen, document, and empathize, but do not judge. Always treat the interviewee with respect.

DISCUSSION QUESTIONS

1. Active listening is an important part of effective communication skills. However, some argue that it is inappropriate to use active listening during client interviews because it interjects too much emotion into what should be a professional setting. Do you agree?

2. What, if any, cultural or gender differences do you think exist with respect to verbal and nonverbal communications? To what extent should they affect one's interview style?

PRACTICE TIP

Keep tissues nearby for emotional interviews. Offer water, a private moment, or the rest room to help clients recover their dignity. But if you really need to obtain information from the client, once the client is able, you must quietly persist with the interview. It is also often useful to acknowledge to the client that you are asking difficult questions and remind the client why you need to do so.

5. Establishing a Comfortable Interview Setting

Communication can be improved by having the interview take place in a comfortable and quiet private location. Such surroundings help establish good rapport. Avoiding interruptions from telephone calls and others shows respect for the interviewee and helps build trust.

Before meeting with a new client or witness, ascertain whether the client has any physical disabilities or other problems that may make access to the office difficult. You can do this by describing the office, stairs, and the like and then asking if anything you described will cause problems for the interviewee. Consider either making a home visit to the disabled or elderly or borrowing more accessible space.

Communication can be facilitated or impeded by a circumstance as simple as where the parties sit during the interview. There is no one right seating arrangement, but be aware that the one you choose will send a message. Which one you choose will depend on how you want the other person to perceive you, who that other person is (new client, established client, hostile witness, etc.), and why that person has come to the firm (ax murderer or elderly gentleman seeking tax advice).

Figure 16-1 shows the basic seating arrangements available in most offices. In the traditional arrangement the lawyer sits behind a large imposing desk, reinforcing the authority image. The client sits on the other side of the desk—usually in a chair that is lower than that of the interviewer. Traditionally, such a seating arrangement is thought to intimidate clients and to make them uneasy. However, there may be times when you want that extra authority image that such a seating arrangement can provide, for example, when meeting with a representative from the opposing side. Once you have established a good working relationship, you might then consider one of the other possible seating arrangements.

At the opposite end of the spectrum from the authority image evoked by arrangement A, arrangement D strikes a very casual tone. The interviewer leaves the desk behind and uses chairs placed around a low table of some sort. This arrangement places you and the interviewee on an equal level at a distance that facilitates personal communication. It also has the advantage of providing comfortable eye contact; it allows the two parties either to look directly at each other

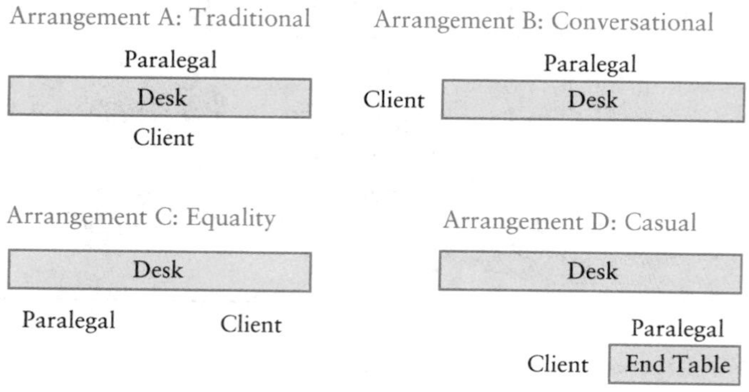

Figure 16-1   Alternative Seating Arrangements for interviews

or to easily glance away at a 90-degree angle. A major disadvantage is that it will be more difficult for you to take notes. In effect, you will have to balance a note pad on your knee. Also, it may convey too casual an image to a client who, after all, has come to the law firm seeking serious help.

When you have no need for a show of authority and yet do not want to convey too informal an image, arrangement B provides a good compromise. This positioning of client and paralegal offers the same advantages as to distance and eye contact as arrangement D. It also provides the interviewer with a large surface on which to take notes.

Finally, arrangement C, while conveying an image of equality, can be quite awkward for both you and the interviewee. The positioning of the chairs does not allow for any but direct eye contact, and the full body is exposed. Note-taking is also quite awkward, and there is no way to hide any notes you might not want the interviewee to see.

6. Listening as Hard Work

If you are beginning to think that listening is hard work, you are right. It is easy to become so overcome with empathy for the client's plight or so wrapped up in trying to get all of the answers for your intake form that you simply neglect to listen to what the client is telling you. While good interviewing skills come mostly with practice, the techniques we have discussed can help you develop the art of listening.

B. THE INITIAL CLIENT INTERVIEW

In this section we will be focusing on the initial client interview. However, much of this discussion is also relevant to witness and follow-up client interviews.

The two main goals of an initial client interview are

1. to obtain information that is legally relevant, complete, and reliable; and
2. to establish a relationship of trust with the client so that the client will feel sufficiently comfortable to convey the needed information.

You may not always be able to attain the first goal for any number of reasons, such as limited time for the interview or lack of knowledge in a particular area of the law. Nonetheless, at a minimum you should leave the interview with enough information to enable your supervising attorney to decide whether the firm should accept the case and formally establish the client-attorney relationship. You should also have a sufficient understanding of the facts to be able to begin working toward an appropriate solution to the client's problems, including deciding what further investigation needs to be done either to corroborate the client's story or to fill in gaps in the client's account.

No matter how productive the initial interview is, it often is necessary to gather additional facts from the client. So long as you accomplished the second goal of establishing a relationship of trust with the client, you can easily gather additional facts by having the client return to the office, by going to the client's home or office, or by using the telephone.

PRACTICE TIP

If there is some time before the initial interview, you should consider sending the client a pre-interview checklist so that even that first meeting can be productive. You can ask for items such as the date of the incident; any documentation; names, addresses, and phone and fax numbers of health care providers; insurance documentation; names, addresses, and phone numbers of witnesses, such as passengers, neighbors, and so on. For wills you will need a list of assets, insurance and bank account numbers, deeds, specific bequests, and guardians' names and addresses. If you would like to have the information before the interview, enclose a self-addressed, stamped envelope to make it easy for the client.

---

1. Starting the Interview

If possible, greet the client in the reception room, and escort the client to the interview location. This will help the client feel welcomed. It also helps preserve other client confidences that a wandering client might accidentally overhear.

Law firms follow any one of three possible approaches regarding the presence of paralegals at the initial client interview. In Mr. Drake's case the law firm preferred to use a paralegal-attorney team. In others the preference is to have a paralegal meet with the client first to collect a considerable amount of information about the client's problems before an attorney meets with the client personally. Finally, there are some law offices where the attorneys prefer to handle the initial interview alone.

The Case of the Distressed Grandfather (continued)

When Mr. Drake appeared for his first appointment at the law office of Darrow and Bryan, the receptionist notified attorney Pat Harper that Mr. Drake had arrived. Pat Harper then went to the reception area, where she greeted Mr. Drake by name, shook his hand, and escorted him to a conference room. When they arrived in the conference room, Chris Kendall was there waiting for them. Pat introduced Mr. Drake to Chris. She explained that Chris was one of the firm's paralegals and would be joining them for the interview.

When an attorney decides to conduct the initial interview, this can be for a variety of reasons. First, it is very likely that a new client is attorney shopping. Therefore, the client will want to interview the attorney, as well as having the attorney interview him or her. Knowing this, the attorney may feel it is important for the client to have the opportunity of meeting with the attorney and deciding whether or not to retain the firm before the firm invests too much time in a case it may ultimately not be handling. Second, because of ethical constraints only the

Only the attorney can establish the attorney-client relationship and negotiate the fee agreement.

Ethics Alert

attorney can establish the attorney-client relationship and negotiate the fee arrangement. Once the attorney-client relationship has been established, the attorney may then bring the paralegal into the interview and ask the paralegal to gather further information about the client's case. Third, as the *People v. Mitchell* case in Chapter 11 illustrated, there may be an issue of whether the attorney-client privilege has been established if the initial interview is conducted solely by a paralegal.

Whenever a paralegal is present at an initial client interview, as part of the introduction process the attorney or paralegal should give a brief explanation of the paralegal's role. The person being interviewed has a right to know who the interviewer is and that the interviewer is not a lawyer. There is no need, however, to launch into a five-minute description of everything that a paralegal can or cannot do. The paralegal's role should be described in relatively simple, positive terms. For example: "I am a paralegal—not an attorney. My job involves gathering the basic facts for (attorney's name). I will be working with him/her on your case."

2. Taking Notes

Although note taking can be distracting, it can actually help to impress on the client the fact that you are taking what he or she is saying seriously. Indeed,

[i]n our culture, when note taking is discriminately handled, it is not resented. On the contrary, its absence may be looked upon as negligence or lack of interest.[6]

In any case note-taking is essential in most legal interviewing situations. The paralegal has to understand the facts and cannot afford to rely on memory until the interview can be written up. If you do not take good notes, you will need to call the client back to fill in the gaps. This irritates the client and needlessly increases the client's billable hours. On the other hand, too much note-taking will mean that you will miss what the client is saying and make the client feel like an object.

The Case of The Distressed Grandfather (continued)

Pat explained to Mr. Drake that while both she and Chris would be asking questions, Chris would also be taking notes so that they would have an accurate record of their meeting.

[6] Benjamin, supra note 2, at 58.

It is an art to be able to take notes and listen at the same time. One method that can help is to always put the same type of information in the same place, such as all potential witness names in the upper right corner of your note pad. To save time, you may want to use abbreviations, such as W. for witness. But make sure you can interpret your handwriting later. This is also where a checklist can prove to be invaluable. Not only will a checklist cut down on the amount of writing that you will have to do, but also it will keep you on track. But be careful that you do not rely so heavily on the checklist that you fail to follow up possibly fruitful areas of inquiry.

3. Asking Questions

Open questions
Broad questions that put few limits on the freedom of the respondent.

Closed questions
Specific questions that usually demand very short or yes-no answers.

A question can take many forms: open, closed (yes-no and narrow), and leading. Consider, for instance, the difference between open and closed questions. **Open questions** such as "How did the accident take place?" focus the interview without greatly limiting the freedom of the respondent. On the other hand, **closed questions** are by their nature very specific and usually demand very short or yes-no answers: "What color was the car that hit you?" "How far in advance did you see it coming?" "Was the sun shining in your face at the time?" Note that if the interviewee, in responding to the general open question, fails to discuss the point at which the other car was first seen, the interviewer can always follow it up with a more specific closed question. However, if the interviewer, in asking a closed question, fails to ask about the condition of the roadway, the information is unlikely to be volunteered by the interviewee.

Compare the information given below by the client in response to the different forms of questions from the paralegal:

Interview No. 1

Paralegal: Did you receive a written eviction notice?
Client: Yes.

Interview No. 2

Paralegal: How did you find out that you were going to be evicted?
Client: The landlord came up to me around 7 o'clock in the evening while I was sitting on the front porch with some other residents. He yelled something about my being a no-good troublemaker because I was always complaining to the city inspections department. Then he stuck this eviction notice in my hand and stomped off.

Better information usually is obtained from open questions. The closed variety should be reserved for pulling together potentially important details that the interviewee may have overlooked.

Therefore, once the client is seated and comfortable, you should begin the interview with an open question and allow the client to introduce the problem in the manner and at the pace most comfortable for him or her. You can, if it seems appropriate, first engage in some small talk about the weather or about the parking situation until the client feels relaxed enough to move on to the nature

of the problem. If after some awkward periods of silence the client seems to have trouble discussing the specific situation, you can then initiate the conversation with an open-ended inquiry, such as "Well, Mr./Mrs. . . . what is it that brings you in to see us?"

The Case of the Distressed Grandfather (continued)

As Mr. Drake entered the office, he seemed somewhat shaky and ill at ease. Because Pat knew Mr. Drake was coming to see them about a matter in relation to his grandson's recent death, Pat felt it best not to spend too much time on small talk. Instead, after asking if she could get Mr. Drake a cup of coffee or tea, she said to Mr. Drake, "I understand you have come to see us regarding an accident that involved your grandson. In what way would you like us to help you?"

Let the client describe the problem independently and not in response to specific questions. Asking a series of narrow questions may lead to the client's answering only the specific questions you ask, thereby causing you to miss valuable information. A further danger is that you will concentrate on framing the next question and will fail to listen to what the client really says.

Avoid **leading questions** because leading questions suggest the answer. For example, after hearing Mr. Drake's story, Chris should not ask, "To have caused such long skid marks, Mrs. Small was probably speeding, wasn't she?" Leading questions are dangerous because they put words in the client's mouth, words that might not otherwise have been there. In trying to give you the answer that they think you want, clients may unconsciously "misremember" the facts. Also, leading questions may cut off what would otherwise be a more helpful and detailed discussion of the event.

"Why" questions can also be dangerous. A good interviewer tries to avoid using "why" questions because the client may view them as suggesting disapproval and displeasure.[7] Although "why" questions have their place, and generally do not harm, even a seemingly innocuous inquiry, such as asking why the client acted in a particular way, can appear to the client as though you are disapproving of her actions (especially if the tone in which you ask conveys total disbelief that anyone could have been so stupid as to have engaged in that particular behavior). "Why" questions put the interviewee on the defensive and erode the relationship of trust that you are trying to build. While there are occasions when you can legitimately ask "why" questions (such as "Why did you move out of your apartment?"), avoid them, especially where matters of values and judgment are involved.[8]

Leading questions Questions that suggest the answer.

---

[7] Id. at 80.

[8] Id. at 85.

> ## PRACTICE TIP
>
> Despite our advice to begin a client interview with open questions, starting off with some very narrow factual information, such as the client's address and phone number, can sometimes be of great assistance, especially in the case of a nervous client (or a nervous interviewer!). However, as soon as the client appears to be at ease, switch to a series of open questions.

DISCUSSION QUESTIONS

3. What are the advantages and disadvantages of having a paralegal rather than the attorney conduct the initial interview with a client?

4. When meeting clients or witnesses for the first time you must be sure they understand your role as a paralegal. At the same time, you do not want to send the message that you are "only the paralegal." Can you think of ways other than that described in the text to accomplish that goal?

5. What do you think is the most important goal to accomplish during the initial client interview: to establish a good rapport with the client or to gather all of the essential facts? Why?

4. Keeping the Interview Going

Once you have elicited the general story through broad, open questions, it is time to move to the second stage of the interview: clarification and verification. During this stage you can use the active listening techniques we discussed earlier to keep the conversation going, to elicit more detail, and to confirm that you have accurately heard what the client has said. Ask questions to clarify areas of ambiguity and help the interviewee tell the story. This approach of starting with broad questions and then progressively narrowing the inquiry is sometimes referred to as the funnel approach, as illustrated in Figure 16-2.

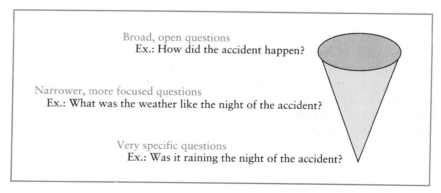

Broad, open questions
Ex.: How did the accident happen?

Narrower, more focused questions
Ex.: What was the weather like the night of the accident?

Very specific questions
Ex.: Was it raining the night of the accident?

Figure16-2   The Funnel Approach

The Case of the Distressed Grandfather (continued)

By the end of the interview, besides obtaining basic information such as Mr. Drake's date of birth, Social Security number, address, phone number, place of employment, health insurance carrier, and details of the accident, Chris also wanted to find out about the extent of Mr. Drake's injuries, any prior medical history, especially involving any heart problems, and his relationship to his grandson (were they close; did they live in the same household; see each other daily, weekly; etc.). Therefore, after Pat and Chris had listened to Mr. Drake's story with a few or no interruptions, Chris told Mr. Drake that he would like to start at the beginning again, but that this time he would stop him occasionally with specific questions in order to help them fill in the details.

For example, Chris pursued the following line of questioning: "Mr. Drake, you said that you and your grandson had started out on your walk because it was such a nice day. Could you tell me a bit more about what the weather conditions were?" Then Chris asked a series of narrow questions, focusing on the details regarding the specifics of the weather that day.

When trying to obtain more details about a subjective condition such as pain, it is sometimes helpful to suggest the use of analogies. Therefore, Chris also asked Mr. Drake to think back to other situations in which he had been hurt and to describe any that were similar.

A good interview checklist can help you keep focused on the necessary facts when you might otherwise have a tendency to get sidetracked. If the client states a conclusion about some person or event, probe to find the specific observations on which that conclusion is based. Distinguish exactly what the client said or heard personally from what he or she learned secondhand. If the client simply conveys to you what someone else told him or her, you may be obtaining inadmissible hearsay evidence. Hearsay testimony is usually not admissible because it is, in effect, someone giving secondhand information. (We discuss hearsay and the rules of evidence in Chapter 17.) If possible, get the name of the person with the firsthand information so that you can interview that person.

DISCUSSION QUESTION

6. If you were interviewing Mr. Drake, what other areas would you want to ask him about? Create an initial interview form that you think would prove helpful in a personal injury case, such as Mr. Drake's, with a short list of questions for each area.

5. Ending the Interview

Near the end of the interview summarize your understanding of the client's problem in order to give the client a chance to add any additional information that may have been overlooked and to correct any misunderstandings you may have. You might also ask the client a very general question, such as "Is there

anything else about this incident that I haven't asked about and that you think I should know?" This sometimes elicits important information; sometimes not. This is also the time to double-check to make sure you have all of the necessary identifying information, such as the client's phone numbers and addresses, name and phone number of current physician, and so on.

Before the client leaves the office, the attorney must explain the firm's policy regarding the payment of fees and expenses. In addition, most firms will ask the client to sign a retainer agreement. A **retainer agreement** is a written contract that outlines the attorney's duties and the client's obligations regarding payment, on either an hourly or a contingency fee basis, as well as the client's responsibility regarding costs and expenses. The various possible fee arrangements used in law offices will be discussed in Chapter 16. Standard retainer agreements are usually stored as word processing templates, with all of the variable information left blank. With a keyboard merge the word processing program stops at each place where the paralegal or secretary needs to insert specific client information.

Retainer agreement
A contract that outlines the attorney's duties and the client's obligations regarding payment, on either an hourly or a contingency fee basis, as well as the client's responsibility regarding costs and expenses.

The Case of the Distressed Grandfather (continued)

At the end of the interview, attorney Harper told Mr. Drake that the firm would be happy to help him if it could but also briefly explained the possible legal problems that might be encountered in his case. She then explained the firm's policy of charging on a contingency basis in personal injury cases and asked Mr. Drake whether he would like to retain the firm. When he said that he would, she asked him to sign a retainer agreement.

Before leaving, the client should also be informed of what, if any, followup will be necessary. Do documents need to be brought in? Should another appointment be scheduled? When should the client expect to hear from the firm? To ensure that you remember to give the client all of the necessary follow-up instructions, it is helpful to make a checklist for the client. For example, on the checklist you can remind the client to bring certain items to the next appointment, to start a journal detailing how the client's daily activities have been curtailed by his or her injuries, and to begin keeping copies of all medical bills.

Once these steps have been completed, collect, or make arrangements to collect, copies of all relevant legal documents. Photocopy and return them to the client as soon as possible. If the client needs to sign authorization forms so that the firm can obtain medical or employment records, explain the purpose of the forms to the client, and have the client sign them. Alternatively, the forms can be given to the client along with a self-addressed, stamped envelope so that they can be easily mailed back to the firm. Exhibit 16-1 on page 491 illustrates a typical release form.

It is also important at this stage to remember the ethical prohibitions that apply to a paralegal's role. Clients often attempt to elicit advice and opinions about their cases from paralegals, but paralegals are not allowed to give legal advice. Also, the clients should not be given false expectations about the outcomes of their cases either by the attorney or by the paralegal. If things do not

---

Darrow & Bryan
Attorneys at Law
333 Main St.
Springfield, MA 01009
413-999-9999

AUTHORIZATION

To: Dr. George Boothby

I hereby authorize you to release a copy of my medical records to Pat Harper
of Darrow & Bryan, or her representative. This authorization is effective
immediately and remains in effect until I revoke it in writing.

_____*Donald Drake*_____

Donald Drake
79 Sycamore Lane, South Hadley, MA 00107
D.O.B. 4/27/29
S.S.N. 364-77-8948

Witnessed by me this_4th_day of_May 2007_.

_____*Chris Kendall*_____

Exhibit 16-1 Sample Release

turn out as hoped, not only will you have a disappointed client, but also you may
have a potential malpractice claim. Finally, do not get trapped by questions that
place you between your attorney and the client. For example, it is not uncommon
for a client to ask the paralegal, "Do you think the attorney really can help?"

6. After the Interview Is Over

As soon as possible after the interview, review the notes you took during the
interview, and type them in a form that can be understood by your supervising
attorney. These notes, along with the copies that were made of relevant documents, should then be placed in the appropriate office file. A more formal
approach is to write a follow-up memorandum addressed to the attorney or to
the file. Such a memo should include the date and time of the interview, basic
background information on the client (name, address, Social Security number,
etc.), information on the reason the client is seeking legal advice, a list of tasks
that need to be completed for the client, a notation as to what the client was asked
to do next, any record of lost business or wages, and the total medical bills to date.

It is also good practice to always follow office appointments with a brief
letter to the client. After a brief introduction stating that the attorney or paralegal enjoyed meeting with the client, the body of the letter should include the
following information:

- You were in the office on . . .
- We discussed . . .
- You decided . . .
- I will . . . by this date
- You will . . . by this date
- We'll meet on . . . to do . . .

Ethics Alert

Even though a client may pressure you with repeated requests of "Please, just tell me. What would you do if you were in my position?" remember that only the client can decide on the appropriate course of action for himself or herself. No matter how much you may empathize, you simply are not in the client's position and so cannot decide for the client.

Enclose a self-addressed and stamped envelope to make it easy for the client to return the information requested. For Mr. Drake, Chris drafted the letter in Exhibit 16-2 for attorney Harper's signature.

Exhibit 16-2 Follow-up Client Letter

Darrow & Bryan
Attorneys at Law
333 Main St.
Springfield, MA 01009
413-999-9999

May 9, 2007

Mr. Donald Drake
79 Sycamore Lane
South Hadley, MA 00107

Dear Mr. Drake:

It was a pleasure meeting with you last Friday. At that time we discussed the accident last September when your grandson was killed and you suffered a heart attack. We decided that before proceeding to file a lawsuit, we should first engage in some legal and factual investigation. To assist us with that investigation you agreed to furnish us with the names, addresses, and phone numbers of all physicians who have treated you within the last ten years. We will also plan to meet again here in the office on July 19, at 2:00 p.m. By that time, we will have had an opportunity to engage in some preliminary legal research to better assess the likelihood of the court's willingness to consider your case.

Thank you again for retaining our firm. If you have any questions or have a need to contact us before your next appointment, please feel free to call either myself or Chris at the above number.

Sincerely,

Pat Harper, Esq.

Pat Harper, Esq.

If a client decides not to retain the firm or the firm decides not to accept the case, you should still send a follow-up letter documenting that fact. The letter should contain basic information regarding the date of the interview and whether the client stated he or she would not be retaining the firm or the firm declined to accept the case. Many attorneys also include a statement regarding the statute of limitations on the claim.

In conclusion, the initial client interview consists of three major stages. First, you must consider the location of the interview and gather as much information as possible before the interview. Second is the actual interview itself. Third, you must follow through by sending the client a follow-up letter and summarizing the interview for your files. Figure 16-3 summarizes the three interviewing stages.

Your supervising attorney may also ask you to develop an investigation plan based on what you have learned. This investigation plan could include interviewing witnesses and gathering documentary and physical evidence. In the next section of this chapter we will discuss witness interviews. In Chapter 17 we will discuss the process of gathering physical and documentary evidence.

DISCUSSION QUESTION

7. Attorney Jones met with Ms. Brown about an injury she received at work. After about half an hour of discussion Ms. Brown said that she would have to think it over before deciding whether to retain the firm. Attorney Jones wrote a quick memo summarizing their discussion and filed it. He never heard from Ms. Brown again and took no action on her case. What ethical problems do you think attorney Jones may have created for himself?

Figure 16-3 Interviewing Stages

A. Before the Interview
   1. Consider the best place to meet, including any client special needs.
   2. Gather all information you can before the interview.
B. During the Interview
   1. Use the funnel approach: Start with open questions, and then use various forms of narrow questions to gather detail and clarify ambiguities.
   2. Use active listening.
   3. Do not judge the client.
   4. Be aware of how racial, cultural, and gender differences between you and your client may affect your ability to communicate.
   5. Give the client a checklist outlining the next steps the client should take.
C. After the Interview
   1. Send the client a follow-up letter.
   2. Summarize the interview.
   3. Develop an investigation plan.

C. INTERVIEWING WITNESSES

After completing the initial client interview, the attorney and the paralegal should have a basic understanding of the facts of the case. It is important to remember, however, the client seldom knows all of the relevant facts and sometimes has an inaccurate perception of the facts that are remembered. Therefore, the attorney or paralegal will need to verify the client's rendering of the facts and to fill in any gaps. One way to do this is through the examination of witnesses. In addition to providing key testimonial evidence regarding disputed facts, witnesses can also identify other witnesses and other sources of evidence that can help you prove your case.

1. Types of Witnesses

Lay witness
A witness who has not been shown to have any special expertise.

Courts distinguish between lay witnesses and expert witnesses. We will address the reasons for this distinction more fully in Chapter 15 when we discuss the rules of evidence. For now, it is important to understand that **lay witnesses** are "regular people" who do not have any special expertise on the subject on which they are testifying and are allowed to testify only as to what they personally observed. **Expert witnesses,** on the other hand, possess some special knowledge that goes beyond what the average person would possess. These expert witnesses are allowed to give an opinion as to what may have happened or what might have caused it to occur even when they were not present to personally observe the event in question. For example, in a medical malpractice case a doctor might be asked to testify as to whether the surgeon who operated on the plaintiff followed good medical practice when he failed to remove what appeared to be a benign tumor.

Expert witness
A witness who possesses skill and knowledge beyond that of the average person.

2. Locating Lay Witnesses

During the initial interview the client should be asked to supply as much information as possible about both the identity and the possible location of relevant witnesses. Depending on the type of event involved, police reports or newspaper articles should be checked for information about possible witnesses.

Do not forget that the media are often the first on the accident scene. Check newspaper archives to see whether there were any reports of the accident. There may also be photos and even videos. If possible, locate and interview eyewitnesses as soon after the incident as possible. The longer the delay is, the more difficult it will be to find them and the less likely it is that they will accurately remember the incident.

Whenever there is a chance that someone who lives or works nearby may have seen or heard something related to the event in question, check with the occupants of all nearby buildings. In investigating an event that took place at a particular intersection at a particular time, observe and record the license numbers of automobiles that go through that intersection at approximately the same time every day. There is a good chance that the drivers of some of those vehicles may have seen at least something relevant to the event in question. Sometimes the search for witnesses may also involve posting a notice in the area or even taking out a display advertisement in a local newspaper.

Occasionally, you will have a witness's name but will be unable to locate that witness because the address is either missing or incorrect. When this occurs,

the telephone book and the city directory are good starting points. If the person has moved, landlords, utility companies, neighbors, and relatives often know the person's new address. If you have a phone number, a reverse directory is especially useful.

3. Locating Expert Witnesses

In addition to locating lay witnesses, you may need to contact expert witnesses. When trying to find expert witnesses, besides looking through advertisements in legal newspapers and journals, you can search in specialized or technical journals, geared toward a readership of the type of expert you are seeking. Also, most associations have listings of their members. Finally, two of the most widely used resources that list experienced expert witnesses and their fields of expertise are H. Philo, D. Robb, and R. Goodman, Lawyers' Desk Reference: Technical Sources for Conducting a Personal Injury Action, and the Directory of Expert Witnesses in Technology, both of which are updated periodically.

You will want to contact expert witnesses early enough so that they can give advice as to the types of factual material that should be gathered. In fact, in some cases, such as medical malpractice, you will need the services of an expert to help determine whether your client even has a viable cause of action.

Although expert witnesses may be used in almost any type of case, they are most likely to be found in products liability and professional malpractice cases. An expert is usually needed to testify about the generally accepted practices and standards of that industry or profession. For example, in product liability cases the plaintiff must show that there was a defect in the design or manufacture of the product. To qualify as an expert in a product liability case, an engineer must demonstrate sufficient technical familiarity with the general type or class of product or equipment under consideration. He or she must also be able to demonstrate knowledge of the pertinent industry at or before the date of manufacture of the product and often must have conducted appropriate tests with the product in question.

Study the curriculum vitae of any potential expert witnesses to make sure that they are qualified and that they have the specialized knowledge your case requires. For example, a general practitioner would not be the best choice to discuss a gynecological problem. When judging the value of various expert witnesses, one should consider such things as their education and degrees, their membership in relevant professional societies, their familiarity with standard reference works, their field experience, and their courtroom experience. Perhaps the most important qualification, however, is the individual's ability to present his or her knowledge in an understandable way to the jury.

> **P R A C T I C E**
> **T I P**
>
> Just prior to trial, require experts to update their curricula vitae and their publications lists to catch any recent accomplishments and avoid any new problems.

NETNOTE

You can search for expert witnesses on the Internet. A good starting place is www.findlaw.com. Click on the tab "For Legal Professionals." Then click on "Consultants & Experts."

4. Setting Up Appointments

On occasion it is best to appear at the witness's doorstep without advance notice. This is particularly true when there is reason to believe that the person might rehearse a story with someone else. Generally, however, it is best to make advance arrangements to ensure that the time available is adequate and convenient for the witness. You need the witness's cooperation and should therefore make every effort to accommodate the witness's needs.

5. Location of the Interview

Initial client interviews are usually held in the attorney's office. There is no standard practice for interviewing witnesses. Therefore, before interviewing a witness, you should consider how and where you want to conduct the interview. Using the telephone is less expensive, but unless the nature of the information to be provided is routine and unlikely to be contested, whenever possible arrange to meet the witness in person. Not only may the witness be more willing to talk to you in person, but also you will be given a better opportunity to assess the witness's credibility.

> **PRACTICE TIP**
>
> While investigating away from the office, always be mindful of personal safety issues for yourself and your witnesses.

The interview can take place in the law office, in the witness's home, or even at the witness's place of work. One way of making sure that you inconvenience witnesses as little as possible is to offer to come to them rather than asking them to come to your office. This is especially appropriate in the case of those who may have a physical disability, the very young, and the very old. As with client interviews, whatever location you choose, make sure it is a relatively private setting where interruptions can be minimized. If possible, the interview should take place out of the presence of friends, family, or co-workers. One exception to this rule is when a young child is being interviewed if having a parent present helps put the child at ease. It is always possible, however, that children may be willing to tell the interviewer something that they would not tell their parents. Another exception is the situation in which an interpreter is needed because the witness cannot speak English.

6. Interview Format

At the beginning of a witness interview always be sure to explain who you are and your role in the investigation. From Chapter 11 recall that it is unethical to ever misrepresent yourself. And once again courtesy can be your best ally. The witness is probably busy and would much rather be doing something else other than helping you. Therefore, you want to assure the witness that you appreciate the time the witness is giving you.

While you will have to provide certain background information to set up the interview and establish your credibility, it is essential that you not give away vital information about the client's case during the course of the interviews. This admonition is especially true when dealing with insurance company representatives and parties that are closely allied with the opposing party.

The Case of the Distressed Grandfather (continued)

While talking to an insurance agent, the agent told Chris how awful it must have been for Mr. Drake to have suffered a heart attack so soon after his first one. Chris was about to reply, "Yes, especially as after his first attack, the doctor told him he should stop smoking." But he suspected that the agent was bluffing with no actual knowledge of any prior heart attack and wisely said nothing.

As with client interviews, begin the witness interview with open questions. Then employ the same types of feedback mechanisms discussed earlier in this chapter—giving nonverbal encouragement, paraphrasing, and reflecting feelings. As the interview progresses, use closed questions to extract the essential details.

As you conduct the interview, carefully evaluate the person's potential strengths and weaknesses as a witness in the courtroom: How convincing will the witness be on the witness stand? Will the witness be able to follow the questions easily, or will the witness become confused? If the interviewee was an eyewitness or overheard something, you may want to subtly test the witness's eyesight or hearing. If a person wears eyeglasses, it is wise to determine the type of prescription and whether the eyeglasses were worn at the time of the incident about which the witness will be testifying.

Make sure you record the actual events witnessed—the facts—as opposed to the opinions the witness formed based on those facts. While lay witnesses are often allowed to testify as to opinions that are formed in everyday life—the man was staggering and reeked of alcohol; therefore, he was intoxicated—do not rely on it. Be sure you have the facts—exactly what the witness means by staggering and how the witness knows the man reeked of alcohol (distance from the man, prior familiarity with the smell of alcohol, etc.).

When interviewing friendly witnesses, be especially careful not to use leading questions, and guard against the witness who embellishes the truth to win approval or help a friend. Finally, do not forget to ask the witnesses if they know of anyone else who could provide information.

7. Reluctant and Hostile Witnesses

Generally speaking, you should attempt to interview hostile witnesses first. Statements from such adverse witnesses can indicate problem areas that your attorney may have when preparing the case and can provide clues for the type of information needed to impeach that testimony.

The conventional wisdom dictates that interviewing a hostile witness is one of those situations mentioned earlier when it is sometimes better to interview the witness without making an appointment in advance. Such a strategy reduces the chance that the witness will carefully rehearse a story before your arrival. However, in this context we are using the term hostile in the legal sense to mean a witness who simply is not in favor of your client's position. Such a strategy might place you in danger if the witness is truly hostile. If there is any chance that the witness could prove to be hostile in the conventional sense of being potentially violent, showing up unannounced and alone may be the last

PRACTICE TIP

When going out on investigations, bring a good supply of business cards. They provide a form of identification and set a professional tone. Also, you can leave them with witnesses with a reminder on the back that they should contact you if they recall additional information.

thing you want to do. In any event be prepared for any eventuality because you probably will have only one opportunity to talk to the hostile witness.

When witnesses appear to be reluctant to cooperate, attempt to determine the cause for this reluctance: Are they friends of the other party or the victim? Do they fear some sort of retaliation? Are they simply afraid of being called to testify at the trial stage? Point out that by giving a statement now, they may be able to avoid having to testify at a trial.

If an adverse witness has consulted with a lawyer, the attorney probably told the witness not to say anything to an investigator. And if a witness has retained an attorney, remember that the rules of ethics forbid you from talking to that witness. All communications must be with the witness's attorney.

8. Taking Statements from Witnesses

As with interviewing clients, it is helpful to use a checklist, such as is illustrated in Figure 16-4 on page 499. At the end of the interview some interviewers ask for a formal statement. This statement cannot be used as direct evidence at the trial, but it can be used to refresh the witness's memory. It may also form the basis for impeaching a hostile witness's testimony by demonstrating that the testimony given in court is inconsistent with statements that the witness made in the earlier statement. (*Note:* As we will discuss in more detail in the next chapter, this type of out-of-court statement does not violate the rule against hearsay because the statement is being offered not to prove its truth but rather to impeach the witness. In other words, it does not matter whether the witness was telling the truth then or telling the truth now. All that matters is that at some point the witness lied.) However, many attorneys would prefer that you only summarize the interview. A verbatim statement may not be protected by the attorney-client work product privilege. This would mean that the opposing side could obtain it as a part of a discovery request.

The first section of your statement should supply as much information as possible about the witness. In addition to such items as name, address, and phone number, it should include information about employer, relatives, professional group memberships, social clubs, and even hobbies. Most of this information is simply for the purpose of making it possible to locate the witness in case of a move prior to the trial. This first section also should include the date and location where the statement was given. If others are present during the interview, mention that also.

The heart of the summary is the description of whatever it is that the witness observed. Usually, you will want to present the events in chronological

Ethics Alert

If the opposing party is represented by an attorney, you may not speak with that party without that attorney's permission.

1. *Identity of the witness*
   Name
   Age, sex, and marital status
   Occupation and employer
   Residence and business address, phone numbers
   Organizational affiliations and other items that will help locate the person in the
   future, such as children and their ages and schools
2. *Identification of the accident*
   Date, day of the week, time
   Location of the accident
   Type of accident
   Identification of parties involved (drivers, passengers, etc.)
   Were parties traveling as part of their job?
   Description of vehicles involved (owner, make, model, color, year, license number,
   serial number)
   Identification of potential witnesses
3. *Detailed description of the scene of the accident*
   Description of streets and highways
       Direction
       Width
       Number of lanes
       Grade
       Speed limit
       Traffic controls
       Type and condition of surface
   Weather conditions
   Buildings and other objects that could obstruct one's view
4. *Detailed description of the accident*
   Direction and speed of vehicles, pedestrians
   Status of traffic signals
   Evasive action
   Point of impact (on roadway and on each vehicle)
   Final resting place of vehicles
   Skid marks and debris
   Statements made
   Location of witnesses
5. *Bodily injuries (for each person injured)*
   Part of body injured
   Extent of injury
   Nature of treatment (ambulance, hospital, doctor)
   Nature of disability
   Occupation and salary
   Preexisting medical problems
6. *Property damage*
   To vehicles, to buildings, etc.

Figure 16-4 Interviewing Checklist

order. In addition to describing the events themselves, it is important to have the witness carefully describe the environment in which those events took place. Thus in an automobile accident case ask the witness to describe such matters as the weather and the existence of any temporary obstructions to a driver's view.

DISCUSSION QUESTION

8. You are interviewing a witness who observed an automobile accident. He was sitting in his car waiting for a red light when he saw your client's car hit from the rear. What questions might you ask to find out as much as you can from the witness as to exactly what happened?

SUMMARY

The key to successful interviewing is the development of good communication skills. Good communication is a two-way street that requires active listening and attention to nonverbal as well as verbal signals. Be extremely cautious about approaching an interview with preconceived ideas and biases, and be conscious of ethnic, racial, and gender differences in communication styles.

Interviews should take place in a comfortable and quiet location in which there will be privacy and no interruptions. The seating arrangement should be one that facilitates personal communication rather than one that intimidates the person being interviewed.

Begin the interview by explaining the paralegal's role in terms that the client will understand. Then use open questions to give the client the opportunity to describe the problem in his or her own terms. Ask direct questions in order to clarify areas of ambiguity and to assist the client who becomes bogged down or forgets a train of thought. Gentle encouragement to talk, paraphrasing, and reflections of feelings are useful techniques for keeping the interview moving ahead constructively. Above all, do not be judgmental. Listen, record, empathize, but do not judge.

When bringing the interview to an end it is wise to summarize your understanding of what the client has said in order to ensure accuracy and to give the client a chance to add information that might have been overlooked. Collect copies of all relevant documents, and have the client sign appropriate authorization forms. Immediately afterward, review your notes from the interview, and write your summary while the matter is still fresh.

Interviewing witnesses requires the use of many of the same communication skills as those used in client interviews. In cases that lend themselves to the use of expert witnesses, identify appropriate individuals, and enlist their support. These experts then can be used as resources for the investigation, as well as witnesses at the trial.

At all times remember that paralegals are representatives of the firm. Act in a professional and courteous manner. Using common courtesy is one of the most effective ways to get the cooperation of clients as well as others.

REVIEW QUESTIONS

Pages 477 through 483

1. What is meant by saying that communication is a "two-way street"?
2. When interviewing clients and others, why is it generally a good idea to keep legal jargon out of the conversation?
3. Give some examples of nonverbal communication.
4. What is active listening, and why is it important?
5. How are the interviewer's and the client's race, ethnicity, and gender related to the interviewing process?
6. How can the seating arrangement impede or facilitate conversation?

Pages 483 through 493

7. What are the two main goals of the client interview?
8. What are some of the reasons an attorney may prefer to handle the initial interview?
9. Describe the funnel approach to interviewing.
10. What are the advantages and disadvantages of open questions? Of closed questions?
11. Generally, why is it not a good idea to use leading questions when interviewing clients?
12. Why should the interviewer avoid the use of "why" questions?
13. When interviewing clients or witnesses, why is it important to find out the facts that support the client's or witness's conclusions?
14. What should be done at the end of a client interview?
15. After meeting with a client, what information should you include in a follow-up letter?
16. What should you include in a letter you sent to a potential client who decides not to retain the firm?

Pages 494 through 500

17. What are the most common means of locating lay witnesses? Expert witnesses?
18. In what types of cases are you most likely to need expert witnesses?
19. Why do many attorneys prefer witness statements in summary form only?
20. What types of information should be included in a summary of a witness statement?

Chapter 17

Evidence and Investigations

I think there is no sense in forming an opinion when there is no evidence to form it on.
Recollections of Joan of Arc

INTRODUCTION

In the last chapter we looked at how an attorney or a paralegal initially learns of the facts through a client interview. We also saw how interviewing witnesses is one method for confirming the facts as related by the client and for learning additional information relevant to the case. In this chapter we will continue our discussion of fact gathering through investigation. The process of factual investigation begins with an investigation plan that outlines the types of information that need to be obtained and the methods for obtaining it. For example, much information can be learned through documents, such as medical and police records. At times personal observations, such as visiting the scene of an accident, are also necessary. We will also continue following the case of Mr. Drake, the grandfather who suffered as a result of seeing his six-year-old grandson struck and killed by an automobile, and learn how Chris Kendall, the firm's paralegal, proceeded with his investigation.

At times a paralegal is personally involved in the investigative process. In other cases when the initial investigative work is done outside the law office, paralegals are frequently used to coordinate the information gained from these outside sources and to prepare it for presentation in the courtroom. In either case it is important to understand the basic concepts and techniques that go into conducting investigations.

Because the purpose of a factual investigation is to locate information that can be used as evidence in support of settlement negotiations or at trial, when

Fact
An actual incident or
condition; not a legal
consequence.

Evidence
Information that can be
presented in a court of
law as proof of some
fact.

Rules of evidence
Federal and state rules
that govern the admissi-
bility of evidence in
court.

conducting an investigation it is important to understand that not all information is necessarily admissible as evidence in court. Therefore, before we can discuss how you gather information, we need to take a short digression into the rules of evidence.

A. RULES OF EVIDENCE

In the legal context the terms *fact* and *evidence* have very precise meanings. A **fact** is defined as an actual incident or condition that is distinguished from its legal consequence. For example, a plaintiff's assertion that the defendant ran a red light is an alleged fact. The plaintiff's assertion that the defendant's running a red light constituted negligence is the legal conclusion or consequence. **Evidence** is information that can be presented in a court of law as proof of some fact. Courtroom evidence can take the form of testimony from witnesses or the introduction of written documents, diagrams, and physical objects. To continue with our red light example, evidence could come in the form of eye-witness testimony provided by the plaintiff and others at the scene of the accident. The **rules of evidence** determine what types of information can be used and what the lawyers must do in order to get evidence admitted.

The federal courts follow the Federal Rules of Evidence, first adopted by Congress in 1975. Most states have used the Federal Rules as the basis for adopting their own evidence codes. Because there is variation among the states and from the Federal Rules, you should always research the specific rules that apply to your state courts.

While you do not have to be an expert on every esoteric aspect of the rules of evidence, you should have a basic understanding of the general principles behind them. This knowledge should affect the manner in which you gather and preserve information. The following provides a general overview of some of the most important principles reflected in the rules of evidence.

NETNOTE

You can locate the Federal Rules of Evidence at several locations. To view them in html format go to *www.law.cornell.edu/rules/fre/overview.html*. To view them as a pdf file go to *judiciary.house.gov/media/pdfs/printers/108th/evid2004.pdf*

1. Forms of Evidence

Evidence is usually categorized into one of four distinct forms:

real or physical evidence,
documentary evidence,
testimonial evidence, and
judicial notice.

Form	Examples
Real or physical evidence	Knife; gun; shoe
Documentary evidence	Contract to purchase refrigerators; apartment lease
Testimonial evidence	On the stand, John says, "I saw Jim shoot Joe."
Judicial notice	Christmas falls on December 25

Figure 17-1   Forms of Evidence

Real or physical evidence is any tangible object, like a knife or a gun. **Documentary evidence** consists of records, contracts, leases, wills, and other written instruments. **Testimonial evidence** consists of the description of events that a witness testifies to under oath in a legal proceeding. Before real and documentary evidence can be introduced, testimonial evidence is often used to establish the foundation or background information necessary to introduce and **authenticate** the evidence. Sometimes through a process known as **judicial notice,** a judge will formally recognize something as being a fact without requiring the attorneys to prove it through the introduction of other evidence. In effect, the judge acknowledges that the information is so well known that specific proof is not required. For example, a judge might take judicial notice of the fact that August 23, 1989, fell on a Wednesday or that a city lies within a particular county. However, if a fact goes to your cause of action, do not rely on judicial notice. Be prepared to prove all of the facts. For example, if it is necessary to show that an accident happened on a public way, get the documents to prove both where the accident happened and that the place was a public way. These various forms of evidence are summarized in Figure 17-1.

Real or physical evidence
Any tangible object, like a bloody glove.

Documentary evidence
Consists of records, contracts, leases, wills, and other written instruments.

Testimonial evidence
Consists of the description of events that a witness testifies to under oath in a legal proceeding.

Authentication
Proof that the evidence is what it is said to be.

Judicial notice
When a judge formally recognizes something as being a fact without requiring the attorneys to prove it through the introduction of other evidence.

The Case of the Distressed Grandfather (continued)

In Mr. Drake's case Chris did not think there would be much physical evidence. The car had been so badly damaged in the accident that it had been towed to a junkyard and demolished for scrap. However, there was a wealth of documentary evidence that he needed to collect, including all of the medical records beginning with Mr. Drake's ambulance ride to the hospital, the hospital records themselves, and his treating physician's notes. Other documentary evidence included the police report made at the scene of the accident and the certification from the registry of motor vehicles that Mrs. Small was indeed the owner of the car she was driving. Chris was also busy organizing potential testimonial evidence from Mr. Drake, the police officers who were at the scene, eyewitnesses to the accident, Mr. Drake's treating physician, and a medical expert who could give testimony on how severe emotional distress can cause heart attacks.

DISCUSSION QUESTION

1. Which type of evidence (testimonial, documentary, or physical) do you think is the most reliable? Which is the least reliable? Describe the potential advantages and disadvantages of each.

2. Types of Evidence

Evidence can also be classified in terms of its being any one of the following:

> direct,
> circumstantial,
> cumulative, or
> corroborative.

Direct evidence
Establishes a direct link to the event that must be proven.

Direct evidence establishes a direct link to the event that must be proven. For example, a witness's testimony that "I saw the defendant shoot the victim" is direct evidence. Circumstantial evidence, on the other hand, provides information that only implies that something took place. It does not directly prove it. A police officer who did not witness the crime but who testifies that the defendant was found with powder burns on his hands consistent with having fired a weapon provides **circumstantial evidence**. While the powder burns do not directly prove the defendant shot the victim, they do create a possibility that he did. There is no requirement that any of the evidence admitted be direct

Circumstantial evidence
Indirect evidence, used to prove facts by implication.

Legal Reasoning Exercise

1. Assume you want to prove that the mail carrier left mail in the mailbox at 67 Dressel Avenue. The first witness you call is Mrs. Baker, who lives at that address. She testifies that at 11:00 a.m. she went to the mailbox, found mail, and brought it into her house. The next witness is Mr. Baker. He testifies that he checked the mailbox when he left for work at 9:00 a.m. and it was empty. Mrs. Brown, a next door neighbor, then testifies that at 9:30 a.m. she saw two sets of footprints in the snow in the Baker yard. One set led up to the mailbox, and one set led away. Mrs. Williams, a relative of the Bakers, testifies that she was walking down the street that morning and saw the mail carrier delivering mail to the house next door at 67 Dressel Avenue. Mr. Grimes, who lives across the street, testifies that he saw the mail carrier put mail in the mailbox at 9:15 a.m. Mr. Smith, another neighbor, testifies that he saw the mail carrier put mail in the mailbox but is not sure of the time. Ms. Williams, the mail carrier's supervisor, testifies that he left the post office at 8:00 a.m. with mail for everyone on Dressel Avenue and that late in the afternoon he returned with an empty mailbag.

Label each piece of testimony as direct, circumstantial, cumulative, or corroborative testimony.

Type of Evidence	Examples
Direct	On the witness stand, John says, "I saw Jim shoot Joe."
Circumstantial	A police officer testifies he saw skid marks on the pavement.
Cumulative	The fifth witness in a row testifies he saw Jim at Jake's Donut Shop at the same time the murder was occurring on the other side of town.
Corroborative	Janet from Security-Is-Us authenticates a surveillance tape taken at Jake's Donut Shop showing Jim entering the shop at the same time the murder was occurring on the other side of town.

Figure 17-2 Types of Evidence

evidence. Sufficient circumstantial evidence can be enough to find liability in a civil case or to convict a defendant in a criminal case.

Cumulative evidence is evidence that does not add any new information but that confirms facts that already have been established. For example, if two people both testify that they saw the defendant make a phone call, the second witness would be providing cumulative evidence. Such evidence may be excluded if in the court's opinion it will add nothing to what has been already presented. In most trials the quality of the evidence is more important than the quantity. A single unbiased eyewitness carries more weight than a series of witnesses who have inherent biases or who tell conflicting stories. The concept of **corroborative evidence** is very similar in that it also supports previous testimony. The difference is that corroborative evidence comes in a different form. For example, telephone company billing records can be introduced to support a statement by a witness that he made a phone call to a certain party on a certain date. Figure 17-2 summarizes the various types of evidence.

3. Relevance and Materiality

Before any information can be introduced as evidence, it must be shown to be both relevant and material. **Relevancy** refers to the "probative value" of the evidence: Does the presentation of this evidence lead one to logically conclude that an asserted fact is either more probable or less probable? For example, that the plaintiff suffered an injury in a previous automobile accident would be relevant only if the injury had been to the same part of the body injured in the present case.[1] **Materiality** is usually thought of as either a subcategory of relevancy or simply another word for relevancy. Often it is stated as requiring that the evidence be more probative than prejudicial. That is, relevancy alone does not ensure admissibility. Thus a gruesome photograph of the condition of the victim

Cumulative evidence
Evidence that does not add any new information but that confirms facts that already have been established.

Corroborative evidence
Evidence that supports previous testimony but that comes in a different form.

Relevancy
Determined by whether the evidence leads one to logically conclude that an asserted fact is either more or less probable.

Materiality
Either a subcategory of relevancy or simply another word for relevancy, the requirement that the evidence be more probative than prejudicial.

[1] W. Rutter, Evidence 12 (8th ed. 1973).

of a mutilation murder may be relevant yet be excluded because of the probability that it would inflame the jury.[2]

4. Competency

Competency
Relates to the ability of a witness to testify; generally, the witness must be capable of being understood by the jury; must understand the duty to tell the truth; and if a lay witness, must give testimony based on personal knowledge.

In addition to being relevant, the evidence must be **competent.** With respect to oral testimony from a witness it must be established that the witness can be understood by the jury (possibly through an interpreter), understands the duty to tell the truth, and in the case of a **lay witness** is testifying to personal knowledge regarding the particular matter about which he or she is called to testify. The first two factors usually involve the age or mental condition of the witness. The third involves the meaning of hearsay evidence.

5. Hearsay and Its Exceptions

Lay witness
A witness who has not been shown to have any special expertise.

Hearsay
Someone in court testifying to what someone said out of court for the purpose of establishing the truth of what was said.

In nontechnical terms **hearsay** is secondhand information. It is someone in court testifying to what someone said out of court for the purpose of establishing the truth of what was said. Imagine, for example, a situation in which Doris tells Sue that she saw Bill, the defendant in a divorce suit, check into a motel with his secretary. She would not be allowed to testify about what her friend Doris has told her. Sue has no personal knowledge about Bill's activities. She herself did not see Bill and his secretary. The person with the firsthand information who should be on the stand testifying is Doris. We want Doris on the stand so that she can be questioned and evaluated by the trier of fact as to her credibility. This includes needing to know whether she is being truthful and whether she had the ability to accurately report what she thought she saw. Figure 17-3, on page 509, diagrams this illustration of Sue repeating what Doris said to her.

Not every out-of-court statement is hearsay. To be hearsay, the statement must be offered to prove the truth of the matter stated. One prime use of out-of-court statements is to impeach the credibility of a witness. Imagine that right after an accident an eyewitness told a police officer that he saw a red car run the stop sign. On the witness stand that same witness testifies that the car was blue. The witness's prior out-of-court statement about the color of the car can be introduced not to prove its color, but to show that the witness is unreliable.

Another twist involves admissions by party-opponents. According to the Federal Rules of Evidence even though an out-of-court statement by a party-opponent is hearsay, it is to be treated as nonhearsay. That is, a party's own statements, offered against the party, can be admitted for their truth, and yet they are not considered to be hearsay. Usually, the statement is harmful to the person who made it, but that is not a requirement.

Declarant
The person who made the statement.

Also, even though evidence remains labeled as hearsay evidence, it may be admissible under one of many exceptions. One set of exceptions relates to when the **declarant,** the person who made the statement, is not available to testify—for example, when the declarant is dead. The second set of exceptions covers a wide range of other circumstances in which it is thought that the nature of the statement itself indicates its trustworthiness. Such exceptions include excited utterances (the witness testifies: "I heard a bystander say, 'Oh, no, she just ran

---

[2] Id. at 25.

1. Doris sees Bill and his secretary enter a motel

2. Doris SAYS to Sue

3. On the witness stand Sue says

Figure 17-3 Example of Hearsay Evidence

over that boy!'"), business records, and statements regarding the declarant's mental, emotional, or physical condition (the witness testifies: "I heard Mr. Drake say, 'My heart is pounding.'").

One way of understanding why some hearsay evidence is allowed while other hearsay evidence is not is to first assume the witness is truthfully recounting what the witness heard. The only question is, Assuming the statement was really made, do we need any further information to evaluate its worth? In the example above we would want to ask Doris how she knew it was Bill that she saw. How well did she know Bill? How far from the entrance to the motel was she standing? Does she wear glasses? Was she wearing them when she thought she saw Bill? In some cases, however, we can assume the declarant's statements are trustworthy without the need for further examination. For example, if Sue

Legal Reasoning Exercise

2. Hearsay is defined in the Federal Rules of Evidence as "[a] statement, other than one made by the declarant while testifying at the trial or hearing, offered in evidence to prove the truth of the matter asserted. . . . A statement is not hearsay if [it is an admission by a party-opponent and the] statement is offered against [the] party." FRE 801.

Ms. Small has been sued for negligently causing the death of Philip Drake in a motor vehicle accident. Evaluate each of the following statements as to whether they would be admissible or inadmissible as hearsay.

a. John just testified that Philip was still alive when the police arrived. When the attorney asked him how he knew that, he said, "Because the poor little guy had just whispered in my ear 'Why did that lady in the red car run me down?'"

b. Mary testified, "John told me just yesterday all about how he saw Mrs. Small's car jump the curb and run over Philip."

c. The first police officer at the scene is on the witness stand. When asked, he testifies that he interviewed John at the scene and John told him that he saw Mrs. Small's car jump the curb and run down Philip.

d. A bystander who was at the scene of the accident testifies that right after the accident he heard Mrs. Small cry out, "Oh, no, I can't afford another speeding ticket."

were also to say, "Doris said that it was very cold out that night," cross-examination of Doris as to why she thought it was cold out would probably not be necessary.

Figure 17-4, on page 511, lists some of the more common hearsay exceptions that are found in the Federal Rules of Evidence, here abbreviated as FRE. Remember these are hearsay statements that the court allows to be heard as evidence of the truth of the matter stated. This is to be contrasted with the rule mentioned earlier allowing out-of-court statements for impeachment purposes.

6. Facts versus Opinions

You must be aware of the differences between facts and opinions. A witness who testifies that he saw the defendant's automobile strike the plaintiff's car broadside is testifying about a fact he observed. But when that same witness states that the defendant was driving too fast for the icy condition of the road, he is stating an opinion.

Generally, everyone is allowed to testify to personal knowledge about basic facts of life. Lay witnesses (regular witnesses who have not been shown to have any special expertise) can give opinions on such subjects as the speed of moving vehicles, the similarity of a person's voice or handwriting to that of someone's voice or handwriting with which they are familiar, and whether or not a person is

FRE 803(1) Present sense impression	The declarant describes the event as it is being perceived.	The bystander said, "It is raining."
FRE 803(2) Excited utterance	The declarant responds to a startling event.	The bystander said, "The driver of that car is out of control!"
FRE 803(3) Then existing mental, emotional, or physical condition	The declarant describes his or her feelings, state of mind, or physical condition.	The driver of the car said, "I feel dizzy."
FRE 804(4) Medical diagnosis or treatment	The declarant's statements were made for the purpose of medical diagnosis or treatment.	A physician testifies, "Mr. Drake told me he often suffered from heart pain."
FRE 803 Records	Various records, including business records, public records, vital statistics, and marriage certificates, are admissible.	Mr. Drake's hospital records are introduced.
FRE 804(b)(1) Former testimony	Former testimony under oath is admissible if the declarant is unavailable.	At a deposition, a witness to the accident stated, "I saw the defendant's car jump the curb and hit the little boy." The witness has since died. The deposition testimony is admissible.
FRE 804(b)(2) Dying declaration	Statements made when the declarant thought he or she was dying are admissible if the declarant is unavailable.	A witness at the scene heard Mr. Drake say, "I saw that woman's car run down my grandchild." If Mr. Drake died before trial, the witness could testify as to what Mr. Drake said.
FRE 804(b)(3) Statement against interest	Statements made by the declarant that are against that person's financial interests or that would expose the declarant to civil or criminal liability are admissible if the declarant is unavailable.	The day after the accident Mrs. Small told her neighbor, "I just looked down at my map for a minute, and the next thing I knew I realized my car had left the road." If Mrs. Small were to refuse to testify, the neighbor could testify as to what Mrs. Small said.
FRE 803(24) and 804(b)(5) Statements not otherwise covered	If a statement does not fall under a specific exception but it relates to a material fact, it is more probative than any other evidence, and the interests of justice so dictate, it may be admitted.	

Figure 17-4 Hearsay Exceptions

angry or intoxicated. In order to be allowed to venture such opinions, the trial judge must be satisfied that

1. The witness personally observed or perceived that on which he renders an opinion,
2. The matter must be one about which normal persons regularly form opinions (speed, size, sound, color, etc.), and
3. Giving an opinion is the best way of getting the matter to the jury (i.e., the facts on which the opinion rests are not as meaningful as the opinion itself).[3]

---

[3] Id. at 72.

Expert witness
A witness who possesses skill and knowledge beyond that of the average person.

An **expert witness** is "a person who possesses skill and knowledge in some art, trade, science, or profession that is beyond and above that of the *average* man."[4] For purposes of giving testimony, it is vital to understand that a witness is not an expert, no matter how impressive the credentials, unless the attorney first lays a foundation to prove the expertise to the court and unless the court then accepts the person as an expert.

The Case of the Distressed Grandfather (continued)

In Mr. Drake's case Chris was hard at work developing the expert witness list. This list included Mr. Drake's treating physician, as well as other doctors hired to look at his records and give their opinion as to the cause of his heart attack and his prognosis. Chris knows that in each case Pat Harper will first have to convince the court of the doctor's expertise, so he has asked each of them to prepare an extensive **curriculum vitae**, which he will then review with the attorney.

While jurors are usually impressed by the amount of formal education a witness has and are especially impressed when the witness has authored books or articles on the subject, formal education itself is not a requirement for being an expert witness.[5] For example, a burglar could testify as an expert witness on the techniques for breaking and entering so long as the court made a ruling that the burglar was an expert witness. Without establishing his expert status, the burglar could testify regarding locks and various security devices as to which he has personal knowledge. However, he could not testify as to whether the security was breached in that particular case unless he was first qualified as an expert.

If the expert witness has personal knowledge of the facts on which the opinion is based (as in the case of a physician who has treated an injury personally), the expert can testify about that opinion directly. If the expert has no such personal knowledge (as in the case of a physician who did not treat an injury personally but is called to give an expert opinion on this injury's ramifications), the attorney must present the witness with a series of hypothetical questions. These hypotheticals ask the witness to express an opinion on the basis of the information provided by the attorney during the questioning.

7. Authentication

Lay a foundation
The process of properly identifying and authenticating evidence so that it can be introduced.

Before physical and documentary evidence can be introduced, witnesses must be called to **lay a proper foundation.** The testimony must establish the relevancy and materiality of the evidence. It must also properly identify and authenticate it.

> **PRACTICE TIP**
>
> Keep curricula vitae of all experts on file in a central location for use on future cases.

---

[4] A. Golec, Techniques of Legal Investigation 53 (1976).

[5] F. Bailey and H. Rothblatt, Fundamentals of Criminal Advocacy 123 (1974).

Legal Reasoning Exercise

3. Determine whether you think the following testimony would be allowed in Mr. Drake's case. If not, state the appropriate objection.

a. An eyewitness stated, "I heard the brakes squeal, and then the car jumped the curb. To my horror, I saw the car hit a little boy."

b. A second eyewitness testified, "That red car was going at least 80 miles an hour just before it swerved onto the sidewalk."

c. Mrs. Small's husband is on the stand. He is asked what, if anything, Mrs. Small told him about how the accident occurred.

d. The plaintiff's attorney wants to show a video taken of Mr. Drake's heart valve repair, necessitated by his heart attack.

e. The plaintiff's attorney wants to introduce color pictures of the grandchild, taken at the accident scene, showing the boy crushed under the front wheels of the defendant's car.

f. The defendant's attorney wants to introduce a sketch of the accident scene that he drew based on the statements given to him by his client.

There are many books that you can consult to help with sample questions that need to be asked to lay the proper foundation. You should use these books to assist the attorney with drafting the foundation questions and writing those questions in the trial notebook so that in the heat of the courtroom none of the questions will be forgotten. If the right questions are not asked and the proper authentication is not made, the court will not accept the evidence. For example, in order to properly authenticate physical evidence, the investigator should be asked whether he or she (1) kept the object in his or her exclusive personal control from the time it was found until the time it is presented in court, (2) maintained a complete record of everyone involved in the chain of possession (i.e., everyone who handled the object from the time it was found to the time it was presented in court), or (3) marked the object in a way that will make it easily distinguishable at a later time.[6]

The rules governing the authentication of photographs differ from one jurisdiction to the next. Most courts simply require that a witness who is familiar with an object or a scene in the photograph testify that it is an accurate representation of that object or scene as it appeared at the time of the incident. On the other hand, a few courts require that the person who actually took the photograph testify about the type of camera and the settings used. Some require testimony relating to the developing process and the chain of possession of the photograph.[7]

Written documents must also be relevant and authentic. According to the **best evidence rule** the original document itself usually must be produced at the trial. Proper testimony must establish that the document presented is in fact what it is purported to be. Under some circumstances, however, a copy may be con-

Best evidence rule
The rule requiring that the original document be produced at trial.

---

[6] G. Stuckey, Evidence for the Law Enforcement Officer 210 (2d ed. 1974).

[7] Rutter, supra note 1, at 25.

sidered admissible. Public records (official governmental documents, as well as private deeds and mortgages that are officially recorded with the government) can be presented through the use of certified copies. In addition to presenting a copy showing an official seal and signature, an affidavit from the record's custodian usually is presented explaining what the record shows and attesting that it is an accurate copy of the one on file.[8]

Copies of private papers may be allowed when the original has been lost or destroyed, is in the hands of an adverse party who has refused to produce it, or is in the hands of a third party who is outside the jurisdiction of the court's subpoena power.[9] In cases where the original is so voluminous that it is impractical to produce it in its entirety, the litigant is allowed to produce a summary.[10]

The best evidence rule also means that when witnesses are called to explain a document, that document should already have been introduced. The witness should not be asked to describe a document not in evidence because as the rule suggests, the best evidence of a document is that document itself. Sometimes you will notice attorneys forgetting this rule when you see them trying to get a witness to testify to the contents of a document rather than introducing the document itself.

B. INVESTIGATION

The goal of factual investigation is to find admissible evidence that will establish the facts necessary to prove the client's case. Therefore, in addition to understanding what types of evidence there are and what makes evidence either admissible or not admissible, you must know what facts are needed to prove the client's case and how to obtain the evidence.

Investigation is often one of the most exciting phases of case preparation. However, at times being an investigator also means having to study what may often be boring and repetitious details. To find all the facts, investigators must be systematic, and yet they cannot just follow a set formula. They must show creativity, imagination, and resourcefulness. Also, as with client interviewing, good communication skills are essential when interviewing potential witnesses and other persons who can help you establish the facts of your case. Finally, good investigators must be able to maintain an open mind. Approach each situation without any preconceived ideas or notions. Never assume anything, and be careful of reaching conclusions that cannot be supported by the facts.

1. Planning an Investigation

The first step in planning an investigation is to determine what evidence already exists in the firm's files. Then you have to develop a strategy for getting other information the attorneys will need to prove the case in court. For example, you may need to conduct additional interviews with the client, interview key witnesses, collect documentary evidence (such as medical records, contracts, and police reports), or visit the scene of the accident.

---

[8] Golec, supra note 4, at 260.

[9] Rutter, supra note 1, at 115.

[10] Id. at 116; Stuckey, supra note 7, at 259.

Generally, the tasks of collecting real evidence (such as a piece of glass found at the accident scene) and going to the scene of the accident should be left in the hands of professional investigators. Similarly, any diagrams or charts should be developed by a professional, such as an expert in accident reconstruction. This is especially true when the case is likely to go to trial or when the case is potentially worth a significant amount of money. Leaving this work to the professional investigator is for practical as well as ethical reasons. If the paralegal is the one who develops the diagram, then the paralegal may be called to the stand to authenticate it. It is much more credible to have a "neutral" investigator testifying than the firm's employee.

Therefore, the first part of any investigation plan should be to decide not only what needs to be done but who will do it. Once this is decided, then a schedule of proposed activities can be developed, including the paralegal's responsibility for locating an investigator and expert witnesses.

Generally speaking, the legal system is a slow-moving process in which delays and continuances are common. For example, it is not uncommon for a period of four to five years to pass between the time of an accident and the eventual courtroom resolution of the negligence and damages issues that arose from the accident. But accident scenes change. Witnesses' memories fade. Witnesses move. Broken parts are repaired or discarded. Injuries heal. Therefore, factual investigation should begin as soon as possible.

a. Identifying Needed Facts

Before beginning the investigation, it is important to discuss the theory of the case with the supervising attorney. For example, if your firm is representing a criminal defendant, you must know the elements of the crime. If your client wants to sue for a personal injury, you will need to know what must be proven to establish a cause of action in a negligence case. You must gather evidence on each element of the case for which your side has the burden of production; otherwise, the other side may move to have the case dismissed.

Attorneys frequently develop a primary theory for their cases, such as negligence, and also alternative theories, such as fraud or another intentional tort, that they might pursue. In addition, the opposition may have yet different theories of the case. Your supervising attorney may want you to gather evidence relevant to all these alternatives.

To help organize the investigation, you may find it useful to begin by chronologically listing the events that the client described. Then attempt to identify evidence that either substantiates or contradicts the client's description of each event. This analysis provides a basis for identifying additional information that you will have to gather. For example, for each event on the list identify witnesses who may have observed it or documents that might substantiate it.

Look for any gaps within this sequence of events. Is it possible that something else could have taken place at that same time? Are there key details that the client cannot remember? Is there something that one would expect to have happened that did not? What was the mental state of the people involved? Who was responsible for creating the conditions that may have contributed to the events that took place? For each gap found, you must identify possible sources of information that could help complete the picture.

The Case of the Distressed Grandfather (continued)

After ending his interview with Mr. Drake, Chris met with Pat Harper, his supervising attorney, and they developed a checklist of the information that they wanted Chris to gather based on what they would have to prove to win a negligence claim against Mrs. Small. First on the list was anything they could find to establish her negligence. This included locating witnesses and documentary evidence, such as the police report, that could show she was speeding immediately prior to the accident, that Philip was on the sidewalk when the car hit him, and that there were no defects in the operation of the automobile. Second, they needed to be able to prove that seeing his grandson's death is what actually caused Mr. Drake's heart attack. For that, Chris would first obtain all medical and hospital records. However, it was likely that they might also need an expert witness to testify that the heart attack was more likely than not caused by seeing the accident. Finally, they needed evidence to prove Mr. Drake's injuries. Again they would rely heavily on medical records, but other witnesses, including Mr. Drake himself, could also provide evidence of the pain and suffering caused by the heart attack and the pain and suffering from seeing his grandson die.

b. Developing a Coordinated Plan

Once you and your supervising attorney have identified the types of information you will need, consider how you might gather it quickly and relatively inexpensively. Often it is cheaper to gather facts informally before litigation is even started rather than waiting until later when you may have to rely on the more formal discovery process. For example, think about whether you can take advantage of investigative work that has already been done by law enforcement agencies and insurance company claims representatives. Then consider how additional evidence should be gathered. Most likely you will be expected to gather documentary evidence and interview possible witnesses. If there is also a need to gather physical evidence, then it may be necessary to hire a private investigator.

DISCUSSION QUESTION

2. Recall the case from Chapter 3 of the waitress who was fired for being pregnant. If you were put in charge of investigating her case, what types of evidence would you look for, and how would you go about collecting it?

2. Gathering Physical Evidence

In criminal cases and those involving accidents or damage to property it is important to visit the scene and to view the damaged property. Because conditions change over time, it is desirable to observe them as soon as possible. If possible, visit the scene at the same time of the day as the matter being

investigated took place and under similar weather conditions. Not only will you get a better perspective on how the accident might have happened, but also you might meet people who frequent that area at that particular time of day and witnessed the accident.

a. Taking Photographs

Photographs are one of the most effective means of gathering and preserving information. While you may want to consider hiring a professional photographer, you should also keep a camera in your office. There will be times when a professional photographer will not be available and waiting for one will not be possible. For example, soft tissue injuries in particular disappear quickly. You may also want to visit the scene of the accident to observe and photograph anything that might help you reconstruct how the accident happened.

When purchasing the camera, consider both a 35mm camera and an instant camera. While a 35mm camera provides a better-quality picture, an instant camera will allow you to immediately check the quality of the shot. Its use also simplifies the problems involved in preserving the chain of evidence.

At times a still picture will not be sufficient. For example, in a personal injury suit brought because the plaintiff has been paralyzed, the plaintiff's lawyer may want to show a "one day in the life of ..." type of movie in order to make the jury more aware of the full implications of the plaintiff's injuries.

b. Preparing Diagrams

In addition to taking photographs of the scene of an accident, it is often useful to make diagrams. Keep in mind, however, that there is a difference between the diagrams you will draw to help you and the witnesses you interview visualize the scene and those your attorney may want to introduce as evidence into trial.

Even if you are creating a diagram only for your own use, record the distances between key points as accurately as possible. Carefully measure everything from the width of the street to the location of various traffic signs.

If there is any possibility the diagram will be used as an exhibit at trial, remember that the diagram cannot be introduced as evidence unless it can be shown to accurately represent the accident scene. The science of accident reconstruction is becoming more sophisticated every day, including the use of computerized re-enactments. To properly present such evidence and exhibits, your firm should consider whether it needs to hire a qualified expert to prepare the evidence and to testify at trial. The success of civil litigation often depends on the quality of the experts hired.

3. Obtaining Documents and Information from Public Records

Depending on the nature of the case, various kinds of documentary evidence may be needed. For example, in personal injury actions the injured party's medical records become an important factor. In a products liability suit information about safety records and industry standards is usually vital to its outcome. Likewise, in many cases information about a company's corporate structure and financial position can be a key element.

Fortunately, this sort of information is usually readily available if you only know where to look for it. Often it is simply a matter of going to the right office and in some cases having the appropriate release form. If the record custodians refuse to cooperate with you, confer with your supervising attorney about using a **subpoena duces tecum** to obtain the records. A subpoena duces tecum is a court order that a person who is not a party to the litigation appear at a trial or deposition and bring requested documents.

When gathering documentary evidence, be sure you are also gathering the information that will be necessary to authenticate the document, that is, to prove it is indeed the document you say it is. Obviously, if the document is not authentic, then it is not relevant to the case. One way to authenticate a document is to have a witness in the position to know testify as to the document's authenticity. For example, a hospital records custodian could testify as to the authenticity of the plaintiff's medical records. In some cases you may be able to avoid having to call a witness by using another method of authentication. For example, the other side may agree to stipulate as to the document's authenticity. If that is not possible, you may be able to get a signed affidavit from the record keeper and have the document certified through that means.

Subpoena duces tecum
A court order that a person who is not a party to the litigation appear at a trial or deposition and bring requested documents.

PRACTICE TIP

Use your word processor to take the drudgery out of creating standardized letters that you routinely use for requests for medical records, releases, letters of representation, and so on. Save these routine documents on disk with space left for the variable information. Type in the information that never varies, and then for the information that does vary (such as the particular client's name, address, etc.), insert codes that will allow you to quickly add that information through a keyboard or secondary merge file. This will allow for immediate and painless action on a new case.

---

a. Medical Records

Medical records can supply information on the diagnosis (the nature and extent of the illness or injuries), the treatment (the drugs, surgery, and so forth used to control or alleviate the condition), and the prognosis (the long-term effect of the condition, including the need for further treatment). Many states have statutes that prescribe what you must do to obtain them and get them admitted. Therefore, it is important to check to see whether your state has any statutes that govern how to obtain medical records. Figure 17-5, on page 519, lists the various types of medical records you may want to review.

If your client was hospitalized, the hospital itself will usually be the best source for information. In order to be accredited by the Joint Commission on Accreditation of Hospitals, hospitals must maintain a complete set of patient records that conform to the commission's specific standards. Private physicians also keep detailed records of the patient's visits. When records are requested for a

Hospital Records
   Admissions form
   History and physical
   Progress notes
   Physician orders
   Lab, x-ray, and ancillary service reports
   Operative report
   Consultant's report
   Discharge summary
Physician's outpatient notes and letters

Figure 17-5   Medical Records

lawsuit, many physicians will send copies of those records or will dictate a letter based on their notes.

Hospital records usually begin with an admissions form, which gives personal data, including date and place of birth, marital status, occupation, religion, former names, relatives, and insurance carrier. At the same time, the doctor is performing a history and physical examination. Based on that and any initial lab work the doctor formulates an initial plan for the patient. Exhibit 17-1, page 520, provides an example history and physical for Mr. Drake's case. The subsequent hospital records include the daily observations of temperature, blood pressure, pulse rate, and skin condition; other observations as required based on the patient's condition; and orders of the physician regarding laboratory tests, medications administered, consultations requested of other doctors, and diagnostic tests.

If an operation was performed, an operative report by the surgeon is included that describes the type of surgical procedure used and what was observed about the patient's condition during the operation.

The discharge summary reviews the patient's condition on admission, progress while in the hospital, results of diagnostic procedures used, condition of the patient on release, any medication that was prescribed for the patient to be taken at home, and a follow-up plan for the patient's post-hospital treatment.

As you can see from Exhibit 17-1, medical reports contain a great deal of technical terminology that is difficult to understand without a medical background. A good medical dictionary; the Physician's Desk Reference (referred to as the PDR), which lists and describes all prescription drugs; and an anatomy book that identifies the parts of the body, refers to the functions of these parts, and discusses the ramifications of injuries to them are extremely useful in helping you decipher the records. There are also books that explain medical terminology written specifically for lawyers. In cases that present unique medical issues, your firm may also want to consider hiring the services of a legal nurse consultant or other medical experts. Finally, if your firm does a great deal of personal injury litigation, you might consider taking a medical terminology or health law course.

MERCY HOSPITAL

HISTORY AND PHYSICAL FORM

PATIENT NAME: Donald Drake
DATE ADMITTED: September 1, 2006

HISTORY

CHIEF COMPLAINT: chest pain, rule out MI
HISTORY OF PRESENT ILLNESS: This 68-yr-old gentleman was brought to the Emergency room by ambulance around 10 am after suffering crushing substernal chest pain, diaphoresis nausea, and weakness. At the time of onset he had been supervising the play of his 5-yr-old grandchild when the child was struck by a passing car. As EMTs were summoned by a passerby, the grandfather tried to revive the child. Help arrived very soon, and EMTs took over treatment and transport to the hospital. Within minutes the patient began having the above-mentioned symptoms and felt very weak and collapsed to the ground. He was still breathing and had a pulse but was unconscious. Another ambulance was summoned, and the patient was brought to hospital ER. At his arrival he was again conscious with oxygen running at 6 liters and Ringer's Lactate at 150 cc/hr. He was immediately evaluated by the ER physician, and the on-call cardiologist was called. The patient was stable at this point with a presumed inferior MI based on EKG and lab findings and was transported to the ICU for further management.
PAST MEDICAL HISTORY: Allergies, Illnesses, Operations, Tobacco, and Alcohol: None.
Family History: Father died at 81 of coronary disease and diabetes. Mother died at 87 of "old age." He has two sons both in good health and 5 grandchildren also in good health except for the above-mentioned accident victim. His wife is alive and well with no current medical problems. Social History: He lives with his wife and two dogs on a farm. He is a retired toolmaker.

PHYSICAL EXAM

Alert 68-yr-old male in mild distress with persistent anterior chest wall pain. Temp 98, pulse 98, resp 28.

HEART: Early mild bilateral cataracts. Otherwise neg. exam with normal EOM and clear fundi.
NECK: Non-tender with no masses or enlarged thyroid. No adenopathy. Oropharynx is clear with good dental hygiene. No dentures.
CHEST: Normal breath sounds, no extra sounds. No shortness of breath or wheezing.
ABDOMEN: Neg exam, no masses, rebound guarding. Normal bowel sounds.
NEURO: Alert and oriented times 3. CN intact. No upper or lower extremity sensory or motor deficits. Reflexes 2+ symmetrical.
LABS: Initial Labs show small Q waves in II, III, and AVF and elevated ST segments in the anterior chest leads. CPK is elevated with MB fraction in the abnormal range. CBC, electrolytes, and chem screen are all in the normal range.
ASSESSMENT: Acute inferior MI.
PLAN: MI management, continued care of his cardiologist.

Exhibit 17-1   Sample History and Physical Examination Section of Hospital Record

PARALEGAL PROFILE

WILLIAM R. MATLOCK
LITIGATION PARALEGAL

I work in a law firm with seven attorneys, six paralegals, and five secretaries. Almost all our work is in the area of personal injury, but our firm also handles other tort cases, such as employment discrimination and medical malpractice, as well as some real estate work, workers' compensation, and social security and disability claims. If you were to ask me what a typical day is like, I would have to say that it is impossible to describe a typical day. No two days are ever alike, and I have never been bored.

The way most of our clients come to us is through an initial phone contact with an attorney. The attorney will then ask the client to come to the office. Often after the attorney handles the initial interview, I will then meet with the client, take pictures if the client has suffered injuries or property damage, and have the client sign all necessary release forms.

The next step I am involved in is the factual investigation of the case. That can include photographing the accident scene; obtaining all of the documents, such as medical records; getting police reports; and interviewing witnesses. I encourage witnesses to speak with me by letting them know that if they help us now, they may not have to appear later for a deposition or for court. However, if they choose not to speak to me, we will subpoena them. But even when I need to appear firm, I always remain respectful and cordial. The case then moves on to a separate department where they try to reach a settlement. One of the most satisfying aspects of the job is seeing a settlement check come in and knowing that the hard work and time I put in to a case helped to settle it. If the case doesn't settle, then it comes back to me to start the litigation process, and I draft the pleadings, such as the complaint and motions. (I enjoy asking interrogatories far more than answering them!)

I use the computer all the time for drafting my documents. In addition, our firm subscribes to our state law on CD-ROM provided by LoisLaw and has an Internet account that allows us to do on-line legal research. I also use the Internet to do searches to find information on corporations and their agents as well as to track down witnesses by using a phone number, address, or any other information I have.

What I like best about my job is the variety—the number of different things I do. In addition to client interviews, document drafting, and investigative work, I assist at depositions and occasionally with arbitrations. One of the unique features of our firm is that we own a twin engine airplane, and we will use it, for example, to take photos through a telephoto lens of an intersection that was the scene of a motor vehicle accident. Aerial photos are intrinsically interesting. We frequently blow them up to poster size to use as an exhibit for a trial or arbitration hearing.

To do this job well, you have to have compassion and be willing to be patient with clients who would rather be doing anything else than answering what they view as very intrusive interrogatory questions. You have to be able to talk but also be able to listen to people. Attention to detail is crucial, especially when drafting documents; I proofread everything two or three times even after I spell check because the documents I send out have to look perfect. It is the best way to let the other side know that we are professionals.

---

b. Government Documents

Government documents can often prove to be very useful. City building departments have information on building construction plans and safety

inspections. Coroners' offices have autopsy and inquest reports. County recorders' offices have information on mortgages, bankruptcies, trusts, and judgments. License bureaus have all sorts of background information on license holders. The secretary of state's office in the relevant state and the federal Securities and Exchange Commission have extensive data about the structure and financial position of corporations.

While the law differs from one state to the next, the general rule is that the public has a right to inspect public records during reasonable business hours. The right to inspect such documents carries with it the right to make copies. For a nominal service fee most offices will provide you with photocopies of the documents you need. At the federal level the Freedom of Information Act requires each agency to make various records available to the public. Exceptions are allowed, however, for such matters as defense and foreign policy secrets, trade secrets, confidential commercial or financial information, personnel and medical files, and investigatory files compiled for law enforcement purposes.

Two state offices most commonly used by paralegal investigators are the secretary of state's office and the agency responsible for licensing occupations. The secretary of state's office maintains a list of all foreign and domestic corporations registered to do business in the state, as well as other business entities. For example, it can provide information as to the official legal names of corporations; the nature of the business the corporation is engaged in; and the names and addresses of its registered agent, its board of directors, and its officers.

The county courthouse also provides a wealth of very useful information. In the office for the registry of deeds you can find information about who owns certain real estate in the county, as well as who holds the mortgages and various liens on the property. You can find additional information on liens in the clerk of the court's office. In the assessor's office you can find information about who pays the taxes on the property and whether any delinquencies exist.

To save yourself a lot of time spent on leg work, think about calling ahead before you go to any of the agencies mentioned in this section. Some governmental agencies do not allow public access on certain days. If you do not know that and go that day, it will simply waste your time. Also find out who at the agency can best help you, and make sure that he or she has the documents you need. Then go to the agency as soon as possible before your newly discovered contact person has a chance to forget you and the purpose of your mission.

> **P R A C T I C E   T I P**
>
> Many governmental agencies have their information available online, either through a commercial service or on their Internet web page.

> **P R A C T I C E   T I P**
>
> If the person being sued is required to obtain some form of licensing, such as an electrician or a beautician, start your investigation with the state licensing board. Not only can you find out the requirements for licensure, but also you may find that the person being sued allowed his or her license to lapse. You may also learn of other complaints pending against that person— a tremendous incentive to the other side for early settlement of the case.

c. Trade Association Documents

In products liability cases you will need to obtain copies of relevant industry standards established by both government agencies and voluntary associations. While the courts of different states vary with regard to their treatment of the admissibility of such codes, the modern trend seems to favor their use. The National Safety Council, the American National Standards Institute, and the American Society of Safety Engineers are some of the most common sources of such standards. The Lawyers' Desk Reference: Technical Sources for Conducting a Personal Injury Action is a handy source for locating relevant organizations. The American National Standards Institute and the Underwriters Laboratories publish catalogs that list the availability of published standards.

4. Researching Miscellaneous Empirical Information

In the process of investigating a specific case, certain types of public information may be helpful. It might be important, for example, to know what the weather conditions were like at the time of an automobile accident. Although a witness might be able to estimate the temperature or the amount of snowfall, the weather bureau's records would be more precise and more reliable. In different contexts it might be useful to know the price that a share of company's stock sold for on a particular day, the latest medical treatment techniques, or the side effects of specific drugs.

a. Library Reference Sources

When seeking information, do not forget to use public libraries. There are also specialized libraries, such as those found at medical schools, that may be able to help you with particular information needs.

Reference librarians have a wealth of knowledge and are often very willing to search out information for you. So if you are looking for information about the weather, information about drugs, or biographical information, the reference desk at the library is a great place to begin. One resource available in most public libraries that you may want to consult is Thomas' Register. It contains information on companies, including names, addresses, and financial data.

b. Computer Databases

Much of the information that formerly had to be gathered through long hours of library research is now readily accessible on personal computers that can be linked with computerized databases. These databases store references to, or summaries of, such information sources as articles in periodicals and journals, books, news stories, and scientific and technical reports. Lexis and Westlaw, the two most prominent legal databases, are covered in the discussion of legal research in Chapter 14. In addition, the Internet is becoming an increasingly important resource.

5. Reporting the Results of the Investigation

Your work will be of little use if you do not communicate it effectively to your attorney. In your report describe what you did, and provide an analysis of the results. Attach statements, diagrams, and photographs. Your supervisor may

want one comprehensive report or, in longer, more complex matters, a series of interim reports.

In the report's analysis section isolate each factual question about which there is some dispute. For each, detail all aspects of the evidence (testimonial, physical, and documentary) that relate to that specific issue. Note any factors that may affect a witness's credibility, such as a witness being hard of hearing or having a surly manner.

Although you should try to present this information in a concise manner, it is important that it be complete. An item might appear to be insignificant at the time the report is being prepared but may become extremely important at some later date.

SUMMARY

In both civil and criminal suits there is usually more of a dispute over what actually took place (the facts) than there is about the meaning of the law. Although on occasion both sides may stipulate to a particular description of the facts, the major part of the attorney's energy goes toward convincing the court to adopt the client's view of the facts rather than the opponent's contrary view. A good paralegal therefore should be a skilled fact finder. At times a paralegal is personally involved in the investigative process. In other cases when the initial investigative work is done outside the law office, the paralegal is frequently used to coordinate the information gained from these outside sources and to prepare it for presentation in the courtroom. In either case it is important to understand the basic concepts and techniques that go into conducting investigations.

To as great an extent as possible, strive to collect information in a form that is admissible in a court of law. Developing a basic understanding of the rules of evidence and what constitutes relevant and competent evidence will assist you in knowing what evidence to gather.

Facts can be obtained through a number of sources, including interviews of clients and witnesses; documentary evidence, such as police reports, hospital and doctor records, employment records, contracts, and photographs; and personal observation, from visiting an accident scene or examining the condition of an apartment.

Begin the investigation as soon after the incident as possible. Physical surroundings change, witnesses' memories fade, and injuries heal. Time is particularly important if you are investigating an automobile accident or similar event in which the physical evidence is likely to change or disappear.

Do not overlook newspapers, periodicals, and other specialized reporting services as sources for locating medical, scientific, or financial information. Computerized databases make such searches much easier and more efficient. Finally, keep your supervising attorney informed about the status of your investigation through reports that effectively summarize and integrate the results of your investigation.

REVIEW QUESTIONS

Pages 503 through 514

•1. How do courts determine what types of information can be used and what the lawyers must do in order to get evidence admitted?

2. Define each of the following: real or physical evidence, documentary evidence, testimonial evidence, and judicial notice.

3. Define each of the following: direct, circumstantial, cumulative, and corroborative evidence.

4. What is the difference between relevancy and materiality?

5. What is hearsay, and under what circumstances is hearsay evidence admissible?

6. Under what circumstances can a lay witness give opinion testimony?

7. Before a person can testify as an expert witness, what must happen?

8. How does the testimony of an expert differ from that of a lay witness?

9. What must be done to properly authenticate real evidence?

10. What impact does the best evidence rule have on the presentation of evidence?

Pages 514 through 524

11. What is the goal of a factual investigation?

12. Why might it sometimes be more appropriate to hire a professional, independent investigator rather than relying on the firm's employees?

13. Before beginning the investigation, why is it important to discuss the theory of the case with the supervising attorney?

14. Describe three different methods for authenticating a document.

Computers and Case Management

A man may as well open an oyster without a knife as a lawyer's mouth without a fee.
Barten Holyday

INTRODUCTION

In addition to assisting with the interviewing and investigative functions discussed in Chapters 16 and 17, paralegals are frequently involved in a variety of case management functions. Case management refers to the record keeping involved in processing a case within the law office. It begins with the initial client interview and continues until the case is formally closed. All documents and case materials must be organized so as to allow for the easy, fast, and accurate retrieval of information.

In the context of the personal injury case we used throughout the last two chapters, case management functions will begin as soon as the firm decides to represent Mr. Drake. Those case management functions include:

- running conflict checks,
- creating various files,
- recording background data,
- entering key dates into a "tickler system,"
- preparing court documents,
- recording time charges, and
- sending out bills.

The Case of the Distressed Grandfather (continued)

At the end of their interview, Chris Kendall escorted Mr. Drake to the door and then settled down to spend the next hour setting up the case file folder. First, he started his timeslips program, a specialized computer program, to begin recording the time he would be spending on Mr. Drake's case. Next, he used his computer to do a conflicts check to ensure that the firm had never represented Mrs. Small or anyone related to her. Third, he set up a case file for the *Drake v. Small* personal injury case. He then switched to his computerized calendaring program to enter the date of Mr. Drake's next appointment; reminders to himself to remind Mr. Drake about updating his information; a list of tasks, such as obtaining the medical records with reminder dates; and most important the relevant statute of limitations along with three reminders, one four weeks prior to the statute of limitations date, one two weeks prior, and one three days prior.

A. PERFORMING A CONFLICTS CHECK

Before a law firm can accept someone as a new client, it must perform a conflicts check. As you will recall from Chapter 11, in order to maintain client confidentiality and to avoid any breach of the fiduciary duty of client trust and loyalty, attorneys cannot accept any case that would involve either a personal conflict or

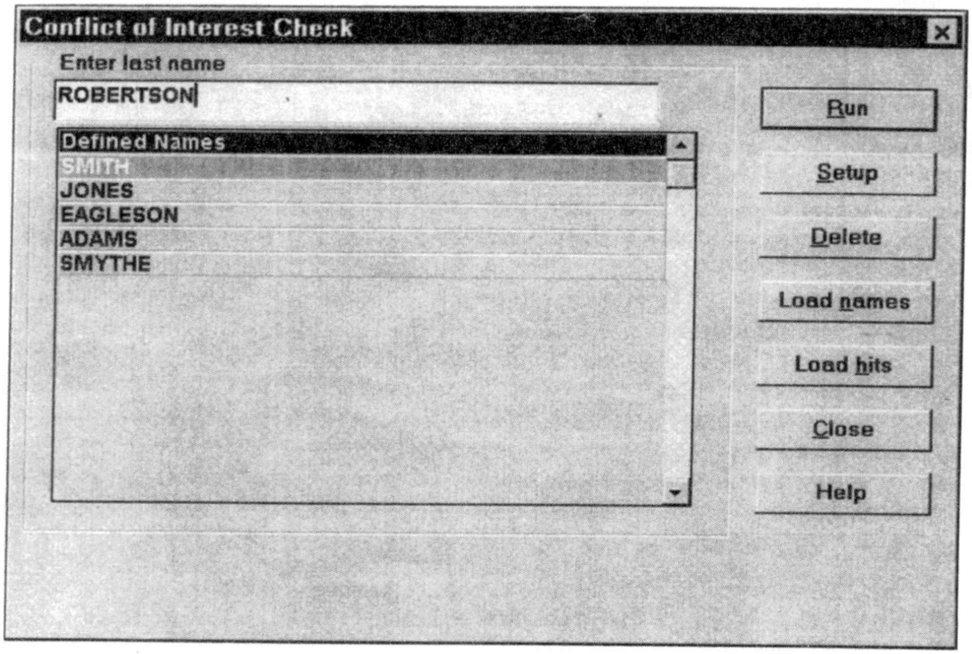

Exhibit 18-1   Computerized Conflict of Interest Checking

a conflict with a prior client. In an increasingly litigious society, conflict checks are becoming more complex. Thus, when a new file is opened, the names of the adverse parties must be cross-referenced with other law firm records.

The best approach is to realize that memories are fallible and that all conflict checking should be done through a computerized system that faithfully records all client names and related parties. Exhibit 18-1, page 528, illustrates how one computer program allows the entry of up to 200 names connected with the case to be checked in a single search. Also, firms frequently circulate memos within the firm to inform all attorneys and paralegals of the firm's new clients.

B. SETTING UP A CLIENT CASE FILE

A law office must maintain complete client files on every case. There are many filing systems in existence. A visit to your local legal supply house will acquaint you with many of them. To help preserve client confidentiality, instead of labeling files with client names, most firms use a numbering system that includes such information as the date the file was opened and a code for the matter type, such as divorce or personal injury.

The type and number of file folders a particular firm uses may vary, but most client files contain

1. background information on the client (including addresses, phone numbers, and billing arrangements);
2. correspondence between the firm and either the client or other outside parties connected to the case;
3. internal office memoranda (including research memos prepared in connection with the case);
4. copies of all pleadings related to the case;
5. copies of relevant contracts, leases, medical reports, laboratory reports, and so forth; and
6. notes by attorneys and paralegals working on the case.

The inside cover often contains the first listed item, that is, the background information, such as phone numbers and addresses for the client, opposing attorney, and insurance carriers. The other materials are often placed in separate subfiles within the larger folder. Within each subfile the materials are arranged in chronological order with the most recent item placed on the top or at the front of the subfile. Firms may store their active client files in a central location and assign a specific individual to set up and maintain these files.

As law firms and legal departments have become increasingly more computerized, many are making greater use of computerized filing systems where client files and other forms of vital information are also stored in an electronic database.

P R A C T I C E   T I P

Keep an up-to-date list of client expenses in an obvious place in the file. This is especially important for immediate access when the insurance company or opposition calls.

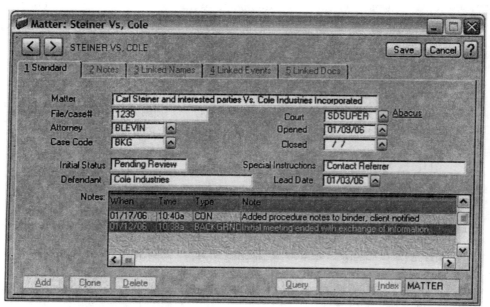

Exhibit 18-2   Case Management Program

Exhibit 18-2 shows the types of information that can be stored in a computerized case management program.

As the case progresses, always get the full name of any insurance or opposition representative who contacts you, and always take notes recording the substance of the conversation and place them in the file. You should make a special place in the file for an ongoing narrative of all the phone calls you have made and received. Then the attorney is never at a disadvantage if you are not around to provide an update yourself.

After the firm's involvement in a matter is completed, a file clerk or secretary officially closes the file. Some materials in the file are returned to the client, some are discarded, and some remain as part of a permanent file. Closed files are frequently stored in a separate, more remote area and eventually may be microfilmed or scanned onto disks in order to cut down on storage costs.

Finally, while the case is still open or shortly before it is closed, many law firms evaluate the various work products, such as complaints, motions, and memoranda of law as to their future usefulness. Legal research can be time consuming, and there is nothing to be gained from duplicating work that already has been done. Rather than beginning from scratch, it would be more efficient if an attorney or a paralegal could review work that someone else had done on a similar topic or problem. Therefore, if a document might serve as a valuable starting point for future work, the document is placed in the firm's work product files. The work product files are typically stored in loose-leaf binders in the library or saved on disk.

C. TIMEKEEPING AND BILLING

As the quotation set out at the beginning of this chapter, written by a British author almost four centuries ago, somewhat drolly suggests, to attorneys and paralegals time is money. In order for a law firm to prosper, not only must it provide quality legal services to a sufficient number of clients, but also it must bill and receive payment for those services. In order to accomplish this, the attorneys and paralegals must keep track of the time they spend on a case. This must be followed by a timely and detailed bill to the client. Studies have shown that the longer the time lapse between the time the legal service is rendered and the time the bill is received, the less likely it is that the client will pay.

1. Alternative Fee Structures

The discussion of fees is an essential element of the initial client interview. Depending on the nature of the case and whether the representation is for a plaintiff or a defendant, attorneys use various methods to bill for their own and their paralegals' time. Before starting work on a case, a law firm may also request an advance in the form of a **retainer** from the client. The word *retainer* has two meanings. The first, as we have already seen in the chapter on client interviewing, refers to the written agreement between the law firm and the client regarding the client's obligations as to the payment of fees and expenses. The second meaning refers to an amount of money the client pays as a type of down payment against future fees and expenses. The firm must deposit such advances in a special client's trust fund and cannot withdraw any of the funds until they have been earned as fees or spent on expenses. All unused funds must be returned to the client at the conclusion of the case.

> **Retainer**
> An advance or down payment that is given to engage the services of an attorney.

    The most common billing methods include

- fixed fee,
- contingency fee, and
- hourly fee.

a. Fixed Fees

Consumers generally pay a set fee for a particular product or service. For example, a physician typically charges a set amount for a routine office call or a specific surgical procedure. Lawyers also price some of their services in this manner and charge a fixed fee. This is especially true of routine tasks, such as drawing up a simple will, incorporating a small business, or handling an uncontested divorce. In many areas real estate closing fees are also billed in this manner.

    When **fixed fees** are used, it is to the firm's advantage to delegate as much work as possible to paralegals because they typically cost the firm less than attorneys do. The decreased overhead that results from such delegation to paralegals should result in higher profits and/or a reduction in the established fee. A fee reduction not only benefits consumers of legal services but also improves the firm's competitive position in the marketplace.

> **Fixed fee**
> A set charge for a specific service, such as drafting a simple will.

b. Contingency Fees

Under a **contingency fee** arrangement the client does not pay the attorney anything by way of attorney fees unless the plaintiff collects some sort of award

> **Contingency fee**
> A fee calculated as a percentage of the settlement or award in the case.

or settlement. However, in most states the client is still responsible for all expenses. If the plaintiff does collect some sort of award or settlement, then the attorney's fee will be calculated as a percentage of the damage award and paid from those funds when the plaintiff receives them. It is common for the law firm to receive 33 percent if a case is settled before it goes to trial, 40 percent if it goes to trial, and 50 percent if the case is appealed.

The plaintiff's attorney in a personal injury suit and attorneys doing collections work are usually hired on a contingency fee basis. On the other hand, this type of fee structure is usually prohibited in divorce and criminal actions. Although percentage fees used to be common in real estate and probate work, the trend in those areas has been to use fixed fees and time charges, respectively.

The use of a contingency fee raises a number of significant issues. Proponents argue that contingency fee agreements allow some clients to bring cases who could not otherwise afford to do so. However, a contingent fee also reduces the amount of the client's award. If the award represents the amount the jury or judge thought adequate to compensate the client for pain and suffering, medical expenses, lost earning capacity, and disfigurement, then any reduction in that award leaves the client without adequate compensation. Also, as the size of the recovery and hence the size of the fee increases, the gap widens between what the attorney would have recovered if charging on an hourly basis and what the attorney actually recovers based on a contingency fee basis. In some states this has been addressed by placing a cap on the amount of contingent fee awards in certain types of cases, such as medical malpractice, so that as the award increases, the attorney's percentage decreases. For example, an attorney might recover 40 percent of any award under $150,000 but only 25 percent of any amount of an award that exceeds $500,000.

As with fixed fees, it is economically advantageous for a law firm to delegate as much work as possible to paralegals. Such delegation reduces costs without affecting the fees received from the case.

c. Hourly Basis

Hourly rate
A fee based on how many hours attorneys or paralegals spend on the case. Different hourly rates are often charged for different attorneys and paralegals within the firm, based on their seniority and experience.

Many legal fees are based on **hourly rates** rather than on percentages or fixed charges. This is particularly true for litigation defense and corporate work. Hourly charges vary depending on whether the work is done by a paralegal, an associate, or a senior partner. The hourly fee may also vary based on the type of activity. For example, court appearances usually command a higher rate than out-of-court work. The client's best interests are served by having less complex matters delegated to paralegals and paying top dollar only for the matters that require the expertise and experience of a senior partner.

The hourly fees established by the firm reflect the firm's overhead costs, the income expectations of its partners, and the competition. Part of the amount collected for an hour of paralegal time pays the paralegal's salary, but part pays for office space and secretarial services, and part is the firm's profit.

Billable hours
The number of hours, or parts of an hour, that can be charged to a specific client.

Both attorneys and clients have attacked the acceptability of billing by the hour. When firms bill by the hour, there is tremendous pressure on lawyers and paralegals to increase their **billable hours.** A report by four sections of the American Bar Association discussed concerns regarding how law is practiced, including the common practice of hourly billing. Specifically, the report detailed complaints from both the clients' and the law firms' points of view.

What are the complaints against hourly billing from a client's standpoint? First, the total cost of representation. Second, the lack of predictability as to the total cost. Third, the lack of any risk sharing between the lawyer and the client, except in contingent fee cases. And, fourth, the lack of any incentive for efficiency or early resolution of the matter. . . .

From the lawyer's perspective, total dependency for revenues on hours billed means that compensation also is totally dependent on hours billed, which in turn means long hours, burnout, increased family problems and personal stress, and decreased morale. The system also is a disincentive for efficiency and creativity because if a matter normally would take 20 hours to do, finding a way of doing it in two hours would result in a drop of income to the firm of 18 billable hours, and thus would place even more pressure on the individual lawyer . . . .[1]

DISCUSSION QUESTIONS

1. A man pulled to the side of the road to help another motorist who was in trouble. While helping her, he was struck by a truck. His resulting injuries have confined him to a wheelchair with no bowel or bladder control. An attorney accepted his case, and they signed a contingency fee agreement whereby the attorney would receive one-third of the recovery. Within a short period of time the case settled for $2,925,000. The trial court, however, refused to approve the attorney fee of $975,000, stating that it was not reasonable. The judge acknowledged that the attorney had handled the case "expeditiously and well," and the client testified that he was satisfied with the fee award. However, when the trial judge considered the attorney's ability and reputation, the time reasonably spent, and the expenses reasonably incurred, he arrived at the figure of $695,000. The case was appealed. How do you think the appellate court resolved it?

2. From the perspective of the client what are the advantages and disadvantages of using a contingency fee structure?

3. In what ways do you think the various methods of billing impact on how willing attorneys are to delegate significant legal work to paralegals?

2. Time and Expense Records

No matter which fee system is used, a law office must maintain adequate time and expense records. If the firm charges at an hourly rate for its services, it must document those charges. In cases where a court may order the payment of attorneys' fees, a specific accounting must be made of the time actually spent on the case by different legal personnel. Even when there is a flat fee, the firm needs to have a record of the time spent on the case so that it can determine whether or not it has set its rates at levels that will produce a reasonable profit. In addition to recording the time spent, the firm must keep track of and bill the client for the firm's expenses, such as photocopying, computerized legal research, and postage.

Several different systems are used for recording how the time is spent. The diary system is probably the simplest. The attorney or paralegal keeps a calendar book that divides the day into time blocks. Hours of the day are typically

---

[1] American Bar Association, The Report of At the Breaking Point, A National Conference on the Emerging Crisis in the Quality of Lawyers' Health and Lives—Its Impact on Law Firms and Client Services (1991).

subdivided into five-, six-, ten-, or fifteen-minute segments. Although a six-minute segment may seem like an awkward number to work with, it represents one-tenth of an hour and thus simplifies calculation of bills by allowing the use of the decimal system. A clerk then copies the information from the diary onto ledger sheets that are maintained for each client. The diary system creates a permanent record of how each person spent the day, and reviewing this record may help that person to become more efficient.

Another variation of timekeeping uses special timeslips. Each timeslip has a space to indicate the date, the name of the client, a description of the nature of the work performed, the initials of the timekeeper, and the time spent on the project. To speed data entry, codes are frequently used for recording services performed. For example, TF might be *telephone call from*; TT, *telephone call to*; LR, *legal research*; FR, *factual research*; P, *preparation of*, and so on. Perforations between the slips allows the slips to be separated, sorted, and placed in the appropriate client files. Carbon paper, situated between the slips and a bottom sheet, means that once the slips have been removed, a permanent daily log is left behind. Exhibit 18-3 shows such a time record with the first three slips completed and ready to be removed to be placed in the appropriate files.

As in other areas of law office administration, specialized computer software has been developed to automate the reporting and integration of this data into the firm's billing and cost accounting systems. Typically, these systems allow the timekeeper (the attorney or paralegal) to directly enter time into the computer, eliminating the necessity for handwritten timeslips. Alternatively, a clerk can enter the information from the attorneys' and paralegals' timesheets into the computer. Exhibit 18-4, on page 535, illustrates such a computerized timeslip. As you can see, the computer automatically takes the time spent and multiplies it by the user's rate to arrive at the amount to bill the client. Whether the timekeeper or a clerk enters the information into the computerized timeslip, the computer then posts those figures to be appropriate client's account, totals the entire amount owed, and prepares an itemized bill. Some systems can also prepare staff paychecks and calculate various partners' contributions to the income of the firm.

Exhibit 18-3   Time Record with Completed Timeslips

TIME RECORD Date	Client/Case	Services Performed	Attorney	Hours	Tenths
9/24	John Brown	TT: Dr. Grant regarding upcoming deposition.	GKB		.1
"	Phyllis Stone	FR: review of medical records	GKB	2	.5
"	John Brown	TF: client. Had questions about his role at the deposition.	GKB		.4

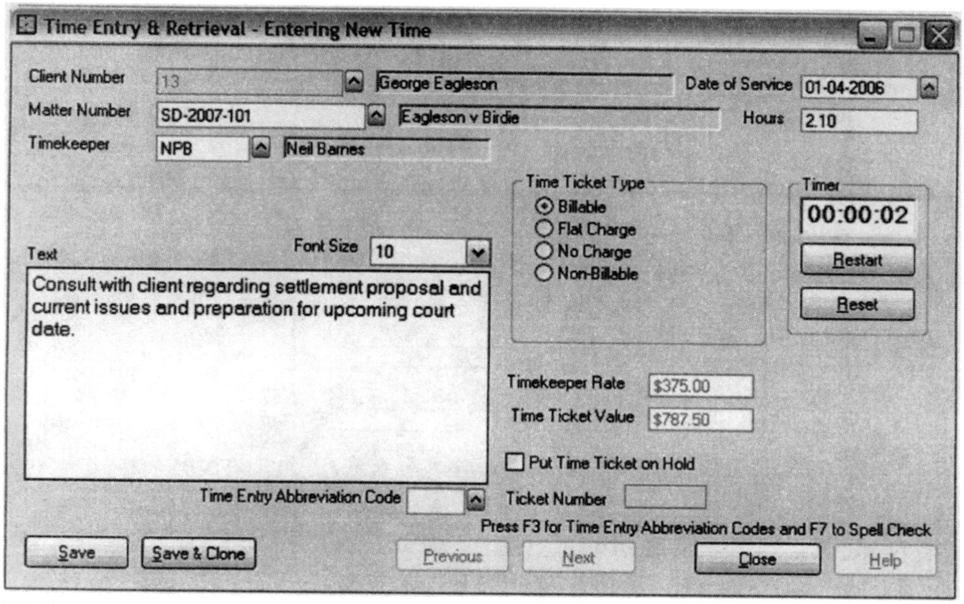

Exhibit 18-4   Computerized Timeslip

D. CALENDARING AND DOCKET CONTROL

The failure to meet deadlines is a leading cause of malpractice claims. Therefore, every law office needs a reliable way to keep track of and give advance warnings of important dates. Probably the most important date is the statute of limitations. If a lawsuit is not filed within the time limits established by the statute of limitations, clients may be barred from going to court. Other dates are also important. For example, once a defendant has been served with a summons, there is a set period of time within which to respond. Every time a motion is filed or an answer is received, another time period begins, and another deadline approaches. If any of these deadlines is missed, the process may have to be started all over, or a default judgment may be rendered against the client. To monitor these important dates, lawyers develop docket control systems, commonly referred to as **tickler systems**.

Tickler system
A calendaring system that records key dates and important deadlines.

P R A C T I C E   T I P

Record your time as close to when you do the work as possible. Later you will find that it is impossible to make an accurate record. This could result in overbilling the client (an obvious ethical problem) or underbilling (a disservice to your firm). Profitable law firms cannot afford to make a regular practice of billing for less time than is actually spent on a case.

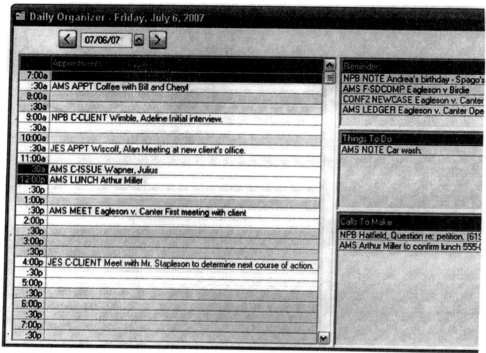

Exhibit 18-5   Docket Control/Calendaring Program

Although a tickler system can be as simple as writing important dates on a desk calendar, most law firms use more complex and more reliable methods. A very elementary version of a tickler system can be set up by using 3 × 5 index cards filed in a set of dividers that are tabbed to reflect day, month, and year. Every time a deadline is established, a separate index card is completed indicating the client's name, file number, and what needs to be done on that date. These cards are then placed behind the proper divider card along with any other cards that also apply to that date. Another variation involves preparing reminder memos that are then filed in file folders marked with a specific day, month, and year.

These manual methods of keeping track of key dates have generally been replaced with new software calendaring programs that automate everything other than the initial entry of the dates. They provide a way to automate a whole series of events, such as the steps required prior to and after a real estate closing or the dates for each step in a court-imposed tracking system for litigation.

Most specialized computer programs will let you enter different types of events, such as priority deadlines (statute of limitations, time by which answers to interrogatories must be filed, etc.), court dates, appointments, and general "to do" information. Then, if you fail to complete a task, most programs will keep reminding you of the missed deadline until you mark the task as completed. These programs will automatically calculate dates that occur a certain number of days before or after any given date and add reminders at any interval you like

prior to the deadline itself. If you should have to change a deadline, the reminders connected to that deadline will automatically change as well. They also allow for the entering of such recurring events as weekly staff meetings or the boss's birthday. Exhibit 18-5, page 536, shows one computer program that mimics the look of the traditional paper daily organizer.

The key to the success of any tickler system is making someone responsible for routinely checking on what needs to be done and circulating that information with sufficient advance notice to the relevant attorney or paralegal.

E. COMPUTERIZED LITIGATION SUPPORT PROGRAMS

As you can now see, through the course of an investigation you are likely to collect a great deal of documentary and witness testimony. In order to organize this so that any item can be retrieved easily, many firms are turning to computerized litigation support systems. These systems can take one of two forms or can be a combination of the two. The first is a **structured database**, in which the paralegal, or someone else delegated within the law office, enters summary information about each document. The second is a **full-text database**, similar to Westlaw or Lexis, in which the entire document or witness transcript is entered into the computer. This allows for full text searching.

The primary advantages of these databases are

- the speed and ease with which information can be retrieved,
- the number of people who can view the same document at the same time from different locations,
- the ease with which you can add or modify information in the file, and
- the decreased amount of physical space required for records storage.

The speed and ease with which these computerized files can be retrieved is one of the most important of these advantages. Rather than walking to the file room and searching through file drawers to locate the precise document required, the paralegal or attorney types identification information, and the computer either displays the requested document on the monitor or produces a written copy on the printer.

Structured database
A computerized database that contains key information about the content of documents, such as medical records.

Full-text database
A computerized database that contains the full text of documents, such as court opinions or depositions.

The Case of the Distressed Grandfather (continued)

During the course of his investigation Chris collected numerous documents. Because his firm uses a computerized litigation support program, as he collected each document, he entered a summary of it into his computer. This enabled him to sort and search through the information contained in those documents. For example, he could easily sort all of Mr. Drake's medical records by date to create a chronology of his medical treatment.

NETNOTE

You can learn more about the software shown in this chapter's exhibits by going to the company's Web site at www.abacuslaw.com.

With paper files the number of people who can view a document at any one time is limited to the number of copies that have been made. However, when an electronic database is made available through a computer network, multiple users can be reading the same document at the same time. Network users can have either "read only" access, which allows them to view but not alter the document, or read/write access, which allows the user to not only read but also make changes in the document.

Finally, the search capabilities of database programs allow you to easily locate that proverbial needle in the haystack. For example, assume you remember that a deponent mentioned that your client had seen a psychiatrist or psychologist. That information had not seemed important at the time, but now your supervising attorney wants to know who said it and in what context. Unfortunately, you do not remember which deponent made that statement, and there were eight deponents who collectively created over a thousand pages of deposition testimony. Using a full-text system, you can type in a search such as psych*. The * is known as a wildcard, and it tells the program to search for all words that begin with the letters "psych." Within seconds the program would search through those hundreds of deposition pages and produce a list of all the question-answer pairs that contain any variation of a word beginning with psych, such as psychiatrist or psychologist. You could then print out those question-answer pairs so that your supervising attorney could see the context in which the word *psychiatrist* or *psychologist* was used.

SUMMARY

Case management refers to the record keeping involved in processing a case within the law office. All documents and case materials must be organized so as to allow for the easy, fast, and accurate retrieval of information. Paralegals must be familiar with the types of records that are kept in most law offices. While naturally there will be variations from one office to the next, the same basic types of files will be kept in most law offices. These include client files, work product files, a tickler system, and timekeeping and billing records.

Sophisticated software programs have greatly increased office automation. This has reduced the number of clerical personnel needed to operate a law office and has opened new opportunities for paralegals to increase their effectiveness.

REVIEW QUESTIONS

Pages 527 through 529

1. What is case management?
2. What is the purpose of performing a conflicts check? Why is a computerized conflicts check more reliable than manual methods?

Pages 529 through 533

3. Why should client files not be labeled with the client name?
4. What should a typical client file contain?
5. Why is it important to bill a client promptly once work is completed?
6. Describe the three traditional billing methods. Give an example of when each type of billing method is most commonly used.
7. What are the problems with hourly billing?
8. What are the problems with contingency fee billing?

Pages 533 through 538

9. Why is it important for paralegals to record the time they spend? Describe the most common ways in which this is done.
10. What is a tickler system, and why is it important? What are the benefits of a computerized tickler system over a manual system?
11. What are the advantages of computerized litigation support programs?

Appendixes

Appendix A

Excerpts from the United States Constitution

Preamble

We the People of the United States, in Order to form a more perfect Union, establish Justice, insure domestic Tranquility, provide for the common defence, promote the general Welfare, and secure the Blessings of Liberty to ourselves and our Posterity, do ordain and establish this Constitution for the United States of America.

Article I

Section 1. All legislative Powers herein granted shall be vested in a Congress of the United States, which shall consist of a Senate and House of Representatives.

Section 2. [*Section 2 describes the composition of and qualifications for the House of Representatives.*]

Section 3. [*Section 3 describes the composition of and the qualifications for the Senate.*]

Section 4. The Times, Places and Manner of holding Elections for Senators and Representatives, shall be prescribed in each State by the Legislature thereof; but the Congress may any time by Law make or alter such Regulations, except as to the Places of chusing Senators. . . .

Section 5. [*Section 5 discusses quorums and the development of procedural rules in the House and the Senate.*]

Section 6. [*Section 6 discusses compensation and legislative privileges.*]

Section 7. [*Section 7 establishes procedures for the passage of laws and presidential vetoes.*]

Section 8. The Congress shall have Power To lay and collect Taxes, Duties, Imposts and Excises, to pay the Debts and provide for the common Defence and general Welfare of the United States; but all Duties, Imposts and Excises shall be uniform throughout the United States;

To borrow Money on the credit of the United States;

To regulate Commerce with foreign Nations, and among the several States, and with the Indian Tribes;

To establish an uniform Rule of Naturalization, and uniform Laws on the subject of Bankruptcies throughout the United States; . . .

To constitute Tribunals inferior to the supreme Court;

To define and punish Piracies and Felonies committed on the high Seas, and Offenses against the Law of Nations; . . .

To make all Laws which shall be necessary and proper for carrying into Execution the foregoing Powers, and all other Powers vested by this Constitution in the Government of the United States, or in any Department or Officer thereof.

Section 9. [*Section 9 imposes several limitations on the federal government, including restrictions against preventing states from importing slaves prior to 1808; suspending the writ of habeas corpus; passing bills of attainder, ex post facto laws, and capitation taxes; and granting titles of nobility.*]

Section 10. [*Section 10 places limitations on the states that include not allowing them to enter into treaties, coin money, tax exports, or engage in war.*]

Article II

Section 1. [*Section 1 describes the qualifications for and procedures to be used in selecting the president. It also discusses compensation and succession if the president dies, resigns, or is unable to perform the duties of the office.*]

Section 2. The President shall be Commander in Chief of the Army and Navy of the United States, and of the Militia of the several States, when called into the actual Service of the United States; he may require the Opinion, in writing, of the principal Officer in each of the executive Departments, upon any Subject relating to the Duties of their respective Offices, and he shall have Power to grant Reprieves and Pardons for Offenses against the United States, except in Cases of Impeachment.

He shall have Power, by and with the Advice and Consent of the Senate, to make Treaties, provided two thirds of the Senators present concur; and he shall nominate, and by and with the Advice and Consent of the Senate, shall appoint Ambassadors, other public Ministers and Consuls, Judges of the supreme Court, and all other Officers of the United States, whose Appointments are not herein otherwise provided for, and which shall be established by Law; but the Congress may by Law vest the Appointment of such inferior Officers, as they think proper, in the President alone, in the Courts of Law, or in the Heads of Departments. . . .

Section 3. [*Section 3 lists duties of the president, including developing a state of the union message to Congress, receiving ambassadors from other countries, and "faithfully execut[ing]" the laws of the country.*]

Section 4. The President, Vice President and all civil Officers of the United States, shall be removed from Office on Impeachment for, and Conviction of, Treason, Bribery, or other high Crimes and Misdemeanors.

Article III

Section 1. The judicial Power of the United States, shall be vested in one supreme Court, and in such inferior Courts as the Congress may from time to time ordain and establish. The Judges, both of the supreme and inferior Courts, shall hold their Offices during good Behaviour, and shall, at stated Times, receive for their Services, a Compensation, which shall not be diminished during their Continuance in Office.

Section 2. The judicial Power shall extend to all Cases, in Law and Equity, arising under this Constitution, the Laws of the United States, and Treaties made, or which shall be made, under their Authority;—to all Cases affecting Ambassadors, other public Ministers and Consuls;—to all Cases of admiralty and maritime Jurisdiction;—to Controversies to which the United States shall be a Party;—to Controversies between two or more States;—between a State and Citizens of another State;—between Citizens of different States;—between Citizens of the same State claiming Lands under Grants of different States, and between a State, or the Citizens thereof, and foreign States, Citizens or Subjects.

In all Cases affecting Ambassadors, other public Ministers and Consuls, and those in which a State shall be Party, the supreme Court shall have original Jurisdiction. In all the other Cases before mentioned, the supreme Court shall have appellate Jurisdiction, both as to Law and Fact, with such Exceptions, and under such Regulations as the Congress shall make.

The Trial of all Crimes, except in Cases of Impeachment, shall be by Jury; and such Trial shall be held in the State where the said Crimes shall have been committed; but when not committed within any State, the Trial shall be at such Place or Places as the Congress shall by Law have directed.

Section 3. Treason against the United States, shall consist only of levying War against them, or in adhering to their Enemies, giving them Aid and Comfort. No Person shall be convicted of Treason unless on the Testimony of two Witnesses to the same overt Act, or on Confession in open Court. . . .

Article IV

Section 1. Full Faith and Credit shall be given in each State to the public Acts, Records, and judicial Proceedings of every other State; And the Congress may by general Laws prescribe the Manner in which such Acts, Records, and Proceedings shall be proved, and the Effect thereof.

Section 2. [*Section 2 discusses extradition for crimes (including escaped slaves).*]

Section 3. [*Section 3 discusses admission of new states into the Union.*]

Section 4. The United States shall guarantee to every State in this Union a Republican Form of Government, and shall protect each of them against Invasion; and on Application of the Legislature, or of the Executive (when the Legislature cannot be convened) against domestic Violence.

Article V

The Congress, whenever two thirds of both Houses shall deem it necessary, shall propose Amendments to this Constitution, or, on the Application of the Legislatures of two thirds of the several States, shall call a Convention for proposing Amendments, which, in either Case, shall be valid to all Intents and Purposes, as Part of this Constitution, when ratified by the Legislatures of three fourths of the several States, or by Conventions in three fourths thereof, as the one or the other Mode of Ratification may be proposed by the Congress. . . . [*This article also contains language designed to protect the importation of slaves until 1808.*]

Article VI

[*Article VI states that debts incurred by the national government under the former Articles of Confederation will be assumed by the new government.*]

This Constitution, and the Laws of the United States which shall be made in Pursuance thereof; and all Treaties made, or which shall be made, under the Authority of the United States, shall be the supreme Law of the Land; and the Judges in every State shall be bound thereby, any Thing in the Constitution or Laws of any State to the Contrary notwithstanding.

[N]o religious Test shall ever be required as a Qualification to any Office or public Trust under the United States.

Article VII

The Ratification of the Conventions of nine States, shall be sufficient for the Establishment of this Constitution between the States so ratifying the Same. . . .

Amendment I[1]

Congress shall make no law respecting an establishment of religion, or prohibiting the free exercise thereof; or abridging the freedom of speech, or of the press, or the right of the people peaceably to assemble, and to petition the Government for a redress of grievances.

Amendment II

A well regulated Militia, being necessary to the security of a free State, the right of the people to keep and bear Arms, shall not be infringed.

Amendment III

No Soldier shall, in time of peace be quartered in any house, without the consent of the Owner, nor in time of war, but in a manner prescribed by law.

Amendment IV

The right of the people to be secure in their persons, houses, papers, and effects, against unreasonable searches and seizures, shall not be violated, and no Warrants shall issue, but upon probable cause, supported by Oath or affirmation, and particularly describing the place to be searched, and the persons or things to be seized.

---

[1] The first ten amendments were ratified in 1791.

Amendment V

No person shall be held to answer for a capital, or otherwise infamous crime, unless on a presentment or indictment of a Grand Jury, except in cases arising in the land or naval forces, or in the Militia, when in actual service in time of War or public danger; nor shall any person be subject for the same offence to be twice put in jeopardy of life or limb, nor shall be compelled in any criminal case to be a witness against himself, nor be deprived of life, liberty, or property, without due process of law; nor shall private property be taken for public use without just compensation.

Amendment VI

In all criminal prosecutions, the accused shall enjoy the right to a speedy and public trial, by an impartial jury of the State and district wherein the crime shall have been committed, which district shall have been previously ascertained by law, and to be informed of the nature and cause of the accusation; to be confronted with the witnesses against him; to have compulsory process for obtaining witnesses in his favor, and to have the assistance of counsel for his defence.

Amendment VII

In Suits at common law, where the value in controversy shall exceed twenty dollars, the right of trial by jury shall be preserved, and no fact tried by a jury shall be otherwise re-examined in any Court of the United States, than according to the rules of the common law.

Amendment VIII

Excessive bail shall not be required, nor excessive fines imposed, nor cruel and unusual punishments inflicted.

Amendment IX

The enumeration in the Constitution of certain rights shall not be construed to deny or disparage others retained by the people.

Amendment X

The powers not delegated to the United States by the Constitution, nor prohibited by it to the States, are reserved to the States respectively, or to the people.

Amendment XI

(ratified in 1798)

The Judicial power of the United States shall not be construed to extend to any suit in law or equity, commenced or prosecuted against one of the United States by Citizens of another State, or by Citizens or Subjects of any Foreign State.

Amendment XII

(ratified in 1804)

[*Amendment XII revises the way in which the electoral college, and in some cases the Congress, votes for the offices of president and vice president.*]

Amendment XIII

(ratified in 1865)

Section 1. Neither slavery nor involuntary servitude, except as a punishment for crime whereof the party shall have been duly convicted, shall exist within the United States, or any place subject to their jurisdiction.

Section 2. Congress shall have power to enforce this article by appropriate legislation.

Amendment XIV

(ratified in 1868)

Section 1. All persons born or naturalized in the United States and subject to the jurisdiction thereof, are citizens of the United States and of the State wherein they reside. No State shall make or enforce any law which shall abridge the privileges or immunities of citizens of the United States; nor shall any State deprive any person of

life, liberty, or property, without due process of law; nor deny to any person within its jurisdiction the equal protection of the laws.

Section 2. [*Section 2 counts former slaves as equal to all other residents in terms of apportioning representation in the House of Representatives.*]

Section 3. [*Section 3 disqualifies those who participate in an insurrection or rebellion against the United States (e.g., the Civil War) from holding public office in the federal government unless Congress votes by a two-thirds majority to remove this disability.*]

Section 4. [*Section 4 states that neither Congress nor any state can be held responsible for debts incurred in aid of an insurrection (e.g., the Civil War).*]

Section 5. The Congress shall have power to enforce, by appropriate legislation, the provisions of this article.

Amendment XV

(ratified in 1870)

Section 1. The right of citizens of the United States to vote shall not be denied or abridged by the United States or by any State on account of race, color, or previous condition of servitude.

Section 2. The Congress shall have power to enforce this article by appropriate legislation.

Amendment XVI

(ratified in 1913)

The Congress shall have power to lay and collect taxes on incomes, from whatever source derived, without apportionment among the several States, and without regard to any census or enumeration.

Amendment XVII

(ratified in 1913)

[*Article XVII changed the method of selecting senators from appointment by state legislatures to direct election by the people of that state.*]

Amendment XVIII

(ratified in 1919)

[*Amendment XVIII the "Prohibition Amendment" prohibited the manufacture, sale, or transportation of intoxicating liquors.*]

Amendment XIX

(ratified in 1920)

Section 1. The right of citizens of the United States to vote shall not be denied or abridged by the United States or by any State on account of sex.

Section 2. Congress shall have power to enforce his article by appropriate legislation.

Amendment XX

(ratified in 1933)

[*Amendment XX changed the starting dates for presidential, vice presidential, and congressional terms. It also sets out procedures for situations in which the president elect dies before he or she actually takes office.*]

Amendment XXI

(ratified in 1933)

[*Amendment XXI repeals Amendment XVIII (Prohibition) but allows states to continue to prohibit the importation of intoxicating liquors across their own borders.*]

Amendment XXII

(ratified in 1951)

[*Amendment XXII imposes a two-term limit on the office of president.*]

Amendment XXIII

(ratified in 1961)

[*Amendment XXIII gives residents of the District of Columbia electors in the electoral college so they are on equal footing with residents of the states in "voting" for the president.*]

Amendment XXIV

(ratified in 1964)

Section 1. The right of citizens of the United States to vote in any primary or other election for President or Vice President, for electors for President or Vice President, or for Senator or Representative in Congress, shall not be denied or abridged by the United States or any State by reason of failure to pay any poll tax or other tax.

Section 2. The Congress shall have power to enforce this article by appropriate legislation.

Amendment XXV

(ratified in 1967)

[*Amendment XXV establishes procedures for selecting a new vice president when the vice president moves up to president upon the death or resignation of a president or when the vice president resigns or dies in office. It also sets out procedures for determining when a sitting president is temporarily unable to fulfill the duties of office.*]

Amendment XXVI

(ratified in 1971)

Section 1. The right of citizens of the United States, who are eighteen years of age or older, to vote shall not be denied or abridged by the United States or by any State on account of age.

Section 2. The Congress shall have power to enforce this article by appropriate legislation.

Amendment XXVII

(ratified in 1992)

No law varying the compensation for the services of the Senators and Representatives shall take effect, until an election of Representatives shall have intervened.

Appendix B

Ethical Codes

NATIONAL ASSOCIATION OF LEGAL ASSISTANTS CODE OF ETHICS AND PROFESSIONAL RESPONSIBILITY

A legal assistant must adhere strictly to the accepted standards of legal ethics and to the general principles of proper conduct. The performance of the duties of the legal assistant shall be governed by specific canons as defined herein so that justice will be served and goals of the profession attained.

The canons of ethics set forth hereafter are adopted by the National Association of Legal Assistants, Inc., as a general guide intended to aid legal assistants and attorneys. The enumeration of these rules does not mean there are not others of equal importance although not specifically mentioned. Court rules, agency rules, and statutes must be taken into consideration when interpreting the canons.

Definition: Legal assistants, also known as paralegals, are a distinguishable group of persons who assist attorneys in the delivery of legal services. Through formal education, training, and experience, legal assistants have knowledge and expertise regarding the legal system and substantive and procedural law which qualify them to do work of a legal nature under the supervision of an attorney.

Canon 1.

A legal assistant must not perform any of the duties that attorneys only may perform nor take any actions that attorneys may not take.

Canon 2.

A legal assistant may perform any task which is properly delegated and supervised by an attorney, as long as the attorney is ultimately responsible to the client, maintains a direct relationship with the client, and assumes professional responsibility for the work product.

Canon 3.

A legal assistant must not: (a) engage in, encourage, or contribute to any act which could constitute the unauthorized practice of law; and (b) establish attorney-client relationships, set fees, give legal opinions or advice or represent a client before a court or agency unless so authorized by that court or agency; and (c) engage in conduct or take any action which would assist or involve the attorney in a violation of professional ethics or give the appearance of professional impropriety.

Canon 4.

A legal assistant must use discretion and professional judgment commensurate with knowledge and experience but must not render independent legal judgment in place of an attorney. The services of an attorney are essential in the public interest whenever such legal judgment is required.

Canon 5.

A legal assistant must disclose his or her status as a legal assistant at the outset of any professional relationship with a client, attorney, a court or administrative agency or personnel thereof, or a member of the general public. A legal assistant must act prudently in determining the extent to which a client may be assisted without the presence of an attorney.

Canon 6.

A legal assistant must strive to maintain integrity and a high degree of competency through education and training with respect to professional responsibility, local rules and practice, and through continuing education in substantive areas of law to better assist the legal profession in fulfilling its duty to provide legal service.

Canon 7.

A legal assistant must protect the confidences of a client and must not violate any rule or statute now in effect or hereafter enacted controlling the doctrine of privileged communications between a client and an attorney.

Canon 8.

A legal assistant must do all other things incidental, necessary, or expedient for the attainment of the ethics and responsibilities as defined by statute or rule of court.

Canon 9.

A legal assistant's conduct is guided by bar associations' codes of professional responsibility and rules of professional conduct.
Adopted: May 1, 1975/Revised, 1979, 1988, and 1995

NFPA MODEL CODE OF ETHICS AND PROFESSIONAL RESPONSIBILITY

Preamble

... In May 1993 NFPA adopted its Model Code of Ethics and Professional Responsibility ("Model Code") to delineate the principles for ethics and conduct to which every paralegal should aspire.

Many paralegal associations throughout the United States have endorsed the concept and content of NFPA's Model Code through the adoption of their own codes. In doing so, paralegals have confirmed the profession's commitment to increase the quality and efficiency of legal services, as well as recognized its responsibilities to the public, the legal community, and colleagues.

Paralegals have recognized, and will continue to recognize, that the profession must continue to evolve to enhance their roles in the delivery of legal services. With increased levels of responsibility comes the need to define and enforce mandatory rules of professional conduct. Enforcement of codes of paralegal conduct is a logical and necessary step to enhance and ensure the confidence of the legal community and the public in the integrity and professional responsibility of paralegals.

In April 1997 NFPA adopted the Model Disciplinary Rules ("Model Rules") to make possible the enforcement of the Canons and Ethical Considerations contained in the NFPA Model Code. A concurrent determination was made that the Model Code of Ethics and Professional Responsibility, formerly aspirational in nature, should be recognized as setting forth the enforceable obligations of all paralegals.

The Model Code and Model Rules offer a framework for professional discipline, either voluntarily or through formal regulatory programs.

1.1 A Paralegal Shall Achieve and Maintain a High Level of Competence.

Ethical Considerations

EC-1.1(a) A paralegal shall achieve competency through education, training, and work experience.

EC-1.1(b) A paralegal shall participate in continuing education to keep informed of current legal, technical, and general developments.

EC-1.1(c) A paralegal shall perform all assignments promptly and efficiently.

1.2 A Paralegal Shall Maintain a High Level of Personal and Professional Integrity.

Ethical Considerations

EC-1.2(a) A paralegal shall not engage in any ex parte communications involving the courts or any other adjudicatory body in an attempt to exert undue influence or to obtain advantage for the benefit of only one party.

EC-1.2(b)   A paralegal shall not communicate, or cause another to communicate, with a party the paralegal knows to be represented by a lawyer in a pending matter without the prior consent of the lawyer representing such other party.

EC-1.2(c)   A paralegal shall ensure that all timekeeping and billing records prepared by the paralegal are thorough, accurate, honest, and complete.

EC-1.2(d)   A paralegal shall not knowingly engage in fraudulent billing practices. Such practices may include, but are not limited to: inflation of hours billed to a client or employer; misrepresentation of the nature of tasks performed; and/or submission of fraudulent expense and disbursement documentation.

EC-1.2(e)   A paralegal shall be scrupulous, thorough, and honest in the identification and maintenance of all funds, securities, and other assets of a client and shall provide accurate accountings as appropriate.

EC-1.2(f)   A paralegal shall advise the proper authority of any dishonest or fraudulent acts by any person pertaining to the handling of the funds, securities or other assets of a client.... Failure to report such knowledge is in itself misconduct and shall be treated as such under these rules.

1.3 A Paralegal Shall Maintain a High Standard of Professional Conduct.

Ethical Considerations

EC-1.3(a)   A paralegal shall refrain from engaging in any conduct that offends the dignity and decorum of proceedings before a court or other adjudicatory body and shall be respectful of all rules and procedures.

EC-1.3(b)   A paralegal shall avoid impropriety and the appearance of impropriety and shall not engage in any conduct that would adversely affect his/her fitness to practice....

EC-1.3(c)   Should a paralegal's fitness to practice be compromised by physical or mental illness, causing that paralegal to commit an act that is in direct violation of the Model Code/Model Rules and/or the rules and/or laws governing the jurisdiction in which the paralegal practices, that paralegal may be protected from sanction upon review of the nature and circumstances of that illness.

EC-1.3(d)   A paralegal shall advise the proper authority of non-confidential knowledge of any action of another legal professional that clearly demonstrates fraud, deceit, dishonesty, or misrepresentation.... Failure to report such knowledge is in itself misconduct and shall be treated as such under these rules.

EC-1.3(e)   A paralegal shall not knowingly assist any individual with the commission of an act that is in direct violation of the Model Code/Model Rules and/or the rules and/or laws governing the jurisdiction in which the paralegal-practices.

EC-1.3(f)   If a paralegal possesses knowledge of future criminal activity, that knowledge must be reported to the appropriate authority immediately.

1.4 A Paralegal Shall Serve the Public Interest by Contributing to the Improvement of the Legal System and Delivery of Quality Legal Services, Including Pro Bono Publico Services.

Ethical Considerations

EC-1.4(a)   A paralegal shall be sensitive to the legal needs of the public and shall promote the development and implementation of programs that address those needs.

EC-1.4(b)   A paralegal shall support efforts to improve the legal system and access thereto and shall assist in making changes.

EC-1.4(c) A paralegal shall support and participate in the delivery of Pro Bono Publico services directed toward implementing and improving access to justice, the law, the legal system, or the paralegal and legal professions.

EC-1.4(d)   A paralegal should aspire annually to contribute twenty-four (24) hours of Pro Bono Publico services under the supervision of an attorney or as authorized by administrative, statutory, or court authority to:

1. persons of limited means; or
2. charitable, religious, civic, community, governmental, and educational organizations in matters that are designed primarily to address the legal needs of persons with limited means; or
3. individuals, groups, or organizations seeking to secure or protect civil rights, civil liberties, or public rights.

1.5 A Paralegal Shall Preserve All Confidential Information Provided by the Client or Acquired from Other Sources Before, During, and After the Course of the Professional Relationship.

Ethical Considerations

EC-1.5(a)   A paralegal shall be aware of and abide by all legal authority governing confidential information in the jurisdiction in which the paralegal practices.

EC-1.5(b)   A paralegal shall not use confidential information to the disadvantage of a client.

EC-1.5(c)   A paralegal shall not use confidential information to the advantage of the paralegal or of a third person.

EC-1.5(d)   A paralegal may reveal confidential information only after full disclosure and with the client's written consent; or, when required by law or court order; or, when necessary to prevent the client from committing an act which could result in death or serious bodily harm.

EC-1.5(e)   A paralegal shall keep those individuals responsible for the legal representation of a client fully informed of any confidential information the paralegal may have pertaining to that client.

EC-1.5(f)   A paralegal shall not engage in any indiscreet communications concerning clients.

1.6 A Paralegal Shall Avoid Conflicts of Interest and Shall Disclose Any Possible Conflict to the Employer or Client, as Well as to the Prospective Employers or Clients.

Ethical Considerations

EC-1.6(a)   A paralegal shall act within the bounds of the law, solely for the benefit of the client, and shall be free of compromising influences and loyalties. Neither the paralegal's personal or business interest, nor those of other clients or third persons, should compromise the paralegal's professional judgment and loyalty to the client.

EC-1.6(b)   A paralegal shall avoid conflicts of interest which may arise from previous assignments, whether for a present or past employer or client.

EC-1.6(c)   A paralegal shall avoid conflicts of interest which may arise from family relationships and from personal and business interests.

EC-1.6(d)   In order to be able to determine whether an actual or potential conflict of interest exists, a paralegal shall create and maintain an effective recordkeeping system that identifies clients, matters, and parties with which the paralegal has worked.

EC-1.6(e)   A paralegal shall reveal sufficient non-confidential information about a client or former client to reasonably ascertain if an actual or potential conflict of interest exists.

EC-1.6(f)   A paralegal shall not participate in or conduct work on any matter where a conflict of interest has been identified.

EC-1.6(g)   In matters where a conflict of interest has been identified and the client consents to continued representation, a paralegal shall comply fully with the implementation and maintenance of an Ethical Wall.

1.7 A Paralegal's Title Shall Be Fully Disclosed.

Ethical Considerations

EC-1.7(a)   A paralegal's title shall clearly indicate the individual's status and shall be disclosed in all business and professional communications to avoid misunderstandings and misconceptions about the paralegal's role and responsibilities.

EC-1.7(b)   A paralegal's title shall be included if the paralegal's name appears on business cards, letterhead, brochures, directories, and advertisements.

EC-1.7(c)   A paralegal shall not use letterhead, business cards, or other promotional materials to create a fraudulent impression of his/her status or ability to practice in the jurisdiction in which the paralegal practices.

EC-1.7(d)   A paralegal shall not practice under color of any record, diploma, or certificate that has been illegally or fraudulently obtained or issued or which is misrepresentative in any way.

EC-1.7(e)   A paralegal shall not participate in the creation, issuance, or dissemination of fraudulent records, diplomas, or certificates.

1.8 A Paralegal Shall Not Engage in the Unauthorized Practice of Law.

Ethical Considerations

EC-1.8(a)   A paralegal shall comply with the applicable legal authority governing the unauthorized practice of law in the jurisdiction in which the paralegal practices.

Appendix C

Fundamentals of Good Writing

*I have made this letter longer than usual, only because
I have not had the time to make it shorter.*
Blaise Pascal

INTRODUCTION

How you say something is often as important as what you say. No matter how insightful and intelligent your thoughts are, if your writing is filled with misspellings and grammar errors, the reader will very likely discount the value of what you are saying. In legal writing, good writing is especially important because people's fortunes often rest on what a lawyer or a paralegal has written. In legal writing therefore it is simply too costly to write in any style other than one that is clear, concise, and grammatically correct.

To be an effective writer, follow these simple rules:

Rule 1   Develop a clear, readable writing style that is appropriate for the audience to whom it is directed. This partly depends on an awareness of the ways in which legal writing differs from more informal writing and speech.

Rule 2   Always use good grammar and proper punctuation. Like it or not, most lawyers, judges, and clients are grammar snobs. If you do not follow the basic conventions of correct spelling and grammar, they will assume you are lazy or stupid, or both.

Rule 3   Carefully proofread what you have written. Take advantage of any spell-checking or grammar programs associated with the word processing software you use, but do not rely on these programs alone. A spell checker will not find correctly spelled but misused words. For example, a spell checker would find nothing wrong with this sentence: "The witness recounted the hole story."

Rule 4   Write and rewrite and then rewrite again. There is no such thing as good writing, only good rewriting. For those of you who suffer from writer's block, this is actually good news. Sometimes people are afraid to start writing because they assume what they initially write will be the final product. It is not.

This appendix is designed to help you improve the style and technical quality of your writing so that your work will be as professional looking as possible.

PART I: GRAMMAR

Good legal writing starts by being good writing. Therefore, to rate as good legal writing, the document must follow the normal rules of grammar and punctuation. The following suggestions should help you correct the most common grammar errors.

A. Use Proper Sentence Structure

Using proper sentence structure will make your writing easier to comprehend. Proper sentence structure means using simple sentence construction, avoiding sentence fragments and run-ons, and using parallel constructions.

1. Use Simple Sentence Construction

Whenever possible, stick to simple sentences. Legal writing is hard enough to read without complicating it further through long, convoluted sentences. Follow these guidelines:

a. Use normal sentence order

Unless there is a good reason to do otherwise, follow normal sentence order: noun, verb, object.

b. One thought per sentence

Have one main thought in a sentence.

c. Limit sentences to twenty-five words

Vary the sentence length but the average sentence should be no longer than twenty-five words.

d. Use tabulations

Divide long sentences using **tabulations**. If the items are complete sentences, use the following format:

1. Begin each item with an upper-case letter.
2. End each item with a period.

If the items are not complete sentences, use the following format:

1. a lower-case letter at the beginning of each item,
2. a semicolon or comma after each item, and
3. an "or" or "and" before the last item.

e. Avoid intrusive phrases

Do not let phrases or clauses intrude between the subject and verb. These **intrusive phrases** disrupt the sentence's logical flow and make it difficult for the reader to follow what is being said.

> **Example:**   The interrogatories sent to our client and received by him at his home three days ago force us to reformulate our defense strategy.

Fourteen words separate the subject, *interrogatories*, from the verb, *force*. This writing style creates several problems. First, until the reader reaches the verb, he or she must wait in suspense as to what is going on with the subject, the interrogatories. Second, the reader must process the new information contained in the intrusive clause while remembering that the main point of the sentence relates to the interrogatories.

If you find yourself writing particularly long sentences, check to see whether your reader may get lost between the beginning and the end. If so, you may have inserted intrusive phrases between your subject and verb. There are two solutions. First, you can simply divide the sentence and create two sentences.

> **Revised:**   Three days ago our client received interrogatories. The interrogatories force us to reformulate our defense strategy.

The other solution is to take the intrusive phrase out of the middle and put it at the beginning or the end.

> **Revised:**   Sent to our client and received by him at his home three days ago, the interrogatories force us to reformulate our defense strategy.

NETNOTE

To find online exercises on run-ons, fragments, and more, go to Grammar Bytes!, *www.chompchomp.com/menu.htm.*

2. Avoid Sentence Fragments

An obvious corollary to the rule that you should use simple sentence construction is the requirement that you write in sentences. A sentence contains a subject and a verb and can stand alone as a complete thought. A sentence can be a single independent clause, two independent clauses joined with a coordinating conjunction, or an independent and a dependent clause.

> **Example:** The man yelled for help.
> (*independent clause*)
>
> The man yelled for help, and the police came running.
> (*two independent clauses*)
>
> Even though the man yelled for help, no one came to his assistance.
> (*dependent clause followed by independent clause*)

Sentence fragment
An incomplete sentence.

Sentence fragments are incomplete sentences and cannot stand alone. One type of sentence fragment is the phrase with no verb.

> **Example:** The doctor in white. (Did what?)

Another type of sentence fragment is the prepositional phrase standing alone.

> **Example:** By six o'clock. (What will happen?)

To correct the first type of fragment, insert a verb.

> **Revised:** The doctor in white *said* that I could go home.

To correct the second type of fragment, attach the prepositional phrase to the rest of the sentence.

> **Revised:** By six o'clock *we should have heard from the doctor.*

The most common type of sentence fragment is the **dependent clause** standing alone. The writer thinks she has written a complete sentence when she has not. The dependent clause does contain a subject and verb, but it cannot stand alone and make sense, as it does not contain a complete thought. When you read a dependent clause that is standing alone, it is as though you are waiting for the other shoe to drop.

> **Example:**   Although the defense attorney asked for a finding of not guilty. (What happened?)

Dependent clauses always begin with what is known as a **subordinating conjunction:** *after, although, as, because, before, even though, if, since, unless, when, where, whereas,* and *while*. To correct a sentence fragment created by a dependent clause standing alone, drop the subordinating conjunction and turn the dependent clause into an independent clause, or add an independent clause.

> **Revised:**   The defense attorney asked for a finding of not guilty. (subordinating conjunction dropped)
>
> Although the defense attorney asked for a finding of not guilty, the jury brought in a guilty verdict. (independent clause added)

3. Avoid Run-On Sentences (Fused Sentences and Comma Splices)

The **run-on sentence** is the opposite of the sentence fragment. Instead of being half a sentence, it is actually two sentences. It can occur either as a comma splice (two independent clauses joined by a comma) or as a fused sentence (two independent clauses with no separating punctuation).

> **Examples:**   The man cried for help, the police came running. (*comma splice*)
>
> The man cried for help the police came running. (*fused sentence*)

Run-on sentences can be corrected in any of the following ways:

> **Revised:**   The man cried for help. The police came running. (divided into two sentences)
>
> The man cried for help; the police came running. (two independent clauses separated by a semicolon, not a comma)
>
> The man cried for help, and the police came running. (two independent clauses joined by a comma and a coordinating conjunction)

Dependent clause
A clause that contains a subject and a verb but that cannot stand alone, as it does not contain a complete thought. A dependent clause always begins with a subordinating conjunction.

Subordinating conjunction
Dependent clauses always begin with subordinating conjunctions: *after, although, as, because, before, even though, if, since, unless, when, where, whereas,* and *while*.

Run-on sentence
Two sentences written as one. It can occur either as a common splice (two independent clauses joined by a comma) or as a fused sentence (two independent clauses with no separating punctuation).

Coordinating conjunction
A coordinating conjunction can join two independent clauses; examples include *and, but, for, nor, or,* and *yet.*

Conjunctive adverbs
Examples include *also, consequently, furthermore, however, moreover, nevertheless, then,* and *therefore.* These should not be used to join two independent clauses.

Parallel construction
Using the same grammatical structure for clauses or phrases that bear the same relationship to some major idea.

As seen above, a comma and a coordinating conjunction can join two independent clauses. **Coordinating conjunctions** include *and, but, for, nor, or,* and *yet.*

However, you cannot use conjunctive adverbs to join two independent clauses. Examples of **conjunctive adverbs** are *also, consequently, furthermore, however, moreover, nevertheless, then,* and *therefore.*

A very common error is to try to use *however* or *therefore* to join two independent clauses. Do not do it.

Incorrect:	The holding in the *Lane* decision would appear to be against our client, however, we do have one counterargument.
Revised:	The holding in the *Lane* decision would appear to be against our client. We do, however, have one counterargument.

4. Use Parallel Construction

Clauses or phrases that bear the same relationship to some major idea should have parallel grammatical structure. When writing lists, be particularly careful about not drifting into variations that lack **parallel construction.**

Incorrect:	The boy ate, he went horseback riding, and he was swimming.
Revised:	The boy ate, went horseback riding, and swam.
Incorrect:	My objections are that the complaint was filed late, no valid cause of action, and the wrong defendant.
Revised:	My objections are that the complaint was filed late, that it does not contain a valid cause of action, and that the plaintiff has sued the wrong defendant.

B. Use the Proper Verb Tense

In legal writing there are two common problems with verb tense: making inappropriate shifts between verb tenses and using present tense for events that happened in the past. The first problem, inappropriate shifts, occurs when a writer begins describing an event in one tense but then, perhaps realizing the wrong tense is being used, switches to another tense. When proofreading, be sure to check for this potential problem.

To correct the second problem, inappropriately using present tense, remember that past tense should always be used for actions that happened in the past. In legal writing these include

1. the facts that make up your client's story,
2. the events that occurred in the cases you read, and
3. what the court said in those cases.

> **Incorrect:**   1. In *Bennett* Mrs. Brown runs home . . . ;
>   2. In *Bennett* a woman sues . . . ; and
>   3. In *Bennett* the court holds that. . . .
> **Revised:**   1. In *Bennett* Mrs. Brown ran home . . . ;
>   2. In *Bennett* a woman sued . . . ; and
>   3. In *Bennett* the court held that. . . .

But use present tense when describing a rule of law.

> **Incorrect:**   In *Bennett* the court held that minors *were* allowed to void contracts that they have signed.
> **Revised:**   In *Bennett* the court held that minors *are* allowed to void contracts that they have signed.

C. Make Sure Pronouns and Antecedents Agree

When you do not want to use a noun, you use a **pronoun** as a substitute. In the following sentence *Mary* is the noun and *her* is the pronoun.

> **Example:**   Mary reviewed her testimony with her attorney.

Because a pronoun (*hers, her, his, him, it, its, them, their, theirs*) substitutes for a noun that has preceded it, the noun is known as an **antecedent**. The pronoun and its antecedent must match as to gender and number. This often becomes a problem when the writer is trying to avoid sexist writing.

> **Incorrect:**   The new computer user may find after many attempts at installing the software by themselves that they need help.

Sometimes you can correct this by making the noun plural.

> **Revised:**   New computer users may find after many attempts at installing the software by themselves that they need help.

Another possibility is to drop the pronoun.

> **Revised:**   The new computer user may find after many attempts at installing the software that help is needed.

Finally, you may need to resort to a "he or she," "his or hers," or "her or him" combination.

> **Revised:**   The new computer user may find after many attempts at installing the software that he or she needs help.

D. Put Modifying Words Close to What They Modify

Misplaced modifiers are a very common problem. Sometimes the result is merely humorous, as in the following example:

> **Example:**   The college has all the money from students deposited in the bank.

Obviously, the college has deposited the money and not the students. Other times, however, a misplaced modifier could cause serious interpretation problems and even litigation. Consider the following example taken from a lease provision:

> **Example:**   If through no fault of Tenant, the apartment becomes uninhabitable, Landlord shall be notified immediately to provide alternative dwelling.

Does this mean that the landlord must be notified immediately or that the landlord must provide an alternative dwelling immediately? In this last example the word *immediately* is referred to as a squinting modifier because you cannot tell if the writer means for it to modify the word that precedes it or the word that follows it. Frequently this happens with the placement of the word *only*.

> **Example:** You may talk with the witness only today.

Does this mean that you can talk with the witness but not with anyone else, such as the defendant, or does this mean that you can talk to the witness today only? Depending on what you mean, you could rewrite the sentence as follows:

> **Example:**   You may talk with only the witness today.
> You may talk with the witness today only.

E. Avoid Punctuation Problems

One area of grammar that may seem the most boring and useless is the area of punctuation. Nothing could be further from the truth. There are too many cases where a comma, or the lack of one, has been the focus of litigation. One example should suffice to emphasize the importance of being careful with punctuation. A will contained the following provision:

> I bequeath and devise my entire estate, both personal and real, . . . in equal shares, absolutely and in fee to my cousin, the said Walter Cassidy; Robert Jamison and William Stivers, tenants on my farm; George E. Smith, who rents my property on Bland Avenue, Shelbyville, Kentucky; and the Kentucky Society for Crippled Children.[1]

Jamison and Stivers argued that they should each receive one-fifth of the bequest. The other three beneficiaries argued that the two men should share one-fourth. Semicolons separated each of the other beneficiaries, whereas Jamison and Stivers were not separated. How would you decide this case? The court awarded the two men one-fifth each. Was the court correct? Only the dead testator knows for sure.

1. Use the Serial Comma

As suggested above, the punctuation problem that gets more attorneys and paralegals into trouble than any other is the one regarding the **serial comma**. In a series of three or more items, use a comma after each item until you reach the final conjunction.

Serial comma
In a series of three or more items use a comma after each item until you reach the final conjunction.

Incorrect:	The boy swam, ran and played.
Revised:	The boy swam, ran, and played.

By always including that final comma you will never have to face the following interpretation problem:

> Sally went to the bookstore to buy book covers in green, red, blue and yellow.

Does this mean she bought three covers: one green, one red, and one blue and yellow? Or did she buy four book covers: one green, one red, one blue, and one yellow?

2. Do Not Use a Comma with Compound Verbs or between a Subject and Its Verb

Do not use a comma with compound subjects, verbs, or objects. Also do not let a comma separate your subject and its verb. Legal writers most often mispunctuate compound verbs.

Incorrect:	The boy ran, and fell down.
Revised:	The boy ran and fell down.

---

[1] Cassidy v. Vanattas, 242 S.W.2d 619, 620 (Ky. App. 1951).

3. Use Commas to Set Off Phrases Containing Nonessential Information

Nonrestrictive phrase
A phrase that is not essential to the sense of a sentence; it should be set off with commas.

Grammarians say that we must set off **nonrestrictive phrases** with commas. What that means is that if the sentence would make sense without the phrase, the phrase is nonrestrictive (i.e., nonessential) and should be set off with commas.

Incorrect:	In the leading case *Dillon v. Legg* the court held that a mother can recover for emotional distress.
Revised:	In the leading case, *Dillon v. Legg,* the court held that a mother can recover for emotional distress.

The sentence would retain its meaning and still make sense without the phrase *Dillon v. Legg.*

A **restrictive phrase** contains essential information.

Restrictive phrase
A phrase that contains essential information; it should not be set off with commas.

Incorrect:	All students, who do not register on time, must pay a $20 late fee.
Revised:	All students who do not register on time must pay a $20 late fee.

Without the phrase "who do not register on time," the sentence reads: "All students must pay a $20 late fee." The phrase contains essential information, the absence of which alters the sentence's meaning. Therefore, it should not be set off with commas.

As a general rule of thumb, use "that" with restrictive phrases and "which" with nonrestrictive phrases.

Example of restrictive:	Courts that recognize spousal immunity usually base their decision on a desire to promote family harmony. (Only some courts recognize spousal immunity.)
Example of nonrestrictive:	Courts, which are forums for justice, decide cases based on the facts presented to them. (All courts are forums for justice.)

4. Forming the Possessive

To form the possessive for singular nouns, use *'s* unless the noun ends in an *s* and it would make the possessive hard to pronounce.

Examples:	child's Bob's James's witness's

Traditionally, however, you should drop the *s* after the apostrophe with some proper names that both end in *s* and have an internal *s* sound.

> **Examples:** Jesus' life

To form the possessive for plural nouns, use *'s* for nouns that do not end in *s* but only an apostrophe for those that end in *s*.

> **Examples:** children's   witnesses'

5. Combining Quotation Marks with Other Punctuation

Periods and commas always belong inside the closing quotation mark.

> **Examples:** The court stated that "the case should be remanded for a new trial."
>
> The court stated that "the case should be remanded for a new trial," and then it reprimanded the prosecuting attorney for his delay tactics.

Semicolons and colons always belong outside the closing quotation mark.

> **Example:** The court stated that "the case should be remanded for a new trial"; the court also reprimanded the prosecuting attorney for his delay tactics.

When they are part of the quotation, place dashes, question marks, and exclamation points inside the closing quotation mark.

> **Example:** The attorney asked his client, "Should we proceed?" before entering the courtroom.

Otherwise, place those marks outside the closing quotation mark.

> **Example:** Did the court state that "the case should be remanded for a new trial"?

PART II: STYLE

> ### Accident Report
>
> The party of the first part hereinafter known as Jack . . . and . . . The party of the second part hereinafter known as Jill . . . Ascended or caused to be ascended an elevation of undetermined height and degree of slope, hereinafter referred to as "hill." Whose purpose it was to obtain, attain, procure, secure, or otherwise gain acquisition to, by any and/or all means available to them a receptacle or container, hereinafter known as "pail," suitable for the transport of a liquid whose chemical properties shall be limited to hydrogen and oxygen, the proportions of which shall not be less than or exceed two parts for the first mentioned element and one part for the latter. Such combination will hereinafter be called "water." On the occasion stated above, it has been established beyond reasonable doubt that Jack did plunge, tumble, topple, or otherwise be caused to lose his footing in a manner that caused his body to be thrust into a downward direction. As a direct result of these combined circumstances, Jack suffered fractures and contusions of his cranial regions. Jill, whether due to Jack's misfortune or not, was known to also tumble in similar fashion after Jack. (Whether the term, "after," shall be interpreted in a spatial or time passage sense, has not been determined.)[2]

Besides following the basic rules of grammar, there are various techniques you can use to increase the clarity and effectiveness of your writing. These techniques include avoiding long paragraphs, using transitions, being concise by eliminating unnecessary words and introductory phrases and by saying it only once, and avoiding the passive voice. This section concludes with some special techniques peculiar to legal writing.

A. Avoid Long Paragraphs

Of course, there is no mechanical rule as to paragraph length. Nonetheless, if you find you have written a paragraph that is over half a page in length, consider whether it is too long. Check to be sure that you have only one major idea in the paragraph.

Trying to develop more than one theme in each paragraph can confuse the reader and require her or him to reread the paragraph. A good check is to

NETNOTE

At the following site, you can find help organized by level: word and sentence, paragraph, and paper: *www.ccc.commnet.edu/grammar/.*

---

[2] The Legal Guide to Mother Goose 7-11 (Don Sandburg trans., 1978).

go back over your document and see whether you can find a topic sentence in each paragraph that states the theme for that paragraph. Then, reading just those sentences from each paragraph, you should be able to follow your argument as it develops throughout your document.

B. Do Not Bury Your Points

A common error is to start a paragraph with "In the case of. . . ." This is a poor writing style for two reasons. First, a reader pays the most attention to the first and last sentences of a paragraph. Therefore, you should place your most important points there rather than burying them in the middle of the paragraph. Second, if you simply start your paragraph with a case description, you have failed to tell the reader why the case is relevant. No one (or at least no one we know) enjoys reading about case law in the abstract. In order to be interested in what you have to say about a given case, the reader must first understand why it is relevant. Lead off with a sentence or clause that will help the reader understand why you will be discussing the next case. At a minimum let the reader know that it is the leading case, the only case, the most recent case, or the like, and place the case citation at the end of the sentence.

Incorrect:	In <u>Bennett v. Bennett</u>, 186 N.E.2d 85 (Mass. 1988), the plaintiff sued to have a contract set aside, arguing that she was only sixteen years old when she signed it.
Revised:	Several cases have dealt with the issue of whether a contract can be set aside if one of the parties was a minor when the contract was signed. For example, in one recent case the plaintiff sued to have the contract set aside, arguing that she was only sixteen years old when she signed it. <u>Bennett v. Bennett</u>, 186 N.E.2d 85 (Mass. 1988).

C. Use Transitions

The type of case introduction in the prior example is one form of **transition**. Transitions help your reader follow the flow of your argument. They provide the link from where you have been to where you are going. On the simplest level, transitions can indicate a sequence: "The first point to be made is. . . . The second point to be made is. . . ." On a more sophisticated level, transitions artfully tie together the preceding thought and the one that follows. Assume a writer has written a paragraph analyzing *Bennett v. Bennett* and the paragraph concludes with the following sentence:

Transition
In writing, a technique used to help your reader move from one thought to the next and to see the connections between them.

> The court therefore held that as the plaintiff was only sixteen at the time she signed the contract, the contract should be set aside as void.

The next paragraph could pick up on the theme presented in the first paragraph by beginning with the following sentence:

> Because Margaret was only fifteen at the time of the contract's formation, her position that her contract should be set aside is consistent with that of the court in <u>Bennett</u>.

D. Be Concise

A taxpayer testified, "As God is my judge, I do not owe this tax." The judge answered, "He's not, I am; and you do."[3] While this may be an extreme example of brevity, it is always a good idea to write concisely so as not to bore your reader. But it is particularly important for lawyers to do so.

One major reason for being as concise as possible is that every unnecessary word serves as a source of potential ambiguity. If you write "null and void" instead of simply "void," you raise the issue of whether there is a difference between something that is only "void" and something that is both "null and void."

Second, those who read an attorney's or paralegal's writing are usually very busy people. Judges, other lawyers, and clients have little time to waste. They want to hear what you have to say and be done with it.

You should remember three guidelines when reviewing something you have written: Eliminate unnecessary words, remove unnecessary introductory phrases, and say it once. By following these guidelines you can condense your writing without sacrificing any of the content.

1. Eliminate Unnecessary Words

There are many compound word combinations that you can replace with a single word. Here are some examples:

At this point in time	Now
At that point in time	Then
Notwithstanding the fact that	Although
There is no doubt but that	Doubtless
The reason why is that	Because
The fact that	(Usually no replacement necessary)

> **Incorrect:** Because of the fact that John shot the victim, he will be found guilty.
>
> **Revised:** Because John shot the victim, he will be found guilty.

---

[3] Judge J. Edgar Murdock of the United States Tax Court, quoted in Brison v. Commissioner of Internal Revenue, T.C. Memo 1983-01, 11.

Finally, there is the attorney's favorite word: *clearly*—as in "Clearly the defendant was negligent." Either the defendant was or was not negligent. Saying the issue is clear will not make it so. In fact, this word often acts as a red flag, raising the reader's suspicions. After all, if you have to bootstrap your argument with words such as *clearly*, perhaps your argument is not that clear.

2. Remove Unnecessary Introductory Phrases

Phrases such as "It is interesting to note that . . ." and "It should be noted in this connection that . . ." are unnecessary filler. When writing a first draft, these phrases are often just what the writer needs to make the pen start moving across the page (or to cause the words to start appearing on the computer monitor). Use these phrases for that purpose, but then go back and strike them out. A good test is this: If the sentence makes sense without the introduction, cross it out.

3. Say It Once

If you find phrases such as "in other words" sprinkled throughout your writing, check to make sure that you are not engaging in some unnecessary duplication. Often a writer will finish a sentence and then think of a better way to say the same thing. We all have doubts now and then about just how clear our points are. Therefore, when this better approach occurs to us, instead of recognizing it as the better alternative we leave in both sentences. Instead try to combine the two approaches, or simply pick the better one and drop the other.

E. Avoid the Passive Voice

Use the active voice whenever possible. The **passive voice** is a weaker form of writing. In the passive voice the subject is acted on, but it is often unclear who is doing the acting.

Passive voice
A form of writing where the subject of the sentence is being acted on; opposite of **active voice.**

> **Examples:** The ball was thrown by Mary. (*passive voice*)
> The ball was thrown. (*passive voice with actor missing so that it is unclear who threw the ball*)
>
> The ruling was made by the trial judge that the defendant was guilty. (*passive voice*)
> The ruling was made that the defendant was guilty. (*passive voice with actor missing so that it is unclear who made the ruling*)

Such ambiguity has its place in legal writing but only if you plan it.

The best clues that you are using the passive voice are the "by" construction, as in the first and third examples ("by Mary," "by the trial judge") and the absence of the actor entirely, as in the second and fourth examples.

Active voice
A form of writing where the subject of the sentence does the acting; opposite of **passive voice**.

Active voice is just that—active. In the **active voice** the subject of the sentence acts.

> **Examples:**   Mary threw the ball.
> The trial judge ruled that the defendant was guilty.

Avoid the passive voice whenever possible. Usually, because of the "by" construction, it adds needless weight to your writing through the addition of useless words. When, to solve that problem, the writer omits the "by" construction, ambiguity often results. Consider the following lease provision, and try to determine who must report what to whom:

> When conditions affecting the habitability of the rental property are discovered, they must be promptly reported and failure to do so shall constitute a material breach of this lease.

Does the landlord have to report defects to the tenant, or does the tenant have to disclose conditions that affect the habitability to the landlord? Perhaps each party must disclose such conditions to the other party. Ambiguity such as this is an open invitation to a lawsuit.

The third reason for avoiding the passive voice is that it is a less powerful form. This becomes particularly important to the legal writer in advocacy writing, but it is something to keep in mind for any form of writing.

There are times when the passive voice is appropriate. But you must know when those times are and then use the passive voice by design and not by inadvertence. Specifically, there are four occasions when you may wish to use the passive voice:

1. When the writer wants to highlight the action instead of the actor.

> **Example:**   The man had been murdered.

2. When the actor is unknown.

> **Example:**   The dead body had been left in the woods.

3. When the writer wants to state a general principle.

> **Example:**   All men are created equal.

4. When the writer wants to disassociate the actor from the statement.

> **Example:** The victim was robbed.
> **Not:** Our client robbed the victim.

F. Special Rules for Legal Writing

As we mentioned at the beginning of this appendix, good legal writing is simply good writing. If you possess a clear, understandable style, you are well on your way to being a good legal writer. However, because you will be writing about the law and the legal system, you need to know a few special rules.

1. Avoid Legalese

Avoid the temptation to use "legalese," archaic legal terminology, to impress your reader. Several states have passed legislation requiring that all legal documents be written in plain English. Although many attorneys are still resisting the plain English movement, you should avoid legalese whenever possible.

Whenever you find yourself tempted to use legal sounding words, such as *wherefore, aforesaid,* and especially **said,** ask yourself if there is a less stilted English word that can serve your purpose better. Consider the following example, and ask yourself whether the word *said* adds anything or actually creates ambiguity.

> **Example:** The defendant was seated inside a station wagon. Parked next to him was a Corvette. Said car was green.

Usually, words such as *said* only give the illusion of precision and bog down the writing with heavy-sounding legal words.

2. Make the Court and Not the Court Opinion the Actor

You can avoid another common writing error if you remember that inanimate objects cannot act. Always make the court and not the court opinion do the holding.

> **Incorrect:** Lewis held that. . . .
> **Revised:** The court in Lewis held that. . . .

3. Avoid Unnecessary Variation

If you have written "the car" four times in a paragraph, you may be tempted to switch to "the motor vehicle." Avoid the temptation. You may

leave your reader wondering if you are talking about both a car and a motor vehicle. As this example illustrates, variation can cause serious interpretation problems if your reader thinks you mean to refer to two separate objects when you mean to refer to only one.

4. Do Not Use the First Person

The generally accepted rule in legal writing is to avoid using the first person. You want the emphasis to be on what you are saying and not on the fact that it is you who is saying it. Whenever you find yourself starting a sentence with a phrase such as "I think the court will hold that . . . ," go back and delete the first two words. Because you are the author, the reader already knows that these are your thoughts and no one else's. The reader also knows that there is no way that you can be 100 percent certain of what you write. Therefore, there is no need to soften the certitude with which you write by inserting "I think."

The one time when you can use the first person is when you are referring to one of your firm's clients, as in "Our client wishes to settle." However, even in that case some purists would prefer to use the client's name, as in "Ms. Brown wishes to settle."

5. Do Not Use Contractions

Legal writing is formal writing, and in formal writing there is no place for contractions. Contractions are acceptable only when you are writing an informal note for someone within the firm or, depending on the policy of your firm, occasionally a letter to a client.

6. Do Not Ask Your Reader Questions

It is your job to provide answers, not to ask your reader questions. There is nothing more annoying than to be reading someone's legal analysis only to be stopped by a series of questions.

> **Example:**   The court in <u>Lewis</u> held that liability is limited to automobile accidents. Will that court extend its holding to our client's facts? Will the court limit its holding to exclude our client's facts?

The reader will probably be thinking, "I don't know. That's what I'm paying you to tell me." When you find yourself posing questions, simply rephrase them as issues.

> **Revised:**   The court in <u>Lewis</u> held that liability is limited to automobile accidents. That raises the issue of whether the court will extend that holding to our client's facts or limit it to the facts of <u>Lewis</u>.

7. That Case/This Case

The convention is to refer to a cited case as **that case** and to your client's case as **this case**.

> **Example:** The court in <u>Lewis</u> held that liability is limited to automobile accidents. In that case the husband had been driving and the wife was a passenger when the accident occurred.

That case
A case that you are citing.

This case
Your client's case.

8. Written Numbers versus Numerals

There are times when you should write out numbers as opposed to using numerals. In text you write out the following numbers:

- zero to ninety-nine;
- any round number, such as one hundred; and
- any number that begins a sentence.

In footnotes you follow the same rules except you write out only the numbers zero through nine. When you have a series of numbers in a sentence, some of which you should write out and some of which you should give as numerals, use all numerals.

> **Example:** There were 2 attorneys, 40 witnesses, and 105 documents.

9. Do Not Eliminate the Articles "A," "An," and "The"

Leaving out articles makes your writing choppy and hard to follow. This style probably comes from students mistakenly thinking that their writing will appear more "lawyerly" if they adopt a headnote style of writing.

> **Example:** A person injured in fall from automobile parking floor to ground below while seeking shelter from rain was at most gratuitous or bare licensee.
>
> **Revised:** A person injured in *a* fall from *an* automobile parking floor to *the* ground below while seeking shelter from *the* rain was at most *a* gratuitous or bare licensee.

PART III: CORRECT WORD USAGE

Correct word usage simply means choosing the correct word to say exactly what you mean. At times this may require you to consult a dictionary or thesaurus. The following is a list of the most commonly misused words.

And/Or

There is much debate as to whether the *and/or* combination is acceptable. Many writers believe it is cumbersome and requires the reader to do too much work to understand its meaning. For example, in the phrase "the husband and/or the wife," the reader must translate that to mean the husband, the wife, or both. Therefore, many writers prefer it to be written just that way.

Because/Since

Because denotes a causal relationship. *Since* refers to time. Using *since* to also denote a causal relationship can cause ambiguity.

> **Examples:** Because he admitted his guilt, he has been held without bail. (The reason he is being held without bail is that he admitted his guilt.)
>
> Since he admitted his guilt, he has been held without bail. (Since the time he admitted his guilt, he has been held without bail.)

Court/court

Unless it starts a sentence, the word *Court* stands for the U.S. Supreme Court. Use *court* when referring to other courts.

Have/Of

In speech it often sounds as though someone is saying "of" when it really is "have." In writing, always use *would have, could have, should have*, not *would of, could of, should of*.

Its/It's

Its is a pronoun. *It's* is a contraction for *it is*.

> **Examples:** The car wobbled on its loose axle.
>
> It's a beautiful day.

That/Which

That is used for restrictive or essential phrases.

> **Example:** He went to the store that was around the corner to buy some bread.

The phrase "that was around the corner" describes which store and is essential for identifying the store.

> **Example:** He went to George's Grocery, which was around the corner, to buy some bread.

The phrase "which was around the corner" simply further describes the store that was already clearly identified as George's Grocery. Therefore, it provides nonessential information.

Their/There/They're *Their* is a possessive pronoun. *There* represents a place. *They're* is a contraction for *they are.*

> **Example:** They're going to their house. Once they are there, they will have supper.

Which/Who Use *which* for things and *who* for people.
Who's/Whose *Who's* is a contraction for *who is. Whose* is a possessive pronoun.

> **Examples:** Who's going to the store?
>
> Whose jacket is this?

Your/You're *Your* is a possessive pronoun. *You're* is a contraction for *you are.*

> **Example:** You're going to have to finish your report.

SUMMARY

Good legal writing starts with good writing. Follow the basic rules of grammar by using proper sentence structure, avoiding sentence fragments and run-on sentences, and using parallel construction. Also use the proper verb tense. Make sure your pronouns agree with your antecedents. Put modifying words close to what they modify, and be aware of common punctuation problems.

While you are encouraged to develop your own style, you should follow certain style guidelines. Avoid long paragraphs, and be careful that you do not bury your points in the middle of your paragraphs. Use transitions between paragraphs. Be concise by eliminating unnecessary words and phrases. Because the active voice is stronger,

use it whenever possible. And when engaged in legal writing, do not fall into the trap of using legalese. Keep the court and not the court opinion the subject of your sentences. Avoid unnecessary variation and the use of the first person. In formal writing do not use contractions, and do not ask your reader questions. Be aware of the differences between "that case" and "this case." Know when to use numerals and when to write numbers out. Finally, do not write like a headnote editor. Include the articles—*a, an,* and *the.*

||| REVIEW QUESTIONS

Pages 557 through 567

Correct the following sentences.

1. On any given day a paralegal can be asked to perform any of the following tasks, to interview clients, research in the library, drafting of documents, filed pleadings, or writing client letters.
2. The complaint, which contains theories based on both tort and contract law, alleging that the product was defective, was filed with the wrong court.
3. Even though the attorney made a long-winded and impassioned plea to the jury at the end of the trial.
4. The attorney made a long-winded and impassioned plea to the jury at the end of the trial the jury found the defendant guilty.
5. In *Jones*, a child is injured by his father's negligence. The court decides that children were able to sue for parental negligence.
6. Even though a criminal defendant may engage in plea bargaining, they still may receive a different sentence from the judge.
7. The judge, denied the plaintiff's request, ordered a new trial and set the new trial date.
8. All paralegals, who are members of the local paralegal association, have access to the job bank information.
9. He went over to Bob Browns house where he saw the Browns collection of stamps.
10. The witness stated that "I ran away from the accident", and he testified that he was "scared".

Pages 568 through 573

Correct the following sentences.

11. In *Black* the court held that only involuntary intoxication could be a defense to the formation of a contract. (first sentence in a paragraph)
12. It is interesting to note that notwithstanding the fact that the defendant was found guilty, at that point in time clearly the defendant still felt his attorney had done a good job of defending him.
13. The decision by the jury to convict the defendant surprised no one.

Pages 573 through 575

Correct the following sentences.

14. In *Jones v. Warner* the court felt that only those who were involuntarily intoxicated could be excused from their contractual obligations.
15. Said court also stated that two beers wouldn't be sufficient to prove intoxication.
16. Will the court in our case say that four beers are sufficient to prove intoxication? Would six be enough? What of two whiskeys?
17. There are 5 cases that deal with intoxication.
18. Defendant driving car after drinking five beers was found to be intoxicated.

Pages 575 through 577

Correct the following sentences.

19. The plaintiff can bring suit for negligence against the city for injuries he sustained in the accident. Even though his contributory negligence may bar him from recovery.
20. The woman was frightened by a man she described as seedy, it was only after she struck him with a rock that she discovered he was an undercover police officer.
21. During an autopsy, looking for the cause of death, the deceased is examined by the pathologist.
22. The new computer system offers four advantages for our firm:
    1. it includes 15 software packages
    2. the warranty extends to 160 days
    3. provides a full-scale training program
    4. state-of-the-art features are included.
23. The enclosed forms should be completed by you no later than August 15.
24. The depositions proved to be very revealing, however, our client has decided to settle.
25. *Dillon* holds that under certain circumstances a bystander may recover for emotional distress.

Appendix D

NetNotes

BUSINESS INFORMATION

Business ownership information, such as the names of the resident agent and the corporate officers—Go to *www.westlaw.com* (Westlaw) or *www.lexis.com* (Lexis).

The Electronic Data Gathering, Analysis, and Retrieval (EDGAR) system—Go to either *www.sec.gov/edgar/searchedgar/webusers.html* or *www.freeedgar.com*.

Information on the Americans with Disabilities Act—Go to the U.S. Department of Justice site at *www.usdoj.gov/crt/ada/adahom1.htm* or the Americans with Disabilities Act Document Center at *www.jan.wvu.edu/links/adalinks.htm*.

CITATION RULES

You can find additional material, examples, updates, and a Frequently Asked Questions list at the ALWD Citation Manual's web site, *www.alwd.org*.

"Introduction to Basic Legal Citation," an on-line tutorial designed to teach the Bluebook rules—Go to *www.law.cornell.edu/citation*.

COMMERCIAL ON-LINE PROVIDERS

Lexis—*www.lexis.com* or *www.lexisone.com*.

Westlaw—*www.westlaw.com*.

Findlaw—*www.findlaw.com*.

VersusLaw—*www.versuslaw.com*.

Loislaw—*www.loislaw.com*.

COURT SYSTEM

Map of the federal circuits with links to their cases—Go to *www.law.emory.edu/ FEDCTS*. Note that FEDCTS must be typed in all caps.

Biographies of the U.S. Supreme Court justices—Go to *http://supremecourtus. gov/about/biographiescurrent.pdf*.

Information on specific state courts—Go to the National Center for State Courts, *www.ncsconline.org/D_KIS/info_court_web_sites.html*.

Information on federal courts—Go to either the federal judiciary home page at *www.uscourts.gov* or the Federal Judicial Center home page at *www.fjc.gov*.

The U.S. Supreme Court—Go to *www.supremecourtus.gov*.

Read about and see video clips of current trials at *www.courttv.com*.

CRIMINAL LAW

Information on hate crimes and the Laramie Project can be found at a web site supported by the Southern Poverty Law Center—Go to *www.tolerance.org*.

The American Anti-Defamation League has an article on hate crimes on its web site at *www.adl.org/99hatecrime/intro.asp*.

The Southern Center for Human Rights represents defendants facing the death penalty. To read about the center's work in that and other areas of criminal law—Go to *www.schr.org*.

The U.S. Department of Justice maintains statistics about crimes and victims at *www.ojp.usdoj.gov/bjs*.

GOVERNMENT SITES

The EEOC home page is located at *www.eeoc.gov*.

The FBI maintains a web site at *www.fbi.gov*.

The White House's web site is *www.whitehouse.gov*.

Both the House and Senate maintain web sites at *www.house.gov* and *www.senate.gov*.

The U.S. Supreme Court's web site is located at *http://supremecourtus.gov*.

GRAMMAR

Grammar Bytes! at *www.chompchomp.com/menu.htm*.

Help organized by level: word and sentence, paragraph, and paper at *www.ccc. commnet.edu/grammar*.

LEGAL ETHICS

Developments in legal ethics and links to the states' Rules of Professional Conduct or Code of Professional Responsibility and to their ethics opinions— Go to *www.law.cornell.edu/ethics* and *www.legalethics.com*.

You can locate the ABA Model Rules of Professional Conduct at *www.abanet. org/cpr/mrpc/mrpc_toc.html*.

NALA's Code of Ethics and Professional Responsibility—Go to *www.nala.org/ 98model.htm*.

NFPA's Model Code of Ethics—Go to NFPA's home page, *www.paralegals.org*, and click on "Professional Development."

To view the ABA Model Guidelines on the Utilization of Paralegal Services—Go to *www.abanet.org/legalservices/paralegals*.

LEGAL NEWS

Start at Findlaw for Legal Professionals: *www.findlaw.com*.

LEGAL SEARCH ENGINES

There are various search engines that can assist you with your Internet legal research. Two that have been designed specifically for legal research are *www.lawcrawler.com* and *http://www.lawguru.com/search/lawsearch.html*.

ORGANIZATIONS

American Arbitration Association—*www.adr.org*.

American Association for Paralegal Education (AAfPE)—*www.aafpe.org*.

American Bar Association (ABA)—*www.abanet.org*.

American Civil Liberties Union—*www.aclu.org*.

Court Appointed Special Advocates (CASA)—*www.nationalcasa.org*.

International Paralegal Management Association (IPMA)—*www.paralegalmana gement.org*.

National Association of Legal Assistants (NALA)—*www.nala.org.*

National Federation of Paralegal Associations (NFPA)—*www.paralegals.org.*

PRIMARY MATERIAL

U.S. Supreme Court opinions dating back to the 1800s—Start at Findlaw: *www.findlaw.com/casecode/supreme.html.*

Federal appellate court opinions—Start at Findlaw: *www.findlaw.com/casecode/index.html.* Select your circuit.

State court opinions—Start at Findlaw: *www.findlaw.com/casecode/index.html.* Select your state.

Federal statutes and regulations—Start at Findlaw: *www.findlaw.com.casecode/index.html.* Select the US Code or the Code of Federal Regulation.

State statutes and regulations—Start at Findlaw: *www.findlaw.com/casecode/index.html.* Select your state.

Current information on federal legislation—A good source is *http://thomas.loc.gov*, provided by the Library of Congress.

The Declaration of Independence—Go to the National Archives web site: *www.archives.gov/national_archives_experience/charters/declaration.html.*

The Constitution at *www.archives.gov/national_archives_experience/charters/constitution.html* or *http://caselaw.findlaw.com/data/constitution/articles.html.*

The Bill of Rights at *www.archives.gov/national_archives_experience/charters/bill_of_rights.html* or *http://caselaw.findlaw.com/data/constitution/amendments.html.*

The Federal Rules of Evidence—*www.law.cornell.edu/rules/fre/overview.html* or *judiciary.house.gov/media/pdfs/printers/108th/evid2004.pdf.*

TORTS

Expert witnesses—A feature of Findlaw, go to *http://marketcenter.findlaw.com/expert_witnesses.html.*

Medical information—You can find current medical news at *www.medscape.com.* The Cancer Web at *cancerweb.ncl.ac.uk/omd* contains an on-line medical dictionary.

Consumer Product Safety Commission—*www.cpsc.gov.*

UNIFORM LAWS

The Uniform Commercial Code as revised through 1992—Go to *www.law. cornell.edu/ucc/ucc.table.html.*

The Uniform Probate Code—Go to *www.law.cornell.edu/uniform/probate. html.*

Various uniform laws governing the family, such as the Uniform Child Custody Jurisdiction Act, the Uniform Interstate Family Support Act, the Uniform Premarital Agreement Act, and the Uniform Marriage and Divorce Act—Go to *www.law.cornell.edu/uniform/vol9.html.*

Glossary

Abstract A condensed history of the title to real property, which includes the chain of ownership and a record of all liens, taxes, or other encumbrances that may impair the title.

Abuse of process Misusing the criminal or civil court process.

Acceptance In contract law, an act by the offeree indicating agreement to be bound to the contract.

Accessory Also referred to as an **accomplice**; a person who assists the principal in the preparation of the crime.

Accessory after the fact A person who aids the principal after the commission of the crime.

Accomplice Also known as a *principal in the second degree;* a person who assists the principal with the crime or with the preparation of the crime.

Accord and satisfaction An accord is an agreement to do something different than originally promised. The satisfaction is the performance of the accord.

Acquit To determine that a criminal defendant is not guilty of the crime with which he or she is charged.

Active listening The process of signaling that you are really listening, accomplished by using verbal and nonverbal clues, paraphrasing, and reflecting the client's feelings.

Active voice A form of writing where the subject of the sentence does the acting; opposite of **passive voice.**

Actual cause Also known as **cause in fact;** this is measured by the "but for" standard: But for the defendant's actions, the plaintiff would not have been injured.

Actual damages See **Compensatory damages.**

Actus reus Bad act.

Adhesion contract A contract formed where the weaker party has no realistic bargaining power. Typically a form contract is offered on a "take it or leave it" basis.

Adjudicatory hearing A mechanism through which parties to a dispute can present arguments and evidence about their case to an administrative law judge.

Administrative law Rules and regulations created by administrative agencies.

Administrative law judge Another name for a **hearing officer.**

Administrative regulations Rules, regulations, orders, and decisions created by administrative agencies under their authority to interpret specific statutes.

Administrator/administratrix A person appointed by the court to carry out the directions and requests of someone's will.

ADR See **Alternative dispute resolution.**

Advance sheets The first printing of a court decision before it appears in a hardbound reporter.

Adverse possession A transfer of real property rights that occurs after someone other than the owner has had actual, open, adverse, and exclusive use of the property for a statutorily determined number of years.

Affinity Persons related to the decedent by marriage.

Affirm A decision is affirmed when the litigants appeal the trial court decision and the higher court agrees with what the lower court has done.

Affirmative action plan A temporary plan designed to remedy past discrimination by using race or sex as a "plus factor" in employment settings or admission to educational programs.

Affirmative defense A defense whereby the defendant offers new evidence to avoid judgment.

Agency adoption An adoption in which a licensed agency assumes responsibility for screening adoptive parents and matching them with available children.

Agent Someone who has the power to act in the place of another.

Alibi defense A defense requiring proof that the defendant could not have been at the scene of the crime.

Alien corporation A corporation formed in another country.

Alimony Also known as **maintenance** or **support**; financial support and other forms of assistance required to supply the "necessities" of life.

Alternative dispute resolution (ADR) Techniques for resolving conflicts that are alternatives to full-scale litigation. The two most common are **arbitration** and **mediation.**

American Association for Paralegal Education (AAfPE) A national organization of paralegal programs that promotes high standards for paralegal education.

American Bar Association (ABA) A national voluntary organization of lawyers.

American Bar Association approval A voluntary process; approval by the American Bar Association indicates that a paralegal program meets ABA standards.

American Jurisprudence Second (Am. Jur. 2d) A general legal encyclopedia that summarizes the entire body of American law.

American Law Reports (ALR) ALR contains the full text of leading court opinions, followed by a discussion of the issue with references to cases from around the country. Only selected topics are covered, but they are covered in more depth than you will find in an encyclopedia.

Amicus curiae Someone who, with the court's permission, intervenes in litigation, usually on appeal, to influence the decision. Also known as a **friend of the court.**

Analogize To find similarities between two situations.

Analogous Similar; analogous cases involve similar facts and rules of law.

Annotated codes Private publications that include not only the statutes arranged by subject matter but also editorial material, such as legislative history and summaries of court decisions that have interpreted the statutes.

Annotated statutes See **Annotated codes.**

Annotations Editorial features, such as court decision summaries and references to other sources of information, added by the editor to assist the researcher.

Annulment A legal (or religious) judgment that a valid marriage never existed.

Answer The defendant's reply to the complaint. It may contain statements of denial, admission, or lack of knowledge and affirmative defenses.

Antecedent When a pronoun (*hers, her, his, him, it, its, them, their, theirs*) substitutes for a noun that has preceded it, the noun is known as an antecedent.

Anti-heart-balm statute A law that prohibits lawsuits for such things as breach of a promise of marriage, alienation of affection, and seduction of a person over the legal age of consent.

Appeal To ask a higher court to review the actions of a lower court.

Appealable issues Questions that can form the basis for an appeal.

Appellant or petitioner The party in a lawsuit who has initiated an appeal.

Appellate brief An attorney's written argument presented to an appeals court, setting forth a statement of the law as it should be applied to the client's facts.

Appellate courts Courts that determine whether lower courts have made errors of law.

Appellate jurisdiction The power of a higher court to review and modify the decision of a lower court.

Appellee or respondent The party in a lawsuit against whom an appeal has been filed.

Appropriation An intentional unauthorized exploitive use of another person's personality, name, or picture for the defendant's benefit.

Arbitration An ADR mechanism whereby the parties submit their disagreement to a third party whose decision is binding.

Arraignment A criminal proceeding at which the court informs the defendant of the charges being brought against him or her and the defendant enters a plea.

Arrest Occurs when the police restrain a person's freedom and charge the person with a crime.

Arrest warrant A court order directing the arrest of a person.

Arson The malicious burning of the house or property of another.

Articles of incorporation The primary document needed to form a corporation.

Artisan's lien The right to retain an interest in property until a worker has been paid for his or her labor.

Assault An intentional act that creates a reasonable apprehension of an immediate harmful or offensive physical contact.

Assigned counsel A private attorney paid by the state on a contractual basis to represent an indigent client.

Assignee A person to whom contract rights are assigned.

Assignment The transfer by one of the original parties to the contract of part or all of his or her interest to a third party.

Assignor A person who assigns contract rights.

Assumption In logic, a belief that justifies one in arguing a conclusion.

Assumption of the risk Voluntarily and knowingly subjecting oneself to danger.

At-will employment When an employee has not signed a formal contract with the employer governing the employment relationship.

Attachment If a creditor either possesses the collateral or has a signed **security agreement,** and gave something of value and if the debtor has rights in the collateral, the creditor's interest in the security is said to have attached.

Attorney Lawyer; a person licensed by a court to practice law.

Attorney-client privilege A rule of evidence that prevents an attorney or a paralegal from being compelled to testify about confidential client information.

Attorney general The chief legal officer of the federal or a state government.

Authentication Proof that the evidence is what it is said to be.

Bail Money or something else of value that is held by the government to ensure the defendant's appearance in court.

Bailee The party taking temporary control of personal property during a bailment.

Bailiff An officer of the court who is responsible for maintaining order in the courtroom.

Bailment A temporary transfer of personal property to someone other than the owner for a specified purpose.

Bailor The owner of the personal property that is being temporarily transferred as part of a bailment.

Bankruptcy judges Appointed for set terms, they handle bankruptcy matters.

Battered woman's or spouse's syndrome Being the victim of repeated attacks, self-defense sometimes is allowed to the victim, even when the victim is not in immediate danger.

Battery An intentional act that creates a harmful or offensive physical contact. Can form the basis for either a tort or a criminal action.

Bearer paper Has written on its front a statement that it is payable to cash or payable to the bearer, or has a signature on the back, causing it to be indorsed in blank.

Bench trial A trial conducted without a jury.

Beneficiary The person named in a will, insurance policy, or trust who receives a benefit.

Bequest Also known as a **legacy;** a gift of personal property in a will.

Best evidence rule The rule requiring that the original document be produced at trial.

Beyond a reasonable doubt The standard of proof used in criminal trials. The proof must be so conclusive and complete that all reasonable doubts regarding the facts are removed from the jurors' minds.

Bilateral contract A contract where a promise is exchanged for a promise.

Bill A proposed law as presented to a legislature.

Billable hours The number of hours, or parts of an hour, that can be charged to a specific client.

Bill of Rights The first ten amendments to the U.S. Constitution.

Black letter law Generally accepted legal principles.

Bluebook A book originally written by a group of law students to provide a uniform method for citations in law reviews; contains detailed rules for all forms of citation.

Board of directors The group responsible for the management of a corporation.

Boilerplate Standard language found in a particular type of legal document.

Bona fide occupational qualification (BFOQ) A defense to an overt discrimination claim, alleging that the qualification is necessary to the essence of the business operation.

Booking The process after arrest that includes taking the defendant's personal information, giving the defendant an opportunity to read and sign a *Miranda* card, and allowing the defendant the opportunity to use a telephone.

Bribery Offering something of value to a public official with the purpose of influencing that official's actions.

Brief Either a short written summary of a court opinion or a written argument presented to a court. See **Appellate brief.**

Brief answer In a law office memorandum, the brief answer gives the reader a short, specific answer to the question presented.

Broad holding A statement of the court's decision in which the facts are either omitted or given in very general terms so that it will apply to a wider range of cases.

Burden of production   The necessity to produce some evidence, but it need not be so strong as to convince the trier of fact of its truth.

Burden of proof   The necessity of proving the truth of the matter asserted.

Bureau of National Affairs (BNA)   A private publishing company that publishes legal materials, including United States Law Week.

Burglary   Breaking into and entering a building with the intent of committing a felony.

"But for" standard   See **Actual cause**.

Buyer in the ordinary course of business   Someone who buys a product in good faith and without knowledge that someone else has a security interest in the goods.

Canons of construction   General principles that guide the courts in their interpretation of statutes.

Capital crime   A crime for which the death sentence can be imposed.

Caption   The heading section of a pleading that contains the names of the parties, the name of the court, the title of the action, the docket or file number, and the name of the pleading.

Case briefing   A method for summarizing court opinions.

Case citation   Information that tells the reader the name of the case, where it can be located, the court that decided it, and the year it was decided. The Bluebook gives precise rules as to how case citations are to be written.

Case history   Either prior or subsequent procedural history of the case cited.

Case management   Managing the flow of paperwork involved in handling client cases.

Case of first impression   A type of case that the court has never faced before.

Case reporters   Books that contain appellate court decisions. There are both official and unofficial reporters.

Cause of action   A claim that based on the law and the facts is sufficient to support a lawsuit. If the plaintiff does not state a valid cause of action in the complaint, the court will dismiss it.

Cause in fact   See **Actual cause**.

Caveat emptor   Let the buyer beware.

Censure   A public or private statement that an attorney's conduct violated the code of ethics.

Certificated   The status of having received a certificate documenting that the person has successfully completed an educational program.

Certification   A method of recognizing accomplishment administered by nongovernmental bodies.

Certified   The status of being formally recognized by a nongovernmental organization for having met special criteria, such as fulfilling educational requirements and passing an exam, established by that organization.

Certified Legal Assistant   A registered trademark of the National Association of Legal Assistants.

Certiorari   See **Writ of certiorari**.

Challenge for cause   A method for excusing a prospective juror based on the juror's inability to serve in an unbiased manner.

Charging the jury   The judge informs the jurors of the law they need to know to make their decision.

Charitable immunity   The prohibition against suing charitable institutions.

Chattel   Personal property.

Check   A specialized form of a draft in which a bank depositor names a specific payee to whom funds are to be paid from the drawer's account.

Checks and balances   Division among governmental branches so that each branch acts as a check on the power of the other two, thereby maintaining a balance of power among the three branches.

Child abuse   Intentional harm to a child's physical or mental well-being.

Child neglect   The negligent failure to provide a child with the necessaries of life.

Child support   Money that the noncustodial parent contributes to assist the custodial parent in paying for a child's food, shelter, clothing, medical care, and education.

Circumstantial evidence   Indirect evidence, used to prove facts by implication.

Citation   A stylized form for giving the reader information about a legal authority, generally including the name of the authority, its date, and specifics such as volume and page numbers to help the reader locate it. For court opinions, a citation includes the name of the case, where it can be located, the name of the court that decided it, and the year it was decided. A statutory citation is a formalized method for referring to a statute's chapter (or title) and section numbers. The Bluebook gives precise rules as to how citations are to be written. See **Bluebook**.

Cited case   The case you are Shepardizing.

Citing case   A case listed in Shepard's that cites your case.

Civil action   A lawsuit brought to enforce an individual right or gain payment for an individual wrong.

Civil law   Law that deals with harm to an individual.

Class action suit A lawsuit brought by a person as a representative for a group of people who have been similarly injured.

Clear and convincing An evidentiary standard that requires more than a preponderance of the evidence but less than beyond a reasonable doubt.

Clear title Also known as **marketable title**; an ownership right that is free from encumbrances or other defects.

Clearly erroneous Standard used by appellate courts when reviewing a trial court's findings of fact.

Client confidentiality An ethical rule requiring that attorneys and paralegals maintain their clients' secrets.

Client trust account A bank account used to hold money belonging to a client or to a third party.

Closed questions Specific questions that usually demand very short or yes-no answers.

Closely held corporation A relatively small business operation in which one person or the members of a family own all the stock.

Closing statement An itemized allocation of all the costs and moneys exchanged among the various parties, including financial institutions and real estate brokers, when a property is sold.

Closing table A table located in digest volumes and pocket parts indicating the last volume and page numbers for the reporters included in that digest.

Code A compilation of federal or state statutes in which the statutes are organized by subject matter rather than by year of enactment.

Code of Federal Regulations (C.F.R.) A compilation of federal administrative regulations arranged by agency.

Code of Massachusetts Regulations A compilation of Massachusetts administrative regulations arranged by agency.

Codicil A supplement or addition to a will that modifies, explains, or adds to its provisions.

Codification The process of organizing statutes by subject matter.

Codification of the common law The process of legislative enactment of areas of the law previously governed solely by the common law.

Collateral heir One who has the same ancestors, but does not descend from the decedent.

Comma splice A type of run-on sentence; two independent clauses joined by a comma.

Commercial impracticability An argument that a contract has become too costly for one of the parties.

Commercial paper A written promise or order to pay a certain sum of money.

Committee hearing Legislative committees often hold public hearings where interested parties can testify about a proposed law. The transcript of the hearing becomes a part of the statute's legislative history.

Committee report When a legislative committee holds public hearings on proposed legislation, the result of those hearings is sometimes published in a committee report, which becomes part of the statute's legislative history.

Common law Law created by the courts.

Common-law marriage A marriage that has not been solemnized but in which the parties have mutually agreed to enter into a relationship in which they accept all the duties and responsibilities that correspond to those of marriage.

Community property states States that classify all property acquired by either the husband or the wife during the marriage, with the exception of gifts or inheritance, as marital property to be equally distributed between the spouses at the time of the divorce.

Comparative negligence A method for measuring the relative negligence of the plaintiff and the defendant, with a commensurate sharing of the compensation for the injuries.

Compensatory damages Money awarded to a plaintiff in payment for his or her actual losses. Compare **punitive damages**.

Competency Relates to the fitness of a person to perform certain legal actions, such as, meeting the minimum requirements to give testimony in court (must be able to explain to the jury what was seen or heard) or the requirements to serve on a jury (must be able to hear and follow testimony and arguments); the defendant's mental state at the time of the trial (must be able to understand the proceedings and communicate with his or her attorney), a person's mental state at the time a will is signed (must be of "sound mind," know what property he or she possesses and to whom it should go); or a person's ability to make a binding contract (must be an adult without severe mental impairments).

Complaint The pleading that begins a lawsuit.

Complete defense A defense that, if proven, relieves the defendant of all criminal responsibility.

Compulsory joinder When a person must be brought into a lawsuit as either a plaintiff or a defendant.

Concluding paragraph The final paragraph in a written legal analysis that summarizes the writer's conclusions.

Concurrent conflict of interest Simultaneously representing adverse clients.

Concurrent jurisdiction   When more than one court has jurisdiction to hear a case.

Concurring opinion   An opinion that agrees with the majority's result but disagrees with its reasoning.

Conditional fee estate   The current owner of the land retains ownership only as long as certain conditions are met.

Cone of silence   See **Ethical wall.**

Confidentiality   The ethical rule prohibiting attorneys and paralegals from disclosing information regarding a client or a client's case.

Conflict of interest   The ethical rule prohibiting attorneys and paralegals from working for opposing sides in a case.

Conjunctive adverbs   Examples include *also, consequently, furthermore, however, moreover, nevertheless, then,* and *therefore.* These should not be used to join two independent clauses.

Consanguinity   See **Kindred.**

Consequential damages   See **Special damages.**

Consideration   Something of value exchanged to form the basis of a contract; each side must give consideration for a valid contract to exist.

Consortium   See **Loss of consortium.**

Conspiracy   An agreement to commit an unlawful act.

Constitutional court   A court established by Article III of the U.S. Constitution.

Constitutional law   The study of the U.S. Constitution, the legal framework it established, and the rights it protects.

Constructive   Not factually true, but accepted by the courts as being legally true.

Constructive delivery   When actual delivery is impossible but the court decides that enough was done to prove intent to relinquish title and control.

Constructive eviction   An act by a landlord that makes the premises unfit or unsuitable for occupancy.

Constructive knowledge   Not actual knowledge but the knowledge the person should have if reasonable care is taken to be informed.

Content neutrality   Laws may not limit free expression on the basis of whether the speech's content supports or opposes any particular position.

Contextual analysis   A form of statutory analysis in which meaning is inferred from the statement of legislative purpose and other sections of the statute.

Contingency fee   Attorney compensation as a percentage of the amount recovered rather than a flat amount of money or an hourly fee.

Contract   An agreement supported by consideration.

Contract reformation   An equitable remedy that allows the courts to "rewrite" contract provisions.

Contributory negligence   Negligence by the plaintiff that contributed to his or her injury. Normally, any finding of contributory negligence acts as a complete bar to the plaintiff's recovery. See **Comparative negligence.**

Conversion   The taking of someone else's property with the intent of permanently depriving the owner; the civil side of theft.

Coordinating conjunction   A coordinating conjunction can join two independent clauses; examples include *and, but, for, nor, or,* and *yet.*

Copyright   An author or artist's right to control the use of his or her works.

Corporation   A business entity formed by an association of shareholders.

Corpus Juris Secundum (C.J.S.)   West's law encyclopedia. Contains cross-references to West digest topics and key numbers.

Corroborative evidence   Evidence that supports previous testimony but that comes in a different form.

Count   In a complaint, one cause of action.

Counterclaim   A claim by the defendant against the plaintiff. A compulsory counterclaim relates to the facts alleged in the complaint. A permissive counterclaim can relate to an entirely different factual setting.

Court   A unit of the judicial branch of government that has the authority to decide legal disputes.

Court clerk   A court official responsible for keeping the court files in proper condition and ensuring that the various motions filed by lawyers and the actions taken by judges are properly recorded.

Court commissioner   A title given in some states to a public official with limited judicial powers.

Court of record   A court where a permanent record is kept of the testimony, lawyers' remarks, and judges' rulings.

Court reporter   A person trained to take a verbatim transcript of a courtroom proceeding or deposition.

Covenant not to compete   A promise not to compete within a given geographical area for a specific time period.

Cover   Finding substitute goods.

Crime   An activity that has been prohibited by the legislature as violating a duty owed to society and hence prosecutable, with the possibility of resulting incarceration or the payment of a fine.

Criminal complaint   A document charging a person with a crime.

Criminal justice system   Used to refer to a combination of legislative, administrative, and judicial agencies that

are involved in the development and enforcement of criminal law in the United States.

Criminal law   Law that deals with harm to society as a whole.

Criminal procedure   The way in which criminal prosecutions are handled; governed by the federal or state rules of criminal procedure.

Critical Legal Studies (CLS)   An offshoot of legal realism that seeks to identify ways in which the law protects certain groups and ideas at the expense of others.

Cross-claim   A claim by one defendant against another defendant or by one plaintiff against another plaintiff.

Cross-examination   The questioning of an opposing witness.

Cumulative evidence   Evidence that does not add any new information but that confirms facts that already have been established.

Custodial interrogation   Questioning that occurs after a defendant has been deprived of his or her freedom in a significant way.

Custody   Occurs when the defendant has been deprived of freedom in a significant way.

Damages   Monetary compensation, including compensatory, punitive, and nominal damages.

Deadly force   A force that would cause serious bodily injury or death.

Decedent   A person who died.

Declarant   The person who made the statement.

Deductive reasoning   A form of logical reasoning based on a major premise, a minor premise, and a conclusion.

Deed   The legal document that formally conveys title to the property to the new owner.

Defamation   The publication of false statements that harm a person's reputation.

Defamation per se   Remarks considered to be so harmful that they are automatically viewed as defamatory.

Default judgment   A judgment entered against a party who fails to complete a required step, such as answering the complaint.

Defendant   In a lawsuit, the person who is sued; in a criminal case, the person who is charged with a crime.

Defense   A fact or legal argument that would relieve the defendant of liability in a civil case or guilt in a criminal case.

Delegatee   A person who owes an obligation to the obligee in a contractual situation.

Delegation   The transfer by one of the original parties to the contract of his or her obligations to a third party.

Delegator   A person who delegates duties under a contract.

Demand letter   A letter from an attorney demanding that some action be taken, with either an implicit or an explicit threat to take the matter to court if the requested action is not forthcoming.

Dependent clause   A clause that contains a subject and a verb but that cannot stand alone, as it does not contain a complete thought. Dependent clauses always begin with subordinating conjunctions.

Deponent   The person who is being asked questions at a deposition.

Deposition   The pretrial oral questioning of a witness under oath.

Derogation of the common law   Used to describe legislation that changes the common law.

Descendants   Also known as issue; lineal heirs who descend from, or issue from, the decedent, such as children and grandchildren.

Detrimental reliance   See **Promissory estoppel**.

Devise   A gift of real estate that is given to someone through a will.

Dicta   Plural of dictum.

Dictum   A statement in a judicial opinion not necessary for the decision of the case.

Digest   A book that contains court opinion headnotes arranged by subject matter.

Direct appellate review   Occurs when the courts think a case is so significant that the middle step of going through an intermediate appellate court should be skipped; the case proceeds directly from a trial court to the highest appellate court.

Direct evidence   Establishes a direct link to the event that must be proven.

Direct examination   The questioning of your own witness.

Directed verdict   A verdict ordered by a trial judge if the plaintiff fails to present a prima facie case or if the defendant fails to present a necessary defense.

Disability   Under the Americans with Disabilities Act, a physical or mental impairment that substantially limits a major life activity. An individual with a disability is one who has such an impairment, has a record of such an impairment, or is regarded as having such an impairment.

Disaffirm   The ability to take back one's contractual obligations.

Disbarment   The revocation of an attorney's license.

Disclosure   The intentional publication of embarrassing private affairs.

Discovery   The modern pretrial procedure by which one party gains information from the adverse party.

Disillusionment See **divorce**.

Dismissal with prejudice A court order that ends a lawsuit; the suit cannot be refiled by the same parties.

Dismissal without prejudice A court order that ends a lawsuit; the suit can be refiled by the same parties.

Disparate impact The legal theory applied when the use of a neutral standard has a disproportionate impact on one protected group.

Disparate treatment The legal theory applied when a rejected applicant claims the reason for rejection was based on a discriminatory intent but the employer alleges a nondiscriminatory reason.

Disposition The result reached in a particular case.

Dissenting opinion An opinion that disagrees with the majority's decision and reasoning.

Distinguish To find differences (distinctions) between two situations.

Distinguishable Different; distinguishable cases involve dissimilar facts and/or rules of law.

District attorney An attorney appointed to prosecute crimes.

Diversity jurisdiction The power of the federal courts to hear matters of state law if the opposing parties are from different states and the amount in controversy exceeds $75,000.

Divided custody A situation in which the court separates the children so that each parent is awarded custody of one or more of the children.

Dividend A distribution of the corporate profit as ordered by the board of directors.

Divorce Also called disillusionment; a legal judgment that dissolves a marriage.

Doctrine of equitable distribution A system for distributing property acquired during a marriage on the basis of such factors as the contributions of the spouses, the length of the marriage, the age and health of the spouses, and their ability to make a living.

Doctrine of implied powers Powers not stated in the Constitution but that are necessary for Congress to carry out other, expressly granted powers.

Documentary evidence Consists of records, contracts, leases, wills, and other written instruments.

Documents clerk Someone who organizes and files legal documents.

Domestic corporation A corporation doing business in its own state.

Donor Also known as a **grantor** or **settlor**; a person who creates a trust.

Double jeopardy A constitutional protection against being tried twice for the same crime.

Draft A three-party instrument in which the **drawer** orders the drawee, usually a bank, to pay money to the **payee**.

Dramshop laws Statutes making bar owners responsible if intoxicated patrons negligently injure third parties.

Drawee On the face of a check or draft, the party that is ordering payment to be made.

Drawer On the face of a check or draft, the party that is ordered to pay.

Due process Fifth and Fourteenth Amendment guarantees that notice and a hearing must be provided before depriving someone of property or liberty.

Durable power of attorney See **Health care proxy**.

Duress In criminal law, a defense requiring proof that force or a threat of force was used to cause a person to commit a criminal act. In contract law, pressure that is so great as to overwhelm the contracting party's ability to make a free choice.

Earnest money The money the buyer turns over to the real estate agent to be applied to the purchase price of property.

Easement A right to use property owned by another for a limited purpose.

Ejusdem generis A canon of construction meaning "of the same class."

Element A separable part of a statute that must be satisfied for the statute to apply.

Emancipated minor Someone who is still under the legal age of adulthood but who has nevertheless been released from parental authority and given the legal rights of an adult.

Eminent domain The power of government to take private property for public purposes.

Employee A person working for another. Compare **Independent contractor**.

En banc When an appellate court that normally sits in panels sits as a whole.

Enabling act A statute establishing and setting out the powers of an administrative agency.

Encumbrance A lien or other type of security interest that signifies that some other party has a legitimate claim to the property.

Entrapment A defense requiring proof that the defendant would not have committed the crime but for police trickery.

Equity Fairness; a court's power to do justice. Equity powers allow judges to take action when otherwise the law would limit their decisions to monetary awards. Equity powers include a judge's ability to issue an injunction and to order specific performance.

Escheat A reversion of property to the state when there are no heirs.

Escrow account A bank account used to hold money belonging to a client or a third party.

Estate An interest in or title to real property. In probate law, the total property of whatever kind, both real and personal, that a person owns at the time of his or her death.

Ethical wall Also known as a **screen** or **cone of silence**; a system developed to shield an attorney or a paralegal from a case that otherwise would create a conflict of interest.

Evict To remove a tenant from possession of rental property.

Evidence The way in which a question of fact is established. Evidence can consist of witness testimony or documents and exhibits. It is the proof presented at a trial.

Evolutionary approach An approach to constitutional interpretation in which judges seek to determine the underlying purpose that the drafters had in mind at the time they wrote the law and the modern-day option that best advances that purpose.

Exception An attorney's objection to a trial court's ruling in order to preserve it as grounds for an appeal.

Exclusionary rule A rule that states that evidence obtained in violation of an individual's constitutional rights cannot be used against that individual in a criminal trial.

Exclusive jurisdiction when only one court has the power to hear a case.

Exculpatory clause A provision that purports to waive liability.

Exculpatory evidence Evidence that suggests the defendant's innocence; opposite of **inculpatory evidence**.

Execute To perform or to sign; in contract law an executed contract is one that has been completely performed.

Executor/executrix A person appointed by the testator to carry out the directions and requests in his or her will.

Executory contract A contract that has not been fully performed.

Exemplary damages See **Punitive damages**.

Exhaustion The requirement that certain preliminary steps be taken.

Exhaustion of administrative remedies The requirement that relief be sought from an administrative agency before proceeding to court.

Exigent circumstances Generally, an emergency situation that allows a search to proceed without a warrant.

Expert witness A witness who possesses skill and knowledge beyond that of the average person.

Explanatory parenthetical A parenthetical located at the end of a case citation containing information about the case.

Express contracts Contracts that are formed through words, either oral or written.

Express warranty An express warranty or promise can be created by an affirmation of fact or a promise made by the seller, a description of the goods being sold (including technical specifications and blueprints), or a sample or model provided.

Extradition The transportation of an individual from one state to another so that person can be tried on criminal charges.

Fact An actual incident or condition; not a legal consequence.

Fact bound When even a minor change in the facts can change the outcome.

False arrest Occurs when a person is arrested (by either a law officer or a citizen) without probable cause and the arrest is not covered by special privilege.

False imprisonment Occurs whenever one person, through force or the threat of force, unlawfully detains another person against his or her will.

False light The intentional false portrayal of someone in a way that would be offensive to a reasonable person.

Family law The area of the law that covers marriage, divorce, and parent-child relationships.

Federal courts of appeals The intermediate appellate courts in the federal system.

Federal district courts The trial courts in the federal system.

Federal question jurisdiction The power of the federal courts to hear matters of federal law.

Federal Register A daily newspaper in which proposed federal regulations are first printed.

Federal Reporter The West reporter that contains decisions from the U.S. courts of appeals.

Federal Rules of Civil Procedure The rules governing the stages of civil litigation in federal courts.

Federal Sentencing Guidelines Government guidelines that specify an appropriate range of sentences for each class of convicted persons based on factors related to the offense and the offender.

Federal Supplement The West reporter that contains decisions from the U.S. district courts.

Federalism A system of government in which the authority to govern is split between a single, nationwide

central government and several regional governments that control specific geographical areas.

Fee simple absolute estate   An ownership of land that is free from any conditions or restrictions.

Felony   A serious crime, usually carrying a prison sentence of one or more years.

Fiduciary   A person who has a legally imposed obligation to act in the best interests of another party.

Fiduciary duty   A legally imposed obligation to act in the best interests of the party to whom the duty is owed.

Financing statement   A public record of a security interest.

Fine   A penalty requiring the payment of money.

Fixed fee   A set charge for a specific service, such as drafting a simple will.

Floating lien   A security interest in proceeds or after-acquired property.

Floor debate   Debate that takes place in the legislature before a vote is taken on a proposed statute. It becomes part of the statute's legislative history.

Follow precedent   When a court bases its decision on prior similar cases.

Forcible entry and detainer   In some states, a summary civil action by a landlord to regain possession of the premises from a tenant who disputes the landlord's right to possession. Also, an action by anyone with the right to possession who has been unlawfully evicted.

Foreclosure   The process by which a creditor who holds a mortgage or some other form of a lien on real property can force the sale of that property in order to satisfy the debt to the mortgagee or lien holder.

Foreign corporation   A corporation incorporated in one state doing business in another state.

Forfeiture   The loss of money or property as a result of committing a criminal act.

Forgery   The alteration or falsification of documents with the intent to defraud.

Formal contract   A contract requiring certain formalities, such as a seal, to be valid.

Formal will   A will that has been prepared on a word processor or typewriter and that has been properly signed by the testator and the required witnesses.

Fourth branch of government   Administrative agencies.

Fraud   A false representation of facts or intentional perversion of the truth to induce someone to take some action or give up something of value.

Freehold estate   A right of title or ownership to real property that extends for life or some other indeterminate period of time.

Freelance paralegal   A paralegal who works as an independent contractor rather than as an employee of a law firm or corporation.

Friend of the court   See **Amicus curiae.**

Fruit of the poisonous tree doctrine   Evidence that is derived from an illegal search or interrogation is inadmissible.

Full-text database   A computerized database that contains the full text of documents, such as court opinions or depositions.

Full-text search   A computer search that identifies every place in which the search term appears in the actual text of the document being searched.

Fused sentence   A type of run-on sentence; two independent clauses with no separating punctuation.

Garnishment   A process through which a court can require an employer to withhold money from an employee's wages and turn this money over to the party to whom a debt is owed.

General damages   Damages that you would naturally expect to occur given the type of harm suffered.

General intent   An intention to act without regard to the results of the act.

General jurisdiction   A court's power to hear any type of case arising within its geographical area.

General partnership   A type of partnership in which all partners have the right to manage the business.

Grand jury   A group of people, usually twenty-three, whose function is to determine if probable cause exists to believe that a crime has been committed and that the defendant committed it.

Grantor   The prior owner.

Guardian   A person appointed by the court to manage the affairs or property of a person who is incompetent due to age or some other reason.

Guardian ad litem   Someone appointed by the court to speak for the interests of a child.

Guilty   Convicted of a crime.

Harmless error   A trial court error that is not sufficient to warrant reversing the decision.

Hate crime   Crime in which the selection of the victim is based on that person's membership in a protected category, such as race, sex, or sexual orientation.

Hate speech   Speech directed at a particular group or classification of people that involves expressions of hate or intimidation.

Headnote   A summary of one legal point in a court opinion; written by the editors at West.

Health care proxy   Also known as a **durable power of attorney**; a document in which an individual delegates legal authority to make medical or financial decisions for that person if he or she is too incapacitated to make such decisions.

Hearing officer Holds administrative hearings, administers oaths, issues subpoenas, oversees depositions, and holds settlement conferences.

Hearsay Testimony or evidence introduced in court regarding what someone said out of court for the purpose of establishing the truth of what was said.

Heir Someone entitled to inherit property left by the decedent.

History The prior or subsequent history of the case you are Shepardizing. It is always preceded by a one-letter abbreviation.

Holder Someone who receives negotiable paper through proper delivery.

Holder in due course Someone who gives value in good faith (a subjective standard) and without notice that the instrument is overdue or has been dishonored or has any claims against it or defenses to it (an objective standard).

Holding In a case brief, the court's answer to the issue presented to it; the new legal principle established by a court opinion.

Holographic will A will that was handwritten by the testator, without the witness signatures necessary for a formal will; an informal will.

Home page The first page of a web site that has multiple links to other places on the web site and to other web sites.

Homestead exemption A provision in state or local law that provides homeowners with specified types of protection from creditors or special tax deductions.

Homicide The killing of one human being by another.

Hostile work environment Occurs when unwelcome sexual conduct has the purpose or effect of unreasonably interfering with an individual's work performance or creating an intimidating, hostile, or offensive working environment.

Hourly rate A fee based on how many hours attorneys or paralegals spend on the case. Different hourly rates are often charged for different attorneys and paralegals within the firm, based on their seniority and experience.

Hypertext links Computer codes that, when clicked on with a mouse, connect the user to other web pages with related information.

Id. A short citation form indicating reference is to the immediately preceding authority.

Immunity For policy reasons, protection from being sued for negligent acts.

Implied warranty of fitness An implied promise that the goods being sold will satisfy a special purpose.

Implied warranty of habitability A requirement that property be fit for the purpose for which it is being rented. Owners are required to repair and maintain the premises at certain minimum levels.

Implied warranty of merchantability An implied promise that the goods being sold will be usable for the purpose for which they were sold.

Implied-in-fact contracts Contracts formed through conduct.

Inchoate crimes Attempted crimes.

Incidental beneficiary Someone who the original contracting parties did not explicitly intend to benefit from the contract.

Inculpatory evidence Evidence that suggests the defendant's guilt; opposite of **exculpatory evidence.**

Independent adoption An adoption that involves a private agreement between the birth parents and the adoptive parents.

Independent clause A clause that contains a subject and a verb and that can stand alone as a sentence.

Independent contractor A person who works for another but who retains the right to control the manner of producing the end result; not an employee.

Independent paralegal A paralegal working under the supervision of an attorney in a contractual relationship. Sometimes used to refer to a paralegal providing legal services directly to the public without being under the supervision of an attorney.

Indictment A grand jury's written accusation that a given individual has committed a crime. Compare **Presentment.**

Indorsement in blank When an indorser simply signs his or her name and does not specify to whom the instrument is payable.

Infant In the law, a name sometimes used to mean any minor child.

Inference A conclusion reached based on the facts given.

Inferior courts In the federal system, all courts other than the U.S. Supreme Court.

Informal contract A contract not requiring any particular formalities to be valid.

Information A prosecutor's written accusation that a person has committed a crime.

Infra Below; used to refer to authority cited later in the document. May not be used with citations to cases, statutes, or constitutions.

Initial appearance The first court hearing for a person charged with committing a crime.

Injunction A court order requiring a party to perform a specific act or to cease doing a specific act.

Insanity defense   A defense requiring proof that the defendant was not mentally responsible.

Intangible property   Personal property that cannot be touched.

Intellectual property   Intangible assets, such as trademarks, copyrights, and patents.

Intended beneficiary   A person the contractual parties intend to benefit.

Intentional infliction of emotional distress   An intentional tort that occurs through an extreme and outrageous act that causes severe emotional distress.

Intentional tort   A tort committed by one who intends to do the act that creates the harm.

Inter vivos trust   A trust that is created before a person's death.

Interference with a contractual relationship   An intentional tort that occurs if someone induces a party to breach a contract or interferes with the performance of a contract.

International Paralegal Management Association (IPMA)   A national association of paralegal managers.

Internet   A worldwide network of computer networks.

Interrogatories   Written questions sent by one side to the opposing side, answered under oath.

Intestate   When a person dies without a valid will.

Intoxication defense   A defense requiring proof that the defendant was not able to form the requisite mens rea due to intoxication.

Intrusion   The intentional unjustified encroachment into another person's private activities.

Intrusive phrase   A phrase placed between a sentence's subject and verb.

Invasion of privacy   An intentional tort that covers a variety of situations, including disclosure, intrusion, appropriation, and false light.

IRAC   A method for organizing legal writing: issue, rule, analysis, and conclusion.

Irresistible impulse test   A test that provides that the defendant is not guilty due to insanity if, at the time of the killing, the defendant could not control his or her actions.

Irrevocable trust   A form of inter vivos trust that the grantor cannot alter.

Issue   Arises when the law is applied to specific facts and the result is not obvious. In a case brief, the statement of the problem facing the court. In an IRAC analysis, the statement of the client's problem. In probate law, a lineal heir; see **Decedent**.

Issue of first impression   An issue that the court has never faced before.

Jails   City or county places of confinement.

J.N.O.V.   Shorthand for **judgment notwithstanding the verdict**.

Joint and several liability   Liability shared collectively and individually.

Joint legal custody   Both parents have an equal say in making major decisions, such as those regarding the education of the child.

Joint liability   Shared liability, so that if one party is sued, others must be sued also.

Joint tenancy   Ownership by two or more persons who have equal rights in the use of that property. When a joint tenant dies, that person's share passes to the other joint tenant(s).

Joint tenancy with right of survivorship   Another term for **joint tenancy**.

Judge   A court official who presides over courtroom proceedings and decides all legal questions. In a bench trial the judge also decides the facts.

Judgment   The decision of the court regarding the claims of each side. It may be based on a jury's verdict.

Judgment notwithstanding the verdict (J.N.O.V.)   A judgment that reverses the verdict of the jury when the verdict had no reasonable factual support or was contrary to law.

Judgment proof   When the defendant does not have sufficient money or other assets to pay the judgment.

Judicial activism   A judicial philosophy that supports an active role for the judiciary in changing the law.

Judicial history   See **Procedural facts**.

Judicial notice   When a judge formally recognizes something as being a fact without requiring the attorneys to prove it through the introduction of other evidence.

Judicial restraint   A judicial philosophy that supports a limited role for the judiciary in changing the law, including deference to the legislative branch.

Judicial review   The court's power to review statutes to decide if they conform to the U.S. Constitution.

Jurisdiction   The power of a court to hear a case.

Jurisprudence   The study of law and legal philosophy.

Jury trial   When a jury decides the facts and determines liability or guilt.

Just compensation   The amount of money the government must pay the owner of property it seizes through eminent domain.

Justice of the peace   A title given to the presiding officer (judge) in limited jurisdiction minor courts operated by some states.

Kidnapping   An unlawful movement and confinement of the victim.

Kindred Also known as **consanguinity**; persons related to the decedent by blood.

Knowingly Not intending to cause a specific harm but being aware that such harm would be caused.

Land contract An installment contract for the sale of land.

Landmark decision A court opinion that establishes new law in an important area.

Larceny Another term for **theft**.

Last clear chance The doctrine that states that despite the plaintiff's contributory negligence, the defendant should still be liable if the defendant was the last one in a position to avoid the accident.

Law clerk A law student or a recent law school graduate whose duties usually focus on legal research.

Law office memorandum An unbiased analysis of the client's situation.

Law review A journal generally published by a law school editorial board or by a bar association. The articles usually contain in-depth analyses of current legal topics.

Laws Rules of conduct promulgated and enforced by the government, based on policy decisions that determine legal rights and duties between people or between people and the government.

Lay advocate A nonlawyer who provides legal services directly to the public without being under the supervision of an attorney; also known as a **legal technician**. Absent a statute allowing this activity, it constitutes the unauthorized practice of law.

Lay a foundation The process of properly identifying and authenticating evidence so that it can be introduced.

Lay witness A witness who is being called to give testimony about things the person personally saw or heard, rather than as a witness who is being called because of special expertise.

Leading question A question that suggests the answer; generally, leading questions may not be asked during direct examination of a witness.

Lease An agreement in which the property owner gives someone else the right to use that property for a designated period of time.

Leasehold A parcel of real estate held under a lease.

Leasehold estate A right to use real property for a limited period of time.

Legacy See **Bequest**.

Legal aid services See **Legal Services Corporation**.

Legal analysis The process of applying the law to a client's facts. Also known as **legal reasoning**.

Legal assistant Synonym for **paralegal**; may also refer to other nonlawyers who assist attorneys.

Legal Clinic Usually organized as either a partnership or a professional corporation, law clinics provide low-cost legal services on routine matters by stressing low overhead and high volume.

Legal custody The designated parent or guardian who has authority to make legal decisions for the child relating to such matters as health care and education.

Legal fiction An assumption that something that is not real is real—for example, assuming that a corporation is a person for purposes of its being able to sue and be sued.

Legal formalism A legal theory that views the law as a complete and autonomous system of logically consistent principles within which judges find the correct result by simply making logical deductions.

Legal malpractice The failure of an attorney to act reasonably.

Legal positivism A legal theory whose proponents believe that the validity of a law is determined by the process through which it was made rather than by the degree to which it reflects natural law principles.

Legal realism A legal philosophy whose proponents think that judges decide cases based on factors other than logic and preexisting rules, such as economic and sociological factors.

Legal reasoning The application of legal rules to a client's specific factual situation; also known as **legal analysis**.

Legal research The process of finding the law.

Legal scrivener The provider of a typing service.

Legal Services Corporation A federally funded program to deliver legal assistance to the indigent.

Legal Services offices Affiliated with the federal government's **Legal Services Corporation**, these offices serve those who would otherwise be unable to afford legal assistance.

Legal technician A nonlawyer who provides legal services directly to the public without being under the supervision of an attorney; also known as a **lay advocate**. Absent a statute allowing this activity, it constitutes the unauthorized practice of law.

Legal writing Examples of legal writing include case briefs, law office memoranda, and documents filed with the court.

Legislative courts Courts created under Congress's Article I powers.

Legislative history The background documents created during the process of a bill becoming a statute. These documents can include alternative versions of the legislation, proceedings of committee hearings, committee reports, and transcripts of floor debates.

Legislative intent The purpose of the legislature at the time it enacted a statute. In interpreting statutes the role of the court is to try to discover the intent of the legislature at the time it enacted the statute.

Lessee or tenant The person with right of possession during the term of the lease.

Lesser included offense A crime whose elements are contained within a more serious crime. Theft is a lesser included offense of robbery.

Lessor or landlord The owner of the property being leased.

Lexis An on-line legal database containing court decisions and statutes from the entire country, as well as secondary authority; a competitor to **Westlaw.**

Liable A finding in a civil suit that a defendant is responsible.

Libel Written defamation.

Liberal construction An approach whereby the courts give a statute a broad interpretation.

Licensing Governmental permission to engage in a profession.

Life estate An ownership right to real property that lasts only as long as that person, or some other named individual, lives.

Life tenant A person who has ownership under a life estate.

Limited jurisdiction A court's power to hear only specialized cases.

Limited liability company (LLC) A new form of business ownership that gives small businesses the advantage of liability limited to the amount of the owner's investment along with single taxation.

Limited liability partnership (LLP) A form of business ownership similar to a general partnership except the partners do not have unlimited personal liability for the wrongful acts of other partners. Unlike a limited liability company, however, the partners remain personally liable for other business debts, such as rent and utilities.

Limited partnership A partnership of at least one general partner and one or more limited partners. The limited partners' liability is limited to their investments so long as they do not participate in management decisions.

Lineal heir Someone who is a grandparent, parent, child, grandchild, or great-grandchild of the decedent.

Liquidated damages clause A contract provision that specifies what will happen in case of breach.

Listing agreement A document that spells out the nature of the services a real estate agent will perform with respect to selling real property and how the agent will be compensated for those services.

Litigation A lawsuit; a controversy to be settled in a court.

Living Constitution Judicial philosophy that seeks to interpret the Constitution in light of existing societal values.

Living trust A form of inter vivos trust that allows a person, while still living, to benefit another.

Living will Also known as a **medical directive;** a document expressing a person's wishes regarding the withholding or withdrawal of life-support equipment and other heroic measures to sustain life if the individual has an incurable or irreversible condition that will cause death.

Loss of consortium The loss by one spouse of the other spouse's companionship, services, or affection.

Magistrate A title sometimes given to a public official exercising limited judicial power.

Magistrate judges In the federal district courts they supervise court calendars, hear procedural motions, issue subpoenas, hear minor criminal offense cases, and conduct civil pretrial hearings.

Maintenance See **Alimony.**

Major premise In deductive reasoning, the statement of a broad proposition that forms the starting point; in law, the statement of a legal rule that you can find in a statute or court opinion.

Majority opinion An opinion in which a majority of the court joins.

Maker On the face of a note, the person who signs, promising to pay.

Malice Making a defamatory remark either knowing the material was false or acting with a "reckless disregard" for whether or not it was true.

Malicious prosecution A lawsuit that can be brought against someone who unsuccessfully and maliciously brought an action without probable cause.

Mandatory authority or decisions Court decisions from a higher court in the same jurisdiction.

Marital property Property that is subject to court distribution upon termination of the marriage.

Market share theory A legal theory that allows plaintiffs to recover proportionately from a group of manufacturers when the identity of the specific manufacturer responsible for the harm is unknown.

Marketable title See **Clear title.**

Massachusetts Decisions The unofficial reporter published by West covering court decisions from Massachusetts also found in the Northeastern Reporter. The pages containing the court decisions from the other four states reported in the Northeastern Reporter are removed.

Massachusetts Digest A West publication; the digest is a collection of Massachusetts court decision summaries arranged by subject matter.

Massachusetts Digest table of cases An alphabetical listing of court decisions arranged by the plaintiff's last name, giving the citation and relevant topics and key numbers. There is also a defendant-plaintiff table, an alphabetical listing by the defendant's last name.

Massachusetts Practice Series (M.P.S.) A West publication; the Massachusetts equivalent of a legal encyclopedia. Contains cross-references to C.J.S. and Massachusetts Digest topics and key numbers.

Massachusetts Register A biweekly publication listing proposed and new Massachusetts regulations.

Massachusetts Reports The official reporter published by the state of Massachusetts covering Massachusetts Supreme Judicial Court decisions.

Master In law, the name that is sometimes given to an employer.

Material breach Such a grave failure to fulfill the contractual terms that the other party is relieved of all contractual obligations.

Materiality Either a subcategory of relevancy or simply another word for relevancy, the requirement that the evidence be more probative than prejudicial.

Mechanic's lien A claim filed by a contractor or repair person who had done work on a building for which he or she has not been fully paid.

Mediation An ADR mechanism whereby a neutral third party assists the parties in reaching a mutually agreeable, voluntary compromise.

Medical directive See **Living will.**

Mens rea Bad intent.

Merchant's firm offer An offer made by a merchant in a signed writing that assures the buyer that the offer will remain open for a specific period of time. It does not require consideration to be binding.

Mini-digest A digest located in an advance sheet pamphlet or hardbound volume of court decisions published by West. It contains the headnotes for the cases in that single publication.

Minimum contacts A constitutional fairness requirement that a defendant have at least a certain minimum contact with a state before the state courts can have jurisdiction over the defendant.

Minor A child who is under the age of legal competence.

Minor premise In deductive reasoning, the second proposition, which along with the major premise leads to the conclusion; in law, the minor premise consists of the client's facts.

Miranda **warnings** The requirement that defendants be notified of their rights to remain silent and to have an attorney present prior to being questioned by the police.

Mirror image rule The requirement that the acceptance exactly mirror the offer or the acceptance will be viewed as a counteroffer.

Misdemeanor A minor crime not amounting to a felony, usually punishable by a fine or a jail sentence of less than a year.

Misfeasance Acting in an improper or a wrongful way.

Mistrial A trial ended by the judge because of a major problem, such as a prejudicial statement by one of the attorneys.

Mitigation of damages The requirement that the non-breaching party take reasonable steps to limit his or her damages.

M'Naghten test A test that provides that the defendant is not guilty due to insanity if, at the time of the killing, the defendant suffered from a defect or disease of the mind and could not understand whether the act was right or wrong.

Model Code of Professional Responsibility An older set of standards governing attorney ethics developed by the American Bar Association.

Model Penal Code and Commentaries The American Law Institute's proposal for a uniform set of criminal laws; not the law unless adopted by a state's legislature.

Model Rules of Professional Conduct A set of ethical rules developed by the American Bar Association in the 1980s. The Model Rules have been adopted by more than half the states.

Motion A request made to the court.

Motion for acquittal A request that the court end the trial by finding for the defendant.

Motion for a continuance A request that the court postpone the proceeding to a later time.

Motion for a directed verdict A request that the court find for the moving party because either the plaintiff failed to present a prima facie case or the defendant failed to present a necessary defense.

Motion for further appellate review In Massachusetts, the process whereby the Supreme Judicial Court agrees to hear a case.

Motion for judgment notwithstanding the verdict A request that the court reverse the jury's verdict when the verdict had no reasonable factual support or was contrary to law.

Motion for leave to obtain further appellate review In Massachusetts, a request that the Supreme Judicial Court hear a case.

Motion in limine   A request that the court order that certain information not be mentioned in the presence of the jury.

Motion for a new trial   A request that the court order a rehearing of a lawsuit because irregularities, such as errors of the court or jury misconduct, make it probable that an impartial trial did not occur.

Motion to require a finding of not guilty   The defense's request that the court find the prosecution failed to meet its burden and that it remove the case from the jury by finding the defendant not guilty.

Motion to suppress   A request that the court prohibit the use of certain evidence at the trial.

Narrow holding   A statement of the court's decision that contains many of the case's specific facts, thereby limiting its future applicability to a narrow range of cases.

National Association of Legal Assistants (NALA)   A national paralegal association.

National Federation of Paralegal Associations (NFPA)   A national association of paralegal associations.

National Reporter System   West's system for reporting court decisions from every state and the federal courts.

Natural law   A legal philosophy whose proponents think there are ideal laws that can be discovered through careful thought and humanity's innate sense of right and wrong.

Necessaries   Normally food, clothing, shelter, and medical treatment.

Necessity   A defense requiring proof that the defendant was forced to take an action to avoid a greater harm.

Negligence   The failure to act reasonably under the circumstances.

Negotiable instrument   Commercial paper that can be transferred by indorsement or delivery. It must meet the requirements of UCC § 3-104 to be negotiable. If it does not, a transferee cannot become a holder, but only gets the rights along with the liabilities of a contract assignee.

New trial   A rehearing of a lawsuit granted when irregularities such as errors of the court or jury misconduct make it probable that an impartial trial did not occur.

Next friend   A person who represents the interests of someone in court without being that person's legal guardian.

No-fault divorce   A form of divorce that allows a couple to end their marital relationship without having to assess blame for the breakup.

No-knock warrant   A warrant that allows the police to enter without announcing their presence in advance.

Nolo contendere   A defendant's plea meaning that the defendant neither admits nor denies the charges.

Nominal damages   A token sum awarded when liability has been found but monetary damages cannot be shown.

Nonfeasance   Failing to act.

Nonrestrictive phrase   A phrase that is not essential to the sense of a sentence; it should be set off with commas.

North Eastern Reporter   An unofficial regional reporter published by West covering court decisions from Massachusetts, as well as four other states.

Note   A promise to pay money.

Notice   Being informed of some act done or about to be done.

Notice pleading   A method adopted by the federal rules in which the plaintiff simply informs the defendant of the claim and the general basis for it.

Novation   In a contract, when a third party is substituted for one of the original parties.

Nuncupative will   An oral will.

Obiter dictum   See **Dictum**.

Obligee   A person owed a contractual benefit.

Obligor   A person under a contractual obligation.

Obscenity   Sexually explicit material without redeeming artistic, scientific, or political worth.

Offer   In contract law, an indication of a firm desire to enter into an agreement, sufficiently definite that once accepted a contract is formed.

Official reporter   A governmental publication of court opinions.

On all fours   A term used to describe two cases that are almost identical, with similar facts and legal issues.

On point   A term used to describe a case that is similar to another case.

Open questions   Broad questions that put few limits on the freedom of the respondent.

Option contract   A contract in which the buyer gives the seller consideration to keep the offer open for a stated period of time.

Order paper   An instrument that is payable to the order of a specific party.

Ordinance   A local law.

Originalism   An approach to constitutional interpretation that narrowly interprets the text of the Constitution in a manner that is consistent with what most people understood those words to mean at the time that they were written.

Original jurisdiction The authority of a court to hear a case when it is initiated, as opposed to appellate jurisdiction.

Output contract A contract in which one party agrees to deliver its entire output of a particular product to the other party.

Overbreadth A reason for invalidating a statute where it covers both protected and criminal activity.

Overrule A decision is overruled when a court in a later case changes the law so that its prior decision is no longer good law. Compare with **Reverse**.

Overt discrimination When an employer openly refuses to treat all applicants or employees equally.

Paralegal A person who assists an attorney and, working under the attorney's supervision, does tasks that, absent the paralegal, the attorney would do. A paralegal cannot give legal advice or appear in court.

Parallel citation When reference to two or more reporters is required, each citation is known as a parallel citation. For example, 333 Mass. 99 is the parallel citation for 89 N.E.2d 488; the reverse is also true.

Parallel construction Using the some grammatical structure for clauses or phrases that bear the same relationship to some major idea.

Parental immunity The prohibition against allowing children to sue their parents.

Parenthetical The parenthetical that occurs at the end of a court citation always contains the year of decision and also the name of the court if that information is not obvious from the name of the reporter.

Parol evidence rule An evidentiary rule that a written contract cannot be modified or changed by prior verbal agreements.

Parole Conditional early release from custody.

Partial defense A defense that reduces a crime to a lesser included offense.

Partnership A business run by two or more persons as co-owners.

Partnership by estoppel A partnership created by the words or actions of persons acting as though they were a partnership.

Passive voice A form of writing where the subject of the sentence is being acted on; opposite of **active voice**.

Patent A right to exclude others from making, using, or selling one's invention.

Pattern jury instructions A set of standardized jury instructions.

Payee The person who will receive payment.

Penal system Also known as the *correctional system;* the system of jails, prisons, and other places of confinement, as well as the pardon and parole systems.

Per stirpes Also known as the **right of representation;** a method of dividing an intestate estate whereby a person takes in place of the dead ancestor.

Peremptory challenge A method for excusing a prospective juror; no reason need be given.

Perfect tender rule The requirement that the goods delivered exactly meet the contractual specifications.

Perfected security interest A creditor's interest in security is perfected if the creditor possesses the security, files a financing statement, or gives money to purchase consumer goods.

Perfection In secured transactions, a security interest is perfected when notice of an attached security interest has been given, usually by filing a financing statement, thereby protecting the secured party from claims of third parties.

Periodic tenancy A tenancy established at a set interval, such as week to week, month to month, or year to year. At the end of each rental period the lease can be terminated with proper notice.

Perjury Lying to the court while under oath.

Perpetrator A person who commits a crime.

Personal defense In negotiable instrument law, a defense that is good against everyone except a holder in due course. Compare **Real defense**.

Personal jurisdiction The power of a court to force a person to appear before it.

Personal property All property that is not **real property**.

Personal recognizance bond A defendant's personal promise to appear in court.

Persuasive authority or decisions Court decisions from an equal or a lower court from the same jurisdiction or from a higher court in a different jurisdiction. Also includes secondary authority.

Petitioner A person who initiates an appeal.

Physical custody The child lives with and has day-to-day activities supervised by the designated parent or guardian.

Physical evidence See **Real evidence**.

Piercing the corporate veil When a court sets aside the unlimited liability protection normally given to corporate shareholders.

Pinpoint cite The reference to a particular page within an opinion.

Plain meaning A method for interpreting statutes in which the ordinary meaning of the statute's language is examined.

Plain view doctrine   Without the need for a warrant, the police may seize objects that are openly visible.

Plaintiff   A person who initiates a lawsuit.

Plea bargaining   A process whereby the prosecutor and the defendant's attorney agree for the defendant to plead guilty in exchange for the prosecutor's promise to charge him or her with a lesser offense, drop some additional charges, or request a lesser sentence.

Pleading in the alternative   Including more than one count in a complaint; the counts do not need to be consistent.

Pleadings   The papers that begin a lawsuit—generally, the complaint and the answer.

Pocket part   A pamphlet inserted into the back of a book containing information new since the volume was published.

Popular name table   Located in most codified statutes, this table lists statutes by their popular names along with their citations.

Potential conflict   A situation in which a conflict of interest may arise in the future—for example, representing business partners.

Power of judicial review   A court's power to review statutes to decide if they conform to the federal or state constitution.

Power of sale clause   A clause authorizing a private foreclosure sale that does not require court action.

Practice of law   An activity that requires professional judgment, or the educated ability to relate law to a specific legal problem.

Practitioners' Notes   A section of the Bluebook devoted to citation information for the practicing attorney.

Precedent   One or more prior court decisions.

Preemption   The power of the federal government to prevent the states from passing conflicting laws, and sometimes even to prohibit states from passing any laws on a particular subject.

Prejudicial error   A trial court error so serious as to require reversal of the trial court's decision.

Preliminary hearing   The first time a judge considers the criminal charge and decides whether there is enough evidence for the government to continue with the case.

Prenuptial agreement   Also known as an antenuptial agreement; a document that prospective spouses sign prior to marriage regarding financial and other arrangements should the marriage end.

Preponderance of the evidence   The standard of proof used in civil trials. The proof must indicate that it is more likely than not that the defendant committed the wrong.

Presentment   Acting on its own initiative, a grand jury's charging a person with a crime. Compare **Indictment**.

Pretrial conference   A meeting of the attorneys and the judge prior to the beginning of the trial.

Pretrial motion   A motion brought before the beginning of a trial either to eliminate the necessity for a trial or to limit the information that can be heard at the trial.

Prima facie case   What the prosecution or the plaintiff must be able to prove in order for the case to go to the jury—that is, the elements of the prosecution's case or the plaintiff's cause of action.

Primary authority   The law itself, such as statutes and court opinions.

Principal   In agency law, a person who permits or directs another person to act on the principal's behalf; in criminal law, the person who commits the crime.

Prior case history   Information about what happened procedurally to the cited case before it was heard by the cited court. Do not include this information in a citation.

Prisons   Places of confinement for those convicted of the more serious crimes.

Privity of contract   The relationship that exists between the contracting parties.

Pro bono work   Legal representation done without charge.

Probable cause   Not susceptible to a precise definition; a belief based on specific facts that a crime has been or is about to be committed; more than a reasonable suspicion.

Probate   The process of court supervision over the distribution of a deceased person's property.

Probation   An alternative sentence to incarceration that releases the defendant upon agreeing to certain conditions.

Probation officers   Government employees who administer the probation system.

Procedural facts   In a case brief, the facts that relate to what happened procedurally in the lower courts or administrative agencies before the case reached the court issuing the opinion and how the appellate court disposed of the case. Examples include aff'd and rev'd.

Procedural law   Law that regulates how the legal system operates.

Product misuse   When the product was not being used for its intended purpose or was being used in a dangerous manner; it is a defense to a products liability claim so long as the misuse was not foreseeable.

Products liability The theory holding manufacturers and sellers liable for defective products when the defects make the products unreasonably dangerous.

Professional corporation A professional entity in which the stockholders share in the organization's profits but have their liabilities limited to the amount of their investment.

Professional judgment The educated ability to apply law to specific facts.

Promissory estoppel Occurs when the courts allow detrimental reliance to substitute for consideration.

Pronoun A word that substitutes for a noun: *hers, her, his, him, its, them, their, theirs.*

Property A tangible object or a right or ownership interest.

Property law Law dealing with ownership.

Pro se One who represents himself or herself in a legal action.

Prosecuting attorney The attorney responsible for presenting the state's evidence against the defendant; called *United States attorneys* on the federal level and **district attorneys** or **state's attorneys** on the state level.

Prostitution Participating in sexual activity for a fee.

Protected categories Under Title VII, race, color, religion, sex, and national origin.

Protection order A court order issued in domestic violence and abuse cases to keep one spouse away from the other, the children, or the home.

Proving a case within a case The requirement in a legal malpractice case that the plaintiff-client prove that but for the attorney's negligence, the client would have won.

Proximate cause Once actual cause is found, as a policy matter, the court must also find that the act and the resulting harm were so foreseeably related as to justify a finding of liability.

Public defender An attorney employed by the state to represent indigent defendants.

Punitive damages Money awarded to a plaintiff in cases of intentional torts in order to punish the defendant and serve as a warning to others.

Purchase money security interest Arises when a seller gives credit to a debtor so that the debtor can purchase an item.

Purposeful Intending to cause a specific harm.

Qualified individual Under the Americans with Disabilities Act, someone who can perform the essential job functions.

Quasi-contract Although no contract was formed, the courts will fashion an equitable remedy to avoid unjust enrichment.

Question of fact Relates to what happened: who, what, when, where, and how. Disputed factual issues are normally for the jury or trial court to decide and cannot be appealed.

Question of law Relates to the application or interpretation of the law. Disputed legal issues are initially for the trial court to decide but can be appealed.

Question presented In a law office memorandum, the question presented states the legal issue raised by the facts of the problem in as concrete a fashion as possible.

Quid pro quo sexual harassment A situation involving an exchange of sexual favors for employment benefits.

Quiet enjoyment The tenant's right to be free from interference from the landlord with respect to how the property is used.

Quitclaim deed A deed in which the grantor gives up any claims to the property without making any assertions about there being a clear title.

Ratio decidendi The court's reasoning for its decision.

Real defense In negotiable instrument law, a defense inherent in the instrument itself, such as forgery. Compare **Personal defense.**

Real evidence Also referred to as **physical evidence;** Any tangible object, like a bloody glove.

Real estate closing A meeting at which the buyer and the seller or their representatives sign and deliver a variety of legal documents associated with the sale and transfer of the property.

Real property Also known as *real estate;* land and items growing on or permanently attached to that land.

Reasonable accommodation Under the Americans with Disabilities Act, an accommodation that would not create an undue hardship for the employer.

Reasonable suspicion A suspicion based on specific facts; less than probable cause.

Receiving stolen property Knowingly possessing stolen property.

Recidivist A repeat offender; one who continues to commit more crimes.

Recklessness Disregarding a substantial and unjustifiable risk that harm will result.

Reformation An equitable remedy whereby the court rewrites a contract.

Registered agent The person designated to receive service of legal documents.

Registration The process by which individuals or organizations have their names placed on an official

list kept by some private organization or governmental agency.

Regulation A law promulgated by an administrative agency.

Relevancy Determined by whether the evidence leads one to logically conclude that an asserted fact is either more or less probable.

Remand When an appellate court sends a case back to the trial court for a new trial or other action.

Remedial statute A statute enacted to correct a defect in prior law or to provide a remedy where none existed.

Removal The transfer of a case from one state court to another or from state court to federal court.

Reporters Books that contain court decisions. There are both official and unofficial reporters.

Reprimand or censure A public or private statement that an attorney's conduct violated the code of ethics.

Request for admissions A document that lists statements regarding specific items for the other party to admit or deny.

Request for documents A discovery tool whereby one party asks for documents in the other party's possession or control.

Requirements contract A contract in which one party agrees to buy all its requirements for a particular product from the other party.

Res ipsa loquitur "The thing speaks for itself"; the doctrine that suggests negligence can be presumed if an event happens that would not ordinarily happen unless someone was negligent.

Rescission The act of canceling the contract and returning the parties to the positions they were in prior to the contract having been formed.

Respondeat superior The tort theory that an employer can be sued for the negligent acts of its employees.

Respondent The party in a lawsuit against whom an appeal has been filed.

Restatement of the Law of Torts, Second An authoritative secondary source, written by a group of legal scholars, summarizing the existing common law, as well as suggesting what the law should be.

Restatements A series of books—the Restatements of the Law—summarizing the basic principles of the common law, written by the American Law Institute (ALI).

Restitution Repaying the victim for harm caused.

Restrictive covenant A provision in a deed that prohibits specified uses of the property.

Restrictive phrase A phrase that contains essential information; it should not be set off with commas.

Retainer An advance or down payment that is given to engage the services of an attorney.

Retreat exception The rule that in order to claim self-defense there must have been no possibility of retreat.

Reversal When an appellate court reverses a lower court decision.

Reverse A decision is reversed when an appellate court overturns or negates the decision of a lower court. Compare with **Overrule.**

Reversible error An error made by the trial judge sufficiently serious to warrant reversing the trial court's decision.

Revocable trust A form of inter vivos trust that the grantor can alter.

RICO The federal Racketeer Influenced and Corrupt Organizations Act.

Right of representation See **Per stirpes.**

Road map paragraph An introductory paragraph listing issues to be discussed in the order they are to be discussed.

Robbery Theft through the use of force.

Rule In a case brief, the general legal principle in existence before the case began.

Rule 8 The rule of civil procedure that sets forth the general pleading requirements.

Rule 11 A requirement that attorneys sign a pleading only after conducting a reasonable inquiry into the circumstances supporting it.

Rule 56 motion (summary judgment motion) A request that the court grant judgment in favor of the moving party because there is no genuine issue as to any material fact and the moving party is entitled to judgment as a matter of law. It is similar to a **12(b)(6) motion** except that the court also considers matters outside the pleadings.

Rulemaking hearing An administrative agency hearing that resembles a legislative hearing in which interested parties present evidence and arguments to an administrative agency about what the general law should be.

Rules of criminal procedure Federal and state rules that regulate how criminal proceedings are conducted.

Rules of evidence Federal and state rules that govern the admissibility of evidence in court.

Run-on sentence Two sentences written as one. It can occur either as a comma splice (two independent clauses joined by a comma) or as a fused sentence (two independent clauses with no separating punctuation).

Said Legalese for "the."

Screen See **Ethical wall.**

Search engine A computer program that allows the user to retrieve web documents that match the key words entered by the searcher.

Secondary authority Information about the law, such as that contained in encyclopedias and law review articles.

Secured transaction An arrangement whereby a creditor asks for and receives a guarantee of repayment from the debtor in the form of collateral.

Security agreement An agreement granting a creditor a security interest in specific property.

Security deposit An amount of money, usually equal to one month's rent, that is collected at the time the lease is signed and then held by the landlord to cover the cost of repairs that may be needed when the tenant moves out.

Security interest A security interest is created when a debtor agrees to put up something as collateral that the creditor can then claim if the debtor fails to pay the debt.

Self-defense The justified use of force to protect oneself or others.

Self-proving clause A notarized affidavit, signed by the attesting witnesses, that may eliminate the need to call witnesses during the probate process to attest to the validity of the will.

Sentence fragment An incomplete sentence.

Sentencing hearing A hearing held after a finding of guilt to determine the appropriate sentence.

Separation of powers The division of governmental power among the legislative, executive, and judicial branches.

Serial comma In a series of three or more items use a comma after each item until you reach the final conjunction.

Servant In law, an archaic term sometimes used to mean employee.

Service The delivery of a pleading or other paper in a lawsuit to the opposing party.

Service mark A mark used to identify a service-oriented business.

Service of process See **Service**.

Session laws Statutes that are enacted and published for a particular session of the legislature

Settlement An agreement between the parties to end the lawsuit on mutually satisfactory terms.

Settlement agreement A document that contains the arrangements agreed on by the parties to a dispute.

Settlor See **Donor**.

Shareholders The owners of a corporation.

Shepardizing The process of using **Shepard's Citations** to check a court citation to see whether there has been any subsequent history or treatment by other court decisions.

Shepard's Citations A book that contains nothing but citations. It serves three purposes: (1) as a source for parallel citations; (2) as a source for subsequent history for a case or statute; and (3) as a source for treatment by later courts of the case or statute you are Shepardizing.

Short citation form A partial citation that may be used after you have given a complete citation.

Signal A word or a phrase that precedes a citation to indicate the purpose for which the citation is being given.

Simultaneous death clause A clause that states that if a person named as a beneficiary in the will dies within a short period of time after the decedent dies, it will be assumed for purposes of the will that the person in question failed to survive the decedent.

Slander Spoken defamation.

Slip laws A form in which statutes are published; they are printed individually at the time they are first enacted.

Sole custody An individual has both physical and legal custody of the child.

Sole proprietorship A business owned by a single owner.

Solemnized marriage A marriage in which the couple has obtained the proper marriage license from a local government official and has then taken marriage vows before either a recognized member of the clergy or a judge and a designated number of witnesses.

Solicitation Encouraging someone to commit a crime.

Sovereign immunity The prohibition against suing the government without the government's consent.

Special damages Indirect damages that must be foreseeable to be recovered.

Specific intent An intention to act and to cause a specific result.

Specific performance When money damages are inadequate, a court may use this equitable remedy and order the breaching party to perform his or her contractual obligations.

Split custody One parent has both physical and legal custody during one part of the year, and the other parent gets both physical and legal custody during the rest of the year.

Spousal immunity The prohibition against one spouse suing the other.

Stalking The intentional or knowing course of conduct that places a person in fear of imminent physical

injury or death to that person or that person's family.

Standing   The principle that courts cannot decide abstract issues or render advisory opinions; rather they are limited to deciding cases that involve litigants who are personally affected by the court's decision.

Stare decisis   The doctrine stating that normally once a court has decided one way on a particular issue in the past, it and other courts in the same jurisdiction will decide the same way on that issue in future cases given a similar set of facts unless they can be convinced of the need for change.

State's attorney   A law officer who represents the state in criminal cases. Also known as a **district attorney**.

Statute   A law enacted by a state legislature or by Congress.

Statute in derogation of the common law   A statute that changes the common law.

Statute of frauds   A statutory requirement that in order to be enforceable certain contracts must be in writing.

Statute of limitations   The law that sets the length of time from when something happens to when a lawsuit must be filed before the right to bring it is lost.

Statutes at large or session laws   The chronological publication of statutes at the end of a legislative session.

Statutory element   A separable part of a statute that must be satisfied for the statute to apply.

Stay the judgment   A suspension of the judgment. It is often requested when the trial court judgment is being appealed.

Stipulate   To agree.

Stop and frisk   The right of the police to detain an individual for a brief period of time and to search the outside of the person's clothing if the police have a reasonable suspicion that the individual has committed or is about to commit a crime.

Strict construction   An approach whereby the courts give a statute a narrow interpretation.

Strict liability   Liability without having to prove fault.

Strict scrutiny   The standard the courts use in equal protection claims involving race-based decisions or "fundamental rights." The government must prove that the challenged action is designed to achieve a compelling government interest and that there is no reasonable alternative method for achieving it.

String citation   A series of citations in a row.

Structured database   A computerized database that contains key information about the content of documents, such as medical records.

Subject matter jurisdiction   The power of a court to hear a particular type of case.

Subordinating conjunction   Dependent clauses always begin with subordinating conjunctions: *after, although, as, because, before, even though, if, since, unless, when, where, whereas,* and *while.*

Subpoena   A court order requiring a person to appear to testify at a trial or deposition. (Administrative agencies also usually have subpoena powers.)

Subpoena duces tecum   A court order that a person who is not a party to litigation appear at a trial or deposition and bring requested documents.

Subsequent case history   Information about what happened procedurally to the litigation after the case cited. Include this information in a citation.

Substantial capacity test   Part of the Model Penal Code; a test that provides that the defendant is not guilty due to insanity if, at the time of the killing, the defendant lacked either the ability to understand that the act was wrong or the ability to control the behavior.

Substantial performance   Although a breach of contract, performance of all the essential terms of the contract will entitle the breaching party to the contractual price minus any damages caused by the breach.

Substantive facts   In a case brief, facts that deal with what happened to the parties before the litigation began.

Substantive law   Law that creates rights and duties.

Successive conflict of interest   Representing someone who is in a position adverse to a prior client.

Summary judgment   A judgment based on a finding that there is no genuine issue as to any material fact and that the moving party is entitled to judgment as a matter of law.

Summary judgment motion   A request for a summary judgment.

Summary jury trial   A nonbinding process in which attorneys for both sides present synopses of their cases to a jury, which renders an advisory opinion on the basis of these presentations.

Summons   A notice informing the defendant of the lawsuit and requiring the defendant to respond or risk losing the suit.

Superseding cause   In negligence, an intervening cause that relieves the defendant of liability.

Support   See **Alimony**.

Supra   Above; used to refer to authority already cited in the document. May not be used with citations to cases, statutes, or constitutions.

Supreme Court Reporter   A West publication containing U.S. Supreme Court decisions.

Surrogacy contract   A document in which a woman agrees to conceive and give birth to a child, deliver the child to its natural father, and terminate her parental rights so the father's wife can become its adoptive mother.

Suspension   A determination that an attorney may not practice law for a set period of time.

Syllabus   A summary of a court opinion that appears at the beginning of the case.

Synthesis   The process of integrating a series of cases in such a way that their interrelationship is explained to the reader.

Tabulation   A method for writing lists.

Tangible personal property   Also known as **chattel**; personal property that can be touched and moved.

Temporary restraining order (TRO)   A court order of limited duration designed to maintain the status quo pending further court action at a later date.

Tenancy in common   Ownership by two or more people. Ownership shares do not have to be equal, but each has an undivided interest in the property. When a tenant in common dies, that person's share passes either by will or by intestate statute.

Tenancy by the entirety   A special type of joint tenancy applicable only to married couples.

Tenancy at sufferance   A situation in which the person in possession of the land has no legal right to be there.

Tenancy for a term or estate for years   A right to control real property for a set period of time.

Tenancy at will   An arrangement in which no time period is specified and the lessee can leave or the lessor can reclaim the land at any time.

Testamentary capacity   The mental capacity, also known as *sound mind*, whereby the testator understands the nature of his or her property and the identity of those most closely related to him or her.

Testamentary trust   A trust that is created by a will and does not become effective until after the testator's death.

Testator/testatrix   The person making a will to direct how his or her assets will be distributed at death.

Testimonial evidence   Consists of the description of events that a witness testifies to under oath in a legal proceeding.

That case   A case that you are citing.

Theft   Also known as **larceny**; the taking of another's property with the intent to permanently deprive the owner.

Third-party   Someone who is not a party to the agreement or transaction.

Third-party beneficiary   Although not a party to the contract, someone the contracting parties intended to benefit.

Third-party claim   A claim by a defendant against someone in addition to the persons the plaintiff has already sued.

This case   Your client's case.

Tickler system   A calendaring system that records key dates and important deadlines.

Title insurance   Insurance against any loss due to a defective title.

Title search   An examination of documents recording title to a property to ensure the owner has a clear title.

Tort   Harm to a person or a person's property.

Tort law   Law that deals with harm to a person or a person's property.

Tortfeasor   A person who commits a tort.

Trademark   A name, combination of letters or numbers, or logo that identifies a particular product.

Transferred intent   A legal fiction that if a person directs a tortious action toward A but instead harms B, the intent to act against A is transferred to B.

Transition   In writing, a technique used to help your reader move from one thought to the next and to see the connections between them.

Treason   Attempting to overthrow the government or betraying the government to a foreign power.

Treatise   A book that summarizes, interprets, and evaluates the law.

Treatment   How subsequent cases have affected the case you are Shepardizing. It is sometimes indicated by a one-letter abbreviation before the Shepard's citation.

Trespass   The unauthorized intrusion onto the land of another.

Trespass to personal property   Occurs when someone harms or interferes with the owner's exclusive possession of the property but has no intention of keeping the property.

Trial   The process of deciding a dispute by presenting evidence and witness testimony either to a jury or to a judge.

Trial courts   Courts that determine the facts and apply the law to the facts.

Trust   A legal relationship in which one party holds property for the benefit of another.

Trustee   The person appointed to administer a trust.

12(b)(6) motion   A request that the court find the plaintiff has failed to state a valid claim and dismiss the complaint.

Ultrahazardous activities Those activities that have an inherent risk of injury and therefore may result in strict liability.

Unauthorized practice of law When nonlawyers do things that only lawyers are allowed to do. In most states this is a crime.

Unconscionable contract A contract formed between parties of very unequal bargaining power where the terms are so unfair as to "shock the conscience."

Undue influence When one party is in a position of trust and misuses that trust to influence the actions of another.

Unenforceable contract A valid contract that cannot be enforced, for example, because the statute of limitations has passed.

Uniform Commercial Code (UCC) Originally drafted by the National Conference of Commissioners on Uniform State Law, it governs commercial transactions and has been adopted by all states entirely or in part.

Uniform Partnership Act (UPA) Known as a gap filler, the UPA comes into play only if terms are left out of a partnership agreement.

Unilateral contract A contract where a promise is exchanged for an act.

United States Code (U.S.C.) Federal statutes arranged by subject matter.

United States Code Annotated (U.S.C.A.) Federal statutes arranged by subject matter, published by West.

United States Code Service (U.S.C.S.) Federal statutes arranged by subject matter, published by Lexis Law Publishing.

United States Constitution Drafted in 1787, it established the structure of the federal government and the relationship between the federal and state governments.

United States courts of appeals The intermediate appellate courts in the federal system.

United States district courts The general jurisdiction trial courts in the federal system.

United States Law Week BNA's publication of U.S. Supreme Court decisions.

United States Reports The official federal government publication of U.S. Supreme Court decisions.

United States Sentencing Guidelines Government guidelines that specify an appropriate range of sentences for each class of convicted persons based on factors related to the offense and the offender.

United States Supreme Court The highest appellate court in the federal system; consists of nine appointed members; established by Article III of the U.S. Constitution.

United States Supreme Court Reports, Lawyers' Edition U.S. Supreme Court decisions published by Lexis Law Publishing.

Unlawful detainer A civil action brought to recover use of property.

Unofficial reporter A private publication of court opinions—for example, the regional reporters, such as N.E.2d, published by West.

Valid In logic, an argument is considered to be valid or sound if the assumptions underlying the argument are true.

Valid contract A contract having all the essential elements needed for a binding agreement.

Verdict The opinion of a jury on a question of fact.

Verification An affidavit signed by the client indicating that he or she has read the complaint and that its contents are correct.

Vicarious representation The rule whereby all members of a law firm are treated as though they had represented the former client.

Void In law, if an action is void, it has no legal effect.

Void contract A contract that is invalid even if it is not repudiated by either party; for example, a contract formed for an illegal purpose.

Void for vagueness A reason for invalidating a statute where a reasonable person could not determine a statute's meaning.

Void marriage A marriage that is invalid from its inception and that does not require court action for the parties to be free of any marital obligations.

Voidable A valid contract that can be set aside at the option of one of the parties.

Voidable contract A contract that can be disaffirmed by one of the parties.

Voidable marriage A marriage that was valid when it was entered into and that remains valid until either party obtains a court order dissolving it.

Voir dire An examination of a prospective juror to see if he or she is fit to serve as a juror.

Warrant A court's prior permission for the police to search and seize.

Warranty A guarantee, made by the seller or implied by law, regarding the character, quality, or title of the goods being sold.

Warranty deed A deed in which the seller promises clear title to the property.

Web An abbreviation for the World Wide Web, a subset of the Internet. Web sites combine text, pictures, and sometimes even sound with hypertext links to other web pages with related information.

Web browser A computer program that allows users to access and search the web with the click of a mouse.

Web page A computer page, accessible on the Internet, that contains links to other pages.

Web site A location on the Internet that contains a series of web pages that are linked to a home page.

West Group A major private publisher of legal materials. Its logo is the key symbol.

Westlaw An on-line legal database containing court decisions and statutes from the entire country, as well as secondary authority; a competitor to **Lexis**.

Will The document used to express a person's wishes as to how his or her property should be distributed upon death.

Writ A judge's order requiring that something be done.

Writ of certiorari A means of gaining appellate review; in the U.S. Supreme Court the writ is discretionary and will be issued to another court to review a federal question if four of the nine justices vote to hear the case.

Writ of execution A court order authorizing a sheriff to take property in order to enforce a judgment.

Writ of habeas corpus A request that the court release the defendant because of the illegality of the incarceration.

Wrongful birth Also known as *wrongful life;* liability for negligently causing a child's birth.

Table of Cases

Index